ACTA IRANICA

DEUXIÈME SÉRIE
VOLUME II

SOUS LE HAUT PATRONAGE
DE S.M.I. LE SHAHINSHAH ARYAMEHR

ACTA IRANICA

ENCYCLOPÉDIE PERMANENTE DES ÉTUDES IRANIENNES
FONDÉE À L'OCCASION DU 2500ᵉ ANNIVERSAIRE
DE LA FONDATION DE L'EMPIRE PERSE PAR CYRUS LE GRAND

DEUXIÈME SÉRIE

HOMMAGES ET OPERA MINORA

Acta Iranica 5

ÉDITION
BIBLIOTHÈQUE PAHLAVI
TÉHÉRAN-LIÈGE

DIFFUSION
E. J. BRILL
LEIDEN

HOMMAGES ET OPERA MINORA

MONUMENTUM H. S. NYBERG

II

1975

DIFFUSION
E.J. BRILL
LEIDEN

ÉDITION
BIBLIOTHÈQUE PAHLAVI
TÉHÉRAN-LIÈGE

ISBN 90 04 03902 3
90 04 04329 2

TABLE DES MATIÈRES

GILBERT LAZARD

LE PRÉVERBE MOYEN-PERSE *bē/ba*

En persan contemporain, le préfixe verbal *be-* est un élément de la conjugaison : il sert à former le subjonctif et l'impératif; dans certaines formes locales du persan, il apparaît régulièrement aussi au prétérit[1]. En persan ancien, sa fonction était différente : nous croyons avoir montré qu'il est affixé au verbe chaque fois que celui-ci se trouve mis en relief soit par sa position dans la phrase, soit par la volonté de l'auteur de l'énoncé; vraisemblablement, il sert à faire porter un accent sur la forme verbale[2]. L'ancêtre moyen-perse de ce préfixe a en pehlevi la forme *bē* et dans les textes manichéens b' *ba*. Ce morphème a embarrassé les descripteurs et sa valeur reste assez énigmatique.

Dans son *Hilfsbuch*, H. S. Nyberg a décrit en détail avec beaucoup de clarté et de précision les différentes fonctions de *bē*[3]. Il distingue les emplois de *bē* : 1) comme conjonction adversative « mais », 2) comme adverbe « hors », 3) comme préposition « hormis », 4) enfin comme préverbe dans deux séries d'emplois : dans une partie des cas, il est « mit klar fühlbarer Eigenbedeutung ab-, aus-, heraus-, hervor-, weg- », dans les autres il est « einfach perfektivierend », soit avec le prétérit, soit avec le présent « um das Fut. auszudrücken », soit avec l'impératif. La même doctrine, à peu de chose près et avec nombre d'exemples nouveaux, est reprise dans le *Manual*[4].

Laissant de côté les autres emplois, qui sont clairs, nous ne considérerons ici que les emplois préverbaux. Retenons que Nyberg distingue nettement les cas où *bē* est en somme un préverbe ordinaire pourvu d'un sens bien défini et ceux où il sert d'instrument de perfectivation, encore que, comme il est dit dans le *Hilfsbuch* et

---

[1] Ainsi dans le parler du Sistan et dans celui de Qâyen au Khorassan, voir G. Lazard, « Morphologie du verbe dans le parler persan du Sistan », *Studia Iranica* 3 (1974) 65-85, et R. Zomorrodian, « Le système verbal du persan parlé à Qâyen », *ibid.*, 87-112.

[2] Voir notre *Langue des plus anciens monuments de la prose persane* (Paris 1963) 298-326.

[3] *Hilfsbuch des Pehlevi, II. Glossar* (Uppsala 1931), s.v. *bē*.

[4] *A Manual of Pahlavi, Part II : Glossary* (Wiesbaden 1974), s.v. *bē*.

répété dans le *Manual*, les uns et les autres soient souvent difficiles
à séparer. Henning, dans sa description du verbe moyen-perse d'après
les textes manichéens, va plus loin et distingue deux morphèmes
différents, un préverbe *ba* «weg, heraus» et une particule verbale
de même forme qui ne modifie pas sensiblement le sens du verbe :
de cette particule «sind sorgfältig zu trennen b' «aber» ... und das
Präverb b' «weg» [5].

Cette interprétation ne va pas sans difficulté. On a du mal à
admettre que dans un même état de langue il puisse exister, comme
le suppose Henning, deux morphèmes homophones et de même nature
grammaticale, mais de valeur différente, ou encore, ce qu'implique
la présentation de Nyberg, qu'un même morphème dans la même
position puisse avoir deux fonctions différentes. Notons encore que
les spécialistes ne sont pas d'accord sur la valeur de *bē/ba* lorsqu'il
n'a pas clairement le sens de «aus, weg». Henning reprend avec
beaucoup de réserve la formule de Horn, selon laquelle la particule
«der Verbalform eine gewisse Spezialisierung für einen bestimmten
Fall verliehe». Au demeurant, la notion de perfectif, empruntée au
système verbal des langues slaves, est mal définie dès qu'on l'applique
telle quelle à d'autres langues et demande à être précisée rigoureusement
dans le cadre des oppositions propres à chacune des langues con-
sidérées. Le moins qu'on puisse dire est qu'elle n'est pas évidente
en moyen-perse; comment, par exemple, interpréter sur cette base,
dans les textes mêmes du *Hilfsbuch*, *bē ēstēd* dans la phrase suivante,
qui décrit l'épaisseur d'une couche d'eau : ...*aš tā aškamb āb bē
ēstēd pad ān bālāy āb bē tazēd* (imaginons un homme à quatre pattes)
«jusqu'à son ventre l'eau demeure (ne s'écoule pas), à [partir de]
ce niveau elle s'écoule» (Bd 82.8) [6]?

Une question telle que la valeur du préverbe *bē* ne peut être
résolue à l'aide d'un petit nombre d'exemples choisis, mais demande
un examen systématique, sur un corpus assez étendu, de l'ensemble
des occurrences avec et sans *bē* d'une série de verbes. Nous avons
donc tenté d'éclaircir la question par un dépouillement de l'ensemble
des textes du *Hilfsbuch*. Les données présentées ne concernent pas

---

[5] W. B. Henning, «Das Verbum des Mittelpersischen der Turfanfragmente», *Zeit-schrift für Indologie und Iranistik* 9 (1933-34) 158-253, voir p. 231-32 et 247.

[6] Le système des références est celui du *Hilfsbuch II*. Nous transcrivons le pehlevi selon le système de D. N. MacKenzie, *A Concise Pahlavi Dictionary*, London 1971.

tous les verbes, mais un échantillonnage aussi varié que possible : pour les verbes retenus, on a relevé la totalité des occurrences.

Une première constatation est que *bē* a exactement la même syntaxe que les autres préverbes. Comme eux, ordinairement il précède immédiatement le verbe, mais, comme eux, il peut s'en trouver séparé par un complément : *bē ō pēš rōšn ēstād* (Bd 79.2), comp. *abāz ō xwēšīh ī man nē rasēnd* (Bd 66.18). D'autre part la présence de *bē* devant le verbe exclut celle de l'un quelconque des autres préverbes, tout comme ceux-ci s'excluent mutuellement. Il est vrai que *bē* peut coexister avec un autre préverbe, lorsque l'un des deux précède un complément : *abar ō axw ī astōmand bē wašt hēnd* (*Manual*, s.v. *vaštan*), *bē ō ān ī asar rōšnīh ī hamāg xwārīh abar rasēd* (MX 2.146). Mais la même construction se trouve avec d'autres préverbes : *frāz raft Pourušāsp ... abar ō āb ī Dāitī* (*Manual*, s.v. *raftan*). Enfin, si, comme nous le verrons plus bas, il arrive que le même verbe soit employé avec et sans *bē* sensiblement dans le même sens, la même variation apparaît avec *frāz*, par exemple : *nazdist Wahman frāz tāšīd* (Bd 76.10), *panjom gāw ī ēwdād tāšīd* (Bd 83.21).

Il est remarquable d'autre part que les emplois des verbes avec *bē* soient considérablement moins nombreux que les emplois sans *bē*, ce qui suggère fortement que ce morphème n'est pas l'instrument d'une opposition perfectif-imperfectif qui jouerait un rôle important dans le système verbal du moyen-perse. Le tableau suivant présente l'ensemble des occurrences d'une série de verbes respectivement sans préverbe, avec *bē* et avec d'autres préverbes [7].

---

[7] Indiquons ici à titre documentaire les autres formes verbales pourvues du préverbe *bē* (il s'agit des verbes dont nous n'avons pas relevé les occurrences sans *bē* parce qu'ils paraissaient insuffisamment attestés dans le corpus) : *bē abesīhēnēd* Bd 64.6, *bē abesīhēd* Pn 20.21, *bē āmad ēstēd* MX 2.189, *bē āmurzēm* Pn 27.19, *bē bast* MX 2.175, *bē apaydāg burdan* Bd 75.18-19, *bē buxtēm* Kn 2.10, *bē hamōxt* Pn 24.12-13, *bē hamōxtan* Pn 24.11-12, *bē nišānēnd* MX 2.156, *bē nišastan* MX 2.19, *bē pāyēd* Pn 23.9, *bē sōwārēm*(?) Kn 3.15, *bē spōxtan* Kn 1.26, *bē spōzēd* Pn 24.18, *bē tāft* Kn 1.9, *bē tazēd* Bd 82.8, *bē winārd* Bd 82.15, *bē wirēzēd* Kn 1.6, 9, *bē wizīdan* Pn 19.19, *bē xēzēm* Bd 66.8, *bē xuft* Kn 2.3.

	verbe nu	bē	andar	frāz	abāz	frōd	abar
šudan	18	1	2	1	3	1	
raftan	10	2		1			
widardan	3	6					
rasīdan	26	(1) [8]	1	1	1		1 [8]
ōbastan	5	1	1		1		
waštan	3	1			1	1	
hištan	5	3					
murdan	3	1					
ēstādan	11	3	1		2		
ēstādan (auxil.)	31						
zadan	3	3					
guftan	68	1		1	1		
dīdan	29	1					
nigerīdan	1	2					
nimūdan	2	1					
dānistan	17	6					
šnāxtan	1	2					
dādan	49	7		1			
kardan	env. 150	12	1	3			1
būdan	env. 180	3		1			
	env. 612	56	6	9	9	2	2

On voit que, en moyenne, les formes verbales sans *bē* sont environ dix fois plus nombreuses que les formes avec *bē*. En revanche la fréquence de *bē* est largment supérieure à celle des autres préverbes : cette statistique sommaire confirme que, si *bē* se range parmi les préverbes, il n'en occupe pas moins une place à part.

Il faut maintenant examiner la valeur sémantique des verbes considérés, respectivement avec et sans *bē*.

šudan sans *bē* signifie : « aller » (quelque part), presque toujours avec un complément introduit par *ō*, ex. *ō naxčīr ud čōbēgān šawēd* « qu'il aille à la chasse et au polo » Kn 1.28, de même Kn 1.31, 39, 2.3, Pn 20.4, 23.16, 25.2, 17, 26.11, MX 2.58, 159, Bd 65.17 ; avec un complément introduit par *andar* Pn 26.13 ; avec un complément sans préposition, *kadām gyāg šud* « où est-il allé ? » Kn 3.5 ; — « marcher, progresser », *ēdōn čiyōn vād ī ardāg hamē šud* « il allait comme

---

[8] *bē* est ici en combinaison avec *abar* : *bē ō ... abar rasēd*.

un vent impétueux » Kn 3.13; — «parcourir», *tā nūn was frasang zamīg šud* «jusqu'à présent il a parcouru bien des lieues» Kn 3.10. — Il est en liaison étroite avec un autre verbe comme une sorte d'auxiliaire dans *wirēxt šud* «il s'est enfui» Kn 3.3, 6. — Avec préverbe on a *andar š.* «entrer» Kn 2.33, MX 2.58, *frāz š.* «aller» (quelque part) Pn 26.15, *abāz š.* «retourner» (quelque part) Kn 2.12, Pn 17.7, MX 2.13, *frōd š.* «se coucher» (soleil) MX 54.12. — *bē šudan* signifie «s'en aller», *az ēdar tā gēhān girēm bē šawēm* «partons d'ici pour conquérir le monde» Kn 2.9 (texte d'après *Manual* I 5.27); noter aussi *bē-šudag-baxt* «dont la fortune est partie, infortuné» Kn 2.3, et d'autres exemples de *bē šudan* dans le même sens dans *Manual* II, s.v. *šutan* (mais aussi *ka ān damistān šud* «when this winter has gone»!).

raftan sans *bē* signifie: «marcher», ex. *mardē ki 2 dast ō zamīg hilēd ud pad dast ud pāy rawēd* «un homme qui met les deux mains par terre et marche à quatre pattes» Bd 82.7, de même Kn 2.15, 3.13, MX 2.37, Bd 88.2; — «parcourir», *50 frasang raft hēnd* «ils parcoururent cinquante lieues» Kn 3.16; — «se conduire», *abāg dōst pad passand ī dōstān raw* «avec les amis conduis-toi au gré des amis» MX 2.62; — «mener sa vie», *abāg kurdīgān šubānān raft* «il vécut parmi les bergers esclaves» Kn 1.7 (texte d'après *Manual* I, 1.10); — «avoir libre cours», *3000 sāl hamāg kāmag ī Ohrmazd rawēd 3000 sāl andar gumēzišn kāmag ī Ohrmazd ud Ahriman harw 2 rawēd* «pendant trois mille ans la volonté d'O. sera faite et pendant trois mille ans, dans le mélange, la volonté d'O. et celle d'A. seront faites toutes deux» Bd 67-68. — Avec préverbe on a *frāz r.* «s'avancer» MX 2.140. — *bē raftan* signifie: «se mettre en route, s'en aller», *az ānōh pad awištāb bē raft* «il s'en alla de là en hâte» Kn 2.19 (autres exemples dans *Manual* II, s.v. *raftan*); — «parcourir», *pad rōzē 70 frasang bē rawēnd* «ils parcourent soixante-dix lieues par jour» Kn 2.14.

widardan sans *bē* signifie «passer (par)», ex. *andar deh nē bē pad kustag ī deh widard* «il ne passa pas dans le village, mais à la lisière du village» Kn 2.16, de même Kn 3.8, MX 2.123. — *bē widardan* signifie «passer outre, franchir», ex. *gōrē andar dašt bē widard* «un onagre passa dans la plaine» (et s'enfuit) Kn 1.32, de même Kn 1.33, 3.9, 10, 12, MX 2.124 (le contraste est net avec la phrase précédente: *kā ruwān ī ahlaw[ān] pad ān puhl widerēd... ud ān ī ahlaw ruwān pad abāgīh ī Sroš-ahrāy bē widerēd* «quand l'âme du juste passe sur ce pont [il s'élargit...] et elle le franchit en compagnie de S. »); noter aussi *bē-widerišnīh* « passage dans l'au-delà, trépas » Pn 24.1, MX 2.155, et d'autres exemples de *bē w.* « franchir » dans *Manual* I, 101.18, 103.23.

rasīdan sans *bē* signifie : « arriver » (sens propre), ex. *ō Činwar puhl ī buland rasēd* « il arrive au haut pont Č. » MX 2.115, de même Kn 3.15 (2 fois), 20, Pn 27.21, MX 37.2, 57.9; — « arriver » (sens figuré), ex. *ō pādixšāyih ī gēhān rasēd* « il atteindra la souveraineté de l'univers » Kn 1.13, de même Kn 1.23, 24, 2.6, 9, 10, Pn 17.4, 30.2, MX 57.32, Bd 70.14 (?); — « venir » (au secours), ex. *kū-t pad mēnōgān ō frahād rasēd* « afin qu'il vienne à ton aide dans le mēnōg » MX 2.97, de même Kn 2.10, MX 2.166; — « échoir, advenir », ex. *ān ī ... az adān mard az kunišn ī xwēš awiš rasēd* « ce qui arrive à l'ignorant du fait de ses propres actes » Kn 1.43, de même Kn 1.13, MX 2.9, 24, 36, Bd 76.18. — Avec préverbe on a : *andar r.* « survenir » Kn 1.33, *frāz r.* « arriver » (sur les lieux) Kn 1.34, *abāz r.* « rejoindre » Bd 66.19. — *rasīdan* ne se trouve avec *bē* qu'une fois, en combinaison avec *abar* : *čahārom gām bē ō asar rōšnīh ī hamāg xwārīh abar rasēd* « au quatrième pas il atteint la lumière éternelle de toute félicité » MX 2.146.

ōbastan sans *bē* signifie : « tomber » (sens propre), *stūnag ō zamīg ōftēd* « la carcasse tombe sur le sol » MX 2.113; — « se coucher » (astre), **dō-ābdān ōbast* « le Verseau s'est couché » Kn 2.5; — « tomber » (regard), *ka-t čašm ō zrēh ōftēd* « quand tu apercevras la mer » Kn 2.18; — « advenir », *kāhišn ō tan ud ruwān ōftēd* « un dommage advient au corps et à l'âme » MX 2.22; — « venir » (à l'esprit), *u-š hamōyēn wināh ud bazag ō mēnišn ōftēd* « et toute sorte de péchés et de crimes lui viennent à la pensée » MX 2.18. — Avec préverbe on a : *andar ō.* « tomber » (au sens propre) Bd 68.19, *abāz o.* « retomber » Bd 68.14-15. — *bē ōbastan* signifie « tomber hors, se détacher » dans la seule attestation : *ān band az grīw bē ōfted* « cette chaîne [lui] tombe du cou » Pn 24.2; comparer *Manual* I, 102.24 (le Mauvais Esprit *az ēn zamīg... bē ō dušox ōftēd* « tombe = est rejeté de cette terre en enfer »).

waštan sans *bē* signifie : « se détourner », *gannāg mēnōg hagriz az petyārag nē wardēd* « le Mauvais Esprit ne renoncera jamais au mal » Bd 69.17; — « changer », *tis ī Ohrmazd ān ī pad bundahišn dād nē wardēd* « ce qui est d'O. et a été créé à l'origine ne change pas » Bd 70.18., — Il semble fonctionner comme une sorte d'auxiliaire dans *gumēzid wardēd* (?) « se mêle » Bd 71.17. — Avec préverbe on a *abāz w.* « retourner » Kn 3.21, *frōd w.* « descendre » Bd 72.17-18.

— *bē waštan* signifie « dévier », *čand mōyē tāg bē nē wardēd* [la balance divine] « ne dévie pas d'un seul cheveu » MX 2.122; noter aussi *bē-wardišnīh* « séparation » Pn 22.14-15. — Par hasard, le sens banal de « tourner », (probablement sans *bē*) n'est pas attesté dans le corpus. Il semble que *bē waštan* signifie proprement « se détourner »; l'absence de *bē* dans le premier exemple cité ci-dessus (Bd 69.17) est un peu surprenante : ce peut être une faute de copie, car le texte du Bundahišn n'est pas sûr. Le *Manual*, s.v. *vaštan*, donne aussi *bē waštan* (et *frāz w.*) au sens de « se métamorphoser ».

hištan sans *bē* signifie : « laisser » (passer, faire), ex. *Ardaxšīr nē hišt ō asb nišastan* « [il] ne laissa pas A. monter à cheval » Kn 1.38, de même MX 37.24, Bd 81.17; — « mettre », *mardē kē 2 dast ō zamīg hilēd* « un homme qui met les deux mains par terre » Bd 82.6; —« abandonner », *čē-t pad frazām hamāg abāyēd hištan* « car à la fin il te faudra tout abandonner » MX 2.103. — *bē hištan* signifie « abandonner, lâcher » : *tan rāy āzarm i ruwān bē ma hilēd* « n'abandonnez pas pour [le bien] du corps la dignité de l'âme » Pn 29.19, de même Pn 23.6-7; — « négliger, tolérer », *wināh... andar hāsr bē ma hilēd* « ne laissez pas un instant le péché [sans expiation] » Pn 25.2-3. — On remarque que dans le sens d'« abandonner » *hištan* se trouve avec et sans *bē*. Nyberg note dans le *Manual* en tête de l'article *hištan* que ce verbe s'emploie « with and without the prev. *bē* ». Mais, si l'on examine les emplois, on s'aperçoit que la répartition n'est pas entièrement au hasard. *hištan* est régulièrement sans *bē* aux sens de « laisser aller » (*Man.* 11.2, 27.2, 15), « faire aller, lancer » (un cheval) (*Man.* 11.2), « congédier » (*Man.* 109.4), et avec *bē* au sens de « négliger, tolérer » (*Man.* 9.4, 23.23, 109.19). En revanche, aux sens d'« abandonner » et aussi d'« introduire » (quelqu'un ou quelque chose), on trouve en concurrence l'emploi avec *bē* (« abandonner » : *Man.* 19.6, 19, 24.25, 33.22; « introduire » : *Man.* 34.25, 35.1, 101.21) et sans *bē* (« abandonner » : *Man.* 19.3, 18, 34.14; « introduire » : *Man.* 101.21).

murdan « mourir » est employé sans différence de sens appréciable sans *bē*, ex. *ka ōy i druwand mīrēd* « quand le méchant meurt » MX 2.158, de même Kn 1.33, MX 44.30; — et avec *bē*, *ka az gursagīh ud tišnagīh bē nē mīrēnd* « afin qu'ils ne meurent pas de faim et de soif » MX 57.11. — Même variation dans le *Manual* (*tā andar zamān mīrēd* 9.13, *mardom ka bē mīrēnd* 34.13, *kāč... pad xwēš baxt pad rahīgīh bē murd hēm* 21.13).

ēstādan sans *bē* signifie : « se tenir, se trouver », ex. *pērāmōn i Sāsān ēstēnd* «se tiennent autour de S.» Kn 1.10, de même Kn 3.6, Bd 84.12; — «se tenir» (à une attitude), *pad dād i ērīh ēstādan* «se tenir à la loi des Aryens» Pn 21.18 (texte d'après *Manual* I 64.15-16), de même Pn 21.21; — «rester» (dans un état), ex. *pad hamēhamērawišnīh pad harvisp xwārīh ēstēd* «il reste pour l'éternité dans la félicité», MX 2.157, de même Bd. 64.17, 75.11,13, 78.14; — «passer» (à un autre état), *ō wirēg ud nihānrawišnīh ēstād* «il prit la fuite et entra dans la clandestinité» Kn 1.7. — Employé comme auxiliaire du parfait, *ēstādan* est toujours sans *bē*, Kn 1.1, 8, 10, 12, 32, 43, 44, 2.2, 9, 13, 3.18, Pn 17.2-3, 22.19, 26.1-2, 27.18, MX 2.10, 19, 48, 116, 151, 189, 190, 44.2, 9, 57.12, 13, 29, Bd 81.7, 18, 83.10, 88.10. — Avec préverbe on a *andar ē.* «rester» Bd 82.3, *abāz ē.* (*az*) «renier» Pn 22.11, MX 57.24. — *bē ēstādan* signifie : «surgir», *ka bē ō pēš rōšn ēstād* «quand il surgit à la lumière» Bd 79.2; — «demeurer immobile, stagner», *aš tā aškamb āb bē ēstēd pad ān bālāy āb bē tazēd* «jusqu'à son ventre l'eau ne s'écoule pas, à [partir de] ce niveau elle s'écoule» Bd 82.8, de même Bd 83.10. — La différence entre *ēstādan* et *bē ēstādan* apparaît bien dans l'article *ēstātan* du *Manual*, où le verbe sans *bē* est donné comme signifiant «se tenir; rester; être en permanence; passer (à un autre état)», et avec *bē* «se dresser; apparaître; rester immobile; s'arrêter; se garder; s'abstenir».

zadan sans *bē* signifie : «frapper» (quelqu'un), *dēw ān ruwān i druwandān... zanēd ud wināhēd* «le démon bat et tourmente l'âme des méchants» MX 2.164; — «frapper» (les cordes d'un luth), *tanbūr zad* «il jouait du luth» Kn 2.2; — «tirer» (une flèche), *tigrē ēdōn ō gōr zad kū* «il tira une flèche sur l'onagre de telle sorte que...» Kn 1.33. — *bē zadan* signifie «combattre», ex. *ārzōg i abārōn pad xrad bē zanēd* «combattez les mauvais désirs à l'aide de la raison» Pn 25.4, de même Pn 25.8, MX 2.94.

guftan «dire» est presque toujours sans *bē*, soit avec une complétive introduite par *kū* «que», *passim*; — soit avec, pour complément, un mot signifiant «parole», ex. *saxwan društēwāzīhā ō-š guft* «[tu] lui as parlé rudement» Kn 1.42, de même Kn 2.7, MX 2.135, 136, 176, 178, 37.33, 57.30, Bd 68.16, 18, 20 (la parole est ici une prière), 78.6; — soit avec un substantif désignant la chose exprimée, racontée, exposée, etc., ex. *xumr... pēš i awēšān guft* «il leur raconta son rêve» Kn 1.12, de même Kn 1.16, Bd 69.3, 80.20, 85.16, 89.5; — soit au sens de «nommer, appeler», ex. *xešm hāwand i Ahrimam guft ēstēd* «on a appelé la colère l'égale d'A.» MX 2.19, de même Bd 62.14, 63.8, 10, 14, 70.9, 80.5, 87.19, 88.5; — soit absolument au sens de «parler», ex. *im 3 pās i-m guft abar* «ces trois gardes dont j'ai parlé» Pn 23.8, de même MX 2.196. — Avec préverbe on a *frāz g.* «appeler» Bd 73.8, *abāz g.* «rapporter» Kn 2.7. — *bē guftan* ne se trouve qu'une fois au sens de «réciter» (rituellement, solennellement), *yatāhuvairyō... bē guft* «il récita l'Ahuna vairya» Bd 68.7; dans le même sens on a *guft būd* (sans *bē*) quelques lignes plus bas (68.16, 18, 20).

dīdan est généralement sans *bē*: «voir» (quelqu'un ou quelque chose), ex. *ka-š Ardaxšīr dīd šād būd* «quand il vit A., il se réjouit» Kn 1.28, de même Kn 1.12, 13, 28, 34, 41, 2.2, 16, 17, 18, MX 2.128, 160, 169, Bd 65.1, 4, 9, 12, 68.14, 69.15; — «voir» (quelqu'un faire quelque chose), ex. *pad xumr dīd čiyōn ka* «il vit en songe que...» Kn 1.9, de même Kn 1.10, 11, MX 2.131, 132, 172, 174, 176; — «observer», *čē hamē wēnēd pad tis i haftān ud dwāzdahān* «que voyez-vous dans les affaires des sept planètes et des douze constellations?» (question adressée à des astrologues) Kn 2.16; — «subir», *dēr zaman anagih wēnē* «tu souffriras longtemps» MX 2.186. — *dīdan* n'a été relevé qu'une fois avec *bē*, sans qu'une nuance de sens particulière soit perceptible: *Pābag ka-š tanbahr ud čābukīh i Ardaxšīr bē dīd, dānist* «quand P. vit la beauté et l'agilité d'A., il comprit...» Kn 1.21.

nigerīdan «regarder» est sans *bē* dans *niger kū rōz ud šab... ō naxčīr ...nē sawēh* «garde-toi jour et nuit d'aller à la chasse...» Kn 1.39; — mais avec *bē* au sens d'«examiner»: *bē niger tā ān wināhkār... kadām gyāg šud* «examine où est allé ce criminel» Kn 3.5, de même Pn 28.5.

nimūdan «montrer» est sans *bē* au sens d'«indiquer»: *ān warrag i-š abāg pad asp čē nimāyēd* «que signifie ce bélier qui est avec lui sur le cheval?» Kn 3.19, de même KN 2.5; — et avec *bē* au sens de «dévoiler», *u-š frazām pērōzīh ī xwēš bē ō gannāg mēnōg nimūd* «il (Ohrmazd) révéla au Mauvais Esprit sa victoire finale» Bd 68.12.

dānistan est ordinairement sans *bē*: «savoir, comprendre» (en général), ex. *ka-š... bē dīd dānist kū ēn xumr i-m dīd rāst būd* «quand il vit..., il comprit que le songe qu'il avait eu était véridique» Kn 1.21, de même Kn 1.8, 40, 45, 3.3, 14. Bd 64.2, 10, 65.16, 66.20, 67.11, 19, 76.19; — en particulier «savoir, comprendre» (une vérité religieuse, en parlant d'un adepte), ex. *miyānjīgīhā pad dast ī xrad bē abēgumānīhā sazēd dānistan* «on peut savoir médiatement par la raison, mais de science certaine...» Pn 18.13, de même Pn 30.11, MX 57.14; — «être capable» (de): *sērīh nē dānēd* «ne connaît pas la satiété» MX 2.117. — *dānistan* avec *bē* n'a été relevé que dans des phrases où il s'agit de savoir religieux : ex. *ēn and tis bē dānistan abāyēd kū* « il faut savoir ces quelques choses, à savoir... » Pn 17.5, de même Pn 24.6, 9, 25.9, 26.21, MX 57.14.

šnāxtan sans *bē* signìfie « reconnaître » (quelqu'un) dans *tarsīd kū ma agar mardom ī deh wēnēnd šnāsēnd* « il craignit que les gens du village ne [les] voient, ne [les] reconnaissent... » Kn 2.16. — Avec *bē* il signifie « reconnaître, distinguer », ex. *dard ud wēmārīh i mardōmān ud stōrān bē šnāxtan* « connaître les maux et les maladies des hommes et des chevaux » MX 57.18, de même MX 2.87. — Dans le *Manual* on trouve *šnāxtan* au sens de « reconnaître » (quelqu'un) sans *bē* (57.22) et avec *bē* (100.18).

dādan sans *bē* signifie : « donner », ex. *u-š pas duxt ī xwēš pad zanīh dād* « il [lui] donna ensuite sa fille en mariage » Kn 1.20, de même Kn 1.11, 18, 2.5, Pn 27.7, MX 2.133, 135, 174, 175, 176, 177, 192, 37.30, 44.29, 57.25, Bd 65.20 ; — « créer », ex. *u-š nazdist āsmān dād* « et il créa d'abord le ciel » Bd 80.3, de même MX 44.21, 57.5, Bd 70.18, 71.8, 14, 73.20, 74.3, 6, 75.2, 15, 17, 76.1, 3, 5, 13, 80.5, 6, 8, 10, 13, 21, 82.9, 11, 83.2, 11, 16, 84.5, 20, 86.4, 12, 19, 87.5. — Avec préverbe on a *frāz d.* « créer » Bd 70.11. — *bē dādan* signifie « créer », ex. *u-š ēn 6 dahišn pad 6 gāh i gāhānbār bē dād* « et il créa ces six créations pendant les six gāhānbār » Bd 85.11, de même Bd 74.17-18, 76.1-2, 79.8, 81.4, 82.21, 85.8. — L'article *dātan* dans le *Manual* suggère que, au sens de « donner », ce verbe est toujours sans *bē* ; d'autre part les sens de « jeter » (un ennemi à terre) et de « retirer » (des vêtements) ne sont attestés qu'avec *bē*. En revanche, au sens de « créer » et aussi de « déposer, mettre », ce verbe est employé aussi bien avec que sans *bē*.

kardan « faire », dans ses divers et nombreux emplois, est ordinairement sans *bē*, comme l'indique le tableau statistique qu'on a vu plus haut. On a relevé *bē kardan* dans trois emplois différents : « enlever », *ān band... az grīw bē kardan nē tuwān* « on ne peut enlever cette chaîne de son cou » Pn 23.20 ; — « accomplir » (un acte religieux ; comparer plus haut *bē guftan*), *čand yašt bē kardan* « accomplir quelques yašt » Pn 24.5, *hērbedistān* (lire *herbedistānīh*?) *bē kardan* « faire des études religieuses » Pn 24.9 ; — « faire devenir » (avec la nuance : « porter à un degré supérieur »), ex. *ka burzišnīg būd hēm ēg-it burzišnīgtar bē kard hēm ud ka grāmīg būd hēm ēg-it grāmīgtar bē kard hēm* « quand j'étais honorée, tu m'as rendu plus honorée et quand j'étais chérie, tu m'as rendu plus chère » MX 2.137-8, de même MX 2.179-80 (dans une formule parallèle MX 2.139 *bē* est probablement omis par erreur), Bd 69.12, 74.1, et sans doute aussi Bd 86.10 (*āb rōšn bē kard čē nazdist tīrag būd* «il a rendu l'eau lumineuse, car elle était d'abord obscure»). *bē kardan* est surprenant dans *hanbār ī zamestān dāmān i xwēš rāy paydāg bē kard* «il a fait paraître des réserves d'hiver pour ses créatures» Bd 87.12, à moins qu'il ne faille entendre *bē kard* comme «il a fait surgir».

būdan aussi s'emploie très généralement sans *bē*. Trois exemples de *bē būdan* ont été relevés, tous au sens de «devenir»: *Ardaxšīr xurram bē būd* «A. se réjouit» Kn 2.19, *ka zamān tāšēd dām-iz ī Ahriman rawāg bē bawēd* «quand il créera le temps, la création d'A. aussi se mettra en marche» Bd 69.21; *kū akār bē bēd... az ān ī xwēš dāmdahišnīh akār bawēd* Bd 74.7-11 peut se traduire «quand il deviendra (ou sera devenu) impuissant..., il sera impuissant à accomplir sa création».

Quelles conclusions peut-on tirer de cet examen? Sans doute est-il toujours dangereux d'extrapoler à partir d'un corpus relativement restreint. D'autre part, les textes pehlevis ne nous sont parvenus que dans des manuscrits bien postérieurs à la rédaction et dont le texte est sujet à caution. La rédaction elle-même est tardive et peut avoir été influencée par la langue vivante, plus évoluée[9]. Néanmoins, sous ces réserves, on entrevoit certains résultats.

Nous constatons que, pour la plupart des verbes, les emplois avec et sans *bē*, en général, ne sont pas sémantiquement équivalents. Il n'y a de concurrence que dans une minorité de cas: (*bē*) *raftan* «parcourir», (*bē*) *rasīdan* «arriver» (sens propre), (*bē*) *waštan* «se détourner», (*bē*) *hištan* «abandonner» (et «introduire»), (*bē*) *murdan* «mourir», (*bē*) *dīdan* «voir», (*bē*) *dānistan* «savoir», (*bē*) *šnāxtan* «reconnaître», (*bē*) *dādan* «créer» (et «mettre»).

D'autre part, dans la moitié environ de ses emplois, le préverbe *bē* a clairement le sens de «aus, weg»: *bē šudan* «s'en aller», *bē raftan* «se mettre en route», *bē widardan* «passer (outre)», *bē ōbastan* «tomber hors», *bē waštan* «se détourner», *bē hištan* «abandonner» et aussi «tolérer» («laisser de côté»), *bē ēstādan* «surgir», *bē nimūdan* «révéler», *bē šnāxtan* «distinguer», et aussi *bē murdan*

---

[9] P. Gignoux, «Note sur la rédaction de l'Ardāy Virāz Nāmag: l'emploi de hamē et de bē», *ZDMG Supplementa* 1 (1969) 998-1004, indique que la rédaction de l'Ardāy Virāz Nāmag est particulièrement tardive et en voit un indice justement dans la fréquence de *hamē* et de *bē*.

«mourir». Cette même valeur se reconnaît dans une inscription en moyen-perse du IIIe siècle, KKZ ligne 13 : *ān-iz-im bē istad u-m abāz ō xwēš šahr hišt hēnd*» [ce que l'on avait ainsi pillé] je le pris et le rendis à mon propre pays» [10] ; — dans le seul exemple du Psautier : *u-š bē anīd* [*Isr*]*āyīl* «er führte Israel heraus» [11] ; — et dans les textes manichéens : 'c dry'b b' 'škrwst «er kroch aus dem Meer» [12], 'wd ks ny hyl''d 'c 'm'h b' nyydn «und niemandem sie von uns wegführen lassen» [13], 'cyš b' 'wzyh'[d] «wird daraus herauskommen», 'c 'ndr b' wz[yhynd] «von drinnen kamen sie heraus», kym dyw w̌ drwxš 'cyš b' [...] «aus denen ich Teufel und Teufelinnen heraus-[getrieben habe]» [14], h'n knyg 'c zryg b' mwrd «jenes Mädchen vor Qual starb» [15]. — Ce sens de «aus, weg» est évidemment la valeur originelle de la particule *bē*, quelle qu'en soit l'étymologie, comme l'indiquent bien ses autres emplois, comme adverbe et conjonction, et le composé *bērōn* «dehors».

Cependant, dans les autres cas que nous avons passés en revue (la moitié de l'ensemble environ), *bē* exprime des nuances diverses, qu'il est difficile de ramener à l'unité. Ce peut être effectivement parfois quelque chose qui évoque ce qu'on appelle, vaguement, «perfectif», par exemple dans *bē hištan* «abandonner» opposé à *hištan* «laiser (faire)» ou *bē ēstādan* «surgir» opposé à *ēstādan* «se tenir». Mais une telle notion ne s'applique guère à *bē hištan* «tolérer» ou *bē ēstādan* «demeurer immobile». Il vaut mieux admettre que *bē* est susceptible de prendre des valeurs variées qui ne peuvent se définir que par rapport à la sémantique de chaque verbe. Ceci n'est pas étonnant : c'est aussi parfois le cas de *frāz*; et c'est, dans beaucoup de langues, celui de bien des préverbes, dont la signification, très ténue, se dilue dans un jeu d'oppositions fort délicat.

Reste à expliquer la concurrence des emplois d'un même verbe avec et sans *bē* sensiblement dans le même sens. On peut se demander si, comme en persan ancien, *bē* ne vient pas renforcer le verbe lorsque celui-ci ne peut s'appuyer sur un autre mot (un complément

---

[10] Voir P. Gignoux, *Journal Asiatique* 1968, 397.

[11] Voir Andreas-Barr, «Bruchstücke einer Pehlevi-Übersetzung der Psalmen», *Sitzungsber. der pr. Akad. der Wiss., phil.-hist. Kl.* 1933, 115.

[12] Voir Andreas-Henning, «Mitteliranische Manichaica... I», *ibid.*, 1932, 181.

[13] *Ibid.*, 200.

[14] Passages cités par Henning, «Das Verbum...», *op. cit.*, 232.

[15] Voir Andreas et Henning, «Mitteliranische Manichaica... II», *Sitzungsber...* 1933, 306.

notamment) auquel il serait syntaxiquement lié de près, c'est-à-dire lorsqu'il se trouve en position isolée. Mais il ne semble pas que cette explication se vérifie : dans *harw čē tō framāyē kunēm* « je ferai tout ce que tu voudras » Kn 2.11, ou *ud ka mīrēnd ahlaw hēnd* « et quand ils meurent, ils sont bienheureux » MX 44.30, par exemple, le verbe est isolé et sans *bē*. Il faut donc supposer que, dans les cas de concurrence entre les emplois avec et sans *bē*, la différence sémantique est si subtile qu'elle nous échappe. Peut-être même une différence qui avait existé anciennement s'était-elle déjà estompée et les rédacteurs employaient-ils les deux formes indifféremment : dans ce cas le morphème *bē*, dépourvu de signification, se trouvait libre pour une autre fonction, et ainsi s'expliquerait l'évolution ultérieure.

PIERRE LECOQ

LE DIALECTE D'ABU ZEYD ĀBĀD

Le petit village d'Abu Zeyd Ābād se trouve à une trentaine de kilomètres à l'est de Kāšān, relativement isolé dans le désert. Les habitants, environ trois mille, vivent essentiellement du tissage des tapis et de la culture des melons qu'ils font pousser dans des champs parfois assez éloignés du village. Le nom de celui-ci, dans le parler local, est *bīzōvōy* et les habitants s'appellent *bīzōvōyja*. Le dialecte, qui n'a pas de désignation locale particulière, fait partie du vaste ensemble des idiomes iraniens «centraux»[1], mais il présente surtout des affinités avec divers dialectes parlés à Kāšān, Qohrūd, Keše, Zefre[2], Natanz[3], Nāīn[4], Farīzand et Yāran[5], Sō[6], Meyme et Jowšaqān[7], Abyāne[8]. Tous ces dialectes présentent une unité certaine, au point que l'intercompréhension soit relativement aisée. Mais chacun d'eux a gardé des traits archaïques qui ne se retrouvent pas dans les autres. C'est pourquoi nous avons entrepris, dès 1972, une exploration systématique de toute cette région afin de rassembler des matériaux qui permettront de refaire l'histoire d'un groupe dialectal relativement bien délimité. Le présent article n'est toutefois qu'une faible partie des informations recueillies sur place : l'exposé grammatical n'est qu'un compte rendu préliminaire et le texte qui y fait suite a été choisi parmi une dizaine de récits enregistrés sur bandes magnétiques et transcrits avec l'aide des informateurs. Le résultat complet de ces recherches paraîtra ultérieurement[9].

[1] G. Morgenstierne, «Neu-iranische Sprachen», *Handbuch der Orientalistik*, I, IV, 1, Leiden-Köln, 1958, p. 170-172; G. Redard, «Other Iranian Languages», *Current Trends in Linguistics*, vol. 6, The Hague, 1970, p. 109-110. I. M. Oranskij, *Iranskie Jazyki*, Moskva, 1963, p. 154-158.

[2] V. A. Žukovskij, *Materialy dlja izučenija persidskix narečij*, I, Sanktpetersburg, 1888.

[3] O. Mann, *Kurdisch-persische Forschungen*, III, 1, bearb. K. Hadank, Berlin-Leipzig, 1926; A. Christensen. *Contributions à la dialectologie iranienne*, 1, Copenhague, 1930.

[4] O. Mann, *op. cit.*

[5] A. Christensen, *op. cit.*

[6] O. Mann, *op. cit.*; F. C. Andreas, *Iranische Dialektaufzeichnungen*, herausg. A. Christensen, Berlin, 1939.

[7] A. K. S. Lambton, *Three Persian Dialects*, London, 1938.

[8] P. Lecoq, «Le dialecte d'Abyāne», *Studia Iranica*, 1974, p. 51-63.

[9] Nous remercions vivement S. E. Shojaeddin Shafa, Vice-Ministre à la Cour

1. Le système phonologique comprend 39 phonèmes : 25 consonnes et 14 voyelles. Celles-ci, sauf deux, s'opposent en longues et brèves, les premières étant plus fermées que les brèves correspondantes :

	antérieures	intermédiaires	postérieures
fermées	*i* *ī*	*ü* *ǖ*	*u* *ū*
moyennes	*e* *ē*	*ö*	*o* *ō*
ouvertes	*a*	*ä*	*ā*

2. Les 25 phonèmes du système consonantique se répartissent comme suit :

	sourdes	sonores	nasales
bilabiales	*p*	*b*	*m*
labio-vélaire		*w*	
labio-dentales	*f*	*v*	
apicales	*t*	*d*	*n*
latérale		*l*	
vibrante		*r*	
sifflantes	*s*	*z*	
fricative palatale		*y*	
dorsales affriquées	*č*	*j*	
chuintantes	*š*	*ž*	
dorso-vélaires	*k*	*g*	
spirantes vélaires	*x*	*ğ*	
uvulaire	*q*		
glottales	*'*	*h*	

3. En position finale, la dorso-vélaire sonore /g/ tend vers une prononciation uvulaire [G], correspondant à la sourde /q/ :

  reg [rɛG] « veine »

4. Les occlusives sourdes /p/ et /t/ précédées de *s* ou de *š* ont une prononciation plus relâchée qui se rapproche des sonores correspondantes :

  espïda [ɛsbi:da] « blanc »
  büštō [büšdo:] « j'allai »

5. De nombreux phénomènes d'altération se produisent lorsque l'entourage phonétique est modifié. C'est particulièrement le cas dans

Impériale, dont l'aide précieuse et bienveillante a permis la réalisation de ces enquêtes linguistiques.

les formes verbales, où la voyelle des préfixes est instable, en raison du glissement de l'accent vers la syllabe finale.

Le passage de *ā* à *ō* est constant devant *w* :[10]

pā « pied » : *pōwe* « son pied »

hāmōgra « nous prîmes » : *hōwamgra* « je pris »

L'harmonie vocalique est responsable d'un grand nombre de ces altérations. Ainsi, la voyelle *a* s'harmonise fréquemment avec un *ō* de la syllabe suivante dans les préfixes verbaux : *bamka* « je fis » : *bomōka* « nous fîmes » ; *ošō* « je vais » < *ašō; *otō* « je viens » < *atō.

La même voyelle *a* > *e* devant *e*, *ē* ou *i* de la syllabe suivante : *akerē* « il fait » et *akeriyä* « vous faites » du thème *kar-* ; *ešē* « il va » < *ašē; *etē* « il vient » < *atē. De même pour les substantifs, avec le suffixe personnel *-e* : *xar* « âne » : *xere* « son âne »; *sar* « tête » : *sere* « sa tête ». D'autres cas d'altération vocalique ne sont pas abordés ici.

6. Un phénomène de sandhi remarquable est la réapparition d'un *-n* étymologique devant suffixe : *östöxō* « os » : *östöxōn-am* « mon os »; *ōsiōwō* « meunier » : *ōsiōwōn-a* « le meunier ». Le même phénomène a été constaté pour la désinence du pluriel, assez rare, en *-ō* : *valg* « feuille » : *valgō* « feuilles » : *valgōn-e* « ses feuilles ».

7. L'accent d'intensité est très faiblement marqué. C'est à peine si la syllabe finale des substantifs, l'article suffixé (cf. § 9) et la pénultième des formes d'adjectifs en *-a/-e* (cf. § 13) sont accentués.

C'est pourtant l'accent qui cause la chute des voyelles de la première syllabe des formes verbales (sauf celle des temps « narratifs » cf. § 28) et entraîne ainsi une assimilation de sonorité des consonnes mises en contact : des formes de débit lent comme *bösöt*, *baka*, *bäšä* deviennent en débit rapide [psöt], [pka], [pšä]. Seule la finale, c'est-à-dire la désinence des formes de plus de deux syllabes, a un timbre vocalique bien clair, au détriment des voyelles qui précèdent. On comprend mieux, dès lors, les flottements constatés dans certaines formes verbales en débit lent, lorsqu'on veut établir le timbre vocalique des préfixes. A l'opposé, les deux temps « narratifs » ont une initiale claire.

8. Le suffixe *-ē* (*-yē* après voyelle) donne une valeur d'indétermination au substantif. Cette valeur peut être renforcée par l'article indéfini *ī* : *pūr-ē* ou *ī pūr-ē* « un fils ».

---

[10] Le problème de l'hiatus et la manière dont il est évité sont provisoirement laissés de côté.

9. Pour déterminer un substantif, on emploie le suffixe -a (-ya après voyelle): šū-ya «le mari». On trouve ce suffixe en redondance avec l'adjectif démonstratif: nē šūya. Au cas oblique, -a devient -e.

La particule enclitique -ey, correspondant au persan ham, est d'un emploi extrêmement fréquent. Outre les valeurs habituelles du persan ham «aussi, même», cet enclitique s'emploie souvent comme un véritable article défini: xer-ey «l'âne en question» (pour l'harmonie vocalique, cf. § 5). Parfois aussi il est explétif, surtout en combinaison avec d'autres suffixes qui déterminent déjà le nom: bār-ey-e «sa charge».

10. Les substantifs sont soit masculins soit féminins, mais la distinction de genre ne se marque pas par des moyens morphologiques: c'est l'accord d'un adjectif ou d'une forme verbale avec un nom qui permet de décider du genre de ce dernier. Toutefois, les féminins ne se trouvent que pour les êtres animés. La seule exception qui ait été constatée pour les inanimés est le mot ōw «eau», traité comme un féminin.

La distinction de genre est parfois marquée par des oppositions lexicales:

pe «père»	möy «mère»
pūr «fils»	döt «fille»
espa «chien»	lāse «chienne»

Certains noms d'animaux dont le sexe n'est pas précisé sont toujours féminins: mōlji «chat», böz «chèvre», qālā «corbeau».

11. Le pluriel semble être une catégorie grammaticale en voie de disparition. Dans de nombreux cas, c'est la forme du singulier qui est préférée, surtout lorsque la notion de pluriel est explicitée par le contexte:

ma pōwam tar än «j'ai les pieds mouillés», p. من پاهايم خيس است

böz xodō šāxyō jäng akerän «les chèvres se battent avec leurs cornes», p. بزها با شاخهايشان جنك ميكنند

Lorsqu'on veut insister sur l'idée de pluriel, on emploie le mot pāk «tous» qui précède le substantif: pāk reg «veines»; pāk mū «cheveux».

Seuls les substantifs en -a ont bien conservé un pluriel morphologique en -e: lūwa «intestin», lūwe «intestins»; ce pluriel peut être renforcé: pāk lūwe.

On trouve plus rarement un pluriel en -ō (-ōn devant suffixe vocalique, cf. § 6). Les exemples constatés ne concernent pas seulement les êtres animés (cf. pluriel persan -ān) : *valg* «feuille», *valgō* «feuilles», *valgōn-e* «ses feuilles»; *pōwōn-e* «ses pieds».

12.   Le déterminant d'un nom, qu'il soit un nom ou un adjectif ou un pronom, se place directement après le déterminé sans l'intermédiaire d'une particule semblable à l'ezāfe persan : *rūj ayd* «jour de fête»; *das rāšta* «main droite»; *zōmād ma* «mon gendre».

Les substantifs en *-a* ont un traitement plus délicat. Qu'ils soient en position de déterminants, ou déterminés par un adjectif ou par un pronom, qu'ils soient employés avec une préposition ou avec une postposition, ils changent leur finale en *-e* :

körra «poulain»	*körre asp* «petit du cheval»
kara «beurre»	*kere tāza* «beurre frais»
kēya «maison»	*bar kēye* «porte de la maison»
	kēye ma «ma maison»
yörta «chambre»	*ta yörte* «plancher de la chambre»[11]
pänjara «fenêtre»	*var pänjere dä* «près de la femêtre»

Bien attestée, cette règle est parfois négligée par les informateurs jeunes, qui rectifient cependant sans hésitation lorsqu'ils sont sollicités.

13.   L'adjectif distingue le masculin, le féminin et le pluriel. Il possède en outre une forme neutre à désinence zéro lorsqu'il ne se rapporte à aucun déterminé :

	sg.	pl.
m.	*-a*	*-e*
f.	*-e*	*-e*
«neutre»	-∅	

L'accord se fait régulièrement, que l'adjectif soit déterminatif ou attribut. On remarquera en outre que la forme de l'adjectif permet de déterminer le nombre du substantif auquel il se rapporte (cf. § 11) :

na merda nača ha «cet homme est bon»
nön žänge nače ya «cette femme est bonne»
nönü nače yän «ils sont bons»
i merde xōša «un bel homme»
i žänge xōše «une belle femme»
nač a «c'est bien»
šōx a «c'est beau»

---

[11] Pour des raisons étymologiques, *ta* < **tah* n'appartient pas à la catégorie des substantifs en *-a*.

nön gis šōxe dārē « elle a de belles tresses »
šorōw espïda « vin blanc »
šorōw espïde « vins blancs »

14. L'adjectif possède un comparatif en *-tar* qui s'ajoute à la forme neutre, avec parfois des modifications dues à l'assimilation des phonèmes en contact : *görd-a* « grand », *görtar* < **görd-tar* « plus grand »; *vejïj-a* « petit », *vejïštar* < **vejïj-tar* « plus petit »; *nač-a* « bon », *naštar* < **nač-tar* « meilleur ».

Le superlatif en *-terïn* est d'un emploi assez limité.

15. On forme des adjectifs dérivés de substantifs à l'aide d'un suffixe *-ayna* ou *-ïna* :

čū « bois »   *čūw-ayna* « en bois »
mī « milieu »   *mïn-ayna* ou *mïn-ïna* [12] « du milieu »

16. Les démonstratifs, employés comme adjectifs ou comme pronoms, distinguent, au singulier seulement, entre le masculin et le féminin :

	« hic »			« ille »	
	sg.	pl.		sg.	pl.
m.	*nē*	*nömü*	m.	*na*	*nönü*
f.	*nēm*		f.	*nön*	

Suivis d'un enclitique, *nē* et *na* deviennent respectivement *nēm-* et *nam-*.

17. Les pronoms personnels indépendants sont utilisés en fonction de nominatif et d'accusatif, ou encore comme déterminants d'un nom pour marquer la possession. Il n'y a pas, au sg. 3 et pl. 3, de formes distinctes des démonstratifs.

	sg.	pl.
1	*ma*	*hama*
2	*te*	*šama*

Suivi d'un enclitique, *ma* devient *man-* (*men-* par harmonie vocalique, cf. § 5).

Les pronoms personnels enclitiques peuvent, comme en persan, marquer la possession, mais aussi indiquer l'agent des verbes transitifs aux temps du passé. Ils sont alors, soit intégrés à la forme verbale, soit suffixés à un mot qui précède cette forme verbale.

---

[12] Avec *n* étymologique (cf. § 6).

	sg.	pl.
1	-am	-mō
2	-a	-dō
3	-e	-yō

Après voyelle, les formes du sg. sont : 1 -*m*; 2 -*ya* ou -*d*; 3 -*we*.
On peut considérer une troisième série de pronoms personnels qui sont préfixés à l'imparfait des verbes transitifs et qui indiquent l'auteur de l'action. Ajoutés à d'autres formes verbales qui possèdent déjà des indices personnels, ils ont une valeur de datif ou d'accusatif (cf. § 45).

	sg.	pl.
1	*m-*	*mōn-*
2	*d-*	*dōn-*
3	*y-*	*yōn-*

18. Le pronom réfléchi se forme sur la base *xōw-* augmentée des pronoms personnels suffixes : *xōwam, xōwa, xōwe, xōwmōn, xōwdō, xōwyō*.

19. On pourra citer brièvement les autres pronoms, adjectifs-pronoms, adverbes et adverbes-prépositions :

— *ēta* « quelqu'un »; *čē, ečē* « quelque chose »; *ečē yā* « quelque part ».

— *bē, bi* « autre, différent »; *hebē* « autre; encore »; *čän* « quelques »; *čänd-ō-čünd* « environ, quelque »; *ō* « celui de, qui appartient à » (= persan *māl-e*); *pāk* « tous ».

— *kē* « qui ? »; *kī, kīyā* « où ? »; *kīyā dä* « d'où; comment ? »; *čērā, čēčērā, sana* « pourquoi ? »; *se, seni* « comment ? ».

— *än, ändä, änjēje* « ici »; *nidä, nijēje* « là ».

— *hemē, hemēša* « toujours »; *asle* « constamment »; *gāhē* « parfois », *ačārā* « jamais »; *heni* « encore ».

— *alōn, ha* « maintenant »; *ha ba ha* « désormais, à partir de maintenant »; *tā ba ha* « jusqu'à maintenant ».

— *irū* « aujourd'hui »; *ēša* « ce soir »; *harū* « chaque jour »; *heze* « hier »; *hezešow* « hier-soir »; *pere* « avant-hier »; *häyā* « demain »; *peryā* « après-demain »; *pešaryā* « après-après-demain »; *ēsāl* « cette année »; *pār* « l'année dernière ».

— *bē* « de, à partir de »; *bar, bērō* « dehors »; *pēš* « devant; avant »;

— *peš, pesar* « derrière; après »; *ta* « en-bas de »; *šēv, ši* « sous; en-dessous »; *xodō* « avec ».

— *ōhō* « oui »; *varāyā, varyā* « ensemble »

— *dä* « à » (préposition) ou « de » (postposition), s'emploie fréquemment avec d'autres prépositions.

20. Les principaux noms de nombres sont les suivants : 1 *ī*; 2 *dö*; 3 *se*; 4 *čār*; 5 *pay*; 6 *šöš*; 7 *haf*; 8 *haš*; 9 *nöh*; 10 *deh*; 11 *yāzze*; 12 *davāzze*; 13 *sīzze*; 14 *čārde*; 15 *pōnze*; 20 *vīs*; 50 *bänjā*; etc.

Sauf *avval* «premier», les ordinaux se forment avec le suffixe *-ma* (f. *-me*) : *dömma, semma, čārma*, etc.

21. La conjugaison des verbes comprend une voix active et une voix passive; trois modes : indicatif (présent, prétérit, imparfait, parfait, plus-que-parfait, futur, conditionnel[13] et deux temps «narratifs»: prétérit et imparfait), subjonctif (présent) et impératif (présent et futur) : un substantif verbal (infinitif «long»), un infinitif «court» et un participe passé.

22. La formation des diverses conjugaisons s'opère par trois procédés : aspect du thème; préfixes temporels et modaux; pronoms personnels suffixés, infixés ou préfixés.

Partout se manifeste l'opposition des transitifs et des intransitifs aux temps du passé.

1) *Forme du thème.*

Chaque verbe possède deux thèmes différents d'où sont dérivés tous les temps :

thème I : indicatif présent, subjonctif présent, impératif présent et futur, passif, temps «narratifs»;

thème II: prétérit, imparfait, infinitifs, participe, parfait, plus-que-parfait.

2) *Préfixes*

Ponctuel *ba-* (non accentué) : prétérit, parfait, plus-que-parfait;

ba- (accentué) : prétérit narratif;

ba-/be- (non accentué) : subjonctif, impératif.

Duratif *a-* (non accentué) : présent, imparfait;

a- (accentué) : imparfait narratif.

3) *Indices personnels*

Il n'existe qu'une seule série de désinences que l'on trouve à l'indicatif présent et au subjonctif (transitifs et intransitifs); au passif (transitifs); au prétérit et à l'imparfait des intransitifs[14].

---

[13] Appelé ainsi, par commodité, en raison de son sens. La formation n'en fait pas un mode distinct de l'indicatif.

[14] Sg. 3 présente ici une forme apocopée.

	sg.	pl.
1	-ō	-ēm[15]
2	-ē	-iyä
3	-ē	-än

Les autres temps utilisent les pronoms personnels suffixés, infixés ou préfixés[16].

23. Le verbe « être » est conjugué sur deux thèmes : présent *h-* et prétérit *böd-* ; les formes enclitiques sont identiques aux désinences du §22, 3, (sauf le sg. 3) et après voyelle, l'hiatus est évité par l'insertion d'un *-y-*.

	présent[17]	négatif	enclitique	passé	subjonctif	impératif
sg. 1	*hō*	*nohō*	*ō*	*bödō*	*bō*	
2	*hē*	*nehē*	*ē*	*bödē*	*bē*	*bē*
3 m.	*ha*	*naha*	*a*	*bā*	*bē*	
f.	*hasä*[18]			*bädä*		
pl. 1	*hēm*	*nehēm*	*ēm*	*bödēm*	*bēm*	
2	*hiyä*	*nehiyä*	*iyä*	*bödiyä*	*biyä*	*biyä*
3	*hän*	*nehän*	*än*	*bödän*	*bän*	

Le verbe « devenir » est, comme le verbe « être », basé sur un thème *b-/böd-*, mais avec le préfixe ponctuel aux temps du passé.

	prétérit	parfait	présent	subjonctif	impératif
sg. 1	*bäbödō*	*bäböda yō*	*obō*	*bobō*	
2	*bäbödē*	*bäböda yē*	*ebē*	*bebē*	*bäbā*
3 m.	*bābā*	*bäböda*	*ebē*	*bebē*	
f.	*bäbödä*	*bäböde ya*			
1	*bäbödēm*	*bäböde yēm*	*ebēm*	*bebēm*	
2	*bäbödiyä*	*bäböde yiyä*	*ebiyä*	*bebiyä*	*bebiyä*
3	*bäbödän*	*bäböde yän*	*ebän*	*bebän*	

24. *Verbes transitifs*

Le prétérit se forme avec le préfixe *ba-* + pronoms personnels infixés + thème II : (verbe *ka* « faire ») sg. 1 *ba-m-ka* ; (verbe *gra* « prendre ») sg. 1 *ba-m-gra*.

---

[15] Peut être renforcée en *-ēmä*.

[16] Au sg. 2, l'indice personnel *-a-* se fond avec la voyelle du préfixe *ba-*, si bien que cet indice se ramène au morphème zéro.

[17] Les formes du présent peuvent être remforcées par *-ä* (après consonne) et *-nä* (après voyelle).

[18] Assez rare, cette forme peut toujours être remplacée par le m.

Le parfait se forme de la même manière, mais avec le participe passé (cf. § 26) : sg. 1 *ba-m-karda*; *ba-m-grata*. Le plus-que-parfait est identique au parfait suivi du verbe « être », sg. 3 du passé, à toutes les personnes : sg. 1 *ba-m-karda bā*; *ba-m-grata bā*.

A l'imparfait, les indices personnels précèdent le préfixe duratif *a-* : sg. 1 *m-a-ka*; *m-a-gra*.

A côté des formes régulières du prétérit, certains verbes forment le sg. 3 et le pl. 3 sans préfixe *ba-* et avec l'indice personnel suffixé : *bedīd* ou *dīde* « il vit »; *boyōdīd* ou *dīdyō* « ils virent ».

25. *Verbes intransitifs*

Le prétérit se forme avec le préfixe *bā* + thème II + désinences : (verbe *kat* « tomber ») sg. 1 *ba-kat-ō*.

L'imparfait a le préfixe duratif *a-* : sg. 1 *a-kat-ō*.

Le parfait est constitué par le participe passé précédé de *ba-* et suivi du verbe « être » enclitique : sg. 1 *ba-kata yō*. De même le plus-que-parfait où le verbe « être » est au passé : sg. 1 *ba-kata bödō*.

On remarquera dans les paradigmes (voir infra) la distinction de genre au sg. 3 du prétérit et de l'imparfait, ainsi que les variations en genre et en nombre du participe dans les temps composés.

26. Le participe est l'ancienne formation en *-t*, avec la finale *-a* propre aux adjectifs (cf. § 13). Cette terminaison *-ta* ne se maintient qu'après une sourde et devient *-da* après sonore ou simplement *-a* après dentale (simplification de la géminée)[19]. Comme l'adjectif, le participe varie en genre et en nombre : verbe « tomber », m. *kata*, f. *kate*, pl. *kate*.

Parfois, un *r* final a disparu du thème du prétérit et reparaît au participe : *ka* « faire » : *karda* « fait »; *ba* « porter » : *barda* « porté ».

Le verbe « aller » a un deuxième participe *šeda* utilisé seulement en composition.

27. On sait que l'infinitif est souvent difficile à obtenir dans de nombreux dialectes, quand il n'est pas un simple calque de l'infinitif persan. Assez curieusement, les formes recueillies dans le dialecte d'Abu Zeyd Ābād se confondent morphologiquement avec le parfait sg. 2 : *bakarda* « faire », *bagrata* « prendre ». Il s'agit pourtant bien d'un véritable substantif verbal déclinable : *baxmarde ī guhūz* شکستن ; يک گردو *bönōwe ka baxarda* « il se mit à manger ».

---

[19] Après voyelle on trouve *-ta* ou *-da*.

28. La formation du présent, et des temps qui en sont dérivés (thème I), est la même pour les transitifs et les intransitifs. Au présent : préfixe duratif *a-* + thème I + désinences : *a-kor-ō* « je fais »; au subjonctif, le préfixe est *ba-* : *bo-kor-ō* « que je fasse ». On pourra voir dans les paradigmes l'importance de l'harmonie vocalique dans toutes ces formes verbales.

L'impératif présente souvent des formes apocopées au sg. 2.

C'est également le thème du présent qui a servi à former deux temps « narratifs », ainsi appelés parce qu'ils se rencontrent essentiellement dans les récits [20], en remplacement du prétérit et de l'imparfait de l'indicatif. Le prétérit narratif a le préfixe *ba-* et l'imparfait narratif le préfixe *a-*. L'accentuation de ces préfixes est ici capitale, car elle a empêché tout phénomène d'harmonie vocalique qui aurait confondu ces formes avec, respectivement, le subjonctif et le présent de l'indicatif. Exemples pour le verbe « aller » :

prét. indic.	*büštō*	imparf. indic.	*üštō*
subj. pérs.	*bošō*	prés. indic.	*ošō*
prét. narr.	*bašō*	imparf. narr.	*ašō*

29. Le futur et le conditionnel sont des formes périphrastiques formées avec un auxiliaire *kam-* (*kom-* et *kem-* par harmonie vocalique). Au futur, l'auxiliaire conjugué comme un présent [21] est suivi de l'infinitif court (= thème II) : *komō ka* « je ferai », *kemē ka* « tu feras ». Au conditionnel, les transitifs ont *komō(n)-* + suffixes personnels + infinitif court : *komōn-am ka* « je ferais, j'aurais fait », *komōn-a ka* « tu ferais, tu aurais fait »; les intransitifs utilisent *komō(n)* suivi d'un temps du passé : *komō bödō* « je serais, j'aurais été ».

30. L'impératif futur se forme sur le thème du présent avec les désinences sg. 2 *-ā* et pl. 2 *-iyā*. Son emploi est assez restreint et il ne se rencontre pratiquement que dans les interdictions de portée générale :

	impér. prés.	impér. fut.	
sg. 2	*dam na dä*	*dam na dā*	« ne parle pas »
pl. 2	*dam na diyä*	*dam na diyā*	« ne parlez pas »

---

[20] Ces deux temps ne se rencontrent en fait que pour les verbes intransitifs les plus courants.

[21] Mais sg. 1 *komōn* devant voyelle (cf. § 6) : *komōn ama* « je viendrai » et pl. 2 toujours *-ēd*.

31. Le passif se forme sur le thème du présent avec un formant *-iv-*
pour le prétérit et le participe (et par conséquent les temps composés)
et avec le formant *-i(y)-* pour le présent et l'imparfait. La formation
de tous les temps est conforme aux principes énoncés plus haut,
mais on constatera ici que l'imparfait et le futur rentrent dans le
système du présent :

prét.	*bakarivō*	prés.	*akariyō*
parf.	*bakariva yō*	imparf.	*makariyō*
pl. q. pf.	*bakariva bödō*	fut.	*komō kariyō*

32.   « faire »

		prét.	imparf.	parf.	pl. q. p.
sg.	1	*bamka*	*maka*	*bamkarda*	*bamkarda bā*
	2	*baka*	*daka*	*bakarda*	*bakarda bā*
	3	*beka*	*yaka*	*bekarda*	*bekarda bā*
pl.	1	*bomōka*	*mōnaka*	*bomōkarda*	*bomōkarda bā*
	2	*bodōka*	*dōnaka*	*bodōkarda*	*bodōkarda bā*
	3	*boyōka*	*yōnaka*	*boyōkarda*	*boyōkarda bā*

		prés.	subj.	impér.	fut.
sg.	1	*akorō*[22]	*bokorō*		*komō ka*
	2	*akerē*	*bekerē*	*bekä*	*kemē ka*
	3	*akerē*	*bekerē*		*kemē ka*
pl.	1	*akerēm*	*bekerēm*		*kemēm ka*
	2	*akeriyä*	*bekeriyä*	*bekeriyä*	*kemēd ka*
	3	*akerän*	*bekerän*		*kemän ka*

33.   « tomber »

		prét.	imparf.	parf.		pl. q. p.	
				m.	f.	m.	f.
sg.	1	*bakatō*	*akatō*	*bakata yō*	*-te yō*	*bakata bödō*	*-te b.*
	2	*bakatē*	*akatē*	*bakata yē*	*-te yē*	*bakata bödē*	*-te b.*
	3 m.	*bakat*	*akat*	*bakata*		*bakata bā*	
	f.	*bakatä*	*akatä*	*bakate ya*		*bakate bā*	
pl.	1	*bakatēm*	*akatēm*	*bakate yēm*		*bakate bödēm*	
	2	*bakatiyä*	*akatiyä*	*bakate yiyä*		*bakate bödiyä*	
	3	*bakatän*	*akatän*	*bakate yän*		*bakate bödän*	

[22] Ou *äkorō*, etc. (cf. §7).

	prés.	subj.	impér.	prét. narr.	imparf. narr.
sg. 1	okō	bokō		bakō	akō
2	ekē	bekē	beke	bakē	akē
3	ekē	bekē		bakē	akē
pl. 1	ekēm	bekēm		bakēm	akēm
2	ekiyä	bekiyä	bekiyä	bakiyä	akiyä
3	ekän	bekän		bakän	akän

34. Les verbes « aller » et « venir » offrent quelques particularités de
détail, comme le montrent les paradigmes suivants :

« aller »

	prét.	imparf.	prés.	subj.	impér.	prét. n.	imparf. n.
sg. 1	büštō	üštō	ošō	bošō		bašō	ašō
2	büštē	üštē	ešē	bešē	bešä	bašē	ašē
3 m.	bäšā	äšā	ešē	bešē		bašē	ašē
f.	büštä	üštä					
pl. 1	büštēm	üštēm	ešēm	bešēm		bašēm	ašēm
2	büštiyä	üštiyä	ešiyä	bešiyä	bešiyä	bašiyä	ašiyä
3	büštän	üštän	ešän	bešän		bašän	ašän

	parf.		pl. q. p.	
	m.	f.	m.	f.
sg. 1	büšta yō	büšte yō	büšta bödō	büšte bödō
2	büšta yē	büšte yē	etc.	
3	büšta	büšte ya		
pl. 1		büšte yēm	fut.	
2		büšte yiyä	komō šä	
3		büšte yän		

35.   « venir »

	prét.	imparf.	prés.	subj.	impér.	prét. n.	ipf. n.
sg. 1	bamdō	atamdō	otō	begō		batō	atō
2	bamdē	atamdē	etē	begē	burä	batē	atē
3 m.	bama	atama	etē	begē		batē	atē
f.	bam(ö)dä	atamdä					
pl. 1	bamdēm	atamdēm	etēm	begēm		batēm	atēm
2	bamdiyä	atamdiyä	etiyä	begiyä	buriyä	batiyä	atiyä
3	bamdän	atamdän	etän	begän		batän	atän

	parf.		pl.q.p.	
	m.	f.	m.	f.
sg. 1	bamda yō	bamde yō	bamda bödō	bamde bödō
	etc.		etc.	

L'infixe -t- de l'imparfait n'a aucune signification particulière; la forme *amdō* est infiniment plus rare. Cet infixe ne se retrouve que dans le présent *atārō*, du verbe *var* «apporter».

36. Principaux verbes transitifs (l'astérisque indique les thèmes du présent soumis à l'harmonie vocalique) :

	prét. (sg. 1)	participe	infinitif	th. de prés
faire	bamka	karda	ka	*kar-
prendre	bamgra	grata	gra	gēr-
apporter	bamvar	varda	var	atār-
amener	bamvūnīd	vūnīda	vūnīd	vōn-
emporter	bamba	barda	ba	*bar-
dire	bamvā	vāta	vā	vāj-
voir	bamdīd	dīda	dīd	vīn-
frapper	bamves	vesta	ves	vēs-
heurter	bamžat	žata	žat	žen-
trouver	bamyöš	yöšta	yöš	yūz-
manger	bamxa	xarda	xa	xor-
acheter	bamrīd	rīda	rīd	rēn-
appeler	bamxan	xanda	xan	xōn-
coudre	bamdaš	dašta	daš	derz-
traire	bamdöt	döta	döt	dūš-
verser	bamrēt	rēta	rēt	rēj-
fabriquer	bamsāt	sāta	sāt	sāj-
briser	bamxmar	xmarda	xmar	xmar-
laver	bamšöš	šöšta	šöš	šūr-
vendre	bamrūt	rūta	rūt	rūš-

37. Principaux verbes intransitifs :

	prét. (sg. 3) m.	f.	part.	inf.	th. de prés.
aller	bäšā	büštä	büšta	šā	š-
venir	bama	bamdä	bamda	ama	t-
tomber	bakat	bakatä	kata	kat	k-
dormir	baxāt	baxātä	xāta	xāt	xās-
courir	batat	batatä	tata	tat	tej-
brûler	bösöt	bösötä	söta	söt	sūj-
mourir	bamar	bamardä	marda	mar	mēr-
s'asseoir	češ	češtä	česta	češ	čin-

38. Certains verbes intransitifs forment le thème du prétérit (et donc celui de l'imparfait) en ajoutant un suffixe -*ov*- au th. du prés., mais le sg. 3 remplace ce suffixe par -*ā* et coïncide ainsi avec l'infinitif court. Le participe est en -*owa* (Pour le préverbe *hā*, *hōw*, cf. §43).

	prét.		part.	prés.
	sg. 1	sg. 3		
être debout	*hōweštovō*	*hōweštā*	*eštowa*	*hōwayeštō*
revenir	*hāgelovō*	*hāgelā*	*gelowa*	*hōwagelō*
craindre	*batarsovō*	*batarsā*	*tarsowa*	*atarsō*
atteindre	*barasovō*	*barasā*	*rasowa*	*arasō*
pleurer	*bäbörömovō*	*bäbörömā*	*börömowa*	*öbörömō*

39. Certains verbes transitifs, correspondant aux verbes intransitifs précédents, forment le prétérit (et donc l'imparfait) en ajoutant -*ā* au thème du présent. Le participe est aussi en -*owa*

	prét. (sg. 1)	part.	th. de prés.
donner	*bamdā*	*dowa*	*d-*
jeter	*bamparnā*	*parnowa*	*parn-*
envoyer	*bamkīnā*	*kīnowa*	*kīn-*
tirer	*bamkešā*	*kešowa*	*keš-*
mettre	*bamnā*	*nowa*	*n-*

40. Trois verbes défectifs ont un présent et un passé avec sens résultatif, comme le parfait grec. Les désinences sont celles des intransitifs. Ils peuvent se traduire par « se trouver », avec les nuances respectives de « après être tombé », « assis », « debout ».

		« être tombé »	« être assis »		« être debout »	
		prés.	passé	prés.	passé	prés.	passé
sg. 1	*velō*	*ävō*	*avadō*	*eštō*	*eštovō*
2	*velē*	*evē*	*avadē*	*eštē*	*eštovē*
3	*velē*	*evē*	m. *avad*	*eštē*	*eštā*
	etc.	etc.	f. *avadä*	etc.	etc.

41. Deux verbes échappent aux règles de formations décrites jusque ici. Au prétérit, *dard*- « avoir » et *zōnā*- « savoir » n'ont pas de préfixe *ba*- et la personne est indiquée par les pronoms suffixés. En outre, le verbe « avoir » a une forme de passé *da* avec pronoms personnels suffixés au mot qui précède : -*m da* « j'avais », -*a da* « tu avais », -*e da* « il avait »; le présent n'a pas de préfixe et le subjonctif combine le thème du présent avec des formes du verbe « devenir ». Pour le

verbe « savoir », l'imparfait est reformé sur le thème du prétérit avec
préfixe *a-*; le présent est régulier mais le subjonctif est formé comme
pour le verbe « avoir ».

		prét.	prés.	subj.	infin.
« avoir »	sg. 1	*dardam*	*dārō*	*dārobō*	*da*
	2	*darda*	*dārē*	*dārebē*	
	3	*darde*	*dārē*	*dārebē*	
		etc.			
« savoir »	sg. 1	*zōnōwam*	*ozōnō*	*zōnobō*	*zōnā*
	2	*zōnōwa*	*ozōnē*	*zōnebē*	
	3	*zōnōwe*		etc.	
	pl. 1	*zōnāmō*			
		etc.			

42.   Les causatifs se forment sur le thème du présent d'un verbe
simple, auquel s'ajoute le suffixe *-ōn*. Les causatifs se rattachent à
la classe de verbes du § 39.

verbe simple	caus. prét.	prés.	
	(sg. 1)	(sg. 1)	
pač- « cuire »	*bampočōnā*	*opočōnō*	« faire cuire »
pūš- « revêtir »	*bampūšōnā*	*apūšōnō*	« habiller qn. »
tars- « craindre »	*bamtarsōnā*	*atarsōnō*	« effrayer »
ras- « arriver »	*bamrasōnā*	*arasōnō*	« faire arriver »

43.   De nombreux verbes ne s'emploient qu'avec préverbes, ce qui a
contribué à l'affaiblissement sémantique de ceux-ci. Dans la conjugaison,
le préfixe *ba-* disparaît. Au futur, l'auxiliaire *komō* se place entre
le préverbe et le verbe. Les principaux préverbes sont les suivants :
    1. *hā* (*hōw-* devant voyelle, cf. § 5), de loin le plus fréquent et le
moins signifiant. Dans les verbes surcomposés (cf. § 44), il se réduit
à *ā* suffixé au mot précédant le verbe.

	sg. 1 :	prét.	prés.	subj.
« prendre »		*hōwamgra*	*hōwagērō*	*hāgērō*
« donner »		*hōwamdā*	*hōwadō*	*hādō*
« être debout »		*hōweštovō*	*hōwayeštō*	*hōweštō*
« revenir »		*hāgelovō*	*hōwagelō*	*hāgelō*
« dormir »		*hāxātō*	*hōwaxāsō*	*hāxāsō*
« mettre »		*hōwamnā*	*hōwanō*	*hānō*
« s'asseoir »		*hāčeštō*	*hōwačīnō*	*hāčīnō*

2. *pē* « à, vers », souvent combiné avec un pronom suffixe, ou même sans ce pronom, indique que l'action est dirigée vers quelqu'un. Ainsi : *pēy-avā* « il (lui) dit », *pē-yavā* « il lui disait », *pēy-e vā* « dis-lui ».

sg. 1 :	prét.	prés.	subj.
« dire à »	*pēyamvā*	*pēyavājō*	*pēvājō*
« frapper qn. »	*pēyamves*	*pēyavēsō*	*pēvēsō*
« se tourner vers »	*pēyamka*	*pēyakorō*	*pēkorō*

3. *dar* « dans, à, sur »

sg. 1 :	prét.	prés.	subj.
« tomber »	*dar katō*	*dar akō*	*dar kō*
« attacher »	*daram bas*	*dar abändō*	*dar bändō*

4. *ārē* : mouvement vers le bas.

sg. 1 :	prét.	prés.	subj.
« jeter »	*ārēyam vän*	*ārēyavänō*	*ārē vänō*

5. *ār* : mouvement vers le haut.

sg. 1 :	prét.	prés.	subj.
« enlever »	*āram gra*	*ār agērō*	*ār gērō*
« sauter »	*ār derezovō*	*ār aderezō*	*ār derezō*

44.   Il existe aussi des verbes qui forment une unité sémantique avec un substantif, un adjectif, etc. Comme pour les verbes précédents, le préfixe *ba-* disparaît. Cette catégorie de verbes peut également être employée avec un préverbe ; *hā* se réduit à *ā* (*ōw-* devant voyelle).

sg. 1 :	prét.	prés.	subj.
« obtenir »	*gēram vūnīd*	*gēr avōnō*	*gēr vōnō*
« commencer à »	*bönōwam ka*	*bönōwakorō*	*bänā korō*
« ouvrir »	*dāǧam nā*	*dāǧ anō*	*dāǧ nō*
« nettoyer »	*pākōwam ka*	*pākōwakorō*	*pākā korō*
« demander »	*sārāǧam ār gra*	*sārāǧ ār agērō*	*sārāǧ ār gērō*

45.   On rencontre souvent les pronoms préfixés à des formes verbales déjà pourvues d'indices personnels. Ces pronoms supplémentaires ont alors une valeur de datif ou d'accusatif. Leur emploi, théoriquement possible à toutes les personnes, est en fait limité par l'usage, par les possibilités phonétiques ou par le sens.

Ainsi, avec *atama* « il venait » et *atē* « id. » (imparf. narr.), on peut former les paradigmes suivants :

matama	*matē*	venait à moi
datama	*datē*	venait à toi
yatama	*yatē*	venait à lui
mōnatama	*mōnatē*	venait à nous
dōnatama	*dōnatē*	venait à vous
yōnatama	*yōnatē*	venait à eux

46.   La syntaxe est, en gros, celle du persan. Elle en diffère cependant
sur un point important : la construction « ergative » des verbes transitifs
aux temps du passé. L'accord du verbe, en genre et en nombre,
se fait régulièrement avec le substantif sur lequel porte l'action et qui
est ainsi considéré comme le sujet grammatical. Exemples :

　　gāyō hā döte « ils (*-yō*) ont trait (f. sg.) la vache (f.) »
　　gōwe hā döte « il (*-e*) a trait (f. sg.) la vache (f.) ».
　　i kūftāram gēr vūnīde « j' (*-am*) ai attrapé (f. sg.) un ramier (f.) ».

Parfois, lorsque l'objet est un pluriel, le verbe transitif prend les
désinences des verbes intransitifs :

　　dö espe... āre gratän, bevūnīdän « il (*-e*) prit (pl.), amena (pl.)
les deux chiens ».

Texte

1) ī žänge bädä. nēn xēli dä šǖye vad yatama. ettefāqan nē šǖye
ačarā kēya dä bar näšā, tā nē ke ī rūj dä nē šǖya yavā ke « čāǧ a,
te bešä ōsiōw, ārt nadārēmä ». — 2) pēyavā « xēli xop ». nē xere bār
ka vō dä xar yavā « bešä ōsiōw mīnīne, masalan dä ōsiōwōna vā :
« fälān kas yavā : nē bār bahar. ō dö bāra kä vō burä ». — 3) xerey ke
ma'mūlan čē sere hā nabē, bäšā. ī nafar nē xere bagra vō bāreye
zemīne nā vō dö rū se rū bekešä vō nē xar nama. — 4) žänge dīde bāzam
nē bar našē. pēyavā ke « čerā našē, čö jǖrē, bābā, čēčērā nüštē
ōsiōw fälān ». pēyavā « xaram bekīnowa, möntāhā namda heni ».
— 5) pēyavā « xēli xop. ha dö bāra ošō särāǧe ». pā bā, bäšā vō bäšā var
ōsiōwōne. pēyavā : « nē xar ma bamkīnā änjēje dä bār baharē. čēčērā
bāre nahar, begē ». — 6) ōsiōwōna befamīd ke nē čē sere hā nabē.
pēyavā : « ohō, ohō, vīram hā šeda, ēša hā xās änjēje dä, āxar ševa
bāra harō, pā bē, bešä ». säbā vāje pē ka, pēyavā : « xara bāre bāreyam
ka, bäšā, pā bē, pēye ras ». — 7) na ke nē rū ōsiōw dä hā xāta bā, sar
ō kallaye ārti bäböda bā vō masalan ōsiōw mīnayne dä bama merzowa
nōǧa. — 8) säbā zū bäböda bā, bama dam jū dä, das ō dǖme bušūrē. dīde
ōsiōwōna ha. yavā « e, nē aveze nē ke vāj dä ma kerē, vāje dä xōwe karda.

ma ke ma nohō». — 9) dö bāra hā gelā, bäšā nījēje. pēyavā : «merde hösöbi, te avezē nē ke vāj dä ma kerē, vāja dä xōwa karda». pēyavā : «ohō, ma eštebōwam karda. — 10) te čēčē kä, bešä, hā xās änjēje dä, säbā vāj dä te akorō, bešä». säbā vāje pē ka vō nē pā bā, bama kēya vō dä žäne yavā ke : «xar bama änjēje». — 11) žäne pēyavā «bābā, xar kēyā dä atē, te čēčērā nänja čē sara hā nabē. xar ke hā rōwa ka, pey kāre ašē. yagērē, bāre zemīn anē fälān». 12) nē jeriyān ändä tämōm bābā. nēm dīde hebē ečē jūri ya herīf nē merde nabē bere kerē. — 13) ī rūj büštä kēye hamsōwe, pēyavā «hama nē če bekerēm ke ečē jūri ya bar našē ändä». pēyavā «bešä, pēye vā : bešä espohō dä, ī dēg hā gērē, begē». pēyavā «xēli xop». — 14) bamdä kēya, pēyavā ke «bešä espohō dä, hama dēg nadārēm, ī dēg hā gē, burä». nē bäšä espohō dä, zarfe čän rū, az nē ke yagā zū hā gelē, nē dēge hā gra vō bama, — 15) dīde masalan nēm žänge yagā ī mā bekešē. bäšä, dö rūa dä bama. büštä var hamsōwe. pēyavā «nē dö rū bekešä, bäšä, bama dö bāra, hebē čē bokorō» — 16) pēyavā «särāğe pē ār gē. pēye vā : namak nē dēga särāğ ār grata baynē čänja namaki ya? ägar särāğa ār nagrata, hā gel dö bāra, nemeke särāğe pē ār gē, čōn dēgē ke ādam nemeke nozōnē be čänja ha, ba dard naxorē». — 17) bamdä kēya, pēyavā ke «nē dēg nemeke ke särāğa ār nagrata, dēgē ke ādam nemeke nozōnē bē čänja ha, ba dardē naxorē». nē dö bāra hā gelā, bäšä espohō, — 18) bäšä var merde, pēyavā «merde hösöbi, te dēg hōwadē, navājē čänja namaki abē». pēyavā «hō hō, vīram hā šeda bā, nemeke alōn pēd avājō». — 19) pēyavā «bavā». pēyavā «na kam na zeyād, ī möš, ī möšt ō nīm, nänja namak nē dēg a». nēmey tarsē nē ke vīre hā šē, hey yavā vō atama «na kam na zeyād, ī möš, ī möšt ō nīm». — 20) bama tā ī yāē dä, xarmäyō baharda bā. na rūjē bā ke pākā yōnaka vō nömühō. nē hey yavā «na kam na zeyād, ī möš ī möšt ō nīm». — 21) nēm ke xarmäyō baharda bā, xēli nārāhat hā bödän, böyōgra, ī fasl dereyō mōlīd. pēyōnavā «nē čē gafē te ekešē». — 22) pēyavā «pas čēčē bavājō». pēyavā «har yā ešē, bayvā : ī dūna hazār dūna bebē, nay vā ī möš ī möšt ō nīm, nē edbār a». pēyavā «xēli xop, dä ma nomōliyä, ma nam avājō». — 23) rā kat dö bārayey darde atama, yavā «ī dūna hazār dūna bebän». bama tā ī golē dä, dīde ī bamarda vō kūlyō grata vō dömmālaye zōri vō börōma akerän atän, — 24) nē kalama yavā «ī dūna hazār dūna bebän, ī dūna hazār bebän». azādāre bamdän ō dä jūne katän, bänāyō ka dereye mōlīda. — 25) pēyōnavā «pe bösöta, hama īyēye bamarda, nänja azādār ēm ō nārāhat ēm, te avājē hazāre bemērän». pēyavā «pas čö jūrē bävājō». — 26) pēyavā «har yā ke ešē, bavā ke «xodāvand rahmat akerē, fāteha böxōniyä, merde načeyē bā»». yavā «xēli xop». nē äšā vō har yā arasā, yavā «fāteha böxōniyä, xodāvand rahmat akerē, merde načeyē bā». — 27) bäšā ī gūša dä, ōrūsi bā, bäzän ō bekūbä bā, sörnā vō dād döhöl ō nēmey hamē nē kalama yavā «fāteha böxōniyä, xodāvand rahmat akerē, merde načeyē bā». — 28) āğā, ändey dä boyōgra, ī fasl dereyō mōlīd. pēyavā «pas ma čö korō, āxar raftār ma, čö jūri yay bā». pēyōnavā «har yā ke ešē, kölōwa hāvā ves, baraxs, šabā bekä, līli bekä, šōdi bekä». — 29) pēyavā «xēli xop». nē rā kat ō bönōwe ka kölōwe hāvā vesta vō baraxsowa vō ser-e-sodā bar varda. ettefāqan dä ī golē barasā, ke ī sayyād a, kemī češta bā. — 30) masalan ī farzē kä ke mosammā yā ī qālā, kūftar, masalan bäbāğovē ha āmāda bäböda bā, ke kemī dä avad, ke pēyevēsē, ke kölōwe hāvōwe ves ō bänōwe ka ār derezowa vō līli bakarda vō šabā bakarda. — 31) nēm beveretä vō pā bädä, büštä. āğā, bama, nē kữn qöndāq tafange bekešā vō dä jūne bönōwe ka pēye vesta. pēyavā ke «nē raftār ādam neyay bā, ma säbā ta nänja zahmatam bekešowa tā ī mosammōwam gēr vūnīde yā ī kūftaram gēr vūnīde. — 32) te ha dārē kölōwa hāvōw avēsē». pēyavā «pas čö korō». pēyavā «har yā ke ešē, döllā bešä, rū jū-vō-jar bē bešä, peš kal ō kulū bē bešä, kallad hey ār dā vō ta dā». na yavā «xēli xop». — 33) bönōwe ka rū jū bē büšta, kallaye hey bālā vō ta barda. ettefāqan ī golē dä, ī qāfala ārē vända bā vō bāre šekasseni bā. čōn nē hey döllā vō rāšt dowa bā, qāfala reme ka, vō pā bā, färāre ka vō nē šekasseni pāke xūrdā bā. — 34) reyīs qāfele vō qāfeledāre bamdän ō dä jūne katān, ī fasle ändä dereyō mōlīd. nē vossā löse baxarda bā, esme xōwe vīre hā šeda bā. — 35) xolāsa bama bar kēye nēsfe šev ō bere bežat. žäne bā nē ke ozōnowe ya nam a, čōn dä nē xoše natama, yagā bar dä bē. pēyavā «burä, bar dāğ nä». — 36) pēyavā «te kē yē». esme vīre hā šeda bā. pēyavā «ma šữd ō». pēyavā «ägar šữ men ē, esma bavā». pēyavā «ma šữya yō, burä peš bar». pēyavā «ägar šữ ma komō bödē, esma komōna zōnā. — 37) šữ ma büšta espohō dä, namak dēg särāğ ār gērē, qarār naha begē». har čē eltēmāsē baka, nēm bere dāğ nanā, tā nē ke nāčārän bama, — 38) bäšā rū masjede, hā xāt nīdä. čē nabā dä šīv sere, nē qorōne dä šīv sere nā, hā xāt. ettefāqan ī neza-ādā mad āğā ke masjedi bā, bama säbā vō dīde ī nafar dữm qorō dä xāta. — 39) vāje pē ka vō ī möš jänge pē ka vō fālān. pēyavā «ādam, ī varaq kāğazey avīnē, dä rū kal anē, xōne kal anē». pēyavā «xēli xop, ma ha baha nē kār äkorō». — 40) mem bad bama vō rū kữče dä ettefāqan dīde ī

teke kāğaz velē. az nē ke na bevāta bā dä xōne kal yay nā, bama.
har yā begelā, ī xōneye nayöš, ke dä rū nē xōne nē. — 41) bama rū
garmuwe vō ettefāqan dallāke salmūni ya ke sar atarāšē vō ma'mūlan
rīš atarāšē, döllā peš eštā. nē fekre baka ke «čāğ a, dä lev hazāre
nē nēm», — 42) čōn xōneye gēr namda bā, tā bäšā dä lev hazāre nē nē.
dallāka dar gelā vō pēyavā «yār qoli, čērā nē jūr akerē» vō nē esme
xōwe vīre yama vō bönōwe ka batata vō «vīr mama, vīr mama».
— 43) bama bar kēye, pēyavā «burä, bar dāğ nä, ma šǖya yō, vō
yār qoli esmem a». žänge bamdä, bere dāğ nā. dar hālē ke nē
šǖve ke sālam büšta bā, leh-ō-lah varda vō darb-ō-dāğō bamda bā.

Traduction

1) Il y avait une femme. Son mari lui déplaisait beaucoup. Il se fait
que son mari ne sortait jamais de la maison, jusqu'à ce que un jour,
elle dit à ce mari : «C'est bien, va au moulin, nous n'avons pas de
farine». — 2) «Très bien» dit-il. Il chargea son âne et lui dit :
«Va au moulin du milieu, ensuite, dis au meunier : 'Un tel a dit :
mouds cette charge (de froment)'. Et reprends ta charge et reviens».
— 3) L'âne, qui d'habitude ne comprenait rien, s'en alla. Un homme
prit cet âne et déposa le froment sur le sol, et deux jours, trois jours
passèrent et cet âne ne revenait pas. — 4) La femme vit que, à nouveau,
(son mari) ne sortait pas. Elle dit : «Pourquoi ne partais-tu pas,
qu'est-ce que c'est que ça, mon vieux, pourquoi n'es-tu pas allé au
moulin un tel?» Il répondit : «J'ai envoyé mon âne, mais il n'est pas
encore revenu». — 5) Il reprit : «Très bien. Maintenant je vais
repartir à sa recherche». Il se leva, s'en alla péniblement chez le
meunier. Il dit : «J'ai envoyé mon âne ici pour que tu moules le
froment. Pourquoi ne l'as-tu pas moulu, (pour qu') il revienne?»
— 6) Le meunier se rendit compte qu'il ne comprenait rien. Il dit :
«Oui, oui, j'ai oublié; ce soir, dors ici, alors je moudrai ton froment
pendant la nuit, (puis) lève-toi (et) pars». Le matin, il l'appela et
dit : «J'ai chargé le froment sur ton âne, il est parti; lève-toi,
rattrape-le». — 7) Comme il avait dormi dans le moulin, toute sa
tête était blanche de farine (litt. «était devenue farineuse») et alors,
il alla du moulin central au Nouveau Champ. — 8) C'était tôt le
matin, il arriva au bord du ruisseau, pour se laver les mains et la
figure. (En se regardant dans l'eau) il vit le meunier (litt. que c'est
le meunier). Il dit : «Eh, lui, au lieu de m'appeler, il s'est appelé
lui-même. Je ne suis pas moi!» — 9) Il revint, repartit là-bas. Il

dit : «Homme d'estime, toi, au lieu de m'appeler, c'est toi qui t'es appelé ». (L'autre) répondit : «Oui, j'ai fait une erreur. — 10) Tu vas faire ceci (litt. fais quelque chose) : dors ici, le matin je t'appellerai, (ensuite), pars». Le matin il l'appela et celui-ci se leva, arriva à sa maison et dit à sa femme : «L'âne est-il venu ici?» — 11) Sa femme répondit : «Mon vieux, l'âne comment (litt. d'où) serait-il venu? Pourquoi es-tu si stupide? L'âne que tu as laissé partir, irait-il à son travail? Quelqu'un l'a pris (et) a mis le froment par terre». — 12) Cette affaire en resta là. Elle vit qu'il n'y avait plus aucun moyen d'être à la taille de cet homme, pour le faire sortir. — 13) Un jour, elle alla à la maison du voisin (et) lui dit : «Qu'allons-nous faire? Il n'y a aucun moyen pour qu'il sorte d'ici». (Le voisin) dit : «Va, dis-lui : va à Ispahan, achète une marmite (et) reviens». Elle dit : «Très bien». — 14) Elle revint à sa maison et dit : «Va à Ispahan, nous n'avons pas de marmite. Achète une marmite (et) reviens». Celui-ci s'en alla à Ispahan; en l'espace de quelques jours, comme il voulait revenir vite, il acheta la marmite et arriva (chez lui). — 15) Il comprit alors que cette femme voulait que cela dure un mois. (Donc), il partit (et) revint après deux jours. Elle alla chez le voisin (et) dit : «Cela a duré deux jours, il est parti, il est revenu. Que vais-je encore faire?» — 16) (Le voisin) répondit : «Va le trouver. Dis-lui : es-tu allé chercher le sel pour cette marmite, pour voir combien de sel elle peut contenir? (litt. combien elle est salée, sc. si elle convient). Si tu n'es pas allé en acheter, retourne encore, va chercher du (litt. son) sel, car la marmite dont on ignore combien de sel elle fait, ne sert à rien». — 17) Elle revint à la maison, dit : «Tu n'as pas acheté de sel pour cette marmite. La marmite dont on ne sait pas combien de sel elle contient ne sert à rien». Il repartit encore, alla à Ispahan, — 18) arriva chez l'homme (qui lui avait vendu la marmite). Il dit : «Homme d'estime, toi tu donnes une marmite, (mais) tu ne dis pas combien de sel elle fait». (L'homme) répondit : «Oui, oui, j'avais oublié, maintenant je vais te dire combien de sel elle fait (litt. son sel)». — 19) «Parle». «Pas peu, pas beaucoup, une poignée, une poignée et demie, tant est le sel de cette marmite». Alors lui, de peur d'oublier, il s'en allait répétant : «Pas un peu, pas beaucoup, une poignée, une poignée et demie». — 20) Il arriva à un endroit (où) on avait (commencé) de battre le grain. C'était le jour où on nettoyait, etc. Lui, il répétait : «Pas un peu, pas beaucoup, une poignée, une poignée et demie». — 21) Ceux qui avaient battu le grain furent fort irrités. Ils (le) prirent et lui donnèrent une bonne raclée. Ils dirent :

«Que sont ces paroles que tu dis?» — 22) Il répondit : «Alors qu'est-ce que je dois dire?» Ils répondirent : «Partout où tu vas, dis : qu'il y en ait un, qu'il y en ait mille; il ne faut pas dire : une poignée, une poignée et demie; c'est mauvais». Il dit : «Très bien, ne me battez pas, je vais dire cela». — 23) Il se mit en route à nouveau, il allait disant : «Qu'il y en ait un, qu'il y en ait mille». Il arriva à un endroit. Il vit (qu'il y avait) un mort, (des gens le) portaient sur le dos et (d'autres personnes) les suivaient en se lamentant et en pleurant. — 24) Et lui disait ces mots : «Qu'il y en ait un, qu'il y en ait mille». Les gens en deuil s'approchèrent et lui tombèrent dessus (litt. sur son âme) et se mirent à le frapper. — 25) Ils dirent : «Fils de damné, l'un de nous est mort, nous sommes tellement affligés et abattus, et toi, tu dis : qu'il y en ait mille à mourir». Il dit : «Alors, comment dois-je dire?» — 26) Il dit : «Partout où tu vas, dis : le Seigneur fera miséricorde, lisez la Fâtiha, c'était un brave homme». Il dit : «Très bien». Il s'en allait (donc) et partout où il arrivait, il disait : «Lisez la Fâtiha, le Seigneur fera miséricorde, c'était un brave homme». — 27) Il arriva dans un endroit où il y avait un mariage. On battait des mains, (on jouait) du hautbois et du tambour, et lui, il répétait toujours : «Lisez la Fâtiha, le Seigneur fera miséricorde, c'était un brave homme». — 28) Holà! Ici aussi on le prit, on lui administra une bonne raclée. Il dit : «Alors, que dois-je faire, finalement, comment faut-il que je me comporte?» Ils dirent : «Partout où tu vas, jette ton chapeau en l'air, danse, pousse des cris de joie, saute, réjouis-toi». — 29) Il dit : «Très bien». Il se mit en route et commença à jeter son chapeau en l'air, à danser, à faire du bruit. Or, il arriva dans un endroit où il y avait un chasseur qui se trouvait à l'affût. — 30) Imagine, par exemple, (qu'il y avait) une perdrix (?) ou un ramier, ensuite, il s'était préparé à frapper. Alors qu'il était à l'affût, pour tirer (le gibier), voilà que (notre homme) jette (litt. jeta) son chapeau en l'air et commence à sauter, à bondir et à pousser des cris de joie. — 31) Ces (oiseaux) s'enfuirent et s'envolèrent, partirent. Holà, ce (chasseur) prit le bas de la crosse de son fusil et se mit à frapper (l'homme). Il dit : «Ceci n'est pas le comportement d'un humain. Moi, depuis le matin, j'ai tant peiné pour attraper une perdrix (?) ou un ramier. — 32) Toi, maintenant, tu es en train de jeter ton chapeau en l'air». Il répondit : «Alors, que dois-je faire?» Il dit : «Partout où tu vas, baisse la tête, traverse les ruisseaux, etc., va par derrière les murs de terre, lève et abaisse tout le temps la tête». Il dit : «Très bien». — 33) Il se mit à passer par les ruisseaux,

à lever et abaisser la tête constamment. Or, à un endroit, il y avait
une caravane qui avait dételé et qui avait des marchandises fragiles.
Comme lui se baissait et se redressait sans cesse, les chameaux prirent
peur, se levèrent et s'enfuirent. Alors les marchandises fragiles furent
toutes en morceaux. — 34) Le chef de la caravane et les caravaniers
arrivèrent et lui tombèrent dessus, lui administrèrent un bonne raclée.
Il reçut tellement de coups qu'il oublia son propre nom. — 35) Finalement, il arriva à sa maison, au milieu de la nuit, et frappa à la porte.
Sa femme, bien qu'elle sût que c'était lui, comme elle n'était pas
contente, elle voulait qu'il reste dehors. Il dit : « Viens, ouvre la
porte ». — 36) Elle dit : « Qui es-tu ? » Il avait oublié son nom !
Il répondit : « Je suis ton mari ». Elle dit : « Si tu es mon mari, dis
ton nom ». Il reprit : « Je suis ton mari, viens derrière la porte ».
Elle dit : « Si tu étais mon mari, tu saurais ton nom. — 37) Mon mari
est allé à Ispahan pour acheter le sel de la marmite, il n'est pas
convenu qu'il revienne ». Il eut beau supplier, elle n'ouvrit pas la porte,
de sorte qu'il fut forcé de repartir. — 38) Il alla dans une mosquée
(et) s'y coucha. (Comme) il n'y avait rien (pour se mettre) sous la tête,
il y mit un Coran (et) il s'endormit. Or, une espèce de bigot qui
était un (pilier) de mosquée vint le matin et vit un homme endormi
sur un Coran. — 39) Il l'appela et le querella un peu, etc. Il dit :
« (Si) tu vois une feuille de papier, tu la mettras dans le mur, dans
le trou du mur ». Il répliqua : « Très bien, dès maintenant je vais
faire cette affaire ». — 40) Ensuite il vint dans la rue et, par hasard,
il vit un morceau de papier (qui) se trouvait (là). Comme (l'homme)
avait dit qu'il fallait le mettre dans le trou du mur, il s'approcha.
Partout où il chercha, il ne trouva pas de trou pour y mettre (le
papier). — 41) Il vint dans l'établissement de bains et, par hasard,
se trouvait (là) le barbier qui d'habitude lui rasait la tête et la barbe.
Il pensa : « C'est bien, mettons-le dans le pli de son pagne de bain ».
— 42) Comme il n'avait pas trouvé de trou, il alla mettre ce (papier)
dans le pli de son pagne. Le barbier se redressa et dit : « Yâr Qoli,
pourquoi agis-tu ainsi ? » et (alors) il se rappela son nom, se mit
à courir et (il se disait) : « Je me rappelle, je me rappelle ». — 43) Il
arriva à sa maison (et) il dit : « Viens, ouvre la porte, je suis ton mari
et mon nom est Yâr Qoli ». Sa femme vint, ouvrit la porte. Bien
que son mari fût revenu sain et sauf, il était abattu et meurtri.

DAVID W. MAC DOWALL

THE COPPER DENOMINATIONS OF MENANDER *

In addition to an enigmatic monogram, some of the square copper coins of the Graeco-Bactrian king Menander which circulated in Western Afghanistan and North West India also have a single Greek letter in the reverse field. Although there is as yet no general agreement on the interpretation and significance of the monograms of the Graeco-Bactrian coinages [1], it has been common ground, since the fact was pointed out by M. Raoul-Rochette, that each monogram is composed of a certain number of Greek (or Kharoshthī) letters. In fact in some cases two constituent letters in a monogram may be almost separate; so that the use of an additional single Greek letter with a monogram *may* be no more than an extension of a complex system of mint marks. But on the coper coins of Menander all the single Greek letters represent low numbers; and this led Cunningham [2] to suggest that they probably denote the current years of the reign of the king. Dr. A.D.H. Bivar [3], moreover, in his recent study of Menander's silver drachms points out that eight numismatic phases can be detected in the silver coinage; the isolated Greek letters on the copper coins of Menander run from *alpha* to *theta* so that if interpreted as dates they would cover regnal years 1 to 9; and he argues that this close correspondence supports the belief that each phase represents the currency of a single year.

If Cunningham's suggestion can be substantiated, it would provide an important chronological framework for the arrangement of Menander's copper coinages. I have therefore tried to collect and analyse the material that is now available to test the hypothesis.

All the copper coins of Menander which have separate Greek letters in the reverse field have the same legends in Greek on the observe:–

---

* I am indebted to Dr. A.D.H. Bivar and Mr. G.K. Jenkins for several discussions on the problems of the coinages of Menander.

[1] A.N. Lahiri *Corpus of Indo-Greek Coins*, 52-62 summarises the principal explanations that have been proffered.

[2] *NC* 1845 (vol VIII), 178.

[3] *JRAS* 1970, 131 ff.

ΒΑΣΙΛΕΩΣ ΣΩΤΗΡΟΣ ΜΕΝΑΝΔΡΟΥ

arranged $\uparrow$ $\rightarrow$ $\downarrow$ as an upright box; and in Kharoshṭhī on the reverse:–

MAHARAJASA TRATARASA MENADRASA

arranged $\downarrow$ $\leftarrow$ $\uparrow$ as an upright box.

Except for this uniformity they have a wide variety of types, sizes, denominations and monograms.

TYPE 1   A in field   — small coins

Obv.   Head of Elephant   r.
RRev.   Club of Herakles placed upright
(a) Rev.   to l.,   [4]   to r.,   A

BMC 67		2.48 gm.		Fig. n° 1
BMC 68		2.78 gm.	BMC Pl. XII, 6.	
BM		2.23 gm.		
BM	ex Whitehead	2.52 gm.		
Oxford		2.87 gm.		
Oxford		2.93 gm.		
Oxford		2.62 gm.		
Cambridge		2.44 gm.		
Cambridge	ex Masson	2.24 gm.	from Begram	
Cambridge	ex Masson	2.91 gm.	from Begram	
Cambridge	ex Masson	3.18 gm.	from Begram	
Cambridge	ex Masson	2.68 gm.	from Begram	
Cambridge	ex Masson	3.60 gm.	from Begram	
PMC 507		2.46 gm.		
PMC 508		[2.5 gm.]		
PMC 509		[2.5 gm.]		
IMC 89		3.05 gm.		
IMC 90		3.05 gm.		
IMC 93		2.57 gm.		
Copenhagen		3.14 gm.	SNG Pl. 10, 308.	
Copenhagen		3.39 gm.	SNG Pl. 10, 310.	
Kabul		3.15 gm.		
Hadda		2.5 gm.	from 1968 Hadda excavations.	

[4] This monogram sometimes appears in slightly different forms, but they seem to belong to the same group.

(b) *Rev.*   to l., A   to r., ⟁

BMC 69		3.16 gm.	
BMC 70		2.62 gm.	
BM	ex Cunningham	2.66 gm.	
BM	ex Cunningham	3.54 gm.	
Oxford		2.60 gm.	
Oxford	ex Cunningham	2.63 gm.	
Cambridge	ex Masson	2.73 gm.	from Begram.
Cambridge	ex Masson	2.55 gm.	from Begram.
PMC 514		[2.5 gm.]	
IMC 92		2.52 gm.	*IMC* Pl. V, 10.
Copenhagen		2.71 gm.	*SNG* Pl. 10, 309.

(c) *Rev.*   to l., A   to r., ⨝

BM	ex Cunningham	2.35 gm.	*CASE* Pl. XII, 11.

(d) *Rev.*   Apparemtly no monogram   to r., A

Cambridge		3.16 gm.	
Cambridge	ex Masson	3.86 gm.	from Begram.
Cambridge	ex Masson	3.53 gm.	from Begram.
PMC 510		[2.5 gm.]	

(e) *Obv.*   A below type   *Rev.* Þ to r.

BMC 71	2.98 gm.	
Oxford	1.91 gm.	
Oxford	3.00 gm.	
Oxford	2.93 gm.	
Oxford	2.46 gm.	
Cambridge ex Masson	2.30 gm.	from Begram.
PMC 511	[2.5 gm.]	
PMC 512	[2.5 gm.]	
PMC 513	[2.5 gm.]	
IMC 91	1.68 gm.	

TYPE 2   B in reverse field.

Obv.   Bust of Pallas r. wearing a crested helmet.

Rev.   Nike standing l. holding a wreath and palm.

(a)   to l., ⧓   to r., B

BMC 56	I.O.C.	6.29 gm.	
Cunningham		5.89 gm.	*CASE* 249, 10.

(b)   to l., ⟁   to r.,   B

BMC 57		5.24 gm.	*BMC* Pl. XII, 1. Fig. n° 2

(c)   to l., B

BMC 58	I.O.C.	4.99 gm.

TYPE 3   Δ in reverse field.
Obv.   Indian elephant standing l.
Rev.   Elephant goad placed upright.
               to l., Δ   to r., ⧇
BM   ex Cunningham 10.80 gm.   *CASE* Pl. XII, 10.
E.C. Bayley   11.40 gm.   *CASE* 250, 15.
Oxford   ex Cuthbert King 10.54 gm.   Fig. n° 3

TYPE 4   H in reverse field
               to l., ⧇   to r.,   H
Obv.   Young laureate male head to r.
Rev.   Dolphin to r.
E.I.C.   *not* in BM   22.02 gm.   *CASE* XII. 6 obtained by
                                                 Masson at Begram, *JASB*
                                                 1836. 22 and Wilson *AA*
                                                 IV. 3.
BM   acquired in 1926 22.21 gm.   *NC* 1950, 214f.
                                                                   Fig. n° 4

TYPE 5   Θ in reverse field.
Obv.   Bactrian camel standing l.
Rev.   Head of bull facing, with long horns and extended ears
               to l., Θ   to r., ⧇
IMC 96   v. worn   19.63 gm.   *IMC* Pl. V. 11. and *CASE*
                                                 Pl. XIII. 8.

TYPE 6   A in obverse field   — large coins
Obv.   Head of bull facing, with long horns and extended ears
Rev.   Tripod lebes
               In obverse field A to r.
               In reverse field ∪ to l. ⧇   to r.
BMC 66   19.99 gm.   *BMC* Pl. XII. 5.
BM   ex Cunningham 19.71 gm.   Fig. n° 5
Oxford   18.89 gm.
Cambridge   20.88 gm.
PMC 500   20.47 gm.
PMC 501   [20 .○ gm.]
PMC 502   [20 .○ gm.] *PMC* Pl. VI. 502.
Kabul   17.25 gm.
Hadda   21.75 gm.   from 1968 Hadda excava-
                                                                   tions.

Taken together as a group, these copper coins with single Greek letters do not seem to constitute a very convincing chronological sequence spanning the whole of the reign. In the coinages of Menander there was a change in format of the Greek legends on both silver and copper which has a chronological significance. Dr. Bivar has shown that the earlier issues of Menander's silver drachms had a *continuous* Greek legend [5], as on the round bilingual silver coins of early Graeco-Bactrian kings such as Apollodotus I [6] and Antimachus [7]; whereas the later issues had a *divided* legend with the titles occupying the upper margin and the king's name placed separately in the exergue [8], as do the silver issues of later Graeco-Bactrian kings [9]. On the square copper coins of Menander there is also a change of format. His earlier coins have the king's name across the obverse so that it can be read as one looks at the type, whereas the later square coppers of Menander have the king's name to the right as the third element in a neat upright box ↑ → ↓ [10]. It is only on the square coppers of early kings such as Agathocles [11], Pantaleon [12], Apollodotus I [13], and sometime Eucratides [14] that one finds the king's name across the obverse so that it can be read with the type. On the square coppers of the later Graeco-Bactrians [15], the king's name is invariably placed to the right of the neat upright box. On the copper coins of Menander with isolated Greek letters, throughout the whole series from *alpha* to *theta* the observe Greek legend appears in the same form and in the same position in the upright box with ΒΑΣΙΛΕΩΣ to the left, ΣΩΤΗΡΟΣ above and ΜΕΝΑΝΔΡΟΥ to the right. This makes it extremely difficult for anyone to claim that the Greek letters represent regnal years or even successive issues.

Menander's copper coins with *alpha* are very common, whereas

[5] *JRAS* 1970, 123 ff.

[6] Lahiri *op. cit.*, Pl. VII, 1-2.

[7] *Ibid.*, Pl. VI. 10.

[8] *JRAS* 1970, 123 ff.

[9] Lahiri *op. cit.* passim.

[10] Lahiri *op. cit.* Pl. XXV. 4. Bivar in *JRAS* 1970, 134. drew attention to this distinction, but regarded the earlier arrangement of legend as the second stage.

[11] Lahiri *op. cit.* Pl. II. 5-7.

[12] *Ibid.* Pl. XXVII. 10-11.

[13] *Ibid.* Pl. VII 6-9.

[14] *Ibid.* Pl. XVI. 7 and XVII. 6.

[15] *Ibid.* passim.

those with *beta, delta, eta* and *theta* are extremely rare. If *alpha* indicated year 1, it would limit the production of most of the common Elephant head/Club small coppers to a single year, which seems most unlikely.

As numerals, the isolated Greek leters do not give us a full numerical sequence. From the examples cited above, it will be seen that we have coins with A for 1, B for 2, Δ for 4, H for 8 and Θ for 9 (as a classical number) or 8 (as the eighth letter of the Greek alphabet at this time when the digamma had fallen out of use as a letter). The sequence on these coins omits 3, 5, 6 and 7.

As a group, the copper coins with separate Greek letters from four distinct denominations. While they are struck *al marco* rather than *al peso*, each denomination covers a relatively narrow range of weights. There is moreover a completely different obverse/reverse type used for each denomination. Except for type 6, to which we shall return, each Greek letter is used on the coins of one denomination only:–

Type 1 has A ie 1 on coins of circa   2.75 gm.
Type 2 has B ie 2 on coins of circa   5.5   gm.
Type 1 has Δ ie 4 on coins of circa 11   gm.
Type 4 has H ie 8 on coins of circa 22   gm.
Type 5 has Θ ie 8 on coins of circa 20   gm.
Type 6 has A ie 1 on coins of circa 20   gm.

We have a well planned and carefully struck system in which the Greek letters correspond numerically to the relative weight standards (and presumably value) of the four denominations. We must therefore regard the single Greek letters not as regnal years but as marks of value, comparable to the marks of value AX, BX and ΔX for one, two and four chalkoi on the copper issues of the Seleucid king Antiochus IV at Seleucia on Tigris [16].

Moreover in the three forms of notation used for the large copper denomination of 20 to 22 gm., we can trace 3 successive stages:–

(a) H when the ordinary Greek numeral was used to indicate 8
(b) Θ when the eighth letter of the current Greek alphabet was used to indicate 8
(c) A when it was intended to emphasise the fact that 8 units of one denomination were equivalent to one unit of a higher denomination.

[16] E.T. Newell *Eastern Seleucid Mints*, 270-274.

This usage of *alpha* on the 20 gm. copper denomination in fact gives us the key to the names of the copper denominations used by Menander. In Bactria the monetary system of the Graeco-Bactrians was derived closely from the Attic system that had been used by Alexander the Great and the Seleucid kings in which 8 chalkoi = 1 obol and 6 obols = 1 drachm [17]. In the coinage of the Seleucids, the copper coins follow closely the weights of the silver denominations, and the unit in copper, the chalkous, was about the same weight as are silver drachm. Throughout the Indo-Greek period successive kings struck silver on the Attic weight standard with legends in Greek alone for territories north of the Hindu-Kush [18] and on the lower Indian weight-standard with bilingual legends in Greek and Kharoshṭhī for territories south of the Hindu-Kush [19]. The introduction of the lower Indian weight standard was necessary to provide a currency that would circulate freely alongside the pre-existing Mauryan currency. Cunningham [20] recognised the purpose of this measure, but regarded the silver coins struck in India as 'didrachms' and 'hemidrachms'; and it was left to Whitehead [21] to show how the Indo-Greek system grew out of the Bactrian with a reduced weight 'tetradrachm' and 'drachm' as the silver denominations. This of course means that the standard silver denomination of the Graeco-Bactrian kings in India was the drachm of circa 2.6 gm. It will also be appreciated that the Indian currency, following the Seleucid and Bactrian pattern, has a standard unit in copper of about the same weight as the silver drachm; and that in the developed system of Menander, this denomination of circa 2.75 gm. bears the unit's mark of value – *alpha* for 'one'. It must therefore be an Indian chalkous, reduced like the Indian silver drachm from the higher Bactrian standard. The 20 to 22 gm. denomination in copper is thus a coin of 8 chalkoi; and 8 chalkoi in the Attic system = 1 obol. The *alpha* that occurs on some coins of this 20 to 22 gm. denomination can therefore be regarded as the mark of value for one Indian obol in copper.

The circumstances of Menander's reign, following that of Apol-

---

[17] A. Cunningham *Coins of Alexander's Successors in the East* 310 ff.

[18] Lahiri *op. cit.*, 14.

[19] *Ibid.* 15 ff.

[20] Cunningham *op. cit.* 333, but he regards the Indian silver drachms as a 'hemidrachm', somewhat heavier than the Bactrian.

[21] The weights of the copper coins of Menander with these types in all collections that I have noted are cited in the appendix.

lodotus I at the beginning of the period of Indo-Greek rule in India, when the Greek coinage was being adjusted to fit in with the pattern of the indigenous Mauryan currency[22], would be sufficient in itself to explain the appearance of this well planned system of four denominations in copper, clearly differentiated by marks of value. But this particular innovation seems to have been intended to cure a muddled situation arising from an earlier emission of copper coins by Menander. The relatively common coins with the types:–

Obv. Helmeted head of Pallas r.
Greek legend ΒΑΣΙΛΕΩΣ to l., ΣΩΤΗΡΟΣ above MENANΔΡΟΥ to r.

Rev. Winged Nike r. holding wreath and palm
Kharoshṭhī legend *Maharajasa* to r., *tratarasa* above *Menadrasa* to l.

are known in a variety of different sizes and weights[23]. Cunningham suggested that they were probably intended to provide 3 different denominations. But there is no type difference or special feature to distinguish one denomination from another, and one has to rely on size and weight alone. While issues with the same monogram might well have been distinguishable at the time they were issued, there are further variations in weight between coins with different monograms. It was presumably to avoid such confusion between different denominations that Menander's mints introduced the features that we see in the issue with separate Greek letters:–

(a) the denominations were struck to a more closely controlled standard.

(b) distinctive obverse and reverse types were employed for different denominations.

(c) each denomination caried a specific mark of value.

Menander's comprehensive system of copper denominations was completed (probably in a different issue, because the coins have no marks of value) by two more denominations, again with obverse and reverse types distinctive to each denomination :–

---

[22] Cunningham, *ibid.*, 249 n° 10, 10a, 10b, 10c.
[23] See the Appendix to this article.

TYPE 7   copper Diobol
Obv.   Helmeted head of Pallas r.
Rev.   Horse rearing to r.
                to r. below, ⊠

BMC 47   35.66 gm.
BM   ex Cunningham   43.98 gm.   Fig. n° 6
Oxford   42.51 gm.
Kabul   37.2 gm.

TYPE 8   copper Hemi-chalkous or lepton
Obv.   Wheel
Rev.   Palm
                to r., ⅊

BMC   ex l.o.c.   1.57 gm.   *BMC* Pl. XII, 7. Fig. n° 7
Taxila   *ASR* 1928/9, p. 65 n° 4,
                                           found at Sirkap.

For the other copper denominations of Menander, we see further emissions of the chalkous, dichalkon, hemiobol and obol, without marks of value, but with distinctive obverse and reverse types, and easily recognisable as further issues of the same denominations as those bearing the marks of value.

I therefore regard the copper coins of Menander with a single Greek letter in the field as the particular issue of a specific period when Menander introduced a comprehensive denominational system; and consider that they served a double purpose. They were designed to show the inter-relationship and relative values of coins in the new system, which had in all six distinct copper denominations. They were also to avoid the confusion that has arisen from the issues of the Pallas/Nike type of Menander. After a relatively short period, the pattern of Menander's denominations was effectively understood; and the two other changes that he had introduced—the use of distinctive types for denominations that might be confused and a narrow weight range for copper coins struck *al marco* were more than enough in themselves to bring order and clarity to copper denominations of different values. Subsequent Indo-Greek kings were able to make orderly issues of copper coins in more than one denomination without the help of value marks.

TABLE OF WEIGHTS

(a) COPPER COINS OF MENANDER Pallas/Nike r. type

GMS.
22
21
20
19
18
17
16   X
15   XXXXX
14   X
13
12   XX
11   X
10   X
9   XXXX
8   XXXXX
7   X
6   XXXXXXX
5   XXXXXXXXX
4   XXXXX
3   X
2
1

Based on the weights of coins listed in the appendix.

(b) COPPER COINS OF MENANDER with single Greek letters

GMS.		
22	HH	α
21		α
20	Θ	ααααα
19		α
18		
17		α
16		
15		
14		
13		
12		
11	ΔΔΔ	
10		
9		
8		
7		
6	B	
5	BBB	
4	AAAA	
3	AAAAAAAAAAAAAAAAAAAAAAAAAAAAAAAAAAAAA	
2	AAAAAAAAA	
1		

Based on the weights of coins listed above in the text:–

A = type 1
B = type 2
Δ = type 3
H = type 4
Θ = type 5
α = type 6

(c) COPPER COINS OF ANTIOCHUS IV with Greek letters

GMS.	
22	
21	
20	Δ
19	
18	Δ
17	ΔΔΔ
16	Δ
15	Δ
14	
13	Δ
12	
11	
10	
9	BB
8	BB
7	BBBB
6	B
5	A
4	AAAAAAAAA
3	AAAAA
2	
1	

Based on the weights of coins cited by E.T. Newell, *The Coinage of the Eastern Seleucid Mints*, 272.

APPENDIX

Copper coins of Menander of the Pallas/Nike r. type
Obv. Helmeted bust of Pallas r.
Rev. Winged Nike standing r. holding wreath and palm branch

(a) ⊕ in reverse field to r.

BMC 49		6.28 gm.	*BMC* Pl. XI. 13
BM	(ex Whitehead)	6.11 gm.	
Copenhagen	*SNG* 306	5.09 gm.	

(b) ⴲ in reverse field to r.

BMC 50		6.32 gm.
BM	(ex Cunningham)	8.62 gm.
BM	(ex Cunningham)	4.91 gm.
BM	(ex Cunningham)	5.88 gm.
BM		5.96 gm.
Cambridge	(ex Masson)	6.59 gm.
Cambridge	(ex Masson)	5.28 gm.
Cambridge	(ex Masson)	2.68 gm.
Cambridge	(ex Masson)	5.76 gm.
Oxford		5.23 gm.
Oxford		5.46 gm.
Oxford		3.79 gm.
PMC 490		4.5 gm.
PMC 491		7.78 gm.
PMG 492		7.5 gm.
PMC 493		7.5 gm.
IMC 78		4.92 gm.
IMC 82		4.21 gm. *IMC* Pl. V. 8

(c) Ř in reverse field to r.

BMC 48		12.09 gm.

(d) ⬠ in reverse field to r.

BMC 51		11.42 gm.
BMC 52		3.87 gm.
BM	(ex Cunningham)	14.18 gm.
BM	(ex Cunningham)	9.57 gm.
Oxford		11.93 gm.
Oxford		15.18 gm.
Oxford		4.90 gm.

	PMC 482	15.55 gm.	
	PMC 483	[15.0 gm.]	
	PMC 484	[15.0 gm.]	
	PMC 487	9.07 gm.	
(e)	ⱈⱈ in reverse field to r.		
	BMC 53	5.61 gm.	
	BMC 54	4.46 gm.	
	Oxford	3.99 gm.	
	PMC 488	4.53 gm.	*PMC* Pl. VI. 488
	PMC 489	[4.5 gm.]	
(f)	ⱈⱈ,ⱈⱈ etc.		
	BMC 55	6.30 gm.	
	BM	8.55 gm.	
	Oxford	8.82 gm.	
	Musée Guimet 44	8.0 gm.	
	PMC 485	[15.0 gm.]	
	PMC 486	[15.0 gm.]	

MANFRED MAYRHOFER

EIN ALTES PROBLEM: »GUŠTĀSP« IM ACHTEN VORCHRISTLICHEN JAHRHUNDERT?

Was ist das Schwerste...?
...ist es das: sich von Eicheln und Gras der
Erkenntnis nähren und um der Wahrheit willen an
der Seele Hunger leiden?
Also sprach Zarathustra (Nietzsche, Werke ed.
Schlechta II 293).

1. In assyrischen Inschriften erscheinen unter den Königen von Kummuḫ, das sich mit dem Gebiet der hellenistischen Kommagene überschneidet[1], zwei Namen, deren Anklang an iranische Namen früh bemerkt worden ist[2]; sie tauchen seitdem immer wieder in der Fachliteratur auf, in der historischen noch mehr als in der linguistischen. Die folgenden Seiten sollen zeigen, daß die Deutungen der beiden Kummuḫ-Namen einer kritischen Überprüfung bedürfen.

1.1 In den Annalen und der Tontafelinschrift Tiglatpilesers III. ist *Ku-uš-ta-aš-pi* von Kummuḫ zu finden[3], dessen Nennungen um das Jahr 740 v.Chr. zu datieren sind; der Anklang an *Guštāsp*, die freilich erst mittelpersische Ausprägung der altpersischen Namensform *Vištāspa-* (awest. *Vištāspa-*), mußte früh auffallen.

1.2 Noch älter, nämlich in das 9. Jahrhundert v.Chr. zu setzen, ist ein bei Salmanassar III. bezeugter *Ku-un-da-aš-pi*[4]. Unter den Bedingungen, unter denen sich *Kuštašpi* zu apers. *Vištāspa-* verhielte,

---

[1] Vgl. L. W. King, Kummukh and Commagene, Journal of the Manchester Egyptian and Oriental Society 1912-1913, 47ff.; F. K. Dörner - T. Goell, Arsameia am Nymphaios (Berlin 1963) 301 u. Anm. 2.

[2] S. die Lit. bei F. Justi, Iranisches Namenbuch (Marburg 1895) 373a.

[3] P. Rost, Die Keilschrifttexte Tiglat-Pilesers III. (Leipzig 1893) 14, 26, 66, 70; P. Naster, L'Asie Mineure et l'Assyrie aux VIIIᵉ et VIIᵉ siècles av.J.-C. (Louvain 1938) 24 Anm.; ältere Lit. bei E. Meyer, KZ 42 (1909) 16f. — Der selbe König erscheint in einer urartäischen Inschrift als *Ku-uš-ta-aš-pi-li*, welche Namensform uns noch beschäftigen wird (s.u. 4.1 u. Anm. 17); vgl. F. W. König, Handbuch der chaldischen Inschriften (AfO Beiheft 8, Teil II, Graz 1957) 123a und 123b Anm. 4.

[4] E. Meyer a.a.O., mit Lit.

wäre er mit einem nicht belegten, aber rekonstruierbaren [5] altiranischen Namen *Vindāspa- zu verbinden.

2. Eine kritische Überlegung zu diesen beiden Namen hat sich zwei Fragen zu stellen: Wie ist das Vorkommen iranischer Namen in Kummuḫ im 9. und 8. Jahrhundert v.Chr. historisch vorstellbar (3.1-2)? Und läßt sich mit linguistischen Mitteln der Zeitraum von fast einem Jahrtausend überbrücken, der zwischen diesen Belegen und der frühesten Bezeugung des mitteliranischen Wandels /vi/ > /gu/ liegt (4.1)?

3.1 Für die geschichtliche Deutung dieser angeblichen Iraniernamen hat sich bis in neuere Zeit ein Vorschlag gehalten, der sich bei näherer Überlegung als reichlich absurd erweist: Die beiden Fürsten »werden Nachkommen der alten Dynastie von Mitanni sein«, meinte Eduard Meyer [6], und noch 1967 stellt sich R. D. Barnett [7] die Frage »are we to interpret this ethnic element as a pre-existent Iranian native element, perhaps deriving from Mitanni, which survived the Mushki pressure?«. Ein Ja auf diese Frage könnte nur unter einer von zwei gleichermaßen unglaubhaften Annahmen ausgesprochen werden. Die eine Annahme ginge davon aus, daß sich unter den Ariern von Mitanni auch eine ausgeprägt iranische Gruppe befunden habe, die so einschneidende Entwicklungen wie das Lautgesetz */śv/ > /sp/ bereits durchgeführt hatte, von dem mitteliranischen /vi/ > /gu/ ganz zu schweigen [8]. Noch weniger greifbar ist die zweite mögliche Annahme: die arische Sprache des Mitannibereiches

---

[5] *Vinda-* als Vorderglied ist mehrfach bezeugt, s. Justi a.a.O. 368b ff., Verf., Onomastica Persepolitana (Wien 1973) 199, 333b; -aspa- ist eines der häufigsten Hinterglieder altiranischer Namen, s. Justi a.a.O. 486, O. Szemerényi, BNF 2 (1950/51) 168, Verf. a.a.O. 259b (°aśba). E. Meyer a.a.O. 17 hat den Namen also mit Berechtigung konstruiert, ihn aber ohne Asterisk abgedruckt, obwohl er in Anm. 1 vermerkt, daß die Form nicht belegt sei; in der Folge wird »*Vindāspa-«* von vielen Autoren leider wie ein belegter Name behandelt.

[6] Geschichte des Altertums II/1[2] (Stuttgart-Berlin 1928) 477 Anm. 1.

[7] Phrygia and the Peoples of Anatolia in the Iron Age. Cambridge Ancient History Vol. II, Chapter XXX (Cambridge 1967 [Vorabdruck]) 7.

[8] Sichere Belege im Mitanni-Arischen reflektieren stets nur urarisches = vedisches (*)aśva- »Pferd«; vgl. die Lit. bei Verf., Die Indo-Arier im Alten Vorderasien (Wiesbaden 1966) 130a, Die Arier im Vorderen Orient — ein Mythos? (Wien 1974) 69. Besonnene Forscher haben darum für Mitanni allenfalls die dem Indoarischen und Iranischen gemeinsame Vorstufe, das Urarische, oder ein dem Urarischen noch nahes »Pre-Iranian« für annehmbar gehalten; der »Nachweis iranischer EN. für die ersten Mitanni-Könige durch P. Kretschmer« kann auf sich beruhen, trotz Kronasser, Μνήμης χάριν I (Wien 1956) 207 Anm. 56.

habe sich im Lauf der Jahrhunderte, die zwischen dem Ende von Mitanni/Ḫanigalbat und den Kummuḫ-Belegen liegt, in diesem Bereich nicht nur erhalten, sondern trotz vermutlicher Isolierung allmählich »iranisiert«[9]. Das ist selbst unter der Voraussetzung eines urarischen oder prä-iranischen Charakters des Arischen von Mitanni schwer vorstellbar — ganz abgesehen davon, daß sich die Forschung heute über die genauere Zuordnung dieser Sprache als »indo-arisch« oder, was davon kaum verschieden ist, »(Ur-)Arisch altindischer Dialektprägung« einig sein dürfte[10].

3.2 Historisch eher akzeptabel ist die Annahme, daß Träger medischer Namen, wie sie uns in diesen Jahrhunderten in assyrischen Quellen bereits begegnen, durch irgendwelche dynastische Verbindungen in die Reihe der Könige von Kummuḫ geraten seien. Das scheint z.B. Kronasser a.a.O. 207, 208 für möglich zu halten, der dies freilich mit der nicht geglückten Annahme verbindet, auch Fürsten späthethitischer Höfe dieser Zeit hätten iranische Namen getragen[11].

4. Die historischen Voraussetzungen für Iraniernamen in Kummuḫ zu Beginn des ersten vorchristlichen Jahrtausends fehlen also nicht ganz; doch sind sie von geringer Wahrscheinlichkeit. Unter diesen Umständen wird die linguistische Überprüfung strenger sein müssen als in Fällen, wo die Volks- oder Gebietskennzeichnung primär an Iranier denken ließe.

4.1 Wer in diesen alten Namen die keilschriftgerechten Wiedergaben von *Vištāspa-* und **Vindāspa-* sehen möchte[12], muß entweder

---

[9] Vgl. die Lit. bei Verf., IF 70 (1965) 158f. Anm. 51; s. besonders B. Landsberger, Samʾal (Ankara 1948) 12 Anm. 27, der unseren beiden Königen sogar »indische Namen« attestiert, »die sich nur aus dem Fortleben der Mitanni-Tradition erklären«. — Ähnlich nebulos äußert sich L. W. King a.a.O. 55 zu den beiden Namen, welche »formed a later ripple of the wave of Aryan migration which seems to have flooded the ... region of Mitanni ...«.

[10] Zum letzteren Terminus, auf dem A. Kammenhuber besteht, s. Verf., AAntH 20 (1972[74]) 280, Die Arier ... (1974) 12f. Anm. 6. — S. noch besonders T. Burrow, The Sanskrit Language³ (London 1973) 29f., 391f.; W. Wüst, Sprache 20 (1974) 159f.

[11] Kronasser a.a.O. 207 zieht vor allem einige Namen auf °s-pa-s heran, die er als iranische -aspa-Komposita zu deuten vorschlägt. Diese Namen enthalten aber sicherlich -tispas = Tešup (E. Laroche, Les noms des Hittites [Paris 1966] 348); »dafür spricht besonders der Name Āhila-tispas Karg. A 8 i ..., der dem mehrmals belegten Ehli-Tešup entsprechen kann« (P. Meriggi, briefl.; s. Laroche a.a.O. 52).

[12] Eine abweichende Auffassung bringt È. A. Grantovskij vor (Drevnij mir [Festschrift Struve, Moskau 1962] 255f.; Rannjaja istorija iranskich plemen Perednej Azii [Moskau 1970] 133), der in *Kundašpi* altiran. **Kundāspa-* (∼ *Kundāgušasp* Fird.,

von einer iranischen Sprache ausgehen, die schon auf archaischer
Stufe /gu/ aus /vi/ entwickelte[13]; oder er muß — im Hinblick auf
die tatsächliche, und zwar erstmals im ersten nachchristlichen
Jahrhundert bezeugte, Entwicklung im Mitteliranischen[14] — die
Erfahrung in Anspruch nehmen, daß Namen mitunter »aus Sozio-
lekten übernommen [werden], in denen sich jüngere Entwicklungen
einer normierten Hochsprache gegenüber vollzogen haben«[15]. Diese
Erfahrung scheint mir im Falle von *Kundašpi* und *Kuštašpi*, in denen
ein Lautwandel neun bzw. acht Jahrhunderte vorweggenommen sein
soll, entschieden überfordert. Ich freue mich, diese Bedenken mit
einer Anzahl besonnener Forscher zu teilen[16]. Es fehlt auch nicht
an Hinweisen, daß diese Namen — trotz der fatalen Ähnlichkeit
von *Kuštašpi* und *Guštāsp* — Erklärungen aus Sprachfamilien finden
könnten, deren Präsenz in Kummuḫ prinzipiell wahrscheinlicher ist
als die des Iranischen[17].

5. Diese Erwägungen können nicht mit mathematischer Sicherheit
den iranischen Charakter der beiden Namen aus Kummuḫ widerlegen; aber sie möchten jene zur Vorsicht mahnen, die ihn ohne
weitere Reflexion für bewiesen ansehen. Es empfiehlt sich, im

---

Justi a.a.O. 120b, 166b) sieht; ebenso geht jetzt J. Harmatta (Studies in the History
and Language of the Sarmatians [Szeged 1970] 104) von **Kundāspa-* und **Kuštāspa-*
aus, ohne das Etymon des letzteren Namens zu erklären.

[13] Kronasser a.a.O. 207 scheint das Medische als mögliche Quelle anzusehen;
es gibt aber kein Indiz dafür, daß diese im Lautstand sonst so archaische
altiranische Sprache diesen Wandel vollzogen habe.

[14] J. Duchesne-Guillemin, AGIt 49 (1964) 116.

[15] Verf., Onomastica Persepolitana (Wien 1973) 312; die Fälle rezenter Züge in
Namen aus achämenidischer Zeit beschränken sich jedoch auf *-iya- -uva-* > *-ī- -ū-*,
-ahya- -aya(:)- > *-ē-*, eventuell *-θr-* > *-hr-* (Verf. a.a.O. 312f.).

[16] Z.B. H. Jacobsohn, KZ 54 (1927) 269 Anm. 1; E. H. Sturtevant, Yale Classical
Studies 1 (1928) 217; W. Eilers, AfO 9 (1933-34) 334b, ZDMG 90 (1936) 173;
J. H. Kramers, Analecta Orientalia (Leiden 1954) 242; Harmatta a.a.O. (gegenüber
seiner früheren Auffassung, a.a.O. 73); s. auch das Zögern von Duchesne-Guillemin
a.a.O. — Über Jacobsohns vernünftige Bedenken schreibt Kronasser a.a.O. 207, sie
seien »durch P. Kretschmer zerstreut« worden. Liest man bei Kretschmer, KZ 55
(1928) 99 Anm. 2 nach, so findet man dort den Hinweis auf »das Zeugnis der
indo-parthischen Münzen des Königs *Gondophares*- Ὑνδοφέρρης (21-ca. 60 n. Chr.)«;
»*Gondo-* = *Vinda-(farna)* bildet die Brücke zu *Kunda-*« — eine zeitliche Brücke
von neun Jahrhunderten!

[17] Vgl. J. Friedrich, Einführung ins Urartäische (MVAeG 37/3, Leipzig 1933) 64
(»Die nunmehr urartäisch belegte Namensform *Kuštašpili* macht... eher einen klein-
asiatischen Eindruck...«); F. W. König, a.a.O. 123b f. Anm.; A. Goetze, JCSt 16
(1962) 56a und Anm. 31.

iranischen Onomastikon den Belegen von uriran. *Višta-aspa- »mit losgebundenen Rossen« (Vīštāspa-, Ὑστάσπης, Guštāsp usw.) den Namen Kuštašpi(li) nur mit äußerster Reserve anzufügen; es empfiehlt sich, einen altiranischen Namen *Vindāspa- nicht wegen Kundašpi für erwiesen zu halten; vor allem aber sei empfohlen, auf kühne historische Schlüsse aus den angeblichen Iranierkönigen von Kummuḫ zu verzichten.

DAVOUD MONCHI-ZADEH

IRANISCHE MISZELLEN

P. *zahār* 'Unterleib, Schamgegend'.

'A. Nūšīn, *Suxan-ī čand dar bāra i Šāh-nāma*, Moskau 1970, S. 40ff, behauptet, dass *axta-zahār* 'kastriert' bedeutet (vgl. 'Abd al-Qādir, *Luγat i Šah-nāma*, ed. Salemann, Petersburg 1895, S. 242). Nach N. ist *zahār* < *zah-āvar* = *farzand-āvar* 'kindererzeuger', also 'Genitalien' (*ālat i tanāsul*).

Šāh-nāma (Mohl) = *ŠnM* 13f, 1543 (*Šn*-Berthels V 172, 1523, 'Abd al-Qādir Nr 2751)

بکردار شیران (گرگان B) بروزشکار برآن بادپایان آهـختـه هار (اختـه زهار B،
هخته زهار A')

Mohl (Üb.) III 432 »semblables à des lions en un jour de chasse, et assis sur des chevaux aux pieds de vent et tendant le cou«. *hār* ist wahrscheinlich nichts anders als hindī *hār* < skr. *hāra-* 'string, necklace of pearls' (vgl. *Tārix i Baihaqī*, ed. Fayyāḍ, Teheran 1945, S. 220 'Halsschmuck'), das Firdausī metaphorisch für 'Mähne' gebraucht haben soll. Somit bedeutet *bād-pāyān i āhixta hār* 'schnellfüssige Rosse mit gesträubten Mähnen', vgl. *āhixta-gōš* 'with ears erect (horse)', Steingass.

zahār (phl. dss. 'womb', MacKenzie, *A concise Phl. Dict.*, London 1971) is 'Unterleib, Bauch, Schamgegend', vgl. *zahār-tang* 'the back girth of the camel', Steingass; und Sōzanī, *Dīwān*, Teheran 1959, u.a. S. 30, 41, 385, 422, 429 (deutlich 'Unterleib' und 'the front of the body'). 'Abd al-Q., ebd., S. 175 meint aber, *hixta-* (bei ihm *huxta*)-*zahār* sei *kašīda-zahār* = arab. *muxṣà* 'kastriert' und *zahār* (= tü. *qasïq* 'Schambein') metaphorisch (*kināya*) für *xāya* ('Hoden') gebraucht. In dem Fall würde *Šn* 13g, 644 (*ŠnB* V 272, 620, 'Abd al-Q., Nr 2550

سواران (ستوران A') چو شیران گشته نهار (آخته زهار B، هخته
زهار A') که باشند پرخشم روز شکار

in der Übersetzung (nach *ŠnB*) lauten: 'Die Reiter wie kastrierte Löwen(!) welche wütend sind bei der Jagd'.

Ich muss erwähnen, dass *hixta-zahār* unter Umständen als 'mit eingezogenem Unterleib' = p. *lāγar-miyān* 'mit schlanke Taille' interpretiert werden kann, vgl. hierzu *Šn* 13, 804 (*ŠnB* IV 59, 791) *kašīda zahār u buland u suturg* '(ein Ross) mit eingezogenem Unterleib, hoch und mächtig'.

Mohl (Üb.) II 501 : »d'encolure (!) fine, ardent et fort«.

M.W. hatte das Wort *zahār* bis jetzt keine Erklärung gefunden. Es entspricht jedoch skr. *jaṭhára-* 'belly, womb, front of the body' Macdonell, welches av. ⁺*zaθara-*, mp., np. *zahār* ergeben wird. Man hat dem skr. Wort bis jetzt nur got. *kliþei* beigelegt, s. Thumb, *Handbuch des Skr.*, § 87 und Mayrhofer, *Kurzgef. etym. Wb. des Altind.* I 414.

* * *

Xurāsānī *xalaj, buz-ī ki gūšhā i zard dārad* 'eine Ziege, die gelbe Ohren hat', Šakūrzāda, *Mardum i Xurāsān*, S. 504, sicher dasselbe wie *Farhang i Jihangīrī* (= *FrJh*) *xalang/j = du-rang* = arab. *ablaq* 'buntscheckig' mit Belegversen von 'Asjadī, Manūčihrī und Bušḥāq; *Burhān* auch *xilanj*. Das ist dasselbe wie Kāšɣarī, *Dīwān Luɣat at-Turk*, Istanbul 1914-18, I 33 *qaδïŋ* (ɣuzz. *qaïŋ*); 297 = arab. *xalanj* 'Birke'. Clauson, *An etym. Dict.*... Oxford 1972, S. 602, hält es für ein eventuelles LW. aus dem P.; ferner osm. *qayïn* (Clauson, ebd.) und 'Abd al-Q, S. 76 : *xadang = qayïn*. FrJh : *xadang nām i diraxt-ē 'st ki az čōb i ān tīr va junāɣ* (Text : *ḥn'y*) *i zēn va amṯāl i ān sāzand* 'x ist Name eines Baumes, aus dessen Holz man Pfeile, Sattelgestelle und dgl. herstellt'. Des öfteren begegnet man dem W. in *Šn*. Die ursprüngliche Bedeutung 'buntscheckig' lässt sich aus einer Stelle Bīrūnī, *Jamāhir*, Hyderabad 1936/7, S. 175 (= *Bīrūnī's Picture of the World*, ed. Togan, Delhi 1937, S. 86 f) herauslesen :

قال حمزة : اسم الجزع بالفارسية قلنج، والبقراني باكرى هلنج، ولفظة خلنج
لايختص بها الجزع ' بل تقع (يقع ;Jam ;so Togan) على كل مخطوط بالوان
واشكال فيوصف (فوصف T) به السنانير والثعالب والزباد والزرافات
وامثالها بل هوبالخشب الذى هو (التى تكون Jam) كذلك اخص ومنها
تنحت المهايد والقعاب والمشارب وامثا لها بارض الترك

'Ḥamza sagt : Onyx heisst p. *qalanj* und *baqarānī* (= die beste Sorte davon, vgl. *Jamāhir* 174, Jāqūt, *Buldān*, ed. Wüstenfeld I 699 : *Baqarān* ein Mixlāf von Jemen, woher das beste *jaz'*, *al-baqarānī*

stammt) heisst (im P.) *bākurī halanj* [1]. Die Bezeichnung *xalanj* beschränkt
sich nicht auf den Onyx, sondern wird gebraucht für alles, was
buntscheckig ist durch Farben und Muster. So werden damit Katzen,
Füchse, Zibetkatzen und Giraffen (auch) bezeichnet. Speziell wird
sie aber für Holz gebraucht, das so (d.i. buntscheckig) ist. Aus diesem
schnitzt man Tabletts, Schüsseln, Trinkgefässe u. ä. im Lande der
Türken'. Hierzu vgl. Dozy, *Suppl. aux Dict. Arabes*, I 192, *mujazza‛*
'tigré, tavelé et moucheté'. Ferner Tōsī, *'Ajā' ib al-Maxluqāt*, ed.
Sutūda, Teheran 1966, S. 312: *xalanj diraxthā 'st bisyār dar bēšahā
i Turkistān tā bilād i Xvārizm ... az ān diraxt ṭabaqhā sāzand va kāsahā
va ɣairuhu 'x.*, das sind Bäume, die in grosser Anzahl in den Wäldern
Turkistans wachsen bis nach Xvārizm hin..., aus jenen Bäumen
schnitzt man Platten, Schüsseln u. dgl.' und ebd., weiter :

خدنگ درختی است بزرگ در ولایتی روس باشد، پوست وی بر غلاف نیزه
پوشند وبعضی باشد که آنرا خدنگ بمهر خوانند وپوست وی منقش بود،
پنداری کی نقاش چین آنرا نگا شته است وآن جنس عزیز باشد، هم چون
آهن گوهر دارد و خدنگ چوبی است نرم و مطیع ازآن تیر تراشند

'*x.* ist ein grosser Baum, der im Lande der Rūs wächst. Mit dessen
Rinde überzieht man Lanzenscheiden (Wohl : Schaften). Es gibt
(davon) eine Art, die man «gestempeltes» *x.* nennt und dessen Rinde
Muster hat, so dass man glauben würde, ein Maler von Čīn hätte
es verziert. Diese Art ist sehr geschätzt und hat Wellenmuster [2]

---

[1] Die Bezeichnung *bākurī* (? < ⁺*bāqurī* < *baqarānī*) hat sich im P. zu *bābāyūrī*
entwickelt. Ḥakīm Mu'min, *Tuḥfa*, Nchdr. Teheran 1959, S. 72: *jaz‛ sang-ē 'st ki az
Yaman va Ḥabaša xēzad va dar ō šabīh ba čašm va ṭabaqāṭ i ō xuṭūṭ i safēd u zard u
surx u siyāh ẓāhir ast. va ba fārsī < yak > qism i ō rā bābāyūrī gōyand '*j. ist ein Stein, der in
Jemen und Abyssinien vorkommt. In ihm sind runde, weisse, gelbe, rote und schwarze
Linien wie in den Augenzonen. Dessen eine Art heisst p. *bābāyūrī*. Dem Wort *b.* werden
Mu'īn, *Farhang i Fārsī*, Teheran 1963-73 (= *FrM*), folgenden Bedeutungen gegeben:
1. Eine Art Blindheit, bei der das Auge schwillt und die Farbe von Schafsaugen
bekommt; 2. Glotzaugen; 3. blind; 4. eine Runde, weiss- und schwarzgerillte Perle,
die gegen den bösen Blick an Kindern angehängt wird. Tōsī, ebd., S. 141, Z. 19 hat
unter den Abarten von *jaz‛*باقرای, das in ⁺*bāqarānī* (< *baqarānī*) zu verbessern ist.

[2] *gōhar*, arabisiert *jauhar* (mp. *gōhr* 'substance, essence, nature; jewel; stock, lineage'
MacKenzie, *Phl. Dict.*, skr. *gotra-* 'Geschlecht, Ursprung') bedeutet in Bezug auf
eine Klinge 'Wellenmuster'. *Burhān* hat unter *jauhar* u.a. *mauj i čōb va ustuxvān*
'Wellenmuster des Holzes und des Knochens (wohl : des Elfenbeins)'. Hier muss ich
auf eine falsche Interpretation aufmerksam machen, die bei Doerfer, *Tü. und mong.
Elemente im Np.*, Wiesbaden 1963-, Nr 765, vorkommt: Es handelt sich um das

wie Stahl (Text: *āhan* 'Eisen'). *x.* ist ein geschmeidiges, leicht zu bearbeitendes Holz, daraus schnitzt man Pfeile'.

xadang, xalanj, ... 'Birke' wird noch *tōz* genannt. Burhān (ed. Mu'īn) unter *tōz* und Anm. 'Birke(nrinde)', atü. *toz* (von Gabain, *Atü. Gram.* Leipzig 1950, S. 343). Dieses setzte ich zu av. *taozya-* (Adj. zu ⁺*Taoza-* 'eine Völkerschaft, die dem Volk vom Av. bekannt war', mp. *Tōz/ž* des öfteren *Šn. twr* geschrieben). *tōz* 'Birke' ist der Baum par excellence jenes Volks und jener Gegend gewesen.

* * *

Xurāsānī *čōlī-qezak, matarsak i sar i jālīz* 'Vogelscheuche der Gurken- und Melonenfelder'. Trotz dieser primären Bedeutung kommt der Verfasser vom *Mard. Xurās.* (S. 270, Anm.) durch den Unsinn, den Malik aš-Šu'arā' Bahār einmal (*Ši'r dar Īrān,* S. 68 nach *Mard. Xurās.*) geschrieben hat, dazu *č.-q.* zu *kōlī-qizak* 'Zigeunermädchen' (*kōlī < kāvulī* 'aus Kabul' + tü. *qïz* 'Mädchen' + p. *-ak*) zu stellen und dieses als eine rätselhafte Umgestaltung der Arədvī Sūrā Anāhitā

Wort *balārak,* das *Tārīx i Waṣṣāf,* Bombay 1852/3, S. 667 wie auch *Tārīx i'Ālam-ārāy i'Abbāsī,* Teheran 1955-6, S. 894 deutlich als *bl'rk* haben, und welches D. *bilärzük* 'Armband, Flintenring' liest. Betreffs *Tārīx i W.* ist zu beanstanden, dass die von D. zitierten Stellen nicht aus dem Werke selbst stammen, sondern aus einem Vokabular, das der Hrsg. *Muḥammad Mahdī* (D.: S. XLI Muhsadī!) im Jahre 1269 d. H. zu seiner Ausgabe schrieb. Ein Zeugnis von Bīrūnī über *b/palārak* findet man *Jamāhir* 254, nachdem er S. 253 sich ausführlich über *firind = jauhar* (in Xurāsān) 'Wellenmuster' und seine Ausarbeitung äusserte :

ولا بأس ان نذكر ماعرفناه من جهة ذوى البصر بجواهر السيوف مستفادة

من الهنود واشرف انواعه (انوعه Text) واسر فها يسمى پلارك بالباء

معربة بالفاء

'Es schadet nicht, wenn wir für diejenigen, welche an *jauhar* der Schwerter interessiert sind, bezüglich der von den Indern hergestellten (Schwerter), was wir wissen, erwähnen : die edelste und stärkeste Sorte nennt man *palārak* mit *p-*'. Dann beschreibt der grosse Xvārizmier, wie die Inder diesen Stahl herstellen. Dass das Wort indischen Ursprungs ist, geht u.a. deutlich aus *Sāmī fī 'l-Asāmī,* Teheran 1967, S. 288 hervor : arab. *muhannad, hindī, hinduwānī* = p. *šamšēr i hindī* 'indisches Schwert', S. 287 arab. *ma'ṭūr* = p. (*šamšēr i*) *gōhar-dār* '(Schwert) mit Wellenmuster', S. 285 arab. *firind* (< p. *parind*), *a/uṭr, rubad* = p. *gōhar i šamšēr* 'Wellenmuster des Schwertes'.

Hindī *phalḍā* 'the blade (of a sword, knife, etc.), Platts, *A Dict. of Urdū, cl. Hindī, and Engl.,* Oxford 1930. D.i. prākr. *phal-ḍo < skr.* ⁺*phal-ra-ka-* mit prākr. *-ḍo = skr. -ra-ka.* Hier haben wir unser *palārak* (skr. *phala-* 'point of arrow; blade or knife' zu √*phal-* 'to burst', Turner, *A comparative Dict. of the Indo-Aryan Languages,* London 1962-6, Nr 9052.

'unbefleckte Göttin der Gewässer' zu betrachten. Dann berichtet er
S. 503 weiter, dass die Kinder bei Dürre und Mangel an Regen einen
Eselschädel schminken, ihn bekleiden, in den Gassen herumtragen
und singen : »Č.-q., lass regnen!«

Dieser Gebrauch in Xurāsān ist schon von Massé, *Croyances et
Coutumes Persanes*, Paris 1938, I 176 bemerkt worden: »L'âne sert
aux mêmes fins dans les villages du Khorasan. Quand on y manque
de pluie, les enfants forment un cortège : ayant mis le crâne d'un
âne au bout d'un bâton, ils le portent devant les maisons et disent :
Tête d'âne! achète du bois (besser : Tête d'âne acheteur du bois!).
De cette manière ils recueillent und grande quantité de bois et font
brûler la tête d'âne au sommet d'une colline«.

Der Verfasser vom *Mard. Xurās.* gibt selber eine Erklärung zu
č.-q. (S. 270, Anm.), die der von Bahār keineswegs nachsteht (übrigens
spricht er an dieser Stelle von einem Esel : *ulāy-ī rā bazak mī-kunand*
'man schminkt einen Esel') : *č.-q.* wäre *kōla* ('gebogen') + (arab.)
quzaḥ ('Genius der Wolken und des Luftraums'). Somit ist nach ihm
č.-q. nichts anderes als 'Regenbogen'!

Man kennt in Persien und den Nachbarländern 2 Typen von
Vogelscheuchen :

1. Eine aus einem Grossviehschädel, meistens Eselschädel, bestehende
(vgl. kurd. LW. aus dem P. *sar i xar*[3] 'Vogelscheuche', Mardūx,
Farhang i Kurdī, Teheran, o.J.).

Wer durch Afganistan wandert, wird stets die Eselschädel in den
Obstgärten bemerken. Sie sind an einem Baum oder an einer Stange
angebracht.

2. Ein Typus, dessen Beschreibung man am besten *Muntahà 'l-Arab*,
Nchdr. Teheran 1957-8, unter *xayāl*, überlässt : *gilīm i siyāh ki dar
kištzār bar čōb-ē kunand tā wuḥūš va ṭuyūr ān rā insān xayāl karda
bi-ramand* 'Ein grobes schwarzes Tuch, das man in Feldern auf eine
Stange steckt, damit die wilden Tiere und Vögel es für Menschen
halten und verscheucht werden'.

---

[3] P. *sar i xar* 'Störenfried, lästiger Mensch' *FrM*, Junker-Alavi, hat vom ursprünglichen
'Vogelscheuche' her dieser Bedeutung erlangt. Sōzanī, *Dīwān* 477 : *bādā ba sān i kalla
i xar kalla i 'adū-š andar miyān i bāy ki gētī ču bāy kard* 'Da er die Welt zu einem
Garten gemacht hat, möge der Kopf seines Feindes wie ein Eselschädel ('Vogelscheuche')
inmitten des Gartens sein'. Ferner Ḥamd-Allāh Mustaufī, *Nuzhat*, Bombay 1893-4,
S. 100 : *sar i xar dar pālēz āvēxtan ṭamara zūd rasānad va čašm i bad va āfāt az pālēz
bāz dārad* 'Eselschädel in Melonenfeldern aufstellen, lässt die Früchte früher reifen
und hält bösen Blick und Schaden fern'.

Mard Xurās. 502f: (*č.-q.*) *čūb-ī ba šakl i ṣalīb ki pārča yā kuhna-ī šabīh ba libās bar ān āvīzand* '(*č.-q.*), ein kreuzförmiges Holzgestell, an welches man ein Tuch oder einen kleiderähnlichen Fetzen hängt'. Osttü. قازق ~ قازوق ~ قازیق ~ قزق 'Pfosten, Pfahl, Pflock, Zaun-pfahl', Zenker, (< *qazγuq* aus *qaz-* 'to dig, dig out', Clauson, *An etym. Dict.* 680b, 682a) ist zusammengesetzt mit tü. *čullu* (<⁺*čul-loq* ⁺*čul-lïq*) 'mit Lappen bedeckt'; *čul* 'Pferdedecke vom groben Wollzeug; Lappen; schlechtes Kleid', Zenker.

Somit bedeutet ⁺*čullu qazïq* (übrigens eine einwandfreie tü. Bildung) 'mit Fetzen bespannte Stange'. Und das ist der 2. Typus von Vogelscheuche. Dass die Vogelscheuche als Wächter der Felder und der Gärten auch für Regen verantwörtlich gemacht wird, ist selbst-verständlich. Die Vogelscheuche (= Eselschädel) wird verbrannt, weil sie ihre Pflicht nicht erfüllt, sodass Dürre herrscht.

* * *

Xurāsānī *xelta*, *kīsa i kūčak* 'kleiner Beutel', *Mard. Xuras.*, 504. Afgp. *xalta* = *xarīṭa*, *kīsa mānand-ē ki az pārča sāzand…* 'eine beutelähnliche (Tasche), die man aus Tüchern anfertigt…', *xalta i mōy* 'Haarbeutel', *xaltagak*, *dāna va amṭāl ān ki āb pur karda va mulā'im šuda bāšad* '*x*. Korn u. dgl., das Wasser eingesaugt hat und weich geworden ist', *bē xalta fair kardan* 'reden ohne erwägen', eigentl. 'ohne Patronentasche (oder: Pulvertasche) Schüsse abfeuern' (*fair* < engl. *fire*), Afγānī-Navīs, *Fārsī i 'āmmiyāna i Afγānistān*, Kabul 1961 (= *FA*).

Zamaxšarī, *Maquddima* (ed. Wetzstein), 50: *xarīṭa* = p. *xalīta* (ed. Teheran 1963, I 267 und II 258 *xlyh*!), *kīsa i muṣḥaf* 'Beutel, Koranbeutel'; *al-xarīṭatu wi'ā'un min adīmin wa min γairihi yusraju* (Teheran: *yušraḥu*!) *'alà mā fīhi 'x*. ist ein Behälter aus Leder u. dgl. der über seinen Inhalt zusammengenäht wird'. Die Reihe enthält *qabāla* 'Urkunde', *ṣakk* 'Scheck, Wertpapier', *ruq'a* 'Brief', *jarīda* 'Heft', *xarīṭa*, …*raqq* 'Pergament', also handelt es sich um Schreib- und Kanzeleizubehör.

Ṣāḥib al-xarīṭa 'Schatzmeister in Tunis', Dozy, *Supplément*, I 363. Ibn Baṭṭūṭa (ed. Paris), III 337, erwähnt »*xarīṭa-dār* 'the master of royal Paper and Pen' was the governor of the territory of Hānsī and Sarastī«, *Hobson-Jobson*, 475.

Xuwārizmī, *Mafātīḥ*, Kairo 1923-4, S. 42, beschreibt *al-uskudār*: *wa huwa mudrajun yukatbu fīhi 'adadu 'l-xarā'iṭi wa 'l-kutubi 'l-wāridati wa 'l-nāfiḏati wa asāmī arbābihā* 'Es ist eine Rolle, in welcher die Zahl der eingehenden und der ausgehenden Briefe wie auch ihre Besitzernamen eingeschrieben wird'. In dieser Bedeutung kommt *xarīṭa, Tārīx i Baihaqī*, 48, vor. Der Hrsg. machte schon auf die Stelle bei Xuwārizmī aufmerksam.

Damit bleibt kein Zweifel übrig, dass *xarīṭa* und *xalīṭa* mindestens in der Bedeutung 'Beutel' zwei Formen desselben Wortes sind. Aber *xarīṭa* bedeutet in modernen tü., p. und arab. Wörterbüchern neben 'Beutel, Sack' auch 'Karte, Plan, Landkarte', s. Zenker, Wehr, *FrM*. In dieser Bedeutung kommt das Wort im Osm. als خارطى ~ خريطه ~ خرطى ~ خارﭡى vor und ist eine neue Entlehnung aus dem Gr. (gr. χαρτής, lat. *charta* 'Karte') wie schon Zenker bemerkte.

Aus dem *AT* kennt man schon חריטים, 2. Könige 5, 23 und Jesaja 3, 22, (beides Mal Dual), nach König, *Hebr.-Aram. Wb.*, arab. *xaraṭa* 'abhäuten' entsprechend.

Gr. χαρτής, sonst dunkler Herkunft, ist am besten aus eben dieser semit. Wurzel herzuleiten, als 'Abgehäutetes, Haut'.

Das nur von Miller, *Persiko-russkij slovar* (vgl. Doerfer, *Tü. und mong. Elemente*, Nr 1360) angeführte *γaltāq* 'patrontaš' ist natürlich dss. wie afgp. *xalta* 'Patronentasche' (s. oben). Das Wort ist in vielen Türksprachen vertreten, ebenso im Russ. (*kalitá*), im Urdū (*xal/rīṭa*). Dagegen ist das von Doerfer, ebd., zu *xal(i)ta* gesetzte osm. حلتا خالطه 'Halsband der Hunde, Pferde' etc. (Zenker 382a 'Halsband der Tiere') natürlich aus arab. *qilāda* (umgp. *γallāda*, s. *FrM* unter *qilāda*, afgp. *γalīda, FA*, < ⁺*qalēda* < *qilāda* 'Halband der Tiere') entstellt.

* * *

Im Dīwān des Sanā'ī, hrsg. von Mudarris i Riḍawī, S. 454, Z. 12-455, Z. 9 kommt eine Erzählung in *xafīf* (‿‿‿‿/ ‿‿‿‿/ ‿‿‿) vor, die in *Kalīla va Dimna* von Abu 'l-Ma'ālī Naṣr-Allāh i Munšī, ed. Mīnovī, 1. Auflage, Teheran 1964, S. 288f Aufnahme gefunden hat. Die Hss. sowohl von *Kalīla* als auch von Sanā'īs *Ḥadīqat al-Ḥaqīqa* stimmen bei einigen Versen dieser Erzählung nicht ganz überein.

F. Meier hatte schon 1963 in seinem Buch *Die schöne Mahsatī*, S. 49ff, eingehend die Probleme dieser Verse behandelt. Doch verliert Mīnovī kein Wort über Meiers Erläuterungen. Merkwürdigerweise stimmen ihre Ansichten über einige Fragen ganz überein.

Meier führt, ebd. in der Rechtschreibung der ältesten Hs. von *Ḥadīqa* (Vehbi (Istanbul) Nr 1672, vollendet 7. Šawwāl 552/16.11.1157) die Erzählung an, deren 1. Vers lautet:

داشت زالی بروستای چکاو   مهستی نام دخترو دوکاو

Demgegenüber hat Mīnovī, *Kalīla*, S. 288, den 2. Halbvers in folgender Form

مهستی نام دختری ودوگاو

Auf diesen Unterschied geht Mīnovī gar nicht ein. Kein Zweifel, dass die erstere die ältere und de echtere ist.

Die Erzählung verläuft folgendermassen :

Eine alte Frau im Dorfe *jk'w* (spätere Hss. *takāv, Fr. Rašīdī* und *Burhān* sogar *xagāv*!) hatte zwei Kühe und eine Tochter, Mahsatī. Diese wurde krank und lag im Bett. Eines Tages steckte eine der Kühe das Maul in einen Kessel. Ihr »verdammter« (*murda-rēg*, Meier, S. 51, Z. 3 übersetzt es mit 'hilflos') Kopf blieb im Kessel stecken. Sie rannte wie ein höllischer Dämon zu der Alten. Diese glaubte, das sei ʿAzrāʾīl ('Todesengel') und schrie :

کای مقلموت من نه مهستیم   مهستی ولت ولت ار نتیم

wofür die späteren Hss. haben

من یکی زال پیر محنتیم   —   —   —

Jedoch nach Meier, S. 51, Anm. 2, bietet Vehbi »die lectio difficilior und verdient den Vorzug vor den geglätteten, hochpersischen Fassungen«.

Mit peinlich genauen Untersuchungen kommt Meier, nachdem er *wl-t*, das metri causa nur *vʾl-t* sein kann, als *vi/ul* (p. *gul*) 'Blume' → 'Geliebte' → 'Freund' und *vil* in der Bedeutung von p. *rahā* 'frei, los' (+ Enkitikon *-t*) in Betracht gezogen hat, und *'r ntym* zu p. *ar na-dahiyam* 'wenn du sie mir nicht schenken (= lassen) willst' gedeutet hat, zu einer Lösung des Rätsels dieses Verses, welche lautet: »O Todesengel, ich bin nicht Mahsatī! Mahsatī steht dir frei, steht dir frei, wenn du sie mir nicht schenken willst (?)«.

Der Rest der Erzählung ist belanglos für unsere Untersuchung. Zu dem Namen des Dorfes, in dem die Alte lebt, schreibt Meier, S. 50, Anm. 1 : »Ich kann den Namen *čakāw* bei keinem Geographen nachweisén. Vieleicht handelt es sich un einem erfundenen Namen, falls er in den Text gehört. Dagegen ist ein ein *Čalāw* in Māzandarān bekannt...«. Ferner erwähnt er zu dem *Takāw* mancher Hss. *Tukāf* oder *Takāb* (Yāqūt, *Buldān* I, 860f). Er nennt auch andere ähnlich aussehende Namen und eine Bemerkung von ʿAbd al-ʿAẓīm Xān i

Garakānī (Meier: Gurgānī) in seiner Ausgabe von *Kalīla va Dimna i Bhrāmšāhī*, Teheran 1351, S. 236, wo das Gedicht zitiert wird, dass es sich um ein früheres Dorf in der Provinz von Ganja handelt. Dabei bemerkt Meier ganz richtig »was aber im Hinblick auf den Heimatsort der Dichterin Mahsatī zu sein scheint«. Doch ist auch daran zu denken, dass sogd. *γzny* bekanntlich p. *ganj-a* ist.

Schliesslich zieht Meier in seiner meisterhaften Übersetzung des Gedichtes vor, wegen *čakāv* 'Lerche' das Dorf als 'Lärchendorf' zu bezeichnen.

Mīnovī, *Kalīla* 288, Anm. 4, schreibt: »Č. ist ein Ortsname, und es ist nicht wichtig, ob es tatsächlich eine Ortschaft mit diesem Namen gegeben hat, oder der Name nur aus Gründen des Reims und des Metrums (erfunden worden) ist«. Weiter erwähnt er die Stelle bei Muqaddasī (ed. De Goeje) S. 316: »... unter den *arbā'* von Naisābūr wird Šāmāt *Takāb* genannt, weil es tiefer liegt als die anderen Rustāq und alles Wasser dahinfliesst ...«

Mehr zu *Čakāv* wissen weder Meier noch Mīnovī. Allein schon *D'Afγānistān juγrāfiyā'ī Qāmūs* II, Kabul 1963 kennt 5 Čakāv, vier Ortschaften und einen Berg:

1. in der Provinz Girišk i a'là (Ober-G.), Gouvernement Nauzād (38,5 km sö. von diesem), L 65° 37′ 1″, B 32° 4′ 18″.

2. in der Provinz Hirāt, Gouvernement Bādγēs (27 km sw. von Qal'a i Nau), L 63° 2′ 13″, B 24° 46′ (Text: 64′!) 19″.

3. in der Provinz Farāh i a'là (Ober-F.), Gouvernement Daulatābād (31,5 km sö. von diesem), L 62° 56′ 5″, B 32° 36′ 6″.

4. in der Provinz Farāh i a'là, Gouvernement Dilārām (25,5 km nö. von diesem), L 63° 38′ 48″, B 32° 17′ 30″.

5. Der Berg (γar) Č., Provinz Farāh i a'là, Gouvernement Qal'a i Jōyan und 837 m hoch.

Das häufige Vorkommen des Namens zeigt, dass es sich um eine alte Bezeichnung handelt. Meiers Č. 'Lerche' in diesem Zusammenhang kann ich weder befürworten noch bestreiten. Es ist auch weniger wichtig. Wichtig ist dass, das Č. von Sanā'ī wirklich eine Ortschaft und keine dichterische Erfindung gewesen ist. Es ist höchstwahrscheinlich die Ortschaft Nr 3 die näher zu Γaznī liegt.

Dass der oben angeführte Vers 9 aus dem Grunde der »sich steigernden Expressivität« in der Mundart jenes Dorfes gefasst ist, sieht man schon sehr deutlich an *maqalmaut* (afgp. *q* des öfteren für p. *k* besonders vor ǎ, ǒ, ǔ, *quštī* 'Ringkampf', *qaf* 'Schaum', *qāγad* 'Papier', *qulūx* 'Erdklumpen').

Bevor ich zur Deutung des Verses übergehe, möchte ich auf eine andere Version desselben aufmerksam machen, welche Mīnovī, *Kalīla*, S. 290, Anm. 1, aus einer Hs. Bibl. Nat., Paris, Ancien fonds pers. 375 = Blochet, *Catalogue des Mss. Persans*, Paris 1905-34, Bd. IV, Nr 2026, geschrieben 6-7 Jh. d. H. anführt[5]. Unser Vers lautet hier:

ولت كزجينك ولت از نتيم   كاى مقلموت ازنه مهستيم

Man sieht deutlich, dass die beiden Halbverse mit *'z nh mhstym* und *'z ntym* statt *mn nh mhstym* und *'r ntym* (s. oben) enden. Es bleibt kein Zweifel, dass ein Abschreiber *az* 'ich'[6] in dem 1. Halbvers durch *man* ersetzt hat. So wird auch in dem 2. Halbvers der 1. Version *'r* ein Fehlschreiben für *'z* sein. Kehren wir jetzt mit diesen neugewonnenen Lesungen zu der 1. Version zurück und setzen wir sie dort ein:

k' ay maqalmaut az na mahsatī om

mahsatī v.l-t, v.l-t az na tī om

Zu dem rätselhaften *wlt* = *v.l-t* (Mīnovī, ebd. vokalisiert *valt*, etwa nach der Hs.?) möchte ich neben den Vorschlägen von Meier, die keinen sehr guten Sinnzusammenhang geben, noch ⁺*vĕl* < ⁺vēl < *vail* (arab. *wail*: *Šn 1*, 40, 45; *12c*, 279; *13f*, 1971; *15*, 346 (Daqīqī), 1766 'Geschrei, Klage' = *vāy* vorschlagen. Die zusammengeschrümpfte dialektische Form *vĕl* + *t* entsricht genau p. *vāy i tu* (Nāṣir i Xusrau, *Dīwān*, Teheran 1965, S. 373: *ay vāy i tu* 'o, wehe dir!', Rūmī (Nicholson) I, Nr 31: *vāy i ō* 'wehe ihm!')

Das Ganze (Version 1) würde in der Übersetzung lauten: 'Sagend (*ki*): O Todesengel, ich bin nicht Mahsatī! Mahsatī! wehe dir, ich bin nicht du!'

In der Pariser Hs. ist der 2. *miṣrā'* vorläufig zu übersetzen: 'Wehe dir *kzjynk*, wehe dir, ich bin nicht du!'

kzjynk entspricht ＿＿＿. Ich schlage vor, das Wort zu *kzxynk* zu emendieren und ⁺*kažxēn-ka* (vgl. afgp. *zan(a)-ka* 'Hure') zu lesen mit *kažxēn* < tü *qazɣan* 'Kessel' (mit sehr häufig afgp. *ā* > *ē*), dessen zahlreiche Nebenformen قازغان ~ غزغان ~ قزغان ~ غزان ~

---

[5] Mīnovī, *Kalila*, S. XIX unvollständige Angabe: *kutub-xāna i millī i Pāris* 375!

[6] *man*, an und für sich Gen. Sg. (ap. *manā*, av. *mana*), hat den Cas. Rect. *az* aus vielen Dialekten vertrieben, doch haben das ältere Gīl., Māz., Tāliši noch *az* gehabt, heute kurd. *az*, simn. *ā* mit Ausfall von *z*, (GrIrPh. I, 2, 82), paštō *zə*, sogd. *'zw* (Morgenstierne, *Etym. Vocab. of Pashto*, S. 101); Osset, *äz*, av. *azəm*, ap. *adam*, ai. *ahám*.

خازقان ~ غزغن ~ غزغند ~ كژغان ~ خاژگان ~ قاژ گان ~ قازقان ~ قزان sind, s. Doerfer, *Tü. und mong. Elemente*, Nr 1390; dazu noch *γazγūn* usw. Nun ist es wichtig, dass in verschiedenen Gegenden von Persien *dēg-ba-sar* 'Kessel-auf-dem-Haupt' ein Schreckgespenst, »der schwarze Mann«, für Kinder ist. Mit dem mir zur Verfügung stehenden Material kann ich leider keinen Beleg im P. finden, jedoch kurd. *qāzāne-sara* (~ *qižne-sara*, das letztere kontaminiert mit *qiž-in* ~ *qiž-ne* 'Haarschopf', s. Mardūx, *Fr. i Kurdī*, unter *pirčīn*) 'Schreckgespenst', ebd. In derselben Bedeutung *kažxēn-ka* 'der mit Kessel' → 'Schreck-gepenst' → 'Todesengel'. Der Halbvers wird dann in der Übersetzung lauten : '(die alte Frau sich an ihre Tochter wended) : Wehe dir, (siehe,) der Todesengel, wehe dir, ich bin nicht du!'

* * *

Xurāsānī *šer-bez* = *alak* (< tü. *elek*) 'feines Sieb', *Mard. Xuras.* 511. In derselben Bedeutung kommt das Wort Amīr-Xusrau, *Hašt-Bihišt*, Moskau 1972, Nr 3395b vor : *mō ba mō šaʿr-bēz karda i ō 'st* 'in (allen) Einzelheiten ist (es) von ihm durchsiebt'.

D.i. *šaʿr* 'Seidenstoff', Zamaxšarī, *Muqaddima* 62 *t̲aubun min al-ibrī-sam* 'Kleiderstoff aus Seide'. Das arab. *šaʿr* ist aber 'Haar; Borste; Fell' → 'grobes Wolltuch' → 'Überwurf'. Vgl. Naṭanzī, *Mirqāt* 84 (Teheran 1967), Anm. 2 *šaʿr* = *jāma az kurk va mō* 'Stoff aus weicher Wolle oder aus Wolle' (nach *Aqrab al-Mawārid*).

Hinter diesem semantischen Wandel steckt p. ⁺*šarak* 'Seide', wie es aus dem chinesischen Namen von Kāšγar *su-leh/su-lek* (< ⁺*šǎrak*) zum ersten Mal von Tomaschek erkannt worden ist, s. Marquart, *Ērānšahr* 283 f und *Wehrot und Arang* 68. Spuren dieses Wortes sind sogar im *Šn.* zu finden, wo in einigen Stellen u.a. *41*, 4406 und *46*, 1392 *šaʿr* unbedingt 'Seide, seiden' bedeutet. Die erstere lautet :
ba gāh i basījīdan i marg may   ču pērāhan i šaʿr bāšad ba day
'Wenn der Tod sich ausrüstet, wird Wein (so ungelegen) sein wie ein Hemd aus *šaʿr* im Monat *day* (1 Wintermonat)'.

An der 2. Stelle handelt es sich um die Verhöhnung des Helden Bahrām i Čōbīn durch Hurmazd, da der König dem siegreichen Heerführer Frauenkleidung und Spindelgerät als Ehrengabe schickt :
ham az šaʿr pērāhan ē lāžavard   yak-ē surx šalvār u miqnāʿ i zard
'Wie auch ein lazurblaues Hemd aus *šaʿr*, ein (Paar) rote Hosen und einen gelben Kopfschleier'. *šaʿr* wird 'Seide' sein, welche den feinsten und femininsten Stoff darstellt.

Ferner lässt Jawāliqī, *Mu'arrab*, Nchdr. Teheran 1966, S. 182 *saraq* = arab. *ḥarīr* 'Seide', das er als arabisiertes *sara* betrachtet (vgl. *Sāmī fī 'l-Asāmī*, Teheran 1967, 158 *saraqa* = *pāra-ē ḥarīr i nēk* 'ein Stück Stoff aus edler Seide' und *Burhān sara* 'Seide') eher auf p. ⁺*šara(k)* schliessen. Während *Burhān šāra* 'tela subtilissima et coloribus distincta, ex qua muliere vestes conficere solent, et laternis inserviens' (nach Vullers) ist⁷, bedeutet p. *ša'r-bāf* (< ⁺*šār/šēr-baf*)⁸ 'Seidenweber', Steingass. Vielleicht ist *šērāza* (so afgp., *FA*, gegen *šī-*, Platts, Vullers, Steingass). 1. 'gesticktes Kapitalband aus farbiger Seide', 2. 'jeder am Rande (der Bekleidungsstücke) mit Seide bestickte Saum (beides *Bahār i 'Ajam* bei Vullers), 3. 'sewing button-holes' (mit Seide natürlich; Platts, Steingass.) zu verstehen aus ⁺*šēr* 'Seide' + *āj/ž(ī)dan*, *āz/ž-* 'stechen, besticken' + *a*, also 'seidenbestickt'.

Selbstverständlich wird ⁺*šār/šēr* eine bestimmte Art von Seide sein wie *qaz* (*kaz/ž*, ... arab. *xazz*) 'Seide minderer Qualität, von Kokons, denen der Falter schon ausgeschlüpft', *abrīšam* (= *ḥarīr*) 'Seide, deren Kokons zwecks der Tötung der Larven mit kochendem Wasser behandelt worden sind', *abrīšam i xām* 'Seide von Kokons, deren Larven nur durch die Sonne getötet worden sind, von bester Qualität', Ḥakīm Mu'min, *Tuḥfa* 11.

Nach Nyberg, *Ordet silke Och dessa historia* (Kungl. Vetenskaps-Soc. Årsbok 1967, S. 29-37), Uppsala 1967, müssen die Zeichen ـسعلـر *Frahang i Pahlavīk*, Kap. IV *šēr-āy* mit aram. adj. Endung gelesen werden. Das Wort entspricht somit gr. σηρ-ικός. Es ist selbst ostasiatischer Herkunft (mong. *sirkek*, korean. *sir*, chin. *ssi*, *ssē*), hat einerseits gr. σηρικόν, lat. *sericum*, frz. *serge* 'Scharsche, Sarsche', andererseits aruss. *šelkŭ*, russ. *šëlk*, apreuss. *silkas*, ags. *sioluc*, engl. *silk*, anord. *silki* ergeben, s. Kluge, *Etym. Wb.*, unter Seide, vgl. Vassmer, *Russ. etym. Wb*, unter »šëlk«.

Auf dem 29. Congrès International des Orientalistes, Paris 1973, schlug M. Navvābī (Universität Teheran) vor, in einer ziemlich schwierigen Stelle von Bundahišn, ed. Anklesaria, S. 104, Z. 4, die Zeichen ـيسبل *šēr* zu lesen und 'Seide' zu deuten. Er stützte sich nur auf p. *ša'r-bāf*.

---

⁷ *Šn 15*, 4202; *35b*, 642; *41*, 3525 »ist vom 'indischen *šāra*' die Rede«. D.i. Sari, hindī *sāṛī*, prakr. *śāḍī* 'Frauenkleid', skr. *śāṭa* 'strip of cloth', Turner, Nr 12381.

⁸ Die Seidenweber, *ša'r-bāf*, von Hirāt versicherten mir (Juni 1974), dass die letztere Bezeichnung aus *šāl/r-bāf* entstellt ist. Der gestreifte, nichtsehr breite Stoff, den sie weben heisst *šāl/r*.

Doch muss die Stelle ganz anderes interpretiert werden.

'pas 'pat šgl a-šān slmk bē tat 'hān i tatak jāmak kart nihuft 'hend

Dieselben Zeichen kommen ebd. 103, Z. 1-2 vor :

'pat šgl frāč' 'ō az-ē i spēt mōy mat'

Es handelt sich um Mašī und Mašyānī, die 30 Tage auf der Suche nach Essen und Kleidung umherliefen, während sie mit Gras bekleidet waren. Nach 30 Tagen kamen sie durch ('pat) šgl zu einer weisshaarigen Ziege, deren Milch sie saugten. Dann kamen sie nach (weiteren) 30 Tagen zu einem Schaf mit weissem Unterkiefer, das sie schlachteten und opferten, indem sie sein Fleisch ins Feuer warfen, das sie unter göttlicher Leitung angezündet hatten. Zuerst zogen sie das Fell und später spannen sie durch ('pat) šgl daraus Fäden und webten aus diesen Kleider.

Dieselbe Geschichte findet man in *Firdaus al-Muršidīya* (ed. F. Meier, Istanbul 1934, S. 283) über das Leben des Šaix Abū Isḥāq Ibrāhīm b. Šahriyār, dessen zoroastrischer Hintergrund durch Abstammung, Jugend und seine späteren dauernden Zusammenstösse mit *Gabrān* ('Zoroastrier') ganz evident ist : Adam und Eva bekleideten sich mit den Blätteren des paradiesischen Baumes (Z. 6). Als sie auf die Erde kamen, begab sich Gabriel zu ihnen und brachte ihnen bei, ein Schaf zu opfern (Z. 8 f). Daraufhin (immer nach den Anweisungen Gabriels) trennten sie die Wolle vom Schafsfell : Eva spann daraus Fäden, und Adam webte diese zu einem Wollkleid.

Gabriels Anweisung entpricht in *Bundahišn* 'pat šgl, welches als sogd. škr, Gershevich, *A Gr. of Man. Sogd.* (§§ 366, 540, 592), šykr (§ 715) 'to lead', škrδ' (§ 726) 'to bring along' und sogd. šqrnyt̲, Pl. (§ 890) anzutreffen ist. Das Wort lebt im Umgp. als *šigird* (*šegerd*) 'Art, Weise, Lebensführung', *FrM*, fort.

Die Zeichen ﺭﻣﻠﻮﻩ an der zuerst angeführten Stelle können nichts anderes darstellen als ein Wort für 'Faden' oder 'Wolle'. Vielleicht sind sie überhaupt aus *lšmk* entstellt, das afgp. (*FA*), kurd, (Mardūx) *rašma*, gabrī (Kirmān, Surūšiyān, *Fr. i Bihdīnān*, Teheran 1956) 'dünner Faden, Schnur', tü. LW. *rešme, irišme* 'Maulkette, Kinnkette' (als Schmuck der Reitpferde), Zenker, entspricht [8].

Die erste Stelle bedeutet somit 'dann spannen sie (es) unter Führung (der Götter) zu Fäden, aus jenem Gesponnenen machten sie Tuch (und) bekleideten sich (damit)'.

---

[9] Vgl. skr. *raśmí*- 'cord, rope; rein; ray,...', Macdonell; hindī 'a rein, a ray of light, ...', Platts.

Die 2. angeführte Stelle lautet in der Übersetzung 'Nach 30 Tagen kamen sie durch Wegweisung (der Götter) zu einer weisshaarigen Ziege'.

* *
*

Xurāsānī *q/xošd/telī* 'Spagetti-Nudel', *Mard. Xurās.* 514. Čaγ., Mahdī Xān Astarbādī, *Sanglāx*, ed. Clauson, London 1960, fol. 288 v : *qoš-deli,*(1) *lisān al-ʿaṣāfir va ān diraxt-ē 'st ʿaẓīm ... ṭamar-aš šabīh ba zabān i gunjišk ...*, (2) *nau-ē az ṭaʿām bāšad va ān čunān ast ki xamīr rā miṯl i zabān i murγ burīda dar rōγan u šakar puxta ba rōy i ṭaʿām afšānand* '(1) Esche (p. *zabān-gunjišk*), sie ist ein grosser Baum... ihre Frucht ähnelt einer Spatzenzunge... (2) eine Art Speise, sie wird auf folgende Weise (zubereitet): man schneidet den Teig wie Vogelzungen, bäckt sie mit Butterschmalz und Zucker und streut sie über Speisen Kāšγarī III, 130: *qīma ügre, ismu nauʿin min al-iṭrīyati yuqṭaʿu ʿajīnuhu muḥarrafan ka-lisāni. 'l-ʿaṣāfiri ʿq.-ü.* (Zamaxšarī, *Muqaddima* 60, اكراء) ist der Name einer Art Spagetti, dessen Teig schräg geschnitten wird wie Spatzenzungen'.

Dass *murγ* (*Sanglāx* : *zabān i m.*) und *gunjišk* in gewissen Kontexten auswechselbar sind, merkt man schon an den Bezeichnungen von Esche(nsamen): *zabān-gunjišk,* = *murγ-zabānak, Burhān.*

Vullers II, 11b (zu *zabān-gunjišk*, aus *Bahār i ʿAjam*) hat ausser a) 'Esche(nsamen)' noch b) »genus panis linguae passeris formam habens alias etiam ﻳﻠﯽ ﺗﻮﺷﻪ«, augenscheinlich verderbt aus ﻗﻮﺷﺪﯾﻠﯽ

* *
*

Xurāsānī *sebrij, ḍarrāt i xākistar u ātaš ki ba hangām i sūxtan i būtahā i xār az dāxil i tanūr ba hawā ṣuʿūd mī-kunand* 'Teilchen von Feuer und von Asche, die beim Brennen der Dornbusche aus den Inneren des Backofens in die Luft steigen', *Mard. Xurās.* 509.

< *si-* (av. *us-, uz-*, ap. *us- ud-* 'hinauf, hinaus', vgl. *si-parī* 'vollendet', phl. *us-purrīk* 'dss.', *GrIrPh* I, 2, 160) + *birēz* : *biruštan*, ai. √ *bhrajj-* 'rösten', über ⁺*us-brēz* 'hinauffröstend'.

* *
*

P. *čalpāsa* 'Eidechse' und Nebenformen. Doerfer, *Tü. LWW. im Tadsch.,* Wiesbaden 1967, Nr 161: tadsch. *kalpas(a), kalpa/ista, kalpesa* 'Eidechse' < özb. dialektisch? Er macht auf Steingass *kalbắsū* aufmerksam und schliesst den Artikel mit dem Satz: »Eine türkische Ursprungform lässt sich daraus schwer ermitteln, ausser das sie mit *kä-* begonnen haben muss; wahrscheinlich liegt Tabuisierung vor. Die persischen und tadschikischen Formen dürften eher auf türkische Dialektformen zurückgehen als umgekehrt«.

Die p. Formen sind (Steingass) *čalpasa, karpās/ša/ū, karbāsak, karpāyaš, karbas(a), karbas/šū, karfaš. Luγat i Furs*, Teheran 1957, S. 62: *karbasa* mit einem Versbeleg von Rūdakī und S. 69 *karbaš* mit einem Versbeleg von 'Unṣurī. Afgp. *čalupāsa, (FA)*, kurd. *karpasa* (Mardūx), sogd. *krps'k* 'lizard', Gershevich, *A Gr. of Man. Sogd.*, §139, vgl. av. *kahrpuna-*, gäbrī (Kirmān), *Fr. Bihdīnān, kerpū* 'Eidechse', phl. *karbōk* 'an Ahrimanic animal, one of the xrafstrs, uncertain which.-Probably a poisonous lizard', Nyberg, *Manual* II.

* * *

P. *jōx* (lexica *jaux*, wegen der arabisierter Form *jauq*, arab. *au* = normale Wiedergabe des p. *ō*; Jawāliqī, *Muʿarrab* 94: *al-jauq, al-jamāʿatu min an-nāsi* 'Menschenmenge') 'Schar, Trupp', Farruxī († 1038), *Dīwān*, Teheran 1970, S. 11, Nr 206b: *ču jōqhā i ḥawāṣil ki bar kašī ba ṭanāb* 'wie Schwärme von Pelikanen, die du auf eine Schnur reihst'; arm. LW. *jok* 'Herde, Schar', *GrIrPh* I, 2, 66. D.i. skr. *yū-thá-* 'herd, flock; host, multitude': √*yu-* 'yoke, harness; bind', Macdonell, Zu *-ō-* vgl. av. √*yaog-* 'anspannen', *AirWb* 1228.

Doerfer, *Tü. und mong. Elem. im Np.*, Nr 1027, schreibt mit Recht, dass das Wort mit tü. *čoq* 'viel' nichts zu tun hat. Aber seine Äusserung »Jedoch stammt das pers. Wort mit Sicherheit aus ar(ab). *ǧau̯q*, cf. u.a. WEHR 134 'Truppe'« kann nicht stimmen.

* * *

P. *xāk-šī/ū, xāk-žī, Burhān*, 'Sisimbrium polyceratium L., vielschotige Raute', Achundow, *Die pharmakologischen Grundsätze des Abu Mansur Muwaffak bin Ali Harawi*, Halle 1893, S. 370, vgl. noch Sontheimer (Ibn al-Baiṭār, *Mufradāt*, Üb., Stuttgart 1840-42), II, 217.

Burhān setzt die oben angebenen Formen arab. *bizr al-ximxim* und *bizr al-xubba* (Text II, 702: *bzr l-jnh!*) gleich. Gemeint ist also der Same und nicht die Staude. Ḥakīm Mu'min, *Tuḥfa* 99 schildert genau die Pflanze und ihre Samen: *xubba ba luγat i Šīrāz šiftarak va ba luγat i Işfahān xākšī va ba turkī šīvaran va dar Māzindarān giyāh i ō rā salam-bī nāmand va ān tuxm-ē 'st bisyār rēza* 'Sisimbrium heisst šīrāzī *š.*, işf. *x.*, tü. *š.* In Māz. nennt man dessen Pflanze *salam-bī* (meine Vokalisierung nach Schlimmer, *Terminologie médico-pharmaceutique*, 3 Aufl., Teheran 1970, S. 510. Māz. *bī* = p. *bēx* 'Wurzel, Stengel, Pflanze'). Es ist ein sehr winziger Same'.

Unter *šiftarak* steht im *Burhān* »es ist das Gewächs vom *xākšī* und nach manchen dessen Same«.

Sanglāx fol. 261 r, 5: *šīvaran*[10] ... *nām i xākšīr bavad va ān rā dar Šīrāz šiftarak gōyand* '*š.* ist Sisimbrium. In Šīrāz nennt man es *šiftarak*'. Hierzu schreibt Clauson, *Sanglāx* S. 103, » *šīwaran* 'the name of a *xākşīr*' (not, as Pavet de Courteille translates 'peach', but some smaller berry; morphologically P(ersian) but not in the dictionaries«. Dies ist wiederum nicht ganz richtig. Der Fehler, *xākšī(r)* als Beere oder Pfirsich zu deuten, ankert in der Verwechslung zwischen *šaftarang* (= *šaft-ālū*, *Luγat i Furs* 112; *šaftalang*, *FrJh*, = *šalīl/r* 'smooth-peach', vgl. Schlimmer, ebd. 94 und Qāsim Abū-Naşrī, *Iršād az-Zirā'a*, Teheran 1967, S. 231, mit *šift-* 'tropfen', *GrIrPh* I, 2, 138; *MirM* III e 37: *šyft-*, av. *xšipta-*, *šuγnī šuwd* 'Milch', *GrIrPh.* I, 2, 308) und *šiftarak* 'Sisimbrium'.

Woher Steingass *šiftarak* 'a red bramble' bezogen hat und warum er die von *FrJh* (unter *xākšī*), *Fr. Ršīdī*, *Burhān*, *Fr. Ānandarāj* angegebene Bedeutung nicht anführt, ist mir nicht klar. Vielleicht hat er *FrJh*: *xākšī/ū tuxm-ē 'st dawā'i ki surx i may-gōn bavad va ba γāyat rēza bāšad* '*x.* ist ein sehr winziger, weinroter, medizischer Same' falsch aufgefasst.

Betrachtet man die Formen *xāk-šī/ū* (~ *xāk-žī*) einerseits und *šif-tarak* andererseits, ist es leicht zu sehen, dass *šif* (⁺*šiv/šu* < ⁺*šīf*) auf Sisimbrium hindeutet, während *xāk-šī* (< ⁺*xāk-šīf*, mit *xāk/g*, p. *xāya* 'Same, Ei', vgl. *tuxm* 'dss.') auf dessen Same und *šif-tarak* (*tara-k* 'Kraut, Grünzeug') auf dessen Pflanze hinweist. Čaγ. *šīvaran* wird dann nichts anderes sein als *šif-tarak*, über eine Form wie ⁺*šiv-taraɲ*.

* *

Xurāsānī *xončeleq/xanjoloq* = p. *višgūn, nīšgūn*, 'Zwicken, Kneifen',

---

[10] Bei den Hazāra in Bāmiyān heisst die Pflanze *šebar* (< *šīvaran*), wie ich in Juni 1974 an Ort und Stelle erfuhr. Danach ist auch der hohe Pass zwischen Čārīkār und Bāmiyān Kotal-i Šebar genannt, wo *š.* in Mengen wächst.

Mard. Xurās. 505, ist auf tü. *qanjalamaq* 'to grapple with a hook; to seize with the bent fingers', Redhouse, zurückzuführen, welches seinerseits ein denom. Verbum aus *qanja/ï* 'Haken, ... Harpune', Zenker, ist. Letzteres hängt mit *qančïq* 'bitch', Clauson, *An etym. Dict.* 634b, zusammen, Hierzu vgl. p. *sag-ak* (*sag* 'Hund') 'eine Art Haken (*qullāb*)', *Burhān*.

Die p. Bezeichnungen *višgūn* (*veš-*), *nišgūn* (*neš-*), mit gelehrter Form *nīš-gūn* 'stachel-ähnlich', gehören zu *šikanj* (s. gleich unten), einmal mit Präfix *vi-*, das andere Mal mit Präfix *ni-*. Die Vokalisierung *niškunj* in *Burhān* ist schon deswegen falsch, weil *Luγat i Furs* in einem Versbeleg von 'Unṣurī *niškanj* mit *nāranj* 'Apfelsine' gereimt bringt, und darüber hinaus *FrJh*, und *Fr. Rašīdī* es ausdrücklich mit *-ka-* angeben. Doch zeigt sie, dass eine *nišgūn* ähnliche Form schon damals vorhanden gewesen ist.

šikank/iškanj (< *škanj*, phl. *škinjak*) ist aber 'Tortur, Buchbinderpresse', *šikanjīdan* 'to put in a press', Steigass; dss. beissen (*gazīden*)', *FrJh*; *niškanjīdan* 'zwicken', *Burhān*; /*schkiga*/ = *(i)škinja*, lat. *turnus* 'Schraubstock', *Codex Cumanicus* 86,25; *Šn.* 20, 1560 *bar-šikanjīdan* 'quälen' (mit *-ka-* in Reimposition), vgl. Zamaxšarī, *Muqaddima* 22, arab. *dahaq* ('Stock, Block (für die Füsse des Verbrechers)'), Wehr = p. *šikanja, iškanja*.

Šn.bar-š. entspricht genau av. *skəndo.-aipi.jati* 'Schlagen, Zufügung eines (körperlichen) Schaden', *AirWb* 1587, und gehört zu /*skand*- 'brechen' schon früh kontaminiert mit √*skamb*- 'stemmen'. Das av. Wort ist übrigens mit phl. *škanāk* wiedergegeben, das Wiederum np. *iškana(k)* 'Daumenschraube', *FrM*, Junker-Alavi, entspricht.

G. MORGENSTIERNE

INDO-EUROPEAN *DHEUGH-* AND *DEUK-* IN INDO-IRANIAN

Latin *mulgeo* "to milk" has cognates as well in all European branches of IE as in Tokh., but the related root Skt. *mr̥j-*, Av. *marəz-* has retained the less specialized meaning of "pulling (off), pressing, making drip", etc.

In Indo-Ar. we find **dh(e)ugh-* "to milk" from the Vedas and down to practically all modern dialects. In fact, Shina *çhau thoiki* "to perform milking" is the only exception known to me. Note also, from Kafiri, Prasun *mim-*?

Already in 1895 Hübschmann [1] was aware of the difficulty of combining phonetically the various Ir. forms. But here, too, either **dheugh-* or **deuk-* can account for the great majority of the words denoting milking. Exceptions are:

Yaghn. *čak(k)-* "to drip, to milk" is probably borrowed from Prs., and the same may perhaps be the case with Wanetsi Psht. *cek-*. But here we find also *lwes-*, related to the ordinary Psht. form, and the relation between these two roots would require further investigation on the spot. Yazghulami differs from its Shughni Group neighbours in having *cəx-*: *coxt*, which according to Sokolova [2] goes back to IE **trenk-* "to compress", cf. Av. **θraxta-* "compressed", a derivation which I am inclined to accept, even if the development of the vocalism is not quite clear to me. Finally I may mention Prs. (acc. to Steingass "Transoxanian") *layzīdan* "to drink, milk" which it would be reckless to take as a corruption of an **l*-dialect form of **duyž-*.

I have not come across the verb "to milk" in Sogd. or Khot., and in OIr. only as a past ptc. in the Av. female name *Duγdō-vā*, with *dugda-* (= Skt. *dugdhá-*) pointing to a pre-Ir. root in **-gh-*.

But we also find numerous forms going back to IE **deuk-*. Henning [3] derives Khwar *δws-*, Oss. *doc-* Prs. *dōš-* [4], Psht *lwas-* < **daučya-*,

---

[1] *Persische Studien*, S. 64.

[2] *Genetičeskie otnošenija jazguljamskogo jazyka i šugnanskoj jazykovoj gruppy*, § 143.

[3] *Mitteliranisch*, 111, n 8.

[4] Tajiki also *jōš-*, with assimilation of *d-* to *-š-*, cf. the parallel development of Khowar *jōš* "ten".

and Benveniste[5] accepts this view as regards Oss. It seems, however, possible that Prs. *š* may go back to *$xš(y?)$* [6].

As for Psht., -*š*- may be derived from either *-*šy*- < (*-*čy*-) or < *-*xšy*-, but the material for comparison is very meagre. A derivation of *wuršō(w)* f. "grazing, meadow" < *fra-čyawā*- is possible but very doubtful, and *mūnğ* "we" probably goes back, with early voicing of -*š*-, to *$mō(n)ẓ$* < *ahmāš(y)a*- < *ahmāčya*- [7].

On the other hand Psht. *wēš* "dividing, division" most probably goes back to *baxšya*-, and the dialect forms like *(a)lwēš*-, *lēš*-, Wan. *lwes*- "to milk" [8] might support the derivation of this word from a form containing a palatalizing *-*xšy*-. But *ē* for *a* occurs, in Psht. dialects, also in words where no palatalization can have taken place (e.g. *wrēj* "day"; *špēğ* "six").

Also Sgl. *dēš*- may be derived from forms in *-*čy*- or *-*xšy*-, and the same may be the case with Orm. K. *dūs*-, L. *duš*-. But as far as I can see, it is not possible to arrive at a certain conclusion.

There can, however, not be any doubt that Wkh. *δic*- and Par. *dūč*- represent OIr. *dauča*-. And it seems probable that this applies also to the Shgh. Group *δŭj*-, etc., and Mj.-Yd. *lūž*-, although in these languages no distinction is made between ancient -*č*- and -*j*- [9].

In EIr. *xt* results in *γd*, and no conclusions can be drawn from modern EIr. forms in *γd*, only Av. *duγda*- testifying to an original group *-*gh* + *t*. Wkh. has, as might be expected, a past ptc. *δaγ-n* [10]. And in Sgl., Bal. etc. we find secondary preterites in -*št*-, etc., and in some dialects also the vowel has been adapted to that of the present.

Ir. *d(a)ug*- is known from various nominal forms: Thus, Prs. *dōγ*, etc.; Wkh. *δiγ* "sour milk"; Psht. *lwaγ* "milking" < *dauga*-, (Skt. *doha*-); cf. Prs. *palūγ* "the act of milking" from an "*l*-dialect". According to Abaev Oss. *doγ*, *donq/γ* "milk from one milking" is derived from *daughna*-, but the vocalism is not easily explained.

Psht. has *lwaγǝy* f. and *lwaγuna* "milk-pail" [11], and it is tempting

---

[5] *Langue oss.*, 137.

[6] V. Zaehner, BSOS, X 616; cf. Duchesne-Guillemin "Pers. *dōšīza*" (Muséon LIX, 575).

[7] Wan. may have split off from ordinary Psht. early enough to retain the *š* in *mōš*.

[8] The Wan. pret. *lwā* < *duxtaka*- shows that *lwes*-, if a lw. from "Psht.," must be an ancient one.

[9] Sokolova's derivation (*op. cit.*, 47) < *dheugh*- cannot be accepted.

[10] Cf. a -*na* also in Yaghn. *čakt/na*.

[11] Poss. contaminated with *γwalūna*, cf. Av. *gaodana*- "id.", and Wan. *γwalūn* "female breast, teat".

to compare *lwaɣza* "(cow/sheep) in milk" with Skt. *doha-ja* "produced by milking" [12].

Psht. *salwāɣa*, etc., "a bucket for drawing water from a well" can be satisfactorily explained as going back to **usa-daugā-* (Skt. **utsa-dohā-*) [13]. This does not imply that the word originally was a "kenning" : "well-milker", but that **daug-* was used in a more general sense. Cf. Benveniste [14] about OPrs. *handugā-* "proclamation" who refers also to Latin *pro-mulgare*.

It is of interest to note that Shgh. has retained a more general meaning of **dauk-* in *wi-δǔj-* "to peel, skin, cleanse (nuts and pease from the husk or pods)" and *war-δǔj-* "to remove the walnut kernel from the husk".

As a finite verb **daug-* appears to be known only from some SE Psht. dialects as *lway-əl* according to various Psht., dictionaries by Afghan authors, and localized to Chaman and Pishin (in the *Quetta-Pishin Gazetteer*, 385).

Theoretically it might be possible to derive forms in -*š*-, etc., < **gh + s*, and such in *xt* < **gh + t* (cf. e.g. Av. *daxša-*, *aoxta*). But Wkh. and Par. *δic-*, *dūč-* must represent IE **deuk-*, and if Henning is right in his derivation of the Khwar., Oss., etc. forms < **daučya-*, this applies also to these languages. As we have seen above it may be possible to derive Psht. *lwaš-*, Sgl. *dēš-* and Orm. *dūs-/düš-* < **dauxšya-*, thus avoiding the necessity of assuming a present in -*ya-* from a strong root **dauč-* But I must leave it to specialists to decide whether a derivation of the Khwar., Oss. forms from **-xšy-* might, after all, be imaginable.

At any rate we must in Ir. reckon with the existence of two roots **dheugh-* and **deuk-* which might in some positions merge phonetically, and which were semantically closely enough related to be attracted to one another.

It seems reasonable to assume that **dheugh-* had acquired the meaning of "milking" already in common Indo-Ir., and *handugā* may represent an ancient relict. There is no trace of **deuk-* in IA, but the root has been plausibly compared with that of Lat. *dūco* [15], cf. also e.g. Alb. *nduk* (dial.) "to suck out".

---

[12] In spite of Mayrhofer, who thinks that the similarity is accidental.

[13] Ir. *usa-* is known only from Av. *an-usavant-* "was kein Aussfluss hat" (Barth.), but may easily have survived in Psht.

[14] BSL, 30, 73, sq.

[15] Acc. to my notes, by Benveniste, but I regret not being able to trace the reference.

But what about Psht. *lwaɣ-* and *lwaš-*? Do they belong to two originally different dialect areas? Or did they once form part of the same paradigm? Since we possess no OIr. finite present forms of the verb, we can only guess at how an original, athematic **daug-di* (Skt. *dógdhi*) was transformed into a thematic **dauga-ti* (not **dauǰa-ti*!).

*Dauxšya- (whether from IE **deuk-*, or **dheugh-* + *sye-*) would phonetically agree completely with Skt. *dhokṣya-*, but this possibility has not been envisaged by Henning, Benveniste and Gershevitch [16]. But I admit that it would be difficult to explain why the future stem gained such a strong foothold in Ir.

---

[16] I have not been able to find a type **CauC-ya-* in Av. or Skt.

JOHANNA NARTEN

AVESTISCH *CIŠ*

Geldner setzt in den Studien zum Avesta I, 1882, p. 68[2], 134 ff. für die Verbalwurzel *ciš* die Bedeutung »versprechen, in Aussicht stellen« an [1]; ebenso Baunack [2]: »in Aussicht stellen«. Dieser Ansatz wird von Bartholomae (AirWb. 429 ff.: [2]*kaēš*), der sich auf Geldner und Baunack bezieht, übernommen — (unter 2:) »in Aussicht stellen, versprechen, zusichern« — und damit für die Folgezeit maßgebend. Doch sieht Bartholomae darin eine Sonderentwicklung der Bedeutung »lehren«, nämlich »spez. in Bezug auf das, was künftig sein oder geschehen wird«. Diese betrachtet er in Übereinstimmung mit der Pahlavi-Übersetzung *čāš*- »lehren« einerseits und im Hinblick auf die zu *ciš* gehörigen Verbalnomina *ṭkaēša*- »Glaubenslehre« und »Glaubenslehrer« andererseits als die Grundbedeutung der Wurzel *čiš*.

An keiner der alt- und jungavestischen Belegstellen des Verbums liegt jedoch die Bedeutung »lehren« klar zutage (zur einzigen von Bartholomae unter 1 genannten Belegstelle, Vr. 12,2 = Y. 27,7, s. unten). Aber ebensowenig auch ergibt sich aus dem Kontext der (unter 2) angeführten Belege von *ciš* eine besondere Beziehung zu dem, »was künftig sein oder geschehen wird«, da von dem Verb kein Objektssatz oder Verbalabstraktum abhängt, mit dem ein künftiges Sein oder Geschehen in Aussicht gestellt würde. Die syntaktische Konstruktion — Dativ der Person, Akkusativ der Sache — entspricht vielmehr jenen Stellen, die Bartholomae unter Ansatz 3 zusammenfaßt: »Jmdm. (Dat.) etwas (Akk.) zuweisen, zuerkennen, zueignen«. Der Unterschied zwischen Gruppe 2 und 3 liegt lediglich darin, ob man das durch *ciš* bezeichnete Übertragen eines Objektes — sei es konkreter oder abstrakter Natur — als künftiges Geschehen auffaßt (= jem. etw. zusichern) oder als durch das Aussprechen symbolisch vollzogen (= jem. etw. bestimmen, zuweisen). Im letzteren Fall läge dann Koinzidenz [3] von Aussprechen und Übertragen einer Sache vor.

---

[1] Justi, Handbuch der Zendsprache, 1864, p. 112: »geben, verkündigen«.

[2] Studien auf dem Gebiete des Griechischen und der arischen Sprachen I 2, 1888, p. 304 ff.

[3] Zur Feststellung des Koinzidenzfalles, bei dem die Handlung im Aussprechen des Satzes besteht, s. Koschmieder, Zur Bestimmung der Funktionen grammatischer

Betrachtet man aber den gesamten altavestischen Belegstand des Verbums, zu dem auch

cəuuištā Y. 34, 13 (für *cōištā : 2. Pl. Inj. Aor.[4], parallel zu 2. Pl. Inj. Aor. *dātā* in Str. 14)

cəuuišī Y. 51, 15 (für *cōišī : 3. Sg. Inj. des Mediopassivaorists[4])

gehören — Formen, die seit Geldner, a.a.O. p. 135 und Darmesteter, Zend-Avesta I, 1893, p. 336[49] wegen ihrer vom Metrum geforderten Zweisilbigkeit und der Pahlavi-Übersetzung *čāš*- immer wieder zu *ciš* gestellt wurden[5], bei Bartholomae aber, der mit Recht eine »graphische Verunstaltung« ablehnt, unter einem eigenen Lemma (doch mit ähnlichem Bedeutungsansatz)[6] verzeichnet sind —, dann fällt auf,

Kategorien, Abh. Bay. Ak. Wiss., NF. 25, 1945, p. 22ff. (= Beiträge zur allgemeinen Syntax p. 26ff.).

[4] Als eine regulär gebildete, zum Wurzelaoristparadigma *cōišəm, cōiš, cōišt* gehörige Form kann *cōištā nur 2. Pl. Inj. Akt. sein (: RV. *ákarta*, vgl. zur Vollstufe der 1. und 2. Pl. des Wurzelaoristaktivs K. Hoffmann, MSS 2, 1952/7, p. 124). Entsprechend ist aus morphologischen Gründen für *cōišī nur Bestimmung als 3. Sg. Inj. des Mediopassivaorists möglich.

[5] Vgl. Tedesco, ZII 2, 1923, p. 48[2], Lommel, NGWG, NF. I 4, 1935, p. 159, Kuryłowicz, Traces de la place tu ton en gathique, 1925, p. 21, L'apophonie en indo-européen, 1956, p. 164, Humbach, MSS 2, 1952/7, p. 14f., Die Gathas des Zarathustra I, 1959, p. 20, Emmerick, TPS, 1966, p. 17ff., Kuiper, IIJ 10, 1967, p. 105f.

[6] AirWb. 442: *'kav*-»versehen«, mit den zusätzlichen Angaben »bestimmen für« und (»in refl. Sinn«) »sicher erwarten, erhoffen«. — Wohlbegründet weist auch Gershevitch, BSOAS 25, 1962, p. 369f. eine Erklärung als »Fehlvokalisation«, damit allerdings auch die Zuordnung zu *ciš* zurück. Die von Geldner in den Text der Edition gestellte v.l. *ciuuĭš*- kann aber nicht mit *juua*-»leben« und *cuuant*- »wie viele« verglichen werden, da hier der scheinbare Schwund des *ī* auf ostiranischem Lautwandel beruht (s. Morgenstierne, NTS 12, 1942, p. 49f., Henning, TPS, 1942, p. 49f., K. Hoffmann, Hb. Or. I, IV 1, 1958, p. 8) und als v.l. wie auch sonst bei nachkonsonantischem -*uu*- nur -*auu*- erscheint. Von einer Basis *čiv- aus führt also kein Weg zu einsilbigem *ciuuĭš*-. *cəuuĭš*- aber, d.h. einsilbiges -*əuui*-, könnte sich als lautliche Erscheinung der traditionellen Avesta-Aussprache erklären. Der uriranische Diphthong -*ai̯*- erscheint in der avestischen Überlieferung in geschlossener Silbe (und auch in anderen Positionen) als -*ōi*-, was sich am leichtesten über eine altavestische Lautung -*ə̄i*- vermitteln läßt (vereinzelt kommt im Altavestischen auch in heterosyllabischer Stellung -*ōii*- statt -*aii*- vor, Lok. Du. *ubōiiō* Y. 41, 2.3, Dat. Sg. *axtōiiōi* Y. 36, 1, 3. Sg. Ipt. *vātōiiōtū* Y. 35, 6, 3. Sg. Inj. *urūdōiiatā* Y. 44, 20, in gleicher Position auch einmal die vorauszusetzende Lautung -*ə̄i*-, 1. Pl. Ind. *vātə̄iiāmahī* Y. 35, 7, wie sie wohl auch für Entwicklung des jungavestischen Dativausgangs -*ə̄e* < -*ə̄i̯ə̄i* < -*ai̯ai̯* (: aav. *axtōiiōi*) der *i*-Stämme angenommen werden muß). Auch für uriran. **čai̯š*- wäre dann mit einer altavestischen Lautform **cə̄iš*- zu rechnen, wofür normalerweise die spätere Lautform *cōiš*- eingeführt wurde. An zwei Stellen (in nachkonsonantischer Position: Zufall?) aber wurde der Diphthong -*ə̄i*- nicht durch -*ōi*- ersetzt, sondern zunächst beibehalten und erst irgendwann im Laufe der traditionellen Avesta-Aussprache zu zweisilbigem -*ə̄u̯i*- (in den Hss. *cə̄uuĭš*-) verändert, vielleicht (als eine Art Hyper-

daß der Prädikatssatz mit dem Dativ der Person und dem Akkusativ der Sache häufig (d.h. in 7 von 13 Fällen)[7] noch eine Ergänzung im Instrumental aufweist. Und zwar handelt es sich bei diesem Instrumental stets um eine Bezeichnung religiös-magischer Kräfte: *vohū manaŋhā* Y. 44, 6; 46, 18; 51, 15, *aṣ̌ā vohūcā manaŋhā* Y. 45, 10, *xšaθrā vohūcā manaŋhā* Y. 50, 3, *aṣ̌ā* Y. 31, 3, *spəṇtā mainiiū* Y. 47, 5.

Wird diese thematisch stark gebundene Ergänzung mit in den Ausdruck einbezogen, dann liegt der Schluß nahe, daß die durch den Instrumental bezeichneten religiös-magischen Kräfte als Mittel zum Vollzug der durch *ciš* bezeichneten Übertragung eines Objektes gedacht wurden. Das erscheint plausibler, wenn diese Übertragung nicht irgendwann in der Zukunft stattfindet (jem. etw. durch religiös-magische Kraft zusichern), sondern — in Koinzidenz — beim Aussprechen des Satzes: jem. etw. durch religiös-magische Kraft bestimmen, zuweisen.

Für diese Auffassung spricht auch, daß in einigen Fällen mit *ciš* das Verbum *dā* in ähnlicher Verwendung (jem. etw. bestimmen, verleihen usw.) parallelgeht. So stimmt Y. 51, 9

> *yąm xšnūtəm rānōibiiā då*
>
>   *θβā āθrā suxrā mazdā*

»die Zufriedenstellung, welche du den beiden Parteien bestimmst durch dein leuchtendes Feuer, o Mazdā« fast wörtlich überein mit Y. 31, 3:

> *yąm då mainiiū āθrācā*
>
>   *aṣ̌ācā cōiš rānōibiiā xšnūtəm*

»die Zufriedenstellung, welche du den beiden Parteien durch (deine) Absicht und (dein) Feuer bestimmst und durch die Wahrheit zuweist«. Auch Y. 34, 13 und 14 stehen beide Verben in ähnlichem Zusammenhang:

> *hiiaṯ cəuuištā hudåbiiō*
>
>   *mīždəm mazdā yehiiā tū daθrəm*

---

gathizismus) in Anlehnung an ein Nebeneinander von -*ōi*- und -*ə̄ui*- in einem Fall wie jav. *yōišta*- »der jüngste« für aav. **yə̄uuišta*- (= ved. *yáviṣṭha*-).

[7] Y. 51, 5 *cistā* gehört aus lautlichen Gründen zu *ciθ* oder *cit* (Humbach, Gathas II p. 87), vgl. Str. 11 *acistā* (AirWb. 428 s.v.*kaēt*-). Y. 32, 5 *fracinas* ist lautlich doppeldeutig (vgl. Humbach, Gathas II p. 33), aber wegen seiner anderen syntaktischen Konstruktion (nur Akk. der Person: *yā fracinas drəguuaṇtəm xšaiiō* »woran der Herrscher den Trughaften erkennt« Humbach) von *ciš* zu trennen, vgl. zum *n*-Infixpräsens von *ciθ* den jav. Konj. *cinaθāmaide* Vr. 12, 4. Dagegen gehört Y. 44, 6 *cinas* zu *ciš*: *taibiiō xšaθrəm vohū cinas manaŋhā* »(Ārmaiti als die rechte, 'durch Taten die Wahrheit festigende' Gesinnung der Menschen) weist dir (Ahura Mazdā) durch das gute Denken die Herrschaft zu«, vgl. Y. 35, 5 *xšaθrəm ..... cīšmahicā* »wir weisen (dem Ahura Mazdā) die Herrschaft zu«.

»den Lohn, den ihr den Gutspendenden zuweist, dessen Bestimmer
du bist, o Mazdā«;

   taṯ zī mazdā vairīm
    astuuaitē uštānāi dātā

»denn diesen wünschenswerten (Lohn), o Mazdā, bestimmt ihr dem
knochenhaften Leben (derer, die ...)«.

An allen vier Stellen steht der Inj. Aor. im generellen Sachverhalt[8];
er bezeichnet das Wirken Ahura Mazdās bzw. Ahura Mazdās und der
anderen ahurischen Wesenheiten, worauf der Plural in 34, 13.14 weist
(vgl. auch *xšmākąm hucistīm ahurā* in Str. 14). Dagegen bezeichnet
die 1. Pl. Ind. Präs. *cīšmahī*[9], von Menschen bei der Verehrung Ahura
Mazdās gesprochen, funktional den Koinzidenzfall[10], ebenso wie die
an allen drei Belegstellen vorausgehende 1. Pl. Ind. Präs. von *dā*:

Y. 35, 5; 41, 1 *dadəmahicā cīšmahicā*

Y. 39, 4   *aθā ... dadəmahī aθā cīšmahī*

»(indem wir dieses aussprechen), bestimmen wir und weisen wir zu
(dem Ahura Mazdā Herrschaft / das, was gut ist / Loblieder usw.)«.

Für *ciš* darf also mit Wahrscheinlichkeit die Bedeutung angesetzt
werden: »jemandem (Dat.) [durch religiös-magische Kraft (Instr.)]
etwas (Akk.) bestimmen, übertragen, zuweisen, zusprechen, zuerkennen«. Damit befindet sich das Verb in der Nähe eines bestimmten
Verwendungsbereiches der Wurzel *dā* (= ai. *dhā*); es unterscheidet
sich hiervon aber durch seine ausschließlich religiös-magische Bedeutungskomponente.

Die semantische Nähe zu *dā* zeigt sich nun auch in einem weiteren
Bereich. Mit Akkusativ und Prädikatsnomen bezeichnet *dā* »jemanden
oder etwas bestimmen zu, einsetzen als« bzw. »etwas bestimmen,
festsetzen als«, vgl. z.B. die mediale 1. Pl. Ind. Präs. — ebenfalls im
Koinzidenzfall — Y. 41, 3:

   humāim θβā ... dadəmaidē

»als Wunderkräftigen bestimmen wir dich (für uns)«. In gleicher

---

[8] Vgl. K. Hoffmann, Der Injunktiv im Veda, 1967, p. 113ff., 135ff.

[9] *cīšmahī* ist Plural zu *cinahmī*, s. J. Schmidt, Die Pluralbildungen der indogermanischen Neutra, 1889, p. 275; falsch Bartholomae, Grundr. Iran. Phil. I 1,
p. 202, AirWb. 429 (Wurzelpräsens). Die Form geht über **číNṣ̌°* zurück auf **činš-masi*;
entsprechend Opt. *cīšiiāṯ* (A. 3, 6) < **cinš-iāt*, Ipt. *cīždī* (Y. 44, 16) < *činž-dʰi*,
vgl. ved. *piṇḍhi* (AV.) < **pinž-dʰi* (: *piṣ* »zerstampfen«; die Durchführung des vedischen
zerebralen *ṣ* in vollstufigen Formen des *n*-Infixpräsens, z.B. RV. *pináṣṭi* gegenüber av.
cinahmī cinasti, ist eine Neuerung des Indoarischen).

[10] Vgl. Koschmieder, a.a.O. (oben Anm. 3).

syntaktischer Konstruktion und ebenfalls im Medium (sonst nur Aktiv belegt; einmal Passiv, s. Anm. 4 zu *c∂uuīšī*) erscheint im Jungavestischen auch zweimal die 1. Pl. Ind. Präs. von *ciš*, und zwar beide Male mit dem gleichen Prädikatsnomen *humāiia-* wie an der letztgennanten Stelle: Vr. 12, 2 = Y. 27, 7

    humaiia upaŋhå cišmaide ahunahe vairiiehe

»als wunderkräftig bestimmen wir das Sichbeschäftigen mit dem Ahuna Vairiia-Gebet«, und zwei Sätze weiter mit vorausgehender 1. Pl. Ind. Präs. von *dā*:

Vr. 12, 4 *humaiia aētā dāmąn daδ∂maide*
           humaiia cišmaide

»als wunderkräftig bestimmen wir diese Geschöpfe, als wunderkräftig bestimmen wir sie (durch diese unsere Worte)«.

Erinnert nun einerseits *humaiia* (A. Pl. n.) ... *daδ∂maide* an das genannte *humāīm* (A. Sg. m.) ... *daδ∂maidē*, so läßt andererseits die Aufeinanderfolge *daδ∂maide cišmaide* unmittelbar an die ebenfalls genannte Aufeinanderfolge *dad∂mahī cišmahī* denken. Das heißt aber: jav. *cišmaide* steht in einem so deutlichen Zusammenhang mit diesen Textstellen, die alle dem wohlbekannten, täglich rezitierten Yasna Haptaŋhāiti angehören, daß hier kaum mit lebendigem Sprachgebrauch zu rechnen ist, sondern eher eine Erscheinung religiöser Epigonensprache angenommen werden darf.

Eben diese textliche Abhängigkeit zeigt auch, daß die Stelle Vr. 12, 2 = Y. 27, 7 nicht mit Bartholomae (AirWb. 429) als Beispiel für die von ihm angenommene Grundbedeutung »lehren« (unter 1 : »etwas lehrend bezeichnen als«) angesehen werden kann. *cišmaide* ist letztlich nicht von den altavestischen Belegen des Verbums, speziell von *cišmahī* im Yasna Haptaŋhāiti, zu trennen und muß von hier aus erklärt werden. Daß das kein Einzelfall ist, zeigt sich auch bei der 1. Sg. *cinahmī* im Glaubensbekenntnis. Auch hier dürfte eine der Stellen aus dem Yasna Haptaŋhāiti das Vorbild geliefert haben, Y. 39, 4: *yaθā tū ī ahurā mazdā ... var∂scā yā vohū aθā tōi dad∂mahī aθā cišmahī ...* »wie du, Ahura Mazdā, das ... tust, was gut ist, so weisen wir (es) dir zu, so bestimmen wir (es dir)«. In lockerer Anlehnung daran dann Y. 12, 1: *ahurāi mazdāi ... vīspā vohū cinahmī* »dem Ahura Mazdā ... bestimme ich alles Gute«. Und eine andere Stelle, Y. 35, 5 *huxšaθrō. t∂māi bā at̰ xšaθr∂m ... dad∂mahicā cišmahicā ... hiiat̰ mazdāi ahurāi ...* »dem am besten Herrschenden weisen wir zu und bestimmen wir die Herrschaft, (nämlich) dem Ahura Mazdā«, diente als Muster für

A. 3, 6 mit der 3. Sg. Opt. Präs.: *huxšaθrō.təmāiciṭ aṭ xšaθrəm cīšiiāṭ yaṭ ahurāi mazdāi.*

Mit diesen beiden Stellen verdichtet sich der Eindruck, daß das Verbum *ciš*, das wohl schon in altavestischer Zeit auf die religiöse Sprache beschränkt war, außerhalb der Gathas und des Yasna Haptaŋhāiti nur mehr in Anlehnung an vorgegebene Muster innerhalb einer bestimmten Textgattung (religiöses Bekenntnis, Verehrungsgebet u.ä.) Verwendung finden konnte.

Dem widerspricht zunächst die in Y. 19 (12-14), 20 (1-3) und 21 (1.2) siebzehnmal vorkommende 3. Sg. *cinasti, para.cinasti.* Es handelt sich bei diesen Textstellen, deren genauer Wortlaut nicht überall klar und verständlich ist, nämlich um alte theologische Kommentarstücke zu den drei Hauptgebeten Ahuna Vairiia, Aṣəm vohū und Yeŋhē hātąm, und *cinasti* bzw. *para.cinasti* fungiert dabei als theologischer Terminus.

Auch hier bemüht sich Bartholomae um eine Vermittlung mit der Bedeutung »lehren«; seine Paraphrase (AirWb. 430, Ansatz 4: »(es) enthält die Lehre von —, bezieht sich inhaltlich auf — (Akk.), ist zu verstehen in Beziehung auf — (Akk.), dass —«) kann jedoch nicht davon überzeugen, daß hier eine von »lehren« ausgegangene Bedeutungsentwicklung vorliegen soll. Außerdem läßt Bartholomaes Übersetzung — und ebenso auch die Geldners[11] (der Wurzel *cit* voraussetzt): »meint, denkt hinzu« — außer acht, daß bei dem größten Teil der Belege nicht nur ein Akkusativobjekt, sondern auch ein Dativobjekt steht. Dieser Tatsache hat offenbar nur Baunack[12] Rechnung getragen, da er *cinasti* mit »stellt in Aussicht, verheißt« übersetzt. Subjekt kann aber nicht, wie Baunack (für Y. 19 und 20) annimmt, Ahura Mazdā sein, da der Gottesname oder ein dafür stehendes Demonstrativpronomen sowohl im Dativ als auch im Akkusativ vorkommt, d.h. als indirektes bzw. direktes Objekt zur Verbalhandlung möglich ist. Geldner hält bei einem Teil der Belege, Bartholomae bei allen die zu kommentierenden Worte selbst für das Subjekt. Diese grammatisch vertretbare Auffassung erschwert es nun aber wieder, eine Verbindung zu den übrigen Belegen des Verbums *ciš* herzustellen, mit dem stets die Handlung von Menschen oder von Ahura Mazdā bzw. ahurischen Wesenheiten bezeichnet wird. So liegt denn die größere Wahrscheinlichkeit bei Geldners zweiter syntaktischer Lö-

---

[11] KZ 27, 1885, p. 246f.
[12] A.a.O. (oben Anm. 2) p. 305.

sung[13], Menschen, d.h. den jeweiligen Sprecher der Gebetsworte, als Subjekt von *cinasti* bzw. *para.cinasti* anzunehmen und dann die zu kommentierenden Worte, etwa *dazda manaŋhō* Y. 19, 13, wie einen Instrumental aufzufassen : »(mit den Worten) *dazdā manaŋhō* ...«.

Geht man nun davon aus, daß der die Gebetsworte Sprechende Subjekt von *cinasti* ist, und berücksichtigt man ferner, daß die syntaktische Konstruktion mit Akkusativ- und Dativobjekt die häufigste ist, dann liegt der Schluß nahe, daß sich *cinasti* semantisch gar nicht so weit von den altavestischen Belegen von *ciš* entfernt hat. Tatsächlich ergibt sich auf diese Weise ein plausibler Sinn : durch das Aussprechen der einzelnen Gebetsworte vollzieht der Sprecher jeweils (wiederum : Koinzidenzfall) eine magische Zuweisung, er »bestimmt jemanden oder etwas (Akk.) für jemanden oder etwas (Dat.)«. Die meisten der siebzehn Belege wären dann etwa nach folgendem Muster zu übersetzen :

Y. 19, 13 '*dazda manaŋhō*' *para īm iδa manaŋhe cinasti yaθa fradaxštārəm manaŋhe* »(mit den Worten) *dazda manaŋhō* bestimmt man ihn (Ahura Mazdā) für das Denken, (so) wie einen Lehrer für das Denken«.

Allerdings finden sich vereinzelte Abweichungen von diesem Muster. So steht Y. 21, 1.2 dreimal nur der Akk. *yasnəm*. Ergänzt man aber aus dem einleitenden Satz *yesnīm vacō ašaonō zaraθuštrahe* '*yeńhe hātąm*' ... »der zur Verehrung gehörige Spruch des ašahaften Zarathustra (lautet :) '*y.h.*' ...« *vacō* als Akkusativobjekt, dann wäre ein Vergleich mit der oben besprochenen Konstruktion mit doppeltem Akkusativ möglich, also die Bedeutung »bestimmen, festsetzen als«; *yasnəm* fungiert dann als Prädikatsnomen : '*yeńhe*' *iδa mazdå yasnəm cinasti* »(mit dem Worte) '*yeńhe*' bestimmt man (den Spruch) als Verehrung Mazdās« usw. — Ohne jedes Objekt steht *cinasti* zweimal in Y. 19, 14. Es wäre aber denkbar, daß in beiden Fällen die (jeweils aus einem Akkusativ und einem Dativ bestehenden) zu kommentierenden Worte selbst gleichzeitig als Akkusativ- und Dativobjekt zu *cinasti* aufgefaßt wurden : '*xšaθrəm ahurāi*' *cinasti* '*tat̰ mazda tauua xšaθrəm*' '*drəgubiiō vāstārəm*' *cinasti yaθa uruuaθəm spitamāi* »(mit den Worten) 'die Herrschaft dem Ahura' bestimmt man (sie ihm), (nach dem Spruch [Y. 53, 9] :) 'das ist deine Herrschaft, o Mazdā'; (mit den Worten) 'den Armen einen Hirten' bestimmt man (ihnen einen solchen), (so) wie einen Freund für Spitama«. — Weniger

---

[13] Vgl. a.a.O. p. 246[3].

durchsichtig ist Y. 20, 3 '*yaṯ ašāi vahištāi ašəm*' *para.cinasti vīspəm mąθrəm vīspəm mąθrāi*. Es wäre denkbar, daß hier beide Konstruktionen, doppelter Akkusativ und Akkusativ mit Dativ, vorliegen : »(mit den Worten) '*yaṯ ašāi vahištāi ašəm*' bestimmt man alles als Spruch, alles für den Spruch«. Wie man die Wendung auch interpretiert, sicher ist das Vorhandensein eines Dativobjektes (*mąθrāi*) neben dem Akkusativ. Entsprechend sind auch die daran anschließenden Vergleichssätze gebaut : *yaθa ašāi xšaθrəm cinasti...* »(so) wie man die Herrschaft für das Aša bestimmt« usw. — Die genannten schwierigen Fälle können jedenfalls kaum widerlegen, daß jav. *cinasti, para.cinasti* sonst nicht nur die gleiche syntaktische Konstruktion (übrigens auch das gleiche semantisch nicht erkennbar differenzierende Präverb *para-* wie in Y. 51, 15 *cōišt parā*), sondern als Theologenterminus auch die alte, religiös-magische Bedeutung der Wurzel *ciš* bewahrt hat : »bestimmen, zuweisen« bzw. »bestimmen, festlegen«.

Daß die 3. Sg. in Y. 19-21 im Unterschied zu den oben besprochenen Belegen, die sich in mehr oder weniger freien Nachbildungen vorgegebener Muster aus dem Yasna Haptaŋhāiti finden, in einem andersgearteten, eigenen Anwendungsbereich steht, liegt an der anderen Textgattung. Der Versuch, eine eigene »exegetische Kunstsprache« mit eigenen »technischen Ausdrücken«[14] zu schaffen, ließ die jungavestischen Theologen auf den älteren religiösen Wortschatz zurückgreifen, aus dem sie ein sonst nicht mehr lebendiges Verb in terminologischem Sinne verwendeten und ihm damit eine — wenn auch begrenzte — neue Existenz verschafften.

Verfolgt man das Verbum *ciš* von altavestischer Zeit bis in seine spätesten Belegstellen, die alten theologischen Kommentarstücke Y. 19-21, dann zeigt sich also ein eng begrenzter Bedeutungs- und Anwendungsbereich, der auf keinen zeitgenössischen profanen Sprachgebrauch schließen läßt. Eben diese Begrenztheit aber spricht dafür, daß *ciš* bereits vor Zarathustra der religiösen Sprache Irans angehörte.

Von hier aus wäre dann auch die Frage nach dem Bedeutungszusammenhang zwischen dem Verbum finitum und dem Nomen actionis *ṯkaēša-* m. (< **káiša-*) »Glaubenslehre« sowie dem Nomen agentis *ṯkaēšá-* m. (< **kaišá-*)[15] »Glaubenslherer« anzugehen. Die beiden Verbalnomina weisen an ihrer einzigen altavestischen Belegstelle, Y. 49, 2.3, eine negative Bedeutungskomponente auf, und zwar beziehen

---

[14] Vgl. Geldner, KZ 27 p. 245.
[15] Zur Akzentdifferenz vgl. Wackernagel-Debrunner, AiG. II 2, p. 98 ff.

sie sich auf Lehre und Lehrer eines der Religion Zarathustras feindlichen
Fürsten. Der dem Nomen actionis ꞇ*kaēša-* sachlich entgegengesetzte
zarathustrische Terminus ist, wie aus Y. 49, 3 hervorgeht, *varəna-* m.
(: *var* »wählen«), das »Glaubensbekenntnis« als Akt persönlicher Wahlentscheidung. Während es sich bei *varəna-*, das im Altindischen kein
Gegenstück hat, um ein Wort — vielleicht sogar eine Wortbildung
(Typ *yasna-)* — der spezifischen Religionsform Zarathustras handelt,
in der die religiöse Wahlentscheidung eine wesentliche Rolle spielt
(Stichworte *var, frauuar, frauuaṣi-* u.a.), dürfte voravestisch **kaiša-*
einer anderen religiösen Konzeption entstammen. Geht man davon
aus, daß die für das Altavestische ermittelte Bedeutung des Verbums
ciš in voravestischer Zeit ähnlich oder gleich war, dann könnte man
für das Nomen actionis etwa mit folgender Bedeutungsentwicklung
rechnen : **kaiša-* bezeichnet zunächst eine magisch wirksame Willens-
äußerung — »Bestimmung« —, durch die jemandem etwas ausdrücklich
übertragen, zugewiesen werden kann oder durch die jemand in eine
bestimmte Stellung eingewiesen bzw. etwas in einer bestimmten
Funktion festgelegt werden kann. Spezialisiert auf Persönlichkeiten
mit besonderem Wirkungsvermögen und Einwirkungskraft auf religiösem Gebiet, also wohl vor allem Priester, konnte **kaiša-* über
»autoritativer, magisch wirksamer Ausspruch« dann schließlich verallgemeinert werden zu »Glaubenssatz, Glaubensinhalt, Glaubenslehre«.
— Entsprechendes wäre für das Nomen agentis **kaiša-* anzunehmen
(religiös-magisch wirkungsvoller, autoritativer »Bestimmer« → »Glaubenslehrer«).

Die an der Gathastelle (Y. 49, 2.3) spürbare negative Bedeutungskomponente der beiden Verbalnomina dürfte dann darin bestehen,
daß **kaiša-* im Unterschied zum Verbum finitum **čiš* wohl schon
vor der Zeit Zarathustras auf bestimmte Personen mit religiöser
Autorität, das heißt also wohl : auf Priester einer vorzarathustrischen
Religionsform spezialisiert war, von denen Zarathustra sich und seine
Nachfolger wahrscheinlich absetzen wollte.

Immerhin entwickelte sich ꞇ*kaēša-* — wohl wegen des stets empfun-
denen Zusammenhangs mit *ciš*, vgl. besonders das Nebeneinander
von ꞇ*kaēša-* und *cinasti* in den theologischen Kommentarstücken Y.
19-21 — nicht zu einem daēvischen Wort. Vielmehr steht es z.B. im
Glaubensbekenntnis im Unterschied zur genannten Gathastelle gleich-
wertig neben *varəna-*, Y. 12, 7 : *yāuuarənō as zaraθuštrō ... tā varənācā
ꞇkaēšācā mazdaiiasnō ahmī* »welchen Bekenntnisses Zarathustra war...,
nach diesem Bekenntnis und (dieser) Glaubenslehre bin ich ein

Mazdayasnier«, könnte allerdings gerade an dieser Stelle wegen der Unproportionalität (*yāuuarənō* : *varənācā ṭkaēšācā*) als späterer Einschub — etwa aus der Zeit, als eine jungavestische Textstelle wie Y. 16, 2 *zaraθuštrahe varənəmca ṭkaēšəmca* verfaßt wurde — erklärt werden.

Vielleicht hängt dem Nomen actionis aber auch im Jungavestischen noch ein letzter Rest seiner Herkunft aus einer vorzarathustrischen Religionsform an, sofern nämlich, worauf Benveniste-Renou[16] hinweisen, der erste Bestandteil in dem jungavestischen Kompositum *ahura.ṭkaēša*- noch der vorzarathustrischen Gottesbenennung — ohne *mazdā*- als Namensteil — entspricht (vgl. auch jav. *āhūiri*- als Epitheton zu *ṭkaēsa*-, allerdings auch zu *frašna*- und *daēnā*-, von denen es aber kein entsprechendes Kompositum gibt).

Man könnte diesen Gedanken noch weiter fortführen. Benveniste-Renou machen darauf aufmerksam, daß sich der ursprüngliche Konflikt zwischen Ahuras und Daivas u.a. auch noch in der festen Verbindung *vīdaēuua- ahura.ṭkaēša*- zeige. Daraus könnte man nun schließen, daß es in vorzarathustrischer Zeit neben **ahura-kaiša*- auch ein **daiua-kaiša*- gegeben hat. Zumindest aber könnte aus dieser Zeit auch ein Kompositum **aniat-kaiša*-»etwas anderes als Glaubenslehre habend«[17] stammen, aus dem vielleicht, wie Hertel[18] darlegt, durch falsche Kompositionsauflösung, d.h. indem man im Vorderglied nicht mehr das Neutrum *aniiaṯ*[19], sondern den Stamm *aniia*- sah, das jungavestische *aniia.ṭkaēša*-, *aniiō.ṭkaēša*- und damit die merkwürdige Lautform *ṭkaēsa*- entstanden ist, für die es keine lautgesetzliche Erklärung gibt. Wann mit dieser Kompositionsauflösung zu rechnen wäre, läßt sich nicht sagen[20]; doch müßte sie in relativ früher Zeit

[16] Vṛtra et Vṛθragna, 1934, p. 47f.

[17] Vgl. zu diesem Kompositionstyp im Vedischen z.B. RV. *tád-anna*- »das als Speise habend«, *yát-kāma*- »was als Wunsch habend«, Wackernagel-Debrunner, AiG. III, p. 438; anders dagegen RV. *anyá-vrata*- »ein anderes Gelübde habend« (TĀ. *anyád-vrata*- ist spätere Mantravariante), p. 592.

[18] WZKM 37, 1931, p. 92f.

[19] *aniiaṯ* (= ved. *anyát*) ist — zufällig — nicht als flektierte Form des Pronominaladjektivs bezeugt, sondern nur als erstarrter Akk. in adverbieller Funktion (jav. *aniiaṯ* »außer, ausgenommen«).

[20] Daß in den Gathas (Y. 49, 2.3) *ṭkaēsa*- überliefert ist, besagt nichts für die Sprache Zarathustras, da die Form auch bei der Textgestaltung durch die orthoepische Diaskeuase anstelle eines sprachwirklich-altavestischen **kaiša*- eingeführt sein kann. Zu den Etappen der Avesta-Überlieferung s. K. Hoffmann, Henning Memorial Volume, 1970, p. 188[2].

stattgefunden haben : im Jungavestischen ist jedenfalls *ṯkaēša-* in dieser Form sprachwirklich, wie aus dem zu *aniiō.ṯkaēša-* hinzugebildeten *aniiō.varəna-* V. 12, 21; 15, 2 hervorgeht.

Daß *ṯkaēša-* im Jungavestischen auch im Zusammenhang mit dem Gerichtswesen verwendet wird, wie das Farhang-i ōīm bezeugt —»Richterspruch« F. 5 (= Ed. Klingenschmitt 276)[21], »Richter« F. 5; 27 b (= 277; 762)[22] —, braucht nicht notwendigerweise auf ursprünglich profanen Gebrauch zurückzugehen, sondern kann auf der nicht unbekannten Praxis beruhen, daß ein Mann mit Autorität auf religiösem Gebiet eben auch eine Funktion auf dem Gebiet des Gerichtswesens ausüben konnte[23].

Wenn nun also *čiš*, wie der Gesamtbefund wahrscheinlich macht, bereits der vorzarathustrischen religiösen Sprache Irans angehörte, dann darf auch mit noch höherem Alter dieses Verbums gerechnet werden, obwohl sich im Altindoarischen keine Spur davon erhalten hat und unmittelbar Vergleichbares auch nicht in anderen altindogermanischen Sprachen zutage liegt. Immerhin darf die Fage gestellt

---

[21] Den Bedeutungsansatz »richterliche Auslegung des Gesetzes, Richterspruch« nimmt Bartholomae, AirWb. 813 für F. 5 (= 276) vor. Die betreffende Belegstelle lautet : *ṯkaēšō plhst gyw'k DYN' BR' 'YT < gyw'k > 'YK d'twbl* »*ṯkaēšō* (bedeutet) an den meisten Stellen *DYN'*, aber es gibt Stellen, wo es Richter (bedeutet)«. Es liegt nahe, daß *DYN'* hier in seiner Bedeutung 'Gerichtsverfahren, Gerichtsentscheid, Urteilsspruch' verwendet ist; aber da die Pahlavi-Übersetzung von *ṯkaēša-* mit *DYN'* aus Stellen wie Y. 12, 7; 16, 2 stammen kann, wo das avestische Wort eindeutig in religiösem Kontext steht, also »Glaubenslehre« bedeutet (*DYN'* hat dann die auch sonst belegte Bedeutung »Entscheidung«), ist trotz der Farhang-i ōīm-Stelle für das Nomen actionis *ṯkaēša-* ein Vorkommen in der Gerichtssprache nicht gesichert. (Hinweis Klingenschmitt).

[22] Für die AirWb. 814 genannten weiteren zwei Belegstellen läßt sich eine Bedeutung »Richter« nicht erweisen. A. 3, 12 spricht der Zusammenhang — Verurteilung zum Verlust »eines ausgesuchten Stücks Großvieh« (*vārəmnəm staorəm,* 10), dann, steigernd, »des zugewiesenen Anteils an Hab und Gut« (*yātəm gaēθanąm,* 11) — dafür, daß die weitere Steigerung (in 12) ebenfalls im Verlust eines Besitzes oder Anteils an etwas besteht. *āhūirīm ṯkaēšəm* bedeutet dann hier ebenso wie an allen übrigen Belegstellen »ahurische Glaubenslehre«, und eine im Verlust der ahurischen Glaubenslehre bestehende Verurteilung bedeutet : Ausschluß aus der mazdayasnischen Glaubensgemeinschaft. — Zu Y. 9, 10 s. folgende Anm.

[23] In diesem Sinne ist auch die Stelle aus dem Hōm-Yašt, Y. 9, 10, zu verstehen, an der *ṯkaēša-* mit dem Attribut *dātō.rāza-* »das Gesetz regelnd« (vom Akk. °*rāzəm* ausgehende Thematisierung eines **dāta.rāz-,* vgl. Yt. 13, 100 *bərəzi-rāz-* »in der Höhe gebietend«, RV. *apna-rāj-* »über Reichtum gebietend«) versehen ist : damit ist nicht gesagt, daß *ṯkaēša-* hier »Richter« heißen muß (so Bartholomae, s. vorige Anm.), sondern nur, daß sich ein mazdayasnischer »Glaubenslehrer« eben auch mit Aufstellung, Begründung und vor allem richtiger Anwendung der Gesetze — die ja weitgehend religiös ausgerichtet waren — befassen konnte oder mußte.

werden, ob nicht mit einer urindogermanischen Verbalwurzel *$kei̯s$
oder *$k^we̯is$ gerechnet werden könnte, die auf arischem Gebiet eine
Bedeutungsverengung auf den religiös-magischen Bereich erfuhr. Hier
bietet sich vielleicht das bislang nicht überzeugend geklärte [24] italische
Verbalnomen *$koi̯sā$- (lat. *cura* »Sorge, Fürsorge«, Denominativ lat.
curare, altlat. *coiraveront*, paelign. *coisatens* »curaverunt«) zum Vergleich. Man hätte dann von einer Wurzel *$kei̯s$ oder $k^we̯is$ [25], wohl mit
transitiver Grundbedeutung, auszugehen, etwa : »etwas bestimmen,
beschaffen, besorgen für« [26]. Daraus ließe sich einerseits die gesamte
Bedeutungsskala von lat. *cura* als des zugehörigen Nomen actionis
erklären; andererseits wäre — unter Einbeziehung einer magischen
Komponente bei Einengung auf den religiösen Bereich — die Bedeutungsentwicklung zu av. *ciš* und den beiden semantisch spezialisierten
Verbalnomina *t̯kaēša*- verständlich.

[24] Vgl. Walde-Hofmann, Lat. etym. Wb. I p. 314, Walde-Pokorny, Vergleich. Wb.
der indogerm. Sprachen I, p. 455, Pokorny, IEW p. 611.

[25] Wenn altlat. *collus* ebenso wie got. *hals* auf ein voreinzelsprachlich aus *k^wol-so-s
(: *k^wel »drehen«) dissimiliertes *$kolsos$ zurückgeht, dann könnte ital. *$koi̯sā$- auch ein
voreinzelsprachlich dissimiliertes *$k^woi̯sā$- zugrunde liegen.

[26] Während *$kei̯s$ wohl keine Analyse mehr erlaubt, ließe sich *$k^wei̯$-s als — bedeu-
tungsdifferenzierte — Wurzelweiterung von *$k^wei̯$ »worauf achten, beobachten« (Walde-
Pokorny I p. 508, Pokorny p. 636) auffassen (ähnlich wohl Hertel a.a.O. p. 91, aber
ohne Stellungnahme zur semantischen Seite; vgl. außerdem auch Humbach, MSS 2,
1952/7, p. 14[13] zu AirWb. 429 [1]*kaēš*-).

MAHYAR NAVVABI

VAXŠĒN KERMAK = SILK WORM

The fourteenth chapter of Bundahishn is : "on the nature (creation) of men" (apar čigonīh i martomān) (TD2, p. 100).

The first couple of human beings, Mahrē and Mahriyanē (Av. mašya- and Mašyāna-) grow up from the earth, attached to each other, in the shape of a *rivas* (= rhubarb) plant. This plant grows from the seed of Gayōmart, discharged when he passes away.

After possessing their material shape and getting in touch with the material world, they try to fulfil their material needs and desires. They milk a white-haired goat which they come across in the desert and drink her milk. Then they kill a sheep and eat its meat.

As to clothing, at first, they put on garments of grass, then of skin and then something woven. Here, showing the step-by-step progress of preparing clothing one comes across an ambiguous passage (TD2, P. 104, L. 4):

و اپ و وهو د ٻپڊ ڪو ٻپ -ريٽ وهلو ا-بسپسپ-سبپ-نن اٻ-نپ وٻسپ

Pas paδ ŠYL 'Š'WW SLMK bē taδ ān(i) taδag yāmag kart...
"Afterwards through (by means of, with) the ŠYL 'Š'WW SLMK, they wove, that which was woven they made clothing..."

B.T. Anklesaria has read and translated this passage thus:
"Pas pa [v]aškar ašan [sarma] bê-tat u ân î tata jâma bê-karta (ni-hûpt-hend). "Then they wove [cotton cloth] in the desert and having prepared garments of the woven-cloth (they-put-them-on).

And Prof. H. Bailey thus : "Pas pat viškar ašān sarmak bē tat ān i tatak yamak kart..." "Afterwards in the wilderness they wove of the sarmak (ivy, orage) tree and made the woof garments..."

In an article published in 'Minovi Nāme' (Festschrift for Prof. Minovi), explaining the word šēr in the compound شیر وشکری šīr- (šēr-) o-šekarī, I have mentioned the ambiguity of this passage in which the word šēr (i.e., ŠYL) is used.

شیر ŠYL could easily be read "šēr" which means silk. It is used as W.B. Henning has mentioned in his article: "Two central Asian words"[1] in the Talmud and its Aramaic translation, together with

[1] Transactions of the Philological Society 1945, pp. 150-62.

parand and parnagan, as šēra paranda and šēra parangān which also means silk.

Modern Persian and Arabic form of this word is شعر šaʿr.

بدرید تاناف شعرِ سیاه   سرازبرج ماهی بر آورد ماه

یکی چادرِ شعرِ برسر کشید   شب تیره زودامن اندرکشید

(Ferdowsi)

Anand Rāy's definition for šaʿr is: "A kind of thin silk clothing which according to certain lexicographers is in black colour".

(نوعی ازجامهٔ باریك ابریشمی که بعضی آنرا سیاه رنگ میدانند.)

F. Wolff in his "Glossar zu Firdosis Schahname", perhaps being influenced by the other meaning of šaʿr in Arabic, i.e., "hair", translates the word as "leichter wollener Überwurf".

In Moqaddemat-ul-adab by Zamakhshari šaʿr is defined as "clothing made of silk" (ثوب من الا بریشم).

It is probable that the word šēr like its other synonyms is an Iranian or east Iranian word borrowed in Aramaic as well as in Arabic. In Arabic al-abrišam, al-farand, al-barand- al-barnakan and aš-šaʿr, all mean silk.

The next word is ⲩⲱ-, 'Š'WW, which, with a very small change, i.e., ⲩⲱ-ⲓ, [W]'Š[Y]WW, could be read "waxšēn".

Waxšēn = waxš-, modern Persian: waxš and waš = Oxus region, + -ēn (suffix): of waxš, from waxš, related to waxš. Mod. Pers. = وشّی wašší.

The following are some examples in which waxš, wašš (the Oxus region) and wašši (silk cloth) are used:

به گامی سپرد ازختا تاختن   به یك تك دوید از بخارا به وخش

šāker i Bakhāri: see Borhān & Loghat i Fors.

شنیدم که درخاك وخش ازمهان   یکی بود درکنج عزلت نهان

Saʿdi, see Būstan. Comment. by Khazāʿeli, p. 206.

شنیدم که بگریست دانای وخش

Būstan, Ibid. p. 206.

چونان کجا زسند ان تیرتو بگذرد   سوزن به جهد نگذرد از وشّی وحریر

Qatran. Jahangīri, (Afifi ed. Mashhad) p. 1412. fn. 3.

وشّی جامه ای داشتی هفت رنگ   چوگل تار وپود ش بر آورده تنگ

Ibid.

همچو خیاط سوزن از وشی   تیر را از وشینه بگذ اری

Jahāngiri, p. 1414.

تا کوه چو مصمت بود اندر مه آذر   تاد شت چو وشّی بود اند رمه آزار

Farrokhi, p. 113. L. 2197.

The third word is سرمک which has been read Sarmak. In Persian
dictionaries we have 'sarmaq' and 'sarmak' (سرمق، سرمک) which mean
some sort of *spinach* or according to some lexicographers '*Kangar*'
(کنگر), a thorny-leaf plant. Neither of them is fit to be woven.
This word with a small change, or even without change, could be
read "kirmak" meaning 'worm, small worm'. Therefore if we read
and translate the whole sentence as the following, it would have a
reasonable meaning :

Pas paδ šēr[i] waxšēn kirmag be taδ ān taδag yāmag kart.

Then with the silk of the worm of Waxš (= silk worm) they wove,
and they made garments out of the woven [stuff].

JEMAL NEBEZ

DIE SCHRIFTSPRACHE DER KURDEN

Die Problematik der kurdischen Schriftsprache- und, damit verbunden, die Entwicklung einer einheitlichen Literatursprache für alle Kurden- gehört zu den Themen, die weder seitens der Kurden selbst, noch seitens der nicht-kurdischen Kurdologen die ihnen gebührende Aufmerksamkeit erlangt haben. Das Ziel dieses Aufsatzes ist es, das vernachlässigte Thema der kurdischen Schriftsprache historisch-systematisch aufzurollen und die wenigen bisherigen Schritte auf diesem Gebiet kritisch zu beschreiben.

Eine einheitliche, von allen Kurden anerkannte und benutzte kurdische Schriftsprache existiert bis jetzt nicht. Dieser Mangel läßt sich sozio-historisch erklären. Den Kurden ist es nicht möglich gewesen, in den letzten 15 Jahrhunderten einen einheitlichen Staat zu gründen, der in der Lage gewesen wäre, einen der vorhandenen Dialekte bzw. eine Mundart offiziell zu adoptieren und zur verbindlichen Staatssprache zu erklären. Erschwerend kam hinzu, daß es auch nie eine einheitliche kurdische Religion gegeben hat. Wenn es sie gegeben hätte, dann hätte sehr wohl einer der kurdischen Dialekte bzw. eine Mundart zur schriftliche Fixierung ihrer Lehre und ihrer heiligen Bücher über die Jahrhunderte verwendet werden können und hätte aufgrund der Allgegenwärtigkeit sehr wohl eine Grundlage für eine allgemein verbindliche kurdische Schriftsprache abgeben können. So entwickelte sich z.B. die arabische Schriftsprache, nämlich aus dem Quraiš-Dialekt, in dem der Koran ursprünglich offenbart wurde. Auch die deutsche Hochsprache entwickelte sich aus der sächsichen Kanzleisprache, nachdem Martin Luther (1483-1546) die Bibel in eben diesen Dialekt übersetzt hatte. Die Religion der Yazīdī *, die zwar die einzige Religion ist, deren heilige Schriften und Litaneien in kurdischer Sprache abgefaßt worden sind, konnte diese übergreifende Rolle ebenfalls nicht spielen, da sie keine allgemein-kurdische und schon gar keine Weltreligion ist. So können der Yazīdī-Religion nur diejenigen angehören, die als Yazīdī geboren worden sind. Die in Kurdistan verbreiteten (spezifisch

---

* Vgl. Nebez, Jemal: Jeziden. In: Lexikon der islamischen Welt. Stuttgart, Kohlhammer Verlag, 1974.

kurdischen) pseudomuslimischen Sekten wie z.B. Ahl-ī Ḥaqq [1] (= Leute der Wahrheit od. Leute Gottes) bzw. Kākayī [2], Šabak [3] ... etc. oder verschiedene Derwischorden wie Naqīšbandī, Qādīrī, Nūrsī konnten diese sprachvereinigende Funktion erst recht nicht erfüllen: Weder sind ihre Lehren auf Kurdisch geschrieben, noch sind sie über eine Minderheitenbedeutung hinaus unter den Kurden verbreitet.

Ein weiterer historischer Grund liegt in der Tatsache, daß fast alle kurdisch-muslimischen Gelehrten der Vergangenheit — im Gegensatz zu ihren persischen und türkischen Kollegen — ihre kurdische Muttersprache total vernachlässigt und nur in der arabischen Sprache bzw. in den Sprachen anderer Nachbarvölker gelehrt und geschrieben haben [4].

Schließlich hat das Bauernvolk der Kurden auch keine Stadt oder Provinz als Haupthandelszentrum für alle Kurden gehabt, so daß es aus diesem wirtschaftlichen Grund heraus von Interesse gewesen wäre, den dortigen Dialekt oder die Mundart jenes Ortes als Schriftsprache anzunehmen.

Es ist nicht genau bekannt, wann man die kurdische Sprache (bzw. welchen Dialekt/Mundart davon) zum ersten Mal niedergeschrieben hat. Obwohl die Kurden mindestens unter dem Namen »Kurd« seit dem 6. Jahrhundert durch das in mittelpersischer Sprache verfasste Buch »Kārnāmak-ī Artaxšīr-ī Pāpakān« (= Tatenbuch des Artaxšīr von Pāpakān) [5] bekannt sind, datieren die ältesten zuverlässigen Dokumente auf Kurdisch erst aus dem 16. Jahrhundert. An der literarischen Spitze dieser Dokumente stehen mystische Epik und Liebesdichtungen von Malē [6] Ğĭzīrī (lebte in der zweiten Hälfte des 16. Jhd.), die im Nordkurmānğī-Dialekt [7] niedergeschrieben worden

---

[1] Vgl. Minorsky, V.: Ahl-i Ḥaḳḳ. In: Handwörterbuch des Islam. Leiden: 1941, S. 19-23.

[2] »Kākayī« ist eine Bezeichnung für die »Ahl-ī Ḥaqq« im irakischen Kurdistan.

[3] Eine im irakischen Kurdistan wohnende und etwa 70.000-100.000 Mitglieder zählende Religionsgemeinschaft, die von manchen Autoren als »Qizilbāš von Kurdistan« betrachtet werden (vgl. Edmonds, C.J.: Kurds, Turks and Arabs. London: 1957, p. 195.

[4] Sāmī, Šems-ettin: Qāmüs ül-E'lām (= Eigennamenverzeichnis), auf Türkisch-Osmanisch. Istanbul: 1314 h. 5 Bd. S. 3842.

[5] Vgl. »The Kârnâmak î Artakhshîr î Pâpakân«. Hrsg. Darab Dastur Peshotan Sanjana. Bombay: 1896. S. 25 (der Pahlawī-Text). S. 22 (die englische Übersetzung).

[6] »Malē (od.) Malā« sind kurdische Bezeichnungen für einen muslimischen Theologen (Vgl. arab. »maulā« mit der Bedeutung »Herr«).

[7] Ich benutze hier das Wort »Kurmānğī« als Synonym für »kurdische Sprache«,

sind[8]. Es scheint, daß diese in Ǧizīra[9]-Mundart geschriebenen Dichtungen des Poeten Malē Ǧizīrī aus dem 16. Jhd., die übrigens noch heute mit Hingabe von den Kurden gesungen werden, den Weg für seine zeitgenössischen Dichter und Denker und dann auch für alle weiteren aus Nord-Kurdistan stammenden Autoren ebneten, um aus der Ǧizīra-Mundart eine Schriftsprache für die Nord-Kurden (d.h. Nordkurmānǧī sprechende Kurden) zu entwickeln. So finden wir die Ǧizīra-Mundart als Literatursprache bei den hervorragendsten Dichtern und Denkern Nord-Kurdistans, wie z.B. ʿAlī Taramāxī (lebte im 16. Jhd.), Verfasser der ersten arabischen Grammatik auf Kurdisch (1000 h. = 1591 n. Chr.)[10]. Aḥmad-ī Xānī (1650-1707), Verfasser der berühmten Liebesdichtung »Mam ū Zīn«[11] (1693/94), Malā Yūnis-ī Halkatainī (starb 1785), Verfasser dreier Aufsätze auf Kurdisch über arabische Syntax[12], Malā Maḥmūd-ī Bāyazīdī (geb. um 1797), der Verfasser des grundlegenden Werkes über »Gewohnheiten und Sitten der kurdischen Volksstämme«[13], und bei anderen, den Kurden wohlbekannten Dichtern wie Faqē Tairān, Malā-i Bātē, ʿAlī Ḥarīrī ... etc. Auch die kurdischen Intelektuellen, die Ende des 19. Jhds. und Anfang des 20. Jhds. an der kulturellen, politischen und sozialen

denn »Kurd« und »Kurmānǧ« sind bei den Kurden ebenfalls Synonym. Danach teile ich die Kurmānǧī-Sprache in folgende Dialektgruppen:
1. Nord-Kurmānǧī.
2. Mittel-Kurmānǧī.
3. Süd-Kurmānǧī.
Nord- und Mittel-Kurmānǧī sind die beiden Hauptdialekte der kurdischen Sprache. Nord-Kurmānǧī enthält folgende Mundarten: Ǧizīrī, Bādīnānī, Bōtānī, Hakārī, Āšitayī. Mittel-Kurmānǧī enthält: Silaimānī- Sōrānī, Piždarī, Arda͡lānī, Mukrī. Süd-Kurmānǧī ist ein Nebendialekt und enthält die Mundarten von Lakī, Ka͡lhufī, Kulyāyī, Kirmānšāhī, Payrāwandī, Failī. Es gibt noch einen weiteren Nebendialekt in Kurdistan, nämlich die »Hawrāmī (Gōrānī) -Zāzāyī« -Dialektgruppe, welche aber von manchen europäischen Philologen als nicht der kurdischen Sprache zugehörig angesehen wird.

[8] Hartmann, Martin: Der kurdische Diwan des Schēch Aḥmad von Ǧezīret ibn ʾOmar genannt Mälāʾi Ǧiziri. Berlin: 1904.

[9] Eine Stadt an der syrisch-türkischen Grenze.

[10] Taramāxī, ʿAlī: Dastūr-ī Zimān-ī ʿArabī ba Kurdī (Grammatik der arabischen Sprache auf Kurdisch). Hrsg. Mārif Xaznadār. Bagdad: 1971.

[11] Vgl. eine deutsche Kurzfassung dieser Dichtung in: Ahmad-i Chanie: »Mam u. Zin«, genannt Romeo und Julia der Kurden, Übersetzung, Vorwort und Kommentare von Jemal Nebez, Publikation der Nukse, München: 1969.

[12] Minorsky, V.: Die Kurden. In: EI.

[13] Mela Maxmud Bayazidi (= Malā Maḥmūd Bāyazīdī): Nravy i Obyčai Kurdov (= Gewohnheiten und Sitten der Kurden). Hrsg. Margarette B. Rudenko, Moskau: 1963 (kurdische Texte mit russischer Übersetzung).

Renaissance ihres Volkes teilnahmen, haben diese Mundart benutzt. So erschien die erste Nummer der ersten kurdischen Zeitung »Kurdĭstān« am 22. April 1898 (in Kairo) in dieser Mundart und danach auch die Zeitungen »Kurd« (Istanbul 1907), »Kurdĭstān« (Urmia 1912-1914),

»Rōž-ī Kurd« (Istanbul 1913), »Hēviyā Kurd« (Istanbul 1913), »Žīn« (Kairo 1916). Nach der Aufteilung Kurdistans als Folge des ersten Weltkrieges blieb die Ğĭzīra-Mundart die Standardsprache für die Nordkurmānğī sprechenden Kurden. So z.B. war die gesamte Literatur der Kurden in Syrien und Libanon (vgl. z.B. die Zeitschriften »Hawar« (1932-1943), »Roja Nû« (1943-1946), »Stêr« (1943), »Ronahî« (1942-1945) und die der Türkei-Kurden (soweit die Benutzung des Kurdischen erlaubt war und ist-vgl. z.B. »Žīn« Istanbul 1919-1920) in dieser Mundart verfaßt. Abgesehen von einigen wenigen Bestrebungen vor allem von Bādīnān-Kurden im Irak in den letzten Jahren, die Bādīnān-Mundart (die ebenfalls eine Mundart des Nord-Kurmānğī-Dialektes ist) zu fördern, kann man sagen, daß die Ğĭzīra-Mundart die überall anerkannte Schriftsprache aller Nord-Kurmānğī sprechenden Kurden war und ist. Natürlich blieb die Ğĭzīra-Mundart in ihrer Entwicklung zu einer Literatursprache nicht von dem Einfluß der angrenzenden Mundarten Hakārī und Bōtānī unberührt, aber sie hat sich immer als eine Standardsprache in Nord-Kurdistan durchsetzen können.

Im mittleren und südlichen Teil Kurdistans war die Lage völlig anders. Die Ğĭzīra-Mundart und ihre Erfolge als Schriftsprache konnte in diesem Teil Kurdistans keine Auswirkungen haben. Die feindseligen Beziehungen zwischen den kurdischen Fürsten einerseits und die Nichtverwendung der kurdischen Sprache in den religiösen Institutionen, den einzigen kulturellen Einrichtungen Kurdistans, andererseits, stellten ein unüberwindliches Hindernis dar. Dort, in Mittel- und Südkurdistan, waren stattdessen die im Lur-Dialekt verfassten Dichtungen populär. Innerhalb dieser Literatur sind die mystischen Dichtungen von Malā Parēšān-ī Kurd (lebte noch 1398/99) besonders erwähnenswert. Bald darauf aber verkündeten die pseudomuslimischen Sekten der »Ahl-ī Ḥaqq« ihre Lehre im Hawrāmī (Gōrānī)-Dialekt und erklärten diesen Dialekt zu ihrer »Heiligen Sprache«, was auch zur Verbreitung dieses Dialektes unter den Mittel-Kurmānğī sprechenden Kurden führte. Schließlich wurde der Gōrānī-Dialekt zur Literatur- und Schriftsprache von Mittel-Kurdistan. Die hervorragenden Dichtungen der Gōrānī sprechenden Kurden wie Malā Mĭstafā-ī Bēsārānī (1641-1702), Xānā-ī Qubādī (1700-1759), Mawlawī Tāwgōzī (1806-1882) und Walī Dēwāna (1826-1881) standen in hohem Ansehen unter den Mittel- und z.T. auch unter den Südkurden[14].

Als Bāba-Ardal sein Fürstentum Ardalān Mitte des 14. Jhds. im Gōrān-Gebiet mit Šārazūr als Hauptstadt errichtete[15], mußte er natürlich den Gōrānī-Dialekt aus religiösen und politischen Gründen respektieren und ihn als Schriftsprache seines Fürstentums anerkennen. Die Gründung der Stadt Sīlaimānī in Mittelkurdistan im Jahre 1784 durch den Bābān-Fürsten Birāyim Pāšā stand in engem Zusammenhang mit der Auswanderung des Ardalān-Fürsten aus Šārazūr als Folge des Angriffes der osmanischen Türken auf Šārazūr[16]. Dies schwächte die Stellung des Gōrānī-Dialektes. Dazu kam auch noch, daß die Eroberer die Ahl-ī Ḥaqq-Religion in Šārazūr gnadenlos bekämpften. Als das Ardalān-Fürstentum 1867 von der Qāǧāren-Dynastie aufgelöst wurde, blieb der Gōrānī-Mundart kein großer Wirkungskreis mehr. So verlor dieser Dialekt Anfang des 20. Jhds. seine Stellung als Literatursprache im Mittleren Kurdistan und wurde »zur Sprache der alten Frauen in den Ecken und Gassen von Sanandağ«[17]. Der Bedeutungsverfall des Gōrānī-Dialektes bahnte den Weg für einen Aufstieg der Sīlaimānī-Mundart, die die Sprache der mächtigen Bābān-Fürsten war. Diese Mundart entstand als Folge der Vermischung der Šārazūr-Mundart (die die Mundart der Ardalān-Kurden war) mit der Qalāčuwālān-Mundart (die die Mundart der früheren Hauptstadt der Bābān-Fürsten war). Dazu ist ein gewisser ergänzender Einfluß des Gōrānī-Dialektes festzustellen. In der Mundart von Sīlaimānī haben die bedeutendsten kurdischen Dichter des 19. Jhds. wie z.B. Nālī (1800-1858), Sālim (1805-1869), Kurdī (1812-1851?), Tālabānī (1837-1909), Maḥwī (1830-1904) geschrieben, die teilweise überhaupt nicht aus dem Sīlaimānī-Gebiet stammen. So konnte sich die Sīlaimānī-Mundart Mitte des 19. Jhds. zur Literatursprache erheben.

Obwohl die osmanischen Türken 1851 endgültig das Bābān-Für-

---

[14] Keine der Mundarten des Süd-Kurmānğīdialektes ist heute zur Literatursprache geworden. Früher schrieben die Sprecher dieser Mundarten nur im Gōrānī-Dialekt. Heute schreiben sie in den Mittel-Kurmānğīmundarten.

[15] Die Ardalān-Fürsten wurden von den Şafawidenkönigen als »Walī« = (Gouverneure) von Kurdistan anerkannt. 1612 machte Ardalān Sanandağ (kurd. »Sina«) zu seiner Hauptstadt.

[16] Nach der Eroberung Šārazūrs durch die Türken wanderten die Ardalān-Fürsten endgültig nach Osten, bauten Sanandağ wieder auf und machten sie wieder zu ihrer Hauptstadt.

[17] Kurdistānī, Sa'īd Xān: Nizānī ((Mizgānī)) (Frohe Kunde). Teheran: 1309 (= 1931). S.b.

stentum erobert und ihrem Reich angegliedert hatten, blieb die
Silaimānī-Mundart die Schriftsprache von Mittel-Kurdistan. Die schö-
nen Dichtungen von Nālī, Kurdī und Sālim wirkten so sehr auch
nach Mukriyān und Ardalān hinein, daß auch die großen unter den
dortigen Dichtern wie z.B. Wafāyī (1844-1914), Sālim-ī Sina (1845-
1909), Maǧdī (1849-1925), Nārī (1874-1944), Adab (starb um 1916)
davon sehr beeinflußt wurden.

Seit Ende des ersten Weltkrieges hat diese Mundart besonders
günstige Bedingungen für ihre Entwicklung vorgefunden. Als der
Kurdenkönig Šēx Maḥmūd (1882-1956) die Stadt Silaimānī zur Hauptstadt seines kurzlebigen Königreiches (1922-1924) machte, und zwar
mit dem Ziel das ganze Kurdistan zu einigen, wurden mehrere kurdische
Zeitungen in dieser Mundart herausgegeben. Als Beispiel erwähne
ich nur »Rōž-ī Kurdīstān« (1922-1923), »Bang-ī Ḥaqq« (1923) und
»Umēd-ī Īstīqlāl« (1923). Diese Mundart wurde auch von der englischen
Besatzungsmacht in Mittelkurdistan (1919-1930) gefördert. Die Werke
des englischen Kurdologen Major Soane*, der gleichzeitig Vertreter
der Besatzungsmacht war, und die von ihm in Silaimānī-Mundart
herausgegebenen Zeitungen »Pēškawtin« (1919-1922) und »Žiyānawa«
(1924) sind nur einige willkürlich ausgewählte Beispiele. Erwähnenswert
ist auch in diesem Zusammenhang, daß einige der hervorragendsten
Dichter des kurdischen Volkes, die nach dem ersten Weltkrieg bekannt
wurden, wie z.B. Gōrān (1904-1962), Pīramērd (1867-1950), Asīrī
(1890-1966), Bēkas (1905-1948), Dîldār (1917-1948), Hardī (geb. 1922)
in dieser Mundart gedichtet haben.

Die Errichtung des Staates Irak aus dem westlichen Teil des mittleren
Kurdistan (also der damaligen osmanischen Mossul-Provinz) und den
arabisch-sprachigen ehemaligen osmanischen Provinzen Baǧdād und
Baṣrah wurde gegen den Willen der Kurden durchgeführt. Jedoch
wurden den Kurden wenigstens in gewisser Hinsicht von der englischen
Mandatsmacht und der neuen arabischen Regierung Konzessionen
gemacht. Es handelte sich dabei um einige kulturelle Zugeständnisse
für die Kurden wie z.B. den Gebrauch der kurdischen Sprache an
den Volksschulen und Gerichtshöfen. Da die Silaimānī-Kurden die
Hauptrolle in der kurdischen Nationalbewegung spielten und ihre
Mundart zudem bis dahin einzige Schriftsprache war, fiel es ihnen
leicht, gerade ihre Sprache als offizielle Schriftsprache für die irakischen

---

* Soane, E. B.: Kitabi Awalamini Qiraati Kurdi (Das kurdische Elementarlesebuch).
Bagdad: 1920.

Kurden durchsetzen. Schulbücher und Zeitungen wurden in dieser Mundart gedruckt und Rundfunkprogramme in ihr gesendet. Erwähnt werden muß aber in diesem Zusammenhang, daß andere Kurden (außerhalb des Irak) seit dem 2. Weltkrieg keine vergleichbare Chance hatten. In Syrien, wo die Kurden im übrigen nur unter der französischen Mandatur (1920-1946) ihre Sprache benutzen durften, ohne Repressionen befürchten zu müssen, pflegte man weiterhin die Ǧizīra-Mundart und nicht die aufblühende Sïlaimānī-Mundart. In der Türkei hat man seit jeher wenig Gelegenheit gehabt, die Kurdische Sprache zu benutzen. Wo man sie aber verwendete, schrieb man eben wie die Syrien-Kurden in der Ǧizīra-Mundart. Als Beispiel kann man hier die Zeitungen »Dicle-Firat« (Istanbul 1962), »Deng« (Istanbul 1962), »Çiya« (Berlin 1965-1970), »Hêviya Welêt« (Berlin 1963-1965) [18] wie auch die Publikationen von Musa Anter [19] und Hemreş Reşo [20] nennen. In der UdSSR schrieben die Kurden ebenfalls in ihrer eigenen Mundart, die aber nur einen geringen Unterschied zur Ǧizīra-Mundart aufweist. In Iran erlebte das Kurdische nur während des zweiten Weltkrieges eine kurze Blütezeit und zwar während der »Mahābād-Republik«, der nur eine kurze Lebenszeit (22.1.1946 bis 16.12.1946) beschieden war. Man gebrauchte die Mukrī-Mundart (d.i. eine Mundart des Mittel-Kurmānǧī Dialektes) zusammen mit Elementen der Sïlaimānī-Mundart, so daß eine Schriftsprache entstand, die kaum einen Unterschied zu der in Sïlaimānī aufwies. Einen guten Vergleich kann man anhand der Zeitschriften und Zeitungen anstellen, die um diese Zeit herausgegeben wurden : Z.B. »Nïštïmān« (Mahābād 1943-1945), »Gïrūgāĺ-ï Mïndāĺān« (Mahābād 1945), »Hāwār-ï Kurd« (Mahābād 1945), »Āwāt« (Mahābād 1945), »Kurdïstān« (Mahābād 1945-1946), »Haĺāĺa« (Bōkān 1946).

Die seit Ende des 2. Weltkrieges ununterbrochene Möglichkeit kultureller Aktivitäten bei den Irak-Kurden — im Gegensatz zur kulturellen Benachteiligung den Kurden in anderen Staaten — setzte die Sïlaimānī-Mundart in eine günstige Situation, und sie konnte sich als Schriftsprache von Mittel-Kurdistan etablieren. Den nächsten Schritt aber, zur einheitlichen Sprache aller Kurden zu werden, konnte die Sïlaimānī-Mundart nicht vollziehen. Zu viele Widerstände standen

---

[18] Die beiden letzten Periodica wurden von dem Exil-Kurden aus der Türkei Hemreş Reşo (= Hemdi Turanli) herausgegeben.

[19] Vgl. Anter, Musa: Birîna Reş/Kara Yara. Istanbul: 1965.

[20] Vgl. Hemreş Reşo (Pseud.): Bakûr (Nordwind). Amsterdam: 1967.

dem bisher entgegen. Da ist zum einen die direkte Bekämpfung der kurdischen Sprache durch einige der Staaten, die sich Kurdistan einverleibten, und zum anderen die Tatsache, daß Millionen der Nord-Kurmānğī sprechenden Kurden in der Türkei leben und ihnen somit die arabische Schrift, in der die irakischen Kurden schreiben, überhaupt nicht vertraut ist.

Von prinzipieller Bedeutung aber ist wohl, daß seit dem ersten Weltkrieg bis heute die Kurden selbst nur gelegentlich zur Frage einer einheitlichen Sprache Überlegungen angestellt haben. Dieses Thema wurde zum ersten Mal anläßlich eines Kongresses der kurdischen Schriftsteller, Dichter und Autoren der UdSSR in Erivan im Jahre 1934 aufgegriffen. Dort wurde beschlossen, die Mundart der Sowjet-Kurden als Schriftsprache für alle Kurden einzuführen[21]. Dieser Beschluß ist natürlich niemals in die Praxis umgesetzt worden.

Nach dem Putsch von General Kassem am 14. Juli 1958 und nach der Ausrufung der Republik im Irak (statt des früheren Königreiches) wurden die Kurden zu »Partnern der Araber im Lande« erklärt[22]. Dies wirkte sich als förderlich für die kurdische Sprache im Irak aus. So wurde ein Lehrstuhl für »kurdologische Studien« an der Universität Bagdad eingerichtet. Mehrere kurdischsprachige Zeitungen wurden lizenziert und die Rundfunkprogramme in Kurdisch in größerer Zahl gestattet. Ein »Generaldirektorat für Kurdische Studien«, das die kurdischen Schulen beaufsichtigen sollte, wurde eingerichtet. Der Sīlaimānī-Mundart, die sich in den letzten 50 Jahren durch die Übernahme vieler Vokabeln, die entweder aus anderen Mundarten oder Dialekten stammten oder neu erfunden wurden, lexikalisch und z.T. auch phonetisch weiterentwickelt hatte (und sich damit von der Sīlaimānī-Umgangssprache entfernt hatte), und die inzwischen den Namen »Sōrānī-Dialekt«[23] oder auch »Kurdī Patī« (reines Kurdisch)

---

[21] Vgl. Vil'čevskij, Oleg: Pervaja Vsesojuznaja Kurdovedčeskaja Konferencija i Probleme Literturnogo Jazyka Kurdov SSSR (= Die erste vereinigte kurdologische Konferenz und das Problem der Literatursprache der Kurden von UdSSR). In: Jazyk i Myšlenie, 1936. Nr. 6-7 (Cronika), S. 333-337. Vgl. auch Vil'čevskj, Ol. L. und Šamilov, A. Š.: O Vesojuznoj Kurdovedčeskoj Konferencii (Über die vereinigte kurdologische Konferenz). In: Problemy istorii dokapitalistíčeskix Obščestv. Leningrad 1934. Nr. 9-10 S. 193-194.

[22] Vgl. § 2 des irakischen Grundverfassung vom 27 Juli 1958. vgl. auch Gstrein, Heinz: Volk ohne Anwalt/Die Kurdenfrage im Mittleren Osten. Freiburg/Schweiz. 1974. S. 24.

[23] Die Bezeichnung »Sōrānī« für die Sīlaimānī-Mundart oder gar für den Mittel-Kurmānğī-Dialekt ist falsch und irreführend. »Sōrānī« ist im eigentlichen Sinne nur

erhalten hatte, wurde nun wieder eine große Chance geboten. Auf einem Kongreß der kurdischen Lehrer, der von der irakischen Lehrergewerkschaft vom 11-13. September 1959 in Šaqĺāwa durchgeführt wurde, wurde beschlossen, den sogenannten Sōrānī-Dialekt als Basis für die einheitliche zukünftige Schriftsprache der Kurden zu nehmen [24]. Da die Lehrergewerkschaft ein amtliches Organ war, wurde dieser Beschluß ohne Aufschub im irakischen Kurdistan durchgeführt. Alle Schulbücher wurden in diesem Dialekt verfasst, doch nahm gleichzeitig die Übernahme von Vokabeln aus anderen kurdischen Dialekten und Mundarten zu (vor allem bei nichtkurdischen Fremdwörtern). Dieser Prozeß entbehrte jedoch jeglicher morphologischer oder phonetischer Regel. Getragen von einer emotionalen Hingabe zur kurdischen Sprache, die — lange unterdrückt — sich endlich entfalten durfte, wurde die Weiterentwicklung des »Sōrānī-Dialektes« in dieser Zeit willkürlich und naiv betrieben.

Auch mit ihren Autonomiebestrebungen im Irak, die von 1961 bis 1970 intensiv betrieben wurden, hatten die Kurden Erfolg. Der Irak erkannte am 11. März 1970 den irakischen Kurden das Recht auf Autonomie zu [25], welche am 11. März 1974 in einem Gesetz niedergelegt wurde [26]. Seit 1968 (besonders von 1970 bis 1974) wurden mehrere kulturelle Einrichtungen entweder wieder belebt oder ganz neu eingerichtet, wie z.B. die Kurdische Universität in Sĭlaimānī (17. Juli 1968), die Kurdische Akademie für Wissenschaften (25. August 1970), die Vereinigung Kurdischer Schriftsteller (10. Februar 1970), das Generaldirektorat zur Pflege der Kurdischen Kultur... etc. Dazu wurde die kurdische Sprache die erste und offizielle Unterrichtssprache für kurdische Schüler an kurdischen Schulen und die zweite (Pflicht) Sprache an arabischen Schulen des Irak. Diese offizielle Förderung der kurdischen Sprache zog die erforderliche Reform der Schriftsprache der irakischen Kurden nach sich. Hinsichtlich dieser Reform ist

die Mundart des Sōrān-Gebietes, einer Landschaft zwischen Groß-Zāb (kurd. »Zē-ī Gawra«) und Klein-Zāb (kurd. »Zē-ī Gĭčka«), deren Hauptstadt Rawāndĭz ist.

[24] Vgl. »Kōngra-ī Māmōstāyān-ī Kurd la Šaqĺāwa« (Kongreß der Kurdischen Lehrer in Šaqĺāwa). In der kurdischen Zeitschrift Hīwā (Hoffnung). Nr. 2 und 3. 3 Jahrg. Dezember 1959 und Januar 1960 S. 99.

[25] Nebez, Jemal: Kurdistan und seine Revolution. Publikation der Nukse. München 1972 S. 231-235.

[26] Die Einzelheiten dieses Gesetzes (Gesetz der Autonomie des irakischen Kurdistans) sind in der Zeitschrift »Sketch«, May 10, 1974, Vol. III. No 5, P. 12-13 nachzulesen. Vgl. auch die halbamtliche irakische Zeitung »al-Ṯawrah« (die Revolution). Bagdad, den 12 März 1974.

besonders zu erwähnen, daß das Präsenspräfix der Sïlaimānï-Mundart
»-a«, das eine Besonderheit der Sïlaimānï-Ardalān-Mundart darstellte,
durch das Präsenspräfix der Sōrānï-Mukrï-Mundart »da-« ersetzt
wurde. Durch diese Änderung, die in einem großen Teil der Schülbücher
und in anderen herausgegebenen Schriften konsequent beachtet wurde,
näherte man sich dem Nord-Kurmānǧï-Dialekt, der das Präsenspräfix
»dï-« benutzt (vgl. z.b. das Nord-Kurmānǧï Verb »dï-čïm« (ich gehe)
mit »da-čïm« und a-čïm«).

Weiterhin ist die Ersetzung des der Sïlaimānï-Ardalān-Mundart
eigenen »hohlen d« (d-ï kulōr) durch das »richtige d« zu erwähnen:
z.b. die Postposition »-dā« in »la šār dā« (in der Stadt). Aufgrund
des »d-ï kulōr« in der Sïlaimānï-Mundart erschien früher in der
Schriftsprache dieser Ausdruck als »la šār ā«. Jetzt wird »la šār dā«
geschrieben.

Durch Assimilation infolge des »d-ï kulōr« war eine Lautung
»-nn-« < »-nd-« sehr häufig in der Sōrānï-Ardalānï-Mundart geworden
(vgl. z.b. den Wandel des eigentlichen »kundababū« (Eule) in »kunna-
babū« und »kunababū«). Dieses »-nn« ist im Laufe der genannten
Reform wieder in »-nd« geändert worden. Lexikalisch gesehen hat
man Vokabeln verschiedener Dialekte und Mundarten übernommen,
ohne sie jedoch vorher phonetisch erforscht zu haben und ohne dabei
einer Regel zu folgen. Was man heute in den Schulbüchern sieht,
ist leider eher eine Verwirrung als ein systematischer Versuch, der
Sache der kurdischen Schriftsprache zu dienen.

So unternahm die »Kurdische Akademie für Wissenschaften« in
Bagdad den Versuch, auf dem Gebiet der Reform der Schriftsprache
einen Beitrag zu leisten. Eines ihrer Mitglieder, Tōfïq Wahbï (= Taufiq
Wahby, geb. 1891), machte in der ersten Nummer der »Zeitschrift
der Kurdischen Akademie für Wissenschaften« (1973)* folgende drei
Vorschläge zur Reform der kurdischen Schriftsprache:

1) (die schon bekannte und eingeführte) Übernahme des »richtigen
d« statt des »d-ï kulōr«,

2) Übernahme des Nord-Kurmānǧï Personalpronomens der 1 Person
Singular »az« (ich) bei casus rectus,

3) Übernahme des Futurs, das im Nord-Kurmānǧï existiert, nicht

---

* Wahbï, Tōfïq: Zïmān-a Adabïya-kamān Čōn Tuwānā ū Āsān-tïr Bïkain (Wie
sollen wir unsere Literatursprache mächtiger und leichter machen?). In: Gōvār-ï
Kōf-ï Zānyārï Kurd (Zeitschrift der Kurdischen Akademie für Wissenschaften). Nr. 1
Teil 1 Bagdad: 1973 S. 29-34.

aber im Mittel-Kurmānǧī, und das dadurch in der heutigen Schriftsprache nicht zu finden ist.

Wichtig zu wissen ist, daß einige kurdische Intellektuelle der Meinung sind, daß die jetzige Schriftsprache der irakischen Kurden die Schriftsprache aller Kurden sein sollte, ohne daß irgendeine Reform nötig sei. Argumentiert wird dabei, daß dieser Schriftsprache der Vorzug zu geben sei, weil sie leicht zu erlernen und in ihr mehr Literatur vorliegt als in anderen Dialekten und Mundarten[27]. Weiter wird argumentiert, daß sich diese Sprache historisch habe bestätigen können[28]. Zweifelsohne ist die Entwicklung einer einheitlichen kurdischen Schriftsprache eine linguistische bzw. kulturelle und auch eine politische Notwendigkeit. Seit langem ist diese für die Kurden zukunftsentscheidende Entwicklung ein wahrhaftes Anliegen des Verfassers. In einer 1957 erschienen Schrift[29] hat er u.a. diese Problematik ausführlich angesprochen und die Gründung einer »Wissenschaftlichen Akademie Kurdistans«[30] vorgeschlagen, im Rahmen derer die Probleme der kurdischen Schriftsprache gründlich behandelt werden sollten, und die möglichst das Kurdische in lateinische Schrift übertragen und propagieren sollte, da diese- nach Meinung des Verfassers damals wie heute- dem kurdischen adäquater wäre als die arabisch-persische oder kyrillische Transkription[31]. Erste Kontakte mit einigen kurdischen Schriftstellern, Dichtern und Philologen zum Zwecke der Gründung einer solchen Akademie hatte der Verfasser schon 1956 aufgenommen[32]. Diese wiederholten Bemühungen scheiterten aber an den politischen Umstände in Kurdistan. Als Folge der erfolgreichen Autonomiebestrebungen der Kurden wurden dann jedoch viele Widerstände ausgeräumt und 14 Jahre später, im Jahre 1970, wurde die »Kurdische

---

[27] Vgl. die Meinung von Kamāl Fuād, dem Direktor des Kurdologischen Instituts an der Universität Sīlaimānī in der Zeitschrift »Rōž-ī Kurdistān« (Sonne Kurdistans). Bagdad: März 1973. Nr. 2.2 Jahrg. S. 7.

[28] Vgl. z.B. die Meinung von 'Izaddīn Mistafā Rasūl, Professor für Kurdische Literatur im Institut für Kurdologische Studien an der Universität Bagdad in seinem Buch »Sarīnǧ-ē la Zīman-ī Adab-ī Yakgirtū Kurdī« (ein Blick auf die einheitliche Sprache der kurdischen Literatur). Bagdad: 1971.

[29] Nebez, Jemal: Xōndawārī ba Zīman-ī Kurdī (Bildung in kurdischer Sprache). Bagdad: 1957.

[30] A.a.O. S. 10 und S. 31-34.

[31] A.a.O. S. 10.

[32] Nebez, Jemal: Nûsînî Kurdî be Latînî (Schreiben des Kurdischen in lateinischer Schrift). Bagdad: 1957. S.w.

Akademie für Wissenschaften« gegründet *. In den dazwischenliegenden Jahren hat sich der Verfasser weiter mit dem Thema einer einheitlichen kurdischen Schriftsprache befaßt und im Februar 1974 in Kurdistan ein Manuskript auf Kurdisch in Druck gegeben. Die darin enthaltene Argumentationslinie bzw. die Alternativvorschläge werden hier in groben Zügen dargelegt:

Ausgegangen wird dabei erstens davon, daß nur die Schriftsprache der irakischen Kurden als Basis für eine einheitliche Literatursprache aller Kurden in Frage kommen kann, denn-realistisch gesehen- nur die Irak-Kurden sind in der Lage, die Verbreitung und Förderung einer kurdischen Schriftsprache zu garantieren. Schließlich ist nur im irakischen Kurdistan die kurdische Sprache Staatssprache. Es ist diese kurdische Sprache, die sich historisch bestätigen und in den letzten 50 Jahren bereichern bzw. erweitern konnte. Unbestrittenerweise hat auch allein sie (wenn man die heutigen Situation Groß-Kurdistans in Betracht zieht) die Möglichkeit zur Weiterentwicklung. Zweitens wird davon ausgegangen, daß -innerhalb der Akzeptation der Schriftsprache der irakischen Kurden als eine einheitliche Literatursprache- weitgehende Reformen unbedingt erforderlich sind, wobei diese Reformen vorher wissenschaftlich-linguistisch analysiert und ausgearbeitet sein müssen, d.h. Fachleute zur Vorbereitung und Durchführung herangezogen werden müssen. Ein grundsätzliches Anliegen sollte es zuerst sein, die kurdische Sprache in allen ihren Dialekten bzw. Mundarten (besonders bei Nord-Kurmānǧī und Mittel-Kurmānǧī) linguistisch zu erforschen, d.h. die morphologischen, phonetischen und lexikalischen Abweichungen untereinander in allen Einzelheiten aufzuführen. Dann erst kann, und zwar im Rahmen der Möglichkeiten, die die Schriftsprache der Irak-Kurden bietet, und im Lichte der Ergebnisse der vorherigen Untersuchungen, an eine echte und dauerhafte Reform gedacht werden.

In dem obengenannten Aufsatz (1974) hat der Verfasser fast alle morphologischen, phonetischen und lexikalischen Unterschiede zwischen den beiden Hauptdialekten besprochen und miteinander verglichen. Im folgenden werden hier nur die Unterschiede angesprochen, die innerhalb einer angezeigten Reform- nach Meinung des Verfassers- für konkrete Vorschläge relevant sind.

---

* In der Zwischenzeit hat der Verfasser eine Chrestomathie zur Schriftsprache der irakischen Kurden vorgelegt (vgl. Nebez, Jemal: Kurdische Schriftsprache, eine Chrestomathie moderner Texte. Hamburg: 1969).

A) MORPHOLOGISCHE REFORMEN

1. *Pronomina*

Der Nord-Kurmānǧī-Dialekt besitzt zwei Arten von Pronomina: 1. Nominalpronomina: az(ich), tu(du), aw(er, sie, es), am (wir), hōn (Ihr), aw(ān) (sie). 2. Posessivpronomina: mǐn (mir), ta(dir), wī(ihm)/wē (ihr), ma(uns), wa(Ihr), wān(ihnen). In dieser Beziehung ist das Nord-Kurmānǧī den altiranischen Sprachen ähnlich. Die Schriftsprache der Irak-Kurden verwendet dagegen, genau wie das Neupersische, nur eine einzige Art von Pronomina: mǐn(ich/mir), tō(du-dir), aw(er, sie, es/ihm, ihr, ihm), ēma(wir/uns), ēwa(Ihr/euch), awān(sie-ihnen). Hier schlägt der Verfasser vor, daß das Personalpronomen der 1 Person Singular bei casus rectus im Nord-Kurmānǧī »az«(ich) das »mǐn«(ich) in der jetzigen Schriftsprache ersetzen sollte, während »mǐn« nur bei casus obliquus verwendet werden sollte. Andere Pronomina der Schriftsprache bei casus rectus, d.h. tō, aw, ēma, ēwa, awān, sollten bestehen bleiben. Folgende Personalpronomina bei casus obliquus im Nord-Kurmānǧī sollten in die Schriftsprache übernommen werden: wī(ihm), wē(ihr), ma(uns), wa(Ihr), wān(ihnen).

Begründet wird dieser Vorschlag dadurch, daß nicht nur die Nord-Kurmānǧī sprechenden Kurden diese Pronomina benutzen, sondern auch die Mehrheit der Mittel-Kurmānǧī sprechenden Kurden verwenden diese Pronomina in ihrer Umgangssprache. Man denke nur als Beispiel an »kuř-ī wī« (»sein Sohn«, wörtl. »Sohn von ihm«) in der Mukrī-Mundart statt »kuř-ī aw« und »mār-ī ma« (»unser Haus«, wörtl. »Haus von uns«) oder »lō ma«[33] (für uns) in manchen Mundarten des Hawler-Gebietes statt »māl̂-ī ēma«[34] und »bō ēma« und »ī wān« (»ihres«, wörtl. »von ihnen«) in der Mukrī-Mundart statt »hī-ī awān« in der Schriftsprache. Außerdem ist die 3 Person Singular bei casus obliquus in der Piždar-Mundart »wī« für Maskulinum und »wē« für Femininum. Ferner sind die Demonstrativpronomen dieser Mundart »awī« (Maskulinum) und »awē« (Femininum) statt »aw« (Fem. und Mask.) in der jetzigen Schriftsprache. Diesen Vorschlag zur Reform unterstützt die Tatsache, daß zwar ein kleiner Teil der Kurden seit kurzem das Personalpronomen der 1. Person Singular

---

[33] lō (Präp.) < la bō.
[34] »r« ersetzt »l̂« in manchen Mundarten von Hawlēr bzw. Kōya.

bei casus rectus »az« vergessen hat [35], ihn aber immer noch unreflektiert in seiner mündlich überlieferten Literatur aufweist [36].

2. *Das Futurum*

Die gegebene Schriftsprache kennt das Futurum nicht, während der Nord-Kurmān̆ī-Dialekt das Futurum sowohl im Indikativ als auch im Konjunktiv kennt: Das Nord-Kurmān̆ī bildet den Indikativ Futurum, indem es das Präsenspräfix »dĭ-« durch »dē« ersetzt, vgl. z.B. »az dĭ-čĭm« (ich gehe) gegenüber »az dē-čĭm« (ich werde gehen). Der Konjunktiv Futurum wird durch Zusetzen von »dē« gebildet, vgl. z.B. »az bĭ-čĭm« (daß ich gehe) mit »az dē-bĭ-čĭm« (daß ich gehen werde). In der gegebenen Schriftsprache bleiben dagegen Präsens und Futurum in beiden Fällen identisch, vgl. z.B. »mĭn a-čĭm« (»ich gehe«, »ich werde gehen = Indikativ) und »mĭn bĭ-čĭm« (»daß ich gehe«, »daß ich gehen werde« = Konjunktiv).

Da das Futurum für ein hochsprachliches und modernes Schrifttum ein sehr wichtiger Tempus ist, ist seine Aufnahme in die gegebene Schriftprache dringlich indiziert, wobei sehr wohl genau wie im Nord-Kurmān̆ī (durch »dē«) verfahren werden sollte*; also: »az da-čĭm« (ich gehe), »az dē-čĭm« (ich werde gehen), »az bĭ-čĭm« (daß ich gehe), »az dē bĭ-čĭm« (daß ich gehen werde).

3. *Genusscheidung*

Die jetzige kurdische Schriftsprache hat (wie das Neupersische) sehr wenig Möglichkeiten zur Genusscheidung. Eine davon ist im Vokativum gegeben: vgl. z.B. »kuř-a« (O Junge!) und »kĭč-ē« (O Mädchen!). Es gibt auch manche Mittel-Kurmān̆ī-Mundarten, die beim Genitiv immer noch einen Rest der Geschlechtscheidung behalten haben, vgl. z.B. »rīš-ī pĭyāw-ī« (der Bart des Mannes) gegenüber »mamk-ī žĭn-ē« (die Brust der Frau) in der Pĭždar-Mundart. Das

---

[35] Als das englische Diplomat Rich Silaimānī im Jahre 1820 besuchte, hörte er die Leute das Lied »az da-nāĺ-ĭm« (ich stöhne) singen.

[36] Vgl. das Sprichwort: »agar zānī az-ĭm, agar na-ī-zānī dĭz-ĭm« (sinngemäße Übersetzung: Sollte ich erkannt werden, zeige ich mich von meiner besten Seite, sollte ich unerkannt bleiben, tue ich das, wonach mir der Sinn steht s. Xāĺ, Šēx Mī̆ḥammad-ī : Pand-ī Pēšīnān (Sprüche der Vorfahren). Sīlaimānī : 1971, 2. Auflage S. 33).

* Das Nord-Kurmān̆ī bildet das Futurum etwa wie das Neupersische (dort durch die 3. Person Singular des Verbes »xwāstan« (»wollen«)). Das Nord-Kurmān̆ī benutzt »dē-«, das vom Verb »vāyĭn« (»wollen«) stammt. vgl. Nordkur. »dīvē(t) und Mittelkur. »dawē« vom »wīstĭn« (»wollen«).

Nord-Kurmānǧī kennt die Genusscheidung in vier Fällen: 1. Im Genitiv: vgl. z.B. »bāv-ē mǐn« (»mein Vater«, wörtl. »Vater von mir«). 2. Im Vokativum: vgl. z.B. »kuῤ-ō!« (O Junge!) mit «kač-ē« (O Mädchen!). 3. Im Akkusativ: vgl. z.B. »az kuῤ-ī dǐ-bīn-ǐm« (»ich sehe den Jungen«) mit »az kač-ē dǐ-bīn-ǐm« (»ich sehe das Mädchen«). Der Verfasser schlägt vor, daß die Genusscheidung systematisch nur in einem einzigen dafür aber dort besonders notwendigen Fall aufgegriffen wird; und zwar dann, wenn das Geschlecht des Substantivs nicht bekannt ist, wie im Fall von »havāl« (Freund), das neutral ist, also Maskulinum oder Femininum sein kann. In solchen Fällen sollte man dem Nord-Kurmānǧī folgen, d.h. man sollte sagen »havāl-ī mǐn« (»mein Freund«), aber »havāl-ā mǐn« (»meine Freudin«). Entsprechend sollte man auch im Vokativ das maskuline Suffix »-ō« (vgl. »kuῤ-ō!«) (»du Junge!«) neben dem maskulinen Suffix »-a« übernehmen.

4. *Komperativendung »-tǐr« und Zahleigenschaftswort »dī«*

Das Kurdische hat das alte Komperativsuffix »-tara« in der Form »-tǐr« bewahrt. »-tǐr«, das in manchen Mittel-Kurmānǧī-Mundarten bzw. auch in der jetzigen Schriftsprache Komperativendung ist, wird auch als Zahleigenschaftswort benutzt. In der Mukrī-Mundart wird das Zahleigenschaftswort »-tǐr« durch »-dīka« (vgl. Np. »digar«)* und im Nord-Kurmānǧī durch »dī« oder »dǐn« ersetzt.

Der Verfasser schlägt vor, daß nur »dī« als Zahleigenschaftswort benutzt wird, während »-tǐr« allein als komperatives Zeichen dienen sollte. Also statt »rōž-ēk-ī tǐr« sollte in der Schriftsprache nur »rōž-ēk-ī dī« (»ein anderer Tag«) benutzt werden.

5. *Agglutination*

Agglutination ist ein bedeutendes Merkmal des Mittel-Kurmānǧī bzw. der gegebenen Schriftsprache. Wenn ein Satz aus einem Verb plus zwei enklitischen Pronomina plus einem Nomen besteht, wechseln die enklitischen Pronomina ihre richtigen Plätze. Aus dieser Regel erwachsen selbst für Kurden anderer Dialekte große Verwirrungen, ganz zu schweigen von den Problemen für diejenigen, für die Kurdisch eine Fremdsprache ist. Wenn man z.B. heute sagt: »pāra-t bō nārd-ǐm«, versteht man darunter logischerweise »ich sandte Geld für dich«.

---

* In der Silaimānī-Mundart und in der jetzigen Schriftsprache kommt auch »-ka« als Zahleigenschaftswort vor, wobei »-ka« aus dem Mukrī-Wort »dīka« entstanden ist.

Die richtige Bedeutung aber ist »du sandtest Geld für mich«, was ja wohl einen erheblichen Unterschied ausmacht! Wenn man sagt: »pāra-m bō nārd-īt«, wird darunter verstanden, daß »du mir Geld sandtest«, während die korrekte Bedeutung ist, daß »ich Geld für dich sandte«. In beiden Fällen sind die enklitischen Pronomina »-t« und »-im« (im ersten Fall) und »-m« und »-īt« (im zweiten Fall) vertauscht worden.

Es gibt noch eine andere Art von Agglutination, die noch verwirrender ist. Hier wird eine vor einem Verb stehende Präposition mit einem enklitischen Pronomen gebunden, wie z.B. »bō-m nūs-īt« und »bō-t nūs-īm«. Im ersten Fall ist die Bedeutung nicht »du schreibst für mich«, wie der Reihenfolge logisch zu entnehmen wäre, sondern »ich schrieb für dich«. Entsprechend ist im zweiten Fall die Bedeutung nicht »ich schrieb für dich« sondern »du schriebst für mich«.

Dieser Bedeutungsverwirrung sollte ein Ende bereitet werden, und der Verfasser schlägt vor, daß man fortan diese Formen in der Schriftsprache konsequent vermeidet und jene Formen benutzt, die heute schon der Klarheit halber in der Umgangssprache Eingang gefunden haben:
»pāra-t bō-m nārd« oder »pāra-t nārd bō-m« statt »pāra-t bō nārd-im«.
»pāra-m bō-t nārd« oder »pāra-m nārd bō-t« statt »pāra-m bō nārd-īt«.
»nūs-īm bō-t« statt »bō-m nūs-īt«.
»nūs-īt bō-m« statt »bō-t nūs-īm«.

B) Phonetische Reformen

1. alveolares »l«

Dieses »l« ist eine Besonderheit des Mittel-Kurmāngī-Dialektes und damit auch der jetzigen Schriftsprache. Das Nord-Kurmāngī kennt dieses »l« nicht. Das Nord-Kurmāngī »l« ist manchmal das Äquivalent für das Mittel-Kurmāngī (alveolare) »l«, vgl. z.B. »dil/dil« (Herz), »gul/gul« (Blume), »bilāv/bilāw« (zerstreut). Das ist aber nicht immer der Fall. Manchmal erweist sich das alveolare »l« in Mittel-Kurmāngī Wörtern als Phonem, vgl. z.B. »kul« (stumpf) gegenüber »kul« (gestutzter Schwanz).

Der Verfasser schlägt vor, zu allererst einmal das alveolare »l« zu erforschen, dazu sollten drei Einzeluntersuchungen angefertigt werden: 1. Die erste sollte alle Wörter aufzählen, die in beiden Dialekten identisch in Bedeutung und Aussprache (einfaches »l«) sind, wie z.B. »šīl« (flüssig, naß), »ğīlk« (Kleidung)... etc.

2. Die zweite enthält dann alle Wörter gleicher Bedeutung, die im Mittel-Kurmānğī mit »Î« und im Nord-Kurmānğī mit »l« ausgesprochen werden.

3. Die dritte bezeichnet dann schließlich jene Wörter, die entweder »l« oder »Î« haben, aber jeweilig nur in einem Dialekt vorhanden sind.

In einem nächsten Schritt-anhand dieser Aufstellung- könnte man dann möglicherweise eine Regel hinsichtlich der Verwendung des alveolaren »l« herausfinden. Die für diese vorgeschlagene Erforschung des alveolaren »l« notwendigerweise aufzubringende Mühe rechtfertigt sich für den Verfasser dadurch, daß dieses »Î« wahrscheinlich eine nicht ohne weiteres zu ersetzende, sinnvolle und bleibende Funktion für die kurdische Sprache hat.

2. *Palatalisiertes »d« (»d-ī kulōr«)*

Der Konsonant »d« wird in der Sīlaimānī-Ardalān-Mundart und danach in der gegebenen Schriftsprache als ein bestimmter palatalisierter Laut wiedergegeben, so daß man dieses »d« als »dē-ī kulōr« (wörtl. »hohles d«) bezeichnet. Hier ist der Verfasser derselben Meinung wie die Schulbuchreformer unter den irakischen Kurden, die alle vorhandenen »d-ī kulōr« durch das stimmlose »d« ersetzt haben, sei es im Präsenspräfix »da« (statt »a-«), oder in der Postposition (vgl. »la šār dā« statt »la šār ā«).

3. *Das labiodentale »v« und das bilabiale »w«*

Im Mittel-Kurmānğī ersetzt das bilabiale »w« das Nord-Kurmānğī labiodentale »v«, vgl. z.B. die Nord-Kurmānğī-Wörter »āv« (Wasser), »haiv« (Mond), »tavir« (Axt) mit den Mittel-Kurmānğī Wörtern »āw«, »haiw«, »tawir«. Im allgemeinen kann man sagen, wenn der Laut »w« im Mittel-Kurmānğī vor oder nach einem langen Vokal steht, wird er im Nord-Kurmānğī zu »v«, vgl. z.B. die Mittel-Kurmānğī-Wörter »čāw« (Auge), »hāwīn« (Sommer), »hīwā« (Hoffnung), »rēwī« (Fuchs), »hawīr« (Teig), »hangwīn« (Honig) mit den entsprechenden Nord-Kurmānğī-Wörtern: »čāv«, »hāvīn«, »hīvī«, »rōvī«, »havīr«, »hangvīn« (od. »hīngīv«). Diese Regel hat aber leider auch Ausnahmen, d.h. nicht jedes »w« im Mittel-Kurmānğī trifft man als »v« im Nord-Ḳurmāngī an. Es gibt Wörter, die in beiden Dialekten als

»w« ausgesprochen werden, wie z.B. »wara« (komme!), »lāw« (Junge), »āwā« (Stil), »walēt/wulât« (Heimatland) *. Es gibt außerdem Wörter, die nur in einem der beiden Dialekte vorkommen und die »w« beinhalten, so z.B. »wēsak« (Drohung)[37] im Nord-Kurmānǧī[38]. Der Verfasser schlägt vor, das labiodentale »v« und das bilabiale »w« zu erforschen. Dazu sollten wiederum Monographien vorgelegt werden: Erstens eine Gegenüberstellung aller Wörter aus beiden Dialekten, wo der eine Laut jeweils den anderen ersetzt. Die zweite Aufstellung sollte alle die Wörter beinhalten, die der eine oder der andere Dialekt mit diesen beiden Lauten überhaupt hat. Eine dritte Aufstellung sollte nur für die Wörter mit dem Laut »w« gemacht werden, sofern es in beiden Dialekten »w« bleibt. Möglicherweise ließe sich daraus eine Regel ableiten, wann die Laute »v« und »w« einander ersetzen. Der Verfasser schlägt vor, in diesen Fällen immer »v« zu schreiben, weil eine solche Nivellierung den Gewohnheiten einer Mehrheit der Kurden bei der Aussprache entspricht und eine gerechtfertigte Vereinfachung hier wünschenswert erscheint.

4. Die Konsonanten »z« und »ž«

Die kurdische Sprache hat (im Gegensatz zum Neupersischen) den iranischen Laut »ž« bewahrt. Das kurdische präpalatale »ž«, das in Verbindung zum avestischen präpalatale »č« (vgl. Av. »raočah-« (= Tag))[39] steht, ist im Neupersischen nur noch »z« (vgl. z.B. die kurdischen Wörter: »rōž« (Tag), »žang« (Rost), »mižda« (frohe Kunde), »žī« (Präp. »von, aus, in«), »žīn« (Leben) mit den persischen Wörtern gleicher Bedeutung: »rūz«, »zang«, »mozd«, »az«, »zistan«. Es gibt aber auch manche Wörter in der gegebenen Schriftsprache die durch den Einfluß des Neupersischen jetzt mit »z« statt mit »ž« ausgesprochen werden, während dieselben Wörter in Nord-Kurmānǧī-Mundarten immer noch auf »ž« lauten. Der Verfasser ist der Meinung, daß

---

* »walēt« und »wulât« sind kurdisierte Formen des arab. Wortes »wilāyah« (hier mit der Bedeutung »Provinz«, »Region«).

[37] Vgl. kurd. »wēsak-šāndin« (wörtl. »Drohung schicken«, d.h. »drohen«).

[38] Die Wörter, die im Nord-Kurmānǧī diesen Laut »w« bewahren, sind meist Wörter mit gutturalem und palatalem »x« im Anlaut, z.B. »xwaš« (angenehm), »xwa« (selbst), »xwastin« (wünschen, verlangen), »xwardiyān« (»Wächter«, vgl. das französische Wort »gardien«), »xwarnūf« (vgl. arab. »xurnūb« (Johannisbrot)). Der Laut »wa-« ist im Mittel-Kurmānǧī häufig zu »ō« geworden (vgl. »xwaš > xōš, xwa > xō«).

[39] Dieses »č« ist immer noch in manchen kurdischen Wörtern vorhanden, vgl. z.B. das Wort »bařōčka« (sonniger Ort).

alle solche Wörter durch Nord-Kurmānǧī-Wörter ersetzt werden sollten, und zwar nicht nur weil dies eine phonetische Annäherung zwischen der Schriftsprache und dem Nord-Kurmānǧī darstellen würde, sondern auch weil dadurch die innere Konsequenz der Sprache und die Homogenität ihrer Grammatik beachtet würde. Wörter wie »dïlsōz« (loyal), »dōzax« (Hölle), »zïrang« (klug), »zīrak« (intelligent), »ḥaz« (Liebe, Begehr) in der gegebenen Schriftsprache sollten danach durch die Nord-Kurmānǧī-Wörter »dïlsōž«, »doža«, »žarang«, »žīrak«, »haž« ersetzt werden.

5. Die Suffixe »gā« und »ga«

»-gā« und »ga« kommen beide in der gegebenen Schriftsprache als Suffixe für Namen vor, woraus der Hinweis auf eine Lokalität entsteht, wie z.B. »laškïr« (Armee), aber »laškïr-gā/ga« (Kaserne). Da im Nord-Kurmānǧī nur »-ga« benutzt wird, schlägt der Verfasser vor, daß in der Schriftsprache auch nur das Suffix »-ga« (und nicht »-gā«) benutzt wird.

C) LEXIKALISCHE REFORMEN

Einige lexikalische Reformen sind nach Ansicht des Verfassers notwendigst angezeigt. Genau wie das Augenmerk derer, denen die kurdische Sprache ein Anliegen ist, auf die grammatikalische Homogenität des Kurdischen gerichtet sein sollte, sollte auch auf eine entsprechende Homogenität in der historischen Entwicklung der Vokale und Konsonanten geachtet werden.

1. Die Vokale »ā« und »ē«

Ein Vergleich zwischen dem Kurdischen und Neupersischen zeigt uns, daß in der Regel der im Neupersischen nach einem Konsonanten kommende lange Vokal »ā« im Kurdischen sein Äquivalent im »ē« hat, vgl. z.B. die neupersischen Wörter: »rāh« (Weg), »ǧā« (Platz), »pā« (Fuß), »darāz« (lang), »bāzār« (Markt) mit den kurdischen Wörtern »rē«, »ǧē«, »pē«, »dïrēž«, »bāžēr̄«. Es gibt aber in der gegebenen Schriftsprache viele Wörter, die sich nicht nach dieser Regel, sondern nach dem neupersischen Einfluß richten, während sie in fast allen Mundarten des Nord-Kurmānǧī-Dialektes und in manchen Mundarten des Mittel-Kurmānǧī durchaus in der richtigen Form vorhanden sind. Deshalb schlägt der Verfasser vor, daß die nicht eigentlich kurdischen Wörter in der jetzigen Schriftsprache durch charakteristisch kurdische Wörter aus anderen Mundarten ersetzt werden. So sollten z.B. die Wörter »nāw« (»Name«, vgl. Np. »nām«), »rābar« (»Wegweiser«, vgl. Np. »rahbar«), »pāitaxt« (»Hauptstadt«, vgl. Np. »pāy-(e)taxt«), »xudā« (»Gott«, vgl. Np. »xodā«) durch die Wörter »nēw« (Mukrī-Mundart), »rēbar« (Badinan-Mundart), »pētaxt« (Mukrī-Mundart), »xōdē« (Nord-Kurmānǧī-Mundart) ersetzt werden.

2. *Die Vokale »a« und »ē«*

Es ist ein Merkmal in der Beziehung zwischen der kurdischen und neupersischen Sprache, daß der einem Konsonanten folgende Vokal »a« im Neupersischen zu einem »ē« im Kurdischen wird, vgl. z.B. die neupersischen Wörter: »zar« (Gold), »mard« (Mann, Ehemann), »panǧ« (fünf), »andak« (bißchen, ein wenig), »mawīz« (schwarze Rosine) mit den kurdischen Wörtern »zēř«, »mērd«, »pēnǧ«, »hēndēk«, »mēwiž«. Wörter, die in der jetzigen Schriftsprache von dieser Regel abweichen, die aber in den anderen Mundarten dieser Regel entsprechen, sollten in der jetzigen Schriftsprache korrigiert werden. So sollte z.B. das Wort »zařangar« (Goldschmied) durch das Mukrī-Wort »zēřīngar« und das Wort »kam« (wenig) durch das Nord-Kurmānǧī-Wort »kēm« ersetzt werden.

3. *Die Vokale »ū« und »ō«*

Ein Vergleich zwischen dem Kurdischen und Neupersischen zeigt uns, daß in der Regel der im Neupersischen einem Konsonanten folgende lange Vokal »ū« im Kurdischen sein Äquivalent im »ō« hat, vgl. z.B. die neupersischen Wörter: »gūšt« (Fleisch), »pīrūz« (siegreich), »pīrūze« (Türkis), »nūš« (Wohlgeschmack), »pūšīdan« (anziehen), »dūǧ« (Buttermilch), »dūst« (Freund) mit den kurdischen Wörtern: »gōšt«, »pīrōz«, »pīrōza«, »nōš«, »pōšīn«, »dō«, »dōst«. Auch die in beiden Sprachen vorkommenden Lehnwörter richten sich häufig nach dieser Regel, vgl. z.B. die arabischen Lehnwörter »rūḥ« (Geist, Seele) und »rūmī« (byzantinisch), die im Neupersischen als »rūḥ« und »rūmī« bleiben, während sie im Kurdischen als »rōḥ« und »rōmī« ausgesprochen werden. Es gibt aber auch Wörter in der Schriftsprache, die von dieser Regel abweichen. Der Verfasser schlägt vor, diese aus der Schriftsprache zu entfernen und sie durch regelrechte Nord-Kurmānǧī-Wörter zu ersetzen.

4. *Die Vokale »ī« und »ē«*

Ein Vergleich zwischen dem Neupersischen und Kurdischen zeigt, daß der Vokal »ī« im Neupersischen (sei es im Anlaut, Inlaut oder Auslaut) im Kurdischen in der Regel als »ē« vorkommt, vgl. z.B. die neupersischen Wörter: »Īrān« (Iran), »šīr« (Milch), »pīš« (vor), »bīgāna« (Fremd), »bī« (Präp. »ohne«) mit denselben kurdischen Wörtern: »Ērān«, »šēr«, »pēš«, »bēgāna«, »bē-«. Der Verfasser schlägt vor, daß alle die von dieser Regel in der Schriftsprache abweichenden Wörter, die aber im Nord-Kurmānǧī oder in anderen Mundarten des Mittel-Kurmānǧī der Regel genügen, von diesen ersetzt werden. So würde dann z.B. statt »rīz« (Reihe) »rēz« und statt »tīž« (scharf) »tēž« benutzt werden müssen.

5. *Die Laute »m« und »w/v«*

Der labiale Konsonant »m« im Neupersischen (besonders wenn er nach den Vokalen »ā«, »í«, »a«, »ī« kommt) hat im Kurdischen sein Äquivalent im bilabialen halbvokalen »w« oder labiodentalen »v«; vgl. z.B. die neupersischen Wörter: »xām« (roh), »dāman« (der untere Teil), »čašīm« (Auge), »namāz« (Gebet), »nām« (Name), »zamīn« (Erde), »nīm« (halb) gegenüber den kurdischen Wörtern: »xāw«, »dāwēn«, »čāw«, »nivēž/nöž«, »nāw/nēw/nāv«, »zawī«, »nīw/v«. Diese Regel findet sich im Kurdischen nicht nur bei den iranischen Wörtern, sondern auch bei den Fremdwörtern, vgl. z.B. die arabischen Wörter: »tamām« (richtig), »salām« (Gruß), »ǧamāᶜah« (Gruppe), »xaimah« (Zelt), »yatīm« (Weise), »dirham« (Geld) mit den kurdischen Wörtern: »tawāw«, »síláw/v«, »ǧivāt«, »xēwat«, »hatīw«, »dirāw/v«. Der Verfasser schlägt hier vor, daß alle solche Wörter, die in der Schriftsprache in der neupersischen Form erscheinen, die aber in der Umgangssprache in der kurdischen Form ausgesprochen werden, durch die letzteren ersetzt werden sollten. Statt der Wörter »dāmudazgā« (Einrichtung, Organisation) und »dam« (Mond) z.B. sollen nur die Wörter »dāwudazgā« und »daw/v« benutzt werden, die außerdem in anderen Mundarten bzw. Dialekten auch tatsächlich vorhanden sind.

6. *Die Konsonanten »d« und »z«*

Es ist eine Besonderheit der kurdischen Sprache, daß sie das »z« des Avestischen (also ein altiranisches Element) immer noch bewahrt hat. Im echt Persischen der SW-Entwicklung stand dem schon im Altpersischen ein »d« gegenüber, vgl. z.B. die kurdischen Wörter: »zāw/vā« (Bräutigam), »zānā« (Gelehrter, Wissenschaftler) mit den neupersischen Wörtern: »dāmād«, »dānā«. Es gibt viele kurdische Wörter, die das avestische »z« aufweisen, so z.B. »az« (»ich«, vgl. Av. »azəm«), »mazin« (»groß«, vgl. Av. »mazant«), »zar« (»Herz«, vgl. Av. »zərəδaya«). Aus dieser Entwicklung heraus findet sich in der kurdischen Sprache die Tendenz, auch bei nicht-iranischen Lehnwörtern »d > z« zu wandeln, vgl. die arabischen Wörter: »xidmah« (Dienst), »kabad« (Leber), »dibs« (Syrup), die zu »xizmat«, »kazab« (vgl. das Wort »kazab-šawāt« mit der Bedeutung »leidenschaftlich« in der ʿĀmūda-Mundart) und »zabaš« (hier mit der Bedeutung »Wassermelone«) werden. So sind auch die arabischen Eigennamen »Šamas ad-dīn« und »Xadīǧah« zu »Šamzīn« und »Xāzē« geworden. Der Verfasser schlägt hier vor, daß alle die Wörter, die neben ihrer lautentwicklungsgeschichtlich »richtigen« Form auch mit »d« in der Schriftsprache gebraucht werden, nicht mehr benutzt werden sollten. Z.B. soll allein das Wort »zaryā« (Meer) in der Schriftsprache benutzt werden und nicht auch das Wort »daryā« (oder »dalyā«) *.

7. *Die Metathesen*

In der jetzigen Schriftsprache werden eine Reihe von Metathesen, falsche wie richtige, parallel gebraucht. So benutzt man z.B. beide Wörter »fīřīn« und »řifīn« (fliegen), »žĭmārdĭn« und »mĭžārdĭn« (zählen), »ǧĭnēw« und »ǧĭwēn« (Schimpf), »yakǧārī« und »yaǧǧārī« (auf einmal). Der Verfasser schlägt vor, bei solchen Wörtern die Etymologie des Wortes in Betracht zu ziehen und dann nur die philologisch richtige Form in der Schriftsprache zu verwenden.

8. *Die Fremdwörter*

Die kurdische Sprache enthält eine relativ geringe Anzahl von semitischen (arabischen, aramäischen und neusyrischen), neupersischen, türkischen und europäischen (englischen, französischen, russischen,

---

* Ein Zeichen dafür, das dieses Wort »zaryā« ein sehr altes kurdisches Wort ist, läßt sich daraus entnehmen, daß der mit einer Legende verknüpfte See in Marīwān immer noch »gōl-ī zīrē-bār« heißt. »zīrē-bār« bezieht sich wohl auf das avestische Wort »*zrayah-pāra« mit der Bedeutung »Küste des Meeres« (vgl. Np. »daryā-bār«).

italienischen, griechischen, deutschen) Fremdwörtern *. Die arabischen und türkischen Lehnwörter werden seit den letzten 40 Jahren von kurdischen Autoren, Schriftstellern und Journalisten systematisch aus der kurdischen Sprache entfernt. An ihrer Stelle werden entweder kurdische Wörter aus anderen Mundarten bzw. Dialekten oder neuerfundene Wörter benutzt. Diese Abneigung gegen arabische und türkische Fremdwörter bei den Kurden hat sicherlich ihre psychologische Erklärung darin, daß die Kurden, deren Nationalbewußtsein sich ebenfalls in den letzten 40 Jahren stärker als je zuvor artikulierte, eine Art von Antipathie gegen die Sprachen ihrer Unterdrücker entwickelt haben. Nichts einzuwenden ist gegen die offizielle Einsetzung von kurdischen Wörtern, dann wenn sie allgemein oder teilweise im kurdischen Sprachgebrauch verwendet werden. Das gilt besonders, wenn sie an Stelle jener Fremdwörter treten, die mit der phonetischen Natur der kurdischen Sprache nicht in Einklang stehen. Die Gefahr liegt aber darin, daß manche Sprachpuristen »selbstgebastelte« Wörter ganz willkürlich einführen, ohne die philologische Struktur des Kurdischen in Betracht zu ziehen. Aus diesem Grunde hat der Verfasser schon früh versucht, seiner Meinung Gehör zu verschaffen, daß doch diejenigen Fremdwörter, die sich in die kurdische Lautlehre gut anpassen und sich dadurch nahtlos in die Sprache einfügen, belassen werden sollten [40]. Außerdem hat er wieder und wieder betont, daß die Erfindung neuer Wörter für Technik und Wissenschaft nur die Sache einer Akademie für kurdische Sprache sein kann und nicht »Hobby« eines jeden beliebigen Sprachliebhabers [41].

Der Verfasser ist auch gegen eine weitere Tendenz, die versucht, alle arabischen Lehnwörter, die nach kurdischer Phonetik ausgesprochen werden, mit arabischer Orthographie zu schreiben. Diese Tendenz ist insofern unsinnig, weil ja dann eine einzige Lautlehre, nämlich die Kurdische, durch zwei Orthographien widergespiegelt werden würde. Wenn also ein arabisches Wort wie »ḍaġṭ« (Druck), das im Kurdischen wie »zaxt« ausgesprochen wird, konsequent arabisch geschrieben werden sollte, so ist das absurd.

---

* Über die Fremdwörter in der kurdischen Sprache liegen vom Verfasser einige Untersuchungen vor, die zu einem späteren Zeitpunkt veröffentlicht werden sollen.

[40] Nebez, Jemal: Wargēfān Hunara (Die Übersetzung ist eine Kunst). Silaimānī: 1958 S. 12-13. Nachdruck vom »Institut für die Kurdologischen Studien der Universität Bagdad« in 1972.

[41] a.a.O. S. 3-4, 16-17.

D) Orthographische Reformen

Der allgemeinen Verbreitung einer kurdischen Schriftsprache steht aber noch ein weiteres erhebliches Hindernis entgegen, und das ist die kurdische Schrift. Gerade dort, wo man heute eine einheitliche kurdische Schriftsprache entwickeln könnte, nämlich im Irak, wird das Kurdische nur in der arabischen Transkription benutzt. Eine andere Schrift zu gebrauchen- vor allem vielleicht gar die lateinische Schrift-, ist aus religiösen und chauvinistischen Gründen seitens der arabisch-irakischen Regierung nicht erlaubt. Obwohl die arabische Schrift von den irakischen Kurden für die Erfordernisse der kurdischen Sprache in den letzten 50 Jahren umfassend reformiert worden ist[*], konnten die Schwierigkeiten, die in der Natur des arabischen Alphabets liegen, nicht ausgeräumt werden. Die Übernahme des lateinischen Alphabets würde dagegen viele Vorteile bringen: Das Erlernen der Sprache würde erleichtert und ihre Verbreitung weitgehend gefördert werden, und das nicht nur im irakischen Kurdistan, sondern auch innerhalb von Groß-Kurdistan; denn sowohl Türkei- wie auch Syrien-Kurden kennen nur das lateinische Alphabet. Die UdSSR-Kurden, die nur widerwillig die kyrillische Schrift benutzen und schon einmal die lateinische Schrift verwendeten, könnten leicht das lateinische Alphabet adaptieren. Ihnen allen, den Türkei-, Syrien- und UdSSR-Kurden ist das arabische Alphabet fremd und schwer — oft unmöglich — zu erlernen. Die Iran-Kurden, die ja durch das Persische die arabische Schrift kennen, würden im großen und ganzen auch nicht benachteiligt werden; denn die kurdische Schriftsprache ist auf der Basis einer Mundart aufgebaut, die ihren beiden Hauptmundarten (d.h. Sīna-Ardalānī und Mukrī) sehr naheliegt. Außerdem ist die lateinische Schrift (durch die Verbreitung der englischen Sprache an der Schulen) ihnen oft wohlbekannt. Der Verfasser kann aus seiner langjährigen Erfahrung beim Lehren der kurdischen Sprache behaupten, daß die Übernahme der lateinischen Schrift der Sache der Schriftsprache im großen Maße dienen würde.

* Nebez, Jemal: Kurdische Schriftsprache. Ibid. S. 13-15.

SCHLUßWORT

Dieser Aufsatz ist naturgemäß eine wissenschaftliche Abhandlung zur Problematik einer einheitlichen kurdischen Schrift- bzw. Hochsprache, aber darüber hinaus möge er als ein Appell an alle Kurden und Kurdologen verstanden sein, daß sie- da die Geschichte selbst noch keine einheitliche kurdische Hochsprache hervorgebracht hat- nicht auf den Advent der »Gott gegebenen Sprachfrüchte« warten, sondern durchdacht, gezielt und systematisch in diesen Prozeß eingreifen und ihn somit beschleunigen, damit auch die Kurden endlich den Anschluß haben, die Privilegien einer *einheitlichen* Hochsprache genießen können.

Es ist wohl richtig, daß jeder Erfolg bei der Reform der kurdischen Schriftsprache und ihre allgemeine Einführung bzw. ihre Vereinheitlichung unumstößlich von den politischen Bedingungen in Kurdistan abhängig ist. Doch muß es klar sein, daß die kurdische Sprache selbst wiederum Einfluß auf die soziale, kulturelle, wissenschaftliche und politische Entwicklung der Kurden hat. Deshalb dürfen wir das Ziel, nämlich die kurdische Sprache zu einem adäquaten, wohlgeformten Instrument für alle Kurden zu machen, nicht aus den Augen verlieren und trotz aller Widrigkeiten stetig und konsequent daran arbeiten.

ANMERKUNGEN

a) *Zur Transkribierung*

Die gesamte Transkribierung der kurdischen, persischen, arabischen und türkischen Worte geschieht nach den bei den Orientalisten üblichen Vorschriften, außer folgenden Besonderheiten:

î — für den persischen »Halb-Murmelvokal« (wie im Wort »čaš(î)m«).

ı — für den kurdischen Murmelvokal.

ŕ — für das kurdische gerollte r. Aber wenn das gerollte r im Anlaut vorkomt, wird es dennoch nur »r« geschrieben, weil jedes »r« im Anlaut gerollt ist.

Î — für das kurdische alveolare l.

N.B. Die Titel der kurdischen Bücher, Artikel oder Zeitungen werden hier so wiedergegeben wie sie im Original erschienen sind.

b) *Abkürzungen*

arab.	arabisch, Arabisch
Av.	avestisch, Avestisch
EI.	Enzyklopädie des Islam
kurd.	kurdisch, Kurdisch
Mittelkur.	Mittel-Kurmānǧī
Nordkur.	Nord-Kurmānǧī
Np.	neupersisch, Neupersisch
SW.	Südwestiranische Sprache

JACOB NEUSNER

THE IDEA OF PURITY IN THE JEWISH LITERATURE OF THE PERIOD OF THE SECOND TEMPLE

The post-biblical history of the concept of purity and impurity is divided by the destruction of the Temple in A.D. 70. Before that time the practical application of the purity-laws in the cult preserved their immediacy and social relevance. Afterward the law remained important, since the menstrual and food rules bore consequences for everyday life. But going to the Temple no longer was an important reason to keep the laws. Evidence on the interpretation of purity before 70 derives from the writings, originating in widely divergent periods and circles, collected in the Apocrypha and Pseudepigrapha, from the Dead Sea Scrolls, from Philo, and from Paul. Three other important sources, completed after 70, contain information on the period during which the Temple stood as well as on the decades immediately thereafter, when the Temple's influence on the Judaic religious imagination remained formative. These are, first, the writings of Josephus, second, the New Testament, and third, the rabbinic traditions about the Pharisees before 70.

These several sources are not wholly comparable. Three tell us about the conceptions of purity of individuals, Paul, Josephus, a priest in Jerusalem, and Philo, a philosopher in Alexandria. Josephus thought of purity primarily in connection with the Temple and the cult. For Philo the Temple was remote and the purity laws were matters for private practice and figurative interpretation. The Dead Sea writings, by contrast, are not to be assigned to an identifiable author; they represent, and were preserved by, a community which saw itself as the holy sanctuary. The rabbinic traditions about the Pharisees and the New Testament Gospels have in common a considerable history of formulation and transmission by people themselves not witnesses to the events they relate and to the opinions they attribute to their predecessors. But the traditions provide a fairly reliable account of the varieties of interpretation of purity in the respective communities which formulated and preserved them.

Specific references to the biblical laws and metaphors of purity in the three centuries before the destruction of the Second Temple were

for the most part routine. Among individual writers, only Philo and
(after 70) the author of Hebrews creatively used and developed the
concept—for their own purposes to be sure. But purity and impurity
played a more central role in the Judaic religious imagination, both
at home and in the diaspora, than the references in the preserved
remains suggest, for many groups within Judaism had to come to
grips with the issues raised by the Temple. In a practical way the
resolution of these issues in part was expressed by the treatment
of the purity-laws. Every important sect had to define its relationship
to the Temple, and one predominant question concerned actually
keeping, or not keeping, the purity laws, making them into a metaphor
for the ethical life, or otherwise reinterpreting them. The only thing
no one could do was ignore them. A group claiming to constitute a
holy community and comparing itself to the Temple would have to
interpret in terms of its life the Temple's chief characteristics, including
purity-rules, cult, and priesthood. Much that is not explicitly said
about purity, therefore, is going to reveal conceptions directly pertinent
to it. Much that is said, furthermore, will adumbrate a broader
polemic, comprehending purity, against the Jerusalem Temple itself;
or, as in the case of Josephus, against people who (in his opinion
falsely) claim to defend the Temple's purity, or, as in the case of the
Christian community, against the common, literalist conception of
the concrete meaning of the laws.

Josephus, the Jewish general and historian who in 75 wrote the
history of the war of 66-73 and about twenty years later published
a history of the Jews, interprets or explains the purity laws primarily
in relationship to the Temple cult. He rarely treats purity in other than
a cultic setting. This viewpoint was natural to him, for he was a priest
and took for granted that the Mosaic legislation about purity applied
primarily to the Temple. In his writings on the Temple, purity and
impurity seldom occur in a metaphorical sense. Josephus's view that
the purity-laws are for the Temple's protection is stated as follows:
"In view of the sacrifices the Law has prescibed purifications for
various occasions, after a funeral, after child-birth, after conjugal
union, and many others" (Against Apion 2: 198).

Since the purity-laws did apply, the defilement of the Temple became
one of the chief accusations against the Zealots, whom Josephus
despised. Zealot blood defiled the sanctuary (War 4: 202). In the civil
war between the Zealots and Ananus, Ananus refrained from assaulting
the Temple portals, for, if he were victorious, he would thereby

"introduce those crowds without previous purifications" (War 4: 205). So the opponents of the Zealots protected the Temple. Josephus cites his own speech to the Zealots. He says that when Titus learned the continual sacrifice had ended in the Temple, he sent Josephus to talk to John of Gischala, the Zealot chief, asking him to leave the city and fight outside of it. "Without involving the city and the sanctuary in his own ruin... He should no longer pollute the Holy Place nor sin against God". Josephus accuses John of not having kept the Temple pure for God, of having defiled the holy place. God has been deprived of his daily food, and the Romans are not at fault. John himself caused the interruption of the sacrifices. The city certainly will fall for "God himself with the Romans is bringing the fire to purge his Temple and exterminate a city laden with pollutions" (War 6: 93-111). John of Gischala not only ate unlawful food, but "abandoned the established rules of purity of our forefathers; so that it could no longer excite surprise that one guilty of such mad impiety towards God failed to observe towards men the offices of gentleness and charity" (War 7: 264). Keeping the purity-laws, seen as an act of piety, is equivalent to deeds of charity, he who does not do the one is unlikely to do the other. Josephus is particularly eager to emphasize the Zealots' indifference to the Temple's purity, because they themselves probably stressed their hope to purify the Temple, as had the Maccabees before them. The Maccabees had purified the land of all pollution (Antiquities 12: 285-6). But God himself turned away from the Temple "because he deemed the Temple to be no longer a clean dwelling place for Him, [he] brought the Romans upon us and purification by fire upon the city... With such pollution did the deeds of the brigands infect the city" (Antiquities 20: 166-7).

The Zealots therefore are shown to have been indifferent to the sanctity of the Temple, while their moderate opponents were scrupulous to preserve its purity. Josephus makes the same point time and again. Ananus and his party "were anxious on their side to preserve the Temple from pollution and that none of their countrymen should fall within its walls" (War 4: 215). "These frenzied men," that is, the Zealots, "stopped short of no impiety". They admitted those who wished to offer sacrifices, carefully searching them, but then many were killed, priests and worshippers alike, by the missiles of war: "The dead bodies of natives and aliens, of priests and laity, were mingled in a mass, and the blood of all manner of corpses formed pools in the courts of God" (War 5: 15-19). What rite of purification follows? Josephus says the Romans entered to purge with fire Jerusalem's internal pollutions (War 5: 19)—a rite of purification no where alluded to in Scripture. So the Zealots' concern for purity—perhaps intended to follow the model of the Maccabees—produced the defilement of the Temple—part of Josephus's broader indictment of Zealotry.

The law against lepers forms part of a considerable polemic, this time against Manetho, an Egyptian anti-Semite. In Antiquities 3 : 265, Josephus refers to the "absurd charge" of those who assert Moses was forced to flee Egypt on account of his being a leper, and was placed in command of all others who had been expelled from the country on the same pretext. In refutation Josephus cites the Mosaic legislation requiring lepers to stay outside of the city and to be treated like corpses. "Moses would never have issued to his own humiliation statutes such as these". Among many nations lepers are honored, not exiled; they may enter sacred courts and Temples (II Kings 5: 1, 18). So Moses and his host could have laid down laws concerning lepers of the most favorable character, instead of imposing any penalty on them (Antiquities 3: 266-8). People who say Moses was a leper are jealous; he acted only for God's honor. In his later treatise, Against Apion ("Or, On the Antiquity of the Jews"), Josephus returns to this theme. The enemies of the Jews assert the libel, motivated by hatred and envy, that the Jews were expelled from Egypt because they were lepers or otherwise polluted. Manetho, to whom this accusation is attributed, says all the maimed people were first segregated, then expelled (Against Apion, 233-236; also Lysimachus, 1: 304-9). But these accusations are ridiculous. Among the many reasons adduced against Manetho's claim is the evidence of the Mosaic laws (Against Apion 1: 279-286). Moses forbids lepers to reside in towns, they have to be solitary vagrants, and whoever touches them or lives under the same roof with is unclean. If the malady passes, the leper has to be purified and offer numerous sacrifices. Would people brought together because they were lepers have enacted laws to their own disgrace and injury?

Josephus refers to purity outside of the Temple cult in only one important context, the purity-rites of the Essenes. They regard oil as defiling and do not use it; they keep dry skin and always dress in white (War 2: 123). "At the fifth hour they gather in one place, gird their loins with linen cloths, bathe their bodies in cold water, then the initiated, now pure, go to the refectory and eat their meal, as in a sacred shrine" (War 2: 129-131). Supper is eaten in the same way. A candidate for admission is kept as a probationer for a year; then he is allowed "to share the purer kind of holy water" (War 2: 138). But before he may touch the common food, he is made to swear oaths regarding piety, justice, and obedience, and so forth. If one is expelled from the group, he still is bound by "their oaths and usages", so he cannot eat other men's food and dies of starvation (War 2: 143-4). The order is divided into four grades; if a junior member touches a senior one, the latter must take a bath, as after contact with an outsider (War 2: 150). Purity does not enter Josephus's account of the sects in *War*. (War 2: 164ff.). In the later description of the sects (Antiquities 18: 12ff.), Josephus says the Essenes send offerings to the Temple, but employ "a different ritual of purification" (Antiquities 18: 19). They therefore are barred from the inner precincts of the Temple frequented by other people, and perform their rites by themselves. The text here is unclear and its sense therefore in doubt. Otherwise, Antiquities 18: 18-22 omits reference to purity-laws. Josephus does not supply the theory according to which the Essenes kept ritually clean outside of the Temple, nor does he remark on the peculiarity of their concern for extra-cultic purity.

Philo takes into account a wide range of biblical purity-laws and pays close attention to their details. He contributes far more than generalized homilies about ethical purity or sexual impurity. To be sure, he makes use of uncleanness in terms entirely divorced from the Scriptural sense. For example he says that all genuine votaries of philosophy discern truths which none of the unclean may touch: "By unclean I mean all those who, without ever tasting education at all... have changed the stamp of wisdom's beauty into the ugliness of sophistry" (Every Good Man is Free 4). The use of "uncleanness" here bears no resemblance to any hitherto examined. But more commonly Philo will resort to Scriptural concepts, even for his more allegorical interpretations of purity. In the prophetic and sapiential tradition, he contrasts purity and wickedness. Wickedness makes purity impure, as it makes truth into falsehood: "Furthermore, they cleanse their bodies with lustrations and purifications, but they neither wish nor practise to wash off from their souls the passions by which life is defiled" (On the Cherubim, 94-5). Here is a second-level metaphor. First, purity is treated as a metaphor for moral cleanness, as in Scripture. But second, it further serves as a metaphor for self-control, since the self-controlled are not 'defiled' by the passions. Without self-control, "A man may submit to sprinklings with holy water and to purifications, befouling his understanding with cleansing his body" (The Worse Attacks the Better 20), a commonplace contrast between cultic purity and "spiritual" impurity.

Philo treats numerous details of the law of leprosy (Lev. 14: 57 ff.) with greatest care. For example, one must remove the houses on which the leprosy-signs appear, because, "When diverse qualities, the handiwork of pleasure and desires and passions... press and weigh down the whole soul... lowering its level, we are to get rid of the principles which cause the infirmity and introduce in their place good healthy principles by means of a training under the law or indeed of a good education" (The Worse Attacks the Better 16). Lamech's name means being brought low. This name has two meanings. The former kind of "being brought low" is a species of leprosy: "For when the uniform and healthy appearance of the flesh is impaired and the mischief is visible below the surface, the lawgiver says the cruel disease of leprosy has set in [Lev. 13: 3]" (The Posterity and Exile of Cain 47). If a living color ("raw flesh") arises in the leper, he is defiled (Lev. 13: 14-15). Now this is opposed to the natural view. Normally, one supposes the healthy are corrupted by diseased or dead things; but the healthy and living do not corrupt their opposites. However, the lawgiver thereby teaches, "It is the healthy and living which produce the condition which is tainted with pollution. For the healthy and living color in the soul, when it makes a genuine appearance upon it, is Conviction. When this Conviction comes to the surface, it makes a record of all the soul's transgressions and rebukes... it almost without ceasing. And the soul then thus convicted sees in their true light its practices... which were contrary to right reason, and then perceives that it is foolish and intemperate and unjust and infected with pollution" (The Unchangeableness of God, 123-6). The paradox is continued: The leper who is only partially a leper is unclean, but if the leprosy spreads throughout, he is clean (Lev. 13: 11-13). Through this paradox the lawgiver shows that "such wrongdoings as are involuntary... are pure and devoid of guilt... but voluntary sins, even though the space they cover be not large, are convicted by the judge within the soul" (Unchangeableness of God, 127-8). Further, the two-natured leprosy, which flowers into two colors, shows voluntary wickedness, "For the soul has within it the healthy, lively upright reason, and yet does not use it as its pilot ... But the leprosy which changes into a single white appearance represents involuntary error, when the mind is throughout bereft of reasoning power ..." (Unchangeableness of God, 129-130).

The founders of the *yahad*, the community at Qumran, were Temple priests, who saw themselves as continuators of the true priestly line, that is, the sons of Zaddok. For them the old Temple service was invalidated because it was defiled. The deliverance would begin with the rise of the sect and the coming of the teacher. They further rejected the calendar then followed in Jerusalem. They therefore set out to create a new Temple until God would come and, through the Messiah in the line of Aaron, establish the Temple once again. The Qumran community believed that the presence of God had left Jerusalem and had come to the Dead Sea. According to Bertil Gärtner, the *community* now constituted the New Temple, just as some elements in early Christianity saw the new Temple in the "body of Christ", in the Church, the Christian community. In some measure, this represents a "spiritualization" of the old Temple, for the Temple now is the community, and the Temple worship is affected through the community's study and fulfillment of the Torah.

While purity is a central issue for the *yahad*, the ideas associated with it do not form an equivalently important concern. The Admonition of the Zadokite Fragments refers (CD 3: 17) to the generation of the wilderness, which was defiled with impiety of man and menstrual impurity (DRKY NDH). Isaiah's prophecy, "Fear and the pit and snare are upon thee", (Is. 24: 17) refers to "whoredom, wealth, and conveying uncleanness to the sanctuary". The one leads to the other (CD 4: 17-8). Isaiah refers to *pahad*, *pahat*, and *pah*, the third meaning "snare". But spelled *pakh*, the word means a flask or jar, very frequently used for oil-jars. Since Josephus says the sect regarded oil as impure (War 2: 123), perhaps the basis for the exegesis before us is a play on the words *pakh* and *pah*.

As to the defiling of the Jerusalem sanctuary, this is explained (CD 5: 6-7) "In as much as they do not keep separate according to the Law but lie with her that sees the blood of flux" (*dam zobah*; Lev. 15: 19). They also "rendered their holy spirits unclean and with a blasphemous tongue opened their mouth against the ordinances of the covenant of God" (CD 5: 11-12). Those brought into the covenant are asked by God "to refrain from the unclean wealth of wickedness acquired by vowing and appropriating the wealth of the sanctuary ... to put a distinction between the unclean and the clean, the holy and the common" (6: 15-18), also "to keep away from all forms of uncleanness in the manner proper for them and not for each man to defile his holy spirit, according as God taught them to distinguish" (CD 7: 3-4). Making the sanctuary unclean recurs (CD 20: 24), without further definition.

What is new in the *yahad's* ideas concerning purity is not the substance, but only the locus of application, of the laws. The priestly code ruled clearly that only the clean might enter the Temple. Cleanness involved morality, not merely taking a bath or refraining from sexual relations with a menstruating woman. Rebellion against God, as in the case of idolatry, was unclean. Water purifies; the sacrifices of the wicked are unacceptable. Creeping things defile. Corpse-uncleanness affects objects in a house. The priests cannot touch corpses. None of these assertions would have surprised the priestly lawyers. Once it is admitted that the community is subject to the purity-laws, it goes without saying that the priestly code will exclude one who despises the law or disobeys God. The cleaning of sins by the 'spirit of holiness' is hardly alien to the imagery of Ezekiel. What would have surprised the priestly authors was the requirement of purity outside of the Jerusalem Temple and to a purpose other than the conduct of the Temple cult. In that sense alone do we find the purity-laws used as part of a much larger metaphor, comparing the Temple to the community; but within that metaphor, purity and impurity are understood in an entirely literal way.

The second innovation in the *yahad's* view of purity seems to me entirely without parallel. Its importance was pointed out to me by Prof. A.R.C. Leaney, Nottingham University, in a lecture at Brown University. The *yahad's* laws treat committing a sin not as a metaphor for becoming unclean, but as an actual source of uncleanness. If one transgresses any part of the law, he is excluded from the "Purity" of the sect. It is not *as if* he were unclean, as with the biblical metaphor. He is *actually* unclean and requires a rite of purification. So the uncleanness is not metaphorical but is treated as equivalent to the impurity imparted by a corpse or a menstrual woman. So 1 QS 5: 13 says the wicked may not touch "the Purity of the holy, for a man is not pure unless he be converted from his malice. For he is defiled for as long as he transgresses His word". Punishments are meted out in terms of periods of uncleanness, symbolized by separation from the Purity of the community. If one speaks angrily against one of the priests, he is excluded for a year; if he speaks arrogantly, it is for six months. Three months' separation punishes foolishness, ten days for interrupting the words of another. One who laughs stupidly and loudly is punished for thirty days. Afterward there is a period of purification, marked by a test of the penitent's spirit. So too in CD (12: 4), if one breaks the Sabbath, he is "watched" for seven years, then allowed to enter the assembly.

Now what makes this view of purity other than metaphorical is the provision of a specific disability consequent on impurity and a rite of purification—whatever it may be. This means the impurity is regarded as effective, the man is really impure and requires cleansing from impurity before he may have contact with the pure objects of the community. This innovation seems to be the ultimate result of the comparison of impurity with sin: it is no longer a matter of comparison at all. One who sins is impure and requires purification; the impurity of the menstrual woman and that of the arrogant person are not distinguished in any way. This last stage in the development of ideas about purity carries to the logical conclusion the interpretations of the priests, both lawyers and prophets, who inaugurated the process by making use of purity as a metaphor for righteousness. For the *yahad*, one cannot distinguish between cultic and moral impurity. In themselves and in their consequences they are identical.

Like the Qumranians, many Christians criticized the Jerusalem Temple and its cult. Both groups in common believed that the last days had begun. Both believed that God had come to dwell with them, as he had once dwelled in the Temple. The sacrifices of the Temple were replaced, therefore, by the sacrifice of a blameless life and by other spiritual deeds. But some Christians differed on one important point. To them, the final sacrifice had already taken place; the perfect priest has offered up the perfect holocaust, his own body. Christ on the cross completed the old law and inaugurated the new. This belief took shape in different ways. For Paul in I Cor. 3: 16-17 the Church is the new Temple. Christ is the foundation of the "spiritual" building. The deuteropauline Ephesians 2: 18 ff. has Christ as the corner-stone of the new building, the company of Christians constituting the Temple. It is within this context that the role of purity in early Christianity is to be interpreted.

The first evidence on Christian views of purity derives from Paul and the Pauline writers. The symbol of purity is routinely alluded to in Romans 1: 24, where impurity is spoken of as "dishonoring their bodies", that is, the transgressors', and in 6: 19, which equates impurity

and iniquity, as against righteousness for sanctification. The use of
purity and impurity in reference to food occurs in Romans 14: 14-23.
Here Paul says, "I am persuaded in the Lord Jesus that nothing is
unclean in itself, but it is unclean for anyone who *thinks* it unclean"—a
highly rabbinic conception as we observed. The context is eating:
"For the kingdom of God does not mean food and drink but
righteousness and peace and joy in the Holy Spirit. Everything is
indeed clean, but it is wrong for anyone to make others fall by what
he eats". I Cor. 6: 12-13 and Gal. 2: 11 likewise allude to the lawfulness
of all food; 8: 1-13 concerns food offered to idols. If a person has a
weak conscience and regards the food as really offered to an idol,
for food has no relationship to God. Idolatry as a source of impurity
is already familiar. The centrality of intention in the determination
of an impure state is, as noted, familiar in Talmudic law. Children may
be "unclean" (I Cor. 7: 14); the child is "holy" if one parent is a
believer, and the couple stays together. Similarly, immorality and all
impurity or covetousness are compared with one another; but here
the meaning is simply filthiness. I Thes. 4: 7 contrasts uncleanness
with holiness, the context being marital relations. Paul therefore uses
the symbol of purity chiefly in respect to food and sex. The former is
no subject to impurity, but the latter certainly is. In Romans and
Corinthians, Paul consistently argues that food is not intrinsically
pure or impure, though an individual may not eat anything he thinks
he should not. There can be no doubt that Paul regards the impurity
decrees in biblical food-laws as suspended. The allusions to purity
otherwise fall wholly within the established biblical framework of
interpretation.

The Synoptic Gospels treat purity in three aspects: bodily afflictions,
unclean hands and food, and ethics. The stories about Jesus emphasize
the first, the sayings attributed to him stress the second and third.

Mark claims that Jesus annulled the purity-rules, that is, the custom
of the Pharisees. The disciples eat with "defiled, that is, unwashed
hands". Jesus is asked why his disciples do not live according to the
tradition of the elders, which is defined as eating with clean hands.
Jesus contrasts obedience to God with the tradition of men, then,
ignoring the issue of the cleanness of *hands*, declares the rules about
the cleanness or uncleanness of *food* are invalid (!). There is nothing
outside a man which by going into him can defile him, but the things
which come out of a man are what defile him (Mk. 7: 15). This then
is explicitly assigned to the problem of food—(7: 19) "Thus he

declared all foods clean". Then the cleanness of food is contrasted with the unclean things in the heart of man which come out and defile: evil thoughts, fornication, theft, murder, and so on. The composite pericope thus links two entirely separate aspects of uncleanness, one concerning the Pharisaic tradition about the hands and washing, the other the biblical rules of food and eating; the former is (correctly) declared to be the work of man, the latter to be unimportant by contrast to inner uncleanness. The metaphorical use of uncleanness to refer to iniquity recurs. But the literal and concrete aspect—the actual uncleanness of certain foods— is at the same time rejected, which is consistent with the picture given by Paul.

Matthew is mostly in harmony with Mark on these points, though he drops the gloss that Jesus had declared all food clean. The washing of the hands is not a divine commandment (Mt. 15: 1-3). It is treated as separate from the cleanness of foods, still in the same context (Mt. 15: 10-19). But then ignoring their differences—the *hands* as a Pharisaic custom, the food as a biblical injunction—Matthew links the two in a curious fusion, "These [namely, iniquitous deeds which come out of a man] are what defile a man, but to eat with unwashed hands does not defile a man". Mark was appropriately silent on the supposed connection between the customary washing of the hands and the mosaic rules on the cleanness of foods, which Matthew has confused. Mk. 7: 23 concludes the pericope, which Mt. 15: 23 further embellishes. It seems to me Matthew has supplied nothing more than a redactional improvement, linking—and mixing up— two quite separate matters in his concluding summary. But the antecedent pericope will have kept them distinct and, correctly, treated them as entirely separate issues. Washing was never part of God's will—the Torah; unclean food was part of the Torah but was meant to teach a moral lesson, and not to be interpreted in a literal way.

Matthew 23: 25-6 (Lk. 11: 39-41) and 23: 27-28 take up and develop the contrast between inside and outside. The Pharisees clean the outside of the cup and plate, but inside they are full of extortion: "First clean the inside of the cup, that the outside also may be clean". Similarly, the scribes and Pharisees are like whitewashed tombs, outwardly beautiful, but inwardly full of uncleanness. Luke 11: 40 adds that God made both the inside and the outside of the cup and dish, a pointless homily. The contrast between impurity and iniquity and purity and righteousness in commonplace. What is more interesting is the problem of the division of the parts of the cup into the insides and the outsides. For Jesus we have here only a metaphor for inner against outer purity. What is to be kept pure is the inside of the man—a play on the theme already introduced in the cleanness of foods. Later rabbinic law distinguished between the inside of the cup, which was highly susceptible to ritual impurity and which, when unclean, rendered the whole cup unclean, and the outside, which was less susceptible and would not impart impurity to the inside. That the same distinction between inside and outside occurs in both rabbinic and Christian material suggests that it was early. But it does not indicate what use was made of it in earlier periods. To be sure, the saying attributes to Jesus the strict view that the inside had to be clean. But the whole saying seems to me solely a metaphor for moral purity and is not built upon exact knowledge of the (possibly later) Pharisaic purity-rule in this connection. If Jesus was supposed to have known the rule and to have treated it literally, and if the Pharisaic law then was the same as the well-attested Yavnean rule later, he could not have told the Pharisees first to cleanse the inside of the cup. That was their rule to begin with, The figurative sense likewise is lost if one really does clean the inside of the cup first of all.

The author of Hebrews, like Philo, is a noteworthy philosopher of the purity-rules. The reason is his view of the abiding importance, even after 70, of the Christians' relationship to Temple, cult, and priesthood. Like Philo, the author of Hebrews treats the purity-rules as metaphorical or figurative of a higher reality. His interpretation is imaginative, original, and wide-ranging. In the important part, Chapters 8-10, the author emphasizes the superiority of Jesus's sacrifice in the heavenly sanctuary to the Levitical priests' sacrifice in the earthly one. In the setting of this extended argument, the author contrasts the sprinking of defiled persons with the blood of goats and with the ashes of a heifer, which sanctifies for the purification of the flesh (Hebrews 9: 13): Then: "How much more shall the blood of the Messiah, who through the eternal Spirit offered himself without blemish to God, purify your conscience from dead works to serve the living God! 9: 14". Jesus' sacrifice here is represented as superior to the sacrifice of the red heifer, which produced the ashes to be mixed with the water for the ceremony of purification. The earthly priests have only the ashes and water. But Christ himself is the heifer. He therefore will more surely effect purification.

The author further alludes to the purity-rite, which was effected by a sprinkling of blood: "Indeed under the law almost everything is purified with blood, and without the shedding of blood there is no forgiveness of sins". The allusions to the priestly law are then given their new meaning: Christ offered himself not repeatedly, but once alone; the blood was not that of a goat, but his own. What is wrong with the earthly cult is that the worshipers, once cleansed, ought no longer have any consciousness of sin (10: 2): "But in these sacrifices there is a reminder of sin year after year". Here the author of Hebrews regards purification as a rite having to do with sin, not with impurity, except as impurity is regarded as a metaphor for sin. He moreover explicitly draws out the ambiguity of the symbol of the blood. Blood-excretions of a human being and of a corpse are a source of impurity, not of purification. The blood of the sacrifice serves to achieve atonement. But the blood of Jesus does *not* defile. It purifies like that of the sacrificial animal: "Let us draw near with a true heart in full assurance of faith, with our hearts sprinkled clean from an evil conscience and our bodies washed with pure water" (10: 22). This is part of Hebrews' larger paradox, that the priest serves also as the oblation.

The third group to whom the laws of purity were important is the Pharisees. Their commune, called *havurah*, which may be translated "fellowship", is described in the law-codes produced by later rabbinic Judaism. We know very little about the Pharisees before the time of Herod. During Maccabean days, according to Josephus, our sole reliable evidence, they appear as a political party, competing with another party, the Sadducees, for control of the court and government. Afterward, as a group they all but fade out of Josephus's narrative. But the later rabbinical literature fills the gap with fanciful stories about Pharisaic masters from Shammai and Hillel to the destruction of the Temple. It also ascribes to pre-70 authorities numerous sayings, particularly on matters of law, both to the masters and to the Houses of Shammai and of Hillel. These circles of disciples seem to have flourished in the first century, down to 70 and for a few years beyond. The legal materials attributed by later rabbis to the pre-70 Pharisees are thematically congruent to the stories and sayings about Pharisees in the New Testament Gospels, and I take them to be accurate in substance, if not in detail, as representations of the main issues of Pharisaic law. After 70, the masters of Yavneh seem to have included a predominant element of Pharisees, and the rabbis after 70 assuredly regarded themselves as the continuators of Pharisaism. Yohanan ben Zakkai, who first stood at the head of the Yavnean group, was later said to have been a disciple of Hillel. More credibly, Gamaliel II, who succeeded Yoḥanan as head of the Yavnean institution, is regarded as the grandson of Gamaliel, Pharisee in the council of the Temple who is mentioned in Acts 5: 34 in connection with the trial of Paul.

The dominant trait of Pharisaism before 70 is depicted both in the rabbinic traditions about the Pharisees and in the Gospels as concern for certain matters of rite. The rite was of eating one's meals in a state of ritual purity as if one were a Temple priest, and carefully giving the required tithes and offerings due to the priesthood. The Gospels' references to Pharisaism also included fasting, Sabbath-observance, vows and oaths, and the like, but the main point was keeping the ritual purity laws outside of the Temple, where the priests had to observe ritual purity when they carried out the requirements of the cult.

The Pharisees, like the Dead Sea commune, believed that one must keep the purity-laws outside of the Temple. Other Jews, following the plain sense of Leviticus, supposed that purity-laws were to be kept only in the Temple. The priests also had to eat their Temple food in a state of ritual purity, but lay people did not. To be sure, everyone who went to the Temple had to be ritually pure, but outside of the Temple, as I said, it was not required that noncultic activities be conducted in a state of Levitical cleanness.

The Pharisees held, to the contrary, that even outside of the Temple, in one's own home, a person had to follow the laws of ritual purity in the only circumstance in which they might apply, namely, at the table. They therefore held that one must eat his secular food, that is, ordinary, everyday meals, in a state of ritual purity *as if one were a Temple priest*. The Pharisees thus arrogated to themselves—and to all Jews equally—the status of Temple priests and did the things which priests must do on account of that status. The table of every Jew in his home was seen to be like the table of the Lord in the Jerusalem Temple. The commandment, "You shall be a kingdom of priests and a holy people", was taken literally. The whole country was holy. The table of every man possessed the same order of sanctity as the table of the cult. At this time, apart from the *yahad*, only the Pharisees held such a viewpoint, and eating unconsecrated food as if one were a Temple priest at the Lord's table thus was one of the two indications that a Jew was a Pharisee, a sectarian.

The other was meticulous tithing. The laws of tithing and related agricultural taboos may have been kept primarily by Pharisees. Here we are not certain. Pharisees clearly regarded keeping the agricultural rules as a chief religious duty. But whether, to what degree, and how other Jews did so, is not clear. Both the agricultural laws and purity rules in the end affected table-fellowship, that is, *How and what one may eat*. That is, they were "dietary laws".

The Dead Sea Sect, the Christian Jews, and the Pharisees all stressed ritual in connection with the eating of meals. The Qumranians and the Christians tended to oppose Temple sacrifice and to prefer to achieve forgiveness of sin through repentence, and, in the case of the Christians, "baptism", a ritual bath. The immersions of the Qumran group were not thought to remove sin but only to give bodily cleanliness, provided the recipient had previously repented and been cleansed by the spirit; on this the Manual of Discipline is explicit and emphatic.

By contrast, the Pharisees before 70 continued to revere the Temple and its cult. While the early Christians gathered for ritual meals, and made them the climax of their group life, the Pharisees did not. What expressed the Pharisees' sense of self-awareness as a group apparently was not a similarly intense communion-meal. So far as we know, eating was not endowed with mythic elements, even though the Pharisees had liturgies to be said at the meal. No communion-ceremonies, or rites centered on meals, or specifications of meals on holy occasions characterize Pharisaic table-fellowship.

In the Dead Sea commune, table-fellowhip was open upon much the same basis as among the Pharisees: appropriate undertakings to keep ritual purity and to consume properly grown and tithed foods. As we know it, the Qumranian meal was liturgically not much different from the ordinary Pharisaic gathering. The rites pertained to, and derived from, the eating of food and that alone. Both Christians and Pharisees lived among ordinary folk, while the Qumranians did not. In this respect the commonplace character of Pharisaic table-fellowship is all the more striking. The sect ordinarily did not gather *as a group* at all, but in the home. All meals required purity. Pharisaic table-fellowship took place in the same circumstances as did the meals of outsiders. Pharisees were common folk, who ate everyday meals in an everyday way, among ordinary neighbors, not members of the sect. They were engaged in workaday pursuits like everyone else. The setting for law-observance therefore was the field and the kitchen, the bed and the street. The occasion for observance was set every time a person picked up a common nail, which might be unclean, or purchased a *se'ah* of wheat, which had to be tithed—by himself, without priests to bless his deeds or sages to instruct them. Keeping the Pharisaic rule did not require an occasional but exceptional rite at, but external to, the meal. Instead, it imposed the perpetual "ritualization" of daily life, that is, the imposition of the cultic rules outside of the Temple, on the one side, and the constant, inner awareness of the communal order of being, on the other.

I. M. ORANSKIJ

NOTES IRANO-SLAVES
VIEIL IRANIEN *VAR-* / RUSSE DIALECTAL *VAR* [1]

Dans le texte avestique bien connu, Vid. 2, 32 sq., il est raconté que, sur l'ordre d'Ahuramazda, Yima Xšaēta (le futur Jamšīd de l'épopée iranienne) construisit un certain bâtiment appelé *var-* : «... Et Yima fit comme Ahura Mazda lui avait ordonné : il foula la terre avec ses pieds et la pétrit avec ses mains... Et Yima fit un *var* long d'une course de cheval sur chacun des quatre côtés. Il porta là les germes du petit et du gros bétail, et des hommes, des chiens, des oiseaux, et des feux rouges et brûlants. Et Yima fit ce *var* long d'une course de cheval sur chacun des quatre côtés, pour servir d'habitation aux hommes, un *var* long d'une course de cheval sur chacun des quatre côtés, pour servir d'enclos au bétail. Là il fit couler l'eau dans un lit d'un *hāθra* de long. Là il construisit demeures, cave, préau, fortification, enceinte»[2]. Le professeur S. P. Tolstov a identifié cette description avec certains édifices dégagés au cours des fouilles de l'ancien Xwarezm, qu'il a appelés «vestiges à murs d'habitation». Selon lui, ces vestiges, que les céramiques permettent de dater des VIe-Ve siècles avant notre ère, ont la forme d'un quadrilatère assez régulier (ou, selon la conformation de la colline, d'un triangle irrégulier), entouré de puissantes murailles qui comportent des demeures en forme de corridors; la partie centrale des vestiges est restée non bâtie; elle servait vraisemblablement, d'enclos pour le bétail, dont la protection avait conditionné tout leur tracé[3].

---

[1] Communication présentée en septembre 1971, à Léningrad, à la conférence internationale consacrée au 2.500e anniversaire de l'État iranien. Pour information, voir «Narody Azii i Afriki», 1972, n° 3, p. 241 (M. A. Dandamaev, È. A. Grantovskij). Publiée ici avec additions.

[2] Cité d'après *Istorija tadžikskogo naroda*, t. I. S drevnejšix vremjen do V v. n.è. Pod red. B. G. Gafurova i B. A. Litvinskogo, M., Izd. vostoč. liter., 1963, p. 145. Cf. traductions de J. Darmesteter («The Sacred Books of the East», vol. IV, Oxford, 1880, pp. 18-19) et de F. Wolff («Avesta. Die heiligen Bücher der Parsen», Strassburg, 1910, pp. 323-324).

[3] Voir S. P. Tolstov, *Drevnij Xorezm*, Izd. MGU, M., 1948, p. 77-82; id. *Po sledam drevnexorezmijskoj civilizacii*, Izd. AN SSSR, M.-L., 1948, p. 93-96. Sur les établissements fortifiés de type analogue en Iran, Afghanistan et Asie Centrale modernes,

Bartholomae traduisit l'avestique *var-* par «Schloss, Burg», et mit ce mot en relation avec la racine verbale du vieil iranien *var-* «couvrir, envelopper» («hüllend bedecken») [4]. Je ne prendrai ici en considération, laissant de côté de nombreux dérivés de cette racine, relevés en indo-iranien il y a quelques dizaines d'années dans les travaux de E. Benveniste - L. Renou et de H. W. Bailey [5], que quelques mots remontant à l'iranien ancien *var-* et attestés dans les langues iraniennes avec le sens de «lieu entouré, cour, enclos pour le bétail», etc. A côté d'avestique *var-*, nous avons notamment pahlavi *var* «lieu entouré, enclos»; parthe manichéen *'hrywr* = **ahrēvar* (av. *aŋra-var-*) «Géhenne» («Todespfuhl») [6], khotanais *vara* «cour» [7] et, avec allongement vocalique, av. *-vāra-* (comme deuxième terme des composés) : *pairi-vāra-* «garde, protection, enceinte»; *fra-vāra-* «fortification» [8], persan classique *bāra*, *bārū*, persan moderne *bǎru* «mur fortifié (d'une ville), muraille fortifiée avec des tours». G. Morgenstierne a également rapporté à cette racine munjī *pərīvur*, *prīvər* [9] «étable, enclos pour le bétail» (< av. *pairi-vāra-*), persan *parwār* «étable, écurie», en comparant pašto waziri *vrōrai* «refuge pour le bétail dans les montagnes» (<· **frawāraka-*) [10]. D'où peut-être aussi kurde *war* «halte»,

---

voir A. Z. Rozenfel'd, «Qal'a (Kala) – tip ukreplennogo iranskogo poselenija», *Sovetskaja Ètnografija*, 1951, n° I, p. 22-38 (avec illustrations).

[4] Chr. Bartholomae, AiWb., 1363-1364, s.v. [5]*var-*.

[5] Voir E. Benveniste et L. Renou, *Vṛtra et Vṛθragna*, Paris, 1934; H. W. Bailey, «Asica», *TPhS*, 1945, p. 28; id. «Analecta Indoscythica I-II», *JRAS*, 1953, p. 110 sq, 1954, p. 26 sq.; id., «Vāsta», *Acta Orientalia*, XXX, 1966, p. 25 (s.v. *urānāṃ*), p. 37-38 (s.vv. *nyūrra-*, *baṭha-*); id., *Indo-Scythian Studies Being Khotanese Texts*, vol. VI, *Prolexis to the Book of Zambasta*, Cambridge, 1967, p. 222-223 (s.v. *baṭha-*), p. 234 (s.v. *bārmañi jsa*), p. 320-321 (s.v. *vara*).

[6] F. C. Andreas - W. B. Henning, *Mitteliranische Manichaica aus Chinesisch-Turkestan III*, Stzb. d. Preuss. Akad. d. Wiss., Philos.-hist. Kl., 1934, p. 882 (M 104.11), p. 893; H. W. Bailey, *JRAS*, 1954, 27. Dans un travail plus ancien, le prof. Bailey (H. W. Bailey, *BSOS*, VII, 1934, p. 295-296) fournit la lecture *'ḥryvr* (avec référence au texte M 99d 21, 22).

[7] H. W. Bailey, *Indo-Scythian Studies Being Khotanese Texts*, vol. VI, *Prolexis to the Book of Zambasta*, Cambridge, 1967, p. 320-321.

[8] Chr. Bartholomae, AiWb., 866, 996, 1411. Cf. encore vieil ir. **pativāra-*, révélé par arménien *patuar* «mur antérieur, ouvrage avancé» («Aussenwerk»), (voir H. Hübschmann, *Persische Studien*, Strassburg, 1895, p. 22, n° 161).

[9] Le dictionnaire de Grjunberg (A. L. Grjunberg, *Jazyki Vostočnogo Gindukuša. Mundžanskij jazyk*, L., 1972, p. 345) donne mundži *paríwər* (signalé par I. M. Steblin-Kamenskij).

[10] G. Morgenstierne, *Indo-Iranian Frontier Languages*, vol. II, Oslo, 1938, p. 240. En liaison avec persan classique *parvār*, remarquons que le nouveau *Persidsko-russkij*

«camp», «lieu occupé temporairement par les habitants d'un village», *wargä* «camp, campement, refuge», kurde méridional *wartən* «héberger», etc.?[11] Etymologiquement, tous ces mots iraniens sont de la même famille que skr. *vṛṇóti* «couvrir, envelopper, entourer (d'un mur)», remontant à i.-e. **uer-* «fermer, couvrir, défendre»[12], dont plusieurs dérivés signifient ̄«enceinte, lieu entouré, enclos pour le bétail», etc., et sont représentés dans de nombreuses langues indo-européennes[13], notamment en slave. Les dictionnaires étymologiques, et d'autres ouvrages, mentionnent, par exemple, vieux-slave *vreti* «verrouiller», vieux russe *vorъ*, *vora* «palissade, enceinte», *zavorъ* «verrou, enceinte», russe *verét'*, *zaverét'* «verrouiller», *vórok*, *vórak* «étable», etc. [14], qui, apparemment, peuvent être considérés comme les représentants de i.-e. **uer-*. Cependant, à côté de ces mots, nous avons aussi, dans les dialectes russes, *var* «cour à bestiaux, étable, lieu enclos (à ciel ouvert) pour le bétail, enclos, obstacle de pilotis,

slovar' de Ju. A. Rubinčik (t. I, Moskva, 1970, p. 291) cite *pärvar I* avec les sens de 1. «rassasié, obèse, gras»; 2. «emplacement pour l'engraissement du bétail», et *pärvar II* avec les sens de «lieu à découvert en été, balcon, terrasse». En outre, pour autant qu'il soit possible d'en juger par ce dictionnaire et par les autres ouvrages lexicographiques persans et tadžiks, le sens premier de persan *parvār*, tadžik *parvor*, semble être «alimentation, engraissage, engraissement». Contamination avec *parvardan* (?). Dans la toponymie du Tadžikistan, le terme *Parvar* désigne souvent un lieu d'habitation.

[11] Voir Č. X. Bakaev, *Kurdsko-russkij slovar'*, Moskva, 1957, s.v.; K. K. Kurdoev, *Kurdsko-russkij slovar'*, Moskva, 1960, s.v.; T. Wahby and C. J. Edmonds, *A Kurdish-English Dictionary*, Oxford, 1966, s.v. Sur l'emploi de ce mot dans la toponymie de l'Iran, voir V. I. Savina, *Slovar' geografičeskix terminov i drugix slov, formirujuščix toponimiju Irana*, Moskva, 1971, p. 46, s.v. *ver, var*.

[12] Voir J. Pokorny, *Indogermanisches Etymologisches Wörterbuch*, Bd. I, Bern, 1959, p. 1160-1162; M. Mayrhofer, *Etymologisches Wörterbuch des Altindischen*, Lief. 21, Heidelberg, 1970, p. 245-246.

[13] Cf., par exemple, en indo-aryen : v.-ind. **vārtra-*, moyen-indien oriental *vāṭa-* (Mahābhārata), *vāṭī-* (Bhāgavata-Purāṇa) «enceinte, lieu enclos», pāli *vāṭa-* «lieu enclos», hindi *bāṛ* «palissade», sindhi *vāṛo*, lahndā *vāṛā*, panjābī *bāṛā* «enclos pour le bétail», etc. Voir L. R. Turner, *A Comparative Dictionary of the Indo-Aryan Languages*, London, 1966, nᵒˢ 11480, 11565 (cf. aussi nᵒˢ 11370, 12068); M. Mayrhofer *op. cit.*, Lief. 20, Heidelberg, 1968, p. 183 (s.v. *vāṭaḥ*).

[14] Voir, par ex., J. Pokorny, *loc. cit.*; M. Mayrhofer, *op. cit.*, Lief. 21, Heidelberg, 1970, p. 245-246; M. Fasmer (= M. Vasmer), *Étimologičeskij slovar' russkogo jazyka*. Perevod s nemeckogo i dopolnenija O. N. Trubačeva, t. I, M., 1964, p. 293 (s.v. *vérat'*), p. 350 (s.v. *vor II*), p. 353; t. II, M., 1967, p. 71-72; R. Trautmann, *Baltisch-Slavisches Wörterbuch*, Göttingen, 1923, p. 352-353; *Ètimologičeskij slovar' russkogo jazyka*, t. I, vyp. 3. V. Pod rykovodstvom i redakciej N. M. Šanskogo, Izd. MGU, Moskva, 1968, p. 168, s.v. *vorota*; P. S. Kuznecov, «Čeredovanija v obščeslavjanskom jazyke-osnove», *Voprosy slavjanskogo jazykoznanija*, vyp. I, 1954, p. 38.

de pieux, fichés au fond d'un cours d'eau et clissés pour retenir le poisson». D'où viennent *varáč*, *varínka*, *varók*, *varúška*, avec la même signification fondamentale [15]. Le russe dialectal *var* a, bien sûr, attiré l'attention des comparatistes, qui l'ont généralement considéré soit comme un emprunt aux langues germaniques, soit comme étant lié étymologiquement au vieux russe *vorъ* «palissade». Même Dal' estimait que le russe dialectal *var* était de même origine que l'allemand *wahren* «défendre». Preobraženskij, considérant ce mot comme un emprunt au germanique, le rapprochait du gotique *var* «circonspect», se reportant aussi au hongrois *vár* «forteresse», *város* «ville», turc de Turquie *oraš* «ville» (*város*? – I.O.) etc. [16]. Dans le plus récent dictionnaire étymologique de la langue russe de M. Vasmer, le russe dialectal *var* est comparé au lituanien *vãras* «pieu dans une haie», *apìvaras* «enclos pour le bétail», vieux-haut-allemand *wuorī* «digue, remblai», vieil anglais *waru* «jetée, môle», et ce mot est associé au vieux russe *vorъ* «palissade» [17].

Dans aucun des dictionnaires étymologiques qui me sont connus, ne se trouve le moindre rapprochement du russe dialectal *var* avec l'iranien. En attendant, le *a* radical reste, apparemment, sans explication. Or, celle-ci me semble se trouver dans l'idée que le russe dialectal *var* représenterait le développement non pas slave, mais iranien de i.-e. *$\underset{\circ}{u}er$* : il me paraît possible, en effet, de relier le russe dialectal *var* à la famille des mots iraniens (av. *var-*, etc.) cités plus haut et d'y voir un reflet de contacts directs entre langues iraniennes et slaves. Une telle supposition peut, à mon avis, être renforcée par le caractère nettement local de ce mot et par son aire d'extension, qui est principalement le sud de la Russie : les régions de Tambov, Kursk, Orel, Voronež, Rjazan', Astraxan', le bassin du Don et les districts adjacents [18], c'est-à-dire le territoire même où l'on connaît

---

[15] Voir V. Dal', *Tolkovyj slovar' živogo velikorusskogo jazyka*, t. I, Moskva, 1955 (réimpression de la seconde édition de 1880-1882), p. 166-167; s.v. *varjat'*, *varit'*; *Slovar' russkix narodnyx govorov*, pod red. prof. F.P. Filina, vyp. 4, Leningrad, 1969, p. 40, 44, 54, 59-60, 61. A cette famille se rapporte aussi, apparemment, le mot *varki* «parois latérales d'une télègue (qui empêchent le chargement de tomber)» (*ibid.*, vyp. 4, p. 54. Cf., d'ailleurs, *vórki*, id., *ibid.*, vyp. 5, p. 100).

[16] Voir A.G. Preobraženskij, *Ètimologičeskij slovar' russkogo jazyka*, M., 1958 (reproduction des fascicules de 1910-1914 et 1949), p. 65-66.

[17] Voir M. Fasmer, *op. cit.*, t. I, p. 273, 350. Cf. aussi E. Fraenkel, *Litauisches Etymologisches Wörterbuch*, Bd. II, Heidelberg, 1965, s.v. *vãras 2*.

[18] Remarqué aussi dans les régions de Kaluga, Tver' (Kalinin), Tula, Brjansk, Orenburg, dans l'Oural et en Sibérie.

un grand nombre de toponymes et d'hydronymes iraniens et où ont sans doute commencé les contacts linguistiques séculaires entre Iraniens et Slaves.

C'est par ce territoire qu'ont été établis des contacts linguistiques irano (resp. alano-osséto) -hongrois remontant aux VI-IXe siècles de notre ère et que reflètent d'assez nombreux emprunts de l'alain en hongrois[19]. Depuis longtemps, on a exprimé (quelquefois, il est vrai, avec prudence) l'hypothèse selon laquelle les mots hongrois *vár* «forteresse» et *város* «ville» (et les emprunts au hongrois : serbo-croate *város* «ville», bulgare *vàroš* «centre de la ville, ancienne partie fortifiée d'une ville», turc *varoş* «faubourg, banlieue») proviendraient de l'iranien, mais le chaînon intermédiaire restait obscur[20]. C'est l'alain (resp. ossète) qui, selon toute vraisemblance, a pu transmettre le mot iranien considéré aux dialectes russes méridionaux, ainsi qu'au hongrois. Et, bien que l'on ne rencontre pas ce mot dans la langue ossète moderne, il n'est pas exclu qu'il ait existé dans les dialectes alains médiévaux, preuve en est abkhaz *bora*, *gwara*, *g°ara* «lieu entouré, stalle», empruntés, comme le pense le professeur H. W. Bailey, à l'alano-ossète[21].

Si les considérations qui viennent d'être exposées sont exactes, le russe dialectal *var* est un élément de plus dans la longue chaîne des mots qui se sont répandus loin vers l'ouest à partir du vieil iranien *var-*, conservé par l'ancienne légende avestique.

[Traduit du russe par P. Lecoq.]

---

[19] Sur les derniers travaux concernant cette question, voir V. I. Abaev, «K alano-vengerskim leksičeskim svjazjam», in *Europa et Hungaria. Congressus Ethnographicus in Hungaria. Budapest, 16-20. X. 1963*, Budapest, 1965, p. 517-537.

[20] Voir B. Munkáczi, *Árya és kaukázusi elemek a finn-magyar nyelvekben*, Budapest, 1901, p. 623-624; G. Bárczi, *Magyar Szófejtő Szótár*, Budapest, 1941, s.v.; Vl. Georgiev, Iv. Gələbov, J. Zaimov, St. Ilčev, *Bəlgarski etimologičen rečnik*, sv. II, Sofija, 1963, p. 121 s.v. *vàroš*.

[21] Voir H. W. Bailey, *JRAS*, 1954, p. 31-32. V. I. Abaev a comparé abkhaze *g°ara* avec ossète *gæræn* (iron)/*goren* (digor) «palissade d'une cour» (voir V. I. Abaev, *Osetinskij jazyk i fol'klor*, I, 1948, p. 314), en proposant, d'ailleurs, pour ossète *gæræn*/*goren* une autre étymologie (< *karana-*). Voir V. I. Abaev, *Istoriko-ètimologičeskij slovar' osetinskogo jazyka*, I, 1958, p. 515, 524-525.

HERBERT H. PAPER

ISAIAH IN JUDEO-PERSIAN
(Chapters 1 and 2)

It seems wholly appropriate to offer to the memory of H.S. Nyberg a scholarly effort that combines reference to his contributions to both biblical and Iranian studies. For this purpose, I have chosen a selection of a larger work still in progress that presents two quite independent Judeo-Persian translations of the Book of Isaiah. This is part of my research in the large domain of JP Bible translations, a bibliography of which is appended to this article. In making these texts available, as I have indicated on other occasions, it is my hope that others will be attracted to these materials in order to focus more directly on them and to make it possible for more detailed study of the individual characteristics of each text.

At this time, two texts of Isaiah are presented in transliteration/ transcription for ease and speed of reproduction. The two Isaiah translations into JP are the following:

1. The Paris manuscript published in Paul de Lagarde, *Persische Studien* (Göttingen 1884).

2. The JP translation (more properly perhaps, Judeo-Tajik) of Reb Shimon Ḥakham, *Sefer yəšayahu vətafsir* (Jerusalem 1914).

Throughout this sample of Chapters 1 and 2 of these two translations, the material is presented as follows:

> *line 1*: Hebrew — the original in full transcription
> *line 2*: Paris text — the Lagarde text in transliteration
> *line 3*: J'lem text — the ŠḤ text in transcription

The Paris text is a manuscript version and contains only a Hebrew consonantal orthography with no vocalization. However, the ŠḤ translation is from a carefully printed edition *with full Tiberian vocalization*, as was his standard practice in almost all of the JP texts he published. His translation of Isaiah (he only lived to complete the middle of Chapter 41) was part of a grand plan to translate the entire Bible into JP. He did complete and see to final printed form the entire Pentateuch, Joshua, Judges, and Samuel. In connection with his translation of the Passover Haggadah, R. Shimon Ḥakham also published his translation of the Song of Songs. For the full story of his many publications, the following valuable account should be consulted: Avraham Yaari, *Sifrey yəhudey bukhara* (1942)—comprising a reprint of two lengthy articles from the biblio-graphical journal *Kiryat Sefer*, vols. 18 and 19.

In the present publication, the two first chapters of Isaiah are given verse by verse and word by word, with the translations immediately beneath the Hebrew original and spaced so as to show exactly what pertains as translation to each Hebrew word. It is abundantly clear that in these translations, as in so many others of the biblical text and into other languages as well, the original sacred text is followed extremely closely in a word for word rendition. The ŠḤ version occasionally contains a form in parentheses (cf. 1: 2, 4, 5, 6 et passim). Here ŠḤ follows a practice that he very specifically refers to in the introduction to his JP Pentateuch translation. He consciously desired to produce a Persian translation that was more widely intelligible by Persian-speaking Jews from Iran and Afghanistan as well as by his Bokharan boothers. (The term 'Bokharan Jews' is to be understood as referring to Jews from Uzbekistan and Tajikistan). Therefore, the translator included forms (in parentheses) in numerous places in the text in order to show what "our teachers in Bokhara used to use". These ŠḤ translations are, as a result, doubly valuable since they essentially document specifically Bokharan (Tajik) renditions together with what ŠḤ conceived to be more generally standard Persian forms.

The Lagarde text is also clearly a closely literal translation. More detailed study shows that this manuscript contains much additional material of three sorts : a. synonym translations; b. translation of entire verses or parts of verses from the Targum; c. supplementary explanations of a commentary nature. In the two chapters given here there is only one example of type c in 2:20 for Heb. laḥpor perōθ, which is first translated and then followed by the phrase 'whose name is l. p.' An example of the synonym-translation of type a can be cited from Isaiah 3:16 for Hebrew wəṭāfōf, vdf znꞌ vrqṣ kvnꞌ.

The transliterations are fairly straightforward and traditional, require no special comment, and are easily convertible to the Hebrew consonant-letter original, especially in the case of the Lagarde-Paris text. The ŠḤ text is, as was noted above, fully vocalized. No attempt was made to provide an exact transliteration. And the following should be noted: x̱ a, x̱ ā, x̱ x̯ e, x̱ ə, x̱ ɪx u, x̱ ꞌx̱ i, ẋ ɪx o.

There is at least one other JP translation of Isaiah known to me but it has been impossible to include it here. It is found in a manuscript newly acquired from Iran in the manuscript collection of the Ben-Zvi Institute in Jerusalem. The manuscript volume also contains a JP Pentateuch translation as well as one of the Minor Prophets.

The following is a list of other JP biblical texts that I have published in recent years:

"The Vatican Judeo-Persian Pentateuch" [= Vat. Pers. 61]
  Genesis   Acta Orientalia (Copenhagen) 28.263-340 (1964-65)
  Exodus and Leviticus   ibid., 29.75-181 (1965)
  Numbers   ibid., 29.253-310 (1966)
  Deuteronomy   ibid., 31.55-113 (1968)
A Judeo-Persian Pentateuch (Jerusalem: Ben-Zvi Institute, Hebrew
  University 1972) [= British Museum ms Or 5446].
"Another Judeo-Persian Pentateuch Translation:
  Ms HUC 2193", Hebrew Union College Annual 43.207-281 (1972).
"Ecclesiastes in Judeo-Persian", Orientalia 42.328-337 (1973).
Biblia Judaeo-Persica: Editio Variorum (Ann Arbor: Monograph
  Series, University Microfilms, 1973) [in microfilm]—contains a
  verse by verse presentation of a number of JP Pentateuch trans-
  lations, including various manuscript versions, plus the Tavus text
  (Constantinople 1546) and the Shimon Ḥakham, Jerusalem 1904,
  printed version. Corrections to the previously published British
  Museum and Vatican texts are included.

Isaiah

1: 1	ḥazōn	yəšaʿyāhū	βɛn	ʾāmōṣ	ʾàšɛr
	nbbvt	yšʿyhu	pvsr	ʾmvṣ	ʾnčy
	karāmāt didani	yəšaʿyāhu	pisari	āmoṣ	ānči

ḥāzā	ʿal	yəhūδā	wīrūšālāyim	bīme	ʿuziyyā
nbvvt krd	ʾβr	yhvdh	vyrvšlm	brvzygʾrʾn	ʿzyhu
kərāmāt did	abar	yəhudā	virušālayim	dar ayyāmi	ʿuziyāhu

yōθām	ʾāḥāz	yəḥizqīyāhū	maləχē	yəhūδā:
yvtm	ʾḥz	yḥzqyhv	pʾdšʾhʾn	yhvdh:
yotām	ʾāḥāz	yəḥizqiyāhu	pādšāhāni	yəhudā:

1: 2	šimʿū	šāmayīm		wəhaʾàzīnī	ʾɛrɛṣ
	by ʾšnvvyd	ʾsmʾn		vhʾz gvš kvny	zmyn
	bišnaved	āsmān (āsmāniyān)		vəguš andāz	(ʾhly) zəmin

kī	yhvh	dibber	bānīm	giddaltī
ky	xvdʾy	sxvn gvft	pvsrʾn	bvzvrg krdm
ko	ḥazrati adonāy	suxan guft	farzandān	buzurg kardam

wərōmamtī   wəhem pāšʿū
v?βr?šth krdm   v?yš?n ?st?rygy krdnd
vəparvariš (vblnd) kardam vəešān taqṣirāt (tmrvd) krdnd

bī:
bmn:
dar man:

1: 3 yāδaʿ   šōr   qonehū   waḥàmōr   ?eβūs   bəʿālāw
        šn?xt   g?v   xryd?r ?vy   vxr   ?xvr   s?l?r ?vy
        bidānist gāv   xəridahi xud   vəxar   āxuri   ṣāḥibi xud

yiśrā?el lo?   yāδaʿ   ʿammī   lo?   hiθbōnān:
yśr?l   nh   šn?xt   qvvm mn   nh   fhm krd ?yš?n r?:
yiśrāel   na   bidānist   qaumi man   na   fahm kard:

1: 4 hōy   gōy   ḥoṭe?   ʿam   kεβεδ   ʿāwōn
        ?y v?y   qvvm   xṭ? kvn?   qvvm   sngyn   gvn?h
        ho   ṭāyifahi xəṭā gār   qaumi   garān (bsy?r)   gunāh

zεraʿ   məreʿīm   bānīm   mašḥīθīm   ʿāzəβū
nsl   bd k?r?n   pvsr?n   tβ?hy kvn??n   rh? krdnd
naṣli   bad kirdārān farzandāni tabāh kunandagān tark kardand

?εθ   yhvh   ni?àṣū   ?εθ   qəδōš
mr   xvd?y   rd krdnd   mr   x?ṣgy
azmar   ʿibādati adonāy buqs āvarānidand azmar xāṣi

yiśrā?el nāzorū   ?āḥōr:
yśr?l   jvd? švdnd   trps:
yśr?l   parhezidand (ps gštnd) bəʿaqib:

1: 5 ʿal   mε   θukkū   ʿōδ   tōsīfū
        ?βr   čy   zdh ?mdnd hnvz   by ?fzvdnd
        abar   či   zada šuded hanuz (b?z) me?afzāyed

sārā   kol rōš lāḥòlī   wəχol leβāβ dawwāy:
gštygy   hmh sry brnjvry   vhmh   dly   ?ndvhgyn:
maʿṣiyat (šr?rty) har sar bəbemāri   vəhar dil   ranjur:

1: 6 mikkaf   rεγεl   wəʿaδ   rōš ?ēn   bō   məθom   pεṣaʿ
        ?z kf   p?y   vt?   sr   nyst b?vy tm?my   šk?fth
        az kafi pā   vətā   sar nest dar o siḥati yara dār

wəḥabbūrā   umakkā   ṭeriyyā   loʔ   zorū   wəloʔ
vjrʔḥt   vzxm   tʔzh   nh   gštnd   vnh
vəxun basta vəzarbi   muraṭab   na   dāru pāšida šudand vəna

ḥubbāšū   wəloʔ   rukkeχā   bašāmɛn:
mvdʔvʕt švdh ʔmdnd   vnh   šksth ʔmd   brvγn:
marḥam basta šudand   vəna   narm karda šud   dar ravγan:

1: 7 ʔarṣəχɛm   šəmāmā   ʕārēχɛm   śərufōθ
        zmyn šumā   frvmgyn   šhrhʔ švmʔ   svxtygʔn
        zamini šumā   furogin   šahr hāyi šumā   soxta šudagāni

ʔeš   ʔaδmaθχɛm   lənɛγdəχɛm   zārīm
bʔtš   zmyn švmʔ   bmvqʔbl švmʔ   bygʔnygʔn
ātaš   ḥāṣili zamini šumā   bəmuqābili čašmi šumā   begāna hā

ʔoχlīm   ʔoθāh   ušəmāmā   kəmahpeχaθ   zārīm:
xvvrʔʔn   ʔnrʔ   vfrvmgyn   čvn zyr ʔz vr gšth   bygʔnygʔn:
xoraān   ān rā   vəfurogin   čun vājgun šudahe   bəbegāna hā:

1: 8 wənōθrā   βaθ   ṣiyyōn   kəsukkā   βəχārɛm
        vbʔqy mʔndh ʔmd jmʔʕt   ṣyvn   čvn sʔyh   brzstʔn
        vəbāqi mānda   šahri   ṣiyon   čvn kāzahe dar raʔz

kiməlūnā   βəmiqšā   kəʕīr   nəṣūrā:
čvn mnzl gʔh   bxrbvzh   čvn šhr   nygh dʔšth:
čun manzil jāye dar pālez   čun šahri qabal šoda:

1: 6 lūlē   yhvh   ṣəβaʔōθ   hōθīr
        ʔgr nh ʔydr   xvdʔy   rb ʔljyvš   bʔqy hšt
        agar na   ḥazrati adonāy   parvardigār   bāqi me mānānid

lānū   śārīδ   kiməʕāṭ   kisədom   hāyyīnū
bʔymʔ   rsth   čvn ʔndk   čvn sdvm   bvdym
bəemā   bāqiyyāt   čun andak   čun sədom   buda mešudem

laʕàmorā   dāmīnū:
bʕmrh   xvmʔnʔ bvdym:
baʕàmorā   mānand mešudem:

1: 10 šimʕū   δəβar   yhvh   qəṣīnē   sədom
         by ʔšnvvyd sxvn   xvdʔy   ʔy ʔmyrʔn   sdvm
         bišnaved   suxani   adonāy   e sayyidāni (ʔmyrʔny) sədom

haʔàzīnū tōraθ ʔɛ̀lohēnū ʕam ʕàmorā:
hʔz gvš kvnyd tvrh xvdʔy ʔymʔ ʔy qvvm ʕmrh:
goš kuned fatvāyi (tvvrʔty) xudāyi emā qaumi ʕàmorā:

1: 11 lāmma- llī roβ ziβhēχɛm yoʔmar
čyrʔ hst bmn bsyʔry dbyhthʔ švmʔ hmy gvyd
čərā bəman bisyāriyi zabh hāyi šumā megōyad

yhvh śāβaʕtī ʕolōθ ʔēlīm wəhelɛβ
xvdʔy syr švdm qrbn ʕvlhʔ nr myšān vpy
adonāy ser šudaham qārbān ʕōlā hāyi qučān vəčarbuyi

mərīʔīm wədam pārīm uχəβāśīm
gʔv myšān vxvn gʔvʔn vbrygʔn
navāla xurdagān (gʔv myšʔn) vəxuni gāvān vəbara gān

wəʕatūδīm loʔ hāfāstī:
vtrvšʔn nh mvrʔd dʔštm:
vənar buzān na murād (xʔhyš) dārm:

1: 12 kī θāβoʔū lerāʔōθ pānāy mī
ky by ʔyyd bdydʔr ʔmdn dr pyš mn kh
ko biʔāyed bəziyyārat kardan bədargāhi man ki

βiqqeš zoθ miyyɛδχɛm rəmos hàṣerāy:
tlb kvnd ʔyn ʔz dst švmʔ xvrd krdn srʔ mn:
talab kard in rā az dasti šumā bəpāyəxust kardan hauliyi man:

1: 13 loʔ θōsīfū hāβīʔ minhaθ šāwʔ
nh ʔfzʔyyd bʔvvrdn hdyh gzʔft
na biʔafzāyed bəʔāvardan qārbān minhāhi (hdyyhy) bevuda

qətorɛθ tōʕɛβā hīʔ lī hoδɛš wəšabbāθ
dvxnh zšty hst ʔn bmn nv mʔh všbt
duxna makrō ānast bəman qurbāni nav māh vəšabāt

qəroʔ miqrāʔ loʔ ʔūχal ʔāwɛn
frʔz rsydn frʔz rsš ntvʔnm dydn gvnʔh
xāndani sabaq (xʔnyš) na tāqat metavānam fitna angezi

waʕàṣārā:
vjmʕ švdn:
vəjamʕiyyat šudan (vʕzʔrh):

1: 14 ḥoδšēχεm umō͡ʕàδēχεm śānəʔā
mhyʔnhʔ švmʔ vjšnhʔ švmʔ dvšmn dʔšt
nav māh hāyi šumā vəʕid hāyi šumā rā dušman dāšt

nafšī hāyū ʕālay lāṭoraḥ
mvrʔd mn bvdnd ʔβr mn bzḥmt
jāni man buda šudand abar man bəzaḥmat (bʕzʔb)

nilʔeθī nəśoʔ :
ʕʔjz švdm bvr dʔštn :
xasta (ʕʔjyz) šudam az bardāštan :

1: 15 uβəfārišχεm kappēχεm
vbgvstrʔnydn švmʔ dsthʔ švmʔ
vədar pahn kardani šumā kafāni šumā

ʔaʕlīm ʕēnay mikkεm gam
by pvšm čšmʔn mn ʔz švmʔ ʔnyz
taγāful (γayb; mxfy) mesāzam nazari xud rā az šumā niz

kī θarbū θəfilā ʔēnεnnī šomeʕa
ky bsyʔr kvnyd nvmʔz nyst mn ʔšnvvʔ
har čande bisyār kuned namāz nestam man qabul kunā

yəδēχεm dāmīm māleʔū :
dsthʔ švmʔ xvnhʔ pvr krdnd :
dastāni šumā xun hāyi nāḥaq pur šudahand :

1: 16 raḥàṣū hizakkū hāsīrū roʕa
by švryd pʔkyzh bʔšyd d̥vr kvnyd bdy
šusta šaved munaza (pʔk) šaved dur kuned badiyi

maʕaləlēχεm minnεγεδ ʕēnāy ḥiδlū
krdʔrhʔ švmʔ ʔz mvqʔbl čšmʔn mn bʔz ʔystyd
kirdār hāyi šumā az muqābili nazari man dar isted

hāreʕa :
ʔz bdy krdn :
az badi kardan :

1: 17 limmǝδū hēṭeβ dirǝšū mišpāṭ
by ʔmvzyd nyky ṭlb kvnyd ḥvkm
biʔāmozed nekōyi bipursed (svrʔq kunyd) šariʕat (ḥvkm)

ʔašrū   ḥāmōṣ   šifṭū   yāθōm
bngryd   ḥʔkm   ḥvkm kvnyd ytym
šayista (hmvvʔr) kuned   sitam kašida rā   šarʕ pursid   yatim rā

rīβū   ʔalmānā:
j̇ng kvnyd   byvh:
daʕvā (dyn) pursed   beva rā:

1: 18 ləχū   nāʔ   wəniwwāχəhā   yoʔmar
     by ʔyyd   nvn   vtvbyx krdʔyym   gvftʔr
     ravāna šaved   aknun   vəmunāzira mekunem   me goyad

yhvh   ʔim   yihyū   ḥàṭāʔēχem   kaššānīm   kaššεlεγ
xvdʔy   agr   bʔšnd   xṭʔhʔ švmʔ   čvn krmyz   čvn brf
adonāy   agare   bāšand   xəṭā hāyi šumā   čun rangin hā   čun barf

yalbīnū   ʔim   yaʔdīmū   χatōlāʕ   kaṣemεr
svfyd bʔšnd   ʔgr   svrx bʔšnd   čvn rng   čvn pšm
səfed šavand   agare   surx bāšand   čun qirmiz   čun pašmi səfed

yihyū:
bʔšnd:
buda šavand:

1: 19 ʔim   toʔβū   ušəmaʕtεm   ṭūβ
    ʔgr   mvrʔd dʔryd   vby ʔšnvvyd   nʕmt
    agare   košiš kuned   vəbišnaved   neʕmati (xubyy)

hāʔārεṣ   toʔχelū:
ʔn zmyn   by xvvryd:
ān zamin rā   mexured:

1: 20 wəʔim   təmāʔànū   umərīθεm   ḥεrεβ
    vʔgr   nʔkʔm hyd   vʕʔṣyty kvnyd   šmšyr
    vəagare   nā kāmi kuned   vəāṣi šaved   bəšamšir

təʔukkəlū   kī   pī   yhvh   dibber:
xvvryd   ky   ʔmr   xvdʔy   sxvn gvft:
xorda mešaved   ko   amri   adonāy   suxan guft:

1: 21 ʔēχā   hāyəθā   ləzōnā   qiryā   nεʔεmānā
    čy gvnh   bvd   bzn byrʔh   šhr   ʔvstvʔr
    či guna (čytv)   buda šud   bəzinā kār   qariyahi   muʕtabar

məle'àθī	mišpaṭ	ṣεδεq	yālīn	bāh
pvr	hvkm	r'sty	mnzl gyrd	dr 'n
pur budahi	šariᶜat (ḥvkm)	ᶜadālat	manzil me girift	dar ān

wə'attā   mərassəḥīm:
v'knvn   qṭl kvn''n:
vəaknun   qaṭāli kunaān:

1: 22

kaspeχ	hāyā	ləsīggīm	sāβ'eχ	māhūl
sym tv	bvd	bqlbyh'	yyn tv	'myxth
nuqrahi tu	buda šud	bəyaš hā	bādahi tu	qəṭi šuda

bammāyīm:
b'b:
dar āb:

1: 23

śārayiχ	sōrərīm	wəhaβrē	γannāβīm	kullō
srhng'n tv	gštygy kvn''n	vrfyq'n	dvzd'n	jvmlh 'vy
amirāni tu	šarirān	vərafiqāni	duzd hā	jumlahi o

'oheβ	šoḥaδ	wəroδef	šalmonīm	yāθōm	lo'
dvst d'r'	rvšvh	vt'xtn br'	sl'mtyh'	ytym	nh
dost dāštahi	rišva	vətāzandahi	bāz xāsti hā	yatim rā	na

		wərīβ	'almānā	lo'	yāβō'
yišpoṭū		vjng	byvh	nh	'yyd
ḥvkm kvnnd		vədaᶜvāyi	beva	na	me āyad
šarᶜ (ḥukm) mepursand					

'alēhεm:
nzd 'yš'n:
bənazdi ešān:

1: 24

lāχen	nə'um	hā'āδōn	yhvh
b'yn sbb	gvft'r	xvd'vnd	xvd'y
binā bar in	nazmi	ān xidevand	ḥazrati adonāy

ṣəβā'ōθ	'āβīr	yiśrā'el	hōy	'εnāḥem
rb 'ljyvš	švβ'n	yśr'l	'y v'y	kmyn kvnm
parvardigār	jəlili	yiśrāel	hō	tasalā meyābam

missāray	wə'innāqmā	me'ōyəβāy:
'z ᶜdvy'n mn	vmvk'f't xv'hm	'z dvšmn'n mn:
az ᶜaduyāni man	vəintiqām megiram	az raqibāni man:

1: 25 wəʾāšīβā yāδī ʿālayiχ wəʾɛṣrof
    vbʾz grdʾnm zxm mn ʾβr tv vby pʾlʾym
    vəbāz me gardānam zarbi man abar tu vəgah me bandam

kabbor sīggāyiχ wəʾāsīrā kol
čvn nvqrh qlby tv vdvr kvnm hmh
čun sābun ɣaš hāyi tu vədur mekunam ǰumlahi

bəδīlāyiχ:
qlʿy tv:
surb (qlʾyy) hāyi tu:

1: 26 wəʾāšīβā šofṭayiχ kəβārišonā
    vbʾz grdʾnm ḥʾkmʾn tv čvn ʾvvlyn
    vəbāz megardānam qāziyāni tu cun dar avalin

wəyoʿàṣayiχ kəβaṭhilā ʾaḥàrē χen
vmšvvrt kvnʾʾn tv čvn qdym bʿd čvnyn
vətadbir dihandagāni tu čun dar ibtidā baʿdi inčunin

yiqqāreʾ lāχ ʿīr haṣṣeδɛq qiryā nɛʾɛ̀mānā:
xʾndʾyd btv šhr rʾst mulk ʾvstvʾr:
xānda āyad bətu šahri ān ʿadālat qariyahi moʿtabar:

1: 27 ṣiyyōn bəmišpāṭ tippāδɛ
    ṣyvn bḥvkm bʾz xrydʾyd
    ṣiyon dar ḥukmi šarʿ vā xəriš meyābad

wəšāβɛhā biṣəδāqā:
vbrdygʾn tv brʾsty:
vəbāz me gaštagāni ān dar ʿadālat:

1: 28 wəšɛβɛr pošʿīm wəḥaṭṭāʾīm yaḥdāw
    vškn ʾstʾrygʾn vxṭʾgʾrʾn yk jʾy
    vəšikasti taqṣir kārān uxəṭā kārān yak jāya

wəʿozəβē yhvh yiχlū:
vrhʾ kvnʾʾn xvdʾy ʾnjʾfth švvnd:
vətark kunandagāni ʿibādati adonāy panā mešavand:

1: 29 kī yeβošū meʾēlīm ʾàšɛr
    ky šrmsʾr švvyd ʾz drxtʾn ʾnčy
    ko šarmanda mešaved az ilɣay daraxtān ānči

hàmaδtεm   wətaḥpəru   mehagannōθ   ʔàšεr
ʔrzvy krdyd vrvy syʔh švvyd   ʔz bvstʔnhʔ   ʔnčy
ārzu burded vəro siyāh mešaved az ān bostān hā ānči

bəḥartεm:
ʔxtyʔr krdyd:
bar guzided:

1:30 kī   θihyū   kəʔelā   noβεlεθ   ʕālεhā
       ky   bʔšyd   čvn drxt   blʔyh švvʔ brgʔn
       ko   buda mešaved čun daraxti   pajmurda   bar hāyi ān

uχəγannā   ʔàšεr mayyīm ʔēn   lāh:
včvn bvstʔny ʔnčy   ʔb   nyst bʔn:
vəčun bostāne ānči   āb   neste bəān:

1:31 wəhāyā   hεḥāson   linəʕorεθ
       vbʔšd   ʔn pʔdyʔvnd   bʔfsʔndn
       vəbuda mešavad ān katāni qavi   bəpakāli ṭafaq karda

ufoʕàlo   lənīṣōṣ   uβāʕàrū
vkrdʔr ʔvy   bgvlhʔ   vdr ʔβruxtnd
vəfeʕl kardahi un bəgul rezi   vədar afroxta mešavand

šənēhεm   yaḥdāw   wəʔēn   məχabbε:
hr dvʔn ʔyšʔn <yk jʔy>   vnyst   frv nšʔnʔyy:
harduyi ešān yak jāya   vəneste   xāmoš kunanda:

2:1 haddāβār ʔàšεr ḥāzā   yəšaʕyāhū bεn   ʔāmōṣ
      ʔn sxvn   ʔnčy   nbvvt krd   yšʕyhv   pvsr   ʔmvṣ
      ān suxan ānči   kərāmāt did   yəšaʕyāhu pisari āmoṣ

ʕal   yəhūδā   wīrūšālāyīm:
ʔβr   yhvdh   vyrvšlm:
abar   yəhudā   virušālayim:

2:2 wəhāyā   bəʔahàrīθ hayyāmīm   nāχōn   yihyε
      vbʔšd   bʔxrt   rvzygʔrʔn   ʔrʔsth   bʔšd
      vəbuda mešavad   dar āxiri   ān ruzgārān   ārasta   me šavad

har   bēθ   yhvh   bərōš   hεhārīm
kvh   xʔnh   xvdʔy   bsr   kvhhʔ
kohi xānahi adonāy   dar sardāri   koh hā

wəniśśā^ʔ	miggəβāʕōθ	wənāhàrū	ʔelāw
vbr d^ʔšth švv^ʔ	^ʔz ǰyγ^ʔdh^ʔ	vby dvvnd	b^ʔvy
vəmartaba mebardārad	az ǰaqāṭa hā	vəǰāri mešavand	bā un

kol   haggōyīm:
hmh   qvvm^ʔn:
ǰumlahi ān ṭāyifa hā:

2: 3 vəhāləχū   ʕammīm   rabbīm
      vby rvvnd   qvvm^ʔn   bsy^ʔr^ʔn
      vəmeravand qaumāni   bisyārān

wə^ʔāmərū   ləχū   wənaʕàlɛ   ʔɛl har
vby gvynd   by ^ʔyyd   vr švvym   bkvh
vəme goyand rəvān šaved vəme barāyem bā kohi

yhvh   ʔɛl bēθ   ʔɛ̀lohē yaʕàqoβ
xvd^ʔy   bx^ʔnh   xvd^ʔy   yʕqb
ḥazrati adonāy bā xānahi xudāyi yaʕàqob

wəyorenū   middərāχāw   wəneləχā
vby ^ʔmvzym   ^ʔz r^ʔh^ʔ ^ʔvy   vby rvvym
vətaʕlim āmozad emā rā az rāh hāyi o vəraviš mekunem

bə^ʔorḥōθāw   kī   miṣṣiyyōn teṣe^ʔ   θōrā
bṭryqh^ʔ ^ʔvy   ky   ^ʔz ṣyvn   byrvn ^ʔmd   tvr^ʔ
dar ǰa^ʔda hāyi o ko   az ṣiyon berun me^ʔāyad taʕlimi fatvā

uδəβar   yhvh   mīrūšālāyīm:
vsxvn   xvd^ʔy   ^ʔz yrvšlm:
vəsuxani adonāy   az yərušālāyim:

2: 4 wəšāfaṭ   bēn   haggōyīm
      vḥvkm kvnd   my^ʔn   qvvm^ʔn
      vəqāzigi mekunad mābayni ān ṭāyifa hā

wəhōχīaḥ   lə^ʕammīm   rabbīm
vtvbyx kvnd   bqvvm^ʔn   bsy^ʔr^ʔn
vəmunāzira (vnṣyḥt) mekunad bəqaumāni bisyārān

wəχittəθū   ḥarəβōθām   lə^ʔittīm
vby kvβnd   šmšyrh^ʔ ^ʔyš^ʔn   bbyrh^ʔ
vemayda mekunand šamšer hāyi xud rā bərāyi taš hā

waḥànīθōθēhɛm   ləmazmerōθ   lo^ʔ yiśśā^ʔ
vnyyzh^ʔ ^ʔyš^ʔn   b^ʔrh^ʔ   nh vr d^ʔrd
vəxanǰar hāyi xud rā bərāyi dāṣ (kč k^ʔrd) hā na mebardārad

γōy	ʔɛl gōy	ḥɛrɛβ	wəloʔ	yilməδū	ʕōδ	milḥāmā:
qvvm	bqvvm	šmšyr	vnh	ʔmvznd	hnvz	kʔrzʔr:
ṭāyifa	bā ṭāyifahi	šamšer	vəna	me āmozand	digar	kārzār:

2:5

bēθ	yaʕàqoβ	ləχū		wəneləχā	bəʔōr
xʔndʔn	yʕqβ	by ʔyyd		vby rvvym	brvšnʔyy
xāna dāni	yaʕàqob	ravān šaved		vəmeravem	dar nuri

yhvh:
xvdʔy:
ḥazrati adonāy:

2:6

kī	nāṭaštā	ʕamməχā	bēθ	yaʕàqoβ	kī
ky	rhʔ krdy	qvvm tv	xʔndʔn	yʕqβ	ky
ko	partāb kardi	qaumi tu	xāna dāni	yaʕàqob rā	ko

māləʔū	miqqɛδem	wəʕonənīm
pvr švdnd	ʔz qdym	vʔxtrdʔrʔn
pur šudahand	jādu gari az ahli mašriq	vəčašm bandi hā

kappəlištīm	uβəyaləδē	noχrīm
čvn plštʔʔn	vbkvdkʔn	bygʔnygʔn
čun pəlištim	vədar bača (ʔndyšh) hāyi	begānagān

yaśpīqū:
by kvbnd:
kifāyat (qʔnyʕ) mekunand:

2:7

wattimmāleʔ	ʔarṣō	kɛsɛf	wəzāhāβ	wəʔēn	qeṣɛ
vpvr švdʔyd	zmyn ʔvy	sym	vzr	vnyst	frjʔm
vəpur šudahast	zamini o	nuqra	vətilāh	vəneste	farjām

ləʔosroθāw	wattimmāleʔ	ʔarṣō	sūsīm	wəʔēn	qeṣɛ
bʔmbʔrhʔ ʔvy	vpvr švdʔyd	zmyn ʔvy	ʔspʔn	vnyst	frjʔm
bəxazina hāyi o	vəpur šudast	zamini o	asp hā	vəneste	farjām

ləmarkəβoθāw:
bmrkbhʔ ʔvy:
bəsuvāriš hāyi o:

2:8

wattimmāleʔ	ʔarṣō	ʔɛ̀līlīm	ləmaʕàśe	yāδāw
vpvr švdyd	zmyn ʔvy	bvtʔn	bʕml	dsthʔ ʔvy
vəpur šudahast	zamini o	but hā	bəʕamalāti	dastāni xvd

yištaḥàwū	laʔàšer	ʕāśū	ʔɛṣbəʕoθāw:
sjdh brnd	bʔnč	krdnd	ʔngvštʔn ʔvy:
sajda mebarand	bəān čize	ki bikardahand	anguštāni o:

2 : 9 wayyiššaḥ   ʔāδām   wayyišpal   ʔīš   wəʔal
         vdvlʔ švvd   ʔdm   vʔvβsth kvnd   mrd   vnh
         vədutāh šùd   ādami zād   vəpast šud   mard   vəna

tiśśāʔ   lāhɛm :
ʔzrm dʔrd   bʔyšʔn :
maᶜāf mekuni   bəešān :

2 : 10 bō̄ʔ   basṣūr   wəhiṭṭāmen   bɛᶜāfār
         by švvd   bkmr   vnhʔn kvnd   bxʔk
         bəāmadan   dar kamar   ubənihān šudan   dar xāk

mippənē   paḥaδ   yhvh   umehàδar   gəʔonō̄ :
ʔz pyš   shm   xvdʔy   vʔz škvt   γšy ʔvy :
az jihati (pyšy) sahmi   adonāy   yəaz šavkati takaburi o :

2 : 11 ᶜēnē   gaβəhūθ   ʔāδām   šāfel
         čšmʔn   bvlndy   mrdvmʔn   ʔvβsth *x* **i** kvnd
         čašmāni   balandi   ādami zād   past mešavad

vəšaḥ   rūm   ʔànāšīm   wəniśgaβ
vdvlʔβ švvd   bvlndy   mrdvmʔn   vpʔdyʔvnd bʔšd
vədutāh mešavad fərāziyi   mardūmān   vəmanšur buda

yhvh   ləβaδō̄   bayyōm   hahū̄ʔ :
xvdʔy   btnhʔyy ʔvy brvz   ʔvy :
ḥazrati adonāy bətanhāyi o   dar rōzi   ān un :

2 : 12 kī   yōm   layhvh   ṣəβāʔō̄θ   ᶜal   kol
         ky   rvzy hst   bxvdʔy   rb ʔljyvš   ʔβr   hmh
         ko   rōzest   bəhazrati adonāy   parvardigār   abar   jumlahi

geʔɛ   wārām   wəᶜal   kol   niśśāʔ
γšy   vbvlnd   vʔβr   hmh   bvlnd švdh
mutakabir   vəsar afrāz vəabar   jumlahi   martaba dār

wəšāfel :
vʔvβsth švvd :
vəpast :

2 : 13 wəᶜal   kol   ʔarzē   halləβānōn   hārāmīm
         vʔβr   hmh   srvvhʔ   byšhstʔn   bvlndʔn
         vəabar   jumlahi   sarv hāyi   ān bešahistān ān sar fərāzidagān

wəhanniśśā'īm   wə'al   kol   'allōnē
v'βr'štyg'n   v'βr   hmh   drxth'
vəān baland bardāšta šudagān vəabar jumlahi daraxtāni

habbāšān:
byšhst'n:
ān bāšān:

2:14 wə'al   kol   hɛhārīm   hārāmīm   wə'al
     v'βr   hmh   kvhh'   bvlnd'n   v'βr
     vəabar   jumlahi ān kuh hāyi ān balandān vəabar

kol   haggəβā'ōθ   hanniśśā'ōθ:
hmh   jyγ'dh'   'βr'štyg'n:
jumlahi ān jaqāṭa hāyi baland bardāšta šudagān:

2:15 wə'al   kol   miγdāl   gāβōah we'al
     v'βr   hmh   kvšk   bvlnd   v'βr
     vəabar   jumlahi munārahi (kvšky) baland vəabar

kol   ḥōmā   βəṣūrā:
hmh   b'rvy   bx'r' sng:
jumlahi qal'ahi ḥiṣār dār:

2:16 wə'al   kol   'òniyyōθ   taršīš wə'al   kol
     v'βr   hmh   kštyh'   trsvs   v'βr   hmh
     vəabar   jumlahi kišti hāyi tarsus vəabar   jumlahi

śəχiyyōθ   haḥɛmdā:
nqšh'   'rzvymnd:
farš hāyi   ān ārzumand:

2:17 wəšaḥ   gaβəhūθ   hā'āδām   wəšafel
     vdvl'b švvd   bvlndy   mrdvm   v'vβsth švvd
     vədutāh mešavad < balandi > ān ādami zād   vəpast mešavad

rūm   'ànāšīm   wəniśgaβ   yhvh
p'dy'vndy   mrdvm'n   vbvlnd švvd   xvd'y
sar farāziyi mardumān   vəmanṣur buda ḥazrati adonāy

ləβaddō   bayyōm   hahū':
btnh'yy 'vy brvz   'vy:
bətanhāyi o dar rozi ān un:

2: 18 wəhā^ʔɛlīlīm   kālīl   yaḥàlof:

v^ʔn bvt^ʔn   tm^ʔm   mvbdl švvd:

vəān but hā   ǰumlagi   barham (gvzšth) mešavad:

2: 19 uβā^ʔū   bimə^ʕārōθ   ṣurīm

vby švvnd   bšk^ʔfth^ʔ   kvhh^ʔ

vədāxil mešavand   dar maɣāra hāyi kamar hā

uβimḥillōθ   ^ʕāfār   mippənē   paḥaδ   yhvh

vb^ʔdvft ǰ^ʔyh^ʔ   x^ʔk   ^ʔz pyš   shm   xvd^ʔy

vədar kāvāki hāyi   xāk   az ǰihati (pyšy) sahmi   adonāy

umehàδar   gə^ʔōnō   bəqūmō   la^ʕàroṣ

v^ʔz škvh   ɣšy ^ʔvy   bvr x^ʔstn ^ʔvy   bškstn

veaz šavkati   takaburi o   dar bar xestani o   bəšikast dādan

hā^ʔērɛṣ :

^ʔn zmyn:

ahli zamin rā:

2: 20 bayyōm   hahū^ʔ   yašlīχ   hā^ʔāδām   ^ʔeθ

brvz   ^ʔvy   by ^ʔfgnd   mrdvm   mr

dar rozi   ān un   me^ʔafkanad ān ādami zād azmar

^ʔɛlīlē   χaspō   wə^ʔeθ   ^ʔɛlīlē   zəhāβō   ^ʔàšɛr

bvt^ʔn   symyn ^ʔvy   vmr   bvt^ʔn   zryn ^ʔvy   ^ʔnčy

but hāyi   nuqrahi o   vəazmar   but hāyi   tilāhi o   ānči

^ʕāsū   lō   ləhištaḥàwōθ   laḥpor

krdnd   b^ʔvy   bsǰdh bvrdn   bmvrɣɣ ky kn^ʔ

karda bāsand   bəxud   bəsaǰda burdan   bəxandaq

perōθ   wəlā^ʕàṭallefīm:

br drxt^ʔn vn^ʔm ^ʔvy lḥpr pyrvt   vbṣnmh^ʔ:

(bkvr muš) hā   ubəkor šapalak hā:

2: 21 lāβō^ʔ   bəniqrōθ   haṣṣurīm   uβisə^ʕifē

bšvdn   bmvɣ^ʔrh^ʔ   kmrh^ʔ   vbdnd^ʔnh^ʔ

bədāxil šudan   dar kandahi   ān kamar hā vədar dandāna hāyi

hassəlā^ʕīm   mippənē   paḥaδ yhvh   umehàδar   gə^ʔōnō

km^ʔzh^ʔ   ^ʔz pyš   shm   xvd^ʔy   v^ʔz škvh   ɣšy ^ʔvy

ān ṣaxra hā   az peši   sahmi adonāy   yəaz šavkati takaburi o

bəqūmō   laᶜàroṣ   hāʔārɛṣ:
bvr xʔstn ʔvy   bškstn   pʔdyʔvndʔn zmyn:
dar bar xestani o bəšikast dādan ahli zamin rā:

2: 22 hiðlū   lāχɛm   min hāʔāðām   ʔàšɛr   nəšāmā
     bʔz ʔystyd bšvmʔ ʔz   ʔn mrdvm ʔnčy   nfst
     dar isted bəšumā az   ān ādami zād ānči   nafas (rmq)

bəʔappō   kī   βammɛ hɛhšāβ hūʔ:
bbyny ʔvy   ky   bčy   hsʔbst   ʔvy:
dar dimāɣi o ko   dar čist hisāb šuda o:

VITTORE PISANI

AVEST. *HIZUMA-*, *STAMAN-* UND VERWANDTES

Für *hizuma-* m. (nur Vd. 3, 14) gibt Bartholomae, Air. Wb. 1816 die Bedeutung »Mund« und fügt hinzu: »Ich nehme diese Bedeutung an -geg. Pü., die »Zunge« will-, weil von den neun Öffnungen des menschlichen Leibes die Rede ist«. Und ich glaube er habe Recht, auch weil die von der Pehlevi-Übersetzung angenommene Bedeutung zweifellos auf dem Gleichklang mit *hizū-* »Zunge« beruht.

Wie ist doch dieses Wort etymologisch aufzufassen? Dass es *hizū-* irgendwie enthält, wie Bartholomae kurz andeutet, ist m. E. nicht zu bestreiten; nur darf man mit ihm von »Ableit. aus *hizū-*« sprechen? Das scheint mir wenigstens fragwürdig.

Ich glaube eher, dass es sich um Kreuzung von *hizū-* mit *staman-* handelt. Davon schreibt Bartholomae ebda. 1592: »j. *staman-* m. 'Maul', nur von dem des Hunds«. Diese Feststellung ist von den zwei Stellen (Vd. 13, 30 und 15, 4), wo das Wort vorkommt, geboten; das bedeutet doch durchaus nicht, dass es nicht in einem allgemeineren Sinn gebraucht war. Richtig vergleicht Bartholomae griech. στόμα, so auch Frisk, Griechisches etymologisches Wörterbuch II 801, der auch die Übereinstimmung in der Stammbildung hervorhebt: »Aber der *n*-Stamm [d.h. von στόμα] ist an sich alt und findet sich nicht nur in av. *staman-* m. 'Maul (des Hundes)' sondern auch im Keltischen, z.B. kymr *safn* 'Kinnlade'«. Nichtsdestoweniger beruft sich Frisk auf Georgakas, 'Glotta' 36, 163 (aber 183), der behauptete, Bildungen wie στόμιον, στομίς, στόμις, στωμύλος, στομοδόκος, στομώδης, στομόω »point to a noun *στομ or *στομος or *στόμα f., as mod. dial. στόμη (in Symi) may indicate. Both nouns στόμα and δῶμα ⟨......⟩joined secondarily the formations in -μα (cf. Schwyzer 1. 524³, 5« [1]. Ob der Übergang zu den *n*-Stämmen unabhängig im Avestischen und im Griechischen vor sich gegangen ist, oder es sich um eine alte Isoglosse handelt, bleibe dahingestellt. Dass jedenfalls neben dem *n*- der *o*-Stamm

---

[1] Ich möchte hier daran erinnern, da Frisk es nicht bucht, dass ich in meiner Schrift Uxor (Miscellanea G. Galbiati III 34f.) στόμαχος »Speiseröhre« als haplologische Hypostasis eines στόμα μαχοῦ betrachtet habe, in ⟨*⟩μαχός eine Entsprechung von dt. *Magen* erkennend.

im Avestischen noch überlebte zeigt wohl unser *hizuma-*, wenn meine Vermutung richtig ist.

Immerhin besitzt m. E. das Sanskrit eine Entsprechung mit *n* im Hapax *stāmán-* m. von AV V 13,5. Im pw. VII, 202 liest man: »*stāman-* m. etwa *Weg*. Roth vermuthet *strāman-*«, und noch Mayrhofer, Kurzgefasstes etymologisches Wörterbuch des Altindischen II 513 schreibt: »*stāmán-* m. (nur AV 5, 13, 5 °*ā́nam*), unklar«. Der Hymnus ist gegen Schlangengift gerichtet und dessen Strophe 5 lautet folgendermassen:

káirāta pŕ̥çna úpatr̥ṇyà bábhra ā́ me çr̥ṇutā́sitā alīkā́ḥ
mā́ me sákhyuḥ stā́mánam ápi ṣṭhātā́çrāvā́yanto ní viṣé ramadhvam,

was Whitney (Atharva-Veda-Samhita. Translated with a Critical and Exegetical Commentary, 1905) so übersetzt I 243: »O Kairātan, O spotted one, O grass-haunter (?), O brown one! listen ye to me, O black serpents, offensive ones! stand ye not upon the track (? *stāmán*) of my comrade; calling out (*ā-çravay*), rest quiet in poison«. Dazu bemerkt er: »It is hardly possible to avoid emending *stāmā́nam* in c to *sthámānam* ['station'] or *srámāṇam* ['course', from *sr̥* 'run' -but not quotable]; Ppp. is very corrupt in c, d, but seems to intend no variants«. Nun wage ich *stāmā́nam* m. -mit *ā* gleich ω in griech. στωμύλος? s. doch weiter unten- zu av. *staman-* gr. στόμα zu stellen und die AVStelle so aufzufassen, dass die Schlangen angewiesen werden, hörend auf dem Mund des »Gesellen« nicht zu verweilen. Dazu bemerke ich: ob der Stamm *stāmán-* oder *stāmána-* ist, kann man nicht feststellen: im ersteren Fall wäre der Genus- und Akzentwechsel zu gr. στόμα derselbe wie in sanskrit *brahmán-* m. »Opferpriester« usw. neben *bráhman-* n. »Opfergebet« usw.; im zweiten Fall könnte man das Maskulinum *brāhmaṇá-* »Opferpriester« vergleichen, dessen *ā* von lat. *flāmen* als sehr alt erwiesen zu sein scheint: wie dem auch sei, weist das Maskulinum von sanskr. *stāmā́nam* und avest. *stamanəm* auf eine »persönliche« Auffassung des Mundes hin entgegen der »sachlichen« von gr. στόμα.

HANS-PETER SCHMIDT

IS VEDIC *DHÉNĀ* RELATED TO AVESTAN *DAĒNĀ*?

1. It is one of the many merits of H.S. Nyberg that he has decisively furthered the understanding of the Avestan term *daēnā* [1]. Though one will not agree with all the details of his interpretation, he has settled some fundamental problems. Thus he has shown, more clearly than any of his predecessors, that Bartholomae's [2] assumption of two lemmata *daēnā* (1. das Ich, das Innerste der Persönlichkeit, das himmlische Wesen im Menschen, 2. Religion) is not justified. The word is derived from the root *dāy* 'to see' and means exclusively the religious vision and the organ with which man experiences the divine.

In a recent publication I have myself dealt with *daēnā* by trying to show that the 'cow' (*gav*) in the Gathas of Zarathustra is a metaphor for the 'good vision' (*vaŋuhī daēnā*) [3]. Here I propose to tackle a related problem, the Vedic term *dhénā* which has frequently been identified with Avestan *daēnā*. I think a fresh investigation is called for since some recent statements are apt to confuse the issue.

Thus G. Widengren [4] rejects the derivation of *daēnā* from *dāy* 'to see' and identifies it with Ved. *dhénā* which he derives from *dhā(y)* 'to nourish', attributing to it the literal meaning 'the nourishing one' as a designation for 'woman' and 'cow', meanings he has taken over from older scholars without checking the evidence. His arguments need be discussed: The simple experiment of substituting the supposed meaning in the overwhelming majority of the Avestan passages would have shown him that his hypothesis is wrong.

In a recent article on "Baltic evidence and the Indo-Iranian prayer" B.L. Ogibenin brings up anew the supposed etymological relationship between Lithuanian *dainà*, Av. *daēnā* and Ved. *dhénā* [5]. With S.G.

---

[1] Die Religionen des alten Iran (Leipzig 1938. Reprint Osnabrück 1966) 114ff.

[2] Altiranisches Wörterbuch (Strassburg 1904) s.v.

[3] Neue Methodologie in der Iranistik, hrsg. v. R.N. Frye (Wiesbaden 1974) 323ff. A more detailed study is to appear elsewhere.

[4] Die Religionen Irans (Stuttgart 1965) 46.85.

[5] The Journal of Indo-European Studies 2, 1974, 23-45.

Oliphant[6], M. Bloomfield[7], and M. Molé[8] he derives the word from *dhī* 'to see', but also stresses the close relationship between *dhénā* and *dhenú* 'milch-cow', for which he refers to L. Renou[9]. He makes the astonishing statement that "one should renounce attempts to discover a single meaning for the words *dhenā, dhenu*: their denotata belong to the mythological reality in which 'speech', especially 'sacred speech', and 'milch-cow' are one and the same complex functional unity" (p. 26). Since nowhere in his article, which otherwise contains some observations worthy of consideration, any proper demonstration is to be found as to how this principle is to be applied, it is difficult to enter into a discussion. If it implies that there is no difference in meaning between *dhénā*, supposedly 'poetic vision', and *dhenú* 'milch-cow' for Vedic man, it is linguistically without value. Imagery is after all based on the fact that the terms substituted for each other denote different things and are identified because of some similarity or analogy. It is the specific analogy which gives the image its pregnancy. Also as to Lith. *dainà* the author leaves us wondering, and it is hoped that he will clarify his position by showing how the Baltic words for 'to dance and to sing' with their derived meanings 'to dress up', 'to brag', 'to seduce' etc. can be made compatible with the Indo-Iranian 'to see'. That the Vedic Uṣas is concerned with visions on the one hand, dancing, dressing up etc. on the other, has linguistically no probative force since for all these activities different words are used. It is true that in semantic development everything is possible, but if and how it happened in a particular case, must be demonstrated with at least some plausibility.

Before we can consider the relationship between *dhénā* and *daēnā*, it is necessary to know what the former actually means. *dhénā* has been a problem child of Vedic lexicography. R. Roth attributed to it the meaning 'milchende Kuh, pl. Milchtrank'[10]. K.F. Geldner dedicated a detailed study to the word[11], trying to vindicate the various meanings given by the commentator Sāyaṇa: 1. Schwester, vielleicht auch Geliebte, Frau. 2. weibliches Tier, Kuh. 3a. b. Stimme, Rede, Lob. He assumed several etymologically unrelated homonyms.

---

[6] Journal of the American Oriental Society (= JAOS), 32, 1912, 393-414.

[7] JAOS 46, 1926, 303-308.

[8] Revue de l'histoire des religions 157, 1960, 182ff.

[9] Études védiques et pāṇinéennes (= EVP) I-XVII (Paris 1955-1969) I 10f.

[10] O. Böhtlingk- R. Roth, Sanskrit Wörterbuch (St. Petersburg 1955-75) s.v.

[11] R. Pischel- K. Geldner, Vedische Studien I-III (Stuttgart 1889-1901) III 35-43.

This was rejected by H. Oldenberg who was of the opinion that *dhénā* has only one meaning: 'Milchstrom'[12]. Oldenberg's view was in turn refuted by S.G. Oliphant and M. Bloomfield (quoted above) who plead for the meaning 'song, prayer', considering the word as an exact equivalent of Av. *daēnā*. The identity of *dhénā* and *daēnā* was also claimed by J. Hertel[13], who, in consonance with his 'Aryan fire-doctrine', assumed the meanings 'flame', 'heavenly fire, heavenly light' for the Vedic word, 'heavenly fire' and 'fire of the heart' for the Avestan. J. Charpentier refuted Hertel's view and came to the conclusion that there are two homonyms, the one meaning 'cow, milk', the other 'spirit' identical with Av. *daēnā*[14]. This view has gained some prominence by being endorsed in the grammar of J. Wackernagel and A. Debrunner[15], and considered in the etymological dictionary of M. Mayrhofer[16].

Geldner has revised his interpretation of the word in his translation of the Ṛgveda[17]. Though he sticks to assuming different meanings, he now tries to derive all from the same root *dhā(y)* 'to suck, to nourish': a) die Saugende = Lippe (of which 'Stimme, Rede' may be a tropos); b) die Säugende = Weib (ad 1.2.3cd); c) Strom (ad 7.21.3c). He explicitly rejects the equation with Av. *daēnā* because of the irreconcilable difference in meaning and because *daēnā* in the Gathas is trisyllabic (**dayanā*).

L. Renou considered the word while dealing with the metaphorical uses of the cow terminology:[18]

"De *gó-* le sens de 'prière' est passé par contamination à *dhenú-* que les Nigh. rangent avec *gaurí-* parmi les *vāṅnāman*,... en effet impliqué... RV. III 58 1,... 57 1,... IV 41 5... ainsi que... ŚB. XIV 8 9 1 = BĀU. V 8 1... Il ne faut dès lors plus hésiter à rattacher à la même racine *dhénā-*... qui a évolué plus nettement vers le sens de 'prière' (cf. Bloomfield JAOS. XLVI p. 303, pour qui le duel *dhéne* désigne elliptiquement 'prière' et 'libation'), tout en y combinant les représentations du 'fleuve', s'il faut en croire O. Vedaforschung p. 97".

---

[12] Vedaforschung (Stuttgart-Berlin 1905) 93-100.

[13] Die arische Feuerlehre I (Leipzig 1925) 63-115.

[14] Brahman (Uppsala Universitets Årskrift 1932.8) 44-55.

[15] Altindische Grammatik II 2 (Göttingen 1954) 733.

[16] Kurzgefasstes Wörterbuch des Altindischen (Heidelberg 1953ff.) s.v. The Elamite *te-nu-m* quoted there as a loan from Old Persian **daina* should be dropped: see W. Hinz, Neue Wege im Altpersischen (Wiesbaden 1973) 50f.

[17] Der Rig-Veda aus dem Sanskrit ins Deutsche übersetzt I-IV (Cambridge/Mass. 1951-57). Cf. also the Nachträge in vol. IV ad 5.31.9; 5.62.2; 7.21.3; 7.24.2; 8.32.22.

[18] Journal asiatique 231, 1939, 354f.

A later statement of Renou's follows a similar line of reasoning:[19]

"A côté de *dhenú* se situe la variante ambiguë *dhénā*, de nouveau un mot pour lequel on ne sait si l'on peut instaurer en acception authentique, linguistiquement valable, des valeurs qui d'abord semblent simplement sous-jacentes et figuratives. G. (ad 1.2,3 7.21,3 8.32,22) nous paraît avec raison maintenir, partiellement, le sens de 'discours': l'Indra qui fait attention aux *dhénā* et aux *dhí* 10.104,3 (analogue 10), n'est sans doute pas différent du dieu avide de poèmes qu'on représente en tant d'autres passages; l'épithète *vísṛṣṭadhenā* du nom *suvṛktí* 7.42,2 vise la masse oratoire qui se trouve libérée dès lors qu'on presse le soma. Ce sont certainement les *dhénā* 'prières' qui 4.58,6 sont dites 'couler' comme des rivières, cf. *gíro arṣanti sasrútaḥ* ('d'un même cours') 9.34,6. Il semble donc que, de ce biais, et malgré la difficulté phonique plus apparente que réelle, le lien de *dhénā* avec av. *daēnā* puisse et doive être maintenu".

These statements are somewhat elusive. It is not clear whether Renou wanted to indicate by 'ambiguous variant' also the etymological relationship of *dhénā* with *dhenú* or only the semantic one with *dhenú* in its figurative sense. If the first were true, he would also have considered Av. *daēnā* as an etymological relative of *dhenú*. The passage rather reads as if he had not yet come to grips with the problem.

In the later fascicles of EVP Renou has translated and/or commented upon most of the passages that contain *dhénā*, and we get a clearer picture of his views as they developed in the last decade of his life. Since it is the authority of Renou, on the basis of the passage just quoted, that has been appealed to in support of the equation *dhénā* = *daēnā*, it may be useful to take his later interpretations as a guideline for the following presentation of the material and to make another attempt at a proper evaluation of the evidence[20].

2. Renou translates 5.62.2c *víśvāḥ pinvathaḥ svásarasya dhénāḥ* by "Vous [Mitra-Varuṇa] faites gonfler les coulées (émanant) du pâturage" (EVP V 78) and in his commentary he considers this as a paradox based on the contradiction between *pinv* and *dhénā* since one cannot make swell what is already flowing abundantly (EVP VII 40). He

---

[19] EVP I 11.
[20] I have refrained from mentioning all stray remarks on *dhénā* by other scholars. —J. Gonda, The Vision of the Vedic Poets (The Hague 1963) has left the 'etymologically and semantically difficult *dhénā*' out of consideration in his study on *dhí* (p. 11 n. 10), but translates 'prayers' (p. 94) and 'words of religious inspiration' (p. 278).—I renounce my remarks in Zeitschrift der Deutschen Morgenländischen Gesellschaft 109, 1959, 445, made at the time under the impression of Oliphant's seemingly overwhelming mass of plausible parallels.

explicitly rejects Geldner's interpretation "alle weiblichen Tiere (Reden)" (Nachträge 255), stating that *víśvāḥ ... dhénāḥ* depends on *viśvádhena,* an epithet of the rivers in 4.19.2 and 6, 'comportant toutes coulées'. Obviously he has joined Oldenberg. It is not necessary to enter into a discussion of the figurative and paradoxical sense Renou considers since in the context of the stanza and the hymn concrete interpretation is fully satisfactory. The meaning of the preceding pāda b has been clarified by J. Narten[21] by establishing the correct meaning of *irmá:* *irmá tasthúṣīr áhabhir duduhre* "standing still (the cows) have given milk every day", which refers to the normal behaviour of cows during milking, and in all probability it alludes to the miracle of the cows' daily giving of milk. Pāda c then attributes the swelling of the milk-streams to Mitra-Varuṇa's activity. This may be further supported by 3c *vardháyatam óṣadhīḥ pínvatam gáḥ* "let the plants grow, make the cows swell!" Oldenberg (Vedaforschung 95) had started his study with 5,62,2, and it does indeed offer the most obvious arguments for his thesis. His specific 'milk-stream' is in fact more appropriate in the context than Renou's general 'coulée'. The implication is that the milk-streams are nourishing, and the same implication is present in *viśvádhena* as an epithet of the streams (*vartanīḥ*) freed by Indra's feat of killing the serpent (4.19.2) and the great river (*aváni*) Indra makes stand still for Turvīti and Vayya (4.19.6), where Geldner has "alltränkend". *viśvádhena* may be compared with the etymologically related[22] *viśvádhāyas* 'all-nourishing', especially in 10.122.6a *íṣam duhán sudúghām viśvádhāyasam* "(Agni) milking the refreshment, easy to milk, all-nourishing" (cf. Renou, EVP XIV 28.97). That in case of the rivers rather *dhénā* than *dháyas* was used, may have its motivation in the fact that *dhénā* contains itself the semantic element 'stream'.

3. 1.141.1d *ṛtásya dhénā anayanta sasrútaḥ.* Renou (EVP XII 33) translates "(Les chanteurs) ont dirigé les effluves de l'Ordre-sacré (en sorte) qu'ils écoulent ensemble", and comments (p. 101): "*dhénā* mot controversé: ces coulées de Ṛta (cf. *ṛtásya dhárāḥ,* passim, terme prob. de même origine) sont les paroles sacrales, cf. aussi *gírah ... sasrútaḥ* 9.34.6". Here we have of course no further contextual evidence to settle the meaning of *dhénā.* Taking the parallel *ṛtásya dhītí* (9.97.34)

---

[21] Indo-Iranian Journal 10, 1968, 244f.
[22] Cf. Mayrhofer, Etym. Wörterb. s.v. *dháyati.*

as the basis of interpretation, would make sense as well. That Renou does not even mention it, clearly shows that he had made up his mind in favour of Oldenberg's view. The translation of the pāda as a whole is not unproblematic regarding subject and object and the meaning of *sasrút*. For the latter Bloomfield had suggested 'together with oblations' (JAOS 46, 306). I would rather suggest 'in full flow' which fits well in 4.28.1 where Indra makes the waters to have full flow for Manu. Instead of supplying the subject (the singers) we may rather supply the object: "In full flow the milk-streams of truth have led (Agni)".

4. In 3.1.9ab Renou (EVP XII 49) follows Oldenberg's translation literally: *pitúṣ cid údhar janúṣā viveda vy àsya dhénā asrjad ví dhénāḥ* "(Agni comme éclair) a découvert (le nuage) mamelle du Père (Ciel) lui même (et cela) dès sa naissance; il a libéré les coulées, les flots-de-lait de cette (mamelle)". In the commentary (p. 113) he gives a reference to Lüders [23] without any further remark though he rejected Geldner's view, followed by Renou, that Agni is here the fire of lightning and *údhan* the cloud. Lüders interpreted the heavenly *údhan* as the primordial source of the waters; the implications of Lüders' interpretation and theory have, however, no direct influence on the meaning of *dhénā* and can be left out of consideration here. It seems in any case unobjectionable to understand pāda b as referring to the waters as streams (*dhárā*) being further specified as milk-streams or nourishing streams.

5. 7.94.4 *índre agnā́ námo bṛhát suvṛktím érayāmahe, dhiyā́ dhénā avasyávaḥ* "En Indra, en Agni (est notre) haut hommage: nous mettons en branle l'hymne-bien-tourné,/ les coulées (de prière réalisées) par la vision-poétique, nous qui cherchons (votre) assistance". (EVP XIV 56) In the commentary he says (p. 127: "... *dhénā* étant un aspect poétique de *vā́c* (Gld. ad 8.32.22)... les deux mots (*dhénābhiḥ*... *dhíbhíḥ*) se retrouvent ensemble 10.104.3. L'image qui est à la base de *dhénā* est déjà préparée par *pī-* 2c". These terse remarks leave much of the reasoning behind them unexpressed. It is not clear what is meant by 'aspect poétique'. Clearly, and without doubt correctly, Renou implies that the poet has associated *dhénā* with *dhī́* pseudo-etymologically.

The pāda 2c *īśāná pipyataṃ dhíyaḥ* "having power over it, make

[23] Varuṇa I-II hrsg. v. L. Alsdorf (Göttingen 1951-59) 390.

the visions swell" recalls immediately *pinvathaḥ ... dhénāḥ* 5.62.2c where we could, however, not find any figurative use of *dhénā*. It can hardly be a mere coincidence that the root *pī* 'to swell' has quite frequently *dhī́* as object. 7.94.2c is identical with 5.71.2c, addressed to Mitra-Varuṇa,ₐ and 9.19.2c, addressed to Indra and Soma who are called *svàrpatī* and *gópatī* in the preceding pāda. The phrase *pinvataṃ dhíyaḥ* "you two make the visions swell" occurs three times (1.151.6; 7.82.3; 10.39.2). In 8.95.5 the *dhī́* is swollen with or abounding in truth (*r̥tásya pipyúṣī*; cf. Lüders, Varuṇa 421), and in 8.6.43 in honey and ghee (*mádhor ghr̥tásya pipyúṣī*) [24].

This tropos is quite clearly derived from the common simile "to make visions swell like cows". 9.94.2c *dhíyaḥ pinvānā́ḥ svásare ná gā́vaḥ* "the visions swelling like cows on the pasture". 10.64.12 *yám me dhíyam ... devā́ adadāta ... tā́m pīpayata páyaseva dhenúm ...* "that vision which you gods have given me ... make it swell like a milch-cow with milk". 2.34.6cd *áśvām iva pipyata dhenúm ū́dhani kártā dhíyaṃ jaritré vā́japeśasam* "make (our vision) swell like a milk-giving mare in her udder; make the vision adorned with victory prizes for the singer!" [25]

The simile then also yielded the straight forward identification: 2.2.9 *evā́ no agne amŕ̥teṣu pūrvya dhī́ṣ pīpāya br̥háddiveṣu mā́nuṣā, dúhānā dhenúr vr̥jáneṣu kāráve tmánā śatínam pururū́pam iṣáṇi* "Thus the human vision has become swollen among the immortals dwelling in the high heavens, o primordial Agni: A milk-giving milch-cow in the (terrestrial) settlements for the bard to incite by herself hundredfold, multiformed (gain)". The assonantic collocation of *dhī́* and *dhenú* is also found in the other passage where an identification of the 'vision' and the 'cow' is given: 4.41.5 *índrā yuváṃ varuṇā bhūtám asyā́ dhiyáḥ pretā́rā vr̥ṣabhéva dhenóḥ, sā́ no duhīyad yávaseva gatvī́ sahásradhārā páyasā mahī́ gaúḥ* "O Indra, o Varuṇa, you two become the lovers of this vision, as two bulls of a milch-cow! May she (the vision) give us milk as if she had gone to pasture, by her milk a great cow of a thousand streams!" Actually we have here a mixture of figures, simile and identification side by side and intertwined, as if the poet did not quite dare to use a clear-cut

---

[24] Geldner compares aptly 8.12.13 *yám viprā ukthávāhaso 'bhipramandúr āyávaḥ, ghr̥tám ná pipya āsány r̥tásya yát*, on which cf. Lüders, Varuṇa 450.

[25] Cf. Renou, EVP X 76. Compare also 1.169.4 *stútaś ca ... stánaṃ ná mádhvaḥ pīpayanta vā́jaiḥ* "Let the songs of praise swell with victory prizes like the breast with sweet (milk)".

metaphor. Compared with the number of times *dhī́* is connected with *pī*, the number of occurrences of *pī* with other terms referring to poetry is very small [26], and in the similes *dhī́* appears only once with *gó* alone, everywhere else *dhenú* is present.

The association of the 'vision' with the 'milch-cow' had become standard in Vedic poetic language because of the assonance which allowed a subtle play. This play does of course not allow us to postulate a semantic unity of the roots *dhī* 'to see' and *dhā(y)* 'to suck, to nourish'—as Ogibenin's assertions tend to imply (cf. § 1)—, it is rather based on their discrepancy. The tertium comparationis is the fact that the proper poetic vision—like the other manifestations of poetic speech in the ritual context—is supposed magically to create nourishment or to induce the gods to do so. This nourishing quality is particularly germane to the milch-cow and her milk, and both offered themselves for comparison and metaphorical identification. The assonance of *dhenú* and *dhénā* with *dhī́* certainly has aided this process, though not necessarily triggered it.

To return to 7.94.4, it should be noted that *dhénā* cannot be understood as a metaphor of *dhī́* itself but rather as the milk-stream of speech that results from the vision. The literal translation of the passage would of course also allow to understand *dhénā* as the real milk-stream. The same is true of 7.24.2c *vísr̥ṣṭadhenā bharate suvr̥ktíḥ* "the well-turned hymn is offered with the milk-streams released"; *dhénā* could refer to the milk offerings accompanying the hymn. However, the context especially of 7.94.4 strongly favours the figurative interpretation, and even Oldenberg (Vedaforschung 98) admitted that here *dhénā* could mean the song insofar as it is conceived as an offering; in fact he was here quite close to the solution of the problem which was in practice solved by Renou. The closest parallel for songs as streams is probably 10.89.4ab where we have a kind of *luptopamā* or implicit comparison: *índrāya gíro ániṣitasargā apáḥ prérayaṃ ságarasya budhnát* "I drive the songs to Indra, the waters (pouring) in restless outpour from the bottom of the ocean". As

---

[26] Cf. the preceding note. Further: 1.181.8 *utá syā́ vāṃ ... gī́ḥ ... pinvate ... vŕ̥ṣā vām meghó ... pīpā́ya gór ná séke mā́nuṣo daśasyán"* And this song swells for you two (Aśvins), ... your bull(-like) cloud has become swollen, ... satisfying men at its outpouring of, as it were, milk". 10.31.11 *prá kr̥ṣṇā́ya rúśad apinvatódhar r̥tám átra nákir asmā apīpet* is obscure according to Lüders, Varuṇa 618f. Renou EVP XVI 130 suggests plausibly: "nul ne l'a aidé dans la composition poétique". *dhenú* as metaphor for 'speech' also in 6.48.12-13: cf. Geldner and Renou EVP 144f.

Geldner has correctly seen, the bottom of the ocean is here a metaphor for the heart; a similar idea occurs in 4.58.5 (cf. § 7). As an alternative interpretation of 7.94.4 one could think of intentional ambiguity, *amphibolia* or *śleṣa*. We shall see in § 7 that *dhénā* actually offers itself for this figure of speech.

6. Also in 10.104.3, the second passage where *dhénā* and *dhī́* appear collocated, both interpretations, 'nourishing stream (of soma)' or 'nourishing stream (of speech)' make sense: *prógrám pītíṃ vṛ́ṣṇa iyarmi satyáṃ prayaí sutásya haryaśva túbhyam, ₁indra dhénābhir ihá mādayasva dhībhír víśvābhiḥ śácyā gṛṇānáḥ* "I drive a strong drink to the bull, a real one of pressed (soma) to you, (driver) of fallow horses, so that you go forth, o Indra; revel here in the nourishing streams (of soma or speech), being lauded mightily by all the poetic visions". The same goes of course for 10b *utápi dhénā puruhūtám īṭṭe* "and also the stream (of soma or speech) implores him who is much called". Oliphant (JAOS 32,396) quotes the passages where the root *íḍ* occurs with terms for 'song' etc which outnumber those with terms for 'libation' etc. It should be obvious that statistics alone cannot have probative force in a case like this.

7. On 4.58.6ab Renou remarks (EVP XVI, 106): " 'Reden' [Geldner] n'est nullement assuré. On a un passage analogue 1.141.1 où *sasrút* figure près de *dhᵒ* comme ici *sarít*", which is nothing but a variation on Oldenberg (Vedaforschung 97) without taking a clear position [27]. Still, this passage is of particular interest since it belongs to a hymn which is a eulogy of the *ghṛtá*, explicitly mentioning three forms of it, the third of which "the gods fashioned by their own power from the seer" (4d *venád ékaṃ svadháyā níṣ tatakṣuḥ*). The whole stanza 5 speaks of *ghṛtá* as poetry: *etá arṣanti hṛ́dyāt samudrác chatávrajā ripúṇā návacákṣe, ghṛtásya dhárā abhí cākaśīmi hiraṇyáyo vetasó mádhya āsām* "These (streams of ghṛta) flow from the ocean in the heart, protected by a hundred fences in order not to be seen by the rascal. I see the streams of ghṛta clearly. The golden reed is in the middle of them". Geldner sees in the golden reed an allusion to soma, Renou (Hymnes spéculatifs 232 f.) takes up this idea and comments: "le soma comme fécondateur des pensées (avec jeu sur le mot *vetasa* 'verge', à la fois bâton et organe viril" [28]. Certainty in this matter

---

[27] Earlier (Hymnes spéculatifs du Véda, Paris 1956, 34) he had 'paroles'.
[28] Based on the sense of *vaitasá* in 10.95.4,5.

is hardly attainable; *vetasá* could also refer to the main artery. For
4.58.6ab we have also an interpretation of P. Thieme:[29] *samyák
sravanti saríto ná dhénā antár hŕdá mánasā pūyámānāḥ* "Die Milchströme
fliessen zusammen, indem sie sich innen durch Herz und Denken
(zur heiligen Dichtung) reinigen, wie die Ströme [zusammenfliessen]"
—zu ergänzen ist offenbar: 'im Meer'". He refers to the archaic
view according to which the heart was the organ of digestion.
Accordingly the 'milk-streams' are digested ('purified') in the heart
and then further transformed into poems by the organ of thinking in
a mystical purification process. As a parallel he adduces ChU 6.8.2...
annasyāśyamānasya yō 'ṇimā sa ūrdhvaḥ samudīṣati, tan mano bhavati
"was die Feinheit der gegessenen Speise ist, die entweicht nach oben.
Dann wird sie zum Denken/Denkorgan". Oliphant (JAOS 32,401)
had quoted 1.61.1 *índrāya hŕdá mánasā maniṣá pratnáya pátye dhíyo
marjayanta* "They cleanse the visions for Indra, their primordial
husband, by the heart, thinking, and enthusiasm". Still closer is the
idea of the filter in 9.73.7-9: 7 *sahásradhāre vítate pavítra á vácam
punanti kaváyo maníṣiṇaḥ* "The enthusiastic poets purify the speech
in the outspread filter of a thousand streams", 8 *ṛtásya gopá... trí
ṣá pavítrā hŕdy àntár á dadhe* "The guardian of truth... puts three
filters in his heart", 9 *ṛtásya tántur vítataḥ pavítra á jihváyā ágre
várunasya māyáyā* "The thread of truth is spread on the filter, on
the tip of the tongue through the magic power of Varuṇa". Lüders
(Varuṇa 470f.) explains that Soma is the filter that guarantees the
truth of the speech, but at the same time the poet thinks of himself
in whose heart soma is doing his purifying which then results in the
utterance of the speech by the tongue controlled by the same filter.
This parallel which shows that speech it self is purified in the heart
leaves room to understand the *dhénāḥ* in 4.58.6 as streams of speech
and may tend to make Thieme's interpretation dispensible. However,
I think that Thieme is right. His interpretation actually implies the
conclusion to which our study leads us almost unavoidably: The
word *dhénā* was chosen by the poet because it conveys both senses,
the stream of milk and the stream of speech.

8. The only case where Renou deviates considerably from the
meaning 'stream' is in his translation of 1.2.3: *váyo táva pvapŕñcatí
dhénā jigāti dāśúṣe, urūcí sómapītaye* "O Vāyu, ta langue s'avance,

---

[29] ZDMG 111, 1961, 96 = Kleine Schriften (Wiesbaden 1971) 172.

comblant (de biens), vers l'adorateur, se faisant-large pour boire le soma". (EVP XV 98) In his note he refers, without discussion, to Geldner, Oldenberg (Vedaforschung 98), and Mayrhofer, and to *urūcí* as an epithet of the tongue (*jihvā́*) of Agni 5.57.5. It is obvious that such a parallel is in itself incapable of proving anything; it can only show that the meaning is thinkable. A reference to *urūcí gaúḥ* (3.31.11) or to Indra as a great stream of wealth (*rāyò 'vánir mahā́n* 8.32.13) would have as little force. The meaning of *dhénā* in the present passage must be compatible with that established for the other passages, and this cannot be demonstrated for 'tongue'. Oliphant (JAOS 32,407) translates *prapṛñcatí dhénā* by 'penetrating voice', which comes in reply to the *ukthá* in stanza 2, and he refers to TĀ 3.9.1 where Vāk is the wife of Vāyu. This makes sense, but since I hope to have shown that 'voice' or 'speech' is not the primary meaning of the word, I prefer to look for the solution in the opposite direction. I propose to translate: "O Vāyu, your nourishing stream, filling (the space with goods) for the worshipper, comes expanding widely to drink soma". That Vāyu is visualized as having a nourishing stream or rather being a stream, is hardly a far-fetched image. He fills the space (*rájas*)[30], empty without him, carrying goods[31] for the worshipper, and the stream is widely expanding because it is reaching over the whole expanse of the earth (cf. *urú vā́ta* 1.25.9; 9.22.2). The nourishing, fecundating powers of Vāyu are referred to e.g. in 1.135.8 *sākám gā́vaḥ súvate pácyate yáo ná te vāya úpa dasyanti dhenávo nápa dasyanti dhenávaḥ* "Simultaneously the cows give birth, the barley ripens, your milch-cows do not dry up, your milch-cows do not dry out".

9. Of the Indra-hymns of the first three maṇḍalas we have only Renou's translation, not his commentary. His renderings show that he had settled for the meaning 'stream', though not always in the literal sense as Oldenberg. 1.55.4 *sá íd váne namasyúbhir vacasyate cáru jáneṣu prabruvāṇá indriyám, vṛ́ṣā chándur bhavati haryató vṛ́ṣā kṣémeṇa dhénām maghávā yád ínvati* "Lui seul dans la (marche en) forêt fait-entendre-sa-voix par ceux qui rendent hommage, en proclamant parmis les hommes (son) précieux (nom) d'Indra. (Le dieu) mâle (est)

---

[30] Cf. *á pṛc* with *rájas* (of Sūrya with his beams) 1.84.1.

[31] Cf. Renou's translation and his study of the word *pṛc*: Études sur le vocabulaire du Ṛgveda I (Pondichéry 1958) 95f.

plaisant, (le dieu) mâle (est) désirable quand lui, le Libéral, par (l'œuvre de) paix met en mouvement le cours (de la parole)". (EVP XVII 21) Renou's decision for 'stream of speech' may have been influenced by Geldner's translation, but also by the reference to speech and the dear (name) of Indra in ab: Indra, by his friendly behaviour, incites man to praise him. 1.18.7c *sá dhīnām̐ yógam invati* "He (Sadasaspati = Bṛhaspati[32]) drives (incites) the yoking of the poetic visions", can be cited in support. However, this is not the only interpretation possible. As Geldner has correctly pointed out, the next stanze speaks, in opposition to the peaceful relations of Indra to man in 4, of his habit to instigate fights (5ab *sá ín mahā́ni samithā́ni... kṛṇóti... jánebhyaḥ*). In his paeceful activity Indra incites the abundant flow of milk, as a bull (*vṛ́ṣan*) he makes the cows swell with milk.

10. 3.34.3cd *áhan vyáṃsam uśádhag váneṣu āvír dhénā akṛṇod rāmyā́ṇām* "il a tué Vyaṃsa, brûlant a son gré dans les bois; il a rendu manifeste les effluves des nuits". (EVP XVII 76) The image makes perfect sense. When killing the serpent (*áhi*) Vṛtra, more specifically identified as a cobra (*vyáṃsa*)[33], Indra also frees the dawns visualized as milk-streams emerging out of the dark of the night. In any case it seems preferable to assume here the primary meaning of *dhénā* than to think, with Geldner, of the voices of the cows or the Aṅgiras imprisoned in the dark of the night, or, with Oliphant (who refers to 2.2.2; 9.96.1 : JAOS 32,408), of the voices of the nights themselves.

11. 1.101.10 *madáyasva háribhir yé ta indra ví ṣyasva śípre ví sṛjasva dhéne, ā́ tvā suśipra hárayo vahantu uśán havyā́ni práti no juṣasva* "Laisse toi enivrer avec les alezans qui (sont) tiens, ô Indra! Délie tes lèvres, laisse couler les deux courants (de soma)! O (dieu) aux belles lèvres, que les alezans te convoient ici; accueille de bonne grâce nos oblations;" (EVP XVII 36) This, and the second passage with the dual *dhéne*, have been embarrassing to most interpreters. I do not think that Renou has found the solution either; at least I do not see to which two particular streams of soma the poet is supposed to refer. Bloomfield (JAOS 46,307f.) had proposed to understand it as

---

[32] Cf. H.P. Schmidt, Bṛhaspati und Indra (Wiesbaden 1968) 98f.
[33] Cf. H.P. Schmidt, Zeitschrift für vergleichende Sprachforschung 78, 1963, 297-304.

an elliptic dual, referring to the prayers and the libations (expressed by *dhénā* and *dhárā* respectively in 3.1.9). This would, mutatis mutandis, be possible also if my interpretation of the meaning is adopted: Both connotations, the literal and the figurative, could be implied. Note that in 9 the poets have pressed soma and Indra is called *bráhmavāhas*.

12. 5.30.9 *stríyo hí dāsá áyudhāni cakré kím mā karann abalá asya sénāḥ, antár hy ákhyad ubhé asya dhéne áthópa praíd yudháye dásyum índraḥ* "For the dāsa had made women his weapons: 'What shall the powerless armies do to me?' (asked Indra). Since he had recognized the two nourishing streams within, Indra then went forth to fight the dasyu". The stanza refers, like the two preceding ones, to the Namuci myth, and this prompted Oldenberg (Vedaforschung 99) to identify *ubhé dhéne* with soma and surā. Geldner sees in them the two women of Namuci, referring to the *kúyavasya yóṣe* (1.104.3). However, neither can Kuyava be identified with Namuci, as Geldner considers[34], nor is there any evidence that *sánāmānā* in 10.73.6 refers to women at all. Geldner's view is of course also influenced by pāda a, but we do not know the precise sense of this expression; it may be an idiom[35]. Bloomfield interprets as follows (JAOS 46,308): "Indra looked upon (considered) both the songs and libations within (him) and then went forth to fight the demon". He understands this in the sense that Indra takes courage from the hymns and soma libations. It is impossible to decide if the Vedic usage would allow supplying 'him(self)' with *antár khyā*; in the only other occurrence (1.81.9) Indra recognizes the possessions of the non-worshipper 'within' (*antár hí khyó... védo ádāśuṣām*), referring to their hiding-places. This parallel could be cited in favour of Oldenberg's view since in the Namuci myth Indra wants to obtain soma and surā which are in possession of Namuci.

13. 7.21.3 *tvám indra srávitavā apás kaḥ páriṣṭhitā áhinā śūra pūrvíḥ, tvád vāvakre rathyò ná dhénā réjante víśvā kṛtrímāṇi bhīṣá* "You, o Indra, make the waters flow, the many encircled by the serpent, o hero. From you the nourishing streams have meandered away,

---

[34] In Vedische Studien III 36f. Geldner identified Kuyava with Śuṣṇa; thus also K. Rönnow, Trita Āptya (Uppsala 1927) 78f.

[35] A similar locution is found in 10.27.10 in a non-mythological context.

all the artificial (fortifications) tremble for fear (from you)". Also
Geldner has 'stream' here; for the fear of the waters he refers to
4.22.6cd *ádha ha tvád vṛṣamaṇo bhiyānā́ḥ prá síndhavo jávasā cakramanta*
"Then the rivers ran quickly away for fear from you, who are of the
spirit of a bull". In 7.21.3 *tvát* and *bhīṣā́* must be construed with
both pādas; this is stylistically emphasized by their respective position
at the beginning and the end. This leaves no room for Oliphant's
interpretation (JAOS 46,405). The comparison of the streams with
charioteers is not hard to understand: they circumvent the obstacle,
Indra, who is standing in front of the rock, since they cannot overrun
him. Cf. also the comparison of the chariot (*rátha*) with a stream
(*aváni*) in 1.181.3; 1.186.8.

14. 8.32.22 *ihí tisráḥ parāváta ihí páñca jánāṁ áti, dhénā indrāvacā́kaśat*
"Pass by the three distances, pass by the five peoples, observing
the nourishing streams, o Indra?" Here we can of course think of the
streams of soma as well as of the streams of speech. Geldner has
'Reden'. In the same tṛca we have in 23 a reference to the songs
(*gíraḥ*) which shall bring Indra hither, and in 24 to soma that is
to be offered to him. Parallels, again, cannot have any probative
force. The same goes for 10.43.6ab *víśaṁ-víśam maghávā páry aśāyata
jánānām* "The liberal one reaches around from clan to clan, the bull
observing the nourishing streams of the people".

15. In later Vedic texts the word *dhenā* occurs only sporadically,
both in its initial meaning and in its figurative sense. The latter is
present in TĀ 3.9.1 *senedrasya dhenā bṛhaspateḥ* "Senā (is the wife)
of Indra, Dhenā of Bṛhaspati". Bloomfield and Oliphant were obviously
right in maintaining that not the sacrificial milk libation but rather
a form of speech would be chosen as the wife of the "Lord of Praise"
(JAOS 32,411. 46,305).
Also in MS 4.13.4. KS 16.21. TB 3.6.5.1 *dhénābhiḥ kálpamānaḥ*
the figurative sense is possible though by no means evident. The
context does not yield any clue which could help to settle the question [36].
KS 35.9. ĀpŚS 14.28.4 *vísṛṣṭadhenās salilā́ ghṛraścyútaḥ* "The waters,
their nourishing streams released, sprinkling ghee" hardly allows
of an interpretation "streams of song outpoured" (Oliphant, JAOS

---

[36] W. Caland, Śāṅkhāyana-Śrautasūtra transl. (Nagpur 1953) 131 ad 5.16.9 considers
the meaning as not clear.

32,410) because of the context which either calls the waters along with the seasons or identifies the seasons with the waters, as W. Caland's translation seems to imply [37].

16. The discussion of the evidence has, on the whole, yielded a vindication of Oldenberg's view, though it has also shown that he failed to recognize the figurative use of the word. In the latter respect Geldner has seen much clearer though he resorted to somewhat tortuous means to force disparate meanings he assumed in single contexts into a semantic unity. Renou's contribution was to bring the figurative use and its implications into better focus though his first attempts remained vague and impressionistic, and he also jumped to premature conclusions without weighing the evidence as a whole. In his later interpretations he had, inspite of occasional inconsistencies, arrived at the correct solution of the problem. The result that *dhénā* means primarily 'milk-stream, nourishing stream' and figuratively 'nourishing stream of speech' places the term in the multifaceted cow and milk imagery of the Ṛgveda. The two senses of the word never became dissociated, the 'stream of speech' did not develop into a homonym. In all probability, however, it gave rise to intentional ambiguities, *śleṣa* (§ 5 and 7). The use of the word in both literal and figurative sense also accounts for the bewildering fact that in most cases we find parallels which tend to support the meanings 'stream' as well as 'speech'. Bloomfield's and Oliphant's error was that they overestimated the weight of the parallels from the semantic sphere of speech, obviously also influenced by the game the Vedic poets play with the assonance of *dhénā* and *dhī́* 'vision'. This led further to the identification of *dhénā* with Avestan *daēnā*, Zarathustra's 'religious vision'. Since the latter was demonstrably still pronounced **dayanā* by Zarathustra himself, the equation should never have been made; it is linguistically untenable. That the Avestan *daēnā* also happens to be involved in cow imagery, is a coincidence. In the Avesta this has developed from the imagery connected with the Indo-Iranian Goddess Uṣas, Dawn, and it may be mentioned that the Vedic *dhénā* has no particular links with Uṣas; only in one single passage does it figuratively refer to the dawn (§10). In summa: Equating Vedic *dhénā* with Avestan *daēnā* amounts to following a will-o'-the-wisp.

---

[37] Das Śrautasūtra des Āpastaba. Achtes bis fünfzehntes Buch (Amsterdam Akad. Verband. Afd. Letterkunde N.R. XXIV 2.1924) 414.

RÜDIGER SCHMITT

NUGAE BAGISTANENSES ALTERAE

Dem Gedenken des grossen Iranisten und Semitisten Henrik Samuel Nyberg, der auch auf dem Gebiet der Erforschung der *alt*iranischen Sprachen reiche Ernte gehalten hat [1], widme ich diese gelegentlichen Notizen, die eine erste Reihe solcher »Nugae Bagistanenses« [2] fortsetzen.

1. *DB I 21 usw.* <*a-ta-ra*>

Die Interpretation dieser Präposition als /antar/ »in, unter« — an der genannten Stelle z.B. *antar imā dahyāva* »in diesen Ländern« — stand bis vor kurzem ausser Zweifel. Die völlige Gleichsetzung mit avest. *antarə̄* und ved. *antár* war, im Verein mit der all diesen Formen gemeinsamen Akkusativ-Rektion, ein zu gewichtiges Argument gewesen. An dieser Gleichung rüttelte aber nun Henrik Samuel Nyberg in seinem gleichsam als sein Vermächtnis — das Vorwort ist von seinem Todestag, dem 9. Februar 1974, datiert — erschienenen grossen *Manual of Pahlavi. Part II: Glossary* (Wiesbaden 1974), S. 18 b: Mittelpers. *andar* wird dort zwar auf altpers. *antar* zurückgeführt, doch zu diesem findet sich dann die Bemerkung »better read *antarᵃ*« [3]. Eine Begründung gibt Nyberg nicht, doch ist sie unschwer zu erraten: Wenn die Präposition (bzw. das Adverb) mittelpers. *tar* »durch, über« auf altpers. <*ta-ra*> /tarah/ [4] (= avest. *tarō* = ved. *tirás*) zurückgeht, muss *andar* auf ein damit reimendes /*antarah/ zurückgeführt werden. Die Argumentation zugunsten dieses Ansatzes ist also rein 'diachronisch-retrospektiv' [5]: Da eine synchronische Beweisführung entfällt und die

---

[1] Vgl. hierzu die Bibliographie von Christopher Toll, *Professor H. S. Nybergs författarskap* (Stockholm 1959), v.a. S. 28-32 »Iranica«.

[2] Erschienen in *MSS* 30 (1972) 139-154.

[3] Diese Bemerkung findet sich noch nicht in dem älteren *Hilfsbuch des Pehlevi. II: Glossar* (Uppsala 1931) des gleichen Verfassers.

[4] Belegt nur DZc 12 *ta[raʰ imā]m yauviyām* »durch diesen Kanal«. Altpersische Inschriften zitiere ich (samt dem dort verwendeten Siglensystem) nach Roland G. Kent, *Old Persian. Grammar, texts, lexicon* (New Haven, Conn. ²1953).

[5] Zu diesem Terminus vgl. Verf., Der »Adler« im Alten Iran. Möglichkeiten und Grenzen der Erschliessung verlorenen Wortgutes, *Sprache* 16 (1970) 63f.

diachronisch-prospektive (extern-vergleichende) ihr widerspricht (vgl. oben), ist sie auf ihre Tragfähigkeit hin zu überprüfen.

Es stellt sich also die Frage, ob die mittelpersische Form *andar* eine altiranische Grundlage zwingend erfordert, die auf das /-r/ noch eine Silbe folgen liess. Bei blosser Anwendung der Lautgesetze, d.h. hier: des 'Auslautgesetzes' müsste diese Frage ohne Zweifel bejaht werden, doch ist gerade bei einer Präposition oder einem Präverb mit besonderen Entwicklungen im Satzsandhi ('Akzenteinheit' von Präposition und regiertem Nomen bzw. Pronomen) bzw. in der Komposition zu rechnen. Gerade im Mittelpersischen sind derartige Fälle auch schon früh beobachtet worden. Im übrigen ist aber die Entwicklung altpers. *antar* > mittelpers. *andar* auch gar nicht ohne Parallele: Im gleichen Verhältnis stehen zueinander avest. *avarə̄* »herab, hinab« (= ved. *avár*; im Altpersischen unbelegt) und mittelpers. *ăvar* »hierher! komm!«[6]. Es besteht also kein Anlass, die traditionelle Interpretation von altpers. < a-ta-ra > als /antar/ in Zweifel zu ziehen.

2. *DB I 40 usw.* < *ha-mi-i-ça-i-ya* >

Die sprachgeschichtliche Interpretation dieses etwa vier Dutzend Male bezeugten (z.T. substantivierten) Adjektivs mit der Bedeutung »abtrünnig, aufständisch, rebellisch, feindlich« ist noch nicht zu einer in jeglicher Hinsicht befriedigenden Lösung gekommen. Gegen die traditionelle Erklärung als »verschworen, *coniūrātus*, σύνορκος«, die auch in sämtliche neueren Handbücher[7] Eingang gefunden hat, wandten sich insbesondere Vittore Pisani und Paul Thieme : Pisani[8] ging von der letztgenannten Bedeutung »feindlich« (italien. *ostile*) aus und sah in *hamiçiya-* das Äquivalent des rigvedischen *a-mitr-íya-* »feindlich«; »il *h* iniziale avrà origine nell'analogia delle numerose parole con *ha-* o *ham-*, sopratutto di *ham-arana-* 'battaglia', che appartiene alla stessa cerchia semantica«. Eine Analogie-Einwirkung als *deus ex machina* ist allerdings wenig befriedigend, und dass man in einem so durchsichtigen und jederzeit leicht verständlichen Wort wie uriran. **a-miθr-iya-* »feindlich« (: **a-miθra-* »Feind«) diese

---

[6] Vgl. dazu Nyberg, *Manual. II* (vgl. oben im Text), S. 36 a.

[7] Ich nenne nur Kent, *op. cit.*, S. 213 b; Wilhelm Brandenstein-Manfred Mayrhofer, *Handbuch des Altpersischen* (Wiesbaden 1964), S. 124; Walther Hinz, *Neue Wege im Altpersischen* (Wiesbaden 1973), S. 136.

[8] Vittore Pisani, Intorno alle antiche iscrizioni persiane, *RSO* 19 (1941) 96.

Durchsichtigkeit bewusst preisgegeben hätte, ist gar völlig unglaubhaft. Im übrigen führte ein Primärbedeutungsansatz »feindlich« zu Interpretationsschwierigkeiten bei den nicht wenigen Textstellen, wo das Adjektiv mit *hačā-ma* »von mir« in der Phrase *NN hačāma hamiçiya abava* »NN wurde von mir abtrünnig« verbunden ist.

Thieme[9] dagegen vermutete in dem anlautenden *ha-* »ein altes idg. *se* 'ohne'« und betrachtete *hamiçiya-* dementsprechend als »Weiterbildung zu *ha-miça-* 'ohne Vertrag', d.h. 'treulos'«. Dieser Vorschlag steht und fällt mit dem angenommenen *se, für das bislang ausserhalb des Lateinischen sichere Nachweise noch nicht gelungen sind. Aus dem Dilemma 'Verschworener' oder 'Treuloser' hilft aber auch eine Betrachtung der inschriftlichen Belege, die sich fast durchwegs auf der Behistūn-Trilingue finden, nicht heraus: *hamiçiya-* heissen Länder im allgemeinen oder besonderen (etwa *Bābiruš, Marguš*), deren Bewohner (etwa *Ūvjiyā, Bābiruviyā*), ein einzelner (*Čiçantaxma*), gegebenenfalls mit seinen Anhängern (mehrfach »sammeln sich« die Rebellen [*hamiçiyā*] und »ziehen in die Schlacht«), und sehr häufig auch der *kāra*; an mehreren Stellen geht unmittelbar voran oder folgt ein Satz, in dem über das gleiche Subjekt gesagt wird, dass es zu einem anderen, einem Usurpator »übergelaufen« sei (*abiy NN ašiyava*); an näheren Angaben finden sich sonst nur noch, dass irgendwer von jemandem (meist »von mir [= Dareios]« = *hačā-ma*, zweimal [DB II 79, III 11] auch »mir« *-maiy*) abtrünnig geworden sei, oder dass einer jemanden »abtrünnig gemacht« habe (*hamiçiyam kar*): DB IV 9f. (*Gaumāta...*) *Pārsam hamiçiyam akunauš* »G. machte Persien abtrünnig« und entsprechend DB IV 12-31 über die acht anderen Usurpatoren (einmal, DB IV 12, mit folgendem *manā*: »NN machte *mir* XY abtrünnig«) sowie DB IV 34 *drauga di[š hamiçiy]ā akunauš* »der Trug machte sie [= all diese Länder] abtrünnig«.

Da ich eine bessere Lösung als die, die mit der (etymologiae causa) angenommenen Grundbedeutung »coniūrātus« rechnet, noch nicht zu erkennen vermag, bemühe ich mich, diese im Formalen weiter auszubauen und vielleicht auch in semasiologischer Hinsicht stärker zu spezifizieren. Eines Kommentars bedürfen dabei das Kompositionsvorderglied, wo sich die Handbücher von Kent und Brandenstein-Mayrhofer nicht zwischen *ha-* < idg. *sṃ- und *ham-* < idg. *sem-* (beide:) »zusammen« entscheiden[10], und das Kompositionssuffix *-iya-*, zu dem

---

[9] Paul Thieme, Besprechung von Brandenstein-Mayrhofer, op. cit., *KZ* 85 (1971) 298.
[10] Hinz, *op. cit.* geht von *ham-* aus.

nur Meillet-Benveniste[11] bemerken, dass es hier zur Bildung eines *nomen agentis* diene. Ohne auf die Frage einzugehen, ob sich hinter < ha-m° > tatsächlich /ham-/ und /hamm-/ verbergen können[12], will ich gleich eine dritte Möglichkeit zur Diskussion stellen: *hama-*»derselbe, gleich« < idg. *somó-* (> ved. *samá-*, avest. *hama-*, griech. ὁμός), mit der Folge, dass Haplologie *hamamiç° → *hamiç° anzunehmen ist (wofür *hamātar-*»von der gleichen Mutter abstammend« < *hama-mātar-* als Gegenstück zu [daneben belegtem] *hama-pitar-*»vom gleichen Vater abstammend« eine vollständige Parallele bietet). Ich fasse demnach *hamiçiya-* < *hama-miç-iya-*, dessen Grundwort ja zweifelsohne altpers. *miça-* = avest. *miθra-*, mask. = ved. *mitrá-*, ntr. »Vertrag, Kontrakt« ist[13], als ein 'Ableitungskompositum' genau des zweiten Typs, den Ernst Risch[14] seinerzeit herausgearbeitet hatte. Es liegt eine Zugehörigkeitsbezeichnung (»zum gleichen Vertrag gehörig«) vor, die morphologisch völlig Risch's Musterwort ὁμο-γάστρ-ιος »aus dem gleichen Mutterleib stammend« entspricht und einer Reihe weiterer griechischer Wörter : teils desselben Bedeutungsfeldes (Abstammungsangabe) wie ὁμο-πάτρ-ιος (ab Aischylos, Herodot), ὁμο-μήτρ-ιος (ab Herodot, Aristophanes), aber auch ὁμ-αίμ-ιος »von gleichem Blut« (Pindar, *Nem.* 6, 16), teils weiter abstehend wie ὁμο-βώμ-ιος (Thukydides 3, 59, 2 von »den gemeinsamen Göttern der Griechen« [θεοὶ … κοινοὶ τῶν Ἑλλήνων], die »am gleichen Altar verehrt« werden) oder ὁμ-ωρόφ-ιος »unter demselben Dache wohnend« (ab Antiphon, Demosthenes). Die hier vorgeschlagene Analyse führt zu einer Ausgangsbedeutung des Kompositums als »zum gleichen Vertrag gehörig«, die in gewissem Sinne ambivalent ist: im Positiven → »*Bundesgenosse«, im Negativen → »Feind«, je nach dem Aspekt des Betrachters[15].

---

[11] A. Meillet, *Grammaire du Vieux-Perse. Deuxième édition…* par E. Benveniste (Paris 1931), S. 153 § 261 d.

[12] Dazu vgl. Verf., Besprechung von Walther Hinz, Altiranische Funde und Forschungen, *Kratylos* 14 (1969) 58 f.

[13] Das Genus des altpersischen Wortes ist nicht feststellbar, und darauf kommt hier auch nicht viel an. Zu dem Genus-Gegensatz zwischen der Avesta- und der Vedaform vgl. etwa Paul Thieme, *Mitra and Aryaman* (New Haven, Conn. 1957), S. 20. — Die Ausgangsposition Kents (*op. cit.*), »*miça-* 'friend'«, ist falsch, da altindoar. *mitrá-*, mask. »Freund« eine indoarische Sonderentwicklung ist: vgl. Thieme, ebenda.

[14] Ernst Risch, Griechische Komposita vom Typus μεσο-νύκτιος und ὁμο-γάστριος, *Museum Helveticum* 2 (1945) 15-27, v.a. S. 21.

[15] Man denke an idg. *ghostis*, das für latein. *hostis* »Feind« ebenso die Grundlage bildet wie für german. *gastiz* »Gast« und ursprünglich einfach den »Fremden« bezeichnet hat, oder an ved. *arí-*, für das erst Paul Thieme, *Der Fremdling im Ṛgveda* (Leipzig 1938) beide Aspekte klar herauszuarbeiten verstand.

Sie würde es also gestatten, die Vorstellung vom »coniūrātus«, die Thieme[16] »immer noch nicht einleuchte(te)« und für die die Kontexte in der Tat nicht den geringsten Anhalt bieten, durch eine 'neutralere' zu ersetzen.

3. *DB I 77 usw.* <*ba-a-ba-i-ru-u-vi-i-ya*>

Dass dieses neunmal auf Dareios-Inschriften bezeugte Ethnikon von dem Stadt- und Landesnamen *Bābiru-* »Babylon(ien)« mittels Suffix »-*(i)ia*-« (so Kent[17]) abgeleitet ist, steht ausser Zweifel. Auffallen muss diese Ableitung aber trotzdem, denn hinter dem Vokalstamm *Bābiru-* erwartete man das Suffix in der Form *-ya-* und also **Bābiru-ya-*. Die stattdessen tatsächlich belegte Bildung /ba:- biruviya-/ ist also ein weiteres Beweisstück dafür, dass das hier vorliegende Suffix in der Form *-iya-* im Altpersischen produktiv geworden ist: Zugrunde liegt ja nicht /°uv + ya/, das dann <°u-vi-i-ya> geschrieben worden ist, sondern vielmehr /°u + iya/. Für ein solches produktives *-iya-* sind andere Beispiele bereits aufgezeigt worden, da die Frage mehrfach im Zusammenhang mit der sogenannten 'Sievers'schen Regel' erörtert wurde: Jerzy Kuryłowicz[18] und, ihm folgend, Manfred Mayrhofer[19] sowie Elmar Seebold[20] führten als Beweisstücke *Harauvatiya-* »Arachosier«, *Ākaufačiya-* »Bergbewohner (?)« und *Mačiya-* »Maker« an. Die beiden letzten erfordern diese Annahme wirklich, da nur aus /°k + iya/ (Auslaut der Grundwörter **Ākaufaka-* bzw. *Maka-*), nicht aber aus /°k + ya/ palatalisiertes /°čiya/ entstehen konnte. Bei dem ersten Beispiel *Harauvatīya-* übersahen jedoch alle, dass das *-ī-* Stammauslaut von *Harauvatī* sein kann und in dem erwähnten Zusammenhang keinerlei Entscheidungskraft besitzt, zumal die Form mit dem Fluch belegt ist, nur auf A?P (dazu vgl. gleich unten) zu begegnen.

Dass auf der Throntägerinschrift am Artaxerxes-Grab (Artaxerxes' II. oder III.?) A?P, die etliche Hapax-Ethnika enthält, tatsächlich

---

[16] Vgl. Anm. 9.

[17] Kent, *op. cit.*, S. 50 §144; ebendort §144. III »*Bābiruv-iya*-«, das das Problem selbst ebenso verschleiert wie des Verfassers Stellungnahme dazu.

[18] Jerzy Kuryłowicz, Zur altpersischen Keilschrift, *ZPhon* 17 (1964) 567; Erstabdruck in dess. *Esquisses linguistiques* (Wrocław-Kraków 1960), S. 278.

[19] Manfred Mayrhofer, Die Rekonstruktion des Medischen, *AÖAW* 105 (1968) 9 Anm. 40.

[20] Elmar Seebold, *Das System der indogermanischen Halbvokale* (Heidelberg 1972), S. 103.

/hinduya/ »Inder«, mit Suffix -*ya*-, nicht -*iya*-, belegt ist (A?P 13),
darf als Gegenargument gegen die versuchte Erklärung der Form
*Bābiruviya- nicht verwendet werden. Der Sprachzustand dieses Textes
spricht bekanntlich allen grammatischen Regeln der Dareios-Zeit in
einem Ausmasse Hohn, dass man Mühe bei der Abgrenzung hat,
wo die Steinmetzfehler aufhören und fehlende Sprachbeherrschung
beginnt: Zu den -*u*-stämmigen Toponymen stehen als Ethnonyme
auf dieser späten Inschrift nebeneinander (A?P 13 bzw. 11 und 16)
Hinduya- (: *Hindu*- »Indien«), *θataguiya*- (: *θatagu*- »Sattagydien«)[21]
und (weder *Bābiruya- noch *Bābiruviya*- — sondern) *Bābiruš*.

4. *Zum Worttrenner*

So bedeutsam die Worttrennung der altpersischen Inschriften auf
der einen Seite ist — die Feststellung der Funktion des Worttrenners
durch Olav Gerhard Tychsen war 1798 der erste Schritt zur Entzifferung
der Schrift überhaupt gewesen —, so unscheinbar ist sie auf der
anderen: Nur so jedenfalls ist es zu erklären, dass erst 1942 die
Erkenntnis in ein Handbuch[22] eingedrungen ist, dass es sogar zwei
verschiedene Formen dieses Zeichens gibt, am Behistūn-Felsen einen
(nach rechts offenen) Winkelhaken, in den übrigen Texten aber einen
(nach rechts unten gerichteten) Schrägkeil. Und erst Walther Hinz[23]
ist es in allerjüngster Zeit gewesen, der anhand prächtiger und deutlicher
Photographien der Behistūn-Inschrift[24] nachweisen konnte, dass dieser
Behistūn-Worttrenner »nur ungefähr halbe Zeilenhöhe hat« und in
Wirklichkeit gar »kein Winkelhaken, sondern ein kurzer Schrägkeil
ist«. Der Gegensatz zwischen den Behistūn- und allen übrigen Inschriften
ist also kein Gegensatz der Zeichen*form*, sondern bloss einer der
Zeichen*grösse*: Der halbhohe Schrägkeil wurde in den nach Behistūn

---

[21] Ausser den von Kent, *op. cit.*, S. 50 § 144. III und S. 187 b angestellten Erwägungen,
von denen allein »error for -*uviya*-« plausibel erscheint (vgl. Verf., Medisches und
persisches Sprachgut bei Herodot, *ZDMG* 117, 1967, 125 Anm. 55), wäre denkbar,
dass diese Form (<θa-ta-gu-u-i-ya >) für (*Hinduya*- paralleles) *θatagu-ya (<θa-ta-gu-
u-ya >) stünde und in sie jenes <i > versehentlich eingedrungen sei, das dem unmittelbar
danebenstehenden Ethnikon <ga-da-a-ra-ya > »Gandarier« (statt regelrechtem * <ga-
da-a-ra-i-ya >) fehlt.

[22] Walther Hinz, *Altpersischer Wortschatz* (Leipzig 1942), S. 11; seitdem vgl.
v.a. Kent, *op. cit.*, S. 19 § 44.

[23] Hinz, *op. cit.* (Anm. 7), S. 24.

[24] Den grössten Teil von DB I zeigt die von Hinz, *op. cit.* publizierte Tafel 10
(gegenüber S. 17).

entstandenen Texten der gewöhnlichen Zeichenhöhe angepasst und auf die ganze Zeilenhöhe verlängert.

Bei der gleichen Gelegenheit gelang es Hinz (ebenda), einen zweiten, völlig entsprechenden Unterschied der beiden Inschriftengruppen festzustellen: Der erste Keil des Zeichens < ya >, der normalerweise ein die ganze Zeilenhöhe füllender senkrechter Keil ist und so auch in Behistūn allgemein gelesen worden war, reicht dort tatsächlich aber nur über die halbe Zeilenhöhe. Auch in diesem Punkt ergibt sich also ein Gegensatz in der Zeichengrösse zwischen Behistūn und den restlichen Texten.

Mit diesen formalen Unterschieden, deren Beseitigung dann natürlich zu einem harmonischeren Schriftbild führte, hat es nun aber noch nicht sein Bewenden: Wie schon längst beobachtet worden ist [25], steht der sogenannte 'Worttrenner' auf den Behistūn-Inschriften auch an unerwarteten Stellen, am Beginn jeder einzelnen Kolumne der Inschrift und am Beginn jedes 'Paragraphen', wobei die einzelnen Abschnitte ja zusätzlich noch durch ein Spatium charakterisiert sind. Nach diesen Spatien setzt der Text des neuen Paragraphen jeweils auffallenderweise mit dem 'Worttrenner' ein, dem dann erst die stereotype Einleitungsformel θātiy Dārayavauš xšāyaθiya folgt. Daraus ergibt sich zwingend, so will mir scheinen, dass die Funktion dieses sogenannten 'Worttrenners' der Behistūn-Inschriften jedenfalls nicht die Worttrennung gewesen sein kann. Seine Verwendung ist nur dann verständlich, wenn man annimmt, dass dieser halbhohe Schrägkeil ein graphisches Signal ist, das den *Wortbeginn* anzeigt. Damit ergibt sich weiter, dass zwischen den Behistūn- und den anderen Inschriften nicht nur ein formaler, sondern auch ein funktionaler Gegensatz besteht: Es wurde nicht bloss der halbhohe Schrägkeil nach oben hin verlängert, vielmehr wurde das (halbhohe) Wortbeginn-Markierungszeichen — um es mit einem Modewort zu benennen — 'umfunktioniert' zum (zu Recht so genannten) Worttrenner. Übrigens ist, da also nicht nur ein formaler, sondern auch ein funktionaler Unterschied besteht, im Sinne einer ein-eindeutigen, voll reversiblen Transliteration die konsequente Wiedergabe dieser beiden Keile durch zwei verschiedene Zeichen, wie sie jüngst Christoph Hauri [26] zuerst praktiziert hat

---

[25] Vgl. am eingehendsten Kent, *op. cit.*, S. 19 § 44, aber auch schon dens., *The Textual Criticism of Inscriptions* (s.l. 1926), S. 11.

[26] Christoph Hauri, *Das pentathematische Schema der altpersischen Inschriften* (Wiesbaden 1973), S. 26 mit Anm. 46.

— Schrägkeil = Punkt (.), 'Winkelhaken' = Doppelpunkt (:) —,
erst recht zu fordern!

Die Erkenntnis der ursprünglichen Funktion des sogenannten 'Worttrenners' als eigentliches Wortbeginn-Markierungszeichen (oder: graphisches Anlautsignal) steht zugleich in vollem Einklang mit der
Vermutung, die zuletzt etwa Hinz[27] geäussert hat, dass »der altpersische
Worttrenner lediglich eine Abwandlung der in Keilschriften seit langem
üblichen Determinative« sei. Der Abstand zwischen dem Determinativ-
Gebrauch der anderen Keilschriftsysteme und dem Worttrenner der
altpersischen Keilschrift (einem ihrer charakteristischen Merkmale!)
verringert sich auf diese Weise jedenfalls in entscheidendem Masse.

Schliesslich ist diese 'Umfunktionierung' des Anlaut-»markers«
zum (nachbagistanensischen) Worttrenner eine tiefer, als es nach aussen
hin den Anschein hat, in das Schrift*system* eingreifende Veränderung
und als solche in meinen Augen auch ein gewichtiges weiteres Argument
in dem (heute aber einer Klärung rasch näherkommenden) Streit
um die Frage nach Ursprung und Entstehungszeit der altpersischen
Keilschrift[28]. Die festgestellten nicht nur formalen, sondern — wie
gezeigt — auch funktionalen Unterschiede innerhalb der altpersischen
Inschriften werden leicht verständlich, wenn man sie sich so erklärt,
dass das theoretisch (gewissermassen 'am Schreibtisch') und, wie die
Entstehungsgeschichte von Relief und Inschrift am Behistūn-Felsen
zeigt[29], auch unter enormem Zeitdruck entworfene Schriftsystem nach
seiner *ersten* praktischen Verwendung am Behistūn-Felsen nach den
dabei gemachten Erfahrungen verändert worden ist.

5. DB § 59 (IV 50-52) und sein neuester Interpret

Während der Niederschrift dieser »Nugae« kommt ein bemerkens-
werter Aufsatz mit »Beobachtungen zur Lexicographie und Grammatik
der achämenidischen Königsinschriften« von Wilhelm Th. in der Smitten[30] zu meiner Kenntnis, der eines Kommentars deshalb bedarf,
weil die eine Hälfte der dort gegebenen Erklärungen evident falsch

---

[27] Hinz, *op. cit.* (Anm. 7), S. 23f.

[28] Über den Diskussionsstand und die Fortschritte der letzten zehn Jahre informieren
am besten Manfred Mayrhofer, Das Altpersische seit 1964, *W.B. Henning Memorial
Volume* (London 1970), S. 280f., ders., Neuere Forschungen zum Altpersischen, *Donum
Indogermanicum. Festgabe für Anton Scherer* (Heidelberg 1971), S. 44f. und Hinz,
op. cit. (Anm. 7), S. 15-21.

[29] Vgl. die Literaturhinweise in den oben Anm. 28 genannten Arbeiten.

[30] Erschienen in *BiOr* 30 (1973) 366-367.

ist und die andere nichts Neues enthält. Um meine völlig negative Einschätzung dieser wertlosen Arbeit — in Abwandlung des geflügelten Wortes des hier zu ehrenden Verewigten[31] könnte man über ihren Verfasser sagen, dass das Altpersische kein für ihn geeignetes Forschungsgebiet zu sein scheint! — zu belegen, greife ich die Besprechung der Passage DB IV 50-52 heraus, wo das sonderbare Verständnis des Autors von dieser Sprache und seine mangelnde Vertrautheit mit ihren Problemen und der einschlägigen Fachliteratur kumuliert in Erscheinung treten.

Der Text dieses Abschnittes (§ 59) ist zumindest in der altpersischen Fassung in seinem Bestand unproblematisch:

θātiy Dārayavauš xšāyaθiya: tayaiy (51) *paruvā xšāyaθiy[ā] yātā āha avaišām avā naiy astiy kṛ*(52)*tam yaθā manā va[šnā] Auramazdāha hamahyāyā θarda kṛtam.*

In der Interpretation ist zwar eine *communis opinio* über das 'Gemeinte' erreicht worden, doch gehen die einzelnen vorgelegten Übersetzungen noch in mancher Hinsicht auseinander. Man halte nebeneinander die Versuche von

Weissbach[32]: "So lange die früheren Könige waren, ist von diesen das nicht getan worden, wie von mir nach dem Willen Ahuramazdas in einem und demselben Jahre getan worden ist«,

König[33] : »Noch nimmer wurde so vieles vollbracht
von den früheren Herrschern, so viel' ihrer warn,
wie ich es vollbracht in dem einen Jahr
nach Willen und Wollen des Ōramazdấ«,

Sen[34]: »Those former kings who had been so long, by them such has never been done as by me, by the will of Ahuramazda, (has) been done in (course of) the same year«,

Kent[35]: »Those who were the former kings, as long as they lived,

---

[31] H. S. Nyberg, Besprechung von Franz Altheim-Ruth Stiehl, Supplementum Aramaicum, *Kratylos* 7 (1962) 145.

[32] F. H. Weissbach, *Die Keilinschriften der Achämeniden* (Leipzig 1911, Nachdruck 1968), S. 65. Die vorausliegende Literatur darf wegen der seinerzeitigen ungenügenden Textgestaltung unberücksichtigt bleiben. — Die Übersetzungsvorschläge der Einleitungsformel *θātiy Dārayavauš xšāyaθiya* lasse ich beiseite.

[33] Friedrich Wilhelm König, *Relief und Inschrift des Koenigs Dareios I am Felsen von Bagistan* (Leiden 1938), S. 54.

[34] Sukumar Sen, *Old Persian Inscriptions of the Achaemenian Emperors* (Calcutta 1941), S. 70.

[35] Kent, *op. cit.* (Anm. 4), S. 132 a.

by them was not done thus as by the favor of Ahuramazda was done by me in one and the same year«,

Asmussen [36] : »Af de tidligere konger er der, så længe de var (konger), ikke blevet udrettet noget tilsvarende, som der af mig ved Ahuramazdās velsignelse er blevet udrettet inden for ét og samme år«

und Dandamaev [37] : »Te, kto prežde byli carjami (v tečenie vsej ich) žizni, ne sdelali stol'ko, skol'ko mnoju sdelano v tečenie odnogo i togo že goda«.

Demgegenüber bedeutet es einen gewaltigen Rückschrift, wenn in der Smitten [38] in dieser Passage »Anakoluth und asyndetisch-parataktische Konstruktionen« findet und sie folgendermassen übersetzt: »Von jenen, welche früher die waren, welche Könige waren [39], ist nicht jenes gemacht (worden) in einem von ihren Jahren[,] wie von mir gemacht (ist) durch den Beistand Auramazdas«. Das unfreiwillige Eingeständnis dafür, dass hier etwas nicht in Ordnung ist, bietet in der Smitten selbst, wenn er fortfährt: »Überträgt man diese Übersetzung zurück ins Altpersische, so ergibt sich folgendes zu erwartende Satzgefüge: *avaišām tayaiy paruvā xšāyaθiyā naiy astiy kr̥tam hamahyāyā θarda yātā āha, yaθā manā kr̥tam vašnā Auramazdāha*« [40]. Was in der Smitten uns hier zumutet und als etwas völlig Neues und Beispielloses in die altpersische Grammatik (oder Stilistik?) einführt, erinnert an die Rätselgattung des 'Rösselsprunges'. Zur Verdeutlichung: Zählt man die Wörter des überlieferten Textes von 1 bis 17 durch, so stellt sich das »zu erwartende Satzgefüge« für in der Smittens Übersetzung so dar: 6-1-2-3-8-9-10-15-16-4-5-11-12-17-13-14, und Wort Nr. 7 *avā* fehlt, vielleicht nur durch ein Versehen, denn übersetzt (»jenes«) scheint es sehr wohl worden zu sein.

Dies im einzelnen in seiner Haltlosigkeit zu widerlegen, erscheint mir wenig sinnvoll. Ich setze deshalb umgekehrt meine Interpretation des Satzes [41] an dessen Stelle und lasse ihr einzelne, vor allem syntaktische Bemerkungen folgen:

---

[36] Jes Peter Asmussen, *Historiske tekster fra Achæmenidetiden* (s.l. 1960), S. 63.

[37] M.A. Dandamaev, *Iran pri pervych Achemenidach* (*VI v. do n.è.*) (Moskva 1963), S. 268.

[38] In der Smitten, *op. cit.*, S. 367 b.

[39] Ebenda Anm. 6 findet sich der Alternativvorschlag »welche früher das waren, was Könige sind«!

[40] Die Transliteration habe ich der oben im Text gegebenen angepasst.

[41] Ich bemerke gleich hier, dass die elamische Version des Textes nichts beiträgt; und die babylonische Fassung ist zu lückenhaft.

»Es verkündet Dārayavauš, der König: Von jenen, die früher (oder: die die früheren) Könige (waren), ist, solange sie (es) waren, so viel (oder: etwas so Grosses) nicht vollbracht worden, wie von mir nach dem Willen Auramazdās in ein und demselben Jahr vollbracht worden ist«.

Die Struktur der Passage als ganzer ist klar: Durch *yaθā* »wie« wird ein Komparativsatz eingeleitet, dessen einzelne Glieder ausser dem Verbum (dem kopulalosen Passivpartizip *kṛtam*[42]) die Agensbezeichnung (Genetivus subiectivus *manā*) sowie eine kausale (*vašnā Auramazdāha*) und eine temporale Umstandsbestimmung (*hamahyāyā θarda*) enthalten. Diesen Genetivus temporis hat in der Smitten offenbar völlig verkannt (er übersetzt »in einem von ihren Jahren«): < θa-ra-da > = *θarda* ist Gen. Sing. fem. des Konsonantstammes *θard-*, näher charakterisiert durch den Genetiv des Pronominaladjektivs *hama-*. Zu dieser Form bemerkt Verfasser an anderer Stelle (S. 366 b), dass sie »grammatikalisch höchst sonderbar« sei; »es scheint sich dabei um eine Dittographie der Genetivendung zu handeln«. Diese Erklärung übersieht jedoch (a) die fünfmalige Bezeugung der Form *hamahyāyā* in DB IV 4, 41, 45, 52, 60, (b) ihre Gegenstücke *haruvahyāyā* und *ahyāyā* sowie (c) das nach DB V 2f.[43] nachweislich feminine Genus von *θard-* »Jahr«.

Der vorangehende Hauptsatz ist seinerseits wiederum mehrgliedrig, wie die korrelativen *tayaiy — avaišām* zeigen : Der eigentliche Hauptsatz setzt zumindest (vgl. unten) mit dem Demonstrativum *avaišām* ein; man vergleiche aus einer Vielzahl von Beispielen etwa DB I 19f. [*taya*]*šām hačāma aθa^{n}hya*[44], *xšapavā raučapativā, ava akunavaya^{n}tā* »was ihnen von mir gesagt wurde, nachts oder tags, das taten sie«, DB I 22 *haya arīka āha, avam ufrastam apṛsam* »der nicht loyal (?) war, den bestrafte ich gründlich«. Er enthält ausser negiertem, wiederum passivischem Verbum (*astiy kṛtam*, hier mit Kopula) und Agensbezeichnung (Genetivus subiectivus *avaišām*) nur die Form *avā*, die

---

[42] Das entspricht ganz der Regel: vgl. Kent, *op. cit.* (Anm. 4), S. 88 § 276. Den Sinn der Bemerkung in der Smittens (*op. cit.*, S. 367 Anm. 7) »Beim P.P.P. fehlt öfter eine Form des Hilfszeitwortes *ah-* 'sein', wodurch sich nicht entscheiden lässt, ob es sich um Zustandsperfekt oder Resultativperfekt handelt« vermag ich nicht zu erkennen.

[43] Zu der Stelle vgl. Verf., Ein altpersisches *ghostword* und das sog. 'inverse *ca*', *Orientalia* N.S. 32 (1963) 437-440.

[44] Zu dieser Normalisierung (mit Wurzelvollstufe) vgl. Verf., Altpersische Minutien, *KZ* 81 (1967) 60f. und 62.

allgemein, wenn auch im einzelnen verschieden, als Adverb betrachtet wird[45]. Hiergegen spricht aber — und dies ist bisher nirgendwo ausdrücklich hervorgehoben worden —, dass der Satz dann eines Subjekts ermangelt, ein Faktum, das für das Passiv *kr̥tam* ansonsten — von dem Sonderfall des hier folgenden *yaθā*-Satzes abgesehen[46] — unerhört ist. Vielleicht war dies der Grund, der in der Smitten[47] das angenommene Adverb hat ablehnen lassen; die von ihm vorgebrachte Erklärung der Form als »Neutrum *Plural* [Hervorhebung von mir: R. Schm.] des Pronomens [scil.: *ava-* »jener«], bei dem die Endlänge nach Analogie des Relativpronomens im Nominativ Plural fem. und neutr. *tayā* ... eingetreten ist« scheitert aber selbstverständlich an der fehlenden Kongruenz mit *kr̥tam*[48]. Wer ein Subjekt für den Hauptsatz dieses § 59 sucht, kann aber — so scheint mir — *avā* auch als Nom. Sing. ntr. zu dem Stamm **avant-* »so viel, so gross« auffassen: Diese Kasusform zu diesem Stamm, der avest. *avant-* »tantus«[49] entspricht, muss natürlich nach aller Regel ar. **avat* > altpers. **<a-va>* */avat/* lauten[50]. Doch dieses */avat/* »so gross, so viel« hätte in der Schrift zusammenfallen müssen mit dem häufig bezeugten <a-va> /avad/ »jenes, das« (:*ava-*). Als Behelf zur graphischen Differenzierung der beiden Formen, die phonetisch und phonemisch wohlunterschieden waren, /avad/ und /avat/, erscheint eine 'Pleneschreibung' <a-va-a> statt <a-va> für die zweite Form durchaus denkbar; im Prinzip ist dies nichts anderes als die Unterscheidung des Genetivs <ča-i-ša-

---

[45] E. Benveniste, Études sur le vieux-perse, *BSL* 47 (1951) 31 f. (dazu vgl. Eric P. Hamp, Old Persian *avā*, *KZ* 75, 1958, 239), akzeptiert von Brandenstein-Mayrhofer, *op. cit.*, S. 108 und Hinz, *op. cit.* (Anm. 7), S. 126; Kent, *op. cit.* (Anm. 4), S. 172 a u.a. halten dagegen an der Annahme eines Steinmetzfehlers <a-va-a> /avā/ für <a-va-θa-a> /avaθā/ »so« fest.

[46] Als modale Konjunktion kann *yaθā* (ebenso wie avest. *yaθā̆* und ved. *yáthā*) mit einem Demonstrativpronomen, also gegebenenfalls dem Subjekt oder Objekt eines Satzes, korrelieren!

[47] In der Smitten, *op. cit.*, S. 366 ab.

[48] Ob die sicher grundsprachlich-indogermanische Regel τὰ ζῷα τρέχει ('singularisches Prädikat bei neutralem pluralischem Subjekt') auch fürs Altpersische galt, lässt sich mangels Zeugnissen weder beweisen noch widerlegen.

[49] Vgl. Christian Bartholomae, *Altiranisches Wörterbuch* (Strassburg 1904, Berlin ²1961), Sp. 174f.; besonders hinweisen möchte ich auf die Belege für Korrelation mit *yaθa*!

[50] Benveniste, *op. cit.* (Anm. 45), S. 31 f. versuchte nachzuweisen, dass »la finale *-ā* répond à i[ndo-]ir[anien] *-ant*«; als Stütze führte er die Nominative *tunuvā* »stark« und *ạrtāvā* »selig (o.ä.)« an, die aber natürlich Dehnstufe zeigen und auf ar. **-ānt-s* zurückgehen.

pa-i-ša > /čišpaiš/ (AmH 3, DBa 8) vom Nominativ < ča-i-ša-pa-i-ša >
/čišpiš/ (DB I 5 ergänzt, DBa 8) durch Einführung von <a> in
< ča-i-ša-pa-a-i-ša > = quasi */čišpāiš/ (DB I 5f.) [51].
Der *avaišām* angegliederte Relativsatz steht ganz regelgemäss voran
(vgl. die Beispiele oben S. 191; er ist ein Nominalsatz (ohne Kopula
also) — *tayaiy paruvā xšāyaθiyā* »die die früheren Könige (waren)«—,
auch dies etwas ganz Geläufiges. So verbleibt nur die Zeitangabe
yātā āha noch in das Satzganze einzufügen: Hierbei handelt es sich
um einen temporalen Konjunktionalsatz, eingeleitet mit der erst jüngst
von Hauri[52] überzeugend erklärten Konjunktion *yātā* »solange (als),
(solange) bis«, der sachlich natürlich — als Gegenstück zu der
temporalen Umstandsbestimmung *hamahyāyā θarda* — in den Hauptsatz
gehört. Das würde bedeuten, dass der eigentliche Hauptsatz schon
mit diesen Worten einsetzt, dass also die Zeitangabe dem Demonstrativum vorausgeht. Dafür scheint mir der bereits oben S. 191 zitierte
Satz DB I 19f. eine Parallele zu bieten: [*taya*]*šām hačāma aθa^{n}hya*,
xšapavā raučapativā, ava akunavaya^{n}tā. Hier ist die temporale Umstandsbestimmung *xšapavā raučapativā* in ihrer Beziehung zu den anderen
Satzteilen zumindest ambivalent: (a) »was ihnen von mir nachts oder
tags gesagt wurde, das taten sie« oder (b) »was ihnen von mir gesagt
wurde, das taten sie nachts oder tags«. Der Gesamtzusammenhang
scheint jedoch der Interpretation (b) den Vorzug zu geben, da es
hier um die Ergebenheit der Reichsländer geht, die dem Dareios
patiyāiša (wohl: »entgegenschritten«), die seine *ba^{n}dakā* (»Vasallen«)
waren und ihm Tribut brachten. Der Nachdruck liegt hier auf dem
Verhalten der Länder, nicht dem des Herrschers, und in diesem Kontext
ist dann auch eine Betonung dessen sinnvoll, dass sie Tag und Nacht
des Grosskönigs Befehle ausführten. Die Zeitangabe *xšapavā raučapativā*
wäre darnach in den Hauptsatz zu ziehen, die Parallele mit der
Satzstruktur der hier behandelten Stelle wäre vollkommen.

---

[51] Vgl. dazu Kent, *op. cit.* (Anm. 4), S. 14 § 24, S. 22 § 53, S. 61f. § 179.IV.

[52] Vgl. Hauri, *op. cit.*, S. 52, wonach *yātā* kontrahiert ist aus **yāvatā*, adverbiellem
Instrumentalis zu ar. **yāvant-* »wie gross, wie viel« und Gegenstück zu avest. *yauuata*
»dass.«.

MARTIN SCHWARTZ

PROTO-INDO-EUROPEAN √ĜEM

A verb *ōzām-* 'to condemn' is found for Sogdian in the three scripts employed for this language. The word first became known in the Estrangela alphabet, *'wz'm-* translating Syr. √*ḥwb* Pa'. in *Matt.* XX, 18 (*ST i* 17, 4). Later the same spelling was found in texts in Manichean characters (see *GMS* §§ 258 fn. 1; 584). A Nestorian attestation in Sogdian letters, *'wẓ-'m-* (again for Syr. √*ḥwb* Pa'.) is now evidenced in a translation of *Psalm* v, 10, which I have recently discussed in describing the Sogdian Psalter [1].

Khwarezmian, which is closely related to Sogdian, has *'wz'cyk* f. 'culpability, crime, offense' (= Arab. *janiyya, jarīma*, see *Muq.* 152, 8 *bis*; 441, 3). I had analysed this as representing *ūzāt-cīk*, envisioning an OIr. alternation **awa-zata-* (in the Sogd. past stem, Man. *'wzt-GMS* § 838) ∼ **awa-zāta-*, parallel to *yata-* ∼ *yāta-* [2]. A refinement is now possible: *'wz'cyk* f. should be added to the feminine abstract nouns treated by D.N. MacKenzie which have *-cyk* (< **-tīkā*, OIr. *-ti-/-tay-*) replacing, as it were, the *-t/d(y)k* of the past participle [3]. Thus *'wz'cyk* (*ūzācīk*) represents OIr. **awa-zāti-*, to whose *-ā-* I shall later return. For the semantic development cf. Lat. *crimen* 'accusation, reproach' > 'crime'.

---

[1] *Altorientalische Forschungen I (Schriften zur Geschichte und Kultur des alten Orients 11*, Akademie der Wissenschaften der DDR, Zentralinstitut für Alte Geschichte und Archäologie), 1974, 258.

[2] *ZDMG* 120/2, 1970, 304. I take this opportunity to set aright an unfortunate series of errors on p. 298 of that article, relating to 'saddle' etc. One must distinguish *(')stry(y)k* m. 'saddle' (*Muq.* 39, 6; 85, 7 *bis*; 346, 4) from *'stryd* f. 'saddle-*bow*' 39, 7, transcribed correctly by Benzing. The latter form may be from **strayd-*, cf. Khot. **straṃj-* 'to stiffen', **pastraṃj-* 'to restrain' < PIE √*streng* (Emmerick, SGS 79, 135). The foregoing observations I owe to D.N. MacKenzie. While the *-t-* of *(')stry(y)k* may be due to *'stryd*, one may still compare Pashto *sary*, Oss. *sary*, Arab. (< Pers.) *sarj*, Aram.-Syr. *srg*. The latter form shows that Sogd. *sayr-* is metathetic; this eliminates the possibility of derivation from √*sag*, which I also suggested for Khwar. *sym* f. 'camel's saddle' = 'pack-saddle' *Muq.* 47, 5 and 6; 216, 5. What may now be mentioned as the correct etymology of *sym* is of great interest for the history of material culture: *sym* is from Greek σάγμα 'pack-saddle' (whence also Late Latin *sagma*, Germ. *Saum-* etc.). For the pack-saddle of donkeys (and horses) Khwar. uses Pers. *pālān*, see *Muq.* 48, 6 and cf. 37, 1.

[3] *BSOAS* XXXV/1, 1972, 69.

The expected imperf. of Sogd. *ōzām-* is *wāzām-* (*wā-* < **awa-* plus augment), which is attested twice as Man. *w'z'm-* (*GMS* §§ 584; 618). The same form occurs in a Nestorian text, a homily of unidentified authorship published by O. Hansen, *BST ii* 905, 16-32. Here however *w'z'm* has a meaning quite unlike 'condemn'. Since little of the text was correctly understood by Hansen, it is worthwhile to examine the larger context in which the relevant passage. Lines 23b-25a, occurs[4]. LL. 16-23 run as follows:

pr bγ'nyq z'rcnwqy' qy qw sfrywn s' 't (17) pr p'tfr's qy pcyγ'z q'yn 't nwḥ qty'qy ẉyt 't sdwmy (18) [mr]txmyt cn wšnt bẓyqt 'rqty pyd'r oo nwṣ̌y 't z'rcnwq xypθ'wnt (19) bγy ywny cn sf̣rywny ̈γ'z mšt'y xypθ z'rcnwqy' 't šṭytq o 't ny (20) n̩yšt xypθ dstwb'ry 't n̩yst ny wnty xypθ ptqrw o 'y cntn xcy (21) bγ'nyq z'rcnwqy' qy ny prbyrt by o ̈'dm pr xypθ ryž ̈x̣yr pr frm'n (22) 't pθr'wnc xypθ γwbty' o 't bγy pr xypθ z'rcnwqy' šw ptymync (23) w'nc'nw npxštw sty qt wnt' bγy crmnyt qwrθyt 't šw ptymync o

"On God's mercy to creation, and on the punishment which Cain received and the generations of Noah's household[5] and the people

---

[4] The readings here given are based on Hansen's transcription (H.) but with the following differences in word division: L. 17 *qty'qy*: H. *qty' qy*; L. 24 *w'zms*: H. *w'z ms*; L. 28 *ptywšn' qt*: H. *ptywšn'qt*; L. 29 *br' xw*: H. *br'xw*. The crucial *w'zms* was noted without comment by the late W. B. Henning alongside L. 24 in his personal copy of *BST II*. Dr. Gershevitch suggested *br' xw* to me in 1967.

[5] The phrase 'generations of the household of Noah' is based on *Gen.* VI, 9 ('the generations of Noah') and VII, 1 ('go into the ark, you and all your household, for I have seen that you are righteous before me in this generation').

qty'q 'house(hold)' = Syr. **bayt-* is the first Chr. attestation of the word spelled *kty'k(h)* in Buddhist texts, e.g. *γn'kh ZY kty'kh* 'house and home' *P2*, 1064-1065; *cnn kty'ky nyẓty, cnn kty'kyh nyẓ'yt* 'gone / goes from household state', Pali *agārasmā* (*anagāryaṃ*) *pabbajito* (see H.W. Bailey, *BSOAS* XIII/4, 1951, 937); *kty'kδ'r'y Vim.* 126 etc. '*gṛhapati-*' *GMS* § 1136. Misled by Hansen's reading *qty'* (*qy*) Benveniste suggested 'œuvre' (*JA* 1959, 131) which would leave the rest of the sentence inexplicable.

The word *wyt* 'generations' (Syr. *dārē) occurs again in L. 27 of our text. I had established the meaning in my doctoral dissertation, where I showed that *pr s't wyt BST II* 888, 7 renders *bklhwn dï* 'per omnia sæcula' in the Syriac parallel text, and I suggested that the sg. was *wē < OIr. **wayah-*, cognate of Vedic *váyas-* 'vitality, vital force, period of life, age', comparing the semantic development seen in Vedic *ayu-* 'vitality, vital force, duration of life, longevity'; Av. *āyu-* 'duration of life' and 'duration' in general; Khwar. *'y* (with geminate *y*) 'lifetime' *Muq.* 490, 5; MPers. *ē* 'time, epoch'; Sogd. *āy* 'lifetime, period, epoch, eternity' (Benveniste, *JA* 1959, 131), *āikun* 'eternal'. Subsequently Nicholas Sims-Williams brilliantly noted the possibility that the sg. of *wyt* could instead by *wy*, which may be attested in the meaning 'generation' at *BST II* 885, 15 (*Asia Major* XVIII/1, 1973, 98). See further Appendix I [and Addenda].

of Sodom, because of their evil works[6]. The eternal and merciful Lord God right from the beginning of creation showed His mercy, and shows it still. And He does not destroy His handiwork, nor does He annihilate His own image[7]. Ah, how great is God's mercy, which cannot be described! Adam, through his desire, transgressed[8] the commandment and his glory was forfeited[9]. And God in His mercy clothed him, as it is written, 'He made leathern shirts and clothed him'".

From the second half of L. 25 the text continues:

't ptyγwnt xypθ ptq'rw qy wy(d)sntnyq [??] (26) b' o yw'r cw pr ptm'q w'bmsqn bγ'nyq šyr'qty' qy qw ywtr s' (27) xyd qy pr pnmcyqt wyt 't byd'ncyqt 't pr pšycyqt wyrxc' qt' (28) q'mysq nwqr 'y ptγwšn' qt γrḅy bγ'nyq šyr'qty' c'nw ny (29) q'mt pr 'ḍy bžyq 8 ywxs' cn q'yn w'xš p't mnq br' xw [q'yn] (30) 't ptyxw'y hbyl xypθ br't o

"And he *covered[10] His image, which was ... But what can I say in

---

[6] Hansen did not realize that this entire sentence, a rubric, corresponds almost verbatim to the Syriac title in the margin. Hansen, p. 903, gives the latter in Estrangela type as follows:

(1) .[ ].w' dṣ.[ ].ryth w'l msm bryš' dbblw q'yn
(2)]y q'ïšy sdwm mṭl 'qyrwthwn oo

He translated this as '(1)... und über die Strafe Babels und (?) Kains (2)... und der Leute von (?) Sodom wegen ihrer Vernichtung...'. Obviously q'ïšy is a misprint for w'ïšy. With a very few minor changes in the readings one may restore the title thus:

(1) ['l rḥmwth d'l](h)' dṣ[yd] bryth w'l msm bryš' dqblw q'yn
(2) [wdï̈' dbyth dnw](ḥ) w'ïšy sdwm mṭl 'qyrwthwn oo

'On the mercy of God which came unto His creation, and on the punishment Cain and the generations of Noah's household and the people of Sodom received because of their *infamy'. The similarity of the Syr. to the Sogd. was obscured by the introduction of Babel (which is bbyl and not bbylw in Syriac) and the misunderstanding of 'qyrwt-, which is not 'destruction' but the abstract of 'qyr' ('əqīrā), defined by Brockelmann (Lex. Syr. 1928 ed., 544a) as 'delendus, nefandus'.

[7] This sentence was correctly translated by Benveniste, JA 1955, 316. To his collection of forms related to dstwb'ry add now the data I give in Altorientalische Forschungen I, 260. If δstβ'r in δstβ'r ''s- SCE 375 is indeed 'authority', comparison with MPers. dastwar suggests that the Sogd. is δastβār; cf. Man. δstβry nyy's- cited GMS § 1131 fn. 1. [δstβ'r 'authority' Mugh B-γ, R 3].

[8] The basic meaning of āxēr- is 'go' (see e.g. the examples in the St. George Passion); 'xyr pr therefore 'went against', cf. Man. šm'r- pr- 'to plot against', γw'nkryy x- pr 'sin against', prw ... nw'rṭ 'against the exhortations' GMS § 1626.

[9] pθr'wnc: f. of a poss. adj. in -āwand(ē) (GMS § 1091 and cf. § 1092) from *pθr- < Av. pərəθa-'Ausgleichung, Sühne, Strafe'; sugg. Gershevitch 1968, letter. (See Addenda.]

[10] The phrase refers again to God's clothing of Adam, whom God created in His

(proper?) measure of that Divine Grace(,) which poured forth on the first, middle[11], and last generations? Or[12] do you want to know now, o listener, how God's Grace does not desire evil for anyone? Learn from the (scriptural) statement on Cain; [Cain] used deceit and slew his brother Abel...."

We may now examine the intervening passage, LL. 23b-25a:

ny (24) w'zms xw bɣy 'dmy qty'qy ɣnt'q o yw'r w'z'm ɣnt'q pr šyrw (25) w'nc'nw ptɣ'mbry w'xš o

Here we have not only w'z'm but also w'zms, which should be the imperfect of *'wzms-, i.e. *ōzams-, passive to ōzām-, which relationship would parallel patyams-: patyām-; ōrams-: ōrām-; see further GMS § 828. But if we apply to our passage the meaning shown for ōzām- by the attestations mentioned at the outset of this study, we arrive at the absurd translations "God was not condemned by the evil... but He condemned evil by good...". The context requires the following translation: "God was not (properly) requited by the evil of Adam's *deed[13], but He compensated (for) evil by good, as per the statement

---

image (ptq'rw, as in L. 20). ptyɣwnt hapax, imperf. of *ptɣwnt-. √gaud with preverb pati- in Sogd. as Man. ptɣwδ- (past stem Chr. ptɣwst-) 'to hide, conceal'. The latter word may be denominative from patɣōδ, attested as B. ptɣ'wδ 'covering' Dhu. 20; 105; 242 (Skt. nivaraṇa- or āvaraṇa-, Tib. trad. 'obscuration'), since √gaud usually is manifested in verbs as *gunda- throughout Iranian (see the forms given by Bailey, Khot. Texts VI, 27-28). Thus *ptɣwnt- agrees in its stem with Man. "ɣwnd- 'to cover', B. pɣwnt-, Khwar. *baɣwind- 'to uncover' < *apa-gundaya-, Chr. *niɣwe/ind- 'to dress someone', Khwar. *nɣwind- 'cover, hide' < *ni-gundaya- (cf. Henning, "Mitteliranisch", 117), intrans. B. nɣ'wnd-, Yaghnobi nuɣūnt- 'dress oneself', prob. < *ni-gunda-. (See further Appendix II)

[11] Read myd'ncyq? Hansen's byd'ncyt is highly suspect, since m is often easily misread as b, and the BST II MS. has myd'ncyq at 901, 24 and myd'n at 865, 15; 924, 19 and myd'ny at 850, 11; 852, 62; 869, 56; 883, 11; 910, 6; 912, 21; and 925, 10. But βyδ'ncyk 'middle, central' is cited in connection with Yaghnobi bidón(čik) etc. 'id.' by M.S. Andreev and E.M. Peščereva, Jagnobskie teksty, 230. S. βyδ'ncyk (which could mean 'pertaining to a bridle'!) is unknown to me. If it exists in the meaning 'central' it would support Hansen's reading. But such a Sogdian word would give Yaghn. *vidón'. The b in the Yaghn. form must be dissimilated directly from m; cf. Ormuri biyân 'waist' (Morgenstierne, IIFL I, 338). A parallel development may have taken place in Sogdian, where βēδān(čik) could have continued alongside meδān(čik) under influence of βēk(čik) 'out(er)'.

[12] qt' i.e. katā, found throughout PST II in place of earlier katār, cf. sār > sā (s'). [See Addenda].

[13] qty'qy error for qty (nom. qty') under influence of ɣnt'q and qty'qy L. 17? Or sic 'household'?

of the Apostle"[14]. Thus, in addition to ōzām- 'to condemn', Sogd. had ōzām- 'to requite, repay, compensate'.

A search for an OIr. word showing √zam in the latter sense leads to Av. zəmanā 'reward, payment, wages' (3 attestations; Pahl. mizd; see Bartholomae, AIrWb. col. 1690-1691). This is represented in later Iranian by Mugh Sogd. z'mn'k, Pashto zəman, zamne 'payment, wages'[15], to which H.W. Bailey has added Khot. ysaṃtha (/zanθa-/) 'payment for use' (JRAS 1972, 110). Bailey goes further and uses the Iranian root to explain Gr. γαμέω 'marry' as originally referring to the "'payment' by the suitor for the bride, the earliest Indo-European marriage practice".

Bailey's interesting hypothesis faces certain difficulties. For the bridegroom's payment to the bride one finds Gr. ἕδνα (pl.; Hom. ἔεδνα), cognate with OEng. weotuma 'id.' etc., and inseparable from words in the various IE languages referring to marriage and deriving from PIE *wed(h)- 'to lead'[16]. There is also the problem of the relationship of γαμέω to Gr. γαμβρός 'son-in-law (dialectally also 'bridegroom'), brother-in-law, father-in-law', and also 'a male relative'; the question of the relationship of both words to OInd. jāmātar-, Av. zāmātar- 'son-in-law', Av. zāmaoya- 'brother(?) of the son-in-law', Pashto zūm 'son-in-law'; OInd. jāmā 'daughter-in-law'; Lat. gener 'son-in-law' etc. A further complication is the meaning of OInd.

---

[14] w'xš is a calque on Syr. melləta 'word' = 'Biblical passage', as also e.g. at BST II 898, 11 and in L. 25 of our homily. In the present instance, as in the latter reference, we have a broad allusion or paraphrase, rather than a direct citation. By 'the Apostle' surely Paul is meant; the author had in mind the passage concerning Adam in Rom. V, 14-21, but conflated this, via the motifs of divine repayment, requital of evil and substitution of good for evil, with the text of Rom. XII, 19-21.

[15] The connection of ōzām- with these words first became clear to me during a trip to Cambridge in 1971. Shortly after I realized that ōzām- can mean 'to repay' I asked Dr. Gershevitch if he knew of an etymon suiting this sense, and he immediately produced V.A. Livšic's connection of Mugh z'mn'k with zəmāna and zamnə (Sogd. dok. Mug II, 34).

[16] Cf. E. Benveniste, Indo-European Language and Society (1971 trans. by E. Palmer of Le vocabulaire des institutions indo-européennes), 194. The etymon may be more accurately stated as √wed; the -dh- of OInd. vadhū- may be due to the influence of vahate (Mayrhofer, KEW s.v.), although other possibilities may be mentioned: aspirating laryngeal (cf. W. Winter, KZ 1962, 32 on the Toch.); influence of PIE √wedh 'bind' connect, yoke', whence OInd. vivadha- and vadhra-; or, least likely, influence of PIE √wadh 'pledge', whence Eng. wed. [See also J. Puhvel, Language 1953, 23; Winter, Evidence for Laryngeals, 113].

jāmi- : in ŖgVedic 'related as brother and sister'; in Classical Sanskrit 'daughter-in-law'. Moreover both Ir. *z* and Gr. *γ* are ambiguous as to their PIE origin; *z* may be from either PIE $*\hat{g}$ or $*\hat{g}h$, whereas *γ* may be from $*\hat{g}$ or $*g$. Thus in lack of independent evidence *zam-* and γαμέω are not necessarily related.

I believe that a resolution of these issues begins with a closer look at Sogd. *ōzām-*. The different meanings 'compensate' and 'condemn' should not be taken as indicating two homophonic verbs *ōzām-*, but rather two aspects of the fundamental meaning of a single verb. 'Condemn' would be 'force an indemnity or expiation', i.e. 'cause compensation' for a negative act. The derivation of *zəmanā* from the root of *ōzām-* is thus in accord with E. Benveniste's general conclusion that in the earlier stages of Indo-European societies, terms for 'wages' were developed from words meaning 'to compensate'[17]. But Benveniste's researches are of much greater relevance to the issue at hand. He lucidly demonstrated that where Bartholomae assumed two Iranian roots *par*, one meaning 'gleich machen' (further 'vergleichen; gleich machen eine Schuld'), and the other 'verurteilen', there is in reality only one root, cognate with Lat. *pār*[18]. Av. *pairyete* meaning both 'is compensated' and 'is condemned' provides a precise parallel for the semantic range of *ōzams-*. One may now define OIr. √*zam* as 'to be par, to be equal', of which $*(-)zāma(ya)-$ would be the causative stem.

The connection of Iranian √*par* with Lat. *pār* may serve further as an illuminating parallel for penetrating the history of √*zam*. As an adjective *pār păris* means 'equal, matching', and as a neuter noun 'a pair'. This allows the consideration that OIr. √*zam* may originally have had a concrete meaning 'to match, to pair'. Confirmation is found in RV *vijā́man-* 'paired, matching, twin' (of the joints, *paruṣi*, of the knees and feet 7, 50, 2). The *vi-* here may have the original sense of 'twain, in two'; one may also compare the *ví-* of RV *víjāmi-* and *vijāmā́tṛ* (both hapax), whose function seems uncertain. The PIE etymon is therefore $*\hat{g}em-$. OInd. *-jāman-*, which is best derived from $*\hat{g}ome/on-$, is close in meaning to Lat. *geminus*, which may be a thematicization of an *-n-* stem $*\hat{g}eme/on-$. A parallel thematicization of an *-n-* stem is offered by Middle Irish *emon* m., *emuin* f. 'pair of twins',

[17] Benveniste, *op. cit.*, 137.
[18] Benveniste, *op. cit.*, 145-148. Further relevant Iranian forms in Bailey, *Khot. Texts IV*, 56. [See also Fn. 27]

and perhaps Gothic *ibns* 'even', etc., all < PIE √*yem* (whence also Indo-Iranian *yama-* 'twin'). One may suppose that PIE √*yem* and √*ĝem* had come to overlap partially in meaning. Perhaps the earliest words for twinship were from √*ĝem* under the influence of which √*yem*, originally meaning 'to hold, grasp, curb' (thus in Indo-Iranian; cf. also OInd. *yáma-* 'bridle'), came to furnish parallel nominal formations for 'twin'.

The association of √*yem* and √*ĝem* in Indo-Iranian also explains the long *ā* seen in Khwar. *'wz'cyk* < OIr. **awa-zāti-*. For PIIr. one must reconstruct a base *yamH*, since we have OInd. *seṭ* forms (RV *yamīmahi, yamitavāi* etc.) and ppptc. *yāta-* in both Indic and Iranian, against forms in Indic and Iranian without the laryngeal. Thus a **-zāt-* alongside the earlier **-zat-* (in Sogd. *ōzat-*) would be by analogy to *-yāt-* alongside *-yat-*, the *aniṭ* √*yam* itself possibly secondary. Further evidence for √*ĝem* 'to pair' in early Indic may be found in *ájāmi-*, which according to Robert Goldman's analysis of *RV* 10, 10, 9-10 means 'not paired' (rather than 'not fitting for brother and sister')[19].

It is true that the text in which this word is found belongs to one of the later parts of the RgVeda, but the myth with which the passage with *ájāmi-* deals, the possibility of incest ᵒbetween Yama and Yamī, is of Indo-Iranian origin[20], so that the connection of *ájāmi-* with *yamá-* and *yamī́* may conserve a *topos* of great antiquity. The semantic generalization of *jāmí-* *'paired, twin' to 'related as brother and sister, consanguineous, related' is due on the one hand to the replacement of the old functions of *jām°* < √*ĝem-* by *yam°* < √*yem*, and on the other by association with *jan(i)-/jā-* 'be born', cf. Av. *hu-zāmi-* 'easy birth'. Cl. Skt. *jāmí-* could be due to influence of *jāmātṛ-* 'son-in law' and perhaps *jani-* 'woman' (< **gʷen-*) and/or *jā-* 'progeny' etc., or else a continuation of an old feminine to **jāma-* ('son-in-law', whence *jāmātṛ-*; see below), this *jāmi-* (older *jāmī*?) being therefore a (dialectal?) homonym of Ved. *jāmí-* which it eventually replaced.

With the establishment of a PIE root √*ĝem* with the sense of 'to match, (be in a) pair' the etymology of Gr. γαμέω (fut. γαμῶ, aor. ἔγημα) and γάμος[21] becomes clear. The basic idea is simply

[19] *Journal of the Oriental Institute of Baroda* XVIII/4, 1969, 293.
[20] As attested by the (*Avestan) myth of the incest of Jam and Jamīg in Pahlavi sources. See A. Christensen, *Les types du premier homme ... II*, 1934, 29-30; 35-39.
[21] The reader is advised to consult as prolegomenon the discussions of γαμέω,

'to form a pair, to mate with'[22]; one need hardly refer e.g. to Lat. *pār paris* m. 'spouse' etc. for a parallel.

One may ask: if √*ĝem* meant 'marry' in PIE, why is the verb attested only in Greek? Since the meaning 'marry' would have been only one of the meanings of the root, and not the fundamental one, one should rather ask why the verb—with whatever meaning—is limited to Greek and Iranian. I believe that the elimination of √*ĝem* from most of Indo-European is due to the encroachment of two other roots, each differing from √*ĝem* by only one phonological feature, and each having meanings somewhat similar to it. The first of these etyma, √*yem*, has already been mentioned. The second one figures in a number of wrong explanations of γαμέω, γαμβρός etc., as well as of Lat. *geminus*: √*gem*.

The three roots likely had originally quite distinct meanings. √*yem* is attested as a verb only in Indo-Iranian *yamati* and its 'inchoative', for these, taken with their primary noun derivatives (apart from *yama-* 'twin', which was explained above) we have only the meanings 'hold, restrain, keep fast'. Gr. ἥμερός 'tame', if it belongs here, would agree with this meaning. √*gem* would have its original semantic range illustrated by OChSlav. *žъmo* 'I compress', RussChSl. *gomola* 'clumps', Norw. *kamsa* 'to knead', *kumla* 'a clump', Gr. γέμω 'am full', Umbr. *gomia*, kumiaf 'gravidas'; here too may well belong Lith. *gìmti* (*giñti*) 'be born', if it is due to a cross of √*gem* as 'be pregnant' and √*ĝen(H)* 'give birth'.

The same root with meaning 'press' has been noted for Iranian in Parth. *'bj'm-* 'to torture', *'bg'm* 'torment, agony', Sogd. *'wy'm* 'id.'[23]. One may add to this group Khwar. **'nc'my-*: *'nct-* 'to cause anxiety, frighten', see e.g. *Muq.* 307, 5 and 343, 7, and, with the more basic mg., Wakhi *wεzεm-*, *wazεm-* 'to express, squeeze out' (Morgenstierne, *IIFL II*, 551), with *-z-* from **-ǰ-* as in Wakhi *wuzem-* 'to

γάμος and γαμβρός in P. Chantraine, *Dictionnaire étymologique de la langue grecque I*, 1968, *s.vv.* and Hj. Frisk, *Griechisches etymologisches Wörterbuch*, *s.vv.*

[22] It now appears that γαμέω in the mg. 'have sexual intercourse with a woman', which is not only the sole meaning of the verb in presentday spoken Greek but is also well attested alongside 'marry' in the ancient language may be explained, with 'marry', simply from the basic meaning 'to form a couple with, *mate with* a woman', rather than as a euphemistic or ironic development of 'marry'. On the non-marital meanings of γαμέω see L. Robert, *Rev. de Phil.* XLI/1, 77-81; for Homeric Greek, *Od.* 1. 36 is cited p. 78 Fn. 3.

[23] Szemerényi, *ZDMG* 1951, 219; Gershevitch, *Studia... Pagliaro II* 177-178.

bring' < *-jāmaya-, to Parth. žām- 'to conduct' etc.; wɛzɛm- is therefore distinct in etymology from Wakhi vizam-, Sariqoli vizāmb- 'to rub to powder' < OIr. √zamb 'to crush'. OInd. jāmarya-, adj. referring to milk in the distended udders of a cow (RV 4, 3, 9) may now be taken as 'fit to be squeezed out' or, less likely, 'bloating (the udder)'[24].

A departure from the dominant mg. 'press, crowd, squeeze, bunch up' is shown by forms in Greek and Celtic: Hom. γέντο 'grasped', Cypriot ἀπόγεμε · ἄφελκε (Hes.), Salaminian ὕγγεμος · συλλαβή (Hes.); and MIrish gemel, Welsh gefyn 'a fetter'. The meanings 'grasp' and 'fetter' may be explained by contamination of √gem by √yem. In √yem the senses of 'pressure', 'suppression', and 'attachment' were latent in its essential meaning of 'hold, certain, bridle, curb'. A bridge between √gem and √yem was provided by √ĝem, which had great phonological similarity to both roots. Semantically the association of the roots was aided by the idea of 'bring two objects together' inherent in √gem.

An interesting illustration of the association of √gem and √yem may be seen in Arm. čim 'bridle'. Arm. č- usually is found only in words of Iranian origin, but there exists no Iranian etymon for the word in question. One cannot accept the derivation of čim directly from √gem (found e.g. in Pokorny IEW s.v. gem-), since PIE g regularly uields Arm. k. Structural and etymological considerations point to č deriving from a PIE cluster *gy[25]. One may accordingly reconstruct pre-Arm. *gyemo-, which can be explained as the old word for 'bridle' (whence also Vedic yáma- 'id.') blended with *gem-.

It would appear from the examples cited that the erosion of √ĝem by √yem and √gem began already in late Indo-European; the process was carried further by the merger of ĝ and g in some dialects. A further early factor in the disappearance of √ĝem in the sense of 'wed' was due to similarity with √ĝen(H), cf. above on the Albanian, Baltic, Slavic (and Latin) words for 'son-in-law'. The same was probably true for the verb 'to wed' in Indo-Iranian, where however the -m- was preserved in 'son-in-law', perhaps because of

---

[24] Earlier explanations of jāmarya- have involved words for 'earth' and 'kindred', see Mayrhofer KEW s.v.

[25] See R. Godel, Current Trends in Linguistics (ed. T.A. Sebeok), Vol. VI, 1970, 147. A. Meillet, Esquisse d'une grammaire comparée de l'arménien classique, 2nd. ed. 1936, 29, gives only ačem 'grow' with -č- < *-gy- as example of original Arm. č; see Pokorny, IEW 773 (ačem < *əgiō).

the partial maintenance of the root in the sense of 'pair, match'. Even this meaning was generally obsolescent in the Old Iranian period, where (apart from the fixed nominal derivatives with economic reference) it may be assumed only for Sogdiana and Chorasmia, surviving in Middle Iranian as a verb only in Sogdian, where it had the meaning 'compensate' in the ethical sphere.

Our etymology serves to show the γ of γαμέω has *ĝ, which had been uncertain, especially in view of the various attempts to relate the word to *γεμ- 'to grasp' < PIE √gem, on which see below with Fn. 26 (where the formation of γαμέω is also discussed).

Against Benveniste (ref. in my Fn. 16), who maintained that Proto-Indo-European had no word for 'marry', we may now claim our √ĝem to have been that very word, for it explains the older IE terms for 'son-in-law'. It has long been a matter of common consent that PIIr. *ẑāmāt(a)r- is based on *ẑāma- (whence also Av. zāmaoya- < *zāma-wya- prob. 'son-in-law's brother', Pashto zūm 'son-in-law', cf. Parachi zâm id.) to which was added the kinship suffix found in *bhrāt(a)r- etc. The vocalism of γαμβρός would be, as is often proposed, due to the influence of γαμέω and γάμος, while for Lat. gener the explanation by contamination with words like gens and genus holds good: the -e- may have already arisen from the pre-Lat. pres. < √ĝem.

It is reasonable to assume that the Greek and Latin words go back to an old form in *-ro- (this suffixation may have taken place independently in the two languages). We may reconstruct *ĝom(e)ró-, with -ro- from *sweḱuró- 'husband's father', Gr. ἑκυρός, Lat. socer;

---

[26] Szemerenyi, *Syncope in Greek*, 1964, 187, sees difficulty in the relationship between γαμέω and its 'mysterious' aorist ἔγημα (dial. inscr. εγᾱμαντυ). To account for this he offers an explanation (complicated by assumptions of analogy) whereby ἔγημα is the aorist (with IE lengthened grade) of *γέμω 'seize'. Apart from the semantic problems of such a connection, the aorist paradigm of γαμέω can easily be explained as the regular outcome of a sigmatic aorist based on the (zero grade) stem γαμ-: *ε-γαμ-σα > ἔγημα etc., with no need of confusion with forms from *γεμ- or of IE lengthened grade. He takes γαμέω as denominative from γάμος (p. 187, Fn. 5); against this see Chantraine, *DELG* s.v. In spite of the early confusion of denominative and deverbative types of inflection in Greek, γαμέω (with its aorist ἔγημα and its future γαμῶ) is best understood as being of deverbative origin, cf. the forms in Chantraine, *Morphologie historique du grec*, 2nd. ed. §§ 287 and 288; -έω is frequently used to make new presents to old zero grade forms, cf. στυγέω ἔστυγον: ἔστυξα. Szemerenyi is certainly right in rejecting the notion that γαμέω is from a laryngeal base. As has been mentioned above, Ir. √zam is probably also non-laryngeal.

note also the suffix of Gr. πενθερός and Lat. *puer*. Thus one may propose for PIE a single form **ĝomó-* 'he who mates, enters a match', i.e. 'the bridegroom' = 'son-in-law' (the equation found in MPers. *dāmād*, Alb. *dhëndër*, etc.). As uncertain as my solution is, I prefer it to assuming a pre-Gr.-Lat. **ĝm̥ró-*. [Gr. inscr. have γαμερος.] Alb. *dhëndër*, *dhândër*, Lith. *žéntas*, Lett. *znuõts*, and OChSl. *zętĭ* 'son-in-law' probably represent, as many have thought, substitutions of the original etymon by derivatives of √*ĝen(H)* having the sense of 'progenitor' and 'kin'. This took place at an early date, since there are otherwise no clear reflexes of √*ĝen(H)* in these languages.

While γαμβρός can mean not only 'son-in-law' but also 'brother-in-law' and (rarely) even 'father-in-law', and can serve in the general sense of 'kinsman through one's wife', I see no reason to think (with Chantraine, *DELG* 209) that the word was originally 'vague and imprecise'. B. Delbrück gave a clear explanation of how the expansion of meaning would have taken place (*Die indogermanische Verwandtschaftsnamen*, 1889, 522-523, and cf. 517). That γαμβρός expanded its meaning is indicated on the one hand by the meaning 'son-in-law' of the extra-Greek forms, and on the other by the situation of πενθερός. The latter is also a general word for 'kinsman through one's wife'. Here however one may safely assume this broad sense to have been original: we have the cognates OInd. *bandhu-* 'kinsman', Lith. *béndras* 'comrade', and the fact that for PIE no specific word for 'husband's father-in-law' can be reconstructed. The latter meaning is almost always conveyed in Greek by πενθερός, which sometimes is used for 'brother-in-law', but only rarely and late for 'son-in-law'. It is unlikely that PIE had two words for the broader signification. The virtual complementarity of distribution for the specific meanings of πενθερός and γαμβρός indicates again that γαμβρός is fundamentally 'son-in-law'. The fact that γαμβρός means 'bridegroom' in Aeolic and Doric caps this conclusion. The expansion of γαμβρός was aided by the coincidence of -ρός with the productive adj. suffix; γαμβρός could be taken as adj. to γάμος.

The elimination of √*ĝem* as 'to wed' in all languages but Greek was probably motivated also by the ambiguity of the root, which could also mean 'to couple, copulate'. In time √*ĝem* lost out as the word for 'wed' to the root for 'lead' (referring to the transfer to the bridegroom's home), which conveyed the important institutional connotations more clearly than √*ĝem*. The early date of an institutional sense of √*wed(H)* is shown by the words for 'bride's price' in

Germanic and Hellenic (in which languages the verb itself disappeared). It is quite possible that √wed(H) and √ĝem referred to two distinct parts of the marriage rite: the *conduction* (associated with delivery of the bride's price) and the thalamic *consummation*, the actual wedding. In Greek γαμέω survived despite its ambiguity (see Fn. 22), and continued in use for a long period alongside ἄγεσθαι γυναῖκα etc. This may be explained by the association with γάμος 'wedding' (itself perhaps from PIE *ĝómo-, with vocalic influence of γαμέω in avoidance of homophony with γόμος 'load'). By virtue of its specificity γάμος has survived down to present day spoken Greek, in the face of the totally obscene sense to which γαμῶ has become limited. Thus it may be said that Indo-European indeed had a word for 'marry', i.e. 'to wed', which designated an act hallowed by ritual, and which furnished an essential kinship term.

It does not seem possible to find for √ĝem a more basic meaning than 'to pair, match'. This is not true for the etymon of Lat. *par* and Av. √*par*, both involving the notion of 'equalization'. It may first be remarked that PIE √*per* in this sense may be reflected in other languages. Gershevitch, who provides a long discussion of the Av. root and its various derivatives[27], compares Av. *frapərənaoiti* 'declares someone a debtor, declares someone guilty' with OInd. * āpr̥noti, vyāpr̥nute* 'is occupied, engaged in', both having the idea of 'obligation'. From the idea of 'compensation' we may also bring in Vedic *pūrtá-, pūrtí-* 'reward, gift' (the latter formally like Av. *āpərəti-* 'Ausgleichung, Sühne', Sogd. *purč* 'debt'), whose verb fell together with *pr̥n̄áti* 'fills'; this seems preferable to derivation from the idea of 'allotment'[28] or 'portioning'. More clearly yet the Ir. words expressing debt or fault are paralleled by Toch. B *peri*/A *pare* 'debt', attractively compared by K. Schneider (*KZ* LXI, 1939, 253) with Goth. *fairina* 'Schuld'. The Toch. words are hardly from Iranian, which has for 'debt' *-ā- and not *-a- in Av. *pāra-* (: Sogd. *pār*, Psht. *pōr*). Toch. B *e*/A *a*, while possibly reflecting OIr. *a* in a few

---

[27] *The Avestan Hymn to Mithra*, 1967, 245-248. Gershevitch found it difficult to bring Av. √*par* (pres. stem *aipi-pāra-* mid.) 'atone' together with the meanings 'debt' and 'condemnation'. The difficulty is resolved if one takes the middle voice as reflexive of the active sense 'cause payment (for a misdeed)'. The various Iranian meanings were taken together long before Benveniste by Henning and compared with Lat. *par* by Walde-Hofmann (see refs. in Gershevitch, p. 247); thus also Pokorny, *IEW* 817.

[28] F.B.J. Kuiper, *AO* XVI, 313 seq., with Gr. ἔπορον, πεπρωμένος.

scarce examples, cannot be from OIr. or MIr. $\bar{a}$ (nor from MIr. a) and regularly goes back to PIE *o [29].

The idea of 'matching' inherent in these words is but one development of the primitive meaning of PIE /*per(H)* $\sim$ *preH*: 'to move (transitive/ intransitive) beside (i.e. *with focus on the goal*, up to any part but the back)'. This mg. accounts for the entire range of forms, including prepositions (essentially fossilized nouns) [30], given by Pokorny, *IEW* 810-818 [31].

APPENDIX I

'*wayah-
(to Fn. 5)

One could see in *wy' 'generation' the reflex of OIr. *$way\bar{a}$ = Vedic *vayá* 'branch, offspring, progeny', but this is unlikely. Syr. *dārā* means both 'age (epoch)' and 'generation', and it is probable that the use of the Sogd. word in the second mg. is but a calque on the Syriac. In the Sogdian Psalter it is *kwtry* (= B. *kwtr'k*, *kwtry*, also *kwtr*, Man. Chr. *qwtr* 'family' < Skt. *gotra-*) which translates Syr. *dārā* 'generation' in *Ps*. 24, 6. If indeed the Sogd. sg. is *wy'* (*wayā*), this could have developed from *$way\bar{a}h$, the old pl. of *wayah-*, with a restriction on monosyllabic nouns *Cē* (or *Cay-*) as a motivating factor.

Possible evidence for *wayah- is found in the WIr. personal name appearing in Elam. as *Mi-ra-u-da*, *Mi-ru-da*, in Parth. and MPers. as *Wērōd*, in Lat. as *Orodes*, in Arm. as *Viroy*, and in NPers. as *Vērōy*, which Gershevitch traced to an original *$Waya(h)$-rauda-, with a very tentative suggestion of a meaning 'growing into the ether (= exceedingly

---

[29] See my forthcoming article in *Mémorial Jean de Menasce*, ed. P. Gignoux and A. Tafazzoli.

[30] R.S.P. Beekes, *KZ* 87/2, 1973, 215-221.

[31] From this root I would hazard a derivation also of PIE *priyó- (OInd. *priyá-* etc.), which Benveniste, *IE Lang. and Soc.* 262-267, showed to mean basically 'personal, intimate' (whence 'one's own', 'dear', 'beloved', 'noble', 'free' etc.); the etymological sense would be 'that which is at one's side, close by'. This form may be built on a "preposition" (i.e. directional word), cf. Lith. *priē*, OChSl. *pri* 'bei, an'.

---

* But not Proto-Yaghnobi, which shows *t-* and *č-* where Sogdian has resp. *pt-* and *pč-*.

+ For *x* cf. Bal. *hīz*, Oss. *xyzäg*, Khot. *häysä*.

tall)'. As will be presently discussed, the meaning 'ether' for Av. *wayah-, upon which Gershevitch based his conjecture, is suspect. If one attributes to *Wayah- a meaning similar to that of OInd. vayas-, one may translate *Wayah-rauda- as 'growing in vitality' or 'causing vitality to flourish', cf. Vedic vayovŕdh-. In support of this one may compare another OPers. proper name, Wāyaspāra-. According to J. Wackernagel (Kleine Schriften 428), this is a vṛddhi from *wayah- plus *pāra-, 'Kraft fördernd'; H.W. Bailey has explained the same name as 'having an abundance (spāra-) of vitality' (Khotanese Texts VI, 1967, 373). But there is no reason to assume that OIr. *wayah- in these names had the meaning 'vitality'; in light of Sogd. wy(') and the history of āyu- one may take *wayah- as 'duration, longevity' and translate *Wayah-rauda- as 'growing to longevity', and Wāyaspāra- as 'having an abundance of years' (or 'achieving longevity', with -pāra- from Av. ₄√par 'hinübergehen', cf. ₂pāra-, Sogd. -pār 'beyond, over').

It is now possible to hazard the hypothesis that Av. wayąm (var. wayąn) in Ny. 1, 1 means not 'ether, atmosphere', but is a masculine theonym from *wayah- n. 'duration'. Support for this may be seen from the epithet darayō.x^{w}aδāta- 'having long autonomy', which is otherwise attested only for zrwan- 'Time', and which contrasts with x^{w}aδāta- 'autonomous', which qualifies θβāṣa- 'Firmament' and other heavenly entities: the Endless Lights, the Place of Mixture (located between Heaven and Earth), and the Pole-star (Mərəzu). Eventually in Zoroastrianism *Wayah- m. 'Duration' would have been ousted as a divinity of time by Zurwān (for whom R.C. Zaehner, Zurvān 88, proposes a West Iranian homeland) and identified instead with the atmospheric god Wayu, who in turn became a hypostasis of the Void. This may help explain why in the passage attributed by Damascius to Eudemus of Rhodes, the Magi are said to call the first principle variously Space or Time. But a trace of the earlier situation may be found in the phrasing of Gr. Bd. XXVI § 3: ān-īz ī baxšišn pad zamān rasēd kē Wǎy ī Dagrand-Xwadāy hast ī Zurwān zēn hast ī Ōhrmazd 'That which is allotted arrives through time, which is Wǎy of Long Dominion (= wayah- darayō.x^{w}aδāta-), be it the weapon of Zurwān or of Ōhrmazd'. The Avesta shows no evidence of the confusion of Wayu with *Wayah: even in the late text Vd. 19, 13, where Wayu follows 'the Autonomous Firmament (θβāṣa-) and Infinite Time (zrwan-)', his epithet is uparō.kairya- 'of lofty working'. All this is, I think, of great significance for the "dilemma" of the history of Zurwān-specula-tion, raising issues which are worthy of detailed investigation. Suffice it to say for present purposes that the ghost-word *wayah-* m. 'atmosphere' has been laid to rest. The other supposed attestation of such a word was in *Yt. 19*, 82, where *wayą̄m wītāpəm* refers to the place of refuge of the *x^warənah-* from Fraŋrasyan. Already Bartholomae expressed uncertainty that *wayą̄n* means 'Luftraum' (*AIrWb*. col. 1359 *s.v. vayah-* and more skeptically 1441 *s.v. vītāpəm*). H.W. Bailey has most attractively explained the phrase as the '(mountain-) surface of the birds', with *wayą̄n* for *wayą̄m* gen. pl. of *way-* 'bird' (*BSOAS* XXVI, 1963, 86 *seq.*). But Bailey's suggestion that this passage is the basis of *Ny. 1*, 1 is unacceptable.

APPENDIX II

Further on *-gundaya- in Iranian
(to Fn. 11)

An interesting form is Yaghn. *buyúnj/č* inf. *buyúnják*, pptc. *buyúšta* 'to steal'. This is wrongly connected by Andreev-Peščereva 234 with B. *'pyw'yz-* 'to conceal' or alternately with B. *'py'(n)š-* 'to remove'. The latter has *-xaš-* from older *-xarš-* (appearing in B. *py'rš-* '*id.*') from OIr. **karš* (cf. *GMS* § 343 and Andreev-Peščereva 357 s.v. *xaš-*), and cannot be related to the word in question. *'pyw'yž-* (*əpywež-*) < **apa-gauzaya-* is sufficiently different from *buyúnj/č-* and may be excluded as a cognate. Its past stem, Man. and Chr. *pywšt-*, coincided with *buyúšta*, but the latter shows the frequent Yaghnobi replacement of the old past participle, whereby *-j/č-ta* becomes *-š-ta-*; thus e.g. *pač-* 'to cook': *pašta*; *xiníj-* 'to churn': *xiníšta*; and cf. *aryunčók* 'a swing': *aryúšt* 'a dance'. It is difficult to separate *buyúnj/č-* from *buyúnt* 'a pocket' (which shows nominal **-gunda-* as in Sogd. *niyundē* 'overgarment, bedclothes', *GMS* § 963).

This would show a development of **-gundaya-* different from what we have seen in Chr. *nyγwynt* (**niγwe/ind-*). It would attest a dialectal palatalization of **d* found also in Bukharan *'fzγnj* (**'βž/zγnj*) against "Sogdian" *fžγnd* (**βžγnd*) cited by al-Bairūnī as variant names of a plant. As Henning observed, these forms mean 'malodorous'; the Bukharan form **γanj* 'odor' is also found (thrice) in the Buddhist Sogdian text *P 2* (where it is spelled *γnčh*, with *-h* marking feminine gender), this instead of *γnt(h)* i.e. *γand*, the normal Sogdian development; as Henning indicated, both **γanj* and **γand* go back to the same ancient *-i-* stem ("Mitteliranisch", 85). This OIr. etymon is attested in Late Avestan as *ganti-*f., which should represent **gandi-*, cf. OInd. *-gandhi-*, MPers. *gn'g*, Baluchi *gandag. ganti-*, like LAv. *gantuma-* 'wheat', probably has *-nt-* as spelling for **-nd-* due to the MIr. voicing of stops following nasals. An attestation of **γanǰ* seems to be found in the Yaghnobi pass Γančón (*JT* 256), cf. the toponym Γandak in Bamiyan (cited by Morgenstierne, *EVP* 26).

The palatalization of *d* (preserved as a stop after *n*) to *ǰ* should be regarded as connected with the sporadic palatalization of *t* before *i* found e.g. in Sogd. *xrīč* 'buying' < **xrīti-*, and the suffix *-kč* < **-kṛti-* against *(ə)ktyā* 'deed' (*GMS* § 275). The double treatment of *-ti-* may now be viewed as due to dialect mixture. If the preverb *p(a)č* is not from **patiš(-)* but, like *p(a)t-*, from **pati-*, then it could be a dialectal form borrowed into mainstream Sogdian, where it became productive (cf. the forms where the two preverbs convey different meanings when used with the same verbal stem, *GMS* § 273). Individual lexical items with *p(a)č-* could be dialectal loanwords, e.g. *p(a)čkwēr-* 'to fear', which may be derived from **pati-kauraya-*, denominative of an old noun **(pati-)kaura-*, cf. Khwar. *nkwr* 'intention, purpose' (MacKenzie, *Khwar. Dict. Frag.* 43, with comparison to OInd. *ā-kū-*); the basic meaning is 'look out (to, for)', shown by Av. √*kaw* 'versehen', OInd. *kavi-* 'seer', Lat. *caveo* 'beware' etc.; **kaura(-ya)-* also explains Oss. *agūrən* 'to seek', *kūrən* 'to petition, woo' (other hypotheses Abaev, *IESOJ s.vv.*).

For *buγúnǰ/č-* one may reconstruct **upa-gundaya-* with regular assimilatory voicing). Whereas in mainstream Sogdian **-gundaya-* resulted in *-γwe/ind-*, in pre-Yaghnobi the *d* was palatalized, perhaps after *-ay-* went to **-əy-*, *-iy-*. The metathesis of *-y-* after continuants is of fairly late date; its final workings were still taking place during the 8th cent. Thus we have in the Mugh texts the pres. stem *pryšy-* ∼ *pryš-* etc. 'to send', imperf. *pr'(')šy-* ∼ *pr'yš-* etc., confirming *GMS* §§ 129, 198 on *pr''šy VJ*; *'wγzy-* ∼ *'wγyz-* 'to lower'; *'zyh* (*ezyǎ*) 32 times against *'yzh* (*īzǎ*) 22 times in б 1, surely 'leather bag' < **izya-(ka-)* 'goatskin' (cognates *IIFL II*, 195 s.v. *ízë*, further Bailey, *Khot. Texts VI*, 414, to which may be added NPers. *xī(k)*+ < OPers. **iδya-*); elsewhere S. *pδyh*, Man. *pδδy'* > NPers. *pil* 'tendon'; Chr. *mydy'n-* and (S.) *mδy'n-* (*meδyān-*) against *mēδān-* (*Altorientalische Forschungen I*, 260), B. *βyδ'y-* 'be impeded' < **badya-* (*βyδ'yt SCE bis* = *βeδīt*, not *βeδet*); and finally cf. S. *'šcy'n-* against Chr. *'yžn*, Man. *'yjn*, Mugh *'yzn* (*GMS* § 155), indirectly attesting primary *-ǰy-* at the time of the fixation of the Sogdian script.

In Khwar. -*aya*- persisted as -*iy*-, and palatalized preceding -*nd*-, e.g. *βncy*- 'to bind'. Khwar. *nγwind*- is exceptional, and may well be from the Sogdian form. While the word which initiated this digressive note, *ptγwnt-, does not have *mater lectionis y*, it could also have had -*γwe*/*ind*- or a contracted by-form -*γūnd*-, cf. Yagn. *nuyŭnt*- (intrans. < trans.).

ADDENDA

After this article was submitted, I received a draft of N. Sims-Williams' doctoral dissertation, which contains a re-edition of the Chr. Sogd. homily discussed in my opening pages. Mr. Sims-Williams has examined the original fragment, and has produced some important new readings and interpretations. I can now offer the following improvements on my own treatment of this text:

L. 22: In place of *pθr'* S.-W. has a quite different reading, which eliminates 'forfeited' and the etymology in my fn. 9. Hansen's misreading of this word led me to assume the syntactic parallelism of *wyrx* (L. 27), which should be construed with *qt* and translated 'has been poured forth' (as I had considered in my dissertation; thus now S.-W.). While *wt'* is found in many other passages in *BST II* for 'or' (as per my Fn. 12), here *qt'* represents OIr. *kr̥tā* f.; apparently a dialectal conservatism, perhaps with 'Divine Grace' felt as animate (see Gershevitch, *JRAS* 1946, 181 and *GMS* 861 A; for the construction cf. *GMS* 823, 4 and 842).

L. 25: The hapax here must be taken as *wiδ̌esantnik*; the context allows 'conspicuous, open to view' from √ *dais* 'to show'.

LL. 17 and 27: There is no longer any reason to think that *wy̧t* (Fn. 5 and Appendix I) may have had *wy'* as its sg. For *BST II* 885, 15 S.-W. now reports *wy'(br)yny̧t*.. Thus we probably have *wy*- (*way-) < *wayah*-.

SHAUL SHAKED

SOME LEGAL AND ADMINISTRATIVE TERMS OF THE SASANIAN PERIOD

1. *driyōšān jādag-gōw*

The title "advocate (or protector) of the poor" has been the subject of an article by the late J. de Menasce [1]. This scholar showed that the seals with the title *driyōšān jādag-gōw ud dādwar* [2], or *jādag-gōw dādwar ī driyōšān* [3], first noticed by E. Herzfeld [4], are those of *mōbads* of Pārs, on the force of a passage in the law book *Mādīgān ī Hazār Dādestān*:

[I]   When the *mōbads* of Pārs engraved a seal, they called and wrote down the *mōbads* not by the name of the *mōbad* office, but by that of "advocacy of the poor". For this reason it has been written down on seals in the same manner (*MHD* facs. 93.4-9; Bulsara 43.12-13, p. 610f) [5].

The purpose of the following remarks is to try and show that "advocacy of the poor" was not a function, as perhaps Father de Menasce understood the term, but rather a honorific title. I should also like to assume, though it is hard to prove such a contention, that the poor of this title are meant in the literal sense and not in any spiritualized meaning. This does not deny, of course, that there was a religious sense in which 'poverty' (*driyōšīh, driyōšān*) was used in the Sasanian period: the willing renunciation of luxury and extravagance in favour of virtuous modesty is referred to with approval [6].

---

[1] J. de Menasce, "Le protecteur des pauvres dans l'Iran sassanide", *Mélanges Henri Massé*, Teheran 1963, 282-287. On the word *jādag-gōw* cf. Bartholomae, *MirMund*, II, 18ff.; '*ZSR*, II, 13; IV, 52-57; Hübschmann, *ZDMG* XLVI (1892), 324-325; A. Perikhanian, *Sasanidskij sudebnik*, Erevan 1973, 466f.

[2] Seal impression from Qaṣr-i Abū Naṣr, quoted by W.B. Henning, *Asia Major*, II (1951), 144.

[3] Seal of Shiraz, cf. E. Herzfeld, *Transactions of the International Numismatic Congress*, London 1938, 417, and de Menasce, loc. cit.

[4] See preceding note.

[5] Menasce's translation is inaccurate in one point. The latest treatment of the text is by A. Perikhanian, op. cit., p. 270.

[6] This is evident, for example, in *Dk* VI 143, quoted by Menasce.

But this does not seem to be the class of people who particularly required the help of a powerful patron and judge against their oppressors. This sense comes out quite unmistakably in the following text, based on a lost Avestan composition:

[II] Question. Is there any one who is as righteous among *mēnōg* beings by his speech as a propagator (of the religion), and whose word is more truthful among *mēnōg* beings? Answer. No. He by whom more 'advocacy'-judgments [7] have been made gives back to them [8] 'advocacy'-judgment. "And he, too, O Spitama Zarathuštra, shall come here, the best speaker among speakers, [who comes there] to a poor man and a poor woman treated by unjust treatment" [9]. He, too, there, O Spitamān Zardušt, comes most eloquent by eloquence, who here comes as superior speaker to poor men and women (i.e. who has performed more 'advocacy' for poor men and women), who have borne sinful treatment [10] with regard to possessions. (*Pursišnīhā* purs. 25, ed. K.M. Jamaspasa and H. Humbach, p. 40 f.) [11].

The sense of this passage seems to require the assumption that the person who performs 'advocacy'-judgments is the same as the *hāxtār* or propagator of the religion mentioned in the question. The Avestan text places most emphasis on the eloquence of the defence given to the poor against material injustice.

In a similar sense we have a reference to *jādag-gōw* which brings out the general helpfulness which is implied in this term: a person in whose body Wahman resides has, as one of the marks of this situation, the following description: he is a *jādag-gōw* of destitute good people (*ne-angad *wehān jādag-gōw). This is opposed to a man in whom Akōman dwells who is characterized by the words: *ne-angad *weh

---

[7] The editors of *Pursišnīhā* regard *wizīr* as a gloss. However, the combination *jādag-gōwīh wizīr* seems to me quite close to *jādag-gōw dādwar* of the above-quoted seal.

[8] I.e. to the *mēnōg* beings. The editors translated the clause: "shall get back (in the next world) intercession (from the spiritual beings)", but this does not seem to me to go well with the structure of the Pahlavi.

[9] I would prefer to read *araθwyō.*bərəti* and regard this as inst. sg. f. of the abstract noun; cf. *hu-bərəti-* etc.

[10] In the phrase *pad abārōn barišnīh* the preposition is out of place, but seems to reflect the instrumental case which we may assume for *araθwyō.bərəti*.

[11] Facsimile fol. 337v.

peyārag "hostile to the destitute good"[12]. Although we do not have here the wording *driyōšān jādag-gōw*, the sense is practically the same. Two other passages can be adduced to show how 'advocacy', a term often used as a short-hand reference to the full concept of *driyōšān jādag-gōw*, is defined as an attitude and activity which entails being helpful to people in need by speaking on their behalf and giving them material assistance.

[III]   *7om jādag-gōwīh hān bawēd ke zan ī wēbag *ud aburnāyag ī gursag ud ātaxšān ud gāwān ud gōspandān ud abārig a-tawānīgān nāmcišt ruwān ī xwēš rāy saxwan gōwēd* (*Priv* 196, AdPRiv §12).

"The seventh is advocacy. It is this: One who speaks a word on behalf of a widowed woman, a hungry child, fires, cattle, sheep and other helpless creatures, specifically for the sake of his own soul".

The point that proper 'advocacy' is one that is performed for one's own soul, that is to say, for the sake of religion, without hope of material gain, is also made elsewhere[13].

A New Persian text based on the Zand of the Hādōxt Nask gives the following description of *jādag-gōwīh*:

[IV] کسی که جادنگوئ کند واز بهر ایشان چیزی از مردم
فراز گیرد وبایشان رساند بی خیانت چنان باشد که از مال
خویشتن بدو داده باشد[14]. (*Sad-dar Nasr* XXII.3)

A person who performs *jādag-gōwīh* and who receives something from people on their behalf[15], and who hands it over to them without fraud, is (considered) the same as if he gave them from his own property.

Jādag-gōwīh apparently implies here material assistance rendered to priests and people who are worthy of it. It comes here in association with the aministration of money received in charity.

The term *driyōšān-jādag-gōw*, it seems from these quotations, need not imply anything more specific than "one who cares for the poor", as mark of his virtuous character, and should not be taken to refer

---

[12] *Dk* VI 78.

[13] Cf. *Dk* VI 23, 91. J. de Menasce overlooked the force of the expression *ruwān ī xwēš rāy* when he translated it in his article "pour l'âme de celui-là".

[14] Cf. West in *SBE* XXIV, 285f.

[15] I.e. on behalf of *mōbadān va-dastūrān va-arzāniyān* mentioned earlier in the text.

to an office or function. It was evidently used, though, as a complimentary title designating the *mōbads* of Pars in particular.

2. *ērang, ēraxt*

The above word, meaning "condemnation, guilt", is most likely connected with the Old Persian word which underlies Aramaic *'drng* "guarantor"[15a], as already pointed out by A. Perikhanian in her recent and thorough discussion of the word[16]. The semantic development, as recognized by Perikhanian, is from 'debt' to 'guilt', and it recalls by a close analogy the variety of meanings of Mishnaic Hebrew (as well as the similar word in Aramaic and Syriac) *ḥayyāḇ* '1. debtor, 2. guilty, 3. sinner, wicked'. The opposite word, *zakkāy*, means 'free from debt or guilt'. The corresponding Syriac pair, *ḥayyāḇā* and *zakkāyā* have in addition the meanings 'vanquished' and 'victor' respectively, with reference either to the judicial process or to the battle field. For the Persian pair *ēraxt* and *buxt*, the meanings "vanquished, defeated"[17] and "saved, escaped", with reference again both to a court of law and to a battle field, are clearly attested. There is therefore no reason, on semantic grounds, to regard the word as belonging to two different sources[18].

In the early Judaeo-Persian Bible translations the word *'yrxth* and its abstract noun form *'yrxtygy* are extensively illustrated, rendering words like רָשָׁע or אָשֵׁם, which has made Lagarde translate it as 'gottlos'[19]. This is too narrow a rendering. We thus have in *Dk* VI 204 a classification of people into three grades with regard to righteousness: *buxt* 'acquitted', i.e. innocent, righteous; *an-ēraxt* 'not guilty', i.e. only moderately righteous; *ēraxt* 'guilty', i.e. wicked.

A word may be in place to show the verbal associations of this word in some religious (as opposed to legal) texts. In these texts its main connotations are "guilt" and "defeat" in the sense of "going

---

[15a] Cf. B. Porten and J.C. Greenfield, *JAOS* 89 (1969), 154, where Martin Schwartz is quoted for the Sogdian cognate **ptžnq** (Christian), **ptz'nkh** (Mt. Mugh) "earnest money".

[16] *Sasanidskij sudebnik*, 469 ff.

[17] Cf. e.g. the phrase *razm-ērang*, *DkM* 125.4.

[18] This is the position of Nyberg, *Manual* II, 71 f., and perhaps also in MacKenzie, *Glossary*, s.v.

[19] de Lagarde, *Pers. St.*, 71; Horn, *Grundriss der neupersischen Etymologie*, Strassburg 1893, 274.

down, being laid low". The first meaning is illustrated by *Dēnkard* III, chapter 39 [20]. The second meaning emerges from the association of *ērang* with *nigōnīh* "downwardness" [21]. *ērang* and *nigōnīh*, as a pair, come in opposition to *bōzišn* (or *buxtišn*) and *burzišn* [22]. Thus, when the term which completes the couple of *ērangīg* appears to be written *nigōhīdag* "despised", a word which could be *prima facie* acceptable, it nevertheless seems preferable, on the basis of the above observations, to regard it as a mistake for *nigōnihīdag* "cast downwards" [23]. The sense of devastation emerges clearly from a text where the following chain of verbs occurs: *ēraxtan ud škastan ud abāz abgandan az dēn* "to devastate, break, and throw away from the religion" [24].

Texts

[V] *abar pand <ī> mardom pad-eš buxtagīh ud hān ī az-eš ērangīh.*
az nigēz ī weh-dēn.

*hād pand ī mardom ī pad kunišnīh pad-eš buxtagīh hāwand ī ō ohrmazd kām andar xwāyišn ud pursišn ī weh-dēn. (ī) hān ī ohrmazd kām *ēwāz [25] andar weh-dēn *ke [26] āgāhān (ī) pad-eš kunišnīg [27] čiš, hān ī anāgīh az kunišn [28] pahrēzišn.*
(*Dk* III 39; *B facs.* [23]; *DkM*, 31)

The way by which people become righteous and that through which they are condemned. From the instruction of the Good Religion.

The way by which people through action get righteousness is equal to the desire of Ohrmazd in the seeking and the enquiring of the Good Religion. The desire of Ohrmazd is

---

[20] See text V.

[21] Cf. *Dk* III 326 (= text VI). In *Dk* III 324 (text VII) the term which corresponds to the word *nigōnīh* in text VI is *pāšimānīh* (possibly *pāšī<n>mānīh*?) which apparently means "being underfoot" or the like. *nigōnīg* comes in opposition to *burzāwandīh* in *Dk* III 283 (= text VIII).

[22] In texts VI and VIII. In text VII *pāšinmānīh* is opposed to *burzišn*.

[23] *Dk* III 76 (= text IX).

[24] *DkM* 11 f.

[25] MS 'ywp.

[26] MS MN.

[27] MS + *pahrēzišnig*.

[28] MS + W p'.

only that which is in the Good Religion concerning which the wise act, while evil is (that which) they avoid doing [29].

[VI] *ce'ōn ēd ī paydāg ku az hān ī dehbad nēw-kāmīh āwām xwāhrīh, ud az wad-kāmīh āwām duš-āhrīh (?) [30]. ud az-eš xrad-āhangīh hamaragānīhā mardom ō dānāgīh nixwārišn, ud az waran āhangīh ō duš-āgāhīh škarwīdagīh. ud az-eš xēm wirāstagih ud dēn-hu-īh mardom pad wirāst-xēmīh ud hu-dēnīh buxtišn ud burzišn, az xēm ālūdagīh ud dēn dušīh pad winast-xēmīh ud duš-*dēnīh ērang ud nigōnīh. (Dk* III 326; *B facs.* [245]f.; *DkM*, 321)

As that which is manifest: From the good will of the ruler (there comes about) prosperous time, from the ill-will (of the ruler) evil time. From his inclination towards reason the whole mankind rush towards wisdom, from his inclination towards concupiscence there is stumbling towards ignorance. From the ruler's right character and good religion people become righteous and elevated through right character and good religion, and from his corrupt character and evil religion people become wicked and debased [31].

[VII] *hu-xwadāy(īh) abspārišn ī xwadāyīh frazām ō rāmišn ī az hān hu-xwadāyīh bōzišn <ud> burzišn ī pad-eš pad dād nēwag-kardārīh ī abar gēhānīg, ce'ōn yam.*

ud duš-xwadāy abspārišn ī xwadāyīh frazām ō bēš ī az hān duš-xwadāyīh ērang ud *pāšinmānīh [32] ī az-eš *pad a-dād [33] anāg-kardārīh ī abar gēhān, ce'ōn dahāg rāy. az dēn paydāg. (Dk III 324; *B facs.* [245]; *DkM* 320)

To submit the kingship to a good king leads in the end to joy which results from the righteousness which is from the

---

[29] Cf. J. de Menasce, *Le troisième livre du Dēnkart*, Paris 1973, 52, where the translation is somewhat different.

[30] The transcription reflects the spelling, which looks like the opposite of *xwāhrīh*, otherwise unattested in Pahlavi, Av. *duž-āθra-*. The normally attested word in this sense is *duš-xwārīh*, cf. e.g. Nyberg, *Manual*, II, 69.

[31] Cf. de Menasce, *op. cit.*, 305 f., where again the translation is different in some points.

[32] MS p'šym'nyx. The emendation is based on the assumption that what we may expect here is not a word for "regret", but the opposite of *burzišn*. I have thought here of a derivative of *pāšina* (attested only in NP) "heel", Av. *pāšna-*.

[33] MS p'd't'.

good kingship and the elevation which is in it by the lawful doing of good to mankind, as was the case with Yam.

To submit the kingship to an evil king leads in the end to the misery which comes from the wickedness of that evil kingship, and the down-troddenness which comes from it through lawless evil doing to mankind, as happened with Dahāg. A revelation of the Religion [34].

[VIII] *hān ī xwadāyān pad xwadāyīh pahlom xwarr mēhan, ud āsnōxrad dād zahāg, ud ābādānīh gušn, xwadāyīh* **tws wtng** (?), *purr-šnāyišn gēhān frāxwkar ud dām srāyēnīdār, rāmišn bun ud bōzišn bar, dūr-brāz rādīh.*

ud hān ī-šān pad xwadāyīh wattom fradom duš-farragīh āgōš <ī> āz, wiškōf a-rāh waran, a-dād cargār (?) [35], *ud škōhīh *tōhm* [36], *ud dām-nizārēnīdār xwadāyīh-ōš (?)* [37], *ud bazag bun, ud ērangīh *tag (?)* [38], *purr-bēšīh ud gēhān-tangēnīdār hayyār-nizārēnīdār ud hamēmār-nērōgēnīdār ud tēz škarwēnāg panīh.*
(*Dk* III 283; *B facs.* [223]; *DkM* 292-293)

That which is best for kings in kingship is the splendour as home, the law of innate wisdom as parent, prosperity as the male, kingship ... [39], that which has full satisfaction is he who

---

[34] Cf., somewhat differently, de Menasce, *op. cit.*, 304f.

[35] *cargār* occurs in a pejorative sense in several other places. Cf. *DkM* 325.9, where it is applied, among other attributes, to *a-dādīh*, and is, again like here, in contrast to *zahāg*, which stands for "parent" in a good sense. Other instances: *DkM* 206.11; 279.6; 359.19. Cf. Zaehner, *Zurvan*, 376.

[36] MS **twm**.

[37] The reading of the final element is doubtful, but its use as a pejorative suffix in a meaning like "the antagonist of" seems quite well established. Cf. *Yam-ōš*, *DkM* 334.11, an epithet of Dahāk (Molé, *Culte*, 39, translates strangely "qui tua Yam"); *zardušt-tan-ōš*, *DkM* 334.12, an epithet of Tūr ī Brādarōgrēs (Molé, ibid.; "qui tua le corps de Zoroastre"). As a prefix we have *ōš-menišnīh* in *DkM* 686.17. We may possibly have the same word in *MX* 20: 13; 25: 7, where one would expect a bad meaning in the context, since it is applied to *a-xwēškār mard*, "a man who does not fulfil his duty", and to *duš-āgāh* "an ignorant person", though the Pāzand reads it *x^vaš* "good" and it is followed in this interpretation by the Sanskrit version: *sukhaṁ* (Pāzand and Sanskrit are not extant for the second of the passages quoted).

[38] MS **wtng**.

[39] **tws** may be associated with **twšn** in *DkM* 346.3: *az ham-bawišn <ī> xištān ēwag twšn* "from the composition of the bricks a **twšn** [is produced]" (cf. Molé, *Culte*, 413f.; Shaki, *Archiv Orientální* 41 (1973), 147f.; Menasce, *Le troisième livre*, 327-in none of these studies is a satisfactory reading of this phrase offered). The

causes the world to be broad, and the creatures to prosper,
joy is the root and salvation (=righteousness) the fruit,
generosity which is luminous afar.

That which is the worst in kingship is first evil splendour
as the embrace of concupiscence, the blossom is wayless lust,
lawless(ness) is the mother, misery the seed, that which causes
the creatures to be weak is the antithesis of kingship (?), sin
is the root, wickedness the branch (?), complete misery is
stinginess which makes the world narrow, weakens the friend,
strengthens the enemy, and stumbles sharply[40].

[IX] *ud ke āsnōxrad pad abāgīh ī ēn 3 ham-yuxt abzār mad ēstēd
abardar burdār ī āsnōxrad pad-eš buxtag-tar ud burzišnīg-tar
andar mardom.* (*Dk* III 76; *B facsimile* [49]; *DkM* 67)

He who has obtained innate wisdom together with these
three combined instruments–he is the superior carrier of innate
wisdom, and he is most righteous and most honoured through
it among men.

*ud ke waran pad hamīh ī ēn 3 ham-yuxt āhōg dārēd škift-tar
burdār ī a-rāh waran, pad-eš ērangīg-tar nigōhīdag-tar[41] andar
mardomān.* (Same chapter; *B facs.* [50]; *DkM* 68)

He who possesses lust together with these three combined
defects–he is the worst carrier of pathless lust, and he is most
condemned and most despised through it among men[42].

3. *gilag-ōbārīh*

This expression does not properly belong to the realm of legal
terminology, but to that of ethics and manners. Since it is concerned
with the relationship of strife and contention between people it has
also some bearing, though indirectly, on the legal field.

---

meaning of this word may thus be either "wall" or some kind of building. If the word
means "house" we should translate **twšn**-*dārišnīh* (*DkM* 606.20 = *Dk* VII 2:34)
"the keeping [of a small child] in the house". Molé, *Légende*, 21, translates: "en lui
donnant de la nourriture", as if we had here *tōšag* "provision". The same word may
also be present in the seemingly corrupt text of *Dd* 36:39.

[40] Menasce, op. cit., p. 279, has a somewhat different translation.

[41] As pointed out above it seems preferable here to read **nigōnihīdag* "turned
upside down, debased", though the contrast *burzišnig* "honoured" / *nigōhīdag* "despised"
makes perfectly good sense.

[42] The general outline of chapter 76 in *Dk* III is given by Menasce, *Encyclopédie*, 46.

A typical text in which the word occurs is the following:

[X]   *u-šān ēn-ez aʾōn dāšt ku gilag-ōbār ud wēdwar ud pad kirbag tuxšāg ud wistāxw bawišn ud spās az mēnōgān xwāhišn (Dk VI 29)*[43].

They held this too thus: One should be a person who suppresses complaint, patient, diligent and confident in doing good works, and who seeks gratitude from the spirits.

gilag-ōbār is thus one who "swallows" complaint, uncomplaining. For the semantic connection it is possible to compare *kēn gugārdan* "to digest vengeance", i.e. to avoid vengefulness[44], *xešm gugārdan*[45], *anāgīh gugārdan* (?)[46], as well as the Neo-Persian idiom *nāla firū xʷardan*. A similar usage is presented by the verb *jūdan* "to chew", hence "to leave out, to forget"[47]. For the etymology and cognates of *gilag* cf. Bthl., *ZKMirMund.*, VI, 23[48]. The word is variously misspelt in Pahlavi: **gln´, gl´n,** but in view of the frequency of this latter spelling, one ought perhaps to postulate *gilān* as variant of *gilag*.

[XI]   **gilag*[49] *az tan bērōn kun u-t tan wirāst ud ruwān buxt bawēd* (*DkM* 46.12-13; *B facs.* [34]).

Put complaint out of your body , so that your body should become tidy and your soul righteous.

[XII]   *nihān mard hanzamanīg ud tan-*gilag*[50]*-ōbār ahlaw bawēd* (*PRiv* 198.2-3).

A modest man, who attends the assemblies, and is uncomplaining in his body, becomes righteous.

---

[43] For quotations from *Dk* VI see my forthcoming edition of the book.

[44] Cf. *ud gugārēd kēn andar wārom ī xwēš* (*PhlT* 144, *WāzAdMah* § 4) "and digest vengefulness in your mind".

[45] Cf. *Dk* E 19; and similarly: *hān harw tars ud sēž ud dušxwārīh ... mihr ī dēn rāy be gugārēm* (*Dd* IV 4) "I digest all fear, pain and hardship for the love of religion".

[46] This is a doubtful example. The expression occurs in *ZXA* 163.20; *pad xrad be gugārēd*, which corresponds to the parallel text in *GBd* 173 (= text XV below) where however the verb is written *gugānēd* (cf. note 59 below). If the spelling in *ZXA* were correct, this idiom would differ from others in that it would imply resigned acceptance of evil from the outside, rather than suppression of an inner drive.

[47] Cf. *Dk* VI 56.

[48] There is also early Judaeo-Persian **gylh,** attested in *Qiṣṣa-i Dāniyāl*, ed. Zotenberg, *Archiv für wiss. Erforschung des Alten Testaments (Merx Archiv)*, I (1869), 390.6 (not recognized by the editor).

[49] Written **gln´.** J. de Menasce translates "concupiscence", evidently reading *waran*.

[50] MS **gl´n.**

The fact that this passage contains elements which are similar to those of passage XI confirms the reading *gilag in that passage.

[XIII] ud *āwāmīgīh[51] ī pāk az *gilag[52] (DkM 59.7; B facs. [43])[53].
    Acceptance of what comes with time (?) which is free from complaint.

This phrase forms part of one of the lists of virtues and vices in the third book of the Dēnkard. It represents a pair of "backward-inclined" opposites, i.e. qualities which are associated with restraint and withholding rather than with activity and joyousness.

[XIV] ke a-zadār andar-ez wanīh <ī> awe wānīdag, rāstgōwišn andar-ez *gilag-[54] menišnīh ud rād andar-ez gursagīh pad pahlom-cīnīh wizīn abar kard ēstēd (DkM 419.14-16; B facs. [327]).

    A man who is non-violent even at the time of victory[55] over one who is defeated, tells the truth even at the time of plaintive thought[56], and is generous even at the time of hunger, has made a choice in the collection of the best.

[XV] u-š wehīh ēn ku wēdwar ud gilag-[57] ōbār <īh>[58] ēn ku anāgīh ī ō spandarmad zamīg rasēd hamāg be gugānēd[59] (GBd 173.6-8; TD₁ 72b.6-8)[60].

[51] MS 'w'mykyx (one would expect 'wb'm-).

[52] MS gl'n.

[53] No reading of this phrase is offered in Menasce, Encyclopédie, 43 or in Le troisième livre du Dēnkart.

[54] MS gl'n.

[55] The terms wan (= victorious), wanīh (= victory), wānišn (= defeat), wānīdag (= the defeated one) etc. are defined in Dk III 148 from a theological point of view:
    wan pādexšā, wan-tom pādexšā-tom spanāg-mēnōg, ud wanīh pādexšāyīh ī wan. wānišn zanišn spōzišn ī hamēstār az wan wanīh. wānīdag azēr purr-zōr pādexšā-tom spanāg-mēnōg nihān-ōz gannāg-mēnōg. wānīdag-tom ham gannāg-mēnōg ... (DkM 150; B facs. [114]f.)
    wan is the sovereign. The most victorious is the most sovereign, the Sacred Spirit. wanīh is the sovereignty of the victorious one. wānišn is the smiting and rejection of the adversary from the sovereignty of the sovereign. wānīdag is under the most sovereign full-of-power, the Sacred Spirit, whose power is hidden. The most defeated one is the same Wicked Spirit...

[56] The expression gilag-menišnīh occurs also in Dk VI 146.

[57] MS TD₂ has this word written twice.

[58] ZXA has ōbārīh.

[59] ZXA has gugārēd; cf. note 46 above and the following note.

[60] Cf. H.K. Mirza, Dr. J.M. Unvala Mem. Vol., Bombay 1964, 157f. provides a variant of the same text, cf. notes 58, 59.

Her [=Spandarmad's] goodness is this: she is patient; her suppression of complaint is this: she destroys all the evil that comes to the earth Spandarmad.

4. *nēwān pad-tan šābistān*

A Sasanian title *mahist pad-tan šābistān* interpreted by Henning [61] as meaning "chief body eunuch" occurs on a seal from the Hermitage Museum in Leningrad:

dynky ZY MLKTAn MLKTA mxysty PWN tny š'pst'n
(Leningrad Cat. No. 2; Borisov-Lukonin, 48) [62].

Dēnag, who is the chief personal eunuch of the Queen of Queens.

As Henning remarked, the portrait on the seal is that of the queen and not of the bearer of the seal.

Another seal in the same collection has not yet lent itself to complete interpretation. It seems to contain a similar title, and a reading of the first part of that inscription may be attempted:

māhān i p<ad> yazdān wināhgīrīh ud xwadāyīh-eš, ardparwast, husrōw, <ī> māhānān. *nēwān p<ad> tan šābistān [63] ud dar-andarzbad... (Leningrad Cat. No. 46) [64].

Māhān, son of Māhān, who possesses, through the gods, (the ability to) defeat sin and dominion, (who is) enclosed in righteousness and has good fame. Personal eunuch of the brave (?), court counsellor...

The reconstruction offered here is based on two analogies, one already pointed out by Lukonin [65], and the other not noticed so far. The short *andarz* treatise *Ayādgār ī Wuzurgmihr* begins with the following string of titles:

man wuzurgmihr ī buxtagān nēwān p<ad> t<an> šabistān <ī> šahr ī ostīgān-xusrō darīgbad... (*PhlT*, 85).

---

[61] W.B. Henning, "Mitteliranisch", 45.

[62] Lukonin, though referring to Henning's discussion, does not seem to have made full use of this interpretation.

[63] Spelled here **š'pstn**.

[64] A. Mordtmann, *ZDMG*, 18 (1864), 34f.; E. Herzfeld, *Paikuli*, I, Berlin 1924, 81; Henning, "Mitteliranisch", 45 n. 3 (where the reading *pad-tan šābistān* is established); J. Harmatta, *Acta Antiqua Hung.*, 12 (1964), 224; Borisov-Lukonin, 20f. None of the photographs published gives a possibility of reading, and the reconstruction offered here is necessarily conjectural.

[65] Borisov-Lukonin, 21.

I, Wuzurgmihr, son of Buxtag, personal eunuch of the brave (?), *darīgbad*[66] of the town of Ostīgān-Xusrō... [67]

Further evidence for this title occurs seemingly in a recently discovered inscription, to which the following reading may be proposed:

(1) [ZNH] dxmk (2) [ ]wk′ ZY (3) [ ]pk′n ZY (4) [ ]k′ bwm[68] (5) [ ]k l′d (6) [ ](c) nyw′n (7) [PWN tn]š′pst′n (8) [ZY š]trdst′n (9) W byxšpwxl (10) mlcp′n plmwt′ (11) krtn′ W LXNA BYRX (12) ′p′n QDM (13) ŠNT 6 yzdkrt′ (14) MLKAn MLKA (15) W YWM xwl PWN bxt (16) ′ZLWNt′ YWM m′x (17) tn′ ZY xm ′xnk′ (18) ′L dxmk′ XNX < TWN > tk′[69] (19) NKSYA KSP (20) 20 AL < P > [70] mzd (21) plmwt′ YXBWNt < n′ > (Eqlīd)[71].

[This] tomb was ordered to be made[72] by [...] for [73] [...], the [personal] eunuch of the brave, who is *marzbān* of Šahristān and Bēšāpūr[74]. This month Ābān, year 6 of Yazdegerd,

[66] This title means perhaps "chief courtier".

[67] An edition of the text is in the course of preparation.

[68] Harmatta reads **BNH**. The last letter seems to me quite clearly **m**, though a crack in the stone creates the impression of **H**.

[69] The abbreviated spelling on the stone seems to present a case of haplography.

[70] The figures here, as is common with numerals in cursive Pahlavi, are of uncertain significance.

[71] G. Gropp in Hinz, *Altiranische Funde und Forschungen*, Berlin 1969, 240f.; R.N. Frye, *Henning Memorial Volume*, London 1970, 155; J. Harmatta, *Die Sprache*, 19 (1973), 76f.; Gignoux's readings can mostly be reconstructed from the entries in his *Glossaire des inscriptions pehlevies et parthes*, London 1972.

[72] The same formula occurs in other inscriptions published in the same group. The text of Istaxr A (or inscription No. 4 in Gropp's numbering) can be reconstructed as follows:

> (1) ZNH dxmk′ (2) plxwz′t′ ZY (3) wxšt b′(l l′d) (4) mtrpn′x ZY (5) [N](PŠH) dwxt′ (6) plmwt′ (7) (k)rtn′ (Gropp, op. cit., 260; Frye, op. cit., 153; Harmatta, loc. cit., 77). This grave was ordered to be made for Farroxzād, whose lot is in Paradise, by Mihrpanāh, his own daughter.

For the expression *wahišt bār* or *-bahr*, which occurs in two of the other inscriptions and in Bīšāpūr under the formula *wahišt-bār b(aw)ād*, or in Istaxr B (= Gropp's No. 1) as *wahišt ī pahlom bār bād* "May he be of the lot of the best Paradise", we may refer to the Neo-Persian expression *bihištī* for a departed person (cf. *ŠN*, ed. Dabīr-Siyāqī, I, 98, line 884). *wahišt-bār* or *bahr* (spelled alternately in these two manners) occurs also in a Judaeo-Persian document of 951 A.D. perhaps from Ahwāz (cf. Shaked, *Tarbiz*, 41 [1971], 54).

[73] The force of the postposition *rāy* was ignored in Harmatta's treatment of the inscription.

[74] These two geographical names designate one entity. Cf. G. Le Strange, *The lands of the Eastern Caliphate*, London 1906, 262.

King of Kings, the day of Xwar[75], he went to his fate[76]. On the day Māh (his) harmonious (?)[77] body was laid in the tomb.[78]. 20.000 (drahm?) value[79] of property were ordered (to be) given as reward".

Although the interpretation of the title depends here on the way one supplements the missing letters at the beginning of line 7, the presence in close proximity of both **nyw'n** and **š'pst'n** makes it probable that we have here the same title as above.

A title *nēwān* (or *mahist*) *pad-tan šābistān* is thus quite well attested. It looks like a court title, to which one may hazard the literal rendering "personal guardian of the brave", or perhaps rather: "guardian of the body, or person, of the brave". The practical significance of this title is however not yet possible to establish.

[75] *Xwar* represents the 11th, and *Māh* the 12th, days of the month. That the man was buried on the day following his death constitutes a departure from Zoroastrian prescription, where a three day vigil following death is enjoined. Burial in a tomb, if that is what is meant, is another departure from custom. A way can be found to explain these puzzles (one could think of explaining *pad baxt šud* as referring to the final departure of the soul from the body, three days after death, etc.), but unless a firm evidence is produced in an opposite direction, it may be assumed that we have here people who did not observe Zoroastrian practices as we know them.

[76] The expression is attested in *MHD* 66.16; cf. Bartholomae, *zSR*, III, 24.

[77] *tan ī ham-āhang* seems to me a plausible reading of the Pahlavi, though the expression is not otherwise known to me. Gropp's "der Körper in gleicher Weise", Frye's "the body of this one", and Harmatta's "sein mitgeborener Körper" seem to me unsatisfactory. I have been unable to ascertain Gignoux's reading.

[78] A *daxma* could conceivably be any place for the disposal of the dead, including one "where the bones rested after having been cleaned of flesh" (Frye, loc. cit., p. 152), but hardly on the day following death, when the bones are not yet cleaned.

[79] On the ideogram **KSP** and some of its cognates cf. the material gathered by H.K. Mirza, *Sir J.J. Zarthoshti Madressa Centenary Volume*, Bombay 1967, 52 f.

MANSOUR SHAKI

THE CONCEPT OF OBLIGATED SUCCESSORSHIP IN THE MĀDIYĀN Ī HAZĀR DĀDISTĀN

The social relations and proprietary demands of the patriarchal Sasanian society which considered every effort towards the maintenance of succession and preservation of private property a categorical imperative had given rise to a most elaborate system of civil laws regulating succession by substitution or proxy, generally called *stūrīh*. It is for this purpose that the preservation of the generations of the Iranian *wēh-dēns* till the Restoration (*paywand ī fraškard*) is set forth as one of the fundamental commandments of Zoroastrianism. Without man, as an ally of Ohrmazd and instrument in the fight against the Evil Spirit, the victory of Good over Evil cannot be achieved.

It is, therefore, incumbent upon every man to have male issue in the absence of whom his soul will be unable to pass the Činvat Bridge. The great importance attached to the maintenance of succession by the Zoroastrians may be seen from the space devoted to it in Sasanian law, comprising by far the greater chapter of their code, partially preserved in the *Mādiyān ī Hazār Dādistān*.

Thus, the problem which must have engaged the attention of many a Sasanian jurisconsult was the creation of a substitute successor *(stūr)* for an adult Zoroastrian man having died without a male progeny. This implied a marriage institution contracted preferably by one of his nearest agnates, financed by his estate, in order to provide the deceased with a male successor regarded as his legitimate progeny[1].

Within the general system of *stūrīh* the concept of obligated successorship forms a special category in which the *stūr* is called in Avestan legal terminology *yō hē pasčaēta* (lit. he to whom afterwards [i.e. after the decease of the issueless person] descends the obligation of *stūrīh*) and in MP literature *ayōk-hē*, *ayōkēn*, *ayōk*, etc. which is here of concern.

The etymon of the word and partially its denotation had already

---

[1] See. my *Sasanian Matrimonial Relations, ArOr* 39. 1974, p. 326, and A. Perikhanian, *On Some Pahlavi Legal Terms, W.B. Henning Memorial Volume*, p. 353f.

become obscure by the ninth century. Bartholomae who initiated
the first serious study of the *MHD* did not propose a reading,
but interpreted it "Nadelgeld"[2]. West and Dhabhar following the
traditional reading have suggested respectively *yūkān*[3] and *ayōk-āin*
"only child". The idea of an "only child" has also led Bulsara to read
aêvakkîn "marriage in condition of the only child"[4], and de Menasce
ēvakēn "le mariage de la fille unique"[5]. Klingenschmitt in his
otiose translation of this chapter of the *MDH*, gives a transliteration
of its defective form, *'ywkkyn*, and takes it in the sense of "Erbtochter"[6].
is also pointed out by Perikhanian who has come very near to its
true signification, but, unfortunately, has restricted it to its main aspect
ἐπίκληρος[7] (not in the sense of the "Erbtochter" of Klingenschmitt).
Her explaination of the term as a lost Avestan *aēno-kaēna-* "expiator,
redeemer"[8] is untenable. On examining the late B.T. Anklesaria's transcription of the texts of the *Rivāyat ī Ēmēt ī Ašavahištān* and *The Pahlavi
Rivāyat of Āturfarnbag and Farnbag-Srōš* it came to my knowledge
that he had shrewdly observed the correct etymology of our term in
as much as he had transcribed *'ywkyn'* as *ayōkēn*[9], *yō hē*[10], and
ayōhē[11], but left unexplained in the translation.

As I have already pointed out in my previous papers[12] the MP
'ywkhy, corrupted into *'ywkyn'* and *'ywkkyn* by generations of copyists
is coined by the fusion of the beginning words of the original Av.
legal phrase *yō hē pasčaēta* in keeping with the rules of the transcription of Avestan words into Pahlavi script. The establishment
of the equation *yō hē (pasčaēta)* = *ayōk-hē* > *ayōkēn* not only dispels
unnecessary conjectures about the origin of the word but greatly
elucidates its actual legal import. Let us first turn to Pahlavi texts
and find out the status of persons referred to as *yō hē pasčaēta* or
ayōkēn. In the order of priority they are: a virile (*zahāg*) *pādixšāyīhā*

[2] *ZsR*, V. 27-41.
[3] *SBE*, XVIII. 185, n. 3.
[4] *The Laws of the Ancient Persians*, p. 153.
[5] *Feux et fondations pieuses dans le droit sassanide*, 1964, pp. 35-57.
[6] *Münchener Studien zur Sprachwissenschaft*, Heft 21, 1967, pp. 59-70.
[7] *W.B. Henning Memorial Volume*, 1970, p. 352.
[8] *Ibid.*, p. 353.
[9] *REA*, Pursišn 1, p. 3.
[10] *Ibid.*, Pursišn 44, p. 163.
[11] *Pahl, Riv. A-F and F-S*, Pursišn 22, p. 107.
[12] *Some Basic Tenets*, ArOr 38, 1970, p. 289 and *SMR*, p. 332-3.

son who is, naturally, an immediate and direct male progeny[13];
a *pādixšāyīhā* widow who is bound by duty to enter into *stūrīh*
marriage (in her case called *čakarīh*) in order to beget male *stūr*
children for the benefit and in the name of the deceased[14]; further,
an adopted son (*pus ī padīriftag*)[15] and a designate *stūr* (*stūr ī kardag*)[16]
instituted by the deceased in his lifetime to his own *stūrīh* successorship. In default of these the obligation of *stūrīh* descends
either to the eldest *pādixšāyīhā* daughter or sister or to the one
who has not yet married[17]. But if the daughter is already married the
majority of decrees disapprove of the dissolution of her *pādixšāyīhā*
marriage in order to assume her father's *ayōkēnīh*[18]. Perikhanian has
concluded, unwarrantedly, to the contrary[19].

From what has been said it becomes evident that a *yō hē pasčaēta*
or *ayōk-hē* or *ayōkēn* is essentially a person to whom descends the
obligation of successorship, be it a straight male descent, as is
the case with a *pādixšāyīhā* son, or a female descent (daughter),
or a female member of family (sister, wife) or anyone else instituted
a substitute-successor (*stūr*) by the testator himself (a designate *stūr*
or adopted son). As all these persons, except the *pādixšāyīhā* son and
designate *stūr*, are referred to as *būdag stūrs* "obligated, responsible or
lawful substitute-successors"[20] the concept of obligation is inherent in
ayōkēnīh[21]. It is to be noted that in contradistinction to *ayōkēnīh*, the
institution of *stūrīh* includes all forms of substitute-successorships:
obligated (*būdag*), designate (*kardag*) and appointed (*gumārdag*). This
distinguishing feature of *ayōkēnīh* as a special category of *stūrīh* is
emphasized by our texts, since the term almost everywhere occurs in

---

[13] *MHD*, I. 22. 8-9; I. 22. 2-3.

[14] *MHD*, I. 87. 1-2; I. 49. 2-3; *Dd. Pursišn* 55: *REA, Pursišn* 1.

[15] *REA, Pursišn* 1.

[16] *MHD*, I. 47. 7-14; *REA Pursišn* 1.

[17] *MHD*, I. 41. 11-13.

[18] *MHD*, I. 22. 1-2; I. 23. 1-4; *Dd. Pursišn* 53: *ka dūdag kadag bānūg widīred ud
duxtarān šōy kard stūr* [*ih*] *gumārišn.* "If the mistress of the house passes away and
the daughters are married, a *stūr* has to be created by appointment".

[19] *HMV*, p. 352, n. 12.

[20] Pagliaro was the first to explain *būtak*, unwarrantedly, as "naturale", *RSO*,
23. 64, followed by de Menasce "naturel", *Feux et fondations*, 35, and Perikhanian
"*natural*", *HMV*, p. 355. See my *SMR*, p. 328.

[21] Cf. *Dd. Pursišn* 57: *stūr ī būdag ēdōn čēōn zan ī pādixšāyīhā ud duxt ī ayōk-hē
*kē pad x^wad *astišnīh stūr.* "An obligated stur is as a *pādixšāyīhā* wife or an *ayōk-hē*
daughter who is (obliged to assume the) *stūrīh* by her own status".

association with the verbal phrase *abar ōh mānēd* "she/he shall succeed or is bound to remain (a successor)".

Of great interest is the stress laid not only on the preservation of the name (renown) and lineage of the deceased but also on his private property[22] a factor that as often as not lies at the very basis of social laws no matter how far-off they may seem from our material aspects of life. This has found a direct expression in the privilege attached to association in regard to successorship.

An *ayōkēn* marriage contracted by an obligated *stūr* (*stūr i būdag*) enjoys special proprietary rights discussed by me in *SMR*, p. 333. That is the reason why the *ayōkēnīh* is regarded as a special form of marriage in the Marriage Contract[23] and to which has been devoted a separate chapter in the *MDH*. Since an *ayōkēn* daughter succeeds to the *stūrīh* of her deceased father as his *pādixšāyīhā* wife, she inherits like a *pādixšāyīhā* son, viz. two shares from the estate[24]. It is only when she is the only heiress that, naturally, inherits all of the patrimony[25]. A sister succeeding to the *ayōkēnīh* of her brother becomes his associate; a part of his estate, apparently, passes to her in absolute ownership and the other part in trust to be held for the management of his sturih, which is revertible to the *stūr* son on his coming of age. The property made over to a designate *stūr* by the testator will be held by him in usufruct[26].

The following translation of the chapter on *ayōkēnīh* and other passages concerning this subject, occurring in the *MHD*, is a part of my work bearing upon the social and economic relations of the Sasanian era. I have rearranged the paragraphs in order to present them in a more coherent sequence.

MDH, I. 21. 3:
dar i ayōkēn[a]   *yō hē pascaēta*   *ayōk hē*[b] *pascaita*[c]

   [a] MS *'ywk kyn*, obviously a corruption of *'ywkyn'*, which occurs throughout the manuscript.
   [b] MS *h* for *hy* by copyist's error.

---

   [22] Cf. *MHD*, I. 22. 3-6: I. 23. 14-24. 2: *Dd. Pursišn* 55: ... *stūrīh ēdōn bawēd... ku... stūr... pad ān i ōy nāmagānīh ud* +*paywand rāyēnēd ud x*ʷ*āstag dārēd.*+ "*stūrīh* is such that the *stūr* should maintain his name and lineage and administer his property".
   [23] *Pahl. Texts*, II. 141. 3.
   [24] *REA, Pursišn* 44.
   [25] *Ibid.*, 2, 3, 18.
   [26] *MHD*, I. 87. 12-13.

^c MS *psčpyt'* for *pšc'yt'*. The last phrase is a transcription of the Av. formula in Pahlavi script.

Chapter on *ayōkēn* "who to him afterwards".

MHD, I. 21. 5-8:

nibišt ku mard zan ud frazand bē duxt-ē kas nēst ud ān ī ān duxt šōy ān duxt az zanīh bē hilēd^a *ud pad sālārīh abāz ō pid nē dahēd ēg-iš stūrīh ī pid pad x*^w*āhišn. ud ka-š pad sālārīh abāz padīrēd*^b *ēg-iš abar ōh mānēd x*^w*āhišn pad kār <nē>* ^c *abāyēd.*

^a MS *ŠBKWN-x.*
^b MS *MKBLWN-x.*
^c *L'* is essential to a logical sense.

It has been written: A man has no wife and children but a daughter; and the husband of that daughter divorces that daughter, but he does not place her again under the guardianship of the father, thereupon, her assumption of the father's *stūrīh* is optional[27]. And if he (i.e. the father) takes her back under his guardianship, thereupon, she shall succeed to his (*stūrīh*); her consent is not necessary.

MDH, I. 21. 8-10:

Sōšyāns guft ku duxt ī beastān^a *ka-š bē hilēd, ka-š murd pid bē hilēd, ēg-iz-iš ayōkēn*[2] *abar ōh mānēd.*

^a MS *by'st'n*, to my mind from *be-ast-ān*, pronounced *biyastān* (?) (lit. out of the house), a daughter who having come of age marries without the consent of her father or guardian, *REA*, *Pursišn* 30 (fourth definition); see *SMR*, 334-5. Bartholomae reads *baydēspān* "Götterbote", a euphemism for bastard, *ZsR*, V. 30-1, Klingenschmitt *bayaspān* and adds "Die Begleitumstände ... erinnern an die Definition der altindischen *gāndharva-Ehe*", *MSS*, Heft 21, p. 63, and n. 5; Perikhanian *bayaspān* "marriage *sine manu mariti*", *HMV*, 349 f; Bulsara *biyâstân* "immodest", *Code*, 152-3.
2 MS *'ywk kyn'*.

Sōšyāns maintained[28]: If a *beastān* daughter is divorced, (or) when her father is dead she is divorced, she shall succeed to the *ayōkēnīh* of her father.

---

[27] From the context it is not quite clear whose wish or desire (*x*^w*āhišn*) is meant, the daughter's or guardian's. Since divorce is not considered valid without dissolution of guardianship (cf. *MHD*, I. 4. 9-10 : I. 87. 5-6 : I. 87. 6-9 and my *Sasanian Matrimonial Relations*, *ArOr* 39, 1971, p. 340) the *x*^w*āhišn* may refer to the guardian, i.e. the ex-husband.

[28] *guftan* (lit. to say, speak) should be rendered "to maintain, to profess an opinion" in legal terminology, cf. Arab. *qaul*.

MDH, I. 21. 10-15:

nibišt ku[a] *ka frazand ī pas-zād*[b] *duxt ud zīndag pid šōy kunēd, az zanīh hilēd ud abāz šawēd widard stūrīh*[c] *kunēd*[d] *ān stūrīh abar ān duxt ōh mānēd. ud ka-š dādistān aōn i* [+]*stūrīh ī pidar*[+] [e] *andar abāyēd pad ān ī pid ōh gumārišn. ud ast kē ēdōn gōwēd ku ka-z-iš andar ān i ka stūr ī kardag pad baxt šawēd šōy [kardan] nē hišt ēstēd ēg-iz yō hē pasčaita*[f]. *Wahrām guft ku ka-š andar ān ī šōy kard ēdōn abāyēd dāštan čēōn ka nē zindag hē.*

    [a] *'YK* is written over *'MT*.
    [b] MS *YLYDWN-yt*, but cf. *'ḤL YLYDWN-t*, *MHD*, I. 47. 1, and *MHD*, I. 21. 15-16.
    [c] MS has a defective *stwly* for *stwlyh*.
    [d] MS *krt'*, better *kunēd* for concord of tense.
    [e] *'BYtl Y stwl*, evidently by copyist's mistake.
    [f] MS gives *ywk hy psčyt'* which when compared with the *'ywk h<y> psčyt'* of the heading the equivalence of *yō hē = yōk hē = ayōk-hē* becomes evident.

It is written: If the last born child is a girl who marries in the lifetime of the father, the husband divorces her and she goes back and assumes the *stūrīh* of a deceased person, that *stūrīh* remains the duty of that daughter. And if her juridical case is such that she should of necessity assume the *stūrīh* of the father, she ought to be instituted to that *stūrīh*. And there is one (jurisconsult) who maintains thus: Even if the husband has not divorced her when the designate[29] *stūr* passes away, she shall assume the *ayōkēnīh*[30] (i.e. obligated successorship) of her father. Wahram maintained: While she is married it must be so considered, as if she were not alive.

MDH, I. 21. 15-22. 1:

*duxt ī pas-zād kē stūrih abar mānēd az čēōn x*ʷ*ēš, ka stūr < īh >* [a] *abarmānd ī pas < -zād >* [b] *nē bawēd andar-iz abarmānd ī pad stūrīh abarmānd ī pad x*ʷ*ēšīh būd nē šāyēd.*

    [a] MS *stwl* for *stwlyh*.
    [b] *YLYDWN-t* as the second element of the compound *'ḤL-YLYDWN-t* is omitted by copyist's error. Klingenschmitt suggests *'BYtl* for *'ḤL* which is hardly convincing.

The last born daughter who succeeds to the management of the *stūrīh* (of her father) is like (the father's) own (*pādixšāyīhā* wife)[a].

    [29] Because a designated stūr has priority over a daughter in assuming the successorship, i.e. contracting a *stūrīh* marriage for the deceased.
    [30] i.e. *yō hē pasčaēta*.

If the *stūrīh* is not a transmitted obligation of the last-born (daughter) neither there may be an inheritance in absolute ownership included in the inheritance which is to be held for *stūrīh* [b].

[a] The sentence is rather obscure. I cannot think of any better explaination. On her proprietary rights as a *pādixšāyīhā* wife see *REA*, *Pursišn* 44; *SMR*, 333.

[b] i.e. the legacy which is to be held in trust for the management of *stūrīh*.

MHD, I. 22. 1-2:

pad guft ī dastwarān aōn nibišt ku yō hē pasčaita [a] *ka zīndag pid šōy kunēd xūb šud, u-š ān stūrīh pad ān dastwarīh awiš nē rasēd.*

[a] MS *ywk hy pww sčyt'* by copyist's error.

From the dictums of the religious authorities it is so written : If an *ayōkēn* (daughter) marries in the lifetime of the father, her going away is legally sound, and that *stūrīh* on that authority does not devolve upon her.

MHD, I. 23. 1-4:

Wāyayyār nibišt ku ka duxt pad dastwarīh ī pid andar kas kunēd ku tā 10 sāl zan ī tō hom ud pid pēš az 10 sāl mīrēd pid tā 10 sāl stūr uzišn [a] *ud ka 10 sāl uzīd duxt zanīh i kas nēst ud *ayōkēn ī [ud] pid.*

[a] MS *YNPKsšn* for the correct *YNPKWN-šn*, *uzišn*. Bulsara has read *yopsêshn* (!), *Code, 161*, and Klingenschmitt *gowsišn* (!), *SSM*, 21, 61. The emendation, suggested by the following *YNPKWN-t'*, *uzīd*, is essential to the coherent sense of the sentence.

Wāyayyār has written: If a daughter with her father's sanction promises a person : "I shall be your wife for 10 years', and the father dies before the termination of those 10 years, thereupon the *stūrīh* of the father should be suspended till the end of those 10 years, and when the term of 10 years elapses, the daughter is in no one's wedlock and is the *ayōkēn* of the father.

MHD, I. 89. 17-90. 1:

*abāg ān ī guft ku duxt ī pid kard ku zanīh ī Mihrēn kun ka zanīh ī Mihrēn nē kunēd *ayōkēn i pid abar ōh mānēd, abarmānd ōh bawēd.*

In conjunction with that which is said : A daughter whose father has prescribed her : "Enter into marriage with Mihrēn", if she does not assume the wifehood of Mihrēn, she shall succeed to the *ayōkēnīh* of the father; she shall become the successor [31].

[31] *Abarmānd*, pass. pt. of *abar māndan*, literally means "left over", however, in our

MHD, I. 24. 3-7:

būd kē guft ku duxt ī andar xānag ī pidarān zād ēstēd ka-š mād andar zīndagīh ī pid ī mād šōy kard *ayōkēn ī pid ī mād abar nē mānēd. Māhwindād[a] *guft ku duxt ī*[b] *pad ān ēwēn*[c] *ka-š mād andar zīndagānīh ī pid ī mād šōy ayāb margarzān ayāb paratačaiti*[d] *(paratačaita) kard kā-š nēm bahrag ī mād abar nēmānēd ēg-iš*[e] *ka pad *ayōkēn andar abāyēd ā-š *ayōkēn abar ōh mānēd.*

[a] MS *m'hwd't*, Bartholomae *Māhāndāt*, *ZsR*, V, 33, is a corrupt spelling for *m'hwnd't*, "Māhwindād", retraced by an unskilled hand. The name of this famous commentator and jurisprudent appears in many Pahlavi books, see *Vyt*, 3, 3; *Py*, 9, 33; *Š n-Š* (Tavadia), *App*. 2, 2; *MHD*, I. 65. 14, etc.

[b] Bartholomae reads *l*.

[c] MS *'ywkyn'* which with Bartholomae I emend to *'dwyn'*.

[d] Written in Avestan characters followed by its transcription in Pahlavi script.

[e] Bartholomae reads *ēvāč*, perhaps inadvertently.

There was a jurisconsult who maintained: A daughter who is born in the house of the ancestors[32] if her mother marries in the lifetime of the father of (her) mother, she will not succeed to the *ayōkēn* (*stūrīh*) of the father of (her) mother. Māhwindād maintained: If the mother of such a daughter either marries in the lifetime of the father of (her) mother, or commits a *margarzān* (death-deserving) sin, or breach of promise[33] (?) then the half share of her mother does not pass to her; thereupon, if it is binding on her to become the *ayōkēn* (of her grand-father), she should succeed to (his) *āyōkēn* (*stūrīh*).

text not in the sense of "legacy", but "successor", "one who maintains succession". Cf. *MHD*, I. 22. 3: *duxt abarmānd ī pid nē bawēd*, which obviously does not imply that the daughter is not the father's legacy, but rather her not being liable to assume the successorship of the father, i.e. to maintain his lineage by undertaking his *stūrīh*. The use of *abarmānd* in the sense of "uninterrupted tradition, sequence", Skr *pāramparyam* (Neryosang, *ŠGV*) attests our interpretation. Bartholomae's translation "Erbschaft" is hardly justifiable in this context, *ZsR*, V. 4, 27-8. On *abarmānd* as "residuary legacy" see *SMR*, 341-2.

[32] The expression *andar xānag ī pidarān zād* is the same as *andar dūdag zād* "a child born of *stūrīh* marriage for the maintenance of the family", see *SMR*, 331, n. 4: *MHD*, II. 35. 11-16. Therefore, "a daughter born in the house of her ancestors" is in our case a girl born of *stūrīh* or *ayōkēnīh* marriage of her mother to maintain the lineage of her grand-father.

[33] Av. *paratačaiti* (lit. runs away) may be an Avestan term for breach of promise of *stūrīh*, i.e. running away from one's obligation to assume *stūrīh*, which is considered a grave *margarzān* sin: *az wināh ī mardōmān kunēnd ... garāntar ... kē stūr rāyēnītārīh škanēd*, *MX*, 36 Nyberg, *A Manual of Pahlavi I*, p. 82. 4-8: For Bartholomae's translation of this passage see *ZsR*, V. 32-3 and that of Klingenschmitt *SSM*, 21, 67.

MHD, I. 22. 8-9:

yō(k)hē pasčaita[a] *abar pus ud duxt ī pādixšāyihā ī zahāg mānēd.*

[a] MS gives in Pahlavi script *ywk hy psčyt'*.

The obligation of successorship[a] descends to a *pādixšāyihā* son and/or daughter capable of begetting children.

[a] Lit. who to him/her afterwards [(i.e. after the death of the father) descends the obligation of successorship]. In the case of a *pādixšāyihā* (one's own) son the succession is maintained by his natural status, and in the case of a daughter through her undertaking the father's *stūrīh*.

MHD, I. 22. 2-3:

ēn-iz aōn[a] *nibišt ku yō(k)hē pasčaita ka duxt abarmānd ī pid nē bawēd ud ka pus ā-š bawēd.*

[a] *ZNH-č* is superimposed on *'wgwn'*.

It is also so written: Concerning the institution of *ayōkēnīh*, if a daughter cannot become a successor[a] of the father, a son, if (there is one), is (always) liable to it.

[a] For *abarmānd* in the sense of "successor" cf. *MHD*, I. 89. 17-90. 1.

MHD, I. 23. 13-14:

pid kē-š pus ast *ayōkēn abar duxt nē mānēd.

(In the case of a) father who has a son, (his) daughter does not succeed to his *ayōkēnīh* (successorship)[a].

[a] i.e. she is not bound by duty to assume his *ayōkēn stūrīh*, because of his secured succession.

MHD, I. 22. 3-6:

ka [š] brād 2 ud xʷah-ē ān gyāg ud ān [ud] xʷah abāg brād-ē hambāy u-š brād-ē did abar sālār, ud brād 2 har pad ē jār pad baxt šawēnd[a] *pad čāštag ī Abarak sālār, pad ān ī Mēdōgmāh hambāy*[b] *gōwēnd ku ka-š ast ā-š abar mānēd.*

[a] For the translation of this part of the sentence by Bartholomae see *ZsR*, V, 26.
[b] MS *hmb'gyh*.

If there are two brothers and one sister, and that sister is an associate of one of the brothers, and the other brother is her guardian, and both brothers die at the same time, then in accordance with the doctrine of Abarak it is the guardian and that of Mēdōgmāh the associate (brother), if she has had one, to whose (ayōkēn stūrīh) she should succeed [34].

MHD, I. 22. 6-8:
ka mād andar dūdag x^wah stūrīh ī brād abar nē mānēd u-š-iz čim ēn ku x^wah pad zanīh mād be pādixšāy dād pad ān čim sālārīh ī andar brād nē bawandag.

If there is a mother in the family the *stūrīh* of the brother does not devolve upon the sister; the reason for it is this: Because the mother is entitled to give (his) sister in marriage, the (force of) guardianship of the (deceased) brother is not sufficient[a] (complete).

  [a] But according to *MHD*, I. 22. 11-12 a sister would succeed to the *stūrīh* of her guardian-brother.

MHD, I. 22. 11-12:
ka pad sālārīh <ō> brād be dād ēstēd ēg-iz-iš *ayōkēn abar ōh mānēd sālār az x^wēšāwandān ī brād [Y] bawēd.

If she (i.e. the sister) had been placed under the guardianship of the brother, thereupon, she should succeed to his *ayōkēn* (*stūrīh*) and (her new) guardian should be a relative of the brother.

MHD, I. 22. 9-12 :
duxt ī pid pad sālārīh ō mard ī šahr dād ēstēd *ayōkēn ī pid ud brād kam abar nē mānēd, ka-š *ayōkēn ī pid abar mānēd sālār ān ham, ud ka-š ān ī brād abar mānēd sālār az nabānazdištān[a] ī brād bawēd, ka pad sālārīh <ō> brād be dād ēstēd ēg-iz-iš *ayōkēn abar ōh mānēd sālār az x^wēšāwandān ī brād bawēd.

  [a] MS *b'nzšt'n* for *nb'nzdšt* by copyist's error.

The daughter whom the father has left under the guardianship of a townsman will no more succeed to the *ayōkēnīh* of either the father or brother. If the *ayōkēn* (*stūrīh*) of the father should descend to her, the guardian should have been the same, and if that of the brother should descend to her, her guardian should become (someone) from (among) the brother's next of kin; if she had been placed under the guardianship of the brother, thereupon, she should succeed (to his *ayōkēnīh*) and (her) guardian should be (someone) from the brother's (agnatic) relatives.

  [34] The case obviously concerns the preference of a guardian brother over an associate brother and *vice versa* in the institution of *stūrīh* marriage by their sister.

MHD, I. 22. 13-23. 1:

*ka brād 2 ud x^wah-ē ān gyāg ud baxtīgīh kunēnd^a ud brād i kih ud x^wah āginēn bahr girēnd x^wah sālārīh-iz be ō brād ī kih rasēd. abāg-iz ān pas-iz ka brād ī mih pēš mīrēd ēd rāy čē x^wah sālārīh az brād nē pad dād i brād bē nē paykārdan [ī] ka bazišn kard brād abar sālārīh ī x^wah rāy aziš ābār^b būd ēstēd x^wah *ayōkēn ī brād ī mih, ud ka naxust brād ī kih mīrēd ka-z har 2 pad ē tāg mīrēnd x^wah *ayōkēn ī brād ī kih.*

^a Bartholomae has read *kunihēd*, perhaps a *lap. cal.*, *ZsR*, V. 27.

^b MS *'p'l*, with M. Boyce I read *ābār*, *BSOAS*, XXXI, 1968, p. 276, n. 41; see *GrnE*, No. 53; Hübschmann, *Pers. St.* pp. 9-10; cp. NP *āvār*, *BQ*, ed. Mo'īn, p. 65.

If there are two brothers and one sister, and they distribute the estate (patrimony), and the younger brother and sister take their shares in common, thereupon, the guardianship over the sister devolves upon the younger brother[35]. In regard to this (case), if afterwards the elder brother dies prior to the younger one, because the guardianship of the sister (had passed to the younger brother) from the (elder) brother not by its assignment by the (elder) brother, but through (his) not having laid claim (to it) when the estate was being distributed, (and therefore the elder) brother had lost his guardianship over the sister, the sister (succeeds) to the *ayōkēn* (*stūrīh*) of the elder brother. And if the younger brother dies first, or even if both of them die at the same time, the sister (succeeds to) the *ayōkēn* (*stūrīh*) of the younger brother.

MHD, I. 23. 5-10:

*ka mard pad baxt šawēd u-š zan ud frazand [ud bē] x^wah ēg-iš *ayōkēn ī brād abar nē mānēd. ud ka baxtīgīh kard ān ī ōy brād abar mānēd kē-š bahr pad hambāyīh abāg stad ayāb-iš pad abarmānd ī dastwarīh abar sālār būd. ka baxtīgīh kard ud brād-ē ī kē bahr pad hambāyīh abāg stad ud brād-ē <ī> kē-š pad abarmānd ī dastwarīh abar sālār būd frāz raft *ayōkēn ī ōy brād abar mānēd kē-š abar sālār būd ud ka-š abāg brād 2 pad hambāyīh bahr stad ēstēd az pēš paydāg.*

If a man passes away and his is a wife and children, thereupon, the *ayōkēn* (*stūrīh*) of the brother does not descend to the sister; and (after) they have distributed the estate she succeeds to that of that brother with whom she had gone shares[36], or to him who had been her guardian in accordance with the canon laws relative to

---

³⁵ Bartholomae has translated this section correctly, *ZsR*, V. 27.

³⁶ lit. had taken a share in partnership.

succession [37]. If (after) they have distributed the estate, the brother with whom she had gone shares [36] and the brother who had become her guardian in accordance with the canon laws relative to succession both die [38], she succeeds to the *ayōkēnīh* of the brother who had been her guardian; and if she had gone shares with both brothers, her case is clear from what has been said before.

MHD, I. 23. 4:

u-š ēn-iz aōn nibišt ku x^wah *ayōkēn ī brād andar hambāyīh ī brād abar mānēd.

And he[a] also wrote thus : A sister who is the *ayōkēn* (*stūr*) of (her) brother also succeeds to (his *ayōkēnīh*) as his associate.

[a] This sentence following a pronouncement of Wāyayyār (*MHD*, I. 23. 1-4) must also belong to him.

MHD, I. 23. 14-17:

brād-iz ka brād ī hambāy ast *ayōkēn <īh> abar x^wah nē mānēd. Bōzišn[a] aōn dāšt ku hambāy ī zīndag[b] ō kardag nē kard[c] ēstēd hamē sālārīh kār ...[d] ud ka brād ī mih mīrēd ēg-iš *ayōkēn abar mānēd ud ka ān ī kih mīrēd ā-š nē mānēd.

[a] MS *bwhš'n* hardly *be-šān*, Klingenschmitt, *MSS*, 21. 62. It may be a new name Bōxšān. Av. *baoxšna-*, Bulsara, Code, 163, not met with anywhere else. In all likelihood it is a corruption of Bōzišn, the well-known Pahlavi commentator occurring in *MHD*, II. 12. 3 "Dādfarrox ī Farroxzurwān Bōzišn", and *MHD*, I. 40. 3 "Bōzišn". "Bōzan" (?), *Nisā* 1949/4.

[b] MS *zywndk*, cf. *hambāy ī zīndag*, *MHD*, I. 24. 2: Bulsara *zīvandak*, Code, 163, Klingenschmitt *dīnīy* (!), *MSS*, 21. 62.

[c] MS *KBYDWN-t* for *'BYDWN-t* by copyist's error.

[d] A sentence must be missing here, since the following sentence has no bearing on the preceding subject. This is, in fact, the concluding sentence of *MHD*, I. 22. 13-23.1.

Also if a brother has a partner-brother (his) **ayōkēn* (*stūrīh*) does not descend to (his) sister. Bōzišn so maintained: A partner (brother) who has not been established as a designate (*stūr*)[a] in the lifetime (of the deceased) is only liable to the guardianship (over the family of the deceased)... and if the elder brother dies first, thereupon, she succeeds to his *ayōkēn* (*stūrīh*), and if the younger one dies (first), she does not.

[37] On *abarmānd* in the sense of "succession" see above *MHD*, I, 89. 17-90. 1.
[38] Lit. went aloft.

^a On *kardag* "designate" see *SMR*, 328.

Pagliaro interprets the phrase *ō kartak kartan* "actio in ius", *RSO*, 23. 67, and the whole passage of the *MHD*, I. 23. 15-16 as "Da Boxšān era ritenuto che al socio, al quale da vivo non è stata fatta ingiunzione formale, spetta tutta la potesta", *ibid.*, 65-6. However, other considerations apart, *zindag* does not refer to the associate (*hambāy*), but to the principal, i.e. the deceased brother for whom an *ayōkēn stūrīh* is to be instituted, and *ō kardag kardan* should be rendered "to establish as designate (*stūr*)", otherwise, the sentence would make little sense. On the obligation of guardianship by a partner-brother see *MHD*, II. 26. 10-12.

MHD, I. 23. 17-24. 2:

ka pid <ud> duxt-ē ud dūdag ī pus-ē pad ān dūdag x^wāstag 60 ast, duxt sālārīh pad pid, ud ka pid frāz rawēd *ayōkēn ī brād čē widard pid <duxt> ^a *abāg dūdag ī pus hambāy.*

^a The context requires the emendation.

If there is a father, a daughter and the family of a son, and there is a property worth 60 (*satērs*)^a in that family, the guardianship over the daughter rests with the father. And if the father passes away (the daughter succeeds to) the brother's *ayōkēnīh*, since on (her) father's death she becomes an associate of the brother's family.

^a On 60 *satērs* as the minimum capital for establishing a *stūrīh* marriage see *SMR*, 328-30; Perikhanian, *HMV*, 357.

MHD, I. 69. 12:

duxt ī padīriftag *ayōkēn ī brād abar nē mānēd.

An adopted daughter does not succeed to the *ayōkēn* (*stūrīh*) of her brother ³⁹.

MHD, I. 49. 2-3:

zan ī čakar ka barwar^a *ā-š *ayōkēn abar ōh mānēd.*^b *tā dād ī 50*^c *sālāg pad barwar dārišn.*

^a *blwl* is explained by *FP*, Junker 1955, p. 20 as "brother", not attested in any other text. Bartholomae reads *barwar* but interprets "nutzbringend", *ZsR*, V. 29. Bulsara reads correctly *barvar* "fruitful", Code, 298. The word is synonymous with **barōmand* explained by *FO*. 2f as Av. *barəθra-* "pregnant", cf. NP *bārvar*, *bārdār*.

^b MS *YḤWWN-yt*, apparently rewritten by an unskilled hand. The idiomatic phrase requires *QDM KN KTLWN-yt*, *abar ōh mānēd*. Bartholomae *apar ō bovēt*, *ibid.*

^c Modi restores the missing word as *LXX*, but according to the context this cannot be more than *L*, 50, the maximum age for a woman to bear children.

³⁹ i.e. her brother german.
Bartholomae's translation of this sentence is untenable, *ZsR*, V. 29.

If a *čakar*[40] woman is able to bear children, then the *ayōkēn* (*stūrīh*) descends to her. She should be considered able to bear children till the age of 50 (?).

MHD, I. 87. 1-2:
ka gōwēd ku < *-m tā 10 sāl*> [a] *tan pad zanīh ō tō dād ēg-iš andar 10 sāl
ayōkēn abar ōh mānēd.

[a] A gap just wide enough for *m 'D X ŠNT* is recovered in accordance with the tenor of the context.

If one declares: "I give myself to you in marriage for 10 years", thereupon, she succeeds to his *ayōkēn* (*stūrīh*) for those 10 years[a].

[a] i.e. if the husband dies within those 10 years, she is liable to assume his *ayōkēn* (*stūrīh*), in this case *čakarīh*, till the end of that period when her marriage contract ends.

MHD, I. 23. 10-13:
*ka brād 2 ud x^wah-ē ān gyāg x^wah sālārīh pad brād i mih ud būd kē
guft ku ka x^wāstag nēst ēg-iz hambāy ōh bawēd ud ka*[a] *ast ēg-iz pad
rāh ī ham-windišnīh abāz gumēxtēd. abāg-iz ēd ku *ayōkēn x^wāstag
x^wāst nē āmār.*

[a] Better *'MT-š*, where the enclitic pronoun refers to the guardian-brother.

If there are two brothers and one sister, the guardianship over the sister rests with the elder brother. And there was (a jurisconsult) who maintained: If (his) is no property, thereupon, he shall become (her) associate, and if (he) has property, then, it shall, by way of profit-sharing, not be mixed[41]. Also in conjunction with this (case): an *ayōkēn*'s[42] demanding property (from the capital) cannot be taken into account.

MHD, I. 47. 7-14:
Wāyayyār nibišt ku ka mard-ē x^wāstag pad stūrīh ī x^wēš[a] *paydāg kard
ud pad dāštan har sāl ē*[b] *sāl ō Farrox* <*ud*> *ē*[c] *sāl ō Mihrēn dād
Farrox ud Mihrēn jud jud pad ān x^wāstāg yō hē pasčaita*[d] *ōh bawēd,*

---

[40] On *čakar*, a widow assuming the *stūrīh* (in this case leviration) of her issueless deceased husband see *SMR*, 331. Should she be fruitful the obligation of her husband's successorship (*ayōkēnīh*) remains binding on her till the age of 50 (? 70).

[41] It is to be noted that in the second case the profit (*windišn*) and not the capital is mixed.

[42] i.e. a would-be *ayōkēn* (successor by *stūrīh*), in our case the sister.

čē ēd-iz pādixšāy ka frāz az x^wēš be dahēd jud jud zan padiš kard xūb, čē ēd-iz pādixšāy ka be ō zanān dahēd. yō hē pascaita ān bawēd ī pad ān sāl zāyēd ka-š stūrīh pad ō zan pad ān sāl kunišn. kas-š stūrīh padiš ēstēd ka az kūst ī būdag be bawēd ud andar būdagīh pad x^wēšīh be ō mard-ē rasēd az ēn kūst pad x^wēšīh ud az kūst ī did pad stūrīh rawēd.

[a] MS *NPŠH*, Bartholomae unwarrantedly emends to *NYŠH* in order to lend credence to his misinterpreted conception of *stūrīh*, ZsR, V. 39.

[b] MS *ḤD*, *ē*, *ēw*.

[c] MS *ḤN'*, *ēd*, frequently used for *ē* "one".

[d] MS *sčyt'* miswritten for *psčyt'*, in Pahlavi script.

Wāyayyār wrote: If a person has appointed[43] a property to be used for his own *stūrīh*[44] and has given it to be administered (held) of every two years one year by Farrox and one year by Mihrēn, (thereupon) Farrox and Mihrēn separately become his *ayōkēn* (*stūrs*) instituted by that property[45]. It is also possible for him either to assign it to be held after his death in order that they may, one at a time, (i.e. in alternate years) take to themselves a (*stūr*) wife by that (property), which is legally sound, or[46] to assign it for *stūrīh* to the (*stūr*) women. (Then) the obligated *stūr*- successor (*yō hē pascaita* or *ayōkēn*) would be the one who begets (a son) in that year (term) which he has instituted a woman to *stūrīh*[47]. If the *stūrīh* rests with (both of) them, and if one side (party) is a *būdag*[48], the (property) passes to (this) man in absolute ownership for him being a *būdag*, (thus) the property passes to one side in private ownership and to the other side (in trust) for *stūrīh* (in alternate years).

[43] The verbal phrase "*paydāg kardan*" used in legal MP terminology in the sense of "assign, appoint, specify" as well as "show, prove" (*MHD*, II. 6. 1) has continued in classical NP in all these meanings, cf. *Tārix-e Bal'amī*, ed. Bahar, p. 1050, and *Šāhnāme*, ed. Moscow, Vol. 8, p. 183. M. Boyce has taken it in the sense of "to devise" (*BSOAS*, 31 1968 p. 274, n. 25) which, although fitting in reference to a deceased, is not its proper sense.

[44] Bartholomae translates: "für die Pflege seiner Frau", *ibid.*, 39.

[45] Bartholomae's translation ends here.

[46] *QDM ... QDM*, *če ... če* here means "whether (either)... or', as in NP.

[47] Bartholomae's translation of this sentence runs: Als "*yō hē pascaēta*" gilt das, was in dem Jahr anfällt, in welchem Jahr von ihm die Pflege für jene Frau zu führen ist: *ZsR*, V. 40.

[48] For a *stūr ī būdag* "*stūr* at-law" holding the property assigned for *stūrīh* in absolute ownership (*x^wēšīh*) see *SMR*, 329.

MHD, I. 69. 3-9:

*abāg ān ī nibišt ku ka kunēd ku-m ēn anšahrīg har 2 sāl ē^a sāl ō
Mihrēn dād ān anšahrīg bē pad ham-dādistānīh ī āginēn ēnyā āzād
kardan nē pādixšāy ud ka yak bahr ī x^wēš pad hursandīh^b ī ōy ī did
āzād kunēd hamēwēn^c āzād—nigīridan. ⁺ud ka^{+ d} ē sāl pad stūrīh ō
Farrox ud ē sāl ō Mihrēn dād Farrox ud Mihrēn jud jud pad ān x^wāstag
yō hē pasčaita ōh bawēd. ud ka az kūst ī būdag be bawēd^c andar
būdagīh pad x^wēšīh ō mard-ē rasēd az ēn kūst pad x^wēšīh ud az kūst-ē
did pad stūrīh rasēd-nigīridan.*

  ^a Missing in MS Modi, but preserved in DJ *ḤD, ē, ēw*, Bulsara, *Code*, 385.
  ^b The SW form is *hursand* as against the NW *hunsand*, Paz. *hōnsand*. Cf. *hwrsnd* =
hwlsnd, *FP*, Chap. 31. 5 where the *r* is spelt *l*.
  ^c Repeated, the first in a corrupt form.
  ^d MS *ŠNT*, so Bulsara, *Code*, 385, a copyist's mistake when retracing the obliterated
W 'MT.
  ^e MS *YḤWWN-t* for *YḤWWN-yt'*.

In conjunction with that it is written: If a person settles: I have
given this slave to Mihrēn one year of every two years, that slave
may not be set free except by mutual agreement[49]. And if one
of them sets his own share (of the slave) free with the consent of the
other, he shall be free accordingly—(it is to be) deliberated. And
if he assigns him one year to Farrox and one year to Mihrēn for
stūrīh, Farrox and Mihrēn shall separately become *ayōkēn* (*stūrs*) by
that property. And if one side is a *būdag*, the slave passes to that
man in absolute ownership for him being a *būdag* (*stūr*), (thus)
(the slave) passes to one side in private ownership and to the other
side (in trust) for *stūrīh*[50] (in alternate years).

  [49] This section has been translated by Bartholomae, *ZsR*, III. 56.
  [50] i.e. the slave as a property assigned for *stūrīh* is to be held in alternate years by
the *būdag stūr* (*stūr* at-law) in ownership and by the other in usufruct, see *SMR*, 329.

WOJCIECH SKALMOWSKI

TWO STORIES IN AFRIDI DIALECT
FROM F.C. ANDREAS' NOTES

During World War I. the German Ministry of Culture ("das Preussische Kultusministerium") organized a Committee called "Phonographische Kommission" for collecting and recording texts, songs and music pieces from the Allied prisoners of war, who represented various »exotic« cultures. Among them were ca. 40 Pashto-speaking British soldiers from the North-Western Frontier, who were kept in a special POW camp called »Halbmondlager« in Zossen near Berlin. In the spring of 1916 the head of the Committee W. Doegen invited F.C. Andreas, who was at that time teaching in Göttingen, to come to Zossen and to start the collecting of materials; the task was urgent— wrote Doegen in his letter of 20 April 1916—"da die Afghanen voraussichtlich bald nach der Türkei abgeschoben werden". Together with this letter Andreas received 23 cards with personal data of the POWs, who were regarded as most suitable informers because of their literacy, knowledge of their folklore and clear pronounciation.

The results of Andreas' work in Zossen form a part of his unpublished »Nachlass«; they consist of hand-written notes in 8 maps, containing ca. 1550 pages. The material ranges from grammatical notes, paradigms, specialized vocabularies to loose phrases, proverbs and whole stories. Two Pashto dialects, viz. Afridi and Mohmandi, are especially well represented. Some of the material is obviously the product of Andreas' further study of his own notes (the dates on some pages show that he has been working intensively on them in the second half of 1918): the transcription is careful here and certain passages are translated into German; apparently he was preparing them for publication, but he never completed this task.

I had the opportunity to look through all this material during my stay at the Center for Middle Eastern Studies at Harvard University in the academic year 1969/70. Professor R.N. Frye who had brought photocopies of the notes from Hamburg to Harvard entrusted me with sorting out and preparing for publication all those fragments, which for the orientalists would still be of interest, inspite of the lapse of time, i.e. inspite of the progress in the knowledge of Pashto. Because of my other duties at Harvard at that time I could not work full-time at this task—which the mass of material would make necessary—but I realized that the eventual publication would in any case have to proceed in stages and be arranged according to the value of the linguistic material. I concentrated my work on what I considered to have the first priority, i.e. the longer pieces of coherent texts, which could be used for the study of syntax and idiomatics. The foremost reason for assigning morphology and phonetics a lower priority is the transcription used by Andreas, which is often difficult to interpret, sometimes inconsistent and always very complicated from the printer's point of view. Consequently I proposed to Professor Frye to start the editing with a few longer stories and a collection of proverbs, which apparently Andreas himself was intending to publish first. The longest story in the collection, called by Andreas "Hexengeschichte", has been prepared jointly by Professor Frye and me and it will be published elsewhere; the two stories presented here belong to the same kind of naive fairy-tale. They have been narrated (probably even written down and dictated, as the initial words of the second one suggest: yua kisá likū́ de Åpridỗ pä žábe) by Ṣenāb Gol, 35 years old, from the village Ašoxēl in the district of Peshawar; the second informer who probably collaborated in the preparation of the texts and—as is seen from Andreas' notes—commented on the pronounciation was Haḍrat Šāh, 27 years old, from the village Baḍixēl in the district of Kohat.

Both stories, carefully written down in the Latin transcription, have been left by Andreas without translation and have been supplied only by a few remarks on the margin of the page. The first story, called "Stammsage der Apridi, erzählt von Senab Gul" comes from map VI, pp. 65-66; the second one, marked "S.-G. (Åšoxḗl)" comes from the same map, pp. 67-69.

My editorial work consisted in supplying the translations and in simplifying the original transcription according to the following principles: (a) the signs of shortness of the vowels have been left out; (b) short and long rounded **a**-pronounciations (marked å and ǻ) have been retained; (c) other numerous specifications of vowel-pronounciation marked by means of dots, dashes and circles under the signs have been rendered uniformly as umlauts ä, ö, ë, because the phonetic reality behind those graphic variants is unknown. Andreas' remarks to the parts of texts marked by asterisks are given immediately after the texts themselves; there follow a few editorial remarks of mine, which may be useful for the reader of the original texts.

I.

(1) drē wr̩úṇa wū, de Kåból-na rèrëwåṇ̄ū. (2) mášër wróṟē Wazír nåmá wa, de dwåm wróṟē γëlgái nåmá wa, de driëm wróṟē Åprīdái nåmá wa. (3) mañgálō-la tsalór rédzē mazál wo, pa yué miåštē-kē r̩å-wárasēdù. (4) mazál lág wo, xó de dó dzéka iyuá miåštᵉ mazál wó-kr̩ë čē de dó-särá gádē wzé wē. (5) če dó pe yuwó talåo dērá šwū dó meslåtᵉ wó-krë če yua wzá bä alåla kù. (6) aγó wr̩úṇō yua wzá alåla kr̩a biá e bráxe kr̩a. (7) pä lári-kè dwó kåsō īsá wåxësta, ywå kas wå-ná-xësta. (8) Wazír isá wåxësta, Gëlǧí isá wåxësta, drém wróre Åpridí isá wå-ná-xësta. (9) dréwåra xᵉpál xᵉpal kålå-la låū. (10) Åprī-dái če xᵉpàl kålå-la wårasedä xᵉpàle xádze-la wårasedä we-ta wéwe če tå-la må γwéxa råwárie da. (11) dā xádza de då ḍéra xᵒšåla šwa če zå bä γwéx áxorᵊm. (12) áye xádza če γwéxa wåkatà lárai pa-kē ná-wa; de xádze xᵉpàl mērå-la åwe dáγe γwéxe-kè lárai näšta. (13) å we-ta yåyi če må de lári bráxa ná da råwårie. (14) da xádza we-tá yåyi xᵉpal mer̩å-la če lår̩ ša de lári bráxa te råwr̩a! (15) áya biå lår̩ä mášr wrōr-la lår̩ä aγå-la åwe če må-la bráxa de lári r̩å-ka! (16) aγå dzåb då wēr-kr̩ä če bráxa máxke tå náwr̩a* wós näšta. (17) wåpás te lår̩ä xádzē-la ye åwe če må-la wrór dzåb r̩å-kr̩a če bráxa näšta, tsá kᵊm? (18) xádza wē-tá yåyi de tå wr̩úṇa ná di xä če tå-la de lári bráxa dēr-ná-kr̩a. (19) dáγe xádze xᵉpal mer̩å-la åwe če tå-la yè spák nazīr wå-kr̩ä. (20) da xádza we-ta yåyi če tsá če te tsū bál watán-la! (21) óγo wr̩úṇo we-tá åwe če wéle de mú-na tsé? (22) då we-ta åwe če zå dená pa dé xabárē tsᵊm če mú-la de lári bráxa tåso r̩å-ná-kra. (23) wr̩úṇo we-ta åwe če de xádze xabära må-mana; ka tå ḍér xapá we mú ba de-tá bála wzà alåla kù. (24) suålúna yè we-tá ḍér wå-kr̩ū. (25) aγå we-tá åwe če de Paxtåṇó yuá xabára wī; må wéli dī če zä dena tsᵊm. (26) tê rawån šwä, Tirå-la wårasedä, då dwa wr̩úna pä máγ dzåe-yē préxu; Tirå-ke yo kálai ē ǧóṟ krä. (27) pä då *Tirå-ke de då špég zamén wå-šwu.

* *Andreas' remarks:* (16) H.S.: nåxësta (27) dáγ?

Editorial remarks: (3) mañgálo; probably Ar. منزل, taken over as [manġàl], cf. [lᵊġ], pronounced: *lag* in this dialect. (5) talåo, تلاو [taláu] m. "water-reservoir"; meslåtᵉ, مصلحت; alåla kù, from:

حلالول [halālawə́l] "to slaughter (cattle)" (6) bráxē kṛa, برخه کول [bárxa // bráxa kawə́l]; (7) pa lắri-ke, لړی /lə́ray/ m. "stomach, intestines"; īsa, حصه [hissá] f. "part, share"; (19) Aslanov's Dictionary, s.v. سپک /spə́k, spuk/: چاته په سپک نظر کتل "to look at somebody with contempt, to despise"; (23) xapá "angry", cf. پسیدل /pəxedə́l/ "to hiss (like a snake); metaphorically: to be angry", with a metathesis like in پښه /pxa/ f. "foot", Eastern Pashto ښپه /xpa/.

I. *Translation*

(1) There were three brothers—they were on their way (back) from Kabul. (2) The eldest brother's name was Wazir; the second brother's name was Gilzai, the third brother's name was Apridai. (3) There was a distance of four days to (their) homes, (but) they arrived (only) after one month. (4) The distance was small, but they travelled one month because there were (their) sheeps (and) goats with them. (5) When they were camping (one day) at a pond, they decided: "We will slaughter one goat". (6) These brothers slaughtered one goat and divided it. (7) From the intestines two persons got (their) share, (but) one person didn't get (any). (8) Wazir got a part, Gilzai got a part, the third brother Apridai didn't get (any) part. (9) (Thereafter) all three of them went to their cottages. (10) When Apridai got (back) to his village, to his wife, he said to her: "I have brought you (some) meat". (11) This woman became very glad (because) of it, (thinking:) "I will eat meat". (12) When this woman saw that there were no intestines in (that) meat—this woman said to her husband: "There are no intestines in this meat". (13) This (man) says to her: "I haven't received (any) share of the intestines". (14) The woman says to her husband: "Go, bring your part of the intestines!" (15) So this (man) went, he went to (his) eldest brother (and) said to him: "Give me (my) share of the intestines". (16) This answered him so: "You didn't take (your) share before—there is none now". (17) So he went (back) from there (and) he said to (his) wife: "(My) brother answered me: 'There is no part for you'—what should I do?" (18) (His) wife says to him: "Your brothers are not good, since they didn't give you (any) part of the intestines". (19) This woman says to him: "They looked at you with a light eye (= treated you in a despicable way)". (20) (And) this woman says to him: "Come, let's go to (some) other country!" (21) These brothers said to him: "Why do you (want to) go (away) from us?" (22) He said to them: "I'am going (away)

from here for the reason that you didn't give us (our) share of the
intestines". (23) The brothers said to him: "Don't listen to a woman's
word—if you are very angry, we will slaughter another goat for you".
(24) They begged him very (hard) (to stay). (25) He said to them:
"The Afghans have (only) *one* word (and) I have already spoken:
'I (will) go (away) from here'".

(26) He departed from there (and) arrived in Tira—the two (other)
brothers stayed in their previous place—he built a cottage in Tira.
(27) In that Tira (-cottage) from him six sons became (born).

II.

(1) de egǻná xálko wǻ de begǻra xálko kisá.
(2) yo saṛái wǻ, bélkuǎl paisá we-srá ná-wa. (3) aɣǻ ǻwe dostǻno-la
če zǻ ṇdëstǻn-la tsəm, (d)e mǻ-sra paisá nḗšta. (4) dostǻno we-tá ǻwe
če xaṛí mäzdurí délta kawà! (5) aɣǻ wǻ-ná-manǎla*xádze-la ye ǻwe
wǻ zamǻno-la ye ǻwe če tsǒ če tsú! (6) kǎḍa ye wǻ-taṛäla rawàn šwū.
(7) yua rēdz če mazál e wǻ-kṛä yua wána wa (d)eɣé-lǻndē dō derá šwū.
(8) p-áɣe wáne-kè̃ če dǒ te-lǻnde derá wū yo mṛɣái*pa-kè̃ kénästä* de
wáne pä sār-ke. (9) daɣ saṛí xᵉpále xádze-la ǻwe če kaṭáwa ǻwinza
zǎ da mṛɣái wáləm. (10) áɣe xádze ìts* dzawǎb wer-ná-kṛä pōrta šwa
kaṭáwa ye ǻwinzäla. (11) mášër zǒe-la ye ǻwe če tǎ largí rǎwṛa*!
(12) kášër zǒe-la ye ǻwe tǎ wǒr bal kà*! (13) aɣǎ wǒr bál kṛä.
(14) mṛɣí če da tǒle xabǎre wǎ-rwedè̃ mṛɣí ǻwe pä zṛǎ-ke če dǎ xalk
tōl egǎná da. (15) (d)e dé wáne-lǎnde xadzäná* da (16) dǎ we-tá
xáya ka dǎ de we-tá wǎ-ná-xala no wěžni de. (17) we-tá xǎya-ye če
de marga báč še. (18) wǒs aɣ saṛí-la yǎyi de de wáne-lǎnde xädzǎnā
da (19) ka mǎ ǻwalè̃ zǎ mǎṛ šəm pa mǎ-kē pǎö ɣwěxa nḗšta da
(20) (d)e de wanē xǎ wǎ-kana ḍéra xadzǎná da te-lǎnde. (21) aɣ
saṛí éɣe wáne xǎ wǎ-kanēstä xadzǎnǎ ye te wá-xka. (22) xadzǎnǎ
ye rarewǎna kra káli-la, pëstaná* rǎɣai kǎlǎ-la. (23) a dostán-e we-ta
rǎgírd šwū* paxtaná ye te wǎ-kra če tǎ xo lǎnd rǎstǔn šwē? (24) dǎ
we-tá tǒla kisá wǎ-kra láka* da máxke bayǎn me likǎlai; dǎ ye*dostǎno-
la ǻwe. (25) pa dǒ dostǎno-kē ye yo saṛái wǻ če dǎ xabáre ye tǒle
wǎ-rwedè̃. (26) dǎ saṛái kǎlǎ-la lǎṛä aɣǎ xádze-la ǻwe če ëndëstǎn-la
tsǖ če paisá wǎ-gatǖ wǻ rǎ-e-wṛǖ. (27) tǒla kǎḍa ye wǎ-taṛǎla sabǎyi*
rawǎn šwū. (28) yuá rēdz mazál e wǎ-kra de yu(w)é wáne-lǎnde derǎ
šwū. (29) m-áɣa mṛɣái de wáne pä sǎr-ke kénǎstä če áɣ mṛɣí máxke
saṛí-la*xadzǎnǎ xǎlie wa.
(30) dáɣ saṛí xádze-la ǻwe če kaṭáwa ǻwinzà zǎ da mṛɣái wáləm.

(31) xádze dzawãb wér-kṛä mēṛã-la če da mṛɣái tã wĩštai ná-da—tã
pa mã kaṭáwa wínze! (32) zõe-la yè ãwe če largí rãwṛa*! aɣá-m
dzawãb wér-kṛä če mṛɣái nãsta* på wáne-kē wå tã pa mã largí
rãwṛḗ! (34) kášär zõe-la ye ãwe če wõr bãl ka! (35) kãšär zõe dzawãb
wér-kṛä pëlãr-la če mṛɣái pä wáne-kē nãsta wå tã pä mã balawḗ!
(36) mṛɣí če da ṭóle xabãre wã-rwedè mṛɣí we-tá awe dáɣ saṛí-la če
gãṭe kawí ã xalk ṭól egãná wi; (37) tãso egãná nã-yo, tãso begãra yo.
(38) tãso ka ëndëstãn-la lãṛ šo tãso gãṭa bä wã-ná-ko — tãso begãra
yo. (39) tãso de-pãra påedá da če pa xpal watán-la lãṛ šo, pa xpál
watán-ke wõ-so.

* *Andreas' remarks:* (5) Femin(inum), weil an *xabära* zu denken ist.
(8) Plur. mṛɣí, Fem. mṛɣḗ; Plur. masc. kḗnãsũ, fem. —tē. (10) ? *ēts*
mit sehr geschlossen(em) ḗ. (11) rãgírd ka. (12) zà wõr balãm- ich
mache Feuer an. (15) H(aḍrat)Š(āh) : xazãná. (22) *wãpás* (pers.) wäre
mehr Hindustani. (23) Var.: we-tá rãɣlu. (24) Var.: láka pa mã da
wãl ter šáwai da; Var.: dã xabáre yḕ — wã-kṛḗ. (27) dies die Aussprache
der Ašoxḗl, die Āxorwãl sagen nach S.-G.: sëbaī. (29) Var.: aɣ máxke
saṛíla.
(32) Var.: rãgírd ka. (33) nãst + da.

Editorial remarks: (1) egãná, Standard Pashto: حقانه [haqqāná];
begãra, بيگره [begṛã]. (2) bélkuãl, Ar. بالكل [bi-l-kull] (6) kãḍa, كده
[kaḍa], f. "family (of the nomads)". (9) kaṭáwa, كتوى [kaṭwɔ́y] f.; awinza,
from: ...اويزاندول [awezāndawɔ́l]; wúlǝm, from: وهل [wahɔ́l] "to hit,
to beat, etc." (15) xaya, from: سودل [xodɔ́l]. (26) wã-gaṭũ, cf. گنه كول
[gáṭa kawɔ́l], "to earn". (39) wõ-so, from سول [swǝl], "to burn", also
colloquially: "to die (in a miserable way)".

II. *Translation*

(1) A story about good (i.e. hardworking) people and about lazy people.
(2) There was a man—he had no money at all. (3) He said to (his)
friends: "I'm going to India— I have no money". (4) The friends
told him: "(Stay and) do (your) city-labourer's job here!" (5) He
didn't listen (to their talk)—he said to (his) wife, he said to (his) sons:
"Come, let's go!" (6) He packed (his) belongings (and) they set out.
(7) When they had made a one-day way— there was a tree (there),
under which they set up (their) bivouac. (8) On this tree under which
they were camping a bird was sitting—at the top of the tree. (9) The

man said to his wife: "Hang up the kettle—I (am going to) kill this bird". (10) The woman didn't give any answer, (she) stood up (and) hung up the kettle. (11) He said to the elder son: "Bring (some) fire-wood!" (12) He said to the younger son: "Make a fire!" (13) This (boy) made a fire. (14) When the bird heard all those words—the bird said to himself: "These people—all (of them)—are all-right. (15) Under this tree (there) is a treasure (buried). (16) Show it to him—if you don't show it to him, he will kill you— (17) show it to him, so that you will be saved from death". (18) Immediately (the bird) says to the man: "Under this tree is a treasure; (19) if you kill me (and) I'm dead—there is no good meat on me (anyhow). (20) Dig near this tree—there is a great treasure under it".

(21) This man dug near the tree (and) he brought up the treasure from there. (22) He took the treasure (with him) to (his) village; he went back to (his) village.

(23) Those friends of his gathered around him (and) asked: "(Why is it that) you returned so quickly?" (24) This (man) told them the whole story as I had written it before (here)—(this) he told to (his) friends. (25) There was a man among those friends of his who heard all of the story. (26) This man went home (and) said to (his) wife: "We are going to India to earn money and bring it (here)". (27) He packed all (his) belongings (and) in the morning they departed. (28) They made a one-day distance and bivouaced a tree. (29) The same bird was sitting at the top of the tree which had shown the treasure to the first man. (30) This man said to (his) wife: "Hang up the kettle—I (am going to) kill this bird". (31) The woman answered her husband: "You haven't (yet) killed this bird, (so) you (should) hang the kettle up for me". (32) He said to (his) son: "Bring (some) fire-wood!" (33) He also answered him: "The bird is (still) sitting on the tree and (so) you (should) bring wood instead of me (doing it)". (34) He said to (his) younger son: "Make a fire!" (35) The younger son answered (his) father: "The bird is (still) sitting on the tree and (so) you (should) make a fire instead of me". (36) When the bird heard all those talks—the bird said to this man: "(Only) those people earn (money) (who) are— all (of them)— good (= hardworking). (37) You people are not good, you are lazy; (38) if you go to India, you will not earn (anything) (because) you are lazy. (39) For you it is better to go (back) to your own country, to starve in your own country!"

BERTOLD SPULER

DIE ARMENISCHE KIRCHE

Gut 1300 Jahre sind es nun her, dass die Armenier den Namen ihres Katholikos (also ihres obersten Kirchenfürsten) Esra mit nach unten gekehrtem Anfangsbuchstaben schreiben — in unserer Schrift etwa Ǝsra — um dadurch zum Ausdruck zu bringen, dass er sich mit Mächten der Unterwelt zusammengetan und somit den hohen Auftrag, der ihm geworden war, verraten habe. Damit haben die Armenier eines der ausrucksvollsten Symbole der Geschichte geschaffen, das Zeichen des siegreichen »Dennoch«, dem allein sie ihr Weiterleben bis zum heutigen Tage verdanken.

Wie war es zu diesem Geschehen gekommen? Jahrhunderte hindurch hatten die Armenier unter den Angriffen der zoroastrischen Perser Unsägliches zu erleiden gehabt, hatten aber trotz allen blutigen Verlusten, aller Not und allem Leid standgehalten, weil sie sich selbst treu geblieben waren. Freilich waren sie nach dem grossen persischen Angriffe anfangs des 7. Jh.s doch genötigt, nach Hilfe von aussen Ausschau zu halten, da ihre Kraft allein nicht mehr aus-reichte. Bei allem Selbstbewusstsein schien es nicht abwegig, sich nach Mächten umzusehen, die sich der Perser gleichfalls zu erwehren hatten. Vielleicht konnten sie ihnen die Last der Abwehr erleichtern, konnten ihnen möglicherweise sogar die Befreiung schenken. Zu denen, die um 630 so dachten, gehörte der Katholikos Esra. Tat-sächlich fand er bei dem von den Persern gleichfalls hart bedrängten Grenznachbarn in Kleinasien, bei Byzanz nämlich, Gehör, bei einer Macht, die schon seit längerer Zeit versucht hatte, zu einer Zusam-menarbeit mit den Armeniern zu kommen. Esras Verhandlungen gingen ohne wesentliche Schwierigkeiten vor sich, bis er unter dem äusser-sten Drucke jenen Schritt tat, den die Armenier als Verrat an ihrer Existenz, bald auch als eine schlimmere Bedrohung denn die islami-sche Oberherrschaft empfanden. Er liess sich dazu herbei, mit ortho-doxen Hierarchen gemeinsam die Hl. Messe zu feiern. Sie waren die Mächte der Unterwelt, von denen eingangs die Rede war.

Mit Esras Handeln war jenes Unausdenkbare geschehen, dass ein armenischer Katholikos Hilfe beim Auslande um den Preis einer Selbstaufgabe des nationalen Wesens suchte. Die Armenier verstanden, dass dies der Anfang vom Ende war, dass nur integrales Beharren auf ihrer Überlieferung ihrem Volke die Einheit, ihrer Nation die Zukunft sicherte. Esra hatte wie so mancher »Intellektuelle« übersehen, welche Urkräfte in einem Volke leben, und wieviel stärker oft das Gefühl für den Kern einer Sache bei der breiten Masse als bei den reflektierenden Schichten ist. Er hatte nicht geahnt, mit welcher Leidenschaft seine Landsleute davon lebten, eines *nicht* zu sein, einem Begriffe zuwider zu leben und daraus wesentliche Kräfte ihrer Existenz zu beziehen : zuwider eben der Orthodoxie (in konfessionskundlichem Sinne), also dem Dyophysitismus, der Staatsreligion des Oströmischen Reiches. Indem die Armenier den Preis einer Verleugnung ihrer nationalen Kirchengeschichte, d.h. ihrer nationalen Geschichte schlechthin, verweigerten und Esras Namen seit einem Synode-Beschlusse von 651 (nach der arabischen Eroberung) in der oben geschilderten Weise schreiben, haben sie sich ein Symbol ihres Daseins gegeben, das nun schon ein Jahrtausend überdauert hat.

Esra hatte geglaubt, Vergangenes vergessen zu dürfen. Sein Volk hat ihn und die Welt belehrt, dass die Erinnerung an eben diese Vergangenheit, an die Jahrhunderte hindurch immer wieder qualvoll durchlebten Versuche der oströmischen Kirche, ihnen die Beschlüsse von Chalkedon (451) aufzudrängen, ein Wesenszug des armenischen Volkes schon damals geworden war und bis zum heutigen Tage geblieben ist. Wenn wir daran denken, mit welch emotionaler Schärfe das Griechentum auch im Angesichte der türkischen Heere vor Konstantinopel eine Union mit Rom ablehnte, wenn wir uns daran erinnern, was dem Metropoliten Isidor von Kiev (einem Greichen) widerfuhr, als er in Russland die Unionsbeschlüsse des Konzils von Ferrara/Florenz 1438/39 durchzusetzen versuchte, so haben wir bekanntere Parallelen für eben das, was sich damals und seither immer wieder in Armenien abspielte und wofür das armenische Volk das einzige wirklich integrale Beispiel im Raume der morgenländischen Kirchen geworden ist.

Wie in Osteuropa ist auch im Vorderen Orient die Religion eine Macht, die Völker formt, die bisher Getrenntes zusammenschliesst und bisher Vereintes trennt. Das eindrucksvollste Beispiel im Vorderen Orient sind eben die Armenier. Schon zur Zeit des Katholikos Esra fühlten sie ebenso bewusst wie unbewusst, dass ihr Bekenntnis, ihre Zugehörigkeit zum Monophysitismus, ein Kern ihres nationalen Wesens sei. Jeder Angriff auf diese Konfession, jeder Versuch, hierin eine Veränderung herbeizuführen, musste ihnen als ein Angriff höllischer Mächte erscheinen, weil jedes Zurückweichen an dieser Stelle: die Bresche bilden konnte, durch die Fremdes überhaupt eindringen und armenisches Wesen letztlich auslöschen konnte.

Um mit meiner Diktion weiterhin im Bereiche armenischen Denkens zu bleiben, darf ich fortfahren: Der Satan umdrohte die Nation freilich nunmehr auch in einer zweiten Gestalt, in der Form des Islāms, der ihr nun ebenso Nachbar wurde wie der Orthodoxie. In hohen Gebirgstälern wohnend und weithin geschlossen siedelnd, ist es den Armeniern gelungen, auch diesen zweiten Versucher von sich abzuweisen und ihm auch nicht (wie etwa die Georgier) den kleinsten Einbruch zu gestatten. Was das bedeutet, wird klar, wenn man sich — neben dem Jahrhunderte währenden Druck — nur für einen Augenblick der grauenvollen Mordzüge Tīmūrs um 1400 und dann der vielen Armenier-Massaker in den Jahren seit 1895 erinnert. Unter Umständen, wie sie kaum ein anderes christliches Volk (auch in der Gegenwart) erlebt hat, standen sie unter dem Wort der Offenbarung (2, 10): *Sei getreu bis an den Tod, so will ich Dir die Krone des Lebens geben.* Die Armenier haben durch ihre Haltung, durch ihren Bekennermut, als einziges morgenländisches Volk bis zum heutigen Tage erreicht, dass jeder, der sich etwa vom Monophysitismus zugunsten des Islams abwenden sollte (es gibt nur sehr wenige Beispiele eines solchen Übertritts, etwa unter der Todesfurcht der Armenier-Massaker), sich zugleich — und zwar *eben dadurch* — auch vom armenischen Volkstum löst. Die Nachfahren der 3 747 muslimischen Armenier der türkischen Statistik von 1935 (darunter im Wilajet Çoruh: 2029) dürften inzwischen restlos im türkischen Volkstum aufgegangen sein. Angesichts dieser Haltung ist bei den Armeniern allein unter den morgenländischen Völkern die Grenze zu den Nachbarn mit absoluter Schärfe und völliger Klarheit gezogen: noch heute ist ein »muslimischer Armenier« für dieses Volk ebenso eine Contradictio in adiecto wie ein »orthodoxer Armenier«.

Damit sind die Armenier eines der prägnantesten Beispiele, dass ein Thema wie »Kirche und Volkstum im Morgenlande« in vieler Hinsicht nur die Beleuchtung desselben Gegenstandes von zwei Seiten her darstellt und nicht, wie so oft im Abendlande, eine Opposition bildet. Bei ihnen ist das Volkstum die Kirche, die Kirche das Volkstum, und die Armenier haben bis an die Schwelle der Neuzeit diese Gleichheit nicht nur *gelebt*, sondern auch bewusst *erlebt*. Dieser Tatbestand macht das Gefühl verständlich, das dem Katholikos Esra entgegenschlug, als er hier eine Änderung herbeizuführen versuchte, macht auch die

vielen und blutigen Zusammenstösse erklärbar, die seit dem 18 Jh.
das Eindringen abendländischen Kirchentums bei armenischen Splitter-
gruppen auslöste.

Man kann die Armenier von dieser Sicht aus übrigens zu den
osteuropäischen Völkern stellen, wo man Serbe ist, *indem* man
orthodox ist, und Kroate, *indem* man Katholik ist (und wo man als
Kroate zwar alt-katholisch, aber nicht orthodox werden kann); wo
ein Ukrainer zwar orthodox und uniert, aber nicht römischer Katholik
sein kann, und wo ein »katholischer Russe« (wie wenige gibt es doch
davon!) praktisch ausserhalb der Gemeinschaft seines Volkes und
ohne Widerhall bei ihm lebt.

Lassen wir die Frage einer Union mit Rom oder des Anschlusses
an eine evanglische Denomination vorderhand auf sich beruhen, so
können wir feststellen, dass die eben geschilderte religionstypologische
Sonderstellung die Armenier im Raume südöstlich des Abendlandes
nur mit den Griechen auf eine Ebene stellt. Ihnen ist gleichfalls in
langen Auseinandersetzungen die Orthodoxie ebenso Bestandteil ihres
nationalen Seins geworden, wie bei den Armeniern ihr Monophysitismus. Wie bei diesen die Orthodoxie, so wurde bei jenen der
Monophysitismus entweder ausgemerzt oder (in einzelnen Splittern)
eingeschmolzen. Die Zugehörigkeit zu einem der beiden Volkstümer
würde der Zugehörigkeit zum Bekenntnis des Nachbarn radikal
widersprechen. Dieser Umstand ist wohl auch die Ursache dafür,
dass die beiden Völker sich dem Islam gegenüber resistent verhalten
haben. Ein islamischer Grieche ist heutzutage ebenso ein Widerspruch
in sich selbst wie ein monophysitischer Grieche.

Man mag annehmen, dass dieses nationale Gepräge der armenischen
Kirche schon bei ihrer Entstehung vorgezeichnet war. Freilich verlieren sich die ersten Spuren der christlichen Mission hier im Dun-
kel der Frühzeit. Die Kirche selbst äussert sich nicht genauer über
eine angebliche Gründung durch zwei Sendboten aus dem Kreise
der 70 Jünger, hat es doch den Anschein, als ob sich in der Frühzeit
vor allem adoptianische Anschauungen geltend gemacht hätten, also
die Meinung, dass Jesus Christus von Gott Vater nur als Sohn adoptiert
worden sei.

Demgegenüber lässt sich eine wirkliche Durchsetzung des Christentums erst für die Zeit um 300 nachweisen, als sich Einflüsse von
den Metropolen Kaisareia (Caesarea) in Kappadokien, heute Kayseri
im mittleren Anatolien, und von Antiochien trafen, die mit Einwir-
kungen aus dem oströmischen und dem syrischen Raume gleichzusetzen

waren. Im Ringen mit Versuchen der persischen Landesherren, den Armeniern ihr neu-zoroastrisches Bekenntnis aufzuzwingen, gelang es dem Königsspross Gregor, den Herrscher von der Wahrheit des christlichen Bekenntnisses zu überzeugen; er heisst deshalb in seiner Kirche »Der Erleuchter«, lateinisch »Illuminator«, armenisch »Lusaworítsch«. Mit königlicher Hilfe baute Gregor eine kirchliche Organisation und gleichzeitig ein Schulwesen auf, das für eine Erziehung der Jugend im christlichen Sinne wirkte. So wurde Armenien etwa 300 der erste Staat mit einer christlichen Regierung, da sich die Auffassung, Edessa sei Anfang des 3 Jh.s für etwa 15 Jahre ein christlicher Staat gewesen, offenbar nicht halten lässt.

Natürlich hat der christliche Glaube im Sinne der damaligen Reichskirche, also des rechtgläubigen Byzantinertums, sich hier ebenso wenig wie anderswo auf einen Schlag durchgesetzt. Aber das enge Netz von Bistümern, das System kirchlicher Schulen und wohl auch die damalige Erblichkeit des Amtes eines leitenden Bischofs, eines Katholikós, liess die Kirche weithin an Boden gewinnen. Sie konnte sich freilich nur mit Mühe der immer erneuten Eingriffe der zoroastrischen Sassaniden aus Persien erwehren. Dabei erwies sich, dass schon damals Armeniertum und christliches Bekenntnis zusammenfielen, gefördert auch durch die Einführung eines offenbar von Mesrop Maschtotz aus den griechischen Minuskeln entwickelten armenischen Alphabets unter Katholikos Isaak dem Grossen (390-439). Nun wurde unter Überwindung des Gegensatzes zwischen dem Griechischen und dem Syrischen das einheimische Armenische — bekanntlich ein besonderer Zweig des indogermanischen Sprachstammes — zur Kirchensprache. Mit der Übersetzung der Bibel sowie vieler religiöser Schriften begann die Entstehung einer national-armenischen Literatur, die sich bald über den religiösen Bereich hinaus entwickelte und die sich — wenn auch über Perioden eines fast völligen Schweigens hinweg — bis zum heutigen Tage fortlaufend entwickelt hat.

Die damaligen Kämpfe zwischen Ostrom und Persien führten dazu, dass seit 387 das armenische Siedlungsgebiet zwischen diesen beiden Reichen aufgeteilt war. Für die Kirche bedeutete das die Notwendigkeit, sich auf eine unterschiedliche Religionspolitik einzustellen, die gegenüber dem Zoroastrismus in Iran lediglich in der Behauptung des Christentums bestehen konnte, im Byzantinischen Reiche aber eine Einbeziehung in die dogmatischen Auseinandersetzungen zur Folge hatte, die sich damals vor allem um das Wesen Jesu Christi und das Verhältnis der beiden Naturen in ihm entspannen. Man folgte dabei der Reichskirche auf dem Konzil von Ephesos 431, auf dem die armenische Kirche vertreten war und auf dem Nestorios und seine Lehre verurteilt wurde. Die Kirche hatte damit einen Weg eingeschlagen, der für die Mehrzahl der Bewohner des Byzantinischen Reiches geradenwegs zum Monophysitismus führte: trotz dem Konzil von Chalkedon 451, das das Nebeneinander der beiden Naturen im Heilande als richtige Lehre feststellte. Die Ägypter und in ihrem Gefolge die Äthiopier sowie die grosse Masse der Semiten in Syrien und im Zweistromlande liessen sich für diese Entscheidung nicht gewinnen und blieben Monophysiten, wie sie immer gewesen zu sein überzeugt waren und bis zum heutigen Tage sind. Die armenische Kirche war nicht vor diese Entscheidung gestellt, erlebte sie doch in eben diesem Jahre 451 eine furchtbare Niederlage im Kampfe gegen die Perser, die ihr Land greulich verheerten — jegliche Verbindung mit Byzanz war abgerissen. Als sie 484 endlich wiederhergestellt werden konnte, neigten die byzantinischen Kaiser dem Monophysitismus zu, ja bekannten sich bis 518 vielfach offen zu ihm. So passte das Bekenntnis zum Monophysitismus, wie es die Synode von Dwin 506/7 offiziell annahm, ganz in die ungebrochene Überlieferung dieser Kirche. Gestützt auf die felsenfeste Überzeugung vom vollen Besitz der christlichen Wahrheit weigerte sich die Armenische Kirche nach 518, die Wendung Ostroms zum Dyophysitismus oder zu einer zeitweisen Vermittlungs-Theologie mitzumachem, also zum Henotikón von 553 oder zum Monotheletismus um 620, also zur Lehre von nur éinem Willen in Jesus Christus. Man bekräftigte diese Haltung 552 und 729 (?) endgültig und vermochte auch die nordöstlich benachbarten Georgier sowie einen andern kaukasischen Stamm, die Albanier, für ein Einschlagen dieses Weges zu gewinnen. Der Bruch mit der oströmischen Kirche war vollzogen, und er war endgültig bis zum heutigen Tage.

Gewiss blieben Versuche eines Ausgleichs nicht aus: einmal in der Zeit des Arabersturms gegen die Mitte des 7 Jh.s — mit Folgen, die wir eingangs behandelt haben. Auch später noch, im 10 und 12 Jh., kam es zu Bestrebungen nach einem Ausgleiche mit Byzanz, die von einem dem Dyophysitismus angenäherten Verständnisse der mono-physitischen Lehre gefördert wurden. Aber das Volk lehnte sie ab, angefeuert durch Nerses Schnorhalí von Lampron, der 1196 jeglicher Annäherung widerriet, nachdem er sich einige Zeit in Konstantinopel aufgehalten hatte. Man blieb also monophysitisch, wie man es war — und das bedeutete nun, dass man sich in Kaukasien religiös so gut wie völlig isoliert sah. Hatten sich doch die benachbarten Georgier schon 580 für einen Übergang zur Orthodoxie im byzantinischen Sinne gewinnen lassen; sie gehören seither bis heute dieser Kirche an. Die Beziehungen zum Griechentum selbst, an das man im Westen, in Kleinasien, grenzte, waren durch gegenseitige Abneigung bestimmt: beide Nationen schieden sich nun nicht nur durch die Sprache, sondern auch durch die christliche Konfession, zu der sie sich bekannten.

Aber auch die rämliche Verbindung zu den monophysitischen Syrern im S war — wir sahen es schon — durch den Islam fast völlig unterbrochen, der sich inzwischen in Kaukasien ebenso wie im Zweistromlande und in Syrien festgesetzt hatte: auch wenn das Christentum in diesen Ländern damals noch wesentlich stärker war als heute. Doch überwog im nördlichen Zweistromlande der Nestorianismus, dem man besonders fernstand, zahlenmässig den Monophysitismus. Nur in Syrien selbst hatten armenische Streusiedlungen unmittelbaren Kontakt mit andern Monophysiten.

Die räumliche Isolierung bedeutete gleichzeitig, dass man entweder an Christen anderen Bekenntnisses oder an Muslime angrenzte. Unter beiden war eine Mission, eine Werbung für das eigene Bekenntnis, ausgeschlossen. Die armenische Kirche konnte also keine weitausgreifende Mission entfalten, wie andere christliche Bekenntnisse (z.B. der Nestorianismus), wie vor allem auch der Islam, der sich auch als Religion der Staatsmacht ausbreitete.

Die räumliche Isolierung bedeutete freilich keine geistige Vereinsamung. Innerhalb des armenischen Volkes hatte zwar das orthodoxe Bekenntnis (im konfessionskundlichen Sinne) keine Chancen — aber eine Auffassung vom Christentum, die sich gegen Hierarchie und prunkenden Kult, die sich gegen die Sakramente ausser Taufe und Abendmahl wandte, eine Gemeinschaft, die nach ihrem Ursprungsorte Thondraki(an)er genannt wurde, machte sich im 9 Jh. geltend und hat sich trotz allen Anfeindungen in Resten bis ins 19 Jh. gehalten, wo sie uns noch begegnen wird. Daneben trat die in diesem Raume weit verbreitete dualistische Weltsicht, die einem ewigen guten Prinzip ein ebenso ewiges böses gegenüberstellt, wie sie — in verschiedenen Ausprägungen — im Zoroastrismus ebenso lebendig war wie im Manichäismus. Die Paulikianer im Grenzgebiet in Armenien wurden seit dem 7. Jh. von den Byzantinern aufs Nachhaltigste bekämpft und schliesslich in mehreren Schüben Mitte des 8. und in der zweiten Hälfte des 10. Jh.s auf den Balkan verpflanzt, wo sie offensichtlich die Keimzelle der Bogomilen und der von ihnen ausgehenden Be-

wegungen der Patarener in Oberitalien und der Albigenser in Süd-
frankreich wurden. Auch in Armenien selbst sind sie nicht sofort
ausgerottet worden.

Neben ihnen bekannte sich offensichtlich der überwiegende Teil
des armenischen Volkes zum nonophysitischen Christentum — freilich
bedeutete das damals kein einheitliche Bekenntnis, stritt man sich
doch im Rahmen der monophysitischen Kirchen etwa um die Frage, ob
der Leib Jesu Christi erst durch seine Auferstehung oder schon von
seiner Geburt an unverweslich gewesen sei. Der zuletzt genannten
Auffassung hingen viele Armenier in jenen Jahrhunderten an. Aber sie
waren — wie gesagt — geistig nicht isoliert, sie standen — gerade
als Untertanen des Chalifats — mit den Syrern und Kopten in enger
geistiger Verbindung. Auch diese waren ja Untertanen des Herrschers
der Gläubigen in Bagdad. Das führte im 12 Jh. zu einem dogmatischen
Ausgleich auf der Linie einer Verweslichkeit von Jesu Christi Körper
bis zu seiner Auferstehung, auch zu einer Einigung hinsichtlich der
Verwendung von Olivenöl als Salböl und der Benützung von mit
Wasser gemischtem Wein beim Hl. Abendmahle. Seither stellen die
monophysitischen Landeskirchen — ebenso wie die orthodoxen —
unter sich eine dogmatische Einheit dar. Ihre Beziehungen sind seither
stets brüderlich gewesen und haben in einem umfangreichen Austausch
von Briefen, von theologischen Schriften, auch von Theologen und
neuerdings von Studenten ihren Ausdruck gefunden.

Als die Frage eines Ausgleichs mit der griechischen Orthodoxie
zu Ausgang des 12. Jh.s endgültig negativ beantwortet war, trat
in Gestalt der Kreuzfahrer die abendländische Form des Christentums,
der Katholizismus, ins Blickfeld der Armenier, also eine Kirche,
mit der man nicht durch eine jahrhundertelange Fehde während der
Frühzeit getrennt war. Im 9. Jh. hatte sich unter der Dynastie der
Bagratiden ein mehr oder minder selbständiges armenisches Staats-
wesen gebildet, dessen Hauptstadt seit 990 in Ani lag, das mächtig
aufblühte, aber 1065 von den Seldschuken überrannt wurde. Damit
war Gross-Armenien (in Ostanatolien und Kaukasien) erneut muslimischer Oberherrschaft untertan, und die Türken waren als Neubekehrte
besonders eifrige Bekenner der Lehren des Korans. Das veranlasste
viele Armenier zur Auswanderung, insbesondere nach Kilikien am
Südrande Kleinasiens in der Nachbarschaft zu Nordsyrien. Hier
entstand — anfangs von den Byzantinern, dann von den Kreuzfahrern auf der Insel Kypern gestützt — das Reich Klein-Armenien,
seit 1198 ein Königreich von Gnaden des Deutschen Kaisers und mit

den Kreuzfahrern eng verbunden. Mit ihnen kam es nun auch zu Religions-Gesprächen und zu den für die damalige Zeit kennzeichnenden Bestrebungen nach einer Union mit der römischen Kirche. Nach längeren, aufs Ganze gesehen ergebnislosen Verhandlungen gelang es dem Orden der *Unitores*, einem Zweige der Augustiner, Mitte des 13 Jh.s formell eine Union zwischen der armenischen Kirche vor allem in Klein-Armenien und der Kurie herbeizuführen. Dabei kam freilich keine völlige Übereinstimmung des Dogmas zustande; sie wurde offenbar auch nicht wirklich verlangt. Das armenische Kirchenwesen blieb weithin unverändert, und die breite Masse der Gläubigen hatte offensichtlich keine Vorstellung von einer Veränderung ihre Glaubenstandes.

Aber die Kreuzfahrer wurden im Laufe der Zeit — vor allem von Saladin und dann von den ägyptischen Mamlūken — wieder zurückgedrängt; 1291 ging mit Akkon ihr letzter Stützpunkt an der syrischen Küste verloren. 1375 wurde Klein-Armenien von den Mamlūken überrannt, die sich der Mongolen erwehrt hatten, denen sich die klein-armenischen Herrscher zeitweise unterstellt hatten, solange sie die Feinde der Muslime am Nil waren und dem Christentum geneigt zu sein schienen. Damit war auch die Union in Klein-Armenien endgültig erloschen, und die armenische Kirche war erneut auf sich selbst gestellt: nun wieder Hüterin aller nationalen Überlieferungen gegenüber dem Islam, dem man sich nun erneut mit aller Schärfe konfrontiert sah ...

Konfrontiert sah auch in seiner furchtbarsten Form: in Tīmūr, der zwischen 1380 und 1405 die Länder Vorder- und Mittelasiens sowie Osteuropa und Nord-Indien in blutigen Kriegszügen verheerte, deren Schädel-Pyramiden selbst den Muslimen einen Schauder einjagten. Armenien (und ebenso Georgien sowie das syrische Christentum) wurden aufs Schwerste betroffen. Die armenische Kirche musste einen hohen Blutzoll bezahlen. Sie hatte Mühe, sich zu behaupten, und ihre hohe Kultur-Entwicklung, von der zahlreiche Kunst- und literarische Werke zeugen, erlitt einen Rückschlag, der Jahrhunderte dauern sollte.

Doch sie behauptete sich letztlich. Sie war nun voll und ganz der Hort des armenischen Volkes geworden, das sich nur noch in ihr verkörpert sah. Dabei hatte das schwere historische Schicksal der Armenier ihre Aufspaltung auf mehrere Staaten mit sich gebracht; dadurch konnte die organisatorische Einheit der Kirche nicht gewahrt werden. Das Katholikat hatte seinen Sitz — oft auf der Flucht vor den Gegnern des Christentums — mehrfach wechseln müssen und hatte sich schliesslich auf der Insel Aghthamar im Wan-See niedergelassen, wo noch heute die wunderbare Kirche zum Hl. Kreuz steht. Daneben war in Klein-Armenien (Kilikien) ein Katholikat, zuletzt in Sis, entstanden, und 1441 wurde in Ečmiadzín nahe dem Ararat ein weiteres Katholikat begründet, Daneben entstand für das Mamlūken-Reich schon 1311 ein Patriarchat in Jerusalem und etwa 1461 ein solches für die Armenier des Türkischen Reiches in Konstantinopel. Schliesslich war Mittelpunkt der Armenier im persischen Safaviden-Staate ein Erzbistum in Dschulfa, anfangs des 17 Jh.s zeitweise in Iṣfahān. Diese Spaltung hat sich verschiedentlich sehr nachteilig auf die Geschlossenheit des Auftretens der Kirche nach aussen hin ausgewirkt, hat aber glücklicherweise die dogmatische Einheit des armenischen Volkes nicht zerstört.

Diese Aufgliederung der Kirche in einzelne Jurisdiktions-Bezirke zeigt deutlich, wie sehr das armenische Volk schon im Mittelalter auf verschiedene Machtbreiche aufgeteilt war. Das ist bis zum heutigen Tage so geblieben, und wie für die Juden in aller Welt ihr religiöses Bekenntnis die einigende Klammer ist, so ist das auch für die Armenier mit ihrer Nationalkirche der Fall.

Freilich bleib die Kirchliche Einheit des armenischen Volkes nicht völlig erhalten. Doch ist die Zahl derer, die vom Glauben ihrer Väter abliessen, zahlenmässig gering. Wie für die übrigen orientalischen Kirchen, trat auch für die armenische Kirche seit dem Beginne der Neuzeit die Frage einer Regelung des Verhältnisses zum abendländischen Katholizismus ins Blickfeld. Immer wieder versuchten Sendboten der römischen Kurie, einzelne Personen oder auch Gruppen der Kirche zum Anschluss an die Union zu bewegen. Es gelang da und dort, sogar höhere Geistliche für diesen Gedanken zu gewinnen. Das hatte im 18 Jh. zeiweise schwerwiegende innere Auseinandersetzungen zur Folge, umso mehr, als auch die einer Union zuneigenden Glieder des Volkes nach türkischem Staatsrechte dem monophysitischen Katholikos unterstellt blieben. Seit 1740 entstand mit Unterstützung Frankreichs eine geregelte Hierarchie, innerhalb deren sich freilich seit 1831 das Erzbistum Konstantinopel und das unierte Bistum Sis bis zu ihrer Vereinigung 1867 um den Vorrang stritten.

Dieser Eingriff von aussen liess die der gregorianischen Kirche treuen Gläubigen — weitaus die überwiegende Mehrzahl — sich ihrerseits nach einer Hilfe von aussen umsehen. So entstand eine gewisse Hinneigung der Armenier zu den orthodoxen Russen, deren Macht sich immer näher an ihre kaukasische Heimat heranschob, bis 1828 der grössere Teil des armenischen Siedlungsgebietes und 1878 weitere

Teile unter die Herrschaft der Zaren kamen, Gebiete, die bisher zu Persien oder aber zur Türkei gehört hatten. Dabei blieb die Selbständigkeit der Kirche gewahrt, da sie nicht, wie die georgische, orthodox war und also nicht, wie diese, einfach der Jurisdiktion der russischen Kirche unterstellt werden konnte — ein Vorgang, der für Georgien erst nach 1917 rückgängig gemacht und erst 1943 vom Moskauer Patriarchat widerrufen wurde. Immerhin schrieb der Staat der Zaren der armenische Kirche gewisse Formen der inneren Verfassung vor, die nicht immer die Billigung der Gläubigen fanden. 1905 wurde die Vermögensverwaltung der armenischen Kirche endgültig russischer Aufsicht unterstellt.

Inzwischen hatte in der Türkei die uniert-armenische Kirche 1830 auch zivilrechtlich den Status einer eigen Glaubengemeinschaft erhalten, doch verlor sie zwischen 1870 und 1880 durch innere Wirren einen Teil ihrer Anhänger an die angestammte gregorianische Kirche.

Die verhältnismässig günstige Stellung, die die armenische Kirche im Russischen Reiche trotz manchen Beschränkungen besass, verlockte viele Armenier in der Türkei dazu, ihre Blicke dorthin zu wenden und von dort eine »Befreiung« zu erhoffen, wie das die Balkan-Völker zur gleichen Zeit ebenfalls taten. Dass sie dadurch den Türken verdächtig wurde, kann nicht wundernehmen, und so kam es, veranlasst auch durch wirtschaftliche Gründe und wohl auch menschliche Abneigung, in den Jahren 1895/96, 1909 und 1915 zu jenen blutigen Armenier-Verfolgungen, denen insgesamt einige Hunderttausend Menschen zum Opfer fielen; etwa 100 000 Frauen wurden in türkische Harems verschleppt. Eine neue Fluchtwelle der Armenier setzte ein, die sich nun noch weiter in der Welt zerstreuten. Auch in Amerika, besonders in Neuyork und in Kalifornien, entstanden grosse armenische Kolonien, die bald auch eine eigenständige kirchliche Organisation unter mehreren Bischöfen erhielten, deren einer — nach dem Muster der Bischöflichen Kirche Amerikas — zum leitenden Bischof bestimmt wird (meist der Erzbischof von Neuyork).

So lebten viele Armenier am Ende des Ersten und auch des Zweiten Weltkriegs in vielfältiger Zerstreuung: viele von ihnen Gegner des sowjetischen Systems und in eigenen politischen Emigranten-Parteien organisiert, unter denen die Föderationspartei (Daschnakzutiún) die Führung innehatte. Nach dem Ende des Zweiten Weltkrieges und den Schwierigkeiten, die für die Armenier in gar manchem ihrer Gastländer auftraten, stieg bei grösseren Gruppen von ihnen das Heimweh auf, das von der Sowjet-Union geschickt benützt wurde, um mehrere

Zehntausende zu einer Rückkehr nach Sowjet-Armenien zu veranlassen, auch wenn das für viele der Rückkehrer nicht ihre eigentliche Heimat war. Gar manche davon waren bisher uniert gewesen und liessen nun trotz den Warnungen ihres Patriarchen von ihrem unierten Bekenntnis, um in den Rätebund zurückkehren zu können. So war es die Forderung der dortigen Regierung: Heimweh und Hinneigung zur angestammten Kirche bildeten in diesem Falle ein Bündnis.

Es mag durchaus richtig sein, wenn man hört, dass manche der Rückkehrer wenig zufrieden waren. Das war vielleicht nicht anders zu erwarten und hat ihnen das Tor für eine erneute Ausreise doch nicht geöffnet. Die übrigen haben es sich in Sowjet-Armenien so gut eingerichtet, wie es eben möglich war. Die Kirche, im Bewusstsein aller Armenier ein fester Bestandteil des nationalen Erbes, hat hier eben dadurch offenbar eine festere Position als im übrigen Rätebunde. Der Katholikos von Ečmiadzín (seit 1955), Wasgén Baldschián, hat es durch eine im Laufe der Zeit ruhigere und geschickter werdende Haltung verstanden, als der leitende Hierarch seiner Kirche anerkannt zu werden — freilich erst, nachdem das Katholikat von Kilikien (Sis), das seit 1921 in Antelias, einem Vorort von Beirut, residiert — 1956 einen versuchten Eingriff in die Besetzung des Thrones abgewehrt und dadurch seine Selbständigkeit gewahrt hatte. Von ihm hängen die Armenier in Amerika weithin ab. Das Katholikat Aghthamar ist im Übrigen im Zusammenhang mit den Armenier-Verfolgungen 1895 faktisch untergegane.

1962 konnte das Katholikat Ečmiadzín eine Synode aller gregorianischen Armenier einberufen, die tatsächlich auch von vielen Hierarchen aus dem Auslande besucht wurde. Das mag zu einer moralischen Steigerung der armenischen Kirche im Rätebunde beitragen haben, wo ein recht reges kirchliches Leben mit eigenen Ausbildungsmöglichkeiten für Geistliche besteht. Die armenisch-gregorianische Kirche bildet also auch heute über die politischen und weltanschaulichen Grenzen hinweg ein einigendes Band, dem sich selbst Armenier anderer Konfessionen bis zu einem gewissen Grade verbunden fühlen. Es kommt auch ausserhalb des Rätebundes gar nicht so selten vor, dass sie sich dieser ihrer angestammten Mutterkirche wieder zuwenden.

Durch die eben erwähnten Rückwanderer ist die *uniert-armenische* Kirche geschwächt worden, trotz dem hohen Ansehen, das ihr Patriarch (1937-62) Gregor XIV., Petrus XV., Aghadschanián an der Kurie und im Welt-Katholizismus besass, ein Ansehen, das ihn gegen Schluss seines Lebens zum Leiter der Kommission für die Glaubensverbreitung berufen werden liess. Sein Nachfolger als Katholikos, Ignaz Petrus XVI. Batanián (seit 1962), ist nicht so hervorgetreten, und um die etwa 70 000 unierten Armenier (davon 15 000 in Frankreich) ist es stiller geworden, so sehr auch die ihnen zugehörigen Mechitaristen in Venedig und Wien durch ihre rege Publikations-Tätigkeit und durch theologische Arbeiten immer wieder hervortreten.

Auch die *evangelischen* Kirchen haben seit dem 19 Jh. eine Reihe von Armeniern für sich gewinnen können, darunter Reste der Thondrakier, deren wir früher gedachten. Protestantische Konfessionen aus Amerika haben sich dabei hervorgetan. Doch hat die Zahl der evangelischen Christen in diesem Volke die Zahl der Unierten wohl nicht erreicht, und ihre Aufteilung auf einzelne Konfessionen des Protestantismus hat ihre Bedeutung etwas zurückgedrängt, auch wenn in einzelnen armenisch-protestantischen Gemeinschaften ein reges und wohl organisiertes Leben herrscht.

So steht also die gregorianische Kirche mit etwa 4,5 Mio. Gläubigen (?) als die echte National-Kirche der Armenier vor uns, eine Kirche, die fast alle Glieder dieses Volkes über die ganze Welt hin verbindet, eine Kirche, die davon überzeugt ist, die geradlinige, ungebrochene Tradition des Christentums bis zum heutigen Tage fortzuführen, von der die andern Bekennnisse, die Orthodoxen, die Katholiken und noch mehr die Protestanten, im Laufe der Jahrhunderte abgewichen seien. Dieses Bewusstsein einer ungebrochenen Überlieferung, eines dauernden Festhaltens an der Wahrheit des Evangeliums in seiner echten Form lässt die Armenier stolz auf ihre Kirche und auf ihre nationale Überlieferung sein. Jeder, der mit Armeniern, der mit Vertretern ihrer Kirche in Verbindung kommt, wird diesem Stolz auf eine grosse Vergangenheit und ein treues Festhalten an der Wahrheit in der Gegenwart immer wieder begegnen.

KLAUS STRUNK

SEMANTISCHES UND FORMALES ZUM VERHÄLTNIS VON INDOIRAN. *KRÁTU-/XRATU-* UND GR. ΚΡΑΤΥΣ

1. Ein etymologischer Zusammenhang zwischen den gr. Wörtern κράτος, κρατύς samt Zugehörigem und dem Abstraktum ai. *krátu-* (m.), airan. *xratu-* (m.) ist seit langer Zeit angenommen, aber auch verschiedentlich bestritten worden. Die schon bei G. Curtius [1] verzeichnete Verknüpfung wurde beispielsweise von Boisacq [2], p. 511, unter die nicht in Betracht zu ziehenden Kombinationen eingereiht und von Walde-Pokorny [3], I p. 354f., sowie Pokorny [4], I p. 531, abgelehnt – offensichtlich wegen der mit den griechischen Wörtern als unvereinbar angesehenen Bedeutung »geistige Kraft« von ai. *krátu-*, airan. *xratu-*. In neuerer Zeit hat É. Benveniste der griechischen Wortsippe um κράτος ein Kapitel seines zweibändigen Buches »Le vocabulaire des institutions indo-européennes« [5] gewidmet. Er kommt zu dem Ergebnis, daß zwar indoiranisch **kratu-* und gr. κράτος, deren semantischer Kern »puissance«, »prévalence« sei, zusammengehörten, nicht aber indoiranisch **kratu-* und gr. κρατύς einschließlich des davon abgeleiteten Denominativums κρατύνειν (καρτύνειν). Das gr. Adjektiv bedeute vielmehr »dur«, das denominative Verbum »durcir«. Daraus folgert Benveniste eine Verbindung des griechischen mit dem in got. *hardus*, dt. *hart*, engl. *hard* vorliegenden germ. Adjektiv [6] und etymologische Unabhängigkeit dieser Wörter von der zuvor genannten indoiranisch-griechischen Wortgruppe.

2. Wenn diese Analyse Benvenistes richtig sein sollte, so ist sie nicht nur für die Etymologie der betroffenen Wörter von Belang.

[1] G. Curtius, Grundzüge der griechischen Etymologie, 4. Aufl. Leipzig 1873, 154.

[2] É. Boisacq, Dictionnaire étymologique de la langue grecque, 4e édition Heidelberg 1950.

[3] A. Walde-J. Pokorny, Vergleichendes Wörterbuch der indogermanischen Sprachen, Berlin und Leipzig 1927-1932.

[4] J. Pokorny, Indogermanisches etymologisches Wörterbuch, Bern-München 1959.

[5] É. Benveniste, Le vocabulaire des institutions indo-européennes, Paris 1969, II 71-83.

[6] Die griechisch-germanische Etymologie wurde schon von H. Schweizer, KZ 2 (1853) 359, und danach von anderen vertreten. Wer ihr Urheber ist, habe ich nicht ausgekundschaftet. Die ältere Literatur bietet H. Ebeling, Lexicon Homericum, I, Leipzig 1885 (Nachdruck Hildesheim 1963), 888.

Sie hätte auch insofern Konsequenzen, als sie eine Paradereihe für das System der sogenannten »Calandschen Suffixe«[7] weniger ausgeprägt als zuvor gelten ließe. Im Anschluß an die von Caland[8] und Wackernagel[9] für das Iranische, Indische und Griechische gemachten Beobachtungen versteht man unter diesem System einen in den Grundzügen schon voreinzelsprachlich entwickelten Verbund bestimmter nominaler Primärableitungen von jeweils gleicher Wurzel. Wichtig ist hier vor allem die Parallelstellung von a) Adjektivstämmen auf *-u- und/oder *-ro-, b) Neutra auf *-es-/-os-, c) Kompositionsvordergliedern auf *-i-, d) primären Komparativ- und Superlativbildungen der Adjektive. Die im Indo-Iranischen und Griechischen existierenden Beispiele für dieses Nebeneinander besetzen die Positionen des Systems zwar mit unterschiedlicher Dichte und Verteilung, aber im ganzen doch so, daß das Gesamtgefüge als gegeben angesehen werden kann. Im Vergleich etwa mit den ai. Gruppen urú-ḥ »breit«, várīyān, váriṣṭha-ḥ, váraḥ (n.) »Breite« und ugrá-ḥ »stark«, ójīyān, ójiṣṭha-ḥ, ójaḥ (n.) »Stärke« konnte auch die griechische Reihe κρατύ-ς, κρατερό-ς, κρε(ί)σσων, κράτιστος, äol. κρέτος[10] (sonst mit analogisch eingeführter Ablautstufe κράτος) bisher als besonders gut gefüllt gelten. Benvenistes Sondierungen machen ihr implicite streitig die Glieder κρατύς und — jedenfalls partiell — κρατερός (καρτερός), das nun teils an κράτος (in der Bedeutung »überlegen«), teils an κρατύς (in der Bedeutung »hart, grausam«) angeschlossen werden soll.

3. Unter solchen Umständen erscheint es geboten, gerade das Verhältnis zwischen gr. κρατύς (mit κρατύνω, καρτύνω) einerseits und ai. krátu-, iran. xratu- andererseits, die ja auch Benveniste etymologisch zu gr. κράτος und Zubehör stellt, nochmals zu prüfen. Diese Überprüfung soll sowohl nach semantischen als auch nach formalen Kriterien erfolgen. Dabei bleibt vorweg festzuhalten, daß die Wortbildung bzw. die Abgrenzung von Wurzel und Suffix bei ai. krátu-, airan. xratu- ein bisher ungelöstes Problem darstellt.

---

[7] Vgl. E. Risch, Wortbildung der homerischen Sprache, 2. Aufl. Berlin 1974, 65 ff. §§ 28 ff., 218 f. § 79, Tabelle S. 66 f.

[8] KZ 31 (1892) 267 f.; 32 (1893) 592.

[9] J. Wackernagel, Vermischte Beiträge, 8 ff. = Kl. Schr. I 769 ff.

[10] Zu zweistämmigen äolischen Eigennamen auf Lesbos mit -κρέτης (neben -κράτης, -κέρτης) im zweiten Glied neuerdings R. Hodot, BNF 9 (1974) 115 ff.

I

4.1.1 Die neueren etymologischen Wörterbücher des Griechischen von Frisk[11] und Chantraine[12] suchen. eine semantische Brücke zwischen der Wortsippe von gr. κράτος (einschließlich κρατύς) und indoiranisch *krátu-*, *xratu-* durch Verweis auf ags. *cræft* zu schlagen, das einerseits »Kraft, physische Stärke, Macht«, andererseits »Einsicht, Gewandtheit usw.« bedeutet. Diese inhaltliche Spannweite des ags. Abstraktums erweist im Sinne einer allgemeinen Semantik die Möglichkeit, daß derartige Bedeutungskomponenten in einem einzigen Wort vorkommen können. Sie beweist aber nicht, daß semantische Komponenten wie »Einsicht« usw. den griechischen Wörtern um κράτος im allgemeinen und dem Adjektiv κρατύς im besonderen tatsächlich mit zugrunde liegen und damit deren Verknüpfung mit ai. *krátu-*, airan. *xratu-* rechtfertigen. Dieser Nachweis wäre auf der Grundlage einzelsprachlich-griechischer Verwendungsweisen noch zu erbringen. Das Abstraktum κράτος hat Benveniste, l.c. 72ff., zutreffend beurteilt und gegen benachbarte Wörter des Wortfeldes »Macht« wie σθένος, βία, ἴς, ἰσχύς abgegrenzt, unter denen σθένος nur physische Kraft bezeichnet[13]. Wir können uns daher auf das Adjektiv κρατύς samt einem verbalen Derivatum beschränken.

4.1.2 Wer die Bedeutung von gr. κρατύς im überlieferten Corpus festzustellen sucht, sieht sich zunächst folgender Tatsache gegenüber: Das Adjektiv selbst ist altepisch. Dort ist es je zweimal in Ilias und Odysse (Π 181; Ω 345; ε 49; ε 148), fünfmal in den homerischen Hymnen (h. Merc. 294; 414; h. Ven. 129; h. Cer. 346; 377) und nur innerhalb der festen Formel κρατὺς Ἀργεϊφόντης am Versende nach der Hephthemimeres belegt. Diese Indizien besagen, daß das Wort schon zur Zeit der Abfassung der homerischen Epen nicht mehr lebendig war und daß es zum tradierten Formelschatz der voraufgehenden oralen epischen Poesie gehört. Überkommene Versschlußformeln dieser Art, also Junkturen aus Attribut (oder Apposition) und einem Götternamen, sind bei Homer bekanntlich in großer Zahl verwendet. Soweit die Epitheta — vielfach Komposita, aber auch Simplicia — semantisch durchsichtig sind, bezeichnen sie

---

[11] H. Frisk, Griechisches etymologisches Wörterbuch, II, Heidelberg 1970, 10.

[12] P. Chantraine, Dictionnaire étymologique de la langue grecque, II, Paris 1970, 579.

[13] Ausführlich sind diese Wörter (außer ἰσχύς) in der ungedruckten Arbeit von R. Eder, Kraft, Stärke und Macht in der Sprache Homers, Diss. Heidelberg 1939 (maschinenschriftlich) untersucht worden.

charakteristische Eigenschaften der jeweiligen Götter: χάλκεος Ἄρης, ὀξὺν Ἄρηα, θοῦρον Ἄρηα, νεφεληγερέτα Ζεύς, Διὶ τερπικεραύνῳ, Ἄρτεμις ἰοχέαιρα, ἀργυρότοξος Ἀπόλλων, χρυσῆ Ἀφροδίτη (mit Varianten in verschiedenen Kasus), λευκώλενος Ἥρη, ὠκέα Ἶρις usw. Es liegt deshalb nahe, daß auch das Beiwort in der Formel κρατὺς Ἀργεϊφόντης Wesenseigentümlichkeiten des Gottes Hermes (Ἀργεϊφόντης) bezeichnet.

Unter den Eigenschaften des Hermes sticht nun physische »Härte« gewiß nicht hervor, so daß sie für ein stehendes Beiwort in einer solchen Namenformel kaum hätte prägend wirken können. Benvenistes Deutung »hart« für κρατύς findet also an der direkten Bezeugung des Wortes selbst keine Stütze. Die auf Hermes bezogenen Mythen berichten von Taten und Leistungen, die mehr die Kraft und Überlegenheit seiner geistigen Fähigkeiten als physische Härte und Stärke verraten. Im homerischen Hermeshymnus heißt es von ihm:

h. Merc. 43 ὡς δ᾽ ὁπότ᾽ ὠκὺ νόημα διὰ στέρνοιο περήσῃ

44 ἀνέρος ...

45 ....

46 ὡς ἅμ᾽ ἔπος τε καὶ ἔργον ἐμήδετο κύδιμος Ἑρμῆς.

»Wie wenn ein schneller Gedanke die Brust eines Mannes durchzuckt, ... so ersann Wort und Tat zugleich der ruhmvolle Hermes«.

Der gleiche Hymnus schreibt dem Einfallsreichen (αἱμυλομήτην V. 13, ποικιλομῆτα V. 514) seine geistige Beweglichkeit gleichsam von Geburt an zu, wenn er V. 17f. preist, Hermes sei an ein und demselben Tag in der Frühe geboren, habe am Mittag die Leier gespielt und am Abend die Rinder des Apollon entwendet. Indem er mit der Herde rückwärts geht, Vorder- und Hinterhufe vertauscht und mit unter die Füße gebundenem Reisig verwirrende Spuren hinterläßt, sticht Hermes mögliche Verfolger von vornherein aus (V. 75ff.). Er stellt die Leier her (V. 25), die er später dem Apollon im Austausch gegen die Rinder übergibt (V. 496, 509). Sein Denken ist zielbewußt und »praktisch«. Die τέχνη des Leierspiels besitzt er noch vor Apollon (V. 464ff.). Aber er ist nicht nur »der Gott des glücklichen Findens und der Einfälle«, sondern auch »der Gott der klugen Rede«[14]. Nach Hesiod, Op. 77ff., gibt er der Pandora Sprache und Namen.

---

[14] K. Deichgräber, Der listensinnende Trug des Gottes, NAWG N.F.4 (1940-41) 3. »Gott der schlauen Rede« formuliert Deichgräber in der überarbeiteten Fassung dieses Vortrages (Der listensinnende Trug des Gottes. Vier Themen des griechischen Denkens, Göttingen 1952, 110).

Vielfältig sind die behütenden Schutzfunktionen des Hermes als Totenbegleiter, Helfer der Hirten, Wanderer, Diebe (die nicht mit moderner Ethik zu messen sind), Kaufleute, Wettkämpfer (s.u.) usw. Eine besondere Rolle spielt er auf Geheiß des Zeus als Überwinder des Argos, jenes alles sehenden, vieläugigen Wächters, den die eifersüchtige Hera zur Bewachung der kuhgestaltigen Io bestellt hatte. Einem solchen Gegner war wohl nicht nur mit »harter« Gewalt beizukommen. Man hat einem Vasenbild entnommen, daß Hermes ihn mit seinem goldenen Zauberstab zuvor eingeschläfert habe[15]. Jedenfalls hat er den »Panoptes« besiegt, indem er dessen Fähigkeiten durch die seinigen übertraf. Er dürfte ihn schließlich auch getötet haben[16]. Die griechische Tradition seit Hesiod (fr. 126 Merkelbach-West, sodann u.a. Aisch. Suppl. 303) berichtet davon. Der Mythos von Hermes' Sieg über den Argos ist wahrscheinlich nicht in zwei, etwa unterschiedlich alten, Überlieferungsvarianten zu verstehen, deren eine von taktischer, die andere von physischer Überlegenheit des Gottes sprach. Einleuchtender scheint es, daß der Sieger über den Argos seinen Gegner in beiderlei Hinsicht auszuschalten imstande war. Daß ihm neben geistiger auch körperliche Behendigkeit und Kraft zugeschrieben wurde, zeigt u.a. seine spätere Eigenschaft als Schutzgott sportlicher Wettkämpfe in Ringschulen und Gymnasien: Das von den Palästren veranstaltete Fest der attischen Ἑρμαῖα (Platon, Lys. 206 D-E) trägt seinen Namen ebenso wie die inschriftlich bezeugten agonistischen Ἑρμαῖα der Kleruchen von Salamis, in Arkadien usw.[17]. Gerade eine derartige Vielfalt der dem Hermes zu Gebote stehenden Fähigkeiten (erfolgreicher Einfallsreichtum, Behendigkeit, Kraft) dürfte in dem auf ihn bezogenen Beiwort der homerischen Versschlußformel κρατὺς Ἀργεϊφόντης[18] stecken. Denn

[15] U. v. Wilamowitz-Moellendorff, Der Glaube der Hellenen, I, Berlin 1931, 163 Anm. 4 (Nachdruck: Basel 1956, 160 Anm. 2).

[16] Zu dieser Tötung jetzt W. Burkert, Homo necans, Berlin 1972, 185ff.

[17] Dazu M. P. Nilsson, Griechische Feste von religiöser Bedeutung mit Ausschluß der attischen, Leipzig 1906 (Nachdruck Darmstadt 1957), 393f.; L. Deubner, Attische Feste, Berlin 1932 (Nachdruck 1956), 217.

[18] Die alte Streitfrage, ob ἀργεϊφόντης »Argostöter« meint oder nicht (Literatur in den Wörterbüchern von Frisk und Chantraine s.v.), kann hier beiseite bleiben. Daß der Name schon in homerischer Zeit so verstanden wurde, beweist die homerische Nachbildung ἀνδρεϊφόντης, die zuerst U. v. Wilamowitz-Moellendorff, Homerische Untersuchungen, Berlin 1884, 299 Anm. 10, als solche erkannt hat. Das Argument kehrt wieder bei E. Risch, l.c. (Anm. 7), 32 Anm. 28, R. Schmitt, Dichtung

hier wie in den oben genannten vergleichbaren Formeln muß das Epitheton Charakteristisches für den Träger des Götternamens bezeichnen.

4.1.3 Das Verbum κρατύνειν wird als von κρατύς abgeleitetes denominatives Faktitivum wie βαθύνειν »vertiefen« von βαθύς, εὐρύνειν »verbreitern, erweitern« von εὐρύς usw. erklärt[19]. Es ist demnach für die mittelbare Bedeutungsbestimmung von κρατύς mit heranzuziehen. Das gilt auch für den Fall, daß die unten (Abschn. 6.2.2.2) erörterte Alternativmöglichkeit zutrifft, wonach κρατύνειν nicht von κρατύς, sondern von κράτος aus gebildet sein könnte. Denn die folgende Untersuchung wird unabhängig von ihren auf κρατύνειν bezogenen Abschnitten zeigen, daß nicht nur κράτος, wie Benveniste meinte, sondern auch κρατύς von indoiran. krátu-/xratu- nicht zu trennen ist. Damit besteht ein formales und inhaltliches Band auch intern zwischen den beiden griechischen Nomina. Semantische Merkmale selbst eines u.U. von κράτος derivierten κρατύνειν sind deshalb in jedem Falle für κρατύς mit aufschlußreich.

Unter den zahlreichen Bezeugungen des Verbums sind, wie bei vielen Untersuchungen griechischer Wörter, die altepischen als die ältesten von besonderem Gewicht. Die drei Belege aus der Ilias (Λ 215; M 415; Π 563) waren wohl Vorbild für einen weiteren Beleg in der Darstellung der Titanomachie bei Hesiod, Th. 676. An allen vier Stellen handelt es sich wiederum um einen formelhaften Ausdruck, ἐκαρτύναντο φάλαγγας, im Anschluß an die Mittelzäsur nach dem »dritten Trochäus«. Benveniste, l.c. 80, meint — in diesem Punkt schwer verständlich —, das Verbum bezeichne bei Homer »la manœuvre des phalanges«; unmittelbar darauf betont er deutlicher, es handele sich um ein »durcir« der Phalangen, die unter dem Bilde von »corps solide(s) et métallique(s)« verstanden seien.

Bei näherer Betrachtung der in Frage kommenden Verse, i.e. unter Einbeziehung der sie umgebenden Verspartien, erscheint diese Deutung als problematisch. Die geschilderte Gesamtsituation der drei Iliasstellen ist jeweils ähnlich. Überall ist zunächst davon die Rede, daß ἡγήτορες den Kampfeswillen der Kämpfer, ihre Angriffsfreudigkeit oder Abwehrbereitschaft anspornen, indem sie an Erinne-

und Dichtersprache in indogermanischer Zeit, Wiesbaden 1967, 124f., W. Burkert, l.c. (Anm. 16), 186 Anm. 18.

[19] Mehr bei E. Fraenkel, Griechische Denominativa in ihrer geschichtlichen Entwicklung und Verbreitung, Göttingen 1906, 31ff.; E. Schwyzer, Griechische Grammatik I, München 1939, 733.

rungsvermögen, Einsicht und Gesinnung appellieren. Jedesmal steht das Syntagma ἐκαρτύναντο φάλαγγας im textlichen Zusammenhang mit einem solchen Aufruf.

a) In der Teichomachie wendet sich der von Aias und Teukros bei seinem Angriff auf die Mauer aufgehaltene Sarpedon um stärkere Unterstützung an seine Lykier. Er fragt, warum sie ihre kämpferische Gesinnung (θούριδος ἀλκῆς) so vermissen ließen, erklärt, daß es trotz seiner Kraft für ihn allein schwierig sei, einen Durchbruch zu erzwingen und einen Weg zu den Schiffen zu bahnen. Schließlich fordert er sie auf, ihm zu folgen, denn mehreren sei besserer Erfolg beschieden. Die Lykier kommen seinem Aufruf betroffen nach und drängen, um ihn geschart, heftiger gegen die Mauer vor:

M   409 «ὦ Λύκιοι, τί τ' ἄρ' ὧδε μεθίετε θούριδος ἀλκῆς;
410 ἀργαλέον δέ μοί ἐστι καὶ ἰφθίμῳ περ ἐόντι
411 μούνῳ ῥηξαμένῳ θέσθαι παρὰ νηυσὶ κέλευθον·
412 ἀλλ' ἐφομαρτεῖτε· πλεόνων δέ τε ἔργον ἄμεινον».
413 Ὣς ἔφαθ', οἱ δὲ ἄνακτος ὑποδείσαντες ὁμοκλὴν
414 μᾶλλον ἐπέβρισαν βουληφόρον ἀμφὶ ἄνακτα.

Auf der anderen Seite der Mauer werden bei den Griechen entsprechende Maßnahmen getroffen. Das kommt in den beiden nächsten Versen gleichsam gerafft, ohne Erwähnung näherer Einzelheiten, in den als Korrelat zu M 409-412 gesetzten Worten M 415f. zum Ausdruck:

M   415 Ἀργεῖοι δ' ἑτέρωθεν ἐκαρτύναντο φάλαγγας
416 τείχεος ἔντοσθεν, κτλ.

»Auf der anderen Seite festigten die Argiver ihre Schlachtreihen diesseits der Mauer usw.«.

b) Im Λ der Ilias kommt die Formel ebenso im Anschluß an eine Versgruppe vor, die, wenngleich knapper als im M, die von einem Vorkämpfer an die Trojaner gerichtete Ermahnung zu besserer Kampfmoral enthält. Wieder nimmt der folgende — mit M 415 identische — Formelvers Λ 215 Bezug auf entsprechende Vorgänge bei den Griechen.

Λ   211 Ἕκτωρ δ' ἐξ ὀχέων σὺν τεύχεσιν ἆλτο χαμᾶζε,
212 πάλλων δ' ὀξέα δοῦρα κατὰ στρατὸν ᾤχετο πάντη,
213 ὀτρύνων μαχέσασθαι, ἔγειρε δὲ φύλοπιν αἰνήν.
214 οἱ δ' ἐλελίχθησαν καὶ ἐναντίοι ἔσταν Ἀχαιῶν.

»Hektor sprang mit seiner Ausrüstung vom Wagen zu Boden und ging, seine spitzen Lanzen schwingend allenthalben im Heere umher

unter ständigen Mahnungen, den Kampf wieder aufzunehmen; zu fürchter-
lichem Streiten rief er auf.
Da machten sie kehrt und stellten sich den Achäern entgegen«.
Unmittelbar darauf heißt es von den Griechen parallel dazu

Λ   215 Ἀργεῖοι δ᾽ ἑτέρωθεν ἐκαρτύναντο φάλαγγας,
      216 ἀρτύνθη δὲ μάχη, στὰν δ᾽ ἀντίοι · κτλ.

»Auf der anderen Seite festigten die Argiver ihre Schlachtreihen,
die Schlacht bahnte sich an, sie traten sich gegenüber usw.«.

c) Auch in der Patroklie steht die Junktur ἐκαρτύναντο φάλαγγας
im Schlußteil eines ähnlichen Textzusammenhanges, der von Π 532
bis 566 reicht. Zunächst treibt Glaukos bei den Lykiern zum Kampf
um Sarpedons Leichnam an, dann bei den Troern, indem er von
Anführer zu Anführer geht und sich an Poulydamas, Agenor, Aeneas
und Hektor wendet (532-537). In seiner Mahnrede hält er Hektor vor,
die Hilfsvölker vergessen zu haben, die, fern von Freunden und
Heimat, ihr Leben gäben, während Hektor ihnen nicht helfen wolle.
Jetzt liege Sarpedon da, von Patroklos' Speer gefällt. Nun aber
sollten die Troer zur Verteidigung antreten und den Kampfeszorn
in sich entfachen, um die wütenden Myrmidonen an Beraubung
und Schändung der Leiche zu hindern (538-547). Da bemächtigt sich
der Troer tiefe Trauer, und sie folgen unter Hektors Führung
(548-553). In der nächsten Versgruppe spornt Patroklos den Kampfgeist der Griechen an, wendet sich zuerst an die beiden Aias
(553-555) und nennt Gründe für die Gegenwehr : Sarpedon, der als
erster auf die Mauer der Achäer gesprungen sei, liege nun da.
Wie wünschenswert wäre es doch, wenn man seinen Leichnam
ergreifen, mißhandeln und der Rüstung berauben, dazu noch einen
Verteidiger des Körpers niedermachen könnte (556-561). Auf diese
Worte hin werden auch sie (wohl die beiden Aias) kampfbegierig (562).
Hier werden also beiden streitenden Parteien Motive für die
Wiederaufnahme des Gefechtes genannt und haben die beabsichtigte
Wirkung. Dann heißt es weiter :

Π   563 οἱ δ᾽ ἐπεὶ ἀμφωτέρωθεν ἐκαρτύναντο φάλαγγας,
      564 Τρῶες καὶ Λύκιοι καὶ Μυρμιδόνες καὶ Ἀχαιοί,
      565 σύμβαλον ἀμφὶ νέκυι κατατεθνηῶτι μάχεσθαι
      566 δεινὸν ἀΰσαντες · ...

»Nachdem sie auf beiden Seiten ihre Schlachtreihen gefestigt hatten,
Troer, Lykier, Myrmidonen und Achäer,
gingen sie aufeinander los, zu streiten um den Leichnam,
mit gewaltigem Schlachtgeschrei; ...«.

Die Verse 563f. bieten gewissermaßen ein verkürztes Gegenbild zu den voranstehenden. Wie dort Vorkämpfer auf beiden Seiten zur Fortsetzung des Kampfes mahnen und damit neuen Mut wecken, so nennt anschließend der Vers 563 pauschal die entsprechenden Konsequenzen bei den φάλαγγες beider Seiten. Diese Konsequenzen bestehen nicht nur in bloßem Zusammenrücken der φάλαγγες, sondern auch darin, daß diese neuen Anlaß zum Kampf sehen und frischen Mut fassen. Die Formel ἐκαρτύναντο φάλαγγας meint eine Festigung der Schlachtreihen nicht nur im physischen und formationstaktischen Sinne, sondern auch in dem des Kampfwillens.

Diese Deutung stützt sich auf die an sämtlichen drei Stellen der Ilias gegebene und in dieser Regelmäßigkeit kaum zufällige Bindung der Formel an unmittelbar voranstehende Aufforderungen zum Kampf, i.e. auf die textliche Funktion der Formel als Korrelat zu solchen Aufforderungen. Daß eine φάλαγξ in der Ilias nicht als unbelebter »corps solide et métallique« (Benveniste) verstanden ist, der kein spirituelles oder emotionales Reagieren kennen würde, beweisen etwa Verse wie Z 83, αὐτὰρ ἐπεί κε φάλαγγας ἐποτρύνητον ἅπασας (Helenos zu Aeneas und Hektor) oder N 90, ῥεῖα μετεισά-μενος κρατερὰς ὤτρυνε φάλαγγας. Dort ist (ἐπ)οτρύνειν »anspornen, antreiben« ausdrücklich auf φάλαγγας wie sonst auf (meist heraus-ragende) Personen (Θ 92, Λ 213, N 767, P 553 usw.) bezogen. Das homerische ἐκαρτύναντο φάλαγγας meint ein Festigen der Schlachtreihen auch oder gerade unter Wiederherstellung des Abwehr-(Λ 215, M 415) und Angriffsgeistes oder -willens (Π 563). Dieser Kampfgeist heißt ἀλκή [20], die Sarpedon in dem oben zitierten Vers M 409 seinen Lykiern zunächst abspricht, dann aber mit seinen Vorhaltungen in ihnen neu belebt. Bezeichnenderweise wird in einer an Agamemnon gerichteten Schmährede des Diomedes die ἀλκή als »das größte κράτος« bezeichnet: I 39 (Ζεύς) ἀλκὴν δ᾽ οὔ τοι δῶκεν, ὅ τε κράτος ἐστὶ μέγιστον »Kampfgeist aber, der das größte κράτος ist, hat dir (Zeus) nicht verliehen«. Die von Benveniste geleugnete semantische Brücke zwischen κράτος und καρτύνεσθαι (κρατύς) ist damit zumindest in der homerischen Sprache, wenn man die oben festgestellten Kontextstrukturen berücksichtigt, greifbar: mit ἀλκή,

---

[20] B. Snell, Die Entdeckung des Geistes, 3. Aufl. Hamburg 1955, 41, paraphrasiert innerhalb einer Darstellung des homerischen Wortfeldes für »Kraft« die ἀλκή als »Kraft der Abwehr, das Feindliche von sich fernzuhalten«. Benveniste, l.c. 74, definiert sie als »force de l'âme, la *fortitude*, qui ne cède pas devant le danger ...«.

»kämpferischer Gesinnung«, haben beide Wörter zu tun. Nicht nur κράτος hat bei Homer verschiedene semantische Komponenten, »les unes tenant... à l'état physique, les autres à des facultés comme l'*alkē*«, wie Benveniste, l.c. 75, für dieses Wort richtig[21] bemerkt, sondern — entgegen seinem Resultat — in gleicher Weise auch καρτύνεσθαι.

Der spätere Gebrauch des Verbums ist freilich mit dem homerischen nicht mehr gleichzusetzen. Schon Hesiod hat die Formel zwar innerhalb des Verses 676 der Theogonie

Τιτῆνες δ' ἑτέρωθεν ἐκαρτύναντο φάλαγγας

äußerlich traditionsgemäß angewandt, aber nicht mehr genau nach homerischer Art verstanden und in einen weiteren Kontext eingefügt. Auch von ihm werden zwar Vorbereitungen für eine bevorstehende Schlacht geschildert, bei Zeus und seinen Helfern auf der einen und bei den Titanen auf der anderen Seite. Aber es fehlt eine unmittelbar der Formel voranstehende Mahnrede, wie sie in der Ilias regelmäßig und sinnvoll war. Abgesehen davon, daß der Ausdruck φάλαγγας für die Titanen wenig passend scheint, ist das in Homers ἐκαρτύναντο steckende mentale Element nicht mehr hinreichend deutlich. So fügt Hesiod der Formel am Anfang des folgenden Verses 677 eigens das Adverb προφρονέως »bereitwillig, eifrig« hinzu. Derartiges wäre in der Ilias wohl redundant gewesen. M. L. West läßt in seinem Kommentar zu dieser Stelle ein zutreffendes Gespür erkennen, wenn er ohne nähere Erläuterungen von nur vagem Gebrauch der Formel durch Hesiod spricht[22].

Folgerichtig wird das Verbum κρατύνειν in späterer Zeit im weiter verallgemeinerten Sinne von »(ver)stärken, (be)festigen, härten usw.« gebraucht, ohne durch ein selektionales semantisches Merkmal [auf Männer bezogen] bestimmten Kontextbeschränkungen wie noch bei Homer unterworfen zu sein. So kann Thukydides 3,82,6 τὰς ἐς σφᾶς αὐτοὺς πίστεις... ἐκρατύνοντο formulieren und ebensogut 1,69,1 τὴν πόλιν μετὰ τὰ Μηδικὰ κρατῦναι oder 3,18,1 τείχη κρατύναντες sagen. Ganz deutlich zeigt sich der Unterschied zu Homer bei

---

[21] Unzutreffend demgegenüber H. Trümpy, Kriegerische Fachausdrücke im griechischen Epos, Basel 1950, 202, der, offensichtlich unter dem Eindruck der fragwürdigen (dazu weiter unten Abschn. 6.1) etymologischen Verbindung mit got. *hardus* usw. »für κράτος als älteste Bedeutung 'Härte' an(setzt)«.

[22] Hesiod Theogony. Edited with Prolegomena and Commentary by M. L. West, Oxford 1966, zu V. 676-677, S. 348.

Theokrit 22,80. An dieser Stelle seines in epischem Versmaß und epischer Sprache abgefaßten Dioskuren-Gedichtes setzt der hellenistische Dichter die traditionelle mediale Aoristform an ihre traditionelle Stelle im Hexameter und verwendet sie auch inhaltlich für die Darstellung einer Kampfvorbereitung : Polydeukes und Amykos treten zum Faustkampf an. Aber Theokrits ἐκαρτύναντο ist durchaus unhomerisch[23] für eine »handfeste« Verstärkung der Fäuste durch lederne Schlagriemen gebraucht :

22,80ff. οἳ δ᾽ ἐπεὶ οὖν σπείραισιν ἐκαρτύναντο βοείαις
χεῖρας... ἐς μέσσον σύναγον, φόνον ἀλλήλοισι πνέοντες.

»Als sie nun ihre Fäuste mit ledernen Schlagriemen verstärkt hatten..., trafen sie in der Mitte zusammen und schnaubten einander tödlich an«.

In der medizinischen Fachsprache des Hippokrates ist für Zusammenwachsen bzw. Verfestigung gebrochener Unterarmknochen ein Ausdruck wie κρατύνεται ὀστέα (Περὶ ἀγμῶν 7) angemessen, und Xenophon, Λακεδαιμονίων πολιτεία 2,3, gebraucht das Verbum für das Abhärten der Füße beim Barfußlaufen (τοὺς πόδας... ἀνυποδησίᾳ κρατύνειν)[24]. Soweit κρατύνειν auch im Sinne von »herrschen (über)« und »Herr werden über, sich bemächtigen« (u.a. bei Sophokles und Euripides) verwendet wird, scheinen semantische Überkreuzungen mit κράτος[25] und κρατεῖν, κρατῆσαι eingetreten zu sein.

4.1.4 Aus dem unter 4.1.2 und 4.1.3 Dargelegten ergibt sich, daß das ausschließlich homerische κρατύς nicht im stofflichen Sinne

---

[23] Eine aus dem zwischenzeitlichen Bedeutungswandel von κρατύνειν verständliche Mißdeutung des epischen Verbums wie dem Theokrit dürfte noch viel später auch dem Byzantiner Eustathios oder seinem Gewährsmann unterlaufen sein : Während die Scholien A, B, T zu ἐκαρτύναντο an den drei Iliasstellen schweigen, bietet Eustathios 911,37 die Interpretamente πυκνῶσαι, στερεῶσαι, die der homerischen Verbalbedeutung schwerlich gerecht werden. Hesych K 905 καρτύνεσθαι · ἀσφαλίζεσθαι, διισχυρίζεσθαι scheint zwar auf ein D-Scholion zurückzugehen. Aber die beiden Interpretamente verraten eine gewisse Ratlosigkeit des Scholiasten. Das erste bedeutet sonst »sichern, befestigen (etwa τὸν τόπον), schließen (etwa τὴν πύλην: späte Belege), sich hüten vor«, das zweite »sich stützen, verlassen auf, nachdrücklich versichern«.

[24] Die vergleichbare Bedeutungsskala des verwandten Adjektivs κρατερός (καρτερός) ist wohl ähnlich bedingt. Jedenfalls besteht kein Anlaß,. mit Benveniste, l.c. 77ff., für das zur Wortfamilie von κράτος gehörende κρατερός (καρτερός) wegen der von Benveniste unterschiedenen Bedeutungen a) »überlegen« und b) »hart, grausam« eine (inhaltliche) Kontamination mit angeblichem κρατύς »hart« anzunehmen. Selbst κράτος ist an einer Odysseestelle, ι 393, mit einem Bedeutungsübergang »Kraft, Überlegenheit« zu »Härte (des Eisens)« verwendet, was Benveniste übersieht.

[25] Vgl. E. Fraenkel, l.c. (Anm. 19), 35.

»hart« bedeuten konnte. Dafür gab es in der Sprache des alten Epos das Adjektiv στερεός — z.B. τ 494 στερεὴ λίθος ἠὲ σίδηρος —, später auch σκληρός. Im Gegensatz zu Benvenistes Beurteilung ist κρατύς nicht von κράτος zu trennen. In beiden Wörtern einschließlich ihrer Ableitungen kommen Qualitäten wie »Überlegenheit«, »überlegenes Leistungsvermögen«, »siegreicher Kampfgeist« zum Ausdruck. Diese Qualitäten beruhen auf außerordentlichen göttlichen oder menschlichen Fähigkeiten, die nicht, oder jedenfalls nicht primär, physischen Ursprungs sind. Konstitutiv für sie sind vielmehr Fähigkeiten des Geistes und der Gesinnung, ohne daß solche in der Vorstellungswelt des archaischen Adels, aus der unsere Wörter stammen, von körperlichen Vorzügen klar zu scheiden sind.

4.2 Über av. *xratu-* und damit indirekt auch über ai. *krátu-* hat K. F. Geldner vor neunzig Jahren folgendermaßen geurteilt: »*khratu* ist ein so vielseitiges Wort, dass wir im Deutschen nicht mit e i n e r Uebersetzung den Begriff erschöpfen. Es ist jede Art von geistiger Kraft, mag dieselbe in dem Willen oder dem Gedächtniss (sic) oder der Intelligenz sich bethätigen, darunter verstanden«[26]. Ähnliche Ansichten werden auch heute noch vertreten[27]. Ein eindrucksvolles Bild von der Schwierigkeit eines einheitlichen Bedeutungsansatzes vermitteln jedenfalls schon die stark aufgefächerten Angaben der drei wichtigsten einschlägigen Wörterbücher.

So setzt Graßmann in seinem Wörterbuch zum Rigveda s.v. *krátu* (Sp. 353f.) insgesamt 15 Bedeutungsvarianten für das ai. Wort an: »1) *Kraft* oder *Fähigkeit, etwas auszuführen,* oder *durchzusetzen;* 2) *Kraft* ohne Unterscheidung der Geistes- und Leibeskräfte; insbesondere 3) mit bhadrá (heilbringend) verbunden; 4) mit dem ihm in der Bedeutung zunächstkommenden dákṣa verbunden; 5) *Leibeskraft;* 6) *Geisteskraft, Geist* ohne Unterscheidung einzelner Geisteskräfte; insbesondere 7) mit juṣ, die *Geisteskraft,* den *geistigen Einfluss* eines andern schmecken oder sich gefallen lassen; 8) *Verstand, Einsicht;* 9) *Willenskraft, Wille* ...; ... 10) der Instr. krátvā, *willig, bereitwillig;* 11) *Gesinnung, heilige Gesinnung,* wie sie für Gebet und Opferwerk sich eignet; insbesondere 12) mit pū, seinen *Sinn,* seine *Gesinnung* reinigen; 13) *Begeisterung,* die zur Liederfindung geschickt

---

[26] K. F. Geldner, Drei Yasht aus dem Zendavesta übersetzt und erklärt, Stuttgart 1884, 95.

[27] Sinngemäß vergleichbare Feststellungen zur semantischen Komplexität des Wortes in neuerer Literatur z.B. bei G. Widengren, Die Religionen Irans, Stuttgart 1965, 84; Benveniste, l.c., 82.

macht. — Ferner auf Eigenwesen übertragen: 14) der *Krafttrunk*, als der Kraft erregende (vom Soma); 15) der *Starke*, der *Held*, von Göttern und Menschen ...«.

Das Petersburger Wörterbuch s.v. *kratu* (Sp. 472 ff.) unterscheidet 7 Bedeutungen, wobei gegenüber Graßmann im wesentlichen Angaben fehlen, die die »Körperkraft« betreffen: 1) Rathschluss, Plan; Absicht, Vorsatz. 2) Verlangen. 3) Vermögen, Tüchtigkeit, Wirksamkeit. 4) Ueberlegung, Rath; Einsicht, Verstand. 5) Erleuchtung, Begeisterung. 6) Opferhandlung. 7) Kratu, die personifizierte Einsicht.

Für das altiranische Gegenstück *xratu-* gibt Bartholomae, Altiranisches Wörterbuch s.v. *xratav-* (Sp. 535), neun auf zwei Gruppen verteilte Übersetzungen an: 1) Wille, Absicht, Plan, Ratschluss. 2) Geisteskraft, Einsicht, Verstand; Gedächtniskraft, Weisheit.

4.2.1 Eine derartige Vielfalt von Bedeutungsansätzen war und ist hier wie in anderen Fällen unbefriedigend. Dementsprechend hat man immer wieder versucht, den Katalog der in den Wörterbüchern verzeichneten Bedeutungen entweder einzuengen oder durch eine zentrale, sämtlichen Belegstellen im wesentlichen gerecht werdende Sinn-Paraphrase zu ersetzen oder auf einen sogenannten »Grundbegriff« bzw. eine »Grundbedeutung« zurückzuführen, aus der sich die übrigen Nuancen entwickelt hätten. Als Beispiel für ein Bemühen der erstgenannten Art kann etwa Bergaignes früher Versuch genannt werden, für ved. *krátu-* die stark differenzierte Skala Graßmanns (und Ludwigs) unter Streichung der auf »physische Kraft« abhebenden Inhaltsbestimmungen zu reduzieren: »Il paraît désigner dans les hymnes védiques la force intellectuelle ou morale, soit en puissance, soit en acte. On pourra donc le traduire selon les cas 'intelligence, volonté, idée, résolution' ou simplement 'désir'«[28]. Paraphrasen haben etwa Oldenberg und, in neuerer Zeit, Renou als angemessenen Zugang zu einem rechten Verständnis des vedischen Wortes erachtet. So interpretiert Oldenberg es folgendermaßen: »k r a t u berührt sich mit m a n a s (z.B. RV. IV, 33,9, ähnlich im Awesta), hat aber ... mehr die besondere Richtung auf praktische Betätigung. Doch bedeutet es m.E. nicht einfach 'Willen', sondern überhaupt die auf das Handeln gerichtete Seelenfunktion, die Einsicht, daß die Sache s o zu machen ist (z.B. RV. VIII, 70,13) und den Willen sie so zu machen (bz. daß sie so gemacht werde), beides noch undif-

---

[28] A. Bergaigne, La religion védique d'après les hymnes du Rig-Veda, Paris 1878-83 (Nachdruck 1963), III 305.

[29] H. Oldenberg, Vorwissenschaftliche Wissenschaft. Die Weltanschauung der Brāhmaṇatexte, Göttingen 1919, 69 Anm. 2.

[30] L. Renou, Études védiques et pāṇinéennes II, Paris 1956, 58 und IV, 1958, 47.

ferenziert«[29]. Wir werden auf diese Deutung unten noch zurück-
zukommen haben. Renou beschreibt das Wort mit Paraphrasen wie
»*Krátu* souligne la 'qualité requise': la faculté de comprendre, qui
précède immédiatement l'acte créateur (gr. ποίησις)« oder »dispo-
sition d'esprit tournée vers l'agir«[30].
Mit dem »Grundbegriff der 'wirksamen, auch magisch wirksamen
Kraft'« rechnete W. Neisser bei dem ai. Wort[31]. Und eine ganze
auf die 'Grundbedeutung' ausgerichtete Untersuchung bot wenig
später K. Rönnow in seiner auch das avestische Pendant mit
berücksichtigenden Arbeit »Ved. *kratu-*. Eine wortgeschichtliche Untersuchung«[32]. Er definiert darin (S. 3; 72) diese »Grundbedeutung«
wie folgt: »(*kratu*) ist der bestimmende, energische Sinn des mutigen
Kriegers, vor allem Indras, eine Macht in seinem Innern, dank
welcher ihm Sieg und Erfolg geschenkt werden, und die der Gott
seinen Verehrern, die darum bitten, geben kann. Das ist die
Grundbedeutung, und daraus erklären sich die verschiedenen Varia-
tionen: Tapferkeit, Siegeskraft, Majestät, Wille u.s.w.«.
   4.2.2 Wiedergaben eines Wortes wie *krátu-/xratu-* durch mehrere
Wörter oder durch Paraphrasen in der Übersetzungssprache sind
Versuche einer synchronischen Bedeutungsbestimmung, während die
Fahndung nach einer »Grundbedeutung« diachronisch den Ausgangs-
punkt einer Bedeutungsentwicklung zu orten bemüht ist. Diese drei
Verfahrensweisen sind zunächst von je andersartigen Intentionen
geleitet. Die Wörterbücher (von Graßmann, Böhtlingk-Roth, Bartholomae) haben gewissermaßen Übersetzungsmöglichkeiten für alle
Belegstellen anzubieten. Dabei ergibt sich eine Vielfalt von Bedeutungsangaben offenbar deshalb, weil aufgrund dahinter stehender
unterschiedlicher Vorstellungswelten die Inhaltsseite eines indoiranischen Abstraktums wie *krátu-/xratu-* sich nicht total mit der irgen-
deines Wortes der Übersetzungssprache (Deutsch, Französisch usw.)
deckt, sondern bestenfalls Teilausschnitte mit den Inhaltsseiten verschiedener Abstrakta der Übersetzungssprachen gemein hat[33]. Der
nicht vorhandenen Äquivalenz von Wort zu Wort in Ausgangs-
und Zielsprache will die Paraphrase (etwa von Oldenberg und Renou)

---

[31] W. Neisser, Zum Wörterbuch des Rgveda, Zweites Heft, Leipzig 1930, 66.
[32] Le Monde oriental 26-27 (1932-1933) 1-90.
[33] Verschiedene Nuancen von *kratu-* (u.a. als »power of the intellect« oder
»power of the body«) je nach Textumgebung (Bezogenheit auf Indra, Agni usw.)
konstatiert S. Venkateswaran, Siddha-Bhāratī (Papers in Honor of Siddheshwar Varma,
ed. by Vishva-Bandhu, Hoshiarpur 1950), I 189 ff.

Rechnung tragen, ohne doch als solche bei der Übersetzung einzelner Textstellen einfach »eingesetzt« werden zu können. Die diachronische Untersuchungsweise strebt als Fixpunkt die älteste Bedeutung an; dabei gewinnt Rönnow seine recht spezielle »Grundbedeutung«, etwa »Siegeskraft«, im wesentlichen aus einer begrenzten vedischen Textgruppe heraus, den Indra-Hymnen des R̥gveda, während Neisser seinen »Grundbegriff« der »magisch wirksamen Kraft« offenbar als Basis sämtlicher Verwendungen des ai. Wortes versteht.

Es hat den Anschein, daß die bisherigen Deutungen von *krátu-/xratu-* nicht einfach »richtig« oder »falsch« sind, sondern jeweils begrenzt Gültiges, manchmal einander Ergänzendes enthalten. Eine erneute synchronische Untersuchung des altindischen und des altiranischen Wortes könnte vielleicht zusätzliche Klarheit schaffen. Dabei wäre eine systematische Abgrenzung von ai. *krátu-* gegenüber vermutlichen Nachbarwörtern seines Bedeutungsfeldes wie *mánas-* (n.), *manyú-* (m.), *mánman-* (n.), *cítti-* (f.), *dákṣa-* (m.), *ójas-* (n.), *śávas-* (n.), *jaítra-* (n.), *tavá-* (m.), *śúṣma-* (m.) usw., ebenso von airan. *xratu-* gegenüber av. *manah-* (n.), av. *ma(i)niiu-* (m.), *cisti-* (f.), av. *vasna-*, ap. *vašna-* (m.), av. *iš̌-* (f.) usw. zu versuchen. Ferner wäre nach möglicherweise bevorzugten Verbindungen von *krátu-/xratu-* mit bestimmten Verben und Adjektiven im Sinne von W. Porzigs »wesenhaften Bedeutungsbeziehungen«[34] Ausschau zu halten. Eine so umfassende Untersuchung, die möglicherweise auch die diachronische und etymologische Beurteilung von *krátu-/xratu-* auf festere Grundlagen stellen würde, ist im hier gesteckten Rahmen nicht möglich. So bleibt fürs erste nur der Ausweg, die oben angedeuteten vorläufigen Teilergebnisse der bisherigen Forschung dem Vergleich von *krátu-/xratu-* mit dem griechischen Wortmaterial nutzbar zu machen.

4.2.3 Dabei ergeben sich immerhin bemerkenswerte Anknüpfungspunkte nicht nur für κράτος und Zubehör, sondern auch für κρατύς und κρατύνω, die im vorliegenden Zusammenhang besonders interessant sind. Wenn Rönnow, l.c. 72, vor allem auf die Indra-Lieder des R̥gveda gestützt, seine Bestimmung von *krátu-* als »energische(r) Sinn des mutigen Kriegers«, »Siegeskraft«, »Heldenkraft, -sinn, -mut, Mut, Tapferkeit, Kampfeslust, männliche Tüchtigkeit« trifft, so paßt das augenscheinlich gut zu der oben ermittelten Bedeutung »(Schlacht-

---

[34] W. Porzig, Wesenhafte Bedeutungsbeziehungen, PBB 58 (1934) 70-97, abgedruckt in : L. Schmidt (Hrg.), Wortfeldforschung, Darmstadt 1973, 78-103.

reihen) in ihrem Kampfgeist festigen« des Faktitivums καρτύνεσθαι im griechischen Epos. Selbst wenn Rönnow die urarische »Grundbedeutung« in ai. *krátu*- nicht restlos erfaßt haben sollte, so kommen doch wesentliche semantische Komponenten des anzunehmenden Erbwortes in ved. *krátu*- der Indralieder und in hom. καρτύνεσθαι übereinstimmend zum Vorschein.

Wichtig ist ferner das besonders von Oldenberg[35] betonte Verhältnis von ai. *krátu*- zu *mánas*- einerseits und *dákṣa*- andererseits. Textliche Kombinationen von *krátu*- und *mánas*- (*xratu*- und *manah*-) kommen im Vedischen und im Avestischen vor. So heißt es beispielsweise RV. 4,33,9, in einem Lied an die Ṛbhus, *ápo hy èṣām ájuṣanta devá abhí krátvā mánasā dīdhyānāḥ*, was Geldner so übersetzt: »Denn an ihrem Werke fanden die Götter Gefallen, als sie es mit Einsicht und Verstand betrachteten«. Zunächst läßt sich aus solcher Reihung im Satz eine semantische Opposition von *krátu*- und *mánas*- folgern, so daß sie, anders als Hertel meinte[36], gerade nicht als Synonyme gelten können. Die gleiche Reihung beider Wörter bietet im Gāthischen etwa Y. 46,18 *taṭ mōi xratōuš manaŋhascā vīciθəm* »Das ist meines Geistes und meines Gedankens Entscheidung« (Humbach). Nun hat Oldenberg in seinen oben bereits auszugsweise zitierten Darlegungen (l.c.69f. Anm. 2) einleuchtend den Bezug von *krátu*- auf »praktische Betätigung«, »Handeln« usw. unter »Zurücktreten der rein theoretischen Nuance« betont. Dafür sind aufschlußreich erstens Verbindungen wie RV. 8,61,4 *táthéd asad índra krátvā yáthā váśaḥ* »Es soll so sein, Indra, wie du es mit deinem *krátu*- wünschen wirst«, RV. 8,66,4 *karad índraḥ krátvā yáthā váśat* »Indra möge tun, wie er es mit seinem *krátu*- wünschen wird«, RV. 1,165,7 *bhūríṇi hí kṛṇávāma... krátvā... yád váśāma* »Denn vieles werden wir tun,... wenn wir (es) mit dem *krátu*-... wünschen werden«; zweitens Verknüpfungen von *mánas*- und *dhī*- »denken«: RV. 7,90,5 *satyéna mánasā dīdhyānāḥ...* »mit wahrhaftem Denken nachsinnend...« (Geldner), RV. 10,181,3 *tè 'vindan mánasā dīdhyānā yáju...* »Die fanden im Geiste nachsinnend den... Opferspruch...« (Geldner), RV. 1,163,12... *devadrīcā mánasā dīdhyānaḥ...* »mit gottwärts gerichtetem Gedanken sinnend« (Geldner).

Das sind also — in Porzigs späterer Terminologie — »wesenhafte

---

[35] H. Oldenberg, l.c. (Anm. 29), 69f. Anm. 2.
[36] J. Hertel, Yašt 14, 16, 17 Text, Übersetzung und Erläuterung. Mithra und Ǝrəxša, Leipzig 1931, 46 Anm. 4.

Bedeutungsbeziehungen« zwischen *krátu-* und *vaś-* »wünschen, wollen« hier sowie zwischen *mánas-* und *dhī-* »denken« dort. Drittens gibt es die berühmte definitorische Unterscheidung von *krátu-* und *dákṣa-* ŚB. 4,1,4,1 : *sá yád evá mánasā kāmáyata idáṃ me syād idáṃ kurvīyéti sá evá krátur átha yád asmái tát samṛdhyáte sá dákṣo* »Wenn er mit seinem *manas* wünscht : »dies möge mir zuteil werden, dies möge ich tun« : das ist *kratu*. Wenn ihm das aber glückt : das ist *dakṣa*« (Oldenberg). Nach Geldner[37] ist an dieser Stelle *krátu-* als »Wollen« und/oder »Absicht«, *dákṣa-* als »Können« definiert. Oldenberg überträgt *dákṣa-* mit »Tüchtigkeit, Geschicklichkeit« und verweist darauf, daß dieses Wort häufig mit *krátu-*, nicht aber mit *mánas-* kombiniert ist. Während demnach *mánas-* einen übergeordneten Begriff wiedergibt, der neben anderem besonders das »theoretische«, intellektuelle Denken betrifft, bezeichnet *krátu-* nur das »praktische« Denken, das zielgerichtete Planen und Wollen eines Tuns, und meint *dákṣa-* die Fähigkeit zur erfolgreichen Durchführung[38]. In dem oben zitierten Stück RV. 4,33,9 a-b, wo es heißt, daß die Götter am Werk der Ṛbhus Gefallen fanden *abhí krátvā mánasā dídhyānāḥ*, scheint der Pāda b ein Zeugma zu enthalten, in dem das zu *mánasā* passende Partizip *abhí... dídhyānāḥ* auch auf *krátvā* angewandt ist. Wie immer man *krátvā mánasā* im Zusammenhang dieser Stelle auffassen[39] und übersetzen mag, irgendein Gegensatz zwischen *krátvā* und *mánasā* dürfte vorliegen. An der gleichfalls oben angeführten avestischen Gātha-Stelle Y. 46,18 scheint mir dieser Gegensatz bei der vergleichbaren Junktur *xratōuš manaŋhascā* noch deutlicher gegeben zu sein. Denn *xratōuš* ist wohl Korrelat zu dem im Text voranstehenden Akkusativ *vārəm* »Willen«. Zarathustras Worte an Ahura Mazdā, ... *xšmākəm vārəm xšnaošəmnō / taṭ mōi xratōuš manaŋhascā vīciϑəm*, möchte ich etwa folgendermaßen wiedergeben : »...euren Willen erfüllend. Das ist meines (entsprechenden) Wollens und Denkens Entscheidung«[40].

---

[37] Pischel-Geldner, Vedische Studien 1 (1889) 267.

[38] Zum Verhältnis zwischen *dákṣa-* und *krátu-* (in RV. 10,31,2) auch L. Renou, Ét. véd. et paṇ. 16 (1967) 129.

[39] Ist mit *krátvā* ein Begehren (vgl. die Paraphrase *idáṃ me syād* des ŚB.) des Ṛbhu-Werkes im Gegensatz zu dessen bloß sinnender Betrachtung (*mánasā*) durch die Götter gemeint? Non liquet.

[40] Dieser Bezug geht auch bei Bartholomaes Übersetzung, BB 8 (1884) 219f., verloren : »...deinen willen zu erfüllen, das ist meines... verstandes und herzens beschluss«.

Kämpferischer Drang des Kriegers und Wettkämpfers, Wille zur Tat und das Wissen um die Art ihrer Ausführung (vgl. oben S. 277, Oldenberg l.c. zu RV. 8,70,13) sind mithin konstitutive semantische Elemente von ai. *krátu-*. Hinter alledem vermutet Neisser, wie oben bereits vermerkt wurde, ansprechend den ursprünglichen Grundbegriff der magisch wirksamen Kraft, unter anderem auch wegen der Bezüge des *krátu-* zum Opfer und zum Soma [41]. In die gleiche Richtung mag der Umstand deuten, daß die Götter nicht nur *krátu-* haben und den Menschen verleihen, sondern selbst — wie dann auch damit begabte Menschen — geradezu *krátu-* sind : Das lehren die bei Graßmann, Wörterbuch s.v. *krátu*, unter Bedeutung 15) gebuchten Stellen des Ṛgveda.

Iranisch *xratu-* hat die gleichen semantischen Voraussetzungen. Freilich entwickelte sich das Wort im Avestischen innerhalb des zarathustrischen Systems semantisch weiter, wo *xratu-* u.a. als innerer Drang und Wollen der Guten und Bösen (vgl. *duš.xratu-* [42]) verstanden wird, ebenso innerhalb des jüngeren Zoroastrismus, wo es für »(göttliche und priesterliche) Weisheit« steht [43]. Auch im Altpersischen dürfte *xraθu-* DNb 3 / *xratu-* XDNb 3 [44] etwas Ähnliches wie »Weisheit« bedeuten; sie wird dem Großkönig von Auramazdā verliehen. In der Darius-Inschrift (DNb) und in ihrer Xerxes-Dublette (XDNb) steht eigens daneben das sich offenbar davon abhebende und ähnlich wie ved. *dákṣa-* mehr auf praktische Fähigkeit gehende Wort *aruvastam*, etwa »Tüchtigkeit, Tatkraft« [45]. Die akkadische Fassung von DNb gibt das ap. *xraθu-* im Sinne von »geistiger Veranlagung«, »Wille«, »Verstand«, »Denkvermögen«, »schöpferischer Gedanke« [46] wieder. Wahrscheinlich ist der *xratu-* des Großkönigs ein entschlossenes Wissen um das, was zu tun ist, und wie es zu tun ist (vgl. Darius' Aufzählungen seiner Fähigkeiten DNb 31-49).

---

[41] B. Schlerath, Festgabe deutscher Iranisten, Stuttgart 1971, 138, erkennt auch av. *xratu-* als »'geistig-körperliche Kraft und Kraftgefühl', sofern sich *xratu-* nach dem Haomagenuß einstellt«.

[42] *duš.xraθßā* in Y. 49,4 übersetzt B. Schlerath, Antiquitates Indogermanicae (Gedenkschrift Güntert), Innsbruck 1974, 216: »mit (aus dem Haomagenuß herrührendem) schlechtem geistig-körperlichen Kraftgefühl«, vgl. auch oben Anm. 41.

[43] K. Rönnow, l.c. (Anm. 32), 75. Das Kompositum *xratu.kāta-* faßt O. Szemerényi im Sinne von und als Lehnübersetzung aus gr. φιλόσοφος: KZ 76 (1959) 68; bei Altheim-Stiehl, Geschichte Mittelasiens im Altertum, Berlin 1970, 22 Anm. 7.

[44] W. Hinz, Altiranische Funde und Forschungen, Berlin 1969, 46.

[45] Zu ap. *xraθu-* und *aruvastam* vgl. É. Benveniste, TPS 1945, 39f.

[46] E. Herzfeld, Altpersische Inschriften, Berlin 1938, 236f.

So wird man auch in den neuerdings verfügbaren altpersischen Namen der elamischen Hofkammertäfelchen aus Persepolis, soweit sie wie beispielsweise *kur-ra-tu-man-ya*[47] das Wort *xratu-* (*xraθu-*) enthalten[48], letzteres schon als Vorstufe von np. *ḥerad*[49] in diesem Sinne von Weisheit verwertet sehen können.

Die Bedeutungsgeschichte des iranischen Wortes von seinen in der urarischen Herkunft wurzelnden Anfängen bis in spätere Zeit hinein hat in mustergültiger Zusammenfassung H. S. Nyberg dargestellt, dessen wir mit diesem Sammelbande gedenken. Wir können auf seine Ausführungen zurückgreifen :

»Es ist angemessen, hier einige Worte über *Chratu* einzuschalten. Das Wort steht mitunter parallel zu Chšathra: in 45_7 heißt es, daß Ahura Mazdāh Schöpfer durch Chšathra ist, aber in 31_7, daß er Schöpfer des Aša durch seinen Chratu ist. Wie Rönnow nachgewiesen hat ..., liegt in diesem Begriff im ganzen arischen Bereich die Bedeutung einer Kraft oder einer Energie, eines Kraftansatzes und einer Kraftentfaltung. Im Unterschied zu Chšathra ist Chratu jedoch eine *bewußte* Energie, ein Willensakt. Er kann als eine individuelle Seelenkraft oder Teilseele gefaßt werden, parallel zu daēnā (31_{11}); 'mein chratu' 46_{18}, 50_6. Auch die Bösen haben chratu (32_{14}, 49_4). Chratu kann als ein Kraftzentrum aufgefaßt werden und im Lokativ stehen : 'der seinen eigenen Neigungen und Wünschen folgt, wird am letzten Ende in deinem Chratu-Bereich abseits stehen' 48_4 (angeredet ist Ahura Mazdāh). Vohu Manah besitzt chratu; 'Chratu des Lebens' 32_9. Chratu ist das Organ für die Pläne der Götter (49_6) und das Organ, durch das Ahura Mazdāh seine Verheißung kundtut (45_6). In 32_4 steht Mazdāh Ahuras Chratu parallel zu Aša. An einigen Stellen (45_2, 46_3) steht Chratu in naher Verbindung mit *sə̄ngha*, worin wir den Begriff für die Ordalentscheidung der göttlichen Macht fanden. Am 'letzten Wendepunkt der Schöpfung' wird Ārmaiti *ratu*, d.h. göttlicher Vertreter, von Ahura Mazdāhs Chratu sein und die Ordalentscheidung verkünden (43_6).

In Vendidad 18_6 werden wir Chratu als Medium der Ekstase oder Organ für die Verbindung des Menschen mit dem Göttlichen wiederfinden (s. S. 185). Sonst scheint der Begriff in späterer Zeit immer mehr intellektuelle Färbung zu gewinnen und sich der Bedeutung 'Weisheit' anzunähern. Das mitteliranische *chrat* steht nicht weit ab von hebr. *ḥokmā* in der Weisheitsliteratur«[50].

[47] Zur Deutung É. Benveniste, Titres et noms propres en Iranien ancien, Paris 1966, 86; anders R. Schmitt, KZ 84 (1970) 16.

[48] Bei M. Mayrhofer, Onomastica Persepolitana, Wien 1973, sind sie unter den laufenden Nummern 8.30 (S. 122), 8.198 (S. 136: unsicher), 8.584 (S. 164), 8.880 (S. 184), 8.1710 (S. 244), jeweils mit Literatur, gebucht.

[49] Vgl. W. Hinz, Neue Wege im Altpersischen, Wiesbaden 1973, 111.

[50] H. S. Nyberg, Die Religionen des alten Iran. Deutsch von H. H. Schaeder, Leipzig 1938 (Nachdruck Osnabrück 1966), 139f. – Zu vergleichen ist ferner E. Herzfeld, l.c. (Anm. 46), 235ff.

4.3 Es wurde oben bereits bemerkt, daß es inhaltliche Anknüpfungspunkte zwischen den von Rönnow für ai. *krátu-* vor allem in den r̥gvedischen Indraliedern festgestellten Bedeutungen wie »Siegeskraft, männliche Tüchtigkeit usw.« und dem Faktitivum καρτύνεσθαι im altgriechischen Epos gibt. Lassen sich nun ähnliche Beziehungen auch zwischen κρατύς selbst als einer formelhaften homerischen Bezeichnung für den Gott Hermes und dem indoiranischen Appellativum *krátu-/xratu-* ausmachen? Mir scheint, daß diese Frage eindeutig zu bejahen ist.

Zunächst hat sich gezeigt (oben 4.1.2), daß Hermes nach einem außerhalb des homerischen Epos bezeugten Mythos — unabhängig von der Etymologie des Wortes Ἀργεϊφόντης — aufgrund seiner Fähigkeiten Sieger über den Argos geblieben ist. Darin ·liegt ein erster möglicher Anschluß an die vedische Bedeutung von *krátu-*. Nähere Einzelheiten dieses Sieges sind unklar. Eine besonders von Wilamowitz betonte Version des Argos-Hermes-Mythos gründet den Sieg des Hermes auf seinen Zauberstab (ῥάβδος), mit dem er den Argos eingeschläfert haben soll. Demnach hätte Hermes bei dieser Auseinandersetzung Zauberkräfte ausgeübt. Das erinnert an den am deutlichsten von Neisser für *krátu-/xratu-* postulierten »Grundbegriff« der »magisch wirksamen Kraft«. Unabhängig von der Argos-Geschichte in der Io-Sage eignen nun auch sonst dem Hermes im Unterschied zu anderen olympischen Göttern magische Züge. Diese zeigen sich für uns Moderne am auffälligsten an der Verfügungsgewalt über seinen Zauberstab. Mit ihm »verzaubert er die Augen« (ὄμματα θέλγει). Es ist wohl kein Zufall und sollte besonders beachtet werden, daß an zwei der insgesamt vier Homerstellen, die Hermes mit der Formel κρατὺς Ἀργεϊφόντης benennen, unmittelbar auf die im Stab manifestierte magische Kraft Bezug genommen wird:

Ω 343-345 = ε 47-49

εἵλετο δὲ ῥάβδον, τῇ τ᾽ ἀνδρῶν ὄμματα θέλγει
ὧν ἐθέλει, τοὺς δ᾽ αὖτε καὶ ὑπνώοντας ἐγείρει·
τὴν μετὰ χερσὶν ἔχων πέτετο κρατὺς Ἀργεϊφόντης.

»Er ergriff den Stab, mit dem er die Augen der Menschen verzaubert(!), bei welchen auch immer er das will, und sie auch wieder aus dem Schlafe
erweckt;
ihn in Händen haltend flog κρατὺς Ἀργεϊφόντης davon«.

Aber auch andere Eigenschaften des Hermes hat man aus seiner Verwurzelung in der Magie gedeutet: Hermes als Wegegott, als Gott

»vom Steinhaufen«, seine Verfügung über die der Tarnkappe vergleichbare Hadeskappe, sein Mittlertum zwischen Göttern und Menschen usw.[51]. Der ihm in nachhomerischer Zeit als Sohn zugeschriebene Autolykos hat Zauberkräfte wie er. Nach einem Hesiodfragment (67 Merkelbach-West) konnte Autolykos alles, was er berührte, unsichtbar machen :

fr. 67 M.-W. ὅττι κε χερσὶ λάβεσκεν ἀείδελα πάντα τίθεσκεν.

Die sonstigen Fähigkeiten des Hermes, von denen in Abschnitt 3.1.2 die Rede war, sind teilweise ebenfalls Eigenschaften vergleichbar, die im indoiranischen Bereich mit dem Wort *krátu-/xratu-* ausgedrückt werden. Hier wie dort mag es sich um parallel entwickelte — also nicht mehr etwa in gemeinsamer »urindogermanischer« Frühzeit eingetretene — Sublimierungen magischer Kraft in Richtung auf geistiges Vermögen handeln[52]. »Praktisches« Denken, wie es für ved. *krátu-* explizit durch die oben genannte Stelle ŚB. 4,1,4,1 definiert wird und an den weiteren inhaltlichen Nuancen des indischen und iranischen Wortes beteiligt ist, zeichnet auch den griechischen Gott Hermes in hohem Maße aus. So wird in V. 46 des homerischen Hermeshymnus ausdrücklich gesagt, daß der Gott Wort und Tat zugleich ersann (ἅμ᾽ ἔπος τε καὶ ἔργον ἐμήδετο). Nach dem gleichen Hymnus erfindet er die Leier (V. 25) und beherrscht als erster die τέχνη ihres Spiels, die er Apollon lehrt (V. 464ff.). Der Rinderdiebstahl und die Modalitäten seiner Durchführung verraten ebenso »praktisches« und wohl auch willensstarkes, entschlossenes Denken. Man ist fast versucht, mit Hermes als dem Gott der Diebe die eine der beiden Teildefinitionen von ved. *krátu-* an der ŚB.-Stelle zu assoziieren : »Wenn er mit seinem *mánas* wünscht : 'Dies möge mir gehören ...', das ist *krátuḥ*«.

Wie vedische Götter *krátu-* haben, so ist der griechische Gott Hermes κρατύς. Die vedischen Götter besitzen *krátu-* von Geburt an : RV. 2,12,1 (von Indra) *yó jātá evá prathamó mánasvān devó devā́n krátunā paryábhūṣat* ... »Der, eben geboren, als erster mit *mánas* begabter

---

[51] Dazu O. Kern, Die Religion der Griechen, II, Berlin 1935, 18f.; U.v. Wilamowitz-Moellendorff, Der Glaube der Hellenen, Berlin 1931, I 163.
[52] Ob wir ai. *krátu-* als die von Rönnow, l.c. 13ff., herausgestellte Kraft und Schnelligkeit beim sportlichen Wettkampf, vor allem beim Wettrennen, mit dem Epitheton κρατύς des Hermes als des schnellen, Flügelschuhe tragenden Boten und Eponyms agonistischer Spiele in Verbindung bringen dürfen, sei offengelassen. Die Beziehung sportlicher Feste auf Hermes könnte auch sekundärer Natur sein : Vgl. v. Wilamowitz-Moellendorff, l.c. (Anm. 51), I 164 mit Anm. 3.

Gott die Götter mit seinem *krátu-* beschirmte…«; RV. 2,22,3 *sākáṃ jātáḥ krátunā… vavakṣitha…* »Sogleich mit *krátu-* geboren… bist du gewachsen…«; ähnlich (von Agni) 1,69,2; 1,149,9 usw. [53]. Der homerische Hermeshymnus läßt (V. 17f.) Hermes am gleichen Tag morgens geboren sein, mittags die Leier spielen und abends die Rinder stehlen, also gewissermaßen ebenfalls von Geburt an κρατύς sein. Wenn das keine spätere Zutat des Hymnus zu den Hermesmythen oder ein bloß zufälliger Parallelismus ist — beides kann natürlich nicht ausgeschlossen werden —, dann liegt auch darin eine beiläufige Übereinstimmung zwischen dem *krátu-* der vedischen Götter und dem κρατύς- Sein des griechischen Hermes.

II

5. Formal gilt κρατύνειν innerhalb des Griechischen als denominales Faktitivum zu κρατύς (s. oben 4.1.3). Im Gegensatz zu κρατύνειν enthält der epische Aorist καρτύνασθαι im Rahmen der Formel ἐκαρτύναντο φάλαγγας inlautendes -αρ- < *-r̥- vor Konsonant, wie es auch sonst gelegentlich statt oder neben -ρα- vorkommt (vgl. umgekehrt hom. κραδίη neben att. καρδία sowie die unmittelbar verwandten homerischen Varianten κάρτος/κράτος und καρτερός/κρατερός) [54]. Zu beachten bleibt, daß ἐκρατύναντο wegen seiner abweichenden Quantitätstruktur (‒◡‒‒◡ oder, bei kurz gemessenem Kurzvokal vor Muta cum Liquida, ◡◡‒‒◡) in der homerischen Versschlußformel (vor φάλαγγας) unbrauchbar gewesen wäre.

6.1. Bei der formalen Etymologie von gr. κρατύς sind zunächst Bedenken gegen die Zusammenstellung mit dem germ. Adjektiv für »hart« (in got. *hardus* usw.) zu erheben. Zwar rechnen die etymologischen Wörterbücher des Griechischen von Boisacq (S. 511) sowie — mit Vorsicht — Frisk (II S. 10) und Chantraine (II S. 579), des Altenglischen von Holthausen (2. Aufl. 1963, S. 152 s.v. *heard*) und des Deutschen von Kluge (20. Aufl. 1967, S. 290) mit einer Verbindung des griechischen und des germanischen

---

[53] Dazu auch A. Bergaigne, La religion védique, III 310.
[54] Zum Verhältnis von inlautendem -ρα- und -αρ- E. Schwyzer, Griech. Gramm., I 342; M. Lejeune, Phonétique historique du mycénien et du grec ancien, Paris 1972, 196f. § 200; G. Klingenschmitt, Antiquitates Indogermanicae (Gedenkschrift Güntert), Innsbruck 1974, 275.

Wortes. Die indogermanischen vergleichenden Wörterbücher von Walde-Pokorny (I S. 354f.) und Pokorny (S. 531), das Vergleichende Wörterbuch der gotischen Sprache von Feist (3. Aufl. 1939, S. 246f.) sowie Benveniste, l.c. 82, favorisieren die griechisch-germanische Etymologie sogar unter ausdrücklichem Ausschluß von indoiranisch *krátu-/xratu-*. Aber die formale Kette zwischen gr. κρατύς und germ. *χardus* ist kaum haltbarer als die semantische. Gr. κρατύς muß entweder auf älteres **kr̥tús* oder, ganz unwahrscheinlich, auf **kratús* zurückgehen. Beide Vorformen weichen von den theoretisch möglichen Vorgängern des germ. Adjektivs, **kortús*, **kartús*, **kordhus* und **kardhus*, ab. Das gesamte Reservoir allfälliger voreinzelsprachlicher Formen erlaubt rein formal zwei morphologische Segmentierungen. 1) Bei Annahme einer Wurzel **ker-* : Mit Suffix **-tu-*, **kr̥-tú-s* für das griechische, **kor-tú-s* oder **kar-tú-s*(?) für das germanische Wort. Auf griechischer Seite scheidet **kratús* in Ermangelung eines irgendwo belegbaren Suffixes **-ατυ-* aus, auf germanischer Seite entfallen **kordhus* und **kardhus* als unwahrscheinliche Bildungen mit einem Suffix **-dhu-*[55]. Beide Ansätze würden zudem die Etymologie lediglich auf die Gemeinsamkeit einer Wurzel **ker-/kor-* gründen. 2) Bei Annahme einer Wurzel **kert-* : Mit Suffix **-u-*, **kr̥t-ú-s* für das griechische, **kort-ú-s* oder **kart-ú-s*(?) für das germanische Wort. Ausgeschlossen bleiben **kratús* (wegen unmöglicher voreinzelsprachlicher Wurzelstufe **krat-* zur Vollstufe **kert-*), **kordhus* und **kardhus* wegen abweichender Konsonanten im Wurzelauslaut.

Damit verbleiben der behaupteten Etymologie unabhängig von der einen oder anderen zugrunde gelegten Wurzel noch die theoretischen Rekonstrukte **kr̥tú-s* für gr. κρατύς, **kortú-s* oder **kartú-s* für germ. *χardus*. Auch vorgerm. **kartús* sollte wegen seines im Rahmen dieser Etymologie morphonologisch kaum erklärbaren Vokals *-a-* der ersten Stammsilbe gestrichen werden. Mögliche restliche Partner sind also bei diesem Stand der Überlegungen **kr̥tú-s* und **kortú-s*. Während sie als *u*-Stämme und mit ihrem Endakzent[56] übereinstimmen, weichen sie im Ablaut der jeweils ersten, die Wurzel

---

[55] H. Krahe-W. Meid, Germanische Sprachwissenschaft III, Wortbildungslehre, Berlin 1967, 178 § 134, nennen nur ein einziges isoliertes Beispiel für ein allfälliges Suffix **-dhu-*: ae. as. *sidu*, ahd. *situ* »Sitte«. Auch diese mögen jedoch angesichts gr. ἔ-θ-ος und ai. *sva-dhā́* »Gewohnheit, Eigenart« in **s(u̯)e-dh-u-* zu zerlegen sein.

[56] Ein solcher wäre bei **kortús* als Vorfom von germ. *χardus* wegen der dann anzunehmenden Wirkung des Vernerschen Gesetzes gegeben.

enthaltenden Stammsilbe voneinander ab : Schwundstufe im einen, abgetönte *o*-Vollstufe im anderen Falle. Diese Ablautdifferenz ist für die griechisch-germanische Etymologie der Wörterbücher und Benvenistes — abgesehen von den oben behandelten semantischen Diskrepanzen — so lange auch ein formales Hindernis, als nicht voreinzelsprachliche *u*-Stämme mit einer paradigmatischen Ablautalternanz »*o*-Vollstufe/Schwundstufe« der ersten Silbe wahrscheinlich gemacht werden [57], aus denen in der einen Einzelsprache die Schwundstufe wie in gr. κρατύς, in der anderen die *o*-Vollstufe wie in germ. **χardus* sich hätte verfestigen können. Denn ein Ablaut dieser Art müßte morphologisch bedingt sein. Der Nachweis eines derartigen uridg. Deklinationstyps der *u*-Stämme [58] ist aber bisher, soweit ich sehe, nicht erbracht.

6.2 Besser ist die formale Vergleichsmöglichkeit zwischen gr. κρατύς und indoiran. *krátu-/xratu-*. Nach unseren in Teil I angestellten semantischen Überlegungen gehört gr. κρατύς innerhalb des Griechischen zur Wortfamilie von κράτος »Überlegenheit« (bei Homer). Dessen äolische Form κρέτος zeigt die originale, bei *s*-Stämmen des Neutrums wie γένος reguläre Vollstufe der Wurzelsilbe, die auch im Komparativ κρε(ί)σσων, letzlich aus **κρετιοσ-*, auftritt. Die gleiche Vollstufe dürfte in indoiran. *krátu-/xratu-* (m.) gegeben sein. Demnach ist dieses Wort in *krát-u-* zu zerlegen, das heißt, es liegt ein barytoner *u*-Stamm vom »genre animé« wie in ved. *hánu-*, av. *zanu-* (f.) »Kinnlade, Kinn«, ved. *śáru-* (m.f.) »Pfeil« [59], *párśu-* (m.) »Rippe, Seite« vor. Angesichts der semantisch fundierten Zugehörigkeit zu gr. κρέτος (κράτος), κρατύς kommen andere Segmentierungen

[57] Vgl. zu »mobilen« Paradigmen allgemein unten Abschn. 6.2.2.1 und die Anmerkungen 58, 65 und 66.

[58] H. Eichner, Die Sprache 20 (1974) 27f., gibt für das frühe Urindogermanische Deklinationstypen zu bedenken, die lediglich von Akzent und Ablaut, nicht von Stammklassen bestimmt wären. Einen solchen Deklinationstyp (unter mehreren in Betracht kommenden) rekonstruiert er S. 28ff. Im Paradigma dieses rekonstruierten Typs sind keine zwei (oder mehr) Kasus mit einem Wechsel zwischen *o*-Vollstufe und Schwundstufe der ersten Wortsilbe vertreten. – Unter den sonstigen suffigierten Stämmen scheinen dagegen die *-r-/-n*-Heteroklita die Alternanz *-e-/-o-/-∅-* in der Wurzelsilbe (vgl. **u̯ed-/u̯od-/ud-* »Wasser«) tatsächlich gehabt zu haben. Aber sind die Ablautverhältnisse dieser Stamm-Akzent-Ablautklasse wirklich auch unter den *u*-Stämmen (und anderen suffigierten Stämmen [die Wurzelnomina können hier außer Betracht bleiben]) nachzuweisen?

[59] In diese Gruppe auch von J. Wackernagel-A. Debrunner, Altindische Grammatik II 2, 474 § 289 aα, gestellt. Andere Beurteilung S. 169 § 72, eine dritte S. 667 § 491 a, wozu sogleich oben im Text.

des indoiranischen Wortes wie *krá-tu-* mit Suffix -*tu-*[60] oder gar
kr-atu- mit Suffix -*atu-*[61] nicht in Frage. Diese Feststellung läßt
sich auch dann treffen, wenn man sich nicht im Gefolge der
vergleichenden Wurzelwörterbücher von Walde-Pokorny und Pokorny
auf die wenig erfolgversprechende Suche nach einer bestimmten in
diesen Wörtern steckenden Wurzel begibt[62].

Es bieten sich nun zwei differierende Beurteilungen für das
Nebeneinander von indoiran. *krátu-/xratu-* und gr. κρατύς an. Beide
haben ihre Vor- und Nachteile, die es gegeneinander abzuwägen gilt.
Ein strikter Beweis für die Richtigkeit der einen oder der anderen
Lösung läßt sich kaum erbringen.

6.2.1 Die erste Deutung hat mit zwei verschiedenen *u*-Stämmen,
abgeleitet jeweils von der gleichen Wurzel, zu rechnen: einem
substantivischen **krétu-* (m.) > indoiran. *krátu-/xratu-* einerseits
und einem adjektivischen **kr̥tú-* > gr. κρατύς andererseits. Die
semantischen Berührungen zwischen *krátu-/xratu-* und κρατύς beruhen
bei solchen Ansätzen nur auf dem ihnen gemeinsamen präsuffixalen
Element (der vermutlichen Wurzel) mit den Ablautstufen **kret-* und
*kr̥t-. Diese Lösung hat für sich, daß die unterschiedlichen Wortarten
eines substantivischen Abstraktums *krátu-/xratu-* und eines ins
Calandsche Suffixsystem (s. oben Abschnitt 2) passenden Adjektivs
κρατύς (wie θρασύς usw.) durch unterschiedliche voreinzelsprachliche
Wortbildungen motiviert wären. Unbefriedigend ist an einer solchen
Beurteilung des Befundes, daß sie die in beiden Fällen gegebenen
u-Stämme sowie die an ihnen auffallende Wechselbeziehung zwischen
Akzentstelle und Ablautstufe des präsuffixalen Bestandteils (**krétu-* :
*kr̥tú-) außer Betracht läßt und damit zu Zufälligkeiten stempelt.

---

[60] Wackernagel-Debrunner, l.c., 667 § 491 a gegen 474 § 289 aα und gegen
169 § 72; W. Havers, Anthropos 49 (1954) 201: »numinoses« *tu*-Suffix; É. Benveniste, Noms d'agent et noms d'action en indo-européen, Paris 1948, 90.

[61] Wackernagel-Debrunner, l.c., 169 § 72 gegen 474 § 289 aα und gegen 667 § 491 a.
Eine solche isolierte Bildung mit einem Suffix -*atu-* bezweifelte bereits J. Gonda,
Four Studies in the Language of the Veda, 's-Gravenhage 1959, 182 f., Anm. 261.

[62] Gegen die Idee von Rönnow, l.c. (Anm. 32), 76 ff., in *krátu-/xratu-* könne
die Verbalwurzel *kram-* »gehen, schreiten« stecken, erhebt M. Mayrhofer, Kurzgef.
etym. Wb. d. Ai., I 276, den berechtigten Einwand, daß diese *seṭ*-Wurzel statt
dessen ein **krā(n)tu-* hätte ergeben müssen. – Die oft bemühte Verbalwurzel ai. *kr̥-*
»machen, tun« ist nur mit Kunstgriffen wie Annahme von Schwebeablaut **ker-/kre-*
plus Determinativ -*t-* oder einem im Sinne von Benvenistes Wurzeltheorie (Origines
de la formation des noms en indo-européen, Paris 1935, 147 ff.) »suffigierten«
Wurzelgebilde **ker-t/kre-t* (neben **ker-*) auf die griechischen Wörter anzuwenden.

6.2.2.1 Die zweite mögliche Deutung wird zunächst den zuletzt genannten Phänomenen besser gerecht. Rein formal lassen sich *krátu-/xratu-* und κρατύς als im Hinblick auf Akzent und Ablautstufe der ersten Silbe verschiedene Realisierungen eines einzigen voreinzelsprachlichen Wortes verstehen. Dafür gibt es eine ziemlich genaue Parallele in dem Gegensatz zwischen ved. *párśu-* m.f. »Rippe« (seit RV.) und jav. *pərəsu-* m. (V. 8,54-56; V. 9,20) »Rippengegend«, *pərəsu°* (V. 6,16) »Rippe« [63], deren kontrastierende Ablautstufen auch bei dem avestischen Wort einen ursprünglichen Endakzent zumindest nahelegen. Es besteht kein Zweifel, daß das vedische und das avestische Appellativum einen einzigen Vorläufer fortsetzen. Dieses ältere Wort dürfte in einem vorgeschichtlichen mobilen Paradigma bei den verschiedenen Kasus zwischen Wurzelsilbe und folgenden Segmenten (Suffix, eventuell Endung) wechselnden Akzent und — abhängig davon — wechselnde Voll- und Schwundstufen gekannt haben [64]. In den idg. Einzelsprachen sind solche ehemals intraparadigmatischen Ablautalternanzen aufgegeben, wobei im vorliegenden Falle, wie öfter, verschiedene Einzelsprachen auch verschiedene Ablautformen aus dem älteren Paradigma verallgemeinert haben.

Eine derartige Vorgeschichte kann ebenso dem Paar indoiran. *krátu-/xratu-* < **krétu-* und gr. κρατύς < **kr̥tú-* zugrunde liegen. So gesehen stammt die arische Wortgestalt aus Kasus mit betonter vollstufiger Wurzelsilbe, die griechische aus solchen mit unbetonter schwundstufiger Wurzelsilbe eines prähistorischen Paradigmas. Schon F. B. J. Kuiper hat *krátu-/xratu-* auf ein mobiles Paradigma zurückgeführt. Er reihte das Wort in seinen »hysterodynamischen« Typ einer derartigen Deklination mit Voll- und Schwundstufenalternanz zwischen Suffix und Endung ein, vornehmlich aufgrund von Formen wie Gen. Abl. Sg. ved. *krátv-aḥ*, jav. *xraθβ-ō*, Instr. Sg. ved. *krátv-ā*, Dat. Sg. *krátv-e* [65]. Inzwischen ist die Forschung hinsichtlich solcher mobilen Paradigmen zu dem Schluß gekommen, daß wir nicht nur Pedersens und Kuipers »hysterodynamischen« (s.o.) und »proterodynamischen« (Voll-/Schwundstufenwechsel zwischen Wurzel und Suffix) Typ zu unterscheiden, sondern mit einem dritten »amphidynamischen« Typ (Voll-/Schwundstufenwechsel zwischen Wurzel und

---

[63] Auch einmal *pərəsu-* (f.) »Rippe« (Frahang i oīm 3g).

[64] Vgl. zu solchen Deklinationstypen oben Anm. 58 und sogleich im weiteren Text mit Anm. 65 und 66.

[65] F. B. J. Kuiper, Notes on Vedic Noun-Inflexion, Amsterdam 1942, 40ff., bes. 51f.

Endung) zu rechnen haben. Dabei müßten die drei Typen von Flexionsablaut ursprünglich durch drei entsprechende »kinetische« Akzentuierungstypen, »hystero–«. »protero–« und »amphikinetischen« Akzent, bedingt gewesen sein[66]. Der bei ved. *krátu-* in Übereinstimmung mit der Wurzelvollstufe stets auf der ersten Silbe (sekundär) fixierte Akzent, die von Kuiper in Rechnung gestellten vollstufigen Endungen in »schwachen« Kasus und der bei gr. κρατύς mit schwundstufiger Wurzelsilbe harmonierende Endsilbenakzent lassen nun daran denken, daß hier eher ein »amphidynamischer« Deklinationstyp vorauszusetzen ist. Aber auch ein »proterodynamischer« (nach Eichner: »proteroperpendikularer«) Typ ist nicht völlig auszuschließen: Immerhin kennt just der ältere gāthische Dialekt statt der jungavestischen Gen.-Abl.-Sg.-Form *xraθβ-ō* (: ved. *krátv-aḥ*) die »proterodynamische« Form *xratāu-š* (Y. 32,4; 34,14; 43,6; 46,18; 49,6; 50,6), die ebenfalls im Ṛgveda ihr Gegenstück *kráto-r* (RV. 4,10,2) hat; für den Instr. Sg. gibt es gāthisch neben *xraθβ-ā* auch die Form *xratū* (Y. 45,6); und der Ṛgveda bietet neben häufigerem Dat. Sg. *krátve* einmal *krátave* (RV. 10,27,16), wobei freilich die nur einmalige Bezeugung gerade im zehnten Buch auf eine jüngere analogische Bildung deutet.

Ob nun ein »amphidynamisches« oder ein »proterodynamisches« Ausgangsparadigma im Hintergrund der belegten Flexionsformen stehen mag — beide vorgeschichtlichen Deklinationstypen eignen sich gut als Basis für den Ablaut- und Akzentbefund im Verhältnis von indoiran. *krátu-/xratu-* und gr. κρατύς[67].

6.2.2.2 Nach Gesichtspunkten der historischen Morphologie ist demnach ein einziges Grundwort für *krátu-/xratu-* und κρατύς durchaus in Erwägung zu ziehen. Diese Konzeption hat jedoch mit der Schwierigkeit fertig zu werden, daß dann die Wortart eines

[66] H. Eichner, MSS 31 (1972) 91 Anm. 33; Die Sprache 20 (1974) 27f. mit Anm. 1 und 2. An der letztgenannten Stelle schlägt Eichner (um bei der Terminologie speziell für den Ablautwechsel der Beziehung des Terminus »-dynamisch« auf Akzentologisches zu entgehen?) statt »proterodynamisch« usw. eindeutigere, aber etwas überladen anmutende Termini wie »proteroperpendikular« usw. vor.

[67] R. S. P. Beekes, KZ 86 (1972) 49, stellt für »hysterodynamische« *u*-Stämme, zu denen Kuiper indoiran. *krátu-/xratu-* zählte, bei griechischen (substantivischen) Maskulina im Nom. Sg. mit Ausnahme von υἱύς Wurzelbetonung fest. Wenn nach dem oben Gesagten *krátu-/xratu-* und κρατύς nicht zum »hysterodynamischen« Typ gehören, verstößt die Oxytonese des griechischen Wortes nicht gegen die von Beekes festgehaltene Regel. Zum möglichen Substantivcharakter von κρατύς vgl. unten im weiteren Text.

substantivischen Abstraktums im Indoiranischen mit der eines Adjektivs im Griechischen in Einklang gebracht werden muß. Rechnet man mit der Priorität des Adjektiv-Charakters[68], so verträgt sich das zwar gut mit der Stellung von gr. κρατύς innerhalb des »Calandschen« Suffixsystems, die ja alt sein müßte, erschwert aber sehr das Verständnis für die Entstehung der Abstraktum-Funktion im Indischen und Iranischen. Setzt man umgekehrt das Abstraktum an den Anfang der Entwicklung, dann läßt sich daraus nicht ohne weiteres die Rolle von gr. κρατύς als altepisches Attribut neben Ἀργεϊφόντης ableiten. Gelegentliche Adjektivierungen von Substantiven im Griechischen, die man genannt hat[69], sind nicht direkt vergleichbar.

Vielleicht liegt die Lösung dieses Problems in folgenden Erwägungen. Es wurde bereits angedeutet, daß im Ṛgveda die Götter nicht nur *krátu-* haben, sondern selbst *krátu-* sind: so z.B. RV. 3,11,6 *krátur devánām ámṛktaḥ agnís* »der ungebrochene Geist der Götter ist Agni« (Geldner), 9,107,3 *krátur índur* »der Tropfen *krátu* (vom Soma)«, 1,17,5 *índraḥ... váruṇaḥ... krátur bhavaty ukthyáḥ* »Indra... Varuṇa... sind des Lobpreises würdiger *krátu-*«. Weitere, wenngleich teilweise verfehlte und nicht vollständige Stellenangaben zu dieser Verwendung bietet Graßmann im »Wörterbuch zum Rigveda« Sp. 354 unter Nr. 15 seiner Bedeutungsangaben. Die mit *krátu-* bezeichnete »speziell männliche Eigenschaft«[70] konnte also offenbar auch mit (göttlichen) Personen gleichgesetzt werden.

Falls diese Identifizierung des *krátu-* mit dem einen oder anderen durch *krátu-* ausgezeichneten Gott nicht ausschließlich auf brahmanischen Auffassungen beruhen, sondern noch ältere Vorstellungen einer auch in Personen (Göttern) wirkenden magischen Kraft fortsetzen sollte, dann könnte eine archaische homerische Namenformel wie κρατὺς Ἀργεϊφόντης Fügungen aus dem Ṛgveda wie den soeben genannten durchaus vergleichbar sein. Wir wissen schließlich nicht, wie das syntaktische Verhältnis der beiden an der homerischen Junktur beteiligten Wörter zueinander eigentlich ist. Handelt es sich

---

[68] Die oben begründete Annahme einer alten mobilen Deklination dieses Wortes steht seinem allfälligen alten Adjektiv-Charakter nicht im Wege. Denn auch für manche Adjektive wird mobile Flexion angesetzt, so z.B. für ai. *svādú-*, gr. ἡδύς: Kuiper, l.c. (Anm. 65), 34.

[69] E. Schwyzer-A. Debrunner, Griech. Gramm., II, München 1950, 176 mit Material und Literatur.

[70] K. Rönnow, l.c. (Anm. 32), 41, ähnlich 72.

a) um eine Kombination von Epitheton und Eigennamen oder
b) um eine solche von Epitheton und Appellativum? Ist innerhalb
der möglichen Kombination a das erste Glied Beiwort (Attribut)
oder das zweite (Attribut, Apposition)? Die Unsicherheit zwischen
den Möglichkeiten a und b wird dadurch verstärkt, daß die Schreib-
weise der Textüberlieferung keine Entscheidungshilfe bietet. Denn
weder die älteren Majuskel- noch die jüngeren Minuskelschriften
der gesamten Texttradition unterscheiden intern Groß- und Klein-
schreibung, so daß die Wiedergabe κρατὺς Ἀργεϊφόντης mancher
Editoren, eher im Sinne der Lösung a, gegenüber der Schreibung
κρατὺς ἀργεϊφόντης anderer Herausgeber, eher im Sinne der Lösung b,
natürlich nur moderne Graphie ist. Wichtiger als eine Entscheidung
zwischen a und b scheint jedoch die Frage nach dem Beiwort in
der Namenformel zu sein. Üblicherweise faßt man κρατύς als
adjektivisches Attribut. Das ist aber nicht selbstverständlich. Man
denke an eine andere alte, ebenfalls auf den homerischen Versschluß
fixierte Namenformel wie βίη Ἡρακληείη (statt Ἡρακλῆς) der Ilias,
die ein substantivisches Abstraktum an erster und ein als Attribut
fungierendes Glied an zweiter Stelle enthält. Dieser syntaktische
Typus einer Namenformel ist abgewandelt in Verbindungen aus
substantivischem Abstraktum und attributivem Genetiv wie ἱερὸν
μένος Ἀλκινόοιο, ἱερὴ ἲς Τηλεμάχοιο, beide in der Odyssee. Nun
hat man mit Recht darauf hingewiesen, daß die in den Abstrakta
dieser Namenformeln ausgedrückten verschiedenen Nuancen von
»Kraft« wohl auf ältere vorhomerische Orenda-Vorstellungen zurückgehen[71]. B. Snell hat das ergänzt durch den Hinweis darauf, »daß
die adjektivischen (Sperrung von mir) Wendungen wie βίη
Ἡρακληείη bei solchen Namen vorkommen, die nicht dem tro-
janischen Kreis angehören, und wohl der richtige Schluß daraus
gezogen (wird), daß sie aus älteren Epen übernommen sind«[72].
Eben das gilt auch für den κρατὺς Ἀργεϊφόντης: Denn die Beziehung
des Hermes zu Argos (ob nun zur Landschaft oder zum Wächter)
gehört offensichtlich nicht in den troischen Sagenkreis.

Es ist also sehr wohl denkbar, daß κρατὺς Ἀργεϊφόντης historisch, inhaltlich und syntaktisch mit βίη Ἡρακληείη auf eine
Stufe gestellt werden muß. Das aber hat zur Konsequenz, daß sich
eine alte orendistische Vorstellung von in Personen (Göttern, Königen,

---

[71] F. Pfister, in: Pauly-Wissowa, RE XI/22 (1922), Sp. 2117, Z. 31-35.
[72] B. Snell, Die Entdeckung des Geistes, 41.

K. STRUNK

Priestern, Helden) wirkenden magischen Kräften auch in dem dann als Abstraktum zu wertenden, mit Ἀργεϊφόντης in attributiver[73] oder appositioneller[74] Gruppe verknüpften κρατύς als Benennung des Hermes niedergeschlagen hätte. Zu den Interpretationsmöglichkeiten a 1 und b unserer Namenformel kommt damit eine dritte Deutungsmöglichkeit a 2. Alle drei Möglichkeiten seien im folgenden mit typisierenden Übersetzungen noch einmal vorgestellt:

a 1 κρατὺς Ἀργεϊφόντης »der überlegene Argeiphontes«

a 2 κρατὺς Ἀργεϊφόντης »magische Kraft argeiphontisch«[75] oder
»magische Kraft Argeiphontes« =
»magische Kraft des Argeiphontes«

b κρατὺς ἀργεϊφόντης »der überlegene Argosbezwinger«[76].

Wenn die Formel nach der Deutung a 2 statt eines Adjektivs ein Abstraktum κρατύς[77] enthalten sollte, dann hätten wir das mit indoiran. krátu-/xratu- voll übereinstimmende Wort des Griechischen vor uns.

Morphologisch ist der adjektivische Status von κρατύς in der aus vorhomerischer Tradition stammenden Namenformel ebenfalls nicht gesichert. Feminine[78] oder neutrale Formen *κρατεῖα oder *κρατύ wie überhaupt weitere Belege auch des maskulinen Wortes außerhalb der altepischen Versschlußformel fehlen[79]. Die Komparativ- und Superlativformen κρε(ί)σσων, κράτιστος setzen nicht notwendigerweise ein Adjektiv als »Positiv« voraus. Es gibt primäre

[73] Ἀργεϊφόντης Attribut zu κρατύς.

[74] κρατύς Apposition zu Ἀργεϊφόντης.

[75] Ἀργεϊφόντης in adjektivisch-attributiver Funktion wie das ihm nachgestaltete ἀνδρεϊφόντης in der Versschlußformel Ἐνυαλίῳ ἀνδρεϊφόντῃ B 651, H 166, Θ 264, P 259.

[76] Auf eine adäquate Wiedergabe des Problemwortes Ἀργεϊφόντης kommt es hier nicht an, da es nur um Verdeutlichung der syntaktischen Struktur der Formel geht.

[77] Der spätere Deminutivname Κρατύλος muß nicht von adjektivischem κρατύς wie Θρασύλος von θρασύς (so M. Leumann, Glotta 32, 1953, 217 = Kl. Schr. 244) abgeleitet sein. Er läßt sich ebensogut auf τὸ κράτος gründen wie Αἰσχύλος auf τὸ αἶσχος, Πενθύλος auf τὸ πένθος, Ψευδύλος auf τὸ ψεῦδος (vgl. Leumann selbst, l.c. 217 mit Anm. 7, 218 = Kl. Schr. 244 mit Anm. 7, 245).

[78] E. Risch beurteilt jetzt in der 2. Auflage seiner »Wortbildung der homerischen Sprache«, 1974, § 30 a, κραταίη als Nachbildung zu Πλάταια und nicht mehr, wie in der 1. Auflage, als primäre Femininform parallel zu Πλάταια. Noch anders und wahrscheinlicher Frisk, Gr. etym. Wb., II 10. Ein direktes Femininum zu κρατύς hat es also auf keinen Fall gegeben.

[79] E. Schwyzer, Griech. Gramm., I 584, argumentiert mit nicht belegten Flexionsformen, also »ghost-forms«, von κρατύς.

Komparative und Superlative, die sich statt auf einen adjektivischen Positiv u.a. auf einen neutralen s-Stamm beziehen (vgl. Beispiele wie ἀλγίων, ἄλγιστος zu ἄλγος; κερδίων, κέρδιστος zu κέρδος) oder gar keinen adjektivischen oder sonstigen »Positiv« wie μείων, λώϊον, ἀρείων, ἄριστος haben[80]. Wenn auch κρε(ί)σσων, κράτιστος zu diesen Fällen gehören sollten und somit keinerlei Bezug zu κρατύς hätten, dann würde sich zugleich eine alte Schwierigkeit auflösen: Während sonst bei ursprünglicher lautlicher Diskrepanz die primären Komparativformen durchweg dem Vokalismus des zugehörigen Adjektivs im Positiv angeglichen sind[81], steht κρε(ί)σσων in dieser Hinsicht unbeeinflußt von κρατύς da[82]. Ein obsolet gewordenes Abstraktum κρατύς statt des seit jeher angenommenen Adjektivs κρατύς ließe das Ausbleiben eines solchen Einflusses als selbstverständlich erscheinen.

Das denominative κρατύνειν, hom. καρτύνεσθαι gehört zwar offenbar in eine Gruppe von Verben auf -ύνειν, die vor allem von Adjektiven auf -ύς abgeleitet sind (s. oben 4.1.3). Es gibt aber darunter auch, allerdings erst nach Homer belegte, Faktitiva wie μηκύνειν »vergrössern«, καλλύνειν »verschönern«, die neutrale s-Stämme (μῆκος, κάλλος) als Grundlage haben. So kommt auch das formal und inhaltlich mit κρατύς zusammengehörende, vielleicht gar als sein jüngeres Substitut anzusehende Abstraktum κράτος[83] als morphologischer Bezugspunkt für die Bildung des sekundären Verbums in Frage. Im Hinblick auf nachhomerisches κρατύνειν hat das schon E. Fraenkel[84] angenommen. An der homerischen Gestalt des Verbums fällt die mit der Variante κάρτος (P 623,

---

[80] H. Seiler, Die primären griechischen Steigerungsformen, Hamburg 1950, 81 ff., und, zum Grundsätzlichen, Glotta 51 (1973) 96 ff. Ferner E. Risch, l.c. (Anm. 78), [2]89 §33b; O. Szemerényi, in: Studia Mycenaea (ed. A. Bartoněk), Brno 1968, 30.

[81] πολύς stand lautlich so abseits, daß es wohl deshalb ohne Einfluß auf den Vokalismus von πλείων blieb.

[82] Vgl. H. Seiler, l.c. (Anm. 80), 53, mit Literatur und anderem Lösungsversuch.

[83] Im Gegensatz zu neutralen s-Stämmen wie γένος, κλέος auf der einen und — nach den obigen Überlegungen möglicherweise — κρατύς auf der anderen Seite hat κρέτος, κράτος keine genaue außergriechische Entsprechung! Ein Grund für die mögliche Ersetzung des ererbten κρατύς durch κρέτος, κράτος liegt vielleicht darin, daß das Abstraktum κρατύς, auch äußerlich (bzw. bei falscher Suffixabtrennung) im Groben den Verbalabstrakta auf -τῦς (δαιτῦς, βρωτῦς, τανυστῦς usw.) vergleichbar, nicht wie diese Femininum war, keinen Bezug zu primären Verba und keinen gedehnten Suffixvokal hatte und damit gegenüber seiner vermeintlichen Wortklasse isoliert war.

[84] E. Fraenkel, l.c. (Anm. 19), 35.

Λ 9, Ο 108, Ι 254 usw. neben häufigerem κράτος) übereinstimmende Lautfolge καρτ(ύνεσθαι) in Abweichung von der in κρατύς auf. Das deutet zumindest einen Einfluß dieses Abstraktums auf das Zustandekommen des Verbums an. Denn während κράτος und κάρτος, κρατερός und καρτερός in der Sprache des Epos nebeneinander bestehen, kommt dort neben καρτύνεσθαι ein direkt auf κρατύς beziehbares κρατύνεσθαι nicht vor. Vermutlich ist κάρτος sogar die wirkliche morphologische Basis für die epische Verbalableitung.

7. Nach allem spricht einiges dafür, daß es ein als Adjektiv funktionierendes κρατύς im Griechischen niemals wirklich gegeben und die homerische Namenformel statt dessen ein uraltes Abstraktum κρατύς bewahrt hat, das aber, petrifiziert und durch κρέτος, κράτος ersetzt, schon von antiken Homererklärern nicht mehr verstanden wurde, so daß sie es bereits für ein Adjektiv wie θρασύς usw. hielten[85]. In diesem Falle wäre κρατύς auch innerhalb des »Calandschen« Suffixsystems zu streichen, wo κρατερός allein den Platz des Adjektivs einzunehmen hätte. Indoiran. krátu-/xratu- und gr. κρατύς stehen dann im Verhältnis einer sogenannten »Wortgleichung« zueinander. Diese These scheint mir nach Berücksichtigung aller Indizien die wahrscheinlichere zu sein. Andernfalls bliebe mit einem im »Calandschen« System verankerten Adjektiv zu rechnen, das mit indoiran. krátu-/xratu- zwar verwandt, aber mit dessen Wortart eines substantivischen Abstraktums nicht leicht auf einen Nenner zu bringen ist, so daß dann ein Vergleich des indoiranischen und des griechischen Wortes in dem oben (6.2.1) dargelegten Sinne in Frage käme. Eines jedoch dürfte sich mit Sicherheit herausgestellt haben : Während die etymologische Verbindung gr. κρατύς : indoiran. krátu-/xratu- in der einen oder anderen Weise semantisch und formal gut fundiert ist, findet die von manchen Forschern statt ihrer verfochtene Gemeinsamkeit zwischen gr. κρατύς und germ. *χardus »hart« keinen tragfähigen Boden.

[85] Einige Scholien geben das Wort mit adjektivischen Interpretamenten wieder, so ὁ ἰσχυρός (immerhin mit Artikel!) schol. T² Π 181, ἰσχυρός schol. T² Ω 345, κραταιός Ap. Soph. Lex. 103, 29. (Υ 72 wird Hermes mit einem anderen und offenbar mit κρατύς nicht gleichwertigen Adjektiv für »stark«, σῶκος, bezeichnet). Merkwürdig und möglicherweise meiner oben im Text bevorzugten Deutung näherkommend ist eine Paraphrase von κρατύς im schol. B Π 181 : πάντων γὰρ περιγίνεται ὁ λόγος κτλ. Das kann sich kaum auf die varia lectio θρασὺς für κρατὺς in Π 181 beziehen, da diese Lesart nur von drei späten unselbständigen Codices des 15. Jh.s (M¹², P¹, Vi¹, alle aus der Handschriftenklasse h [Siglen nach Allen]) geboten wird und damit als erst mittelalterliche Korruptel anzusehen sein dürfte.

W. SUNDERMANN

ÜBERRESTE MANICHÄISCHER YIMKI-HOMILIEN IN MITTELPERSISCHER SPRACHE?

Die mittelpersischen Fragmente M 433 a, 882 a, 2023, 2451, 3706, 4161, 4168 und 7101 der Turfansammlung der AdW der DDR gehören, wie ihre Schriftart erkennen läßt, *einer* Handschrift an [1]. Vielleicht ist auch M 825, das ich BTT IV, S. 96f. veröffentlichte, ein Teil dieses Manuskripts. Größe und Duktus der Buchstaben, sowie der Zeilenabstand sind in allen Fällen identisch, nur M 882 a bietet Text von etwas gröberer Schriftgestalt, ein Umstand, der die Zugehörigkeit dieses Stückes nicht unmöglich macht und sich durch Abstumpfung des Schreibgerätes erklären ließe. Wenngleich die Fragmente sich wegen ihrer Versehrtheit zumeist einer inhaltlichen Deutung entziehen, erscheint doch ihre erstmalige Veröffentlichung in einem Werk gerechtfertigt, das dem Gedenken eines Gelehrten gewidmet ist, der die Fortschritte der Kenntnis des Mittelpersischen in unserem Jahrhundert mitbestimmte und an der Entwicklung der Manichäismusforschung tätigen Anteil nahm [2].

1

Stück der oberen inneren oder äußeren Ecke eines Blattes. Daß /2.S./1 u. 2/ wahrscheinlich die ersten Zeilen einer Seite sind, wird durch den Umstand nahegelegt, daß die Initialbuchstaben Zierform haben. Die Zeilenbruchstücke des Fragments setzen sich aus M 433 a und M 3706 wie folgt zusammen:

---

[1] Zu den Stücken vgl. M. Boyce, A Catalogue of the Iranian Manuscripts in Manichean Script in the German Turfan Collection, Berlin 1960, S. 28. 60. 85. 91. 97 und 98.

[2] Die in diesem Artikel verwendeten Abkürzungen, Sonderzeichen und technischen Mittel entsprechen grundsätzlich dem in BTT IV (Berliner Turfantexte IV, Berlin 1973) befolgten Verfahren und sind dort S. 7 und S. 144ff. erklärt. Darüberhinaus bedeuten: Hennecke: E. Hennecke, Neutestamentliche Apokryphen in deutscher Übersetzung II, Berlin 1966, MacKenzie: D. N. MacKenzie, A Concise Pahlavi Dictionary, London 1971, Nyberg: H. S. Nyberg, A Manual of Pahlavi II, Wiesbaden 1974, Payne Smith: R. Payne Smith, Thesaurus Syriacus I-II, Oxonii 1879-1901.

/1.S./1-7/ : M 433 a
1-6/ : M 3706

/1.S./1/](') gryyd u
2/] (q)ysr³ pd wzrg
3/](w)n⁴ gwpt kw nwn
4/]](.) 'st 'w pwlys
5/]wyd h'nyš 'w (dst) ⁵
6/](d) oo 'wd ps ny(rwn) ⁶

/2.S./1-7/ : M 433 a
1-6/ : M 3706

]weinte ¹³ und
]der Kaiser ¹⁴ mit großem
] ¹⁵ sprach : « Nun
] ist dem Paulus ¹⁶
] jenes ihm zur Hand
]. Und darauf Nero ¹⁷

---

³ Linkes Ende des q erhalten.

⁴ Nur linkes Ende eines w (kaum ') sichtbar.

⁵ Rechter Teil des t-Rumpfes erhalten.

⁶ Oberteil eines finalen n sichtbar.

¹³ Gryyd ist für das MtT. neben gryyst als Part. Perf. bezeugt in S 9 /d/10/, vgl. Henning, Verbum, S. 204 f., S. 222. Andernfalls 3. Sg. Präs. »er/sie/es weint«.

¹⁴ Vgl. auch 3 /1.S./Ü/, 4 /2.S./6/, 5 /2.S./2/. Die letzte Stelle, zitiert bei M. Boyce, Catalogue, S. 91, war bisher die einzige bekannte mpT.-Bezeugung des Wortes. Sie entspricht mpI. kysly, parthI. kysr (Ph. Gignoux, Glossaire des Inscriptions Pehlevies et Parthes, London 1972, S. 26 u. 56), mpB. kēsar (MacKenzie, S. 51, Nyberg, S. 118), man.-soghd. (soghd. Schrift) kysr (Henning, BSOAS 11 [1945], S. 477 f.), christl.-soghd. qysr (F. W. K. Müller (†), Soghdische Texte II, ed. W. Lentz, SPAW Phil.-hist.Kl. 1934, S. 586), baktr. κησαρο (wozu vgl. Anm. 49). S. ferner H. H. Schaeder, Iranica, AGW Göttingen 1934, S. 35. Die vorliegende Stelle gestattet eine Ergänzung der von Henning a.a.O. über die manichäische Verwendung des Kaisertitels gemachten Bemerkungen insofern, als hier tatsächlich vom Römischen Kaiser als dem obersten Herrscher des Gesamtreiches die Rede ist.

¹⁵ Man wüßte gerne, ob am Zeilenanfang der Name šym](w)n »Simon« (belegt M 18/V/12/ [HR II, S. 36], M 788/R/3/ [Henning, JRAS 1944, S. 142 Anm. 1], ferner M 6281/R/6/ šymwn kyf') verlorengegangen ist. Zu denken wäre in diesem Fall wohl an Simon Petrus. Sollte dagegen Simon Magus gemeint sein, so müßte auf Grund christl. Vermittlung sym](w)n erwartet werden. In beiden Fällen ließse sich an eine den Passiones apostolorum Petri et Pauli (Acta Apostolorum Apocrypha I, ed. R. A. Lipsius, Leipzig 1891, S. 118 ff.) nahestehende Geschichte denken. Aber das ist ganz unsicher, und andere Ergänzungen, z.B. ''wn »so«, sind möglich.

¹⁶ In S /15/ (s.S.) und M 788/R/5/ [Henning, JRAS 1944, S. 142 Anm. 1] p'wlys geschrieben. Dem steht christl. soghd. pwlws (z.B. T III 99² /R/23/) gegenüber. Dieselbe Endung hat das von Menasce aus paz. Pāwarōs hergestellte *Pāwlōs (Škand-Gumānīk Vičār, S. 216 Anm. zu /91/).

¹⁷ Die Schreibung nyrwn deutet auf aram. Vermittlung der gr. Form Νέρων. Da christl. Ursprung zu erwarten ist, so denkt man insbesondere an das Syrische, für das Payne Smith II, S. 2263 aber nur die Schreibung n'rwn (' als Trägerzeichen eines e) belegt. Wahrscheinlich wurde diese Form also in man. Überlieferung umgestaltet und der von Mani selbst verwendeten Orthographie angepaßt, es sei denn, man rechne gemäß dem S. Ausgeführten mit einer christl.-mp. Pahlavischreibung *nylwn o.ä. als unmittelbarer Ausgangsform.

7/	](x)wyš qd(g)[[7]	]eigenes Haus[
/2.S./1/	'wd 'w[	Und zu[
2/	''wryd oo[	bringt. [
3/	''wrd 'ygyš(')[n[8]	gebracht. Darauf sie [
4/	(p)ym'(d) 'wš'n 'w (.)[	abgemessen [18]. Und sie zu [
5/	(g)hy [9] sdwyn' 'wh̲ (g)[wpt [10] kw	Darauf Sdwyn' [19] so s[prach : »
6/	(d)'n(y)m [11] kw hrw ky '(.)[[12]	ich weiß [20], daß jeder, der [
7/	[1-2](r)'d 'yg h[	[ ] darauf [

---

[7] Unterer Teil des g abgerissen, oberer versehrt.

[8] Rechter Arm des zweiten ' erhalten.

[9] Nur unteres Ende eines g sichtbar. Auch z möglich.

[10] Oberteil eines g erhalten.

[11] Nur Kopf eines d erhalten.

[12] Auf ' folgt wahrscheinlich der rechte Arm eines h oder c.

[18] Pym'd dürfte von mpB. und np. *paymūdan* »measure« (MacKenzie, S. 67) nicht zu trennen sein und ihnen gegenüber eine ältere Form des Part. Perf. ebenso bewahren wie mpT. prm'd und mpI. plm't(y), prm't(y) gegen mpB. und np. *framūdan*, bzw. *farmūdan*. In anderen Fällen weisen von *mā*- abgeleitete Partizipien auch bereits im MpT. oder im MpPs. -*ūd* auf (Henning, Verbum, S. 203. 219), während das ParthT. generell -ād bewahrt (Ghilain, Essai, S. 86 f. Henning zitiert Verbum, S. 203 in einem Fall parth. frmwd, vgl. Ghilain, Essai, S. 23, aber ich kann die angeführte Stelle nicht finden). Henning sah in mpT. prm'd daher »wohl nur historische Schreibung« (Verbum, S. 219). Ich halte das für wenig wahrscheinlich, besonders wenn zu mpT. *framād* noch mpT. *parmād* »gedacht« und nun auch *paymād* hinzukommt. Pym'd ist die zu erwartende mpT.-Entsprechung von parthT. pdm'dg (Ghilain, Essai, S. 87. Was bedeutet parthT. pym'dg im M 6090/2/?). Es selbst ist bisher m.W. unbezeugt. Statt seiner führt Henning aber einmal im MpT. pdm'd »measured« mit -d- wie im Parth. an (BSOAS 11 [1943], S. 59 u. 63, Text M 101 h /168/). Daß dort eine noch ältere Form bewahrt oder irrtümlich eine parth. Form verwendet wurde, erscheint schwerlich denkbar. Wie ich mich an Hand des Originaltextes überzeugen konnte, befindet sich zwischen pd und m'd eine deutliche Lücke, so daß die Lesung 'wd zmyg (nicht Hennings wmyg!) pd m'd d'(r)[den Vorzug verdient, und dies bedeutet »und die Erde halt[en wir(?)] für die Mutter«. (Zum Vergleich der Erde mit einer Mutter s. auch M 5265 /V?/4 f./ zmyg m'd qyrbg »die Erde, die wohltätige Mutter«. — Leider gestattet der defekte Kontext des vorgelegten Stückes keine präzise Bedeutungsbestimmung von pym'd. Statt »abgemessen« wäre auch eine Übersetzung »vertraglich festgesetzt, vereinbart« denkbar, wenn man die für mp. *paymān* bestimmten Bedeutungen »measure, period; moderation; treaty« (MacKenzie, S. 67, Nyberg, S. 158) mitberücksichtigt.

[19] Zu Sdwyn' vgl. S.

[20] Oder : wir wissen?

2

M 4168

/1.S./1/	](...) [
2/	]pʾyy(hyst)[²¹	] (beschützt)(?) [²⁸
3/	](.. š)nʾn ʿy z(.)[
4/	](kyr)d ²² hy(nd) ²³ o u ʾ(b)[	]gemacht sind. Und [
5/	](.n) ʿy grʾsmʾ[n	] des Paradies[es ²⁹
6/	](o) ʾ(wd) ²⁴ ʾ(br)[	](und auf)[
/2.S./1/	](w..) [²⁵
2/	m](rd)y(h)n ²⁶ kwnynd[	]begehen (*Unzucht) [
3/	qʾr]ycʾr nsʾẖ[	Kampf]platz(?) Leichnam [
4/	g](h)y ²⁷ lwlynws[	da]rauf(?) *Lūlianus* ³⁰ [
5/	](m)yrd sʾrʾr (p)[	]Mann Befehlshaber [
6/	](.) gwpt ʾ(.)[	] gesprochen [

3

M 2023. Ich veröffentliche das Stück in diesem Zusammenhang, weil es 1. das Wort qysr enthält und 2. auf Grund seiner Schrift und Sprache zur hier vorgelegten Handschrift gehört haben könnte. M 2023 ist Bruchstück des oberen Teiles eines Blattes mit Bewahrung des oberen Randes und eines Seitenrandes. Reste der Überschrift sind erhalten, doch teilweise bis zur Unerkennbarkeit verblaßt.

²¹ Buchstaben durch Abschabung versehrt, nur rechte Spitze und Ende des linken Bogens des s erhalten, t ganz unsicher.

²² Ende der Horizontalen eines k oder x erhalten.

²³ D durch Abschabung fast unkenntlich.

²⁴ Buchstaben stark abgeschabt.

²⁵ Auf w folgt d/r und p/f.

²⁶ Unsicher. Über d Zeichenrest, der aber wohl eher Ende eines Buchstabens der vorangehenden Zeile als ein r-Punkt gewesen sein dürfte.

²⁷ Rechter Arm des h abgeschnitten.

²⁸ Wenn richtig gelesen, so wohl vom pass. Präs. St. pʾyh- (M 36/V/10/ [Mir. Man. II, S. 325]) abgeleitetes Part. Perf.

²⁹ Zum Wort s. Henning TPS 1945, S. 157. Eine Belegstelle bereits Mir. Man. II, S. 340 zitiert. Weiterhin M 28/I/V/I/30/, M 627/1.S./II/5/. Vgl. auch M 325/R/13/ grʾsmʾnyq. Außer den von Henning angeführten Formen läßt sich weiterhin in diesem Zusammenhang vor allem auf mpB. *garasmān* (MacKenzie, S. 35, neben *garōdmān*) hinweisen. Das von D.D. Kapadia, Glossary of Pahlavi Vendidad, Bombay 1953, S. 162 zitierte np. gršmʾn dürfte aus *grsmʾn entstellt sein.

³⁰ Zu *Lūlianus* s. S.

/1.S./Ü/   qys(r pd) bwšy's[p³¹   der Kaiser³³ im Schla[f³⁴
/2.S./Ü/   ]'rd'w('n pr)yst'd(n o)³²   ] die Gerechten schicken.

4

M 882 a
/1.S./1/   ](.) [
     2/   ]m ''stw'ny(ẖ)[   ] Bekenntnis [
     3/   ](')ydr'y bzgyẖ pd 'y(n)[   ]deswegen Sünde diesem [
     4/   ](y)d bwd 'wd mrdyhn 'w(d)[   ] war und *Unzucht⁴² und [
     5/   ]ws kyryhyd oo 'w(d)[   ]viel wird gemacht. Und [
     6/   ]št 'wm py(š .)[   ] und ich vor[
     7/   ](.) [

/2.S./1/   ](.) [
     2/   ](.š)t(.)³⁵ [2-3](.) 'wd 'b('g³⁶ .)[   ]   und (mit) [
     3/   ](z)myg³⁷ ny(ys)³⁸ oo 'wd 'gr 'y(w) [³⁹   ]Erde(lege)⁴³! Und wenn ein(?)[
     4/   ](s)t'ẖ bwd h'nd (')[   ] sie werden geworden sein [
     5/   ]('ndr xwyš)⁴⁰ gryw m'[   ] (im eigenen) Selbst[
     6/   ](ky)sr⁴¹ hy oo (')[   ] Kaiser⁴⁴ bist du. [
     7/   ](ẖ) [

---

³¹ Überschrift in roter Tinte, stark verblaßt.
³² Überschrift in roter Tinte, stark verblaßt.
³³ Zu qysr s. Anm. 14.
³⁴ Zum Wort vgl. Nyberg, S. 51 und BTT IV, S. 120.
³⁵ Buchstaben stark abgeschabt.
³⁶ Nur rechter unterer Ansatz des ', unteres Ende des g erhalten.
³⁷ Verdickter Kopf eines Zeichens vorhanden, das dem Kontext zufolge z sein muß. Eine Lesung](j)myg »Zwilling, Paargenosse« ist auch graphisch unwahrscheinlich.
³⁸ Linksläufige Horizontale des s bis auf den Endpunkt abgeschabt, vom zweiten y nur Spur vorhanden.
³⁹ Nur rechter Aufstrich des w erhalten.
⁴⁰ Buchstaben durch Abschabung fast unkenntlich, Punkt über x abgerissen.
⁴¹ Buchstaben stark abgeschabt.
⁴² Vgl. die M 473 a/V/3/ [HR II, S. 23] belegte Adjektivableitung mrdyhng'n (mit Suff. -agān, nicht Pl.). Ein Deutungsversuch, der meiner Übersetzung zugrunde liegt, bei Ghilain, Le Museon 59 [1946], S. 543 f. Ghilain übersetzt mrdyhng'n als »luxurieux« und bemerkt, daß, die Richtigkeit seiner Etymologie vorausgesetzt, auch für das MpT. eher *mrzyhng'n erwartet werden sollte. Das hier belegte mrdyhn schließt aber jedenfalls die Möglichkeit einfacher Verschreibung aus.
⁴³ Zum Wort s. Henning, Verbum, S. 212. Belege M 454/II/13/, M 736/2/. Von Henning ebenfalls M 570/7/ ergänzt (BSOAS 14 [1952], S. 516).
⁴⁴ Zu kysr s. Anm. 14.

5

M 2451

/1.S./1/	](r)y(št⁴⁵ p.)[⁴⁶	
2/	](o) ʾyg nwy(s)[t	]. Darauf begon[nen
3/	](h)rwm⁴⁷ b[	] Rom⁴⁹ [
4/	](wd ʾ) [	

/1.S./1/   ](r)y(št⁴⁵ p.)[⁴⁶
2/   ](o) ʾyg nwy(s)[t   ]. Darauf begon[nen
3/   ](h)rwm⁴⁷ b[   ] Rom⁴⁹ [
4/   ](wd ʾ) [

/2.S./1/   ](...) [2-3] (....)[
2/   ]qysr[   ] Kaiser⁵⁰ [
3/   ](rʾ)sty[⁴⁸   ](Wahrheit) [
4/   ](.)n(w) [

6

M 7101

/1.S./1/   oo ʾ(wd ..)[(und) [
2/   (ʾw)m(ʾn)[⁵¹   (und uns) [
3/   (.)m[
4/   o[o](..)[

/2.S./1/   ]ʾw(r)myzd⁵²   ] Ormezd(?)⁵⁵
2/   ](s)t ʾb(r)⁵³   ] auf
3/   ]wšg
4/   ](.)d⁵⁴

---

⁴⁵ Fuß des r zerstört, Spur eines diakritischen Punktes erkannbar. Vom t(?) nur linkes Ende des Rumpfes erhalten.

⁴⁶ Wahrscheinlich (pd)[oder (pr)[. Nur untere Horizontale des p erhalten.

⁴⁷ Oberteil des linken h-Armes erhalten.

⁴⁸ Rʾstyy oder rʾsty̱h. Buchstaben durch Abschabung versehrt.

⁴⁹ Zu mpT., mpB. hrōm, parthT. frwm, christl.-soghd. frwmcyq (unpubl. auch frwm) vgl. Schaeder, Iranica, S. 26ff. Ferner mpI. hlwmy, parthI. prwm (Gignoux, Glossaire, S. 23 und 61), man.-soghd. (soghd. Schrift) β(rw)[m](ʾyk) oder β(rw)[m](cyk) »Byzantine« (Henning, Sogdica, London 1940, S. 8f.) und (unpubl.) βrʾwm- »Rom«, baktr. φρομο κησαρο »Kaiser von Rom« (H. Humbach, Baktrische Sprachdenkmäler I, Wiesbaden 1966, S. 64f., 20ff., J. Harmatta, Late Bactrian Inscriptions, Acta Ant. Hung. 17 [1969], S. 411f., 431f.). (Ein Beleg von parthT. frwm mit unversehrter Bewahrung des f in M 5800/4/, zitiert bei M. Boyce, Catalogue, S. 115).

⁵⁰ Zu qysr s. Anm. 14.

⁵¹ Kopf den n verschmutzt, doch kaum (ʾ)[.

⁵² Punkt über r abgerissen. Andernfalls d.

⁵³ Rand des r-Kopfes und diakritischer Punkt erhalten.

⁵⁴](p)d oder](s)d.

⁵⁵ Falls meine Lesung richtig ist (s. Anm. 52), so ʾwrmyzd statt ʾwhrmyzd. Diese

7

M 4161

/1.S./1/	](y) ws[	
2/	]wd (h)ym (p)[	]ich bin[
3/	]'(n) 'yt (pyyš)[	
4/	](w)ysp'n[	]alle[
/2.S./1/	]'wd (g)[	]und [
2/	]'wd (wyš b)[	]und (mehr)(?) [
3/	]'wd pd hrwy(s)[p	]und zu alle[n
4/	](.) 'y mwrdg[	]tot [56] [

Es wäre ein hoffnungsloses Bemühen, den kleinen Fragmenten als sichere Ausbeute mehr abgewinnen zu wollen als einige interessante Namen. Immerhin aber darf gefolgert werden, daß in *1* die Nennung des Paulus wie des Nero Zugehörigkeit zu einer Geschichte über den Apostel Paulus sowie Rom als Ort der Handlung wahrscheinlich macht, daß das Stück also einer Version des Martyriums des Paulus angehörte oder ihm in nicht zu großem Abstand voranging. Es liegt nahe, als Quelle der Erzählung eine apokryphe christliche Paulus-Überlieferung zu postulieren, vorzugsweise die im 2.Jh. entstandenen *Acta Pauli,* die älteste bekannte literarische Ausprägung dieser Tradition, wenn man voraussetzt, daß die Manichäer dieses Werk früh übernahmen [57].

Leider vermag ich den mp. Text aber nicht mit einer der zahlreichen Versionen der gr. und lat. *Acta Pauli, Acta Petri et Pauli* oder der

---

Schreibung, wohl Wiedergabe einer schnellsprachigen Form *Ormezd*, begegnet im MpT. bisweilen sowohl als Gottesname (BTT IV /819/) wie (ebenfalls im ParthT.) als Teil des Namens š'd 'wrmyzd (F. W. K. Müller, Maḥrnâmag, APAW 1912, Berlin 1913 /169/, Waldschmidt-Lentz SJ, S. 60). M. Boyce, Catalogue, S. 129 liest jedoch 'wd myzd »und Lohn«, zweifellos eine einfachere Erklärung der vorhandenen Zeichen, der ich mich nicht angeschlossen habe, weil der Abstand zwischen d/r und m so gering ist, daß eigentlich ein einziges Wort erwartet werden sollte, zumal Anlaß für Zusammenrückung aus Platzmangel am Zeilenende nicht bestand.

[56] Oder: das Tote/ Leichnam (BTT IV, S. 128).

[57] Ein manichäisches Korpus von Apostelakten, zu dem auch die *Acta Pauli* gehörten, ist jedenfalls schon für das 4.Jh. anzunehmen (K. Schaeferdiek bei Hennecke, S. 119, vgl. jetzt P. Nagel, Die apokryphen Apostelakten des 2. und 3. Jahrhunderts in der manichäischen Literatur, in: Gnosis und Neues Testament, ed. K.-W. Tröger, Berlin 1973, S. 152f.

Passiones Pauli (*et Petri*) zu identifizieren, die Lipsius und nach ihm besonders C. Schmidt veröffentlicht hat[58]. Auch bieten weder die *Acta Petri*[59] Vergleichbares noch die von F. Nau publizierten syr. Texte der *Petrus-, Paulus- und Lukas-Martyrien*[60], und dies gilt ebenso für die syr. »*Geschichte des hl. Apostels Paulus*«[61] wie die »*Geschichte von Simon Petrus, dem Haupt der Apostel*«[62] (und übrigens auch für das christl.-soghd. *Simon-Fragment*[63]).

Soweit ich sehe, bieten sich vier Lösungsmöglichkeiten der Herkunftsfrage an, die aber alle ihre eigene Problematik besitzen:

1. Der manichäische Text entstammt einer christlichen Quelle, die nicht zu dem oben umrissenen Literaturkreis gehört, von ihm aber wohl irgendwie abhängig ist.

2. Ausführlichere Erörterung verdient die andere Hypothese, daß die manichäische Erzählung einem verlorengegangenen Teil der Paulusakten entstammt. Bedenkt man, daß der heute bekannte Rest einer Schätzung von Michaelis zufolge kaum die Hälfte des ursprünglichen Bestandes ausmachen dürfte[64], so erscheint diese Möglichkeit beträchtlich. Sie wird aber sehr vermindert, wenn man voraussetzt, daß die im manichäischen Fragment geschilderten Ereignisse zum *Martyrium Pauli* gehören oder jedenfalls zu seinem Italienaufenthalt im weiteren Sinne, denn das Martyrium selbst liegt in einem geschlossenen Text vor, und die vorangehenden Ereignisse der Italienreise sind zwar durch eine Lücke vom Martyrium getrennt, aber über die Größe dieser Lücke besteht keine volle Sicherheit[65].

---

[58] Acta Apostolorum Apocrypha I, ed. R.A. Lipsius, Leipzig 1901, C. Schmidt, Acta Pauli aus der Heidelberger koptischen Papyrushandschrift Nr. 1 herausgegeben, Leipzig 1905, ders., Πράξεις Παύλου, Acta Pauli nach dem Papyrus der Hamburger Staats- und Universitätsbibliothek, Glückstadt und Hamburg 1936. Vgl. dazu bes. W. Schneemelcher bei Hennecke, S. 221 ff.

[59] C. Schmidt, Die alten Petrusakten, Leipzig 1903, W. Schneemelcher bei Hennecke, S. 177 ff.

[60] Revue de l'Orient Chrétien 3 [1898], S. 39 ff., 151 ff.

[61] P. Bedjan, Acta martyrum et sanctorum I, Paris 1890, S. 34 ff. Übers. von L. de Steffani, Giornale della Società Asiatica Italiana 14 [1901], S. 201 ff.

[62] P. Bedjan a.a.O., S. 1 ff.

[63] Müller - Lentz, Soghdische Texte II, S. 528 ff.

[64] W. Michaelis, Die Apokryphen Schriften zum Neuen Testament, Bremen 1956, S. 272.

[65] C. Schmidt, Πράξεις Παύλου, S. 6, rechnet mit 4 fehlenden Seiten. Über Versuche, die Lücke durch weitere kleine — übrigens mit dem man. Fragment nicht identische — Stücke zu füllen s. Schneemelcher bei Hennecke, S. 237. Michaelis, Apokryphe Schriften, S. 273 f., hält es dagegen für möglich, daß die problematische Lücke viel, um 16 oder

3. Der manichäische Text könnte Überlieferungsgut bewahren, das, zum ursprünglichen Bestand der *Acta Pauli* gehörend, in die uns zugänglichen Handschriften dieses Werkes keines Eingang gefunden hat[66].

4. In das manichäische Fragment hat jüngeres ergänzendes christliches Überlieferungsgut von Paulus Aufnahme gefunden.

Leider ist das selbst erklärungsbedürftige, aber sicher lesbare Wort sdwyn', gewiß ein Eigenname, dem Verständnis des Textes nicht förderlich. Ich frage mich, ob sdwyn' eine Entstellung des Namens des philosophischen Lehrers Neros, Seneca, sein könnte. Dieser Gedanke sei aber mit der größten Zurückhaltung ausgesprochen, denn seine Behauptung führt zu Problemen, die zu lösen ich nicht kompetent bin. Hier möchte ich nur daran erinnern, daß ein apokrypher Briefwechsel zwischen Seneca und Paulus seit dem Ende des 4.Jh. bezeugt ist[67]. Eine inhaltlich entsprechende Bemerkung findet sich in der *Passio sancti Pauli apostoli* (*a Lino episcopo conscripta*)[68]. Insbesondere in der Erwähnung des *institutor imperatoris* bzw. des *magister Caesaris*, d.h. Senecas, sah von Harnack das Werk eines «Interpolators der pseudolinischen Passio Pauli, der dem frühen Mittelalter zuzurechnen ist»[69], erwog andererseits aber die Möglichkeit, daß »der Anstoß zu der Fälschung des Paulus-Seneca-Briefwechsels« von den der christlichen Urliteratur zugehörigen Paulusakten ausgegangen sei[70]. Bardenhewer dagegen spricht nur von »älteren Legenden über persönliche Beziehungen zwischen Paulus und Seneca« als Grundlage des Briefwechsels[71], und noch zurückhaltender und unbestimmter drückt sich Vouaux aus[72]. Die alten Paulusakten jedenfalls nennen lediglich »viele Philosophen« in der Umgebung Neros[73].

32 Seiten, größer war. Die von P. Nagel, Apokryphe Apostelakten, S. 154 ausgesprochene Vermutung, »daß die Manichäer nur denjenigen Teil der A[cta] P[auli] übernommen haben, der sich als Acta Pauli et Theclae ... von dem Gesamtwerk verselbständigt hat«, ist natürlich auf der *derzeitigen* Kenntnis der manichäischen Überlieferung begründet.

[66] Vgl. Schneemelcher bei Hennecke, S. 238 f.
[67] A. Kurfess bei Hennecke, S. 85.
[68] Lipsius, Acta Apostolorum I, S. 24, 3 ff., Übersetzung bei Kurfess a.a.O.
[69] A. von Harnack, Geschichte der altchristlichen Literatur bis Eusebius I, 2, Leipzig[2] 1958, S. 764.
[70] Harnack a.a.O., S. 765.
[71] O. Bardenhewer, Geschichte der altkirchlichen Literatur I, Darmstadt 1962 = 1913, S. 608.
[72] L. Vouaux, Les Actes de Paul, Paris 1913, S. 345.
[73] Lipsius, Acta Apostolorum I, S. 42. 116, Schneemelcher bei Hennecke, S. 267.

Viel ferner liegt es m.A.n., sdwyn' als Entstellung des Namens (Poppaea) Sabina der Geliebten und Gattin Neros aufzufassen. Im 5. und 8. Schreiben des Seneca-Paulus-Briefwechsels wird nach allgemeiner Auffassung auf sie angespielt.

Auf den bemerkenswerten Umstand, daß insbesondere die Zeichenfolgen sdwyn' und *synyk' in der Schrift sowohl des Buchpahlavi wie des Pahlavi der mp. Psalterübersetzung sehr ähnlich sind, machte mich Herr Prof. Harmatta aufmerksam :

synyk'   sdwyn'

mpPs.

mpB.

Darf also sdwyn' als eine in einer Pahlavi-Schrift möglich gewordene Entstellung von *synyk' angesehen werden? Eine denkbare Voraussetzung dafür wäre m.A.n., daß der man. Text nicht unmittelbar auf die vermutete syr. Quelle zurückgeht, sondern auf ein aus dem Syr. übersetztes christl. Werk mp. Sprache und in Pahlavi-Schrift, vielleicht eine Übertragung des Ende des 5.Jh. lebenden Maʿnā, der damals angeblich »die gesamte syrische Kirchenliteratur« in das Persische übersetzte (E. Sachau, SPAW Phil.-hist. Kl. 1916, S. 971).

Der in Stück 2 erscheinende Name lwlynws weist auf syr. Literaturtradition hin. Dort bezeichnet, Payne Smith II, S. 1910 zufolge, lwlyn' (Lūliānā) und lwlynws (Lūlianus) den von 361 bis 363 das Gesamtreich beherrschenden römischen Kaiser Julian Apostata. Auch in das Arabische ist durch Rezeption des christlichen Julianus-Romans diese Namensform als lly'ns und lly'nws gedrungen[74]. Es darf dann in der Tat gefragt werden, ob auch eine manichäische Adaptation eben jenes christlichen Julianus-Romans existiert haben könnte, um so mehr, als 2 irgendwie auf kriegerische Ereignisse, wie sie Julians Persienfeldzug darstellt, hinzudeuten scheint. Eine sichere Identifizierung mit den bekannten, von Th. Nöldeke[75] erstmals beschriebenen oder

---

[74] Th. Nöldeke, Über den syrischen Roman von Kaiser Julian, ZDMG 28 [1874], S. 292 Anm. 1, auch S. 663. Vgl. Th. Nöldeke, Geschichte der Perser und Araber zur Zeit der Sasaniden, Leiden 1879, S. 60ff., bes. S. 60 Anm. 1. Die Schreibung lwlynws begegnet in der Ausgabe der syr. Romanfragmente durch Hoffmann (vgl. Anm. 75) nur S. 38, 4 u. 10, S. 244, 28 u. S. 245, 1. Sonst regelmäßig ywlynws und ywlnws.

[75] Th. Nöldeke in ZDMG 28 [1874], S. 263ff. u. S. 660ff. Edition : J. G. E. Hoffmann,

übersetzten Bruchstücken des Romankreises war mir aber nicht möglich. Es bleibt auch unklar, welche Tendenz, ja welchen Sinn wohl eine manichäische Version eines Julianus-Romans besessen haben könnte. Nicht unerwähnt sollten die anderen Möglichkeiten bleiben, daß der christliche Julianus-Roman wie die manichäische Erzählung auf eine gemeinsame ältere Quelle zurückgehen [76] oder daß in *2* Überlieferungsgut von Julian vorliegt, das in die erhaltenen Romanbruchstücke keinen Eingang gefunden hat.

Für wesentlich unwahrscheinlicher sehe ich andere Möglichkeiten an, z.B. daß der genannte lwlynws einen syr. als lwlyn' bezeugten christlichen Märtyrer (Samosata, 9. Dez. 297) bezeichne[77], der gr. »Julianus« und lat. Lollianus heißen soll[78], oder, daß vielleicht gar jener Proconsul von Africa Julianus gemeint sei, der als Adressat des Antimanichäeredikts von 297 bekannt geworden ist[79].

Versuche einer Bestimmung des literarischen Charakters der vorgelegten Fragmente als Teil eines manichäischen Schriftwerkes müssen so hypothetisch bleiben wie die vorausgeschickten Erwägungen zu Inhalt und Herkunft. Was *1* betrifft, so ist es zweifellos die nächstliegende Annahme, dieses Stück dem manichäischen Korpus christlicher Apostelakten zuzuweisen, dessen Existenz seit dem 4.Jh. wenigstens für den westlichen Manichäismus gesichert ist[80]. Auf Kenntnis des Gegenstandes der *Acta Pauli et Theclae* im östlichen Manichäismus läßt wohl eine Nennung beider Namen in einem mp. Fragment der Beschreibung der Offenbarungen des Heiligen Geistes in seinen Aposteln schließen[81]. Kenntnis des Gegenstandes bedeutet aber nicht

---

Julianos der Abtrünnige. Syrische Erzählungen, Leiden 1880. Vollständige Übersetzung: H. Gollancz, Julian the Apostate, London 1928.

[76] Etwa die dem Socrates (1. Hälfte 5. Jh.) zugeschriebene »Erzählung von den Königen Constantin und Jovian«? Nöldeke hielt geradezu für möglich, daß sie mit dem syr. Roman identisch sei (ZDMG 28 [1874], S. 292 Anm. 2). Anders A. Baumstark, Geschichte der syrischen Literatur, Bonn 1922, S. 183.

[77] Payne Smith II, S. 1910.

[78] Vollständiges Heiligen-Lexikon, ed. J.E. Stadler, II, Augsburg 1897, S. 747ff.

[79] E. de Stoop, Essai sur la diffusion du manichéisme dans l'empire romain, Gand 1909, S. 39. 89, P. Brown, The Diffusion of Manichaeism in the Roman Empire, Journal of Roman Studies 1969, S. 92.

[80] K. Schäferdiek bei Hennecke, S. 117ff., P. Nagel, Apokryphe Apostelakten, S. 152f.

[81] M 788, der in diesem Zusammenhang relevante Teil wurde publ. von Henning, JRAS 1944, S. 142 Anm. 1. Das ganze Stück hoffe ich in anderem Zusammenhang vorlegen zu können.

Identität der Texte, und wie ließe sich in diesem Zusammenhang das
Auftauchen des Namens Julianus in Stück *2* rechtfertigen? Auf Grund
der heute bekannten Literaturreste des östlichen Manichäismus jedenfalls halte ich eine andere Möglichkeit für wahrscheinlicher. Beschränkt
man sich bei seiner Suche nach Zugehörigem auf Namenswieder-
holungen und handschriftliche Vergleiche, so stellt man schnell fest,
daß sowohl die Erwähnung des Paulus wie gewisse formale Ähnlich-
keiten der Textbruchstücke auf eine engere Beziehung zu dem bereits
1904 von C. Salemann in Faksimile und Umschrift publizierten
Fragment S (1) hinweisen[82]. Wie Salemann mitteilt, stammt S aus
Turfan wie die Berliner Stücke, und daß Teile desselben Manuskripts
sich heute in Berlin und Leningrad befinden können, wurde bereits
an einem anderen Beispiel festgestellt[83]. Im vorliegenden Fall stimmen
die Sprache und Schriftgröße aller Stücke überein und vielleicht auch
die Blatt- und Kolumnenbreite von S und *3*.

Von einer Identität des Duktus kann dagegen keine Rede sein.
Die Schriftzeichen des Leningrader Fragments sind allgemein feiner
und besser durchgeformt als die der Berliner Stücke. Ein größerer
Unterschied besteht dagegen in der Schreibung von s und 1 (in S ist
der linke s-Bogen höher emporgeführt, der linke 1-Arm bis auf die
Grundlinie hinabgezogen). Ein weiterer, jedoch auch sonst ungewöhn-
licher Umstand ist ferner die Tatsache, daß S, obwohl offenbar Seite
eines Buches in Codex-Format[84], aus einer chinesischen Schriftrolle
herausgeschnitten ist und daher auf seiner Rückseite chinesische
Zeichen trägt.

Eine immerhin mögliche Erklärung dieser eigenartigen Mischung
von Gemeinsamem und Trennendem scheint mir zu sein, daß S ein
Inhaltsverzeichnis des Buches darstellt, zu dem die Berliner Texte
gehörten. Es wurde ihm vielleicht erst nachträglich beigegeben oder
beigeheftet. Aus Sparsamkeitsgründen war es aus einer chinesischen
Schriftrolle herausgeschnitten worden. Vielleicht entstammen die Berliner Texte und S verschiedenen Schreibern.

---

[82] Ein Bruchstük Manichaeischen Schrifttums im Asiatischen Museum, Mém. Acad.
Imp. des Sc. de St.-Pétersbourg, 8ᵉ sér., vol. 6, n° 6, St.-Pétersbourg 1904, S. 1ff.

[83] BTT IV, S. 12f.

[84] Dafür, daß S einem Codex und nicht einer Rolle entstammt, spricht 1. Bewahrung
des oberen Randes und beider Seitenränder, 2. die Tatsache, daß das Stück einseitig
mit chinesischen Zeichen beschrieben ist, jedoch nicht in seiner ursprünglichen Gestalt
benützt, sondern zurechtgeschnitten wurde, 3. Salemann, der mit dem Original von S
arbeitete, die Möglichkeit, daß ein Fragment einer man. Buchrolle vorliegen könnte,
überhaupt nicht erwogen hat.

Noch ein weiterer Umstand ist mit der hier vermuteten Zusammengehörigkeit der behandelten Stücke gut vereinbar. Die für *2* vermutbare christliche Quelle kann keinesfalls vor dem 4.Jh., kaum vor dem 5. entstanden sein. Sie entstammt vielleicht erst dem 6.Jh., und die manichäische Adaptation dieses Stoffes muß noch jünger sein (ca. 5. bis 7.Jh.?). Auch für *1* kann, sollte tatsächlich Seneca erwähnt worden sein, ein spätes Entstehungsdatum angenommen werden. Jedenfalls gehören die Berliner Stücke nicht zum Urbestand des manichäischen Schrifttums. Sie sind vielleicht sogar ein spätes Sondererzeugnis der zentralasiatischen *Dīnāwarīya*-Gemeinde. Ähnliches kann für S vermutet werden. Sein Text läßt auf eine nicht mehr korrekte Beherrschung des Mp. schließen, denn er ist von parth. Wörtern durchsetzt (/1/ hnjft, /17/ (ʾrdʾwyftyg), zu /2/ ymgʾnyg s.Anm. 88). Bemerkenswert ist auch unter den Jesushomilien der Titel ʾbr gwyšn ʾy qynšryy md(.)[»Über die Homilie von Qynšryy/ des Qynšryy…« (S/16/). Qynšryy wurde von Henning, BSOS 9 [1937], S. 84, unter Hinweis auf syr. qnšrʾ »eagle-eyrie (name of a monastery)«, zweifelnd als Personenname bestimmt. Ich vermute, daß die erhaltenen Schrifttreste die Ergänzung qynšryy md(y)[ntʾ] »Sta[dt] *Qenneŝrē*« gestatten, worunter im Zusammenhang der Jesushomilien wohl nur die Stadt jenes Namens am Euphrat verstanden werden kann, in der sich das berühmte *Bar-Aftōnyā*-Kloster befand[85]. Da es erst zu Anfang des 6.Jh. gegründet worden ist, so dürfte weder das Fragment S noch die Homilie von *Qenneŝrē*, auf die sich S bezieht, früheren Datums sein.

Sollte es sich aber doch einmal erweisen, daß S von den Berliner Fragmenten zu trennen ist, so kann m.A.n. das Leningrader Stück immer noch wenigstens zu einer hypothetischen Bestimmung der hier veröffentlichten Textstellen benützt werden.

Wie Henning erkannt hat[86], macht S Angaben über die »days of Yimki-prayers« (vgl. Anm. 88), genauer gesagt, es stellt ein Verzeichnis von Homilien (gwyšnʾn) dar, die aus Anlaß der *Yimki*-Tage der Erzmärtyrer der manichäischen Kirche zu Gehör gebracht werden sollten[87]. Das geht aus den ersten drei Zeilen des Stückes hervor:

/1/ hnjft hynd ʾymyn gwyšnʾn rwšnʾn ʾy
/2/ (ymg)ʾnyg rwcʾn oo ʾwš ʾst ʾc ʾndr pd yk
/3/ m̈r wysp gwšg oo XLV gwyšnʾn ʾy yzdygyrdyy

---

[85] G. Hoffmann, Auszüge aus syrischen Akten persischer Märtyrer, Leipzig 1880, S. 162 Anm. 1260, Payne Smith II, S. 3673.

[86] JRAS 1945, S. 155.

[87] Über den Ritus der *Yimki*-Feiern ist nur wenig und Bruchstückhaftes bekannt (Henning, JRAS 1945, S. 154, Text Nr. 5, vgl. S. 147 f.).

Ich möchte dieses schwierige, m.W. bisher nie vollständig übersetzte
Textstück versuchsweise so wiedergeben :
    Vollendet sind diese leuchtenden Homilien der *Yimki*-Tage[88].
Und in ihm[89] sind in einer *allumfassenden[90] Zusammenrech-
nung(?)[91] 45 Homilien von der Göttlichkeit[92].

[88] Zum Wort s. bes. Henning, BSOS 8 [1936], S. 588 Anm. 3 und JRAS 1945,
S. 155, wo für ymg'nyg rwc'n die Übersetzung »days of Yimki-prayers« gegeben wird.
Das Wort gehört also zu türk. *y(i)mki*, soghd. ymgyy, ymkyy, ymqyy und yymkyy
und parth. ymg, das in der hier geforderten Bedeutung nicht nur aus dem runen-
schriftlichen y²mk² erschlossen werden muß, sondern auch in man. Schrift sicher belegt
ist, nämlich in M 30/R/II/4-7/ pṯ 'ym b'ym rwcg u ymg 'frydg 'g'dg wx'zyd 'c bg
»bei diesem *Bema*-Fasten und gesegneten *Yimki* erbittet vom Gott einen Wunsch«.
Es scheint also, daß der mp. Text S den Namen der Feier in parth. Form verwendet.
Liegt eine sprachechte Entlehnung aus dem Parth. vor oder gehört ymg'nyg zu jenen
parth. Wörtern, die in S inkorrekterweise verwendet werden (vgl. S)? Da weder
der Charakter der *Yimki*- Feiern noch die Bezeichnung derselben völlig klar sind,
behalte ich im deutschen Text ihren Namen in der wohlbekannten Sprachprägung
des türkischen *Xwāstwanīft* bei. Insbesondere unklar ist das Verhältnis von soghd.
ymkyy, parth. ymg »*Yimki*-Feier« zu mpT. jmyg, parthT. ymg »σύζυγος; ἀρχηγός«
und damit zusammengesetzten Bezeichnungen. Ich muß mich in diesem Zusammenhang
darauf beschränken, 1. daran zu erinnern, daß Henning beide Bedeutungsbereiche
voneinander trennte und soghd. ymkyy durch »prayer, prayer of intercession« und
»supplication« übersetzte (JRAS 1945, S. 147 u. 155, vgl. BB, S. 139), während
J. P. Asmussen, Xᵘāstvānīft, S. 226f. die Möglichkeit einer Ableitung von soghd. ymkyy,
parth. ymg »*Yimki*-Feier« von mp./parth. jmyg, ymg »σύζυγος; ἀρχηγός« erwog. 2. Ich
halte die herkömmliche Erklärung von jmyg, ymg als »ἀρχηγός« für sehr zweifelhaft
und glaube, daß Asmussens vorsichtige Umschreibung »a kind of Fravaši« einen
wesentlichen Fortschritt des Wortverständnisses darstellt. 3. Wie immer das sprachgeschichtliche Verhältnis zwischen ymkyy, ymg und jmyg, ymg gewesen sein mag,
in den vorliegenden Texten dürfte jedenfalls ymkyy als ein eigenständiges Wort verstanden worden sein, denn die Bedeutung »σύζυγος; ἀρχηγός« o.ä. läßt sich für ymkyy
nicht nachweisen, und die Schreibung ymgyḫ pŏky'(ḥ) »*Yimki*-Ritus« (M 7950/1/)
zeigt doch wohl, daß dieses Wort als ein Femininum aufgefaßt wurde.
[89] Dem Buch.
[90] H. H. Schaeder, Iranica, S. 5 Anm. 4 meinte, daß wysp gwšg Eigenname in
der Bedeutung »Alles-hörend« sei und auf einen man. Geistlichen hinweise, offenbar
den Verfasser der Homilien. Zu übersetzen wäre also »... des *Wisp-gōšag* 45 Homilien«,
eine Möglichkeit, die aber schon durch Setzung von Interpunktionszeichen zwischen
regens und rectum unwahrscheinlich gemacht wird, um so mehr als eine *Wisp-gōšag*
genannte Persönlichkeit ebensowenig bekannt ist wie ein mp. Verb *gōš-* »hören«.
An Hennings Bemerkung in BSOS 8 [1936], S. 588 Anm. 3 anknüpfend, daß gwšg
vielleicht zu np. *gōšä* »Winkel« gehöre, bzw. zu mpB. *gōšag*, verstehe ich wysp gwšg
als »alleckig, allwinklig« u.ä. (vgl. np. *čahār gūše* »viereckig«), dies wiederum im
Sinne von »allumfassend« oder »insgesamt«, was ausgezeichnet in den vorliegenden
Kontext passen würde.
[91] Hennings zur Stelle gelieferte Teilübersetzung (BSOS 8 [1936], S. 588 Anm. 3)

Unter den Jesus gewidmeten (yyšw'yg) fünf Homilien erscheint als eine Überschrift /15/ 'br gwyšn 'y p'wlys fr(y)[stg] »Über die Homilie vom Apo[stel] Paulus«, bzw. »Über die Predigt des Apo[stels] Paulus«. Die erstere Möglichkeit ist aber die wahrscheinlichere, wenn man andere Überschriften zum Vergleich heranzieht : /8/ 'br gwyšn 'y dw'zdẖ sxwn »Über die Homilie von den zwölf Worten«, /16/ 'br gwyšn 'y qynšryy md(y)[nt'] »Über die Homilie von der Sta[dt] *Qennešrē*«.

»und es (sc. das Buch) enthält in einer Hymne alle *gōšaγ*« setzt doch wohl eine Erklärung von punktiertem mr als verkürzte Schreibung von mhr »Hymne« voraus. Bereits BB, S. 112 wird dagegen dieses mr als »Zahl(?)« übersetzt. Diese Deutung behielt Henning in BSOS 9 [1937], S. 85 bei, bemerkte jedoch mit Recht, daß »number« üblicherweise ohne die zwei Punkte über dem m geschrieben werde. In der Tat bezeichnen die problematischen Punkte in der Regel Kurzschreibung, oft, aber nicht immer, und offenbar auch im vorliegenden Fall nicht, aus Platzmangel. Da sie jedoch zweifellos eine distinktive Bedeutung haben müssen, so erscheint es mir als die nächstliegende Annahme, daß der Schreiber ein ursprünglich in den Text gestelltes mr »Zahl« nachträglich korrigieren wollte, dies aber nicht durch Ergänzungen, Tilgungen oder Neuschreibungen tat, sondern sich auf jene Punkte beschränkte, die dem Leser nur mitteilten, daß Zeichen zu ergänzen seien. Demnach wäre eine Lesung mhr also an sich möglich, ist aber doch kaum sinnvoll, denn S ist ja erklärtermaßen ein Homilienvereichnis, und selbst eine aus 45 Homilien bestehende Hymne kann wohl auch im Manichäismus nicht erwartet werden. Die zweifellos einfachste Ergänzung wäre *m'r *mār*, das im Np. existiert und für das Steingass, S. 1139 u.a. die Bedeutungen »an account-book, register; an accountant« anführt (vgl. auch Vullers II, S. 1114. Nyberg, S. 126 verband damit jüngst das Heterogramm ḤYB des MpB., das dort »times (in multiplication)« bedeute und als dessen Aussprache er *mār* feststellte). M.A.n. kann np. *mār* nicht von *āmār* getrennt werden, auf das es zurückgeht und das im MpB. wie MpT. (M 8172/4/ 'm'r) bezeugt ist. Vgl. ferner in dem soghd. Text T. I 1055 = Ch/U 7117 /1/ [sγ]t'(n)'m'r »Aufzählung/Liste der Tages[da]ten«. Daß 'm'r auch im vorliegenden Fall gemeint war, halte ich für die wahrscheinlichste Möglichkeit.

[92] Salemann las Bruchstück, S. 2 yzdygyrd oo, ebenso MS I, S. 87, und sah darin einen Eigennamen oder ein Adj. »gotterschaffen«. Daß ein solcher Name eines man. Schriftstellers sonst nicht bekannt ist, widerlegt Salemanns Auffassung nicht, wohl aber die im Vergleich mit anderen Interpunktionszeichen zu große Schreibung der letzten Buchstaben, die mithin -yy sein müssen. Zu lesen ist also yzdygyrdyy (so richtig Müller, HR II, S. 110) »Göttlichkeit«, eine Abstraktableitung von yzdygyrd »göttlich« (nicht »gotterschaffen«), die in publ. und unpubl. Texten wiederholt begegnet. Das Wort bezeichnet den vom Erwählten erreichten Zustand der Vollkommenheit, vgl. die Mir. Man. II, S. 347 angeführten Stellen, ferner bes. IB 4974/V/II/17-24/ [Waldschmidt-Lentz, MD, S. 559], das ich so umschreibe und übersetze : ky [pd] wyhyẖ w'(c)'pryd z'ynyy przynd'n pd w'c 'w(š)'n prwryẖ p(d) š(y)r 'y w'xšyg 'wš'n z'm(y)[nyẖ] 'w pym'n ('yg) yzdygyrdyy »Der du (= der Lehrer) [durch] 'wortgeschaffene' Weisheit Kinder gebierst durch < dein > Wort und sie aufziehst mit geistiger Milch

Wenigstens das Fragment *1* könnte dann ein Teil dieser Paulus-homilie sein. In den übrigen Fällen lassen sich nur Aussagen von noch geringerer Sicherheit machen. So frage ich mich, ob die Über-schrift]ʾrdʾw(ʾn pr)ystʾd(n o) in *3* auf eine der »Erwähltenschaft« (ʾrdʾwyftyg) gewidmete Homilie hindeutet, deren Existenz aus S /17/ hervorgeht. Henning meinte, daß die »Erwähltenschaft« mit den »Drei Presbytern« identisch sei, die *Mār Sīsin* in den Tod folgten[93]. Da die andere Seite von *3* einen Kaiser erwähnt, so müßte dann für sie wohl ein zeitweiliges Wirken im Römischen Reich angenommen werden. Völlig unklar bleibt leider insbesondere die genaue literarische Einordnung des lwlynws nennenden Fragments *2*. Da auch S defektiv ist, lassen sich aber nicht einmal aus diesem negativen Umstand sichere Schlüsse ziehen.

[Erst nachträglich werden mir die Fragmente M 4750 und M 4757 zugänglich, die nach Ausweis ihrer Schrift und Sprache zur hier behandelten Handschrift gehören, den Text jedoch nicht wesentlich bereichern.]

und sie gelei[test] zur Reife der Göttlichkeit«. Im Sinne religiöser Vollkommenheit der in den Homilien verherrlichten Märtyrer ist offenbar auch das yzdygyrdyy dieses Textes zu verstehen. Weniger wahrscheinlich ist die Annahme einer zu yzdygyrd hinzutretenden pleonastischen Adjektivbildung *yzdygyrdyg »göttlich« (wie in mpB. *tanigard* und *tanigardig*, MacKenzie, S. 82), die irrtümlich yzdygyrdyy geschrieben sein müßte. Zwar kann mit Fehlern dieser Art gelegentlich gerechnet werden, aber *yzdygyrdyg selbst ist im MpT. nicht sicher bezeugt. M 82/R/11/ bietet zwar tatsächlich yzdygy(r)dyg, der Paralleltext in M 235/V/4/ aber yzdygyrdy für zu erwartendes Abstraktnomen, so daß in diesem Fall nur irrtümliche Ersetzung des Abstraktsuffixes -yh/-yy durch das lautgleiche Adjektivsuffix -yg vorliegt (eine Ausnahme der von Henning, Mitteliranisch, S. 76 Anm. 1 formulierten Regel). In seiner Transkription des Textes normalisierte Henning daher stillschweigend zu *yazdegerdīh* (TPS 1942, S. 56).

[93] JRAS 1945, S. 155 Anm. 3 und S. 148.

OSWALD SZEMERÉNYI

IRANICA V*

(Nos. 59-70)

59. OP xšāyaθya 'king'

The Old Persian noun xšāyaθya undoubtedly meant 'ruler, king'. It survives in the modern title of the ruler of Persia, šāh, as does the frequent OP phrase xšāyaθya xšāyaθyānām 'king of kings' in the modern title šāhanšāh. The source of this noun is also clear: it derives from the verbal root xšai- 'rule' which is attested in the OP participial phrase xšayamna amiy 'I am ruling' (DNb 15, hapax) and the 1. sg. impf. patiyaxšayaiy 'I ruled' (DNa 19; DSe 17-18; XPh 17); it is more remotely connected with OP xšaśa- 'kingship, kingdom', xšaśapāvan- 'satrap'. Cognate forms exist also in Avestan xšayati, xšayamnō, xšaθra-, and Sanskrit kṣayati, kṣatra-.

But while the etymological relations, at least within Indo-Iranian, are tolerably clear, the formation of the word is still not clarified. Bartholomae thought that an OP word could only have the ending (spelt) -θiya if that ending was really disyllabic since a monosyllabic -θya should have developed into -šya, as in hašya- 'true', spelt hašiya-, from early satya-; accordingly, he saw himself forced to trace OP xšāyaθiya- to an Aryan *kšāyathiya- which, in his view, was a derivative formed with the suffix -iya- either from *kšāyatha-, Iran. *xšāyaθa- (from the root *xšāy-), or from the vṛddhied form

---

* The present series is almost exclusively devoted to Old Persian problems which were treated in a seminar at the University of Freiburg in the 1971/72 session, and again in the summer semester of 1974. For earlier parts of this series see *Iranian Studies I* (Nos. 1-8), KZ 76, 1959, 60-77; *Iranica II* (Nos. 9-31), Sprache 12, 1967, 190-226; *Iranica III* (Nos. 32-43), Henning Memorial Volume, 1970, 417-426; *Iranica IV* (Nos. 44-58), Orbis 19, 1971, 500-519.—It should be noted here that a prodromus, as it were, to these studies appeared 1950 under the title *Contributions to Iranian lexicography* (JAOS 70, 226-236; seven items); 1951 as *Iranica* (ZDMG 101, 197-219; six items) and *Vištāspa* (BzN 2, 167-177). The results of the last paper now seem widely accepted. It is all the more surprising that my solution is credited to another scholar at, e.g., Sprache 18, 1972, 50, a practice that is both embarrassing for the recipient and shows little feel for scholarly ethics.

of *kšayatha-, Iran. *xšayaθa-, the basic suffix being in either case
Aryan -atha-, Iran. -aθa- [1].

Most scholars, however, rejected such a quadrisyllabic form, and
maintained that the OP word had the trisyllabic shape xšāyaθya-.
But since they also acknowledged that θy ought to have gone to
OP šy, they assumed that xšāyaθya- was not an indigenous but
a Medic form [2]. This assumption became particularly cogent when
the Manichaean manuscripts found in Chinese Turkestan in the first
decade of our century revealed the existence in the Middle Iranian
period of two Western dialects, Persian and Parthian, of which
the latter appeared to be the Middle Iranian development of Ancient
Medic [3]. For this dichotomy, coupled with the erstwhile supremacy
of the Medes over the Persis, explained how Persian could exhibit
so many non-Persian elements in its lexicon.

It is true, nevertheless, that neither side has been able to produce
decisive arguments in favour of its view. Bartholomae thought [4] that
epigraphic šāhi etc. showed that the OP form ended in -iya, for
only this could yield -ī. Hübschmann, on the other hand, argued [5]
that the form šāh proved that the OP ending could not have been
-iya since in that case -ī would have survived. But there can be
little doubt that Andreas was fundamentally right in holding that
the old -a-stem genitive in -ahya developed into -ē (later -ī), and
thus -∅/-ē, representing the old nom. in -a(h) and the gen. in -ē,
could exist side by side (cf. also duxt-duxtar 'daughter', etc.), and
could lead to the generalization of either form [6]. Benveniste insisted
that "the development seen in šāh indicated a trisyllabic form

---

[1] Cf. Bartholomae 1904, 554; 1919, 29[4]. For earlier treatments see Schmidt 1889,
419; Bartholomae, BB 13, 1888, 75; Hübschmann 1895, 134. Bartholomae's view
was also upheld by Meillet 1915, 77, 140.

[2] See, e.g., Hübschmann, IFA 10, 1899, 121; Foy, KZ 37, 1904, 536; Nyberg
1931, 213; Meillet-Benveniste 1931, 90; Herzfeld, AMI 3, 1931, 97; Gonda 1969, 37;
Benveniste 1969, II 18; Mayrhofer 1971, 47-8; Hinz 1973, 139.—Gershevitch probably
stands alone with his view (TPS 1964, 23f.) that xšāyaθya is a normal Persian form.

[3] Concerning the relation of Parthian to Medic, see Henning 1958, 92f.; Perixanjan,
REArm 3, 1967, 21[7], 24; and in: Etimologija (1966), 1968, 251.

[4] See in particular Bartholomae 1919, 29[4].

[5] Hübschmann, IFA 10, 1899, 121.

[6] Cf. Andreas, Pauly-Wissowas Realencyclopädie s.v. Ambara; Horn 1898, 100-101.
This seems to me still the best explanation, in spite of the inconsistencies in epigraphic
Middle (West) Iranian, due to widespread analogical reorganizations, which Henning
(1958, 64f., 68f.) discussed in such masterly fashion.

accented on the initial syllable, i.e. *xšáyaθya-*, for the accent could not go beyond the antepenult"[7]. But it is quite obvious that *šāh* cannot prove an original accentuation *xšáy-*, and therewith a trisyllabic shape, since a quadrisyllabic *xšāyaθiya-*, accented as *xšāyáθiya*, would also have developed into *šāh* (morphologically reshaped from *šāhē*).

It is indeed quite clear that phonological considerations cannot decide the question whether the primitive form was **xšāyaθya-* or **xšāyaθiya-*. And yet this minute point has momentous consequences. If the primitive form was the quadrisyllabic **xšāyaθiya-*, then the basic form must be posited as (Aryan) **kšāyatha-* or **kšayatha-*, a noun with the suffix *-atha-*. This analysis was long in favour, in fact it can still be said to be favoured by most scholars[8]. And it must indeed be conceded that, even if it cannot be traced to Indo-European, *-atha-* is an Aryan derivational suffix[9]. Indian has such nouns as RV *šapátha-* 'curse', *ucátha-* 'saying, saw' (17 in the RV), and Iranian (Avestan) offers more than half-a-dozen examples, e.g. *mahrkaθa-* 'killing, destroying', *varadaθa-* 'growth', *zbaraθa-* 'foot' (of a daēvic being). But it is surprising all the same that there is only one noun that is found both in Indian and Iranian, and is usually regarded as inherited in both branches, i.e. *vakṣatha-* 'growth' = Av. *vaxšaθa-*. What is more, there is not a single example of a common, i.e. Aryan, derivative in *-ath(i)ya-*, Iran. *-aθ(i)ya-*, which seems to suggest that the type was unknown to the Aryan period.

If the primitive form was the trisyllabic *xšāyaθya-*, then it is unnecessary to postulate an Aryan antecedent **kšāyathya-* since an Aryan **kšāyatya-* would also have developed into the OP form. And some scholars have indeed adopted this solution. If I am not mistaken, Herzfeld was the first to see in *xšāyaθya-* the same suffix as is present in Skt. *satya-*, i.e. *-tya-*, the Iranian correspondence being *-θya-*[10]; it was of course a mistake to cut off in *satya-* a suffix *-tya-* (see below), but then it is well known that grammar was not Herzfeld's *forte*. He was followed by Kent who

---

[7] Meillet-Benveniste 1931, 63.

[8] Cf. Bartholomae 1904, 554; Foy, KZ 37, 1904, 524; Meillet-Benveniste 1931, 63, 153; Wackernagel-Debrunner 1954, 818; Brandenstein-Mayrhofer 1964, 126; Mayrhofer 1968, 9[40], 18, 21[92]; Benveniste 1969, II 18; Gonda 1969, 37.

[9] See Wackernagel-Debrunner 1954, 171-173.

[10] Herzfeld, AMI 3, 1931, 97.

posited Aryan *kšāyatya without explaining the formation[11], and after several false starts they have now been joined by Mayrhofer. This scholar first began to doubt the traditionally reconstructed *xšayaθa- (or *xšāy-) in 1968, and since 1971 has firmly come down in favour of an original form *kšāyatya-[12]; in his most recent work Hinz has also adopted this protoform[13]. But of Herzfeld's followers only Mayrhofer has offered a reason for this assumption: he pointed to Ind. nāsatya- as probably representing the same type of formation, and explained both as vrddhied derivatives of the abstract nouns *kṣayati-, *nasati-[14].

The basic idea of this explanation was taken over from Hermann Güntert who in his famous study, Der arische Weltkönig und Heiland, examined the nature of the Vedic Aśvinā, the divine twins, whose frequent epitheton ornans is nāsatyā (dual, the sg. is found once), although, as is shown by the Mitanni treaties and Iranian nāhaθya (Av. nåŋhaiθya), the form was originally their name, or at least the name of one of them[15]. Güntert showed[16] that the name of the twin gods, whose function is exactly described as 'rescuers, saviours', was, as had been suggested before[17], connected with the Indian verb nasate 'approaches, joins someone'; more precisely, nāsatya- was based on *nasati- 'Rettung durch Herbeieilen', just as ādityá- was derived from áditi-, vāsatya- from vasati-[18].

It is quite clear[19] that the saviour gods derive their name from

[11] Kent 1953, 181.

[12] In Brandenstein-Mayrhofer 126 only xšayaθa- is reported but Mayrhofer 1968, 9[40] and 21[92], it is left open whether *kšāyatya- or *kšāyathya- is to be assumed, at 1970, 289, *kšāyatya is held to be more probable, and 1971, 48, it is the only form quoted.

[13] Hinz 1973, 139.

[14] Mayrhofer 1970, 289.

[15] On this point see D.J. Ward, in: Myth and Law among the Indo-Europeans (ed. J. Puhvel), 1970, 194.

[16] Güntert, o.c., 259. His view was accepted by Porzig, IFA 42, 1924, 19.

[17] Uhlenbeck, Kurzgefaßtes etym. Wb. der altindischen Sprache, Amsterdam 1898-99, 147: 'heilend, errettend', but no word is said about the formation.

[18] Unfortunately, vāsatya- seems a ghost-form. The Nirukta-passage, quoted by Güntert (1923, 258), has vāsātya- which is not from vasati- but from vasāti- 'dawn' (?, but cp. Geldner, in: A. Bertholet, Religionsgeschichtliches Lesebuch, 1908, 94). The Atharvaveda has a derivative vāsatēya- from vasati- but in the sense "zu Obdach berechtigt". It seems then that Güntert made a mistake in operating with vāsatya-.

[19] Lommel, Festschrift W. Schubring, Hamburg 1951, 29-31 (joined by Puhvel, in: Indo-European and Indo-Europeans, Philadelphia 1970, 381 fn. 18) tried to rescue

the IE verbal root *nes- 'save, bring home', in the middle 'be rescued, get home safely, return home', which is particularly clear in Greek νέομαι 'get safely somewhere, return', in the active sense 'rescue' in Νέστωρ 'Heimführer, Retter', Νείλεως (from *Νεε-λᾱϝος) 'der seine Leute gesund heimführt'[20], but also in Gothic ga-nisan 'be saved, recover', OE ge-nesan 'to be saved, preserved; escape from'.

It is, however, quite unlikely that Nāsatya- should be based on an abstract noun nasati-. As is known, nouns in -ti- are formed, as a rule, from the nil-grade of a verbal root, more exceptionally from the full grade. From the root nas- we can expect therefore *asti- (from *n̥s-ti-, cf. asta- from *n̥s-to-) or *nasti- but not *nasati-. To be sure, there is a diminutive group of nouns (perhaps five or six altogether) formed with -ati-, but none of them recurs outside Indian, and therefore all of them seem to represent an Indian innovation; in the case of *nes-, the IE type is represented by Gothic ga-nists 'reaching safety', in the case of *wes- by OE wist 'staying, existence', OIr. fe(i)ss 'staying, sleeping'[21]. Especially unlikely is an abstract noun *kṣayati-, seeing that what we should expect is actually attested in kṣi-ti-[22].

We are thus left with two parallel formations, nāsatya- and *kšāyatya-, which however cannot be based on abstracts of the type *nasati-, *kšayati-. Iranian scholars have tried to add to this group such nouns as *harvaθya- 'the observant one', *isaθya- 'ruler', *garbaθya- 'one who habitually grabs or understands', etc.[23], but

the native etymology from nāsā-tya- 'nose-born'—allegedly referring to the myth, according to which the Aśvins' mother was impregnated by sniffing the spilled sperm of Vivasvant. But quite apart from the unparalleled mode of fecundation, the attempt breaks down on the simple grammatical observation that the suffix -tya- only forms adjectives from adverbs, not from nouns, see Wackernagel-Debrunner 1954, 697f.

[20] For the Greek group see Palmer, Eranos 54, 1956, 8f.; 1st Mycenaean Congress I, 1968, 340; Mühlestein, MH 22, 1965, 155f.; Durante, SMEA 3, 1967, 33f.; Frisk II 304f., III 156.

[21] Cf. Liebert 1949, 52-54, 102; Wackernagel-Debrunner 1954, 628.

[22] There is of course no such difficulty with a form kšayati-ya 'he who has power' (posited by Nagy 1970, 43 fn. 121) but the assumption that this clause could be vr̥ddhied and supply an adjective is not supported by evidence or intrinsic probability.—As to Nāsatya, I have not seen the paper of Michalski, RO 24, 1961, 7-52.

[23] Cf. Henning, Asia Maior 2, 1951, 144; Gershevitch, Studia A. Pagliaro oblata II, 1969, 200; BSOAS 33, 1970, 85-87; Hinz, Neue Wege im Altpersischen (Privat-Vorabdruck), Göttingen 1970, 28. With the exception of *gaubaθya- (reconstructed by Henning), all these names are discussed by Mayrhofer 1973, no. 8.464, 8.516, 8.768.

the newcomers are either intrinsically improbable or ill supported by the Elamite evidence used. On the other hand, a clear and decisive parallel is supplied by Vedic *raivatya-* 'wealth, riches': *raivatyéva máhasā čárava sthana* (RV 10, 94, 10) 'you are lovely (through =) in your wealth (and) might'. For this is indisputably a vṛddhied derivative in *-ya-* of the well-known adjective *revant-* (earlier *rayi-vant-*) 'rich, wealthy', that is *rēiwṇt-yo-*, here used as a substantivized neuter in the instrumental [24].

This means that *nāsatya-* must be interpreted as *nāsṇtya-*, and *xšāyaθya-* as *kšāyṇtya-*. But the simultaneous presence of vṛddhi and suffix *-ya-* is certainly secondary, although the type is probably an innovation of the Aryan period [25]; however, the original principle was suffixation with *-ya-* (IE *-yo-*) *or* vṛddhi, with, if necessary, the addition of simple *-a-* (IE *-o-*, type *swēkuros*), and the new type (vṛddhi *and* suffix *-ya-*) is no doubt a contamination of the two earlier types [26].

The original relations are best represented by such pairs as:

Aryan *sant-*   :   *satyá-* 'existing, true'

IE *sont-*   :   *sṇt-yó-*,

in which the derivative only shows the suffix, no doubt always accented, and so entailing the nil-grade of the preceding morpheme. But the latter principle could be eliminated in favour of the original stem-form. Thus the Rig-Veda offers *sahant-ya-* 'overpowering, powerful' (from *sah-ant-*) without the reduction in the stem-suffix, and the Atharva-Veda presents the vṛddhied *sāhantya-*. Although the meaning of *sahantya-* and *sāhantya-* is identical, this is no doubt the result of a circuitous development: the vṛddhied *sāhantya-* originally meant 'belonging to, characteristic of *sahantya-*', and only later became identical with its source.

---

[24] See Wackernagel-Debrunner 1954, 120, 820-821, 823, 834. Geldner 1951, III 297, takes *raivatyeva* as = *raivatyā(ḥ) iva* which is not only against the syntax and the Padapāṭha but also against the sandhi-rules: I know of only one comparable instance, *bhūmyōpari* (10, 75, 3) which is taken by Wackernagel-Debrunner (1954, 316) as *bhūmyā(s) upari*, but it is quite unnecessary to abandon the Padapāṭha interpretation *bhūmyā upari* since the genitive with *upari* would be just as much a hapax as the instrumental is (although the genitive is of course supported by the post-Vedic usage); cf. Brugmann 1904, 464. On *vṛṣabhéva* see Wackernagel-Debrunner 1957, 316-317 and Nachtrag.

[25] See Wackernagel-Debrunner 1954, 818-819.

[26] See Wackernagel-Debrunner 1954, 819.

Although we have above adhered to the traditional doctrine that vṛddhied derivatives in -ya- are probably an Aryan innovation, it should be mentioned here that a possible counterpart may be seen in Gothic nēhvundja '(thy) neighbour'. It is obviously a -yo- derivative (in Gothic even expanded with -n-) of an original participle nēhvund- (IE -ṇt-), and possibly the long root-vowel, which has so far found no convincing explanation, arose in vṛddhied formations.

We can thus regard as established that xšāyaθya- (and nāsatya-) are based on xšayant- (and nasant- respectively), and not on the unattested *xšayaθa- or *kšayati- (*nasati-). And this base is well attested in Iranian. In the Avesta, xšayant-, the participle of xšayati, is repeatedly found in the sense of 'ruling, ruler, king'. In the Mihir-Yašt we find: miθrǝm... yazamaide... xšayantǝm 'we worship Mithra... who rules'[27]. In the Fravardīn-Yašt we read (Yt. 13,63): yå ahurahe xšayatō dašinąm upa yūiδyeinti 'who fight on the right of the ruling lord'[28]. The phrase xšayąs mazdå ahurō (Yasna 51,17c) is rendered by Hinz as "der selbstherrlich waltende Allweise Herr", by Humbach as "der waltende Kundige Lebensherr", by Bartholomae as "der Herrscher Mazdāh Ahura"[29], and the last seems to me the most accurate. As Gonda says[30], instead of xšāyaθya, "Zarathustra uses either xšaθrǝm or the participle xšayant-. Every king is a xšayant-, but not every xšayant- a king". If we now take into account that an Aryan *kšaya- 'ruler, king' is guaranteed by the agreement of Vedic kṣaya- 'ruler'[31] and Av. xšayō 'id.' (Yt. 13,18), then we can give the following outline-history of our title.

The inherited IE title *rēg-s 'king', which survives in India, was soon ousted in Iran by the Aryan coinage xšaya-, formed from the Aryan verb xšayati 'he rules'. A rival to xšaya- arose in the free use of the participle xšayant- 'ruling, ruler'. But with the creation in the eighth century B.C. of a unified realm of the Medes the need was felt for a new general term, and it was no doubt then that the term xšāyaθya was coined[32] which was later taken over by

[27] Cf. Gershevitch 1959, 90 (Yt. 10, 35).

[28] See Wolff 1910, 238; Lommel 1927, 119.

[29] Cp. Hinz 1961, 203; Humbach 1959, I 155; Bartholomae 1905, 110.—For further examples of xšayant- see Bartholomae 1904, 551 f.

[30] Gonda 1969, 38.

[31] But perhaps RV kṣaya- m. is not as safe as it seems, cf. Mayrhofer I 287.

[32] Cf. Gonda 1969, 38; note also Mayrhofer's statement (1968, 21, fn. 92) that it is most unlikely that the term kšayat(h)ya-, unknown to the cognate languages,

the Persians when they had succeeded in freeing themselves from
the Median yoke [33].

But, as has been stressed by Gonda in recent times [34], Cyrus
the Great (559-529) called himself simply the "Great King, an
Achaemenian" [35], the title "King of Kings" was first assumed
by Darius I (522-486). But when Gonda asserts (p. 41) that
Mesopotamian influence left no traces "upon the royal titles", one
must ask whether Darius is supposed to have invented his titles
ex nihilo. This is irreconcilable with the known facts of Near Eastern
history. To be sure, R.N. Frye has also at first thought that the
title "King of Kings" was unknown in Mesopotamia—where "King
of the world", or "King of the four rims (of the earth)" were
the customary titles—but used in Urartu, so that the OP title was,
via the Medes, to be traced to Urartu [36]. But soon after he realized
his mistake and correctly stated that the title was old and widespread
in the Near East. It could be shown not only that the title (*šar
šarrāni*) was demonstrably used by various Assyrian kings, e.g.
Tiglathpileser (ca. 1100 B.C.), Assurnasirpal (883-859 B.C.), and the
great Assurbanipal (668-626 B.C.), but also that, before the Assyrians,
several pharaohs had used it, e.g. Amosis I, Thutmosis III, and
Amenophis II (16th-14th centuries B.C.) [37].

Since it is not widely known, it is perhaps useful to recall here
that the title "ruler of rulers" ($ḥq^3 \ ḥq^3.w$) was arrogated as early
as the 18th c. B.C. by the King of Byblos [38]; this might suggest
that the title was, ultimately, of Near Eastern, and not Egyptian,
origin. For the other end of the story, more directly relevant to

should have been present in the period preceding our OP documents; and (1971, 48)
that *kšāyatya-* was an innovation which was known in a very limited area only.

[33] The situation is quite different with *Nāsatya-* which was in existence in the
middle of the second millennium B.C. But linguistically this term also represents
a vṛddhied form, this time of **nasatya-*, based on the participle **nasant-* of the
active verb **nas-* (IE **nesō*) 'to save'.

[34] Gonda 1969, 39.

[35] See the Murghab inscriptions, Kent 1953, 116; and on the problems raised
by the OP version, Nylander, Orientalia Suecana 16, 1967, 144-177; Hinz 1973, 15f.

[36] Frye, The charisma of kingship in Ancient Iran (Iranica Antiqua 4, 1964, 36-54)
36-37; and now in: Beiträge zur Achämenidengeschichte, 1972, 85.

[37] Frye, Cama Golden Jubilee Volume, 1969, 144.—But all this was perfectly
well known to earlier scholars, cf., e.g., Wesendonk, Studies Pavry, 1933, 488-490,
esp. 489.

[38] Cf. Albright, BASOR 176, 1964, 41.

the Iranian problem, we now have a useful summing up by
A.K. Grayson who shows that already in the reign of the Assyrian
king Tukulti-Ninurta I (1244-1208 B.C.) "there is a sharp increase
in more general bombastic titles such as 'king of the four quarters'...
and 'king of kings' (*šar šarrāni*)" beside which the titles 'lord of
lords' (*bēl bēlē*) and 'ruler of rulers' (*mālik mālikī*) are also found.
Since there is no clear evidence of Hittite or Mitannian influence
but "abundant examples of Babylonian influence on the Assyrian
concept of sovereignty", Grayson thinks that the titles mentioned
may be Babylonian in origin, although "so far there is no proof" [39].

From all this it emerges that the title "King of Kings" which
in the Near East in all probability was mediated to the Assyrians
by the Babylonians was also taken over from the Assyrians by
the kings of Urartu. Since the Medes were in contact with all three
nations, they no doubt knew the title. If they did not use it,
the explanation is to my mind quite simple: they were throughout
under the suzerainty of the Assyrians, and naturally could not use
such proud titles of themselves. The end of Babylon was brought
about by Cyrus in 539 B.C. After that date the reason just mentioned
was no longer valid, the Persian king could have assumed the title
of his former overlords. Whether Cyrus, or after him Cambyses II.
(529-522 B.C.), did assume the title is not known [40]. New finds
may yet decide this question.

One last question concerns the etymological relations of the verbal
base *xši-*, Ind. *kṣi-*. As is known, the traditional view establishes
a connection with Greek κτάομαι 'I acquire', which requires an IE
root *$qþēi$-/*$qþəi$- [41]. But the semantic difficulty (: acquire-rule) has
forced several scholars to consider alternative solutions. Kuiper,
adopting an idea advanced by Collitz, connects *xšayati* with Greek
ἴφθῑμος 'strong', and κτάομαι with Av. *šaēta-* 'money, possession';
the former is traced to IE *$q^wþhāi$-, the latter to *$kþāi$- [42]. Wüst
thinks that *xšay-* is derived from IE *k^ws-ei- (ultimately from *ok^wes-
'eye', and so also connected with Av. *aiwyāxšayāṯ* 'watch over,

---

[39] See Grayson, The early development of Assyrian monarchy, Ugarit-Forschungen 3,
1972, 311-319, esp. 315-6. Grayson refers (fn. 39) to Brinkman, A political history
of post-Kassite Babylonia, Rome 1968, who was the first to raise (p. 95 and fn. 495,
498) the question of Babylonian origin of *šar šarrāni*.

[40] On Cyrus see Harmatta, Acta Antiqua Hung. 19, 1971, 221.

[41] Cf. Pokorny 626; Frisk II 31 (doubtful); Mayrhofer I 287; Kent 1953, 181.

[42] See Collitz, BB 18, 1892, 227-230; Kuiper, ZII 8, 1931, 245-249.

supervise'), and has nothing to do with κτάομαι[43]. Palmer wants to connect κτάομαι with κτει- in Myc. *ktoinā, ktiyensi*, and thinks that Ind. *kṣayati* can also be connected; he overlooks that Iranian distinguishes *šay-* and *xšay-*[44].

New data were brought into the debate by H.W. Bailey who found that Khotanese *ṣavā-* (from older **xšawā-*) meant 'possession', and was connected with *ṣṣau* 'ruler', originally 'owner' (from **xšāwa-*), and RV *kṣó- : kṣú-* 'possession'; ultimately **xšau-* would be an *-eu*-base beside the *-ei*-base in Av. *xšay-* 'possess, rule'[45].

If this root is rightly extracted from the not always unequivocal Khotanese material, then **kþeu-* 'possess' could be the source of Greek **ktēw-ṛ/*ktēw-ṇos*[46], Homeric κτέαρ, -ατος, earlier κτέαρ, κτέανα, etc. If **ktēw-ṛ* was reinterpreted as **ktē-wṛ*, then Greek could also acquire a new root κτη- from which the Homeric aorist κτήσασθαι, the perfect ἐκτῆσθαι, and the noun κτῆμα could be formed; the meaning of the perfect is in any case 'to own, possess' (cf. Att. κέκτημαι), and the aorist could develop from 'come into possession' into 'acquire, gain'. For the Aryan group of **kšai-* one would have to accept Bailey's suggestion that it is an alternant of **kšau-*.

The appearance of an IE root **kþeu-* would at last bring the long-awaited solution to a further Greek problem. As is known, the Amphictyons appear either as ἀμφικτίονες (Pindar, etc.) or as ἀμφικτύονες (Herodotus, inscriptions). It is usually assumed that the correct form is -κτίονες which is then connected with κτίζω[47]. But in that case the variant -κτύονες remains inexplicable. If, on the other hand, -κτύονες was the original form[48], then -κτίονες could be due to the influence of περικτίονες, attested since Homer. This solution, dictated by the Greek facts, gains welcome support

[43] Wüst, Altpersische Studien, 1966, 83.

[44] Palmer, TPS 1954, 25f., esp. 26[2]; Chantraine, DELG I 590 is inclined to follow him.

[45] Bailey, Asia Maior N.S. 7, 1959, 14-15; add: Corpus Inscriptionum Iranicarum II/V, Text volume, 1968, 29: **xšau-* 'own'.

[46] For the lengthened grade note φρέαρ from **bhrēw-ṛ*, root **bhreu-*, cf. Pokorny 144. For the Greek group see now also Manessy-Guitton, Hommage à P. Fargues, Nice 1974, 99-112; Risch 49, 62, 320, 342.

[47] Cf. Frisk II 35; Chantraine, DELG I 592; Buck, Greek Dialects, [3]1955, 26.

[48] This possibility has been considered by Gunnarsson, NTS 24, 1971, 44-5 (who is mainly concerned with the "interdental spirant") but he draws on Greek ghost-forms.

if Iranian *xšau- justifies the assumption of an IE *kþeu- 'own, possess': ἀμφικτύονες, then, originally meant 'those who have possessions around', practically the same as 'those who live around'[49].

60. OP *haya-* or *hya-*?

The stem of the OP relative pronoun and definite article is spelt h^a-y^a- and t^a-y^a- respectively. The traditional interpretation of these forms used to be *hya-*, *tya-*. I do not have the resources to find out who introduced this interpretation, but it had been established by the end of the last century, and was universally accepted until twenty years ago[50]. The main reason seems to have been the existence of the Vedic demonstrative pronoun *sya, syā, tyad* 'that', which indeed is a very close fit. But the facts could hardly justify the assumption that the Iranian and Indian pronouns derived from an IE demonstrative *syo-, *tyo-[51]. Since Avestan only has the relative *ya-*, and shows no trace of a *hya-* or *θya-*, it would seem to be more reasonable to regard the OP pronoun as of recent date, as an Iranian or even OP coinage. And once the diachronic link with the Vedic *sya* is severed, one can move on to interpreting OP *hya* and *tya* as contaminated from *ha-* + *ya-*, and *ta-* + *ya-* respectively[52].

But this is only a half-way solution if the old reading—*hya, tya*—dictated by an 'alien' consideration (i.e. the Vedic pronouns), is still retained. It is just as well to go the whole hog and adopt the readings *haya-*, *taya-*, which has the added advantage of doing away with the linguistic difficulty implied in the old *tya-* instead of the expected *θya-*. This solution was indeed suggested in 1954 by E. Risch and K. Hoffmann, and soon accepted by others, so that it seems to be the almost universally accepted doctrine of our day[53];

---

[49] Schwyzer's guess (I 597[5]) that κτυ- of our word may be present in τρι-κτύς, also gains in probability.

[50] Cf. Bartholomae 1901, 236; 1904, 658f.; 1842f.; Brugmann 1904, 661; Tolman 1908, 94, 134; 1910, XVII; Meillet 1915, 17, 76, 170; Meillet-Benveniste 1931, 22, 79, 89, 191; Hinz 1942, 92, 131; Kent 1953, 186, 214.—The first mention, known to me, of this equation is at Bopp, Vergl. Gram. II, ³1870, 155.

[51] This was assumed by Bartholomae 1901, 236; Tolman, ll.cc.

[52] This is the analysis suggested by Kent 1953, 186, 214.

[53] See Risch, Asiatische Studien 8, 1954, 149f.; Hoffmann, MSS 9, 1956, 83[5]; R. Schmitt, Orientalia 32, 1963, 439 with fn. 2; Brandenstein-Mayrhofer 1964, 69, 125

accordingly the source of the OP pronoun is to be sought in the combinations *ha ya, ta ya*, which find exact correspondences in Av. *hō yō* and Vedic *sa yaḥ, tad yad*.

Unfortunately, this explanation is not without difficulties either. First of all, the syntagma assumed—the combination of demonstrative and relative pronouns in immediate sequence—is anything but likely. The question has been examined very thoroughly by K. Strunk [54] whose findings can be summarized as follows. In the Rig-Veda, the favoured position of relative clauses is before their main clause (:*ye... te*, etc.), and this type is naturally of no avail. In the reverse sequence, on the other hand, the pronouns are not in contact as a rule: of Grassmann's 150 examples for this type, not one has the immediate sequence *ta- ya-*, and of Porzig's additional instances only one (:*taṁ yaḥ*). In Vedic prose some further isolated instances can be found, but on the whole it can be said that contact position is extremely infrequent.—In the Avesta, too, distance position is favoured, contact position is found three times in the Gāthās (e.g. *tā yā*), and a few more times in the later Avesta.—It is therefore not all that easy to posit contact position as the habitual order for a pre-OP period.

Secondly, the new interpretation stands or falls with the correctness of the assumption that the second part of *hya-, tya-* is the relative pronoun. Now it is true that in the overwhelming majority of instances *hya-* and *tya-* are used either as the relative pronoun (DB 4,3: *ima tya adam akunavam* 'this is what I did'; DB 2,18: *kāra Pārsa... hya upā mām āha* 'the Persian army... which was with me'), or as a definite article, corresponding to the later izāfet (DB 1,50: *Gaumātam tyam Magum* 'Gaumata the Magian'). But there are two instances in which the pronoun is used as a straightforward demonstrative.

In his famous inscription on the building of the palace at Susa, Darius states of his father and grandfather that (DSf 14) *tyā ubā*

(: "wahrscheinlichere Interpretation"), 145; Strunk, KZ 81, 1968, 265-75; 83, 1970, 49-58; Klingenschmitt, MSS 30, 1972, 201; Hauri 1973, 34.—It would, of course, be interesting to know whether the OP combination could have had a Semitic model (which would decide against Aryan or IE origin), but the question is still not settled, see Eilers, KZ 82, 1969, 62f.; Strunk, KZ 83, 1970, 49-58; Degen, KZ 84, 1971, 202-206; Kutscher, in: Current Trends in Linguistics (ed. T.A. Sebeok) 6, 1970, 391-392.

[54] Strunk, KZ 81, 1968, 266-268.

ajīvatam '*they* were both alive (when Ahuramazda made me king on this earth)'. There can be absolutely no doubt that here *tya* is a demonstrative. A likewise unequivocal construction appears in the Behistun-inscription (DB 3,73) where Darius reports that *pasāva Vivāna hadā kārā nipadiy tyaiy ašiyava* 'afterwards Vivāna with his army went off in pursuit of *them*'.

Both arguments are of course circumstantial evidence, although the second would seem to be decisive.

But a third argument, or rather fact, proves conclusively that the reading *haya-* is not correct.

In his excellent survey of Iranian borrowings, found in the Elamite version of Xerxes' Daiva-inscription, Cameron also listed (from line 39) the Elamite transcription *ia* of the OP pronoun *hya*[55]. This clearly excludes an OP *haya*, and is proof of a monosyllabic *hya* whose *h-* is not written. It is interesting to note that in the 50 lines of the Elamite version there are more than 20 Old Persian forms. Of these, seven have the sequence *ya* or *yā* (*ayauda*, *dahyāva*, *dahyāvam*, *dahyāuš*, *brazmaniya*, *šiyātim*, *hya*), the Elamite transcription shows in all of them the sign *ia*[56].

In these circumstances we must return to the old readings *hya*, *tya*. Their linguistic interpretation has been in essence given by Meillet[57]: the OP pronouns, like the Vedic ones, represent derivatives with the suffix *-ya/-iya-* (and not the relative *ya-*) of the demonstrative *ha-*, *ta-*, the form *-iya-* being no doubt the Sievers-variant after a heavy syllable of the suffix *-ya-*; after the development of *ty* > *θy* > OP *šy*, the pronouns acquired the allegro-variants *hya-*, *tya-*, and Kent is no doubt right in holding that the use of the *a*-signs (*t^{a}y^a*, not *t^{a}iya*) originated with *hya* (and, I would add, the thematic genitive ending *-hyā*), where *h^a*, not *h^{a}i* was the normal spelling for *h-ya*[58].

61-64. OP *vašnā – vazraka – vazra – vasaiy*

The phrase *vašnā Auramazdāha* (or *Auramazdāhā*, in the inscriptions of Xerxes and Artaxerxes I also *Auramazdahā*, in one Xerxes-inscription *Aurahya Mazdāha*) occurs over seventy times, 56 times

[55] Cameron, The "Daiva" Inscription of Xerxes in Elamite (Die Welt des Orients 2, 1959, 470-476), 471.

[56] Cp. also Mayrhofer's list of words with initial OP *ya-* (1973, 58, 88).

[57] Meillet 1915, 76, 170.

[58] See Kent 1953, 186, and cp. 14-15. For the general problems of Sievers' law see now E. Seebold, Das System der indogermanischen Halbvokale, Heidelberg 1972.

in the inscriptions of Darius I, 15 times in those of his son, Xerxes;
the additional examples listed in lexica and presented in text-editions
owe their existence, with one exception (A²Sd), to the restorations
of modern scholars.

There is almost complete unanimity in interpreting the form *vašnā*
as the instrumental singular (masc.?[59]) of a noun **vaš-na-* 'will',
derived from the verb (Av.) *vas-* 'to want, wish', cognate with Ind.
vaš- 'id.'; Hitt. *wekmi* 'ask, demand', Greek ἑκών 'willingly'. Accordingly, the phrase in question is translated 'nach dem Willen
Ahuramazdās', 'par la volonté de ...', 'par la grâce ...', 'by the favour
of AM', 'nach dem Willen, durch die Gunst ...'[60]. This interpretation
was no doubt prompted, and supported, by the Avestan *vasnā* which
occurs three times in the Gāthās (Y. 34, 15c; 46, 19b; 50, 11d) and
three times in the later Avesta (Y. 55, 6; Yt. 19, 11 = 19, 19).
This form is also isolated, it looks like the instrumental singular
of an *a*-stem **vasna-*[61], and this like a derivative of the verbal root
vas-, so that in the end OP *vašnā* and Av. *vasnā* can be regarded
as identical, that is as differing only on account of certain dialectal
differences in phonetic development[62], but proved as identical by
the semantic identity, since *vasnā* is also taken to mean 'in accord
with (my, his, their) will', 'nach seinem Willen'[63].

[59] Since only the form *vašnā*, *vasnā* occurs, it is hard to see how the gender
can be determined as masculine as is done by, e.g., Bartholomae 1904, 1393; Hinz
1942, 144; 1961, 230.

[60] Cp. Bartholomae 1904, 1393; Meillet-Benveniste 1931, 71, 155; Kent 1953, 207,
and 116f. *passim*; Brandenstein-Mayrhofer 1964, 152; Hauri 1973, 2, 54f.

[61] Humbach suggests a different analysis: in his view (1959, I 52fn. 58) *vasnā* is
the locative of an *i*-stem (**vasni-*), meaning 'im Wunsche', and so is *vašnā*! Pisani
(Lingua 11, 1962, 329f.) identifies *vašnā* with ONorse *vegna* 'wegen', and traces both
to IE **weḱnō*, although the latter is usually regarded as a borrowing from MLowGerm
(*van ēnes*) *wegene*, cf. de Vries, Altnordisches etym. Wb., ²1962, 650.

[62] The earlier view was that IE *ḱn* and *ǵ(h)n* both developed into Iranian *šn*,
which, however, could be changed to *sn* under the influence of coexistent forms
with *s* from IE *ḱ*; cf. Bartholomae 1901, 14; WZKM 22, 1908, 73f.; Reichelt 1909, 48f.;
Meillet, MSL 17, 1912, 354f.; 1915, 60; Meillet-Benveniste 1931, 69; Kent 1953, 35;
Brandenstein-Mayrhofer 1964, 39. In more recent times the tendency has been to trace
the different developments to different dialects (e.g. OP *šn*, Av. *sn*), but the lines
of division have become blurred rather than cleared, especially with *zn* (OP *šn*, Avest.
sn, Medic *zn* or *nz*, elsewhere, e.g. Sogd., *zn*?), cf. K. Hoffmann, 1958, 4-5; Benveniste,
JA 246, 1958, 51; Henning, Asia Maior 10, 1963, 198; Gershevitch, TPS 1964, 10¹, 24¹.
For the problem of *zn* etc., see also Duchesne-Guillemin, Western response to
Zoroaster, 1957, 56; Widengren, Die Religionen Irans, 1965, 147f.

[63] Cf. M. Smith 1929, 98, 129, 147; Bartholomae 1905, 46, 81, 103; Hinz 1961,
181, 193, 200, 230; and for the Later Avesta the translations of Wolff and Lommel.

For a long time the only dissentient voice came from W. Hinz, who at first rendered the OP *vašnā* as 'mit dem Schutz, Schirm, Segen' and 'mit dem Segen, unter dem Schirme, dem Schutz, durch die Gunst, die Huld'[64]. Particularly interesting is the reasoning in the 1941 paper: "Bisher glaubte man freilich, *vašnā* mit 'nach dem Willen' übersetzen zu sollen. Trotz der möglichen Ableitung aus idg. *wek-* 'wollen' fasse ich *vašnā* auf als 'mit dem Schutz, Schirm, Segen'. Diese Deutung paßt an allen Stellen besser". But his main reason is, of course, that he wishes to interpret *framānā* and *framātam*, theretofore taken to mean 'command' (cf. NP *farmān, farmūdan*), as 'Plan, Entwurf, Absicht, *Wille*, Ratschluß', and therefore wants to avoid a duplication in *vašnā*. A further reason, though not mentioned, may have been that the Akkadian rendering of the OP phrase is *ina ṣilli ša* ᵈ*urimizda*', i.e. 'im Schatten, im Schutze Ahuramazdas'[65].

But since then Hinz has gradually reverted to the traditional position: 'durch die Gnade Ahuramazdas' (1952, 1965), 'mit dem Willen Ahuramazdas' (1967), 'nach dem Willen Ahuramazdas' (1972) are the only slightly varying renderings, although the last pronouncement (1973) is again somewhat ambivalent: 'nach dem Willen, durch den Segen'[66]. This is all the more surprising as his views of the Elamite version have been increasingly diverging from the accepted interpretation. Whereas other scholars still retain for Elamite *zaumin* ᵈ*uramašdana* the translation 'by the aid of Oromazdes', or even 'par la grâce d'Ahuramazda'[67], Hinz has repeatedly stressed that *zaumin* can be neither 'will' nor 'protection' but means something like 'durch die (schwere) Arbeit (Ahuramazdas)' or 'durch die Mühewaltung (von Gott Ahuramazdā)'[68], without asking himself

---

[64] Hinz, ZDMG 95, 1941, 233f.; 1942, 144. Cf. also ZDMG 96, 1942, 327.

[65] Against the form *ṣellu(m)* see Edzard, ZAss 63/2, 1974, 290 with fn. 12; on *ṣillu(m)* 'Schatten, Schirm, Schutz' see now v. Soden 1101; Chicago Assyrian Dictionary, vol. 16, 1962, 190-192.

[66] Hinz, ZDMG 102, 1952, 37; 115, 1965, 240 (§ 8a); Orientalia 36, 1967, 331; AMI N.F. 5, 1972, 244 line 88, 248 lines 7, 32; 1973, 155.—Eilers, Persica 4, 1969, 10-11, also speaks of the protection, "Schutz", of Ahuramazda (*vašnā* = Akk. *ṣillum*), but he does not discuss the point.

[67] Cf. I. M. Diakonov, Acta Antiqua Hung. 17, 1969, 107; F. Vallat, Revue d'Assyriologie 64, 1970, 151 line 8; Syria 48, 1971, 57 (but ibid. 58 the Akkadian version is rendered with 'par la protection d'Ahuramazda'!). R. T. Hallock, Persepolis Fortification Tablets, 1969, 773: "with the cooperation of AM".

[68] Cf. Hinz, Orientalia 36, 1967, 331-332; AMI N.F. 5, 1972, 244 lines 1-2.— R. Schmitt (Göttingische Gelehrte Anzeigen 226, 1974, 98) accepts Hinz's view in

how this divergence between Old Persian and Elamite is to be accounted for. And yet, in view of the close correspondences between the two versions such a question must be put in any case, and if the Elamite really insists on the notion of 'working (hard)', one is naturally tempted to try to find in *vašnā* a derivative of Iranian *varz-*, which means 'to work' in a very general sense, that is, e.g., **va(r)šnā*, the instrumental singular of a noun **varz-an-*.

Although the cluster *ršn* has been reduced to *šn* in various Iranian dialects (e.g. in Arsacid Pahlavi[69]), and in one case at least even in Avestan (:*pāšna-* 'heel', cf. Skt. *pāršṇi-*)[70], on the whole it remained unchanged at the Old Iranian stage; for Old Persian we have the telling evidence of *baršnā* 'in height' (= Av. *barəšna*). We cannot therefore seriously reckon with the possibility that an early *varšnā had been simplified to *vašnā* in Old Persian by the middle of the first millennium B.C.[71]. Nor need this surprise us, for, according to Mary Boyce's apt remark[72], in such translation correspondences (e.g. MIran. *drōd*: Aram. ŠRM, *šalōm*) the equation of the words operates on account of usage, not meaning!

Even so, the traditional interpretation of *vašnā* remains puzzling. The very fact that the OP term, if it really means 'by the will, by the favour', is something quite different from 'the protection' suggested by the Akkadian, and 'the (heavy) work' of the Elamite, shows that the OP term exhibits so idiosyncratic an aspect of Ahuramazda that no direct equivalent could be found in the other cultural environments. No less idiosyncratic is the use of *vašnā* at DB IV 46:

45   *θātiy Dārayavauš xšāya-*
46 *θiya vašnā Auramazdāha utāmaiy aniyaš</čiy vasiy astiy karta*
47 *m*

"Saith Darius the King: By the favour of Ahuramazdā and of me

the form 'unter der Mitwirkung Ahuramazdās' but does not pronounce on the possible consequences for Old Persian of this interpretation.

[69] Cf. Pahl. *gušn* 'male', *tišn* 'thirst' from Av. *varšni-*, *taršna-*, and see Hübschmann 1895, 261; Horn 1898, 89.

[70] But note that the preceding vowel is long here, see Hübschmann, IFA 6, 1896, 35; Reichelt 1909, 57.

[71] Although the extraordinary frequency of the formula, found no doubt not only in the formal style of documents but also in the living speech, could have contributed to a precocious development.

[72] See M. Boyce, BSOAS 31, 1968, 62 fn. 81.

much else was done"[73]. Here one might say that the awkwardness of the translated passage is Kent's fault, who chose the inappropriate word 'favour'. But even 'will' would suggest the theologically doubtful idea that the will of the supreme god can be coupled with that of the king.

Some twenty years ago I noticed that the inscriptions of Urartu pointed the way out of these difficulties. But before drawing on them, it will be useful briefly to survey the range of applications, in which the Old Persian phrase is found. For the sake of economy *v.AM.* will be used for *vašnā Ahuramazdāha.*

I.   I am/was/became king:

v.AM. adam xšāyaθiya a(h)miy, DB I 11; DPd 4-5; AmH 7; A²Hcl6.

v.AM. adamšām xšāyaθiya āham, DB I 13-4; XPh 14-6.

v.AM. adam xšāyaθiya abavam, DB I 59-60; XPf 34-5.

II.   I hold this kingdom, I seized these countries/men:

v.AM. ima xšaśam dārayāmiy, DB I 26; DPe 6-8; AsH 10.

v.AM. imā dahyāva tyā adam agarbāyam, DNa 16-7; DSe 15-16; DB II 3.

III.   I did; I made, built (palace, colonnade):

ava visam v.AM. akunavam/akumā, DNa 49-50; DB I 68, IV 3-5, 40-41, 59-60; DSa 4-5; DSd 3; DSe 34-5; DSf 20-22; DSi 4; XPb 25-7; XPh 43-5. Cf. DNb 47-9; DB IV 52, 88-9, V 16-7 = 32-3; XPa 16-7; XPf 42-3.

v.AM. ima hadiš akunavam/akunauš, XPd 16-7; XPc 10-11; XPg 2-6 = XV 18-20; XSa 1-2; A²Sd 3.

v.AM. imam duvarθim akunavam, XPa 11-3; cf. XPg 7-8.

v.AM. utāmaiy aniyaščiy vasiy astiy kartam, DB IV 46-7.

IV.   I/my army smote the/that army (exceedingly):

v.AM. kāram adam ajanam (vasiy), DB I 94 = II 68-9; cf. DB IV 6; XPh 33-4.

v.AM. kāra hya manā avam kāram aja (vasiy), DB II 25-6, 35-6, 40-1, 45-6, 54-5, 60-1, 86-7, 97-8; III 6-7, 17-8, 37-9, 45-6, 62-3, 67-8; cf. DB III 87-8.

V.   I strove/placed/destroyed:

adam hamataxšaiy v.AM., DB I 70.

v.AM. adamšim gāθavā niyašādayam, DNa 35-6; DSe 42-5.

v.AM. adam avam daivadānam viyakanam, XPh 36-8.

---

[73] There is no doubt now about the reading of *utāmaiy* (instead of, e.g., Weissbach's *apimaiy*), cf. Kent's note p. 130 ad 46. He is also right (p. 218) in arguing against Benveniste's interpretation of *utā.*

VI. I am of such sort/they lived/we crossed over:

v.AM. avākaram amiy, DNb 6-7.

v.AM. ubā ajīvatam, DSf 12-5.

v.AM. Tigrām viyatarayāmā, DB I 88.

VII. Everything is successful, wonderful:

v.AM.... visam učāram āha, DS1 2-5.

v.AM.... visahyā frašam θadayātaiy, DSj 5-6.

VIII. The countries were/lived by...:

v.AM. manā badakā āhatā, DB I 18.

v.AM. imā dahyāva tyanā manā dātā apariyāya, DB I 22.

IX. The Persian fears nobody:

v.AM. manačā Dārayavahauš xšāyaθiyahyā hačā aniyanā naiy tarsatiy, DPd 9-12.

The royal inscriptions of Urartu [74] present surprising similarities in their phraseology. They can be dated between the late 9th century and the middle of the 7th century B.C. Urartean power stood at its highest around the middle of the 8th century B.C., but in 714 B.C. the defeat inflicted on Urartu by Sargon II of Assyria put an end to its aspirations as a great power, and in the 7th century its rulers tried to live with their Assyrian overlords. Whether the kingdom survived the Assyrian empire which after several decisive victories of the Medes — in 614 Assur was sacked, in 612 Ninive was taken—finally collapsed in 609, is uncertain, but some historians think [75] that Urartu found its end somewhat later, around 600 B.C. But the main point is that the Medes had been in close contact with them for over a century by then.

In comparing the Urartean inscriptions, it will again be useful to distinguish certain groups on the basis of the semantics of the expression [76].

I. For the statement:

"By the grace of god X, Y is a great king",

---

[74] On Assyria, Urartu, and the Medes, see, e.g., R. Labat's survey in: Fischer Weltgeschichte IV, 1967, 9-111, on Urartu esp. 44f. Note also the chronological table at p. 111.

[75] Cp., e.g., B.B. Piotrovskij, Il regno di Van-Urartu, Roma 1966, 170.

[76] The inscriptions are quoted from G.A. Melikišvili, Urartskije klinoobraznyje nadpisi (= UKN), Moscow 1960, by page, number, and line-number. For the language see J. Friedrich, Urartäisch, in: Altkleinasiatische Sprachen (Handbuch der Orientalistik I/II/I-II/2, Leiden 1969) 31-53; G.A. Melikišvili, Die urartäische Sprache, Rome 1971. On the style of the Urartean inscriptions see Melikišvili, UKN 93f., esp. 106f.

the following sentence-type is frequently found [77]:

[d]Haldinini alsuišini [l]Menuani LUGAL *DAN.NU* LUGAL *alsuini*
LUGAL [KUR]*Biainae alusi* [URU]*Tušpa* URU

"Through the greatness of (god) Haldi, Menua (is) a mighty king, a great king, king of Biaina, governor of Tušpa-City".

[d]Haldinini ušmašini [l]Išpuinini [ld]Sardurihi LUGAL *DAN.NU* LUGAL
alsuini LUGAL [KUR]*Biainaue alusi* [URU]*Tušpa* URU

"through the might of (god) Haldi, Išpuini, son of Sarduri, (is) a mighty king, a great king, king of Biaina, governor of Tušpa-City".

II. The statement "X says" also frequently occurs with the same kind of phraseology [78]:

[d]Haldinini alsuišini [l]Argištiše ale

"through the greatness of (god) Haldi, Argišti saith".

[d]Haldinini ušmašini [l]Rusaše
[ld]Sardurihiniše ale

"through the might of (god) Haldi, Rusa, son of Sarduri saith".

III. For "X did, made, built" the same types of expression are used [79]:

[d]Haldinini ušmašini [d]Haldie eurie [l]Menuaše
[l]Išpuinihiniše ini susi šidištuni

"through the might of (god) Haldi, Menua, son of Išpuini, built Haldi, (his) master, this *susi*".

[d]Haldinini alsuišini [l]Menuaše [l]Išpuinihiniše
ini É.GAL *zaduni*

"through the greatness of (god) Haldi, Menua, son of Išpuini, built this palace".

[d]Haldinini alsuišini [ld]Sarduriše [l]Argištihiniše
ini [GIŠ]GEŠTIN *teruni*

"through the greatness of (god) Haldi, Sarduri, son of Argišti, placed (planted) this vineyard".

[d]Haldinini ušmašini [l]Menuaše [l]Išpuinihiniše
ini pili aguni

---

[77] Cf. Melikišvili, UKN 152, no. 29, lines 13-5; 142, 25, 2-3.

[78] See Melikišvili, UKN 222, 127, Col. IV, 21-24; 329, 266, 1-2. Cf. also UKN 123, 18, 1-2; 215, 127, Col. II, 37-8. Note that according to Herzfeld (AMI 2, 1930, 120) the phrase "Saith King NN" in Babylonia is from Urartu! Cf. also Kutscher, Current Trends in Linguistics 6, 1970, 391.

[79] Melikišvili, UKN 185, 73, 1-3; 152, 29, 1-3; 313, 167, 1-3; 168, 43, 1-3; 122, 17, 1.

"through the might of (god) Haldi, Menua, son of Išpuini, laid (excavated) this canal".

ᵈHaldinini ušgini ¹Išpuiniš
É ini šidišituni

"through the power of (god) Haldi, Išpuini built this house".

IV. "On account of Haldi's might, Rusa did not fear the battle":

¹Rusani ... ᵈHaldinini ušmašini ... ui
gunuše dirasiabi[80]

V. "By Haldi's might X took the field":

ᵈHaldinini ušmašini uštali ¹Išpuini
ᴵᵈSardurihi ¹Menuani ¹Išpuinihi[81]

These examples will suffice to show that in most turns in which the OP texts have *v.AM.*, the Urartean texts have one of the expressions *Haldinini alsuišini, H. ušmašini, H. ušgini*; the ablatives *alsuišini, ušmašini* are from the abstract nouns *alsuiše, ušmaše*, which are formed with the suffix -*še*- from the adjectives **alsui*- 'great', **ušma*- 'powerful', of which the former is attested in *alsui-(ni-)* 'great'; the internal relations of *ušgi* 'power' are not so clear but it may be connected with *ušmaše*. For our purposes it is important to note that where the OP text is supposed to speak of the will of Ahuramazda, the Urartean refers to "Haldi's greatness, might, or power"[82]. Expressions of this kind, e.g. *ina emuq ᵈAššur* 'by the might of (god) Assur', *ina tukulti ᵈAššur* 'by the aid of Assur', *ina qibît ᵈAššur* 'by the command of Assur', are not alien to the Assyrian and Babylonian inscriptions either; but the frequent repetition of such phrases seems an Urartean peculiarity.

It will have become clear by now that OP *vašnā* is not to be interpreted as 'by the will' but as 'by, through the greatness'.

---

[80] Melikišvili, UKN 324, 264, 24-27.

[81] Melikišvili, UKN 137, 23, 2-3; very frequent, cf. 153, 30, 5f.; 161, 39, 6, etc.

[82] It is interesting that, following in the footsteps of V.V. Struve, I.M. Diakonov has also pointed out (W.B. Henning Memorial Volume, 1970, 121) that 'Saith NN the king' has a parallel in Urartean inscriptions, although he ignores the important fact that, in Urartean, the formula is: "Through the greatness/might of Haldi, NN the king saith". And when Diakonov says that the Achaemenian phrase "by the aid (or: will, approval) of Oromazdes" has an Urartean prototype, he again fails to draw the necessary conclusions from the most interesting part of this information, i.e. that the Urartean has none of the expressions mentioned (: aid, will, etc.) but invariably employs the expressions "by the greatness/might/power of Haldi". My aim, on the other hand, is precisely to show how the Urartean formulae can be used to obtain a clearer insight into the OP expression.

It is, therefore, without doubt to be connected with the adjective *vazraka-* 'great', and may conceivably represent the instrumental singular of a heteroclitic neuter abstract noun *vazar, *vaznah 'greatness'. In the oblique stem-form *vazn-* we find the same development to *vašn-* as in OP *baršnā* from *barz-n-ā, identical with Av. *barəšna*, and in Avestan in *rašnā* (whether this be the instr. sg. of *razan-* 'law'[83] or of *rašnā* 'straightness'[84]) and in *rāšnąm* from *rāzar/rāzn-* 'order'[85].

At first sight it would seem that *vazraka-* is the expanded form (with the suffix *-ka-*) of an original adjective **vazra-*, formed from the nil-grade of *vazar with simple thematization: **vazr-a-*. Unfortunately, the reading of what has above been transcribed as *vazraka-* (v z r k) is by no means certain. In fact, the overwhelming majority of scholars has since the end of the last century maintained that the OP adjective was to be read as *vazr̥ka-*[86]. The main reason for this decision has been the *u* in the second syllable of Pahlavi *wazurg*, MPeT *wazurg*, NP *buzurg*, supported by Arm. *vzowrk* (which points to *wuzurk), which seemed most easily reconciled with an old syllabic *r̥*[87]. Oddly enough, the fact that this interpretation is phonetically possible, made scholars overlook the much more important problem, i.e. whether the morphological structure of the assumed form is possible. As far as I can see, there are no satisfactory parallels either in Iranian or in Indian of such a formation. In the Avesta, there is not a single example of a noun or an adjective in *-r̥-ka-*[88] (*-əraka-*), for *vəhrka-* 'wolf' is, of course, IE **wl̥kʷ-o-*, not **wl̥-ko-*, and in the other words in *-ka-* also *-k-* is part of the root (e.g. *harək-a-*). On the Indian side, the Rigveda only presents *vr̥ka-* 'wolf', which we have just discussed, and *sr̥ka-*

[83] This view is held by Bartholomae 1904, 1514; 1905, 76; Andreas-Lommel 105-6; Hinz 1961, 191, 229.

[84] This is Humbach's interpretation (1959, I 129, II 69).

[85] For this see Bartholomae 1904, 1526; 1905, 45; Humbach 1959, I 108, II 46.

[86] Cf. Hübschmann KZ 27, 1885, 111; 1895, 29; Bartholomae 1904, 1390; 1925, 61; Meillet 1915, 5, 48, 60; Meillet-Benveniste 1931, 8, 13, 53, 68, 85; Nyberg 1931, 237; Monde Oriental 31, 1937, 63[2]; 1974, 207; Henning 1958, 67; Gershevitch, TPS 1964, 12[4]; Brandenstein-Mayrhofer 1964, 153; Mayrhofer 1968, 10[42]; Hinz 1973, 156; Watkins 1973, 200; Hauri 1973, 20[19].—Some scholars prefer a form **vazarka-*, cf. Tolman 1908, 124; Bailey, TPS 1954, 136.

[87] See Hübschmann 1895, 146 (: *r̥* after *t, z, š* went to *ur*), and especially Batholomae 1925, 48 f., 61.

[88] Cf. Bartholomae 1904, 1894.

'arrow, speer' (or just 'sharp point'?) which again represents *sṛk-a-*[89]. In the later language there is a small number of words in *-ṛ-ka-* (e.g. *mātṛka-* 'maternal; maternal uncle'; *paitṛka-* 'belonging to a father, paternal, ancestral'; *hautṛka-* 'belonging to a hotar'), but they make their first appearance in Manu, the Mahābhārata, and Rāmāyaṇa, that is in the last centuries before our era. It is also significant that the compositional *-ka-* is first added to *-ṛ-* in the Sūtras (e.g. *jīva-pitṛ-ka-* 'whose father is alive'), whereas the earlier writings still have forms without it (e.g. RV *sapta-svasṛ-* 'who has seven sisters', AV *hata-mātṛ-* 'whose mother has been slain')[90]. We must therefore conclude that, although in theory there is nothing against expansions in *ṛ-ka* (cf. *-i-ka-*, *-u-ka-*), in actual fact they are not formed until a very late date even in India.

A further point to note is that *-ka-* forms diminutives from nouns (: Av. *mašyāka-* 'homuncio') or adjectives from adjectives (: Av. *apərənāyu-ka-* 'minor'), but not adjectives from nouns. The adjective v z r k demands an adjective as its starting point, and not a noun **vazṛ*.

It was no doubt, partly at least, for this reason that several scholars decided that the OP adjective was to be read as *vazraka-*, a derivative of an earlier adjective **vazra-*[91]. Henning thought that the reading *vazra-* was safely established by the Turfan superlative *vazišt* 'greatest' (cf. *šōž vazurg* 'großer Heiliger': *šōžān vazišt* 'der Heiligen größter', and the adverb *vazištīhā* 'in sehr großer Weise' = 'in umfassendster Weise'), since the gradation was of the same type as that seen in Av. *srīra-* 'beautiful': *sraēšta-*, and Ind. *sthūra-* 'thick': *sthaviṣṭha-*. This *vazraka-* developed, by labial umlaut, into *vuzraγ* (Turfan *wzrg*) which was then assimilated to *vuzruγ* (seen in Arm. *vzrowk*), and by metathesis to *vuzurg* (Pahl. *wčwrg*), the source of NP *buzurg*[92]. Benveniste opted for **vazra-* because he thought that its basis was an *r*-noun **vazar*: the relation was the same as between

[89] H.P. Schmidt, KZ 78, 1963, 16¹, 299; Mayrhofer III 497.

[90] Cf. Wackernagel-Debrunner 1954, 526, 538; Wackernagel 1905, 103.

[91] Among the first to argue for this form were Fr. Müller (WZKM 11, 1897, 200f.) and W. Foy (see KZ 35, 1899, 25), who however later (KZ 37, 1904, 537) changed his view, and under the influence of Τανυοξάρκης, interpreted as *Tanu-vazarka-*, opted for *vazarka*. It is interesting to note that the same name is interpreted by Benveniste (1966, 94) as reflecting *vazraka*.

[92] See Henning, NGGW 1932, 224 with fn. 8, and for the texts E. Waldschmidt-W. Lentz, Die Stellung Jesu im Manichäismus, Berlin 1926, 39.

Av. *ugra-* 'strong' and *aogar-* 'strength'[93]; one would of course, in strict parallelism, expect a form **uzra-* but **vazra,* could be restored after the base-noun.

There can be little doubt that *vazraka-* could be umlauted to **vuzrak,* and this assimilated to **vuzruk:* the first step is clearly demonstrated by the development of old *vazra-* 'club' to later *burz* and *gurz.* The form corresponding to *burz* (i.e. *va-* > *ba-* > *bu-*?) would be *buzurg,* while the form corresponding to *gurz* (i.e. the development *va-* > *vu-* > *gu-*?) would be present in Pāzend *guzurg* and the modern dialect forms which have been collected by Gershevitch: Kermani, Baškardi *gohort,* Farizandi *gōrd* etc.[94]. More difficult would be to explain why a form **vuzrak* or **vuzruk* should have been changed to *vuzurg.* But the gravest difficulty, in fact the fatal objection to the whole explanation, lies in the cluster assumed: if the original form had the group *-zr-,* then the final result should have been the metathetized **burzag* as is clearly shown by *gurz* 'club'. The cluster *zr* is one of the many internal *r*-groups, with *r* as second element, which suffered transposition; cf. the change of *xr, fr. sr, zr, mr* to *rx (lx), rf, rs, rz, rm* in, e.g., *surx, Balx, barf, ars, gurz, narm*[95].

If, then, neither **vazr̥ka-* (or **vazarka-*) nor *vazraka-* are admissible, we are driven to the conclusion that the OP adjective was *vazaraka-.* As far as I can see, Andreas has been the only scholar to draw this conclusion, and no doubt for the same, though unstated, reasons: he suggested (in his peculiar system of vocalization) that the OP adjective (borrowed from Medic) was *vozoroko,* an adjective of appurtenance from **vozor;* this form gave *vuzuruγ,* which was later syncopated to *vuzruγ* (seen in Arm. *vzrowk*), and then metathetized to *vuzurg*[96]. We must rather assume that *vazaraka* became by labial umlaut **vuzaraka,* and later by assimilation **wuzuruk* which was then syncopated to **vuzurk, vuzurg.* This directly accounts for NP *buzurg,* while Arm. *vzrowk* represents an Armenian metathesis

[93] Benveniste, Origines de la formation des noms en indo-européen, 1935, 15; 1966, 94; 1969, II 21. Further advocates of *vazraka-* are: Kent 1953, 207; Liebert, Orientalia Suecana 11, 1962, 153f.; Eilers, Persica 4, 1969, 29 fn. 76.

[94] Gershevitch, TPS 1964, 12[4]. But it is not perhaps necessary to trace these forms to an OP variant *vadr̥ta-* beside *vazr̥ka-:* assimilation of *d-k* to *d-t,* or influence of adjectives in *-ta-* may account for the change.

[95] Cf. Hübschmann 1895, 266. Against **vazraka-* speaks also Sogd. *wz'rk.*

[96] Andreas ap. Lentz, ZII 4, 1926, 284.

from the likewise attested *vzowrk*. An early Iranian syncope is also seen in NP *dāng*, 'sixth of a dram' in Pahlavi, 'sixth of a dīnār' in the Talmud[97]. The original form of the word had long been known from the δανάκη of post-classical Greek authors (e.g. Callimachus)[98] when Cameron happily recognized it in Elamite *danakas* 'one eighth (of a shekel)'[99]. The early date of the syncope is shown by the borrowed forms, e.g. Arm. *dang*[100]. The syncopated *dāng* and *vuzurg* mutually support each other.

It is now time to turn to the problem of origin. There is long-standing agreement that *vaz-* in *vazaraka-*, and in that case, as we now know, also in *vašnā*, has a close cognate in Av. *vazārət-* which is interpreted as 'mit Energie, Kraft, Macht sich aufmachend', i.e. consisting of **vaza-* and a compositional second element formed from ^1ar- 'move, set out', **vaza-* + **r̥t-*[101]. The *ā*, which was a stumbling block to Bartholomae, was correctly explained by Andreas as reflecting the use of *alif* as an indicator of a new word, of juncture, i.e. **vaza-'r̥t-*[102]. The trouble is that this interpretation is by no means safely established. The form *vazārətō* is a *hapax* but since it occurs with four other words exhibiting the same formation, it will be useful to look at the only passage (Yt. 13, 23) where they all occur. "We worship the Fravašis", says the text,

yā̊	ašbərətō	yā̊	uγrārətō
yā̊	hvārətō	yā̊	vazārətō
yā̊	taxmārətō	yā̊	zaoyārətō.

[97] See B. Geiger, Jackson Memorial Volume, 1954, 74-5; and cf. M. Shaki, ArOr 39, 1971, 223.

[98] See Schwyzer, IF 49, 1931, 22; Frisk I 347, III 68; Chantraine I 251.

[99] Cf. Cameron, Persepolis Treasury Tablets, Chicago 1948, 132; Gershevitch, AM 2, 1951, 134; Eilers, WdO 2, 1957, 332f.; Bailey, Khotanese Texts IV, 1961, 10²; Gershevitch, JNES 24, 1965, 184; Belardi, Studia A. Pagliaro oblata I, 1969, 203.

[100] Hübschmann 1897, 134.—Henning thought (BSOAS 18, 1956, 367) that a further example of early syncope was found in Bactrian ΒΑΓΟΛΑΓΓΟ from *baga-dānaka but Morgenstierne (BSOAS 33, 1970, 126¹⁴) thinks that only *-dāna-* need be assumed. See also Henning, ZDMG 115, 1965, 83-84.

[101] Cf. Bartholomae 1904, 1390 and 192; Duchesne-Guillemin 1936, 80 (but 's'ouvrant' is a misunderstanding of 'aufmachen'); Bailey, TPS 1954, 136; Eilers, Añjali-Wijesekera Felicitation Volume, Ceylon 1970, 117; Watkins 1973, 200.—An earlier interpretation is presented by K. Geldner, Über die Metrik des Jüngeren Avesta, Tübingen 1877, 75: "welche rüstigen Ganges, welche ihre eignen Wege gehend, *welche kräftigen* Ganges, welche gewaltigen Ganges, welche raschen Ganges".

[102] Bartholomae 1904, 192; Andreas-Wackernagel 1911, 12-13; Duchesne-Guillemin 1936, 80.

Bartholomae's interpretation of the various terms, accepted by Duchesne-Guillemin (l.c.), can be summed up in Wolff's translation (p. 232): "(Die Fravašis),

   die viel bringen, die sich kräftig aufmachen,

   die sich gut aufmachen, die sich tatkräftig aufmachen,

   die sich kühn aufmachen, die sich auf den Ruf hin aufmachen".

One cannot say that these interpretations are compelling—in spite of the fact that they are (for want of anything better?) taken over and repeated time and again. Yet, Lommel seems to be the only one to have tried a different tack. Rather diffidently, to be sure, he suggested that the second part of the compounds might be *arta-* 'truth', so that the passage would mean: "die starke Wahrheit, eigne(?) Wahrheit haben, *die Wahrheit fördern*, schnelle Wahrheit, anrufende Wahrheit haben" [103]. This would at once remove *vazārət-* from our sphere, but of course the interpretation is none too persuasive, and *artō* as a nom. pl. is rather difficult. For that very reason it is worth recalling the observation that Vedic does not have an agent-noun formation from *r̥-* 'to move' [104]. That suggests that we should take *art-* as a unit, and then perhaps the compounds would contain **art-* 'attack, battle', which appears as *ardīg* 'battle' in the Šāpur-inscription, in Pahlavi, and in the Turfan texts, and is perhaps developed from Av. *ərəti-* 'energy' (? but cf. Ind. *r̥ti-* 'attack') [105]. The resultant bahuvrīhis with 'attack, battle' as their second component would certainly suit the adjectives *ugra-* 'strong' and *taxma-* 'strong, swift' much better than 'going' or 'setting out'. But before concluding this discussion, one final comment: of the five adjectives, three have an adjective as their first member (*ugra-*, *taxma*, and *hu-* or *hva-*?), while the other two show first components otherwise unknown. But this observation shows that the traditional connexion or even identification of *vaza-* as a noun with Ind. *vāja-* (s. fn. 104) cannot be regarded as very likely: if anything, **vaza-* is an adjective, not a noun.

Another adjective, which has been connected with our group, is Av. *vāzišta-*. It occurs six times all told, once with 'name'

---

[103] Lommel, ZII 5, 1927, 86; 1927, 114³.

[104] Wackernagel-Debrunner 1954, 43 top, where *vazārət-* is said to be identical with Ind. **vāja-rt-*.

[105] See Henning, BSOS 9, 1939, 834; and for the Turfan texts most recently W. Sundermann, Mittelpersische und parthische kosmogonische und Parabeltexte der Manichäer, Berlin 1973, 116 B.—For the not undisputed relations of these words

(Y. 36,3), three times with 'guest, companion' (Y. 13,2; 31,22; 70,4), and twice with 'fire' (Y. 17,11; Vid. 19,40). No doubt on account of the perfect formal match, Bartholomae (1904, 1417-8) identified it with RV *vāhiṣṭha-*, and interpreted it as "der am besten vorwärts bringt, der förderlichste, nützlichste". But one cannot feel quite certain that these translation-equivalents really suit the Avesta-passages—it is probably no mere coincidence that Bartholomae gives a translation for 'name' only—and Andreas, doubtless relying on the newly found Turfan *vazišt*, did not hesitate to pronounce that (at Y. 31,22) *vāzišta* certainly did not belong with Ind. *vāh-* but either with *vazrka-* or Ind. *vāja-* 'Energie'; thus for him *tōi vāzištō astiš* is 'dein *mächtigster* Genosse'[106]. Hinz takes the identification of *astiš* with Ind. *atithi-* 'guest' seriously, and therefore guesses from the context that *vāzištō astiš* is 'willkommenster Gast'[107]. More persuasive is Humbach's interpretation 'dein am besten gelabter Gast', partly because it retains the connection with Ind. *vāja-* 'strength', *upa-vājayati* 'kindle, fan', Av. *ātrǝ.vazana-* 'Feuerwedel, bellows', partly because it also offers a new, and more satisfying, solution to a further problem. The line (Y. 44,7c)

kə̄ uzəmə̄m čōrəṯ vyānayā puθrəm piθrē,

rendered by Bartholomae as: "Wer machte mit Weisheit den Sohn ehrerbietig gegen den Vater", and, in essence, accepted by most other scholars, including Andreas[108], is interpreted by Humbach quite differently: "Wer schafft durch seine Fähigkeit dem Vater einen *tüchtigen* Sohn?". The, for us, crucial word *uzəma-* is not taken by him from a root *auz-* 'honour', because the verbal form *uzəmōhī*, a hapax (Y. 46,9), is also interpreted differently; *uzəma-*

---

see H.W. Bailey, R̥gveda *art-*, Annals of the Bhandarkar Or. Research Institute 48-49, 1968, 71-73 (who does not discuss our words), and I. Kühn, MSS 28, 1970, 89-104.

[106] Andreas-Wackernagel 1911, 32 and 29.—B. Geiger, Die Aməša Spəntas, Wien 1916, 193 fn. also denied that *vāzišta* (referring to 'fire') could have anything to do with *vāhiṣṭha-*, and suggested rather that it was to be connected with Agni's epitheton *vājin (tama)-*.

[107] Hinz 1961, 174.—Bartholomae also adopted this etymon (1904, 213), but still retained 'der nützlichste Geselle' (e.g. 1905, 24), echoed by the 'most helpful comrade' of M. Smith 1929, 81.—In Nyberg's view (1938, 458 ad 206), *vāzišta* meant 'auf das heftigste dahinfahrend', and so 'feurigst'. Cf. Henning, ZDMG 115, 1965, 83-84.

[108] Cp. Bartholomae 1905, 60; Smith 1929, 109; Duchesne-Guillemin 1948, 206; Hinz 1961, 185; Andreas-Lommel 1934, 81.

is possibly the positive to the superlative *vāzišta*, and may also be present in the proper name *Usmānara-* (i.e. 'tüchtige Männer habend'?)[109]. On the whole, Humbach's interpretations seem attractive, although I should prefer for *vāzišta* and *uzma-* something nearer to *vazaraka-*, e.g. 'great' or 'grand'.

This survey clearly shows that the two Avesta words compared with *vazaraka-*, that is *vazarət-* and *vāzišta-*, cannot be regarded as safely established. On the other hand, firm ground is once again under our feet when we turn to the Turfan superlative *vazišt* 'greatest'. There can be no doubt that this is closely connected with OP *vazaraka-*.

Outside Iranian, Vedic *vāja-* 'vigour, speed; contest, prize', *vājayati* 'drive, urge', etc., are compared, to which are added from other areas of the IE world: Lat. *vegēre* 'quicken, arouse', *vigēre* 'be lively, active', and the adjectives *vegetus* 'lively', *vigil* 'awake'; Goth. *us-wakjan* 'wake up' (Germ. *wecken*), and the Germanic adjective **wakra-* 'awake, aroused; vigorous' in OE *wacor*, ONorse *vakr*, OHG *wackar* 'wacker'[110]. New material has been brought to bear by Toporov who suggests that ORuss. *vaznь* "sčast'e, udača; doblest', otvaga" ('luck, success; prowess, courage, bravery'), and the derivative *vaznivyj* 'lucky', so far unexplained, can be from a heteroclitic noun seen in *vazarka-* from *vaz-ar-* or *vaz-ra-*, to which *vaznь* brings the *n*-stem; the basic meaning of *vaz-* was 'be strong', as is shown by *vāja-*; *vajra-* 'mace'; *vegēre*, etc.[111]. Although Toporov does not discuss the vocalism, it is clear that a simple juxtaposition of *vazar-ka-: vaz-n-* is impossible: the Russian words would have to have *a* from IE *ō*, i.e. we would have to do with an unusual pattern *weǵ-r: wōǵ-n-*; all the same, the comparison remains attractive.

A word perhaps about the formation of *vazara-(ka-)*. As we have hinted already, **vaza-*, if to be acknowledged at all, would be an adjective rather than a substantive, i.e. 'strong, big'. The expansion by the suffix *-ra-* is known from several examples in both Iranian

---

[109] See Humbach 1959, I 94, II 31; for Y. 44,7, I 118, II 55; and for Y. 46,9, II 70-71.

[110] See Pokorny 1117-8; Mayrhofer III 182; and the attractive paper by Watkins (1973, 195-201), especially the morphologically pleasing derivation of *vegeō* from **wogeyō*.

[111] Toporov, in: Etimologija 1972, Moscow 1974, 18.—A further interesting suggestion is (19 fn. 68) that Lat. *vagārī* may also belong with this group, its meaning having developed *via* 'spread'.

[112] See Benveniste, Asiatica-Festschrift F. Weller, 1954, 33-4.

and Indian. Avestan *bāzura-* '(upper) arm' is form *bāzu-* [112]; *daxšāra-* 'sign' is from an earlier **daxša-*; *javara-* (Y. 48,8), if 'Förderer', is no doubt from *java-*, cf. *java* 'hurry' [113]; *ahura-* is expanded from **ahu-* [114]. On the Indian side we find formations like *dravara-* 'running', *patara-* 'flying', *bhramara-* 'bee', which are expanded from *drava-*, *pata-*, *bhrama-* ('wandering'!); their *-ra-* may be from IE *-lo-* [115], but also from *-ro-*. An Old Iranian **vazara-* may thus imply an earlier **vaza-* 'grown up, strong, big'.

So far we have refrained from introducing Avestan *vazra-* 'mace, club' which has its exact correspondence in Vedic *vajra-*. Almost all scholars think that this—exclusively—Aryan word is closely connected with our *vaz-* 'great' or 'strong', only Bartholomae was decided enough to state that the comparison was neither phonetically nor semantically acceptable [116]. It is hard to see what difficulties the equation would present from the point of view of phonetics, but from the viewpoint of semantics the difficulties are truly overwhelming. The assumption that 'mace, club' derives from an adjective which originally meant 'provided with reproductive power', and later developed the sense 'bull-phallus', 'club or another weapon' [117], is truly staggering, and the statement that a meaning 'mit zeugender Kraft versehen' fits OP *vazraka-* in all its occurrences is simply untrue: as can be seen from the Elamite and Akkadian versions, and the Urartean 'prototypes', *vazaraka-* had in Achaemenid times no other sense but 'great, big' [118].

From W.W. Malandra's study entitled "A glossary of terms for weapons and armor in Old Iranian" [119] it has become clear that, for 'mace', Old Iranian had two expressions: *vazra-* and *vadar-* (l.c., 281-3 and 277-281). It is therefore pertinent to ask whether

[113] See Humbach 1959, II 78, in contrast to Bartholomae 1904, 605. But note that according to K. Hoffmann (Studi A. Pagliaro III, 1969, 17-20) *java* does not exist, it is to be read *jasa*.

[114] Schlerath, Festschrift Kuiper, 1969, 142f., argues for *ah-ura-*, but there can be no doubt about the segmentation *ahu-ra-*.

[115] This is favoured by Wackernagel-Debrunner 1954, 215f.; cf. also 849.—R. Schmitt (BzN N.F. 7, 1972, 341; cf. Hinz, ibid. 9, 1974, 260) sees in *Asara* a correspondence to Ind. *aśva-la-*.

[116] Bartholomae 1904, 1390.—Among those in favour of the connexion, I should mention in more recent times Kent 1953, 207; Bailey, TPS 1954, 136; Mayrhofer Sprache 5, 1959, 86 fn. 43; Eilers, Persica 4, 1969, 29 with fnn. 76, 78.—Against the connexion seem to be Benveniste 1969, II 22; Mayrhofer III 182.

[117] Liebert, Orientalia Suecana 11, 1962, 130, 145, 153.

[118] This is also emphasized by Eilers, Persica 4, 1969, 10[24].

[119] See Malandra, IIJ 15, 1973, 264-289.

the two expressions are independent or connected. In view of the
phonetic similarity a connexion would seem to be *a priori* probable.

According to Bartholomae's law, the original sequence *dh-s-* developed into Aryan *dzh*, and this gave Iranian *z* [120]. A well-known example
of this development is NP *hēzum* 'fuel', which represents **aizma-*,
original **aidh-s-ma-*, from the Aryan root **aidh-* 'kindle'. Accordingly
an Aryan **wadh-s-ra-* had to develop into *vaz-ra-*.

But the early development—in the Aryan community—was slightly
different. The combined evidence of Indian and Iranian shows that
the new sequence *zh* developed into *ž*. This is particularly clear in
Iranian [121]. There the original sequences *bhs, ghs, ǵhs* developed into
bzh, gzh, žzh, and later *bž, gž, ž* (simplified from *žž*); cp. Av.
diwžaidyāi 'to cheat' from **dibh-s-*, *vawžakāiš* 'with spiders' from
*wabž-, early **wabh-s-*, *dafšnyā* 'those cheated' from **dawšnya-*
(unvoiced because of *n*), early **dabž-na-*, original **dhabh-s-na-*; *aoyžā*
'you said, commanded' from **augh-sa*; *uz-važaṭ* 'brought out' from
*važž-, **važzh-*, IE **weǵh-s-*. In Indian, the voiced *z* and *ž* were
eliminated, either by loss (before a voiced consonant) or by loss of
voice (after a voiced consonant). The latter development is quite
clear in Vedic *vakṣat*, corresponding to Av. *-važaṭ*, and representing
IE **weǵh-s-et*; *dakṣi* 'burn' from **dagži*, earlier **dhagzhi*, **dhagh-si*;
Vedic *jakṣat* 'laughing' from **jagž-at*, **jhagh-s-* In *bž*, from *bhs*,
the original sibilant was later restored so that the final result is *ps*
(cf. AV *psā-* from *bhs-*, and RV *-psu-* from *bhs-*), and the same
is true of original *dhs*, cp. *gṛtsa-* 'dexterous, clever' [122]. But the
earlier development was no doubt *bž*, and even *dž*, and the latter
accounts for the fact that the Indian form corresponding to Iranian
vazra- is *vajra-*: it represents **vadž-ra-* which regularly developed
from Aryan **wadh-s-ra-*; the basic word is present in Vedic *vadhar*
'a destructive weapon, esp. the thunderbolt of Indra'. The Aryan
*wadh-s-ra- is of the same build as **aidh-s-ma-* : they are either developed
from an *s*-stem (with the suffix in the nil-grade *-s-*, cf. *uṣas* from
*uṣ-s-as) or are formed with a suffix *-sma-*, *-sra-*. The interesting
thing is that in both branches of Aryan the final development from

---

[120] Cf., for the general problem, Szemerényi 1970, 95-6, 136; P. Kiparsky, Historical
Linguistics (in: Survey of linguistic science, ed. Dingwall, 1972), 627-8; Szemerényi
1972, 146-7. For Iranian, see Bartholomae 1901, 17.

[121] See Bartholomae 1901, 17, 21.

[122] Cf. Wackernagel-Debrunner I, 1957, 131, 239-242; Nachträge 72, 133-135;
Thumb-Hauschild I 1, 300, 310f.

the original consonant cluster collapsed with a sibilant/affricate, which had been lately acquired by the language concerned.

One last point. Among the phrases employing the expression *vašnā Ahuramazdāha* we find fairly frequently the statement "I/my army smote the army exceedingly'—*v.AM. kāram adam ajanam vasiy* (s. type IV above). The "adverb" *vasiy* is also read *vasaiy*, and in either case is, like *vašnā*, usually derived from the verbal root *vas-* 'want, wish' [123]. This derivation is, however, rather unsatisfactory: there are no parallels for 'much, many' being derived from 'want, will', not even from 'according to wish'. Since our discussion has been mainly concerned with the semantic field of 'great, big, mighty', it is reasonable to ask whether 'mighty, mightily; much' does not also belong to it. An encouraging parallel is provided by Latin *validus* 'strong'—*valdē*. The OP *vasaiy* could represent the locative of **vasa-* from **vassa-*, IE **weǵ-sǩo-*; the development would of course be the same as for Kent's **wek-sk-oi*. For the suffix we may refer to ONorse *vaskr* 'munter, flink' from Gmc. **wak-ska-*, IE **woǵ-sǩ-o-*.

To sum up. OP *vašnā Auramazdāha*, hitherto generally taken to mean 'by the will/favour of Ahuramazdā', is shown by the Near Eastern parallels to signify 'by/through the greatness/might of Ahuramazdā'. In consequence, *vašnā* can no longer be derived from *vas-* 'to want, wish' but must be connected with the adjective meaning 'great, big', which so far has been variously read as *vazarka*, *vazrka*, or *vazraka*. It can be shown that none of these forms satisfies the requirements of diachronic phonology and/or morphology, they must be replaced by *vazaraka*, which is expanded from **vazara-*, and this, in its turn, from a basic adjective **vaza-*. OP *vazaraka* seems to have been a defective adjective, confined to the positive; it was in suppletion with the superlative *maθišta* 'greatest', just as Pahlavi *vazurg* formed a suppletive system with *mēh* and *mahist*; but that this cannot have been the whole truth, was shown by the emergence of the Turfan superlative *vazišt-* whatever the niceties of the distribution were [124]. OP **vaza-* and, *via* a heteroclitic **vaz-ar/*vaz-n-*, OP *vašnā*, are both the Iranian representatives of a widely attested IE root **weǵ-* which starting from a basic meaning

---

[123] See Bartholomae 1904, 1384; Kent 1953, 35(**weǩ-sǩoi*), 207 (loc. of root-noun **vas-?*); Brandenstein-Mayrhofer 1964, 152.

[124] Cf. Hauri 1973, 23; and, for Pahlavi, Nyberg 1974, 207.

'grow, be strong' developed the sense 'strong, great', cf. Lithu. *stóras* 'thick', ONorse *stórr* 'strong, great, big'. The same root further supplied OP *vasaiy*, the locative of **vasa-*, (IE) **woǵ-sk̑-o-*, cf. English dialectal *store, stoore* 'sehr, viel', from OE *stór* 'great, strong, violent' [125].

On the other hand, Iran. *vazra-* and Ind. *vajra-* 'mace, club', often combined with *vazaraka*, have nothing to do with this group, they are closely connected with Aryan **wadhar*, and represent the regular developments of a derivative **wadh-s-ra-*.

One last remark about *vasnā*. This form, actually attested in the Avesta, could still be from *vas-* 'will', that is different from OP *vašnā*. On the other hand, since the Avesta always shows *vasnā* in combination with *frašəm*, *fərašō.təməm* '(most) wonderful', Avestan specialists will have to decide whether it is not more appropriate to regard Avestan *vasnā* as identical with OP *vašnā*. But an isolated remnant of a noun **vasna-* 'will' [126] seems, nevertheless, to be acknowledged in the postposition *vasnā* 'for the sake of' which was borrowed in this form into Armenian (*vasn* 'on account of'), survived unchanged in Sogdian (*wsn*), and was blended in Parthian with the old postposition *rādī* to *wasnād* [127].

65. OP *antar*

That Aryan inherited the IE adverb **enter* 'between', attested from the Far East of the IE community (Aryan) to the Far West (Insular Celtic: OIrish *eter*), cannot be doubted. Form and meaning are safely established for Indian from Vedic on: *antar* 'between' appears
(1) with the accusative:
   antar dyāvā 'between heaven and earth' (RV 3, 6, 4)
   ubhē antar rōdasī 'between both worlds' (RV 4, 7, 8)
(2) with the locative:
   ašmanor antar 'between two stones' (RV 2, 12, 3).

[125] Cp. J. de Vries, Altnordisches etym. Wb., ²1962, 551.

[126] It is perhaps worth pointing out that, in Indian, there is no **vasna-* at all; the RV offers *vaša-* 'wish, desire'.

[127] See Szemerényi, Sprache 12, 1967, 214-5.—But CS *pr ... wsyd*, formerly often derived from *vas-*, has nothing to do with 'will', it represents *wi-sēd* from **said-* 'instigate', see Schwartz, JAOS 89, 1969, 445 B. On the other hand, *vas-* probably survives in Khot. *vaska* 'for', see Bailey 1967, 323.

The same is true of Avestan: *antarə* 'between' appears with the accusative:

antarə ząm asmanəmča 'between heaven and earth' (Y. 68, 15; Yt. 10, 95)

antarə måŋhəmča hvarəča 'between the moon and the sun' (Yt. 6,5)

nisāim yim antarə mōurumča bāxδīmča 'Nisāya between Marv and Balx' (Vid. 1, 7).

In these circumstances it is not surprising to find that OP *antar* is listed in grammars and dictionaries with the same meaning. Bartholomae's 'innerhalb, in, unter, zwischen' (1904, 131) is of course inconclusive, seeing that it has to do for both Avestan and Old Persian. But the latter dialect alone is, at least ostensibly, the subject of the following treatments. Tolman gives 'within, among, in' (1908, 61) but his translations of DB II 78 (15: "these I haled within the fortress at Ecbatana") and DB IV 32 (25: "These nine kings I seized within these battles") are in a most peculiar English. Meillet-Benveniste give the translations 'parmi' (82), 'à l'intérieur' (98), 'dans, parmi' (208, 226); the interesting thing is that, when actual passages are to be translated (208, 226), only 'dans', and perhaps 'à l'intérieur' are needed, certainly not 'parmi'. Kent also renders *aⁿtar* with 'within, among' (1953, 166; cf. 86 B) but his translations (:within these battles, within these countries, among the provinces) produce very odd formulations. Brandenstein-Mayrhofer offer the interpretations 'durch, unter' (1964, 103) but the rendering of *antar imā hamaranā* (DB IV 32) as 'durch diese Schlachten' implies the erroneous notion of 'means' where only the 'place where' was intended. Hinz formerly was satisfied with a simple 'in' (1942, 61), but this has now been amplified to 'in, innerhalb, zwischen' (1973, 123).

An inspection of the not very numerous passages in which *antar* occurs will suffice to show that all these interpretations are based on the data of comparative Aryan (and even IE) philology, not on the Old Persian synchrony. The preposition occurs six times all told, four times in Darius' Behistun inscription, twice in Xerxes' Daiva-inscription. The passages are given with the necessary contexts[128]:

(1) DB I 21-2: *a(n)tar imā dahyāva martiya hya āgariya āha avam*

---

[128] Since here we are only concerned with the functions of *antar*, I follow Kent's text even when there might be reason for disagreeing with it.—I ignore here the further question also whether the OP word should be read *antarah* as suggested by Nyberg (1974, 18).

ʰubrtam abaram 'in these countries, the man who was loyal, him I rewarded well';

(2) DB II 77-8: *martiyā tyaiyšaiy fratamā anūšiyā āha(n)tā avaiy Hagmatānaiy a(n)tar didām frāhajam* 'the men who were his foremost followers, those at Ecbatana *in* the fortress I hanged';

(3) DB IV 31-2: *imaiy IX xšāyaθiyā adam agrbāyam a(n)tar imā hamaranā* 'I seized (= took prisoner) these nine kings *in* these battles';

(4) DB IV 91-2: *pasāva i(mā)m dipim adam frāstāyam vispadā a(n)tar dahyāva* 'afterwards I sent off this inscription everywhere *in* the lands';

(5) XPh 29-32: *yaθā tya adam xšāyaθiya abavam astiy a(n)tar aitā dahyāva... ayauda* 'when I became king, there is *in* those lands... (where) there was commotion';

(6) XPh 35-6: *a(n)tar aitā dahyāva āha yadātya paruvam daivā ayadiya(n)* '*in* those lands (there) was (a place) where formerly daivas had been worshipped'.

It is quite clear that in none of these passages is a meaning 'between' tolerable, while a simple 'in' is in each one of them quite appropriate. An interpretation 'within' in (3), as adopted by Kent, is meaningless; in (2), if the hides of the rebels were stuffed and hung out on the walls, the translation 'within the fortress' is not merely quaint but downright ridiculous, and the same applies to 'à l'intérieur'. For (6), 'among' is clearly unacceptable, since one point is specified in the whole expanse of the empire; and this shows that in (5) also *antar* is to be taken in the same sense.

If the fact that OP *antar* means 'in', and nothing else, is disappointing from the point of view of the past, it is only what is to be expected from the point of view of the subsequent development. The fact itself is in a roundabout way corroborated by the use in Pahlavi of Aramaic BYN in the sense of 'in'. In Aramaic, the meaning of BYN is normally 'between'; only as a Pahlavi ideogram had it been known in the sense of 'in', until the fifth century Aramaic letters from the chancery of Aršam, satrap of Egypt, revealed that BYN was in common use in the sense 'in' in the Reichsaramäisch or Official Aramaic of the Achaemenid empire[129]. This will, then, be one of the instances in which the Pahlavi ideograms go back to Achaemenid times[130].

---

[129] On these questions see F. Rosenthal, Die aramaistische Forschung seit Th. Nöldekes Veröffentlichungen, Leiden 1939, 81 (on BYN); on the letters see Rosenthal 37-8;

The close agreement on this point between Reichsaramäisch and Old Persian again (as in the case of *hya* above) prompts the question whether one language influenced the other in triggering off the change from 'between' to 'in'. Since in Aramaic territory only Reichsaramäisch exhibits this feature, while in Aryan both Avestan and Indian show the same development (cf. *antarə təmahe* 'in the dark', N. 68; *viṣveṣu bhuvaneṣu antar* 'in all beings', RV I 157, 5), and the development is well known from other areas as well [131], it is more likely that Aramaic shows with BYN 'in' the influence of Old Persian.

But the diachronic fact which manifests itself as a new fact in OP synchrony, i.e. that *antar* is 'in', not 'between', raises a further question: what was the OP word for 'between'? As far as I can see this question cannot be answered at present. But in view of the fact that in Pahlavi 'between' is *andarg* and *miyān*, we have, *a priori*, a choice between two forms: **madyānai* and **antarkā* (or **antarkam?*) [132]. Only future discoveries will decide what the right answer is to the above question, as also to the further question whether OP *antar* was found in other uses. But on the present evidence our dictionaries and grammars should only list a preposition *antar* 'in'.

66. OP *Sakām*

The form *Sakām* occurs once in the whole of extant Old Persian 'literature', in the fifth column of the Behistun inscription, where we read [133]:

DB V 21-3: *pasāva hadā kārā adam ašiyavam abiy*
         Sakām pasā Sakā tyaiy xaudām tigrām
         bara(n)tiy imaiy Sakā hačāma aiša(n)

G.R. Driver, Aramaic documents of the fifth century B.C., Oxford ²1965 (on BYN p. 104); on Official Aramaic see E.Y. Kutscher, in: Current Trends in Linguistics (ed. T.A. Sebeok) 6, 1970, 361f.

[130] Cf. Kutscher, o.c., 393f. (with references), esp. 398.

[131] Note especially the French preposition *entre* in the meaning *in*, see Vendryes, Choix d'études linguistiques et celtiques, Paris 1952, 175f.

[132] I posit **madyānai* on the strength of Bartholomae's *madyāna-*. But if Humbach should prove right with his claim (Cama Golden Jubilee Volume, 1969, 121) that the Avestan forms represent the consonantal stem *madyān-*, then my form should read **madyāni*.—For **antarkā* see Nyberg 1974, 18, as already Bartholomae, IF 12, 1901, 99² (where also on **antarkam*). MacKenzie's *andarag* (1971, 9) requires an earlier **antarakam* or similar.

[133] Text and translation are again Kent's.

"Afterwards, with an army I went off to Scythia, after the Scythians who wear the pointed cap. These Scythians went from me".

This text (and translation) is, owing to the numerous damages to the rock surface, not completely certain. Kent himself had originally presented a restoration which differed on a number of important points from the text given above[134]. The same applies to the repeated efforts of Hinz of 1939 and 1942 respectively[135]. The decisive change came in 1948 when George G. Cameron had an opportunity of studying the rock-inscriptions with all the helps and aids put at his disposal by modern technology. The results, published in 1951, were important for our passage also; this was his reading[136]:

21 *pa-[sa-a-va : ha-da-]a : ka-[a-ra-a : a]-da-ma : [a-ša]-i-ya-va-ma :*
                                            a-ba-i-ya : sa-ka-
22 *a-ma : pa-sa-[a]-v[a : ...] : ta-i-ga-ra-a-ma : ba-ra-ta-i-*
23 *ya : i-[...]-i-ša,*

and this was put by Kent into the following shape[137]:

21   *pa[sāva : had]ā : k[ārā : a]dam : [aš]iyavam : abiy : Sak-*
22 *ām : pas[ā :] Sa[kā : tyaiy : xaudām] : tigrām : bara(n)ti-*
23 *y : i[maiy : Sakā : hačāma : ā]iša(n).*

As can be seen, there is only one point on which Kent refused to follow Cameron: in line 22, he thought that instead of *v* in *pasa[ ]v[a* the word-divider + *sa* should be read (l.c., 57). The latest revision retains Cameron's *pasāva* in 22, and restores *i[maiy : patiš : mām : ā]iša(n)* in 23[138].

But the main point is now established with certainty: after *adam ašiyavam abiy Sakām* there is *pasā* or *pasāva*, and not *abiy*.

Having established the form *Sakām* and its environment, the next question is: what form is *Sakām*? The answer would seem to be quite clear: the acc.sg.of an *-ā*-stem *Sakā*, to be interpreted as

---

[134] Cf. Kent, Darius' Behistan inscription, Column V (JNES 2, 1943, 105-114), 108, 112. His restorations are criticized by Herzfeld, The Persian Empire, Wiesbaden 1968, 291 fn.

[135] Hinz, ZDMG 93, 1939, 364-369; 96, 1942, 333, 338f.

[136] Cameron, Journal of Cuneiform Studies 5, 1951, 53.

[137] Kent, Journal of Cuneiform Studies 5, 1951, 56-57.—The new readings had been communicated to Kent in advance, so that Kent could print his new text in the revised edition of 1953 (p. 133).

[138] Hinz, Die Zusätze zur Darius-Inschrift von Behistan (AMI N.F. 5, 1972, 243-251) 245-246 and 251.

'land of the Saka'[139]. Unfortunately, there is no feminine *Sakā*. The form *Sakā* occurs frequently (some fifteen times) but it is always masc.nom.pl. or acc.pl. Even *Sakā* at DPe 18, which Hinz (1942, 125) took to be the feminine, is no doubt rightly interpreted by Kent (1953,209) as representing the masc. *Saka*.

And this is indeed the difficulty with *Sakām*: there is no feminine singular *Sakā* for the 'land of the Saka'; for this notion the singular *Saka* or the plural *Sakā* can, and must, be used interchangeably. What is more, there is only one instance of a feminine *-ā*-stem, used as the name of a country or province[140], namely *Aθurā* 'Syria', cf.loc.sg. *Aθurāyā*. And this is patently a quite different formation, it is not from a (non-existent) ethnic **Aθura* 'Assyrian, Syrian' but represents the indigenous name of the province, known to us from Akkadian and Hebrew *Aššur* and Aramaic *Aθur* (: *'twr*). The latter form, with *θ*, even reveals that OP *Aθur-* represents the Aramaic form, as has been argued convincigly by W. Belardi[141]. But we must go a step further: even the ending *-ā* is not an OP addition but part of the Semitic original, either the sign of the status emphaticus known from the later Syriac form *Atūrā*[142], or else the adverbial form in *-ā*, possibly attested in Hebrew *Aššūrāh* (Genesis 25,18)[143]; in the latter case, since the *h* locale normally expresses 'place whither'[144], the borrowing into Old Persian of this form would be comparable to the borrowing of an accusative in such place-names as *Istambul* from εἰς τὴν πόλιν, *Ancona* from acc. Ἀγκῶν-α, etc.

It is thus clear that *Sakā* would be the only form in which the feminine of the ethnic were used for the name of their land. The oddity of such a formation is further highlighted by the observation that wherever we find a true Iranian derivation for a land-

---

[139] Cf. Bartholomae 1904, 1554; Tolman 1908, 31-32; Meillet 1915, 138, 180; Meillet-Benveniste 1931, 151, 202; Hinz 1942, 125; Kent 1953, 209; Hinz 1973, 151.

[140] At Meillet 1915, 138 (also Meillet-Benveniste 1931, 151) two names in *-ā* are mentioned, *Sakā* and *Aθurā*.

[141] Belardi, AION-L 2, 1960, 177f.

[142] See Moscati, An Introduction to the Comparative Grammar of the Semitic Languages, 1969, 98-99.

[143] On the difficulties of this form see Koehler-Baumgartner, Hebräisches und Aramäisches Lexikon zum Alten Testament, 3rd ed., Part I, 1967, 91 A.

[144] On the *h locale* see Gesenius-Kautsch, Hebräische Grammatik, [25]1889, 242f.; C. Steuernagel, Hebr. Gramm., 1953, 86, 103; Beer-Meyer, Hebr. Gram. I, Berlin 1952, 120; Moscati (see fn. 142), 95.

name, the formation is with the feminine suffix -ī-, nom.sg. -iš; cf. *Hᵛārazmiš*[145], *Bāxtriš*, and *Harahvatiš*.

If, then, the general usage only allows the masculine ethnic, whether it be employed in the singular or plural[146], one is led to ask whether *Sakām* is not in fact a plural form, especially as the next lines present the plural *Sakā* at least three times. As is so often the case, once the right question is asked, the correct answer offers automatically: *Sakām* is a sandhi-variant of the accusative plural *Sakān*, and its *m* is due to the accident that it was followed by the labial *p-* at the beginning of the next word.

This kind of assimilation across a juncture is of course well-known from Greek inscriptions, especially in the case of nasals[147], cf. τὴμ πόλιν for *-n p-*, and even in looser combinations, e.g. ἐστὶμ περί, but also from modern publications. I have no handy examples from English newspapers but perhaps the following gleanings from a German daily (Die Welt) will serve my purpose: *vergisst bei seinem Bemühungen kein Detail* (instead of: seinen B-, 11th Sept. 1974, p. 3), *haben einem Bombenanschlag verübt* (: einen B-, 16th Nov. 1974, p. 5). In my view, the OP inscriptions should also be re-examined from this point of view, especially where so far it has been customary to assume a grammatical error. Thus, e.g., at XPh 33 we read:

33   *ava : dahyāvam*
34 *: adam : ajanam : utašim : gāθavā : nīšāda-*
35 *yam :*

"I smote that country and put it down in its place".

According to Kent (1953,23-24) *ava dahyāvam* represents an "error in syntax", concerned with gender: the 'neuter' *ava* is a mistake for *avām*. But the 'magnitude' of the blunder can be kept within reasonable bounds if we assume that *ava dahyāvam* represents *avan dahyāvam*, i.e. an assimilated *avam dahyāvam* (*Add.* p. 394); *avam* can then be for *avām*, with neglect of quantity, or a masculine form although *dahyu-* is normally a feminine. The same explanation would

---

[145] See Szemerényi, Sprache 12, 1967, 194-196.

[146] For the ethnic names see the complete lists at Kent 1953, 56-57; for the most recent find on Darius' statue see JA 260, 1973, 258-9.—In some cases there is reason to believe that a form in *-ā* is not a masc. plural (nor a fem. sg.!) but a mistake for *-a*, cf. *Skudrā* for *Skudra* at XPh 27; *Pārsā* for *Pārsa* in (the late) AmH 2. For the ethnics see also Walser, Die Völkerschaften auf den Reliefs von Persepolis, 1966, 27f.; for the spelling of final *-a*, Weissbach 1911a, 49; Kent 1953, 17 (§36), 22 (§§52 III; 53); Szemerényi, Sprache 12, 1967, 212.

[147] Cf. Buck, The Greek Dialects, 1955, 82.

apply to *tuva kā hya* in line 46 of the same(!) inscription, which naturally represents *tuva(n) kā*. The neglect of quantity curiously contrasts with the overfull spelling *āhām* in lines 15-16 of the same inscription, this time for *āham*.

It will be realized that the new interpretation has a significance far beyond the narrow limits of the sentence in which the form *Sakām* occurs. If it is correct, it is the first time that proof positive has been found for the survival of the case-ending *-n* in the accusative plural of the masculine *-a*-stems [148]. On a previous occasion I showed that the *-i*-stem acc.pl.ending was (for both masculines and feminines) *-īš*, cf. *ārašnīš* [149], and the same will hold for the *-u*-stems [150]. Accordingly, we can now restore for the OP short vocalic stems the following sets of ending:

	-a-	*-i-*	*-u-*
nom.pl.	*-ā(h)*	*-aya(h)*	*-ava(h)*
acc.pl.	*-ān*	*-īš*	*-ūš*.

This still does not enable us to decide what the *-ā*-stem acc.pl. ending was, that is how the attested *aniyā* is to be interpreted. It is to be hoped that future discoveries, or the re-interpretation of well-known facts, will one day allow us to settle this question also.

67. OP *isuvā*?

This word is again a *hapax*, which occurs in the superscription to the bow-bearer of Darius on the monument at Naqš-i-Rustam near Persepolis; the OP text (DNd) reads:

Aspačanā : vašabara : Dārayavahauš :
xšāyaθiyahyā : isuvām : dārayatiy.

This is rendered by Kent (1953,140) as:

"Aspathines, bowbearer, holds the battle-axe of Darius, the King", that is the following identifications are made:

vašabara = 'bowbearer' (*vaša* = 'bow')
isuvā = 'battle-axe'.

[148] I had reached this conclusion when I noticed that in his latest work Hinz gives all *-a*-stem acc. pl. forms with *-ān*, e.g. *xšāyaθiyān*, *marttān* (1973, 139, 144). Upon inquiry, Prof. Hinz kindly informed me (letter of 12. 12. 1974) that his forms rest on the Avestan and Indian evidence. I am glad to see that my interpretation of *Sakām* coincides with his intuitive hunch.

[149] Cf. Szemerényi, Sprache 12, 1967, 196-199. On a-b-i-č-r-i-š see Schmitt, KZ 81, 1967, 56 f.; Prosdocimi, RSO 42, 1967, 42. Bogoljubov's interpretation, VJ 1974(6), 110, is impossible.

[150] The form *dahyāva* is of course the nom. pl. used as an acc. The original form must have been **dahyūš*.

The two terms have been the subject of varied conjectures. For *i-s^a-u-v^a-a* the following suggestions may be recalled—if we ignore the early attempts listed by Weissbach (1911a, 41-42):

'server of the arrows' (Tolman 1908,47,74,99);
'Bogen?' (Weissbach 1911a,43: = Ind.*iṣvāsa-*?);
'Bogenfutteral' (Weissbach 1911b,97);
'arc' ou 'flèche' (Meillet-Benveniste 1931,165);
'bow-cover' (Kent,Lg.15,1939,174);
'Streitaxt, Streitkolben' (Junge, Klio 33,1940,23²);
'Bogenscheide, Bogenhülle' (Hinz 1942,98);
'battle-axe' (Kent, JNES 4,1945,233, after Junge; 1953,174);
'Streitaxt' (Brandenstein-Mayrhofer 1964,127);
'spear' (Wüst, Altpersische Studien, 1966,31);
'Köcher?' (Eilers, Persica 4,1969, 30 fn.);
'bow?' (Malandra, IIJ 15,1973,271);
'Köcher für Bogen und Pfeile, Bogen-Pfeil-Hülle' (Hinz 1973,58-59, 140);
'Köcher' (Hauri 1973,36).

The wildly fluctuating definitions of the meaning, ranging from "arc ou flèche", "bow, bow-case", "Bogen, Bogenfutteral, Bogenhülle, Köcher" to "battle-axe", even "spear", show that they have no secure foundation. This is rather surprising, at first sight, seeing that the sculptured representation would seem to be marvellously clear and helpful: "Aspathines has a heavy bow, or a bow-case, slung over his left shoulder, and holds a battle-ax in his hand" is Kent's description (1953,140), while Olmstead states that Aspačana is "holder of the king's battle-ax and bow case. Over his left shoulder hangs the bow case.... In his right hand is held the *sagaris*, the double battle-ax of the Scythians" [151]. But it is exactly this apparent precision in the representation that is the cause of so much floundering. For the other term in the superscription, *vašabara-*, has received equally, or one should rather say, correspondingly, wide-ranging interpretations: 'Genosse' [152], 'Stabträger' [153], 'bow-bearer' [154], 'battle-axe bearer' [155], and, last not least, 'Gewandträger,

---

[151] A.T. Olmstead, History of the Persian Empire, 1948 (paperback 1966), 218.

[152] Spiegel, see Weissbach 1911a, 41-42.

[153] Justi, see Bartholomae 1904, 1346; Weissbach 1911a, 42; Meillet-Benveniste 1931, 64.

[154] Tolman 1908, 47, 123; Junge, Klio 33, 1940, 23²; Kent, JNES 4, 1945, 233; 1953, 206.

Kämmerer'[156]. The difficulty lies in securing the first step; for if one term is safely identified, the other also becomes clear(er).

This has now been achieved by Rykle Borger in an important paper on "Die Waffenträger des Königs Darius"[157], and that on the only satisfactory basis, the texts of the superscription; he also had the advantage of being able to use the excellent photos of Erich F. Schmidt which yield more than was visible to Weissbach (1911a,30,41f.). As a result, Borger could read in the Akkadian version after the words 'of Darius, the King', ^{kuš}šal-ṭu (: "die Lesung... ist vollkommen sicher", p. 389), which, as shown by the determinative kuš, denotes an object made of *leather*. On the other hand, the reliefs show two weapons: a bow case (Bogen-futteral, Bogenkasten) and a double axe. With the increase in the Akkadian version we now have the following equations for the weapons:

OP *vaša* = Elam. *lipte* = Akk. [...]-*ta*

and

OP *isuvā* = Elam. *apti* = Akk. *šalṭu*.

And Borger can proudly conclude (p. 390): "Das alte Problem, welche von diesen Wörtern die Doppelaxt bzw. den Bogenkasten wiedergeben..., ist durch meine Lesung der babylonischen Fassung entschieden: Das Determinativum kuš vor šal-ṭu deutet einen Gegen-stand aus Leder an, wodurch Doppelaxt und Dolch ausgeschlossen werden. *isuvā* = *apti* = *šalṭu* muss also 'Bogenkasten, Bogenfutteral' bedeuten"[158], which is a kind of combination of quiver and bow case. Borger also shows (391-2) that the Persian bow case is a direct or indirect development of its Assyrian counterpart.

But Borger does more than this: he helps the Iranianist even on his last lap, in his attempt to find the origin of *isuvā* 'bow case', although he is unaware of this kindly service. In order to clinch the main point of his argument—the meaning of Hebrew *šlṭ*—he lists

---

[155] Weissbach 1911b, 97; Hinz 1942, 144; Gershevitch, in: A locust's leg—Studies in honour of S.H. Taqizadeh, 1962, 78[8]; Brandenstein-Mayrhofer 1964, 150 (but "battle-axe" cannot be the meaning of both *vaša-* and *isuvā*!); Widengren, Festschrift Leo Brandt, 1968, 526; Eilers, Persica 4, 1969, 30; Malandra, IIJ 15, 1973, 271, 281.

[156] Hinz 1973, 57-59 (from *vas-tra-); Hauri 1973, 36.

[157] Borger, Vetus Testamentum 22, 1972, 385-398, esp. 389f.

[158] For *vaša-* 'double axe' Borger suggests (p. 390) [paš]ta as the Akkadian equivalent; but if Hinz should prove right in his assumption that *vaša-* is 'garment' (see fn. 156), then the Akkadian equivalent could be [ṣu-ba]-ta (p. 391).

all nine (or ten) occurrences of Akkadian *šal(a)ṭu*, which can all
be dated in the 6th and 5th centuries B.C. It so happens that
two of the passages quoted have a further important term:

UET 4,117,8: ...for a bow, ...for ^kuš^*iš-hi u* ^kuš^*šal-ṭu*, ...for an arrow
(cf. CAD I/J, p. 242a);

BIN 1,172,1: 2 ^kuš^*šá-la-ṭu*, 2 ^kuš^*i-šá-hu* (cf. CAD I/J, p. 242a and Ṣ,
p. 110f.).

If one checks on *iš(a)hu*, which appears side by side with *šalṭu*,
one gets the following information[159]. The word, of unknown
provenience, is first attested in the Alalakh tablets (about the middle
of the 2nd millennium B.C.); the only occurrence gives 1 ^túg^*i-ša-ah-hu*
in an apparently unmilitary context. The next attestations come from
the Neo-Assyrian (after 1000 B.C.) and Late Babylonian periods:

^túg^*iš-he, ana* ^kuš^*iš-hi,* 2 ^kuš^*i-šá-hu.*

It is interesting that the determinatives *túg* (for clothes) and *kuš*
(for leather) can both be applied to this object. For that very
reason one can hardly define its meaning as "Tuch (aus Stoff oder
Leder)" but rather "covering" which can be either of leather or
some textile.

The fact that *iš(a)hu* twice occurs in combination with *šal(a)ṭu*
shows that they are very close in meaning, that they are essentially
identical. And this leads to the last step in our discussion: the
material presented suggests that *išahu* was borowed into Old Persian
as *isahvā*[160]. The writing *i-s^a^-u-v^a^-a* indicates, not *isuvā* or *isvā*,
but *isauvā*[161] which is to be interpreted as *isa^h^uvā*, phonetic *isahvā*.
The OP writing uses here the same orthographical device as in the
case of *mškauva* = *maškāhvā*, *aniyauva* = *anyāhvā*, *mnauv^i^iš*
= *manāhviš*. Two points require further comment.

First, the fact that OP has an -*ā*-stem *isahvā*, and not, say, an
-*u*-stem *isahu*, reveals that the word did not come directly from
Akkadian but *via* Aramaic: its -*ā* is the Aramaic postpositive
article, *isahvā* is the status emphaticus[162]. It is therefore important

---

[159] See v. Soden, Akkadisches Handwörterbuch I, 1959-1965, 394; and cf. CAD s.v.

[160] For the meaning note that, as Hinz (1973, 58-59) rightly emphasizes, *isahvā*
is not simply a "quiver" but "gemäss dem archäologischen Befund jene 'Lederhülle',
in welcher sich Bogen und Pfeile vereint befanden".

[161] It is a pleasant duty to recall that this possibility has been kept alive by
various scholars, cf. Weissbach 1911b, 96 fn. NRd(b); Junge, Klio 33, 1940, 23[2];
Hinz 1942, 98; Brandenstein-Mayrhofer 1964, 127.

[162] The settling of the meaning by Borger, and of the origin of *isahvā* in the

to note that -ā does not indicate a special emphasis or determinate state: it is a well-known fact that in the Aramaic of Behistun the article -ā has already lost its determinative force [163].

Secondly, it has been suggested recently that, contrary to Hinz's view that early *hv* had already in Old Persian developed into *xv*, there was no such change in Old Persian, and, what is more, *hu* had even developed into *u* [164]. We must agree that there was no change *hv* > *xv* because in that case we should expect to find the use of *x* in the cluster. But it is quite impossible to admit the claim that *hu* had gone to *u*. On the one hand, Iranian knows of no such general change, especially not before *u* [165]; and it would be ridiculous to assume that forms like *hunar*, *Xuzistan* etc. do not represent or reflect the OP phonetic shape. On the other hand, our explanation of *isahvā* shows that *hv* existed in OP; there would be no justification for the assumption that a foreign *xv* was changed to *uv* and not taken over as *xv* if *hv* did not exist.

One final word on the Akkadian expressions for 'quiver'. As Borger noted (p. 393), the normal Akkadian word for this object is *išpatu*. If, then, the second word, *šalṭu*, is found in a narrowly limited period only—in the 6th and 5th centuries B.C.—and in Assyria not at all, then it is not impossible that *šalṭu* is a loanword from West Semitic [166]. In view of our results, we have to add a third word with the same general meaning, although in this case, too, foreign borrowing is more than likely. But all three seem to have coexisted in the synchrony of 'Late Akkadian', and this again raises the question what semantic differences there may have been between them, a question that Akkadists may yet be able to solve with the help of new material.

68-70. OP *hazārapatiš* — MP (*h*)*arkapat* — OP **āžarapatiš*

So far as can be ascertained, the 18th century French scholar Maturin Veyssière de *LaCroze*, "Bibliothécaire et Antiquaire du

present paper, disposes of the idea that it might be connected with Greek αἰχμή (Wüst, Altpersische Studien, 1966, 31). Hinz's suggestion (1973, 59) that *isahvā* will be of Medic origin, can only be accepted in the sense that the Aramaic loanword might have passed into Old Persian through Medic.

[163] See Kutscher (fn. 129) 362.

[164] Cf. Hinz 1973, 29; R. Schmitt, Göttingische Gelehrte Anzeigen 226, 1974, 101 with fn. 15.

[165] See Horn 1898, 96.

[166] In v. Soden's Dictionary (Lfg. 12, 1974, 1151) this is already stated as a fact.

Roi de Prusse", was the first to suggest a connexion between the Hesychian gloss ἀζαραπατεῖς· οἱ εἰσαγγελεῖς παρὰ Πέρσαις and the Armenian word *hazarapet* 'chiliarch, chief of a thousand men, governor; steward, major-domo, controller, intendant; house-steward, manager'[167]. As can be seen, the Armenian word has a much wider range than the Persian word. In its 'military' meaning it renders in the Bible[168] the Greek χιλίαρχος e.g. at Mark 6, 21-2: "Herod on his birthday gave a banquet to his chief officials and commanders and the leading men of Galilee", "τοῖς μεγιστᾶσιν αὐτοῦ καὶ τοῖς χιλιάρχοις καὶ τοῖς πρώτοις τῆς Γαλιλαίας", "principibus et tribunis et primis Galilaeae", *naxararac iwroc ew* hazarapetac *ew mecamecac Galileacwoc*. Particularly interesting is the scene described at Acts 21, 31-32, for it displays a contrast between the chiliarch and the subordinate centurions: "the officer commanding the cohort [= chiliarch]... took a force of soldiers with their centurions and came down", "τῷ χιλιάρχῳ... ὃς... παραλαβὼν στρατιώτας καὶ ἑκατοντάρχας κατέδραμεν", "tribuno cohortis... qui statim assumptis militibus et centurionibus decurrit", "hazarapet *gndin... areal zawrakans ew* hariwrapets *dimeac*". In the civilian sphere, *hazarapet* can render 'steward' as, e.g., at 1 Corinth. 4, 1 (and 2): "stewards (of the mysteries of God)", "οἰκονόμους (μυστηρίων θεοῦ)", "dispensatores (mysteriorum Dei)", "hazarapets (*xorhrdocn Astucoy*)"; Luke 8, 3: "Herod's steward", "ἐπιτρόπου Ἡρῴδου", "procuratoris Herodis", "hazarapetin *Herovdi*"; Galat. 4,2: (the heir) "is under guardians and trustees (until the day fixed by his father)", "ὑπὸ ἐπιτρόπους ἐστὶν καὶ οἰκονόμους", "sub tutoribus et actoribus est", "*ənd* hazarapetawk' *ē ew ənd gawarapetawk'*".

In view of the considerable semantic difference it is small wonder that de Lagarde, that opinionated, vain, and quarrelsome but withal exceedingly learned and ingenious cleric, should at first have failed to notice any connexion between the Greek gloss and the Armenian word. In fact, in 1851 he had voiced the opinion that ἀζαρα- was

[167] See Bedrossian, New Dictionary Armenian English, 367, and cf. I. Miskgian, Manuale Lexicon Armeno-Latinum (Rome 1887, repr. Louvain 1966) 165: 'militum tribunus, chiliarchus, procurator; dispensator, tutor; princeps'.

[168] I have used the Armenian Bible in the edition of the American Bible Society (Vienna 1929); for the Greek and Latin New Testament E. Nestle's edition for the Württembergische Bibelanstalt (Stuttgart, [22]1964); for the English translation the Authorized Version as well as the New English Bible (Oxford and Cambridge, 1970).

to be connected with ἀζαβαρίτης—a word reported from Ctesias—
interpreted as 'nuncius tabellarius' and analyzed as *az-*, a variant
of *azd* 'message, report' (without *d* which is a participial suffix!),
and *barit*, Aryan *bhar-it-* (comparable in formation to *sar-it-*!)[169].
But already in 1854, after he had seen the manuscript Armenian
dictionary of LaCroze, he reported the view of that great scholar
which he subsequently upheld on several occasions[170].

The equation was received into Hübschmann's Armenische Grammatik also (see p. 174), though he made a point of stressing that,
while the ordinary *hazarapet* was a chiliarch or a steward—in either
case a (comparatively) small fry—the '*great* hazarapet *of Aryans
and Non-Aryans*' mentioned by Ełišē, and the '*hazarapet of the Aryans*',
so titled by Lazarus of Pharp, was "the highest civilian dignitary
in Persia, the Grand Vizier". An altogether different title, though
also of a high rank, was in his view the (Arm.) *hazarawuxt*,
mentioned by Faustus of Byzantium, Lazarus of Pharp, and the late
writer Thomas Artsruni, which was identical with Persian *hazāraft*,
Syriac *hzrpt*, Greek Ἀζαρέφθης.

It is not quite clear what Hübschmann really meant by saying
that Arm. *hazarapet* and *hazarawuxt* had to be distinguished. In any
case, it is now certain that they reflect different, but Iranian,
developments of the same Iranian term. The Middle Iranian, especially
epigraphic, data, which were available but unknown in Hübschmann's
time, were made available in Herzfeld's trail-blazing Paikuli-edition:
Middle Persian and Parthian were thus shown to have possessed
the forms *ḥz'[lwpty]* and *ḥzrwpty* respectively[171]. Herzfeld assumed
(p. 188) that the dialects differed, that Parthian *ḥzrwpty* contrasted
with Persian *ḥz'[lpt]*, and, what is more, that the *w* between the

---

[169] P. de Lagarde, Arica, 1851 (reprinted as Part IV of his Frühe Schriften,
Osnabrück-Wiesbaden 1967), p. 12. For the passage containing ἀζαβαρίτης, reported
by Photius at 42a 21f., see now the Budé edition of the Bibliotheca by R. Henry,
vol. I, 1959, 124; and F.W. König, Die Persika des Ktesias von Knidos, Graz 1972,
§ 46, p. 18; on the word itself see the text futher on, p. 74.

[170] See P. de Lagarde, Zur Urgeschichte der Armenier, 1854 (reprinted as Part VI
of the Frühe Schriften cited in fn. 169), p. 35 line 978; Gesammelte Abhandlungen,
1866 (reprinted Osnabrück 1966), 186; Armenische Studien (Abhandlungen der Gesellschaft der Wissenschaften, Göttingen, vol. 22), 1877, 81,176. In this last work Lagarde
also speaks (p. 191) about LaCroze, on whose Indological work cp. Windisch,
Geschichte der Sanskrit-Philologie I, 1917, 6.

[171] E. Herzfeld, Paikuli—Monument and inscription of the early history of the
Sasanian Empire, Vol. I, Berlin 1924, p. 101, lines 16 (Pers.) and 15′ (Parth.).

two components of the Parthian form was an "Avestan archaism". But the sensational discovery in 1936 and 1939 of the three versions of the great Šāpūr-inscription on the Kaʿba-i-Zardušt at Persepolis showed that both dialects had the form with *w*: Persian *ḥzʾlwpt* and Parthian *ḥzrwpt*; the Greek version with αζαροπτ and αζαριπτου revealed that the Iranian form was *ḥazāruft* or *ḥazārəft*[172]; the relation of the forms is the same as in the case of Persian-Parthian *dpyrwpt*, Greek διβιρουπτ in the same inscription (line 57).

These forms reveal—what has passed unnoticed so far[173]—that the compounds with *pati-* 'master, head of, commander of' developed in two rather different ways: the second member either developed 'normally' into *-bad* (or *-bud*)[174], or was syncopated after the juncture-vowel (*-u-* owing to the following labial) to *-pt-* which then changed to *-ft-*. Beside *hazārbad* there was also *hazāruft*, beside *dibīrbad* also *dibīruft*. The double development is no doubt connected with the two possible accentuations of this compositional type: the compound could be accented either as *hazára-páti-* (giving *hazārbad*) or with a single accent, according to the three-syllable law[175], as *hazárápati-* which was then syncopated to *hazārápt*, *hazāraft* (and umlauted to *hazāruft*); the syncope is the same as in NP *bīst* '20' from *vísati*, and *duvēst* '200' from *duvḗsatē*.

There can be no doubt that *hazārpat* (or rather *hazārapati-*) is reflected by Arm. *hazarapet*. Arm. *hazarawuxt*, on the other hand,

---

[172] Cf. M. Sprengling, American Journal of Semitic Languages and Literatures 57, 1940, 403.410; and now P. Gignoux, Glossaire des inscriptions pehlevies et parthes, London 1972, 24.54; and for the Greek version, in addition to Sprengling, A. Maricq, RGDS = Res Gestae Divi Saporis (Syria 35, 1958, 295-360) 323.327, lines 56 and 61 respectively.

[173] Eilers (IIJ 5, 1962, 215) did notice the fact but did not attempt an explanation.

[174] See Hübschmann 1895, 126; Horn 1898, 28f.

[175] Cf. Meillet, JA 15, 1900, 254-277; Gauthiot, MSL 20, 1916, 1-25; Szemerényi, Sogdicisms in the Avesta (in: F. Altheim, Aus Spätantike und Christentum, 1951, 153-166; reprinted in F. Altheim-R. Stiehl, Geschichte Mittelasiens im Altertum, 1970, 736-749) 159 (742); Kuryłowicz, L'accentuation des langues indo-européennes, ²1958, 369f.; Indogermanische Grammatik II: Akzent-Ablaut, 1968, 194f.—It is interesting to note that in compounds with a substantive as second member the Rigveda also often shows double accentuation, e.g. *gnás-páti-*, *sádas-páti-*, *śácī-páti-*, while in compounds with a single accent the first member is more frequently found accented than the second, cf. *gṛhá-pati-*, *svá-pati-* but *viś-páti-*, *nṛ-páti-*, see Wackernagel 1905, 262-265; Kuryłowicz, Idg. Gr. II 61. But it is very unlikely that the two Iranian types should have anything to do with this Vedic peculiarity which even in Vedic times gives way to final accentuation.

must be connected with *hazāruft*: in all probability it represents a blend of the two syncopated variants, *hazāraft* and *hazāruft*, i.e. **hazārafuft*. Hübschmann thought (pp. 149-150) that the change from *ft* to *xt* was an Armenian development, paralleled by *zaṙnawuxt* 'silken' which had *wuxt* from Iran. *vaft*. But we now know that this development is no more an Armenian process than the representation of Iran. *fr* by *hr-* in, e.g., Arm. *hraman* 'command', *hramatar* 'commander' from *framān*, *framātār*[176]. A sealstone published in 1960 bears the Bactrian inscription ναζαροχτο, i.e. *hazāruxt*, and the same title, with a slight alteration in the second vowel, had been known for quite some time from another Bactrian seal (probably of the 4th century A.D.) in the form ναζοροχτο, i.e. *hazoruxt*[177].

We can thus conclude that an early Parthian *hazārápati-* was borrowed into Armenian as *hazarapet*; the corresponding Persian form was umlauted to **hazārúpat* which, by about the middle of the third century A.D., was syncopated to *hazāruft*, the form that appears in all three versions of the Šāpūr-inscription. This form then developed (in some Northern dialects?) into *hazāruxt* which was taken over by Bactrians and Armenians alike[178].

Having cleared up the formal side of the equation, we must turn our attention to the *semantic aspect*. We can state first of all that the meaning of the Greek gloss ('gentleman usher') is not matched by either the Armenian or the Iranian word. But Armenian and Iranian do not agree very well between themselves either. As we have seen, Armenian *hazarapet* denotes either a military rank, 'colonel' or sim., or a civilian occupation, 'steward, major-domo, guardian'. The Iranian forms, as we now know, apply to a much higher station in life.

The second part of Šāpūr's trilingual inscription on the Ka'ba-i-Zardušt (ŠKZ), cited already, gives detailed information of the court dignitaries during three generations: his own, his father's and his grandfather's[179]. Since the grandfather, Pāpak, was only a petty

---

[176] See Szemerényi, Orbis 19, 1970, 506-7.

[177] Cf. Henning, ZDMG 115, 1965, 81, who also notes (fn. 37) that *xt* in Arm. *hazaravuxt* is not an Armenian replacement.

[178] It is highly interesting that just as Armenian reflects both *hazārapati* and *hazāruxt*, so Bactrian, too, has not only the latter form but also the former in the form OZOPOBAΔI, found on Hephthalite coins, see Bailey, BSOS 8, 1937, 893.

[179] On the three lists see Henning, in: Jackson Memorial Volume, 1954, 43f.;

king, it is small wonder that his list includes eight persons only, of whom only one, the sixth, is given his title, although this is quite interesting, i.e. *Zīk*, 'master of ceremonies', Pa(rthian) *nivēdpat*, Pe(rsian) *ādēnīk*, Greek δειπνοκλήτωρ 'one who invites to dinner'[180]. His son Ardašīr, the first King of Kings of the Sassanian house (226-240 A.D.), naturally boasts a much fuller court. The thirtyone personages mentioned are listed in the following order:

(1-4)	4	kings (of Abrēnax, Merv, Kirmān, Sīstān respectively),
(5-7)	3	queens (mother, wife, and daughter of Pāpak),
(8)		Ardašīr, *bidaxš* 'vice-roy',
(9)		Pāpak, *hazāruft*,
(10-14)	5	representatives of the great clans,
(15)		Abursām, *framātār*[181],
(16)		Gēlimān of Demāvend,
(17)		Raxš, *spāhbed* (commander of the army),
(18)		Mard, *dibīruft* (chief secretary),
(19)		Pāpak, *nivēdbed*,
(20-22)	3	dignitaries without titles,
(23)		Hōmfrayād, *maigānbed*,
(24)		Dirān, *zēnbed* (chief of armoury),
(25)		Čērīk, *dādvar* (judge),
(26)		Vardān, *āxvarrbed* (master of the horse)[182],
(27-28)	2	dignitaries without titles,

Frye, in: Studi orientalistici in onore di G. Levi della Vida I, 1956, 314-335, esp. 328-334; Maricq, RGDS 322-331; Chaumont, JA 247, 1959, 175-191; 254, 1966, 488-491. For the Greek text see Pugliese Carratelli, La Parola del Passato II/6, 1947, 356-362; E. Honigmann & A. Maricq, Recherches sur les RGDS, 1953, 16-18. For some special problems see Benveniste, Titres et noms propres en iranien ancien, 1966, 11-50.—For a genealogical tree of the early Sassanians see Frye, *o.c.*, 335; Maricq, RGDS 333.

[180] On the terms for this dignitary see Eilers, Der alte Name des persischen Neujahrsfestes, Abh. Akad. Mainz, 1953/2, 67 (33); Frye, *o.c.*, 318; Maricq, RGDS 324; Chaumont, JA 247, 1959, 182, 185. The function of the *nivēdbad* is clarified (as "master of invitations") by Sogd. nw'yδ- 'invite', and especially by Arm. *nuirak* (from *nivēdak*) 'usher, nuncio', i.e. 'he who invites', see Chaumont, *o.c.*, 190 fn. 63. On NP *navīd* see now again Eilers, XVIII. Deutsche Orientalistentagung (1972), 1974, 477.

[181] This famous minister was *framādār* but not *vuzurg framādār*, if the latter title was introduced after Šāpūr's time, cf. Maricq, RGDS 324[1], but also Henning's guess at ZDMG 115, 1965, 81.

[182] See Gershevitch, TPS 1969, 170 (: *āxvarna-pati-* already in Elamite!); Harmatta-Pekáry, in: La Persia nel medioevo, 1971, 470; Widengren, ibid. 742.

(29)   Sagpus, *naxčirbed* (master of the hunt),

(30)   Hōduk, *grstpty* (chief provisioner?),

(31)   Jahēn, *mayār* [183] (cup-bearer).

For us it is of importance to note that at the top of the list, immediately after royalty, are mentioned the *bidaxš* and the *hazāruft*; they are followed by representatives of the great clans (Varāz, Sūrēn, Kārēn), and a long string of various office-holders, among them the *framātār, spāhbed, dibīruft, nivēdbed* (or *ādēnik*), *maigānbed, zēnbed, dādvar, āxvarrbed, naxčirbed*.

Šāpūr's own court-list, in which sixty-six personages are enumerated, shows much the same structure. After the royalty (1-9), come:

(10)   Šāpūr, *bidaxš*,

(11)   Pāpak, *hazāruft*,

(12)   Pērōz, *aspbed* (chief of cavalry);

then, after the great clans (13-16), follow

(17)   Vahunām, *framādār*,

(18)   Frīk [184], *šahrab* (satrap);

then, interrupted only by

(22)   Ardašīr, *satrap*,

follow five untitled officers (19-21 + 23-24). Next come

(25)   Tīr-mihr, *dizbed*

(26)   Zīk, *nivēdbed*,

and, with title-less interruptions (27-29, 32-33, 39-40, 42-43, 48-49, 52, 59-62, 65), there follow

(30)   Vārzan, *satrap*,

(31)   Kirdisrō [185], *bidaxš*,

(34)   Yazdibād, *bānigān handarzbed*(?) [186],

---

[183] For the reading of Pe. *maͬly* see Henning 1958, 65[4].

[184] This form is based on the Greek version; the Iranian versions may offer different forms, Pe. *Friyōg* and Pa. *Friyak*, see Henning 1958, 70; Maricq, RGDS 327[12]; Gignoux, Glossaire 32, 61.

[185] *Kirdisrō* is the interpretation of Pe. *Kltslwby*, Pa. *Krtsrw* based on the Greek version; Gignoux's *Kardsrav* (25,55) ignores this important source.—On Kirdisrō's rank see Hinz [s. fn. 202] 153 fn. 25.

[186] This Persian title, to which the Parthian version offers as correspondence *MLKTHn ḥndrzpty*, i.e. queens' instead of ladies', is generally rendered as 'councillor of the Queen' (Frye, meaning 'counsellor'?), 'conseiller des reines' (Maricq, Gignoux), 'mentor et guide spirituel et, peut-être, aussi, pour les plus jeunes, éducateur' (Chaumont, JNES 22, 1964, 199); it is not translated but merely transliterated as ANΔAPZABIΔ in the Greek version. This surely must mean that the word did not have the easily translatable meaning 'counsellor'. I think that Armenian can

(35)   Pāpak, *šafšilār* (sword-bearer),
(36-7)   two *satraps*,
(38)   Vardbed, *paristag-bed* (master of the household) [187],
(41)   Abursām-šāpūr, *darīgān sālār* (chief of court-personnel).

It will suffice to enumerate the remaining titles:

(44) *grstpty*, (45) *dibīrbed*, (46) *zēndānīg* 'prison governor', (47) *darbed* 'master of the gate' (?), (53) *ganzvar* 'treasurer', (55) *dibīr* 'scribe, secretary', (56, 63) *šābistān* 'harem-ward, eunuch', (57) *vāzārbed* 'supervisor of markets', (64) *dādvar*, (66) *varāz-bed* 'caretaker of boars' (!). It deserves to be mentioned specifically that *Kardīr*, so famous in the church history of the late third century A.D., here comes fiftieth as a modest *magus*; but of course it speaks for the man that he "made it" at all. It is also interesting that in this list there are two *framādār*-s: one is Vahunām who takes the 17th place, the other a Šāpūr who comes 54th.

It is clear from the two lists of ŠKZ, which was engraved shortly after 260 A.D., that the *hazāruft* held a very important office in the first two thirds of the third century A.D. He has a fixed position immediately after the *bidaxš*, and both are at the top of

help us in this question. It has our term both in the (Parthian) form *anderjapet* and in the (Persian) form *handerjapet* (see Hübschmann 1897, 99,179). In the description of Iranian events the first form (once also the second) is used to denote the *andarzpet* of the magi, the court, the nobility, or of Sīstān. The second form, which seems to be the true Armenian form, is used in quite different contexts, as a rendering of 'steward, agent, major-domo'. It seems to me that ŠKZ uses *handarzbed* in this meaning, i.e. Yazdibād was 'the Queen's (or the Queens') steward'.—I am pleased to note here that this seems to have been also the view of the late Nyberg in his excellent Glossary, 1974, 94. He also put a questionmark after *bānigān*, and it seems indeed inevitable to assume that this form is a mistake for the expected *bānūgān*.

[187] This title, correctly rendered by Maricq (RGDS 328) as 'majordome', is by an oversight interpreted as 'chef de la diplomatie' by Gignoux (pp. 31,61), although the Greek version is quite clear with its τοῦ ἐπὶ τῆς ὑπηρεσίας. Even more curious is Harnack's mistake (in: Altheim-Stiehl, Geschichte Mittelasiens im Altertum, 1970, 546-7) who sees that the Iranian expression must mean 'Herr der Diener' but derives it nevertheless from Av. *fraēšta-* 'messenger, herald'. It is, of course, clear that Pe. *plstk* and Pa. *prštk* are the regular representatives of early **parišta-*, BP *paristag* 'servant'; the word is also widely represented in Armenian: *am-parišt*, *am-barišt* 'evil, impious', *bare-parišt* 'good, pious', *bare-pašt-el* 'live a pious life, worship god', *paštel* 'serve'; cf. Bolognesi, Le fonti dialettali degli imprestiti iranici in armeno, 1960, 34-35; Widengren, Iranisch-semitiche Kulturbegegnung in parthischer Zeit, 1960, 84 fn. 294; and especially Nyberg, Glossar, 1931, 170; Glossary, 1974, 151: *paristātan, paristišn*.

the list, immediately after royalty. In Šāpūr's list the *asp-bed* comes after the *hazāruft*, but the *framādār* follows several steps behind, after all the great clans; if he was a court-minister, his position was not a very eminent one [188].

A curious change comes with the Paikuli-inscription of King of Kings Narses (293-302 A.D.) which can be dated ca. 293/4 A.D. The sequence *bitaxš-hazāruft* is still retained but they are both preceded by a new dignitary—ranking immediately after the members of the royal house—who is called *ḥrgwpt* in Persian but *ḥrkpty* in Parthian. Thus for lines 7-8 the following (Pe.) text can be restored:

u pas Šāhpuhrē ī hargubad u Narsahē ī vispuhr ī Sāsānagān u Pābagē ī bidaxšē ud Ardašīr ī hazāruft ud Ardašīr ī Sūrēn u Raxšē ī spāhbad ud Ohormizdē Varāz ī Varhrānīgān x^vadāy ud abārīg vispuhr u vuzurg u kadagx^vadāy ud āzād...

'and afterwards Šāpūr the hargubed, and Prince Narse, son of Sāsān, and Pābag the bidaxš, and Ardašīr the hazāruft, and Ardašīr Sūrēn, and Raxš the army commander, and lord Hormizd-Gurāz son of Varhrān and other princes and magnates and clan-chiefs and noblemen...' [189].

At line 9, after a gap, we find the sequence:

vispuhrān u hargubad u vuzurgān ud āzādān...

'princes and the hargubed and the magnates and noblemen... [190], a sequence which, beginning with *hargubad*, reappears at line 20.

But the most complete list is given at lines 16-17:

ēg Šāhpuhrē ī hargubad u Pērōz ī vispuhr u Narsahē ī vispuhr ī Sāsānagān u Pābagē ī bidaxšē u Ardašīr ī hazāruft ud Ardašīr ī Sūrēn u Ohormizdē [Varāz]... u Kardīr Ohormizdē Mōbed... (17)... u Raxšē ī spāhbed ud Ardašīr ī Taxm-Šāhpuhrē... xšahr-āhmar dibīr u Zōδkardē ī tagarbed u... vuzurg ud āzād u kadagx^vadāy u šahrab u ahmārkar ud abārīg pārs u pahlav az Asūr[istān]...

'thereupon Šāpūr the hargubed, and Prince Pērōz and Prince Narse,

---

[188] There are, of course, several further problems concerning the differing arrangements of the lists. The order of precedence is, according to Maricq (RGDS 335), determined by the position of the family, not by the function of the dignitary named; cf. also Pugliese Carratelli, *o.c.*, 360. Henning thinks (Jackson Mem. Vol., 1954, 44[6]) that the order of the sons is linked to age, in the case of the Great Families (see BSOAS 14, 1952, 510), to the "strict order of precedence".

[189] See Herzfeld, Paikuli 96-97, 173 B.

[190] See Herzfeld, *l.c.*

sons of Sāsān, and Pābag the bidaxš, and Ardašīr the hazāruft, and Ardašīr Sūrēn, and Hormizd-Gurāz... and Kardīr-Hormizd the mōbed... and Raxš the army commander, and Ardašīr Taxm-Šāpūr... and NN secretary of the Imperial Accounts (Office) and Zōδkard the cup-bearer, and... the magnates, and noblemen, and clan-chiefs, and satraps, and bursars, and other Persians and Parthians from Asūristān...'[191].

As will be seen from the diagram below, the three lists available from the third century A.D. present a momentous shift at the end of the century.

Ardašīr	Šāpūr	Narse
1-7 royalty	1-9 royalty	royalty
8 bidaxš	10 bidaxš	hargubed
9 hazāruft	11 hazāruft	....
		bidaxš
		hazāruft.

In Narse's time, then, the hitherto undisputed position of *bidaxš* and *hazāruft* seems overshadowed by a newly emerging dignitary, the *hargubed*. So far the *bidaxš* had been the highest official of the nation. His title is known in many variants, such as, within Iran, the third-century Pe. *btxšy*, Pa. *btxš*, rendered in the Greek version of ŠKZ as πιτυάξου (l. 64), πιτιξιγαν (l. 66), βιδιξ (l. 56), πιτιάξου (l. 61); and, outside Iran, Mtskheta *btxš* and πιτιάξης (Graeco-Aramaic bilingual inscription) and *pytxš* (Aramaic inscription) on the one hand, and Bori (silver dish) *byty'xš* on the other (both in the Soviet Republic of Georgia), Armenian *bdeašx*, Georgian *pitiaxši*, later *patiašxi*, Syriac *p^eṭaḥšā*, *'afṭaḥšā*, Greek πιτιάξης, later βιδαξ(ης), Ammianus Marcellinus: *vitaxa*[192].

The title, which is undoubtedly Iranian, has given rise to a number of interpretations. Andreas at first suggested that it represented an early **pati-axš-tā(r)* 'inspector'[193]; it was no doubt the difficulty of explaining the loss of final -*t* that led him to the later

[191] See Herzfeld, *o.c.*, 100-103; Henning, BSOAS 14, 1952, 518-519.

[192] For these forms see Hübschmann 1897, 120; Nyberg, Eranos 44, 1946, 237; Altheim-Junker-Stiehl, Mélanges Grégoire, 1949, 3, 12; Altheim-Stiehl, Supplementum Aramaicum, 1957, 77; Forschungen und Fortschritte 35, 1961, 172f.; Eilers, IIJ 5, 1962, 209-210.

[193] Andreas ap. Christensen, L'empire des Sassanides, 1907, 11 and 113. Cf. Herzfeld, Paikuli 156 (doubtful), Altpersische Inschriften, 1938, 210 (more enthusiastic).

suggestion that the title derived from *pati-axša-[194], an explanation
apparently found around the same time by others also[195]. Altheim
has repeatedly voiced the view that our title continued an OP
*pati-xšāyaθiya, attested in the name of the magus Πατιζείθης[196].

All these interpretations necessitate the assumption that we can
reconstruct OP pati as the initial part of a compound. This, however,
is quite impossible. To begin with, Hübschmann rightly emphasized
(1897, 120) that the first vowel was, on the showing of our evidence,
i, and therefore he ruled out (l.c., fn. 6) the possibility of comparing
our title with pātšāh (that is OP *pati-xšāyaθiya). Secondly, the
assumption that the initial consonant was p- is quite impossible.
The Iranian forms all show initial b- which is supported even
by the external forms btxš (Mtskheta), byty'xš (Bori), Arm. bdeašx
which presupposes *bidiaxši, and by Late Greek βιδαξ(ης) which
is reflected by Latin vitaxa. An initial p- is only found in Greek
πιτιάξης, Georgian pitiaxši and Mtskheta pytxš, and Syriac pᵉṭaḥšā.
Can it be seriously suggested that the Iranians did not know how
to spell their consonant but some foreigners did? The assumption
is so absurd that it need not detain us[197]. All the same, it is
perhaps worth pointing out that the Greek preference for π- rather
than β- is obviously due to the fact that β had already become v-,
and therefore was not the right letter to render the Iranian stop b-[198].
The Georgian pitiaxši is no doubt borrowed from Arm. *bidiaxši,
and its p- must therefore be due to an internal process, probably
assimilation to the following t, or to the numerous Iranian words
with pati- (note the later full-scale assimilation in patiašxi), and
the Semitic pᵉṭaḥšā (like 'afṭaḥšā) owes the devoicing of the initial
consonant to the syncope of the following vowel.

[194] Andreas(-Wackernagel), Göttinger Gelehrte Nachrichten 1931, 306[1].

[195] Cf. Bailey, BSOS 6, 1930, 64; Pagliaro, RSO 12, 1929, 160f.; Rendiconti
dell'Accademia dei Lincei 8/9, 1954, 141-146 (: 'king's eye' from 'master's eye');
Eilers, IIJ 5, 1962, 209-210 (: 'Aufseher'); Commémoration Cyrus, 1974, 287.

[196] Altheim, in: Mélanges Grégoire (s. fn. 192!) 3-5; Totenklage und Heldenlied
bei den Hunnen, Mededel. Koninkl. Vlaamse Acad. 20, 1958, Nr. 3,10[1]; Altheim-
Stiehl, Supplementum Aramaicum, 1957, 78; Die aramäische Sprache unter den
Achämeniden, 1957-63, 248f.; Die Araber in der Alten Welt I, 1964, 638.

[197] Pagliaro 1954 [s. fn. 195], 144[1], suggested that the Iranian b was due to
(Semitic!) bēt 'house', although this title is never written with an ideogram!

[198] This was rightly stressed by Rundgren (Orientalia Suecana 12, 1964, 91)
who, in the end (p. 98), nevertheless, opts for an initial p-. It is rather surprising
that Benveniste should have allowed himself to be swayed by the spurious evidence
of external p-, see Titres, 1966, 65[2].

There can be no doubt that the Iranian word had the original initial group *bi-*, and Nyberg was right in drawing the conclusion that the primitive form of the title was **bitiyaxša*, a compound whose first member may have been *bitiya-* 'second'; the force of this conclusion was admitted by Henning, too, and it is indeed inescapable[199].

But once the first part is seen to contain the (Parthian!) ordinal *bitiya-*, the second member also becomes clear. In recent years much has been written about the rank of *second king* or *second ruler* in Iranian countries, and the whole evidence is lucidly presented by Benveniste; some corroborative testimony from Armenian has been pointed out by Widengren, and from the Old Testament by Rundgren[200]. It will suffice to recall that the institution goes back to Darius the Great at least: Xerxes reports (XPf 30-32) that *Dārayavahuš hya manā pitā pasā tanūm mām maθištam akunauš* "Darius my father made me the greatest after himself". This concept is also attested by the classical authors of the Hellenistic period who often refer to ὁ δεύτερος μετὰ τὸν βασιλέα or *secundus a rege*, and by Armenian writers. It is a remarkable fact that the institution is stil very much alive in Sogdian literature in the eighth-ninth centuries, long after the fall of the Sassanian empire. The Christian St. George-passion uses the expression *dbtyq xšywny* 'second king, vice-roy', and the Buddhistic Vessantara Jātaka speaks of δγβty γwt'w 'second king' (after me = *secundus a me*).

Widengren thought that the true Iranian expression for the notion was to be seen in Turfan Pe. *ps'gryw* and Sogd. (originally Parthian) *pš'gryw*[201], and Benveniste even assumed that this expression had been coined in Achaemenid times. But the very expression used by Xerxes (*pasā tanūm mām maθištam akunauš*) shows that *pasā tanūm* was an adverbial phrase which, unlike the later *pašāgrīw*, had not yet reached the stage of coalescence into a compound; and the fact that *tanū-*, not *grīw-* is used proves that *pasāgrīw* is a later, post-Achaemenid, coinage. There can be no doubt that

---

[199] Nyberg [s. fn. 192] 237[2]; Henning 1958, 62[2]. — Frye, Oriens 15, 1962, 354, suggests confusion of *bitaxš* (from **bitīya-xšāyaθya*) and *pātaxš* (from **pati-xšāyaθya*) but there is no room for the latter, and the former cannot be right (we would expect **bitaxšāh-ē*).

[200] See Benveniste, Titres, 1966, 51-65: *Le second après le roi*; Widengren [s. fi 187] 27-29; Rundgren [s. fn. 198] 92 f.

[201] Widengren, *l.c.*

the Achaemenid term for 'second king' was *dvitīya xšaya*, as was recognized by Hinz[202]; the interesting conclusion to be drawn from the form *bidaxš* (*dw-* > *b-*) is that this Parthian development demonstrates that the Sassanian title is not a direct continuation of the Old Iranian term (and office) but was taken over from the Arsacid court.

But we can go a step farther. In accord with his title, the *bidaxš* was in the early Sassanid empire the highest dignitary after the reigning monarch. However, we also know from the Paikuli-inscription that this state of affairs changed under Narse at the latest: the *bidaxš* was demoted, and in his place the *hargubed* was elevated to the highest office. This change must be connected with another well-known fact. It is generally thought that, originally, *bidaxš* was the military title of the margraves of Armenia (and Assur)[203]. The fact that an inscription on a silver bowl from Georgia asserts that the bowl was the property of "Pābag the bidaxš, son of Ardašir the bidaxš, son of Šāpūr the bidaxš" has been interpreted by Henning as indicating that in the late third century A.D.—the probable date of the bowl—it was understood that a bidaxš was naturally the bidaxš of Iberia[204]. This would suggest that in the latter part of the third century the essential functions of the bidaxš were given to the hargubed while the bidaxš himself was relegated to a high, but peripheral ofice.

Who is now this mysterious *hargubed* who attained to the highest office of the realm? Current views are generally based on the fact that this title seems to appear at several places and in several contexts.

The earliest mention is seen in ἀρκαπάτης, the rank of the eunuch Phraates, stated in a contract of Dura, dated 121 A.D., and usually interpreted as φρούραρχος[205]. His office is identical with that of the ἀργαπέτης, mentioned several times in inscriptions of Palmyra

---

[202] See Hinz, ZDMG 118, 1969, 433; Altiranische Funde und Forschungen, 1969, 149-153, esp. 153, where also Schmid's analysis is cited.—For *xšaya-* note also what has been said above in the next and in fn. 31a. On the alternation of *-xšē* (from *-xšaya*) and *-xš* (morphologically shortened from *-xšē*) see fn. 6 above!

[203] Cf. Bailey, BSOS 6, 1930, 64; Herzfeld, Altpersische Inschriften, 1938, 210; Frye, Studi Levi della Vida, 1956, 317f.

[204] Henning, BSOAS 24, 1961, 355.

[205] See The Excavations at Dura-Europos, Final Report V/1, 1959, 115 (no. 20, line 4), and cf. LSJ Supplement, 1968, 23.

from the third century A.D. (between 264 and 267 A.D.), and
taken to mean 'commandant of a fort'; the Palmyrene form is
ʾrgbṭ, *argbatā*, which agrees with ʾrqbt of the Jerusalem Talmud,
ʾrqpt, ʾlqpṭ of the Babylonian Talmud, and Syriac ʾlqpt [206]. The
Paikuli-inscription offers, as we have seen, Pe. *ḥlgwpt*, Pa. *ḥrkpty*,
as the title of the highest dignitary, and this is obviously identical
with ἀργαβίδης, ἀρχαπέτης of the Byzantine authors [207]. How are
all these forms to be reconciled?

The most widely held, and now a hundred years old, interpretation
was given by Nöldeke on the strength of Palmyrene ἀργαπέτης
and Tabarī's *arğabeδ*, which he traced to an Iranian prototype
*argabed 'Castellherr', a compound of the earlier form of NP *arg*
'castle' and of *pati-* 'master, lord' [208]. This view was accepted by
many scholars, even after the Paikuli forms had become known [209].
It is perhaps best summed up in Frye's words: "We may tentatively
conclude that the title ἀρκαπάτης originally meant the military
commander of a (frontier?) fortress in Parthian times. With the
rise in importance of the fortress states such as Palmyra, Hatra, etc.,
the title grew in importance. Under Ardašīr and Šāpūr, the title
had not reached the Sassanian court. After the capture of Valerian
and close contact with Palmyra and other states in Šāpūr's westward
campaigns, the title came to be known at the court, and by the time
of Narseh it had become an important title at the Sassanian court.
It does not seem to be equal to the commander-in-chief of the
army, because another man bears the title *spāhpat* in the Paikuli
inscription. Perhaps the title meant commander of the home garrison
or the imperial bodyguard" [210]. And in Mlle Chaumont's view,
from Narse's time on, that is from the end of the third century A.D.,
the *argapat* "occupera le premier degré de la hiérarchie militaire",
although in Pābag's time he was "un simple commandant de
forteresse ou de citadelle" of whom there must have been many

---

[206] Cf. Dittenberger, Orientis Graeci inscriptiones selectae II, 1905 (repr. Hildesheim
1960), 351-2, no. 645; LSJ s.v.

[207] While κ and γ in ἀρκαπάτης, ἀργαπέτης reflect an Iranian development,
ἀρχαπέτης must be due to a Greek 'folk etymology", seeing in the word an ἀρχή.

[208] See Nöldeke, ZDMG 24, 1870, 107f.; Geschichte der Perser und Araber zur
Zeit der Sasaniden—Aus der arabischen Chronik des Tabarī, 1879, 5¹.

[209] Cf. Christensen [s. fn. 193] 27; Telegdi, La phonétique des emprunts iraniens
en araméen talmudique (JA 226, 1935, 117-256) 228.

[210] See Frye, in: The Excavations at Dura-Europos, Final Report V/1, 1959, 112 =
111 fn. 15.

368 O. SZEMERÉNYI

in the Parthian empire[211]; and a few years later she restates her
view that *harkapat* seems to have denoted originally "le commandant
de la garnison affectée à la défense d'un ouvrage ou d'un groupe
d'ouvrages fortifiés: citadelle, forteresse, château fort", and the
promotion of this officer to the first place in the Paikuli inscription
must have been "une promotion récente, aussi éclatante qu'excep-
tionnelle"[212].

This explanation presupposes the existence of an Iranian word
ark 'castle, fortress'. Such a word exists, of course, in New Persian
where *arg* (in the everyday language also *ark*) means 'castle, citadel,
a small citadel within a larger one'[213]. But does it exist early
enough to appear in ἀρκαπάτης in 121 A.D.? This question can
be answered in the affirmative if Foy was right in interpreting
Ar(a)kadriš, the name of a mountain in the Behistun-inscription
(DB 1,37), as containing *ark-* 'castle' (i.e. 'bearing a castle')[214];
but the spelling of Elamite *ha-rak-qa-tar-ri-iš*, and Akkadian *a-ra-
ka-ad-ri-*' suggests *araka-* and thus speaks against the comparison.

In Book Pahlavi the simplex *arg* (or *ark*) does not appear but
the compound *arkpat* is well known. There would, therefore, be
no objection, from the chronological point of view, to Justi's suggestion that *arg* is not, as had been held, a cognate of Lat. *arx*
but a comparatively late borrowing from the Latin word[215]. But,
quite apart from the phonological difficulty to be mentioned presently, it has rightly been pointed out recently that the Roman
frontier fortresses were called *castellum*, not *arx*[216].

At this point it will be as well to lay a ghost. In 1916, Bartholomae
expressed the view that, although *arg* 'castle' was unknown to Book
Pahlavi—where *diz* was used in this sense—the Middle Persian of
Turfan had both *'rk* and *dyz*[217]. This statement has ever since

[211] Chaumont, JA 247, 1959, 177.

[212] Chaumont, JA 250, 1962, 11,14. Cf. also Rundgren [s. fn. 198] 95-96; and
Harnack, ΑΡΚΑΠΑΤΗΣ 'Festungskommandant', in: Altheim & Stiehl [s. fn. 187]
540-544.

[213] Cf. Steingass 38B.

[214] Cf. Foy, KZ 35, 1899, 62; 37, 1904, 532; and cp. Bartholomae 1904, 191;
Altheim-Stiehl, Die Araber in der Alten Welt II, 1965, 569 ad I 636f.; Harnack
[s. fn. 212] 541-2.

[215] See Justi, IFA 17, 1905, 107; and cf. Bartholomae 1906, 116.

[216] See Harnack [fn. 212] 542.

[217] Bartholomae, Zur Kenntnis der mitteliranischen Mundarten I, 1961, 16.

been quoted as a statement of fact, even with the implication that *ark* 'castle' occurs frequently[218]. In point of fact *there is no such word in the Turfan texts.*

Bartholomae referred for his statement to two passages of the *Mahrnāmag* published shortly before[219], in which F.W.K. Müller had indeed interpreted *ark* in this way. The passages were (with Müller's translation):

p. 11, line 88: *'wd hm 'rkčyq xwt'w* 'dazu den Burgherrn';

p. 16, line 187: *pd m'nyst'n 'y 'rk* 'in dem Wohnraum der Burg'.

But as far back as 1938, Henning showed that *Ark* was a place name (= Qarašahr!), and the passages meant 'in the monastery of Ark' (l. 187) and 'the king of Ark' respectively[220].

No wonder that, having banished the 'castle' from Turfan, Henning should have concluded that a 'lord of the castle' had no room in the Sassanian empire either; in his view, *harkapat* (or *hargubed*) was 'Tributherr, Fronfürst', and its first element, *hark*, was identical with Arm. *hark* 'tribute, work, corvée', Niya *harga* 'tax', and Pahl. *harg* 'duty, tribute; work, effort'[221]. Dissatisfaction with the interpretation 'lord of the castle' (and Justi's derivation of *ark* from the Latin) had been expressed long before by Herzfeld in his Paikuli-edition (193A). And nearly a quarter of a century later, in Zoroaster, he advanced his new view that *arka-* was 'the tribute owed by the vassal', and the *arkapat* the 'chief collector of taxes'[222].

[218] Cf. Telegdi [fn. 206] 228; Widengren, Orientalia Suecana 5, 1956, 158; Chaumont, JA 250, 1962, 12; Harnack [fn. 212] 542.

[219] See F.W.K. Müller, Ein Doppelblatt aus einem manichäischen Hymnenbuch (Mahrnāmag), Abh. Preuss. Akad. 1912/V.

[220] Cf. Henning, BSOS 9, 1938, 565-6, and the interesting note (at 566[1]) that Schaeder had, orally, already proposed that *ark* was a place-name, and not 'castle'.

[221] See Henning 1958, 41 with fn. 4, where Henning insists that the word interpreted by Bartholomae [s. fn. 217] as BP *ark* 'Arbeit' was in fact *hark*, denoting 'tribute' *and* 'corvée', which ultimately derives from Akkadian *ilku*, as does the form *harāg*. For a linguistic discussion of *harg* and *harāg* see also Henning's early treatment at Orientalia 4, 1935, 291-293 (OP *harāka* 'Grundsteuer'), and Bailey, Asia Maior 7, 1959, 18. In view of the varying forms *hark-* and *ark-*, collected by Benveniste (JA 247, 1959, 125-126), it is perhaps, *pace* Henning, useful to distinguish *hark* 'tribute' and *ark* 'work'; for the latter see the large material mustered by Bailey, Zoroastrian problems in the ninth-century books, [2]1971, XIX-XXII. For the revenue aspects of *harg*/*harāg* see also Altheim-Stiehl, in: Jahrbuch für Wirtschaftsgeschichte 1967, Part II, 311-312, where the authors reaffirm the meaning 'Grundsteuer' for Pe. *harāg*, and its derivation from Aram. *ḥᵃlāk* in the sense of 'was weggeht' or 'was davongetragen wird', and Araber V/2, 1969, 215-7.

[222] Herzfeld, Zoroaster and his world I, 1947, 128.

The interpretation first given by Herzfeld, and then again discovered by Henning, is now codified in Gignoux's Glossaire (23,52) who defines the *hargubed* as 'chef des impôts' [223].

And the choice is indeed narrowed down to the alternative 'lord of the castle' or something like 'inspector of revenue'. A derivation from **harva-ka-pati-* 'leader of the guards' (to be connected with Avest. *har-* 'protect, watch over') is just as impossible as the assumption that the first part might contain Aramaic *'arqā* 'land (i.e. *hargubed* = 'land lord'!) [224].

At this juncture, we must have a closer look at form and meaning of the title in question. As has been noticed already, the Iranian forms always show *hark-/harg-* as the first part [225]; only the foreign forms (Greek, Talmudic, Syriac) offer *ark-* instead, but that again without exception [226]. Thus we find ourselves in the same position as with the initial consonant of *bidaxš* above, and here again there can be no doubt that the native spelling must be "right"; as Herzfeld put it (Paikuli 193A), "we must assume *harkapati* as the original form". The loss of initial *h-* being confined to a small number of unstressed words or particles (*agar* 'if', *az* 'from', *am/an-* for *ham/han-* etc.) [227], we could not account for the reduction in

---

[223] It is interesting that Frye, who at Oriens 15, 1962, 353 judged that the derivation of Dura ἀρκαπάτης from an Iranian 'tax collector' was unacceptable, in The Heritage of Persia, also published in 1962, should have admitted (279 fn. 56) that the title might have a first part *ark/hark* similar in meaning to Akkadian *ilku*, and that it might have had an antecedent in an OP **haraka pati* 'lord of tribute', "or perhaps really the local tax farmer rather than the official tax collector (the *hamārakar*?)".

[224] The former seems to have been Frye's favourite, but the latter is also his idea, see Oriens 15, 1962, 353. Cf. also Altheim-Stiehl, Araber [fn. 196] I, 1964, 636.

[225] The only exception would be the form *'rkpty* read by Herzfeld on "a curious small epigraphical monument" (Paikuli 193A), and accepted by Henning (1958, 41), but it obviously cannot outweigh the massive evidence of Paikuli, and, in spite of Herzfeld's reassurance, the reading does not seem above doubt, so that the "monument" would deserve to be re-examined; cf. also Chaumont, JA 250, 1962, 19 fn. 2.

[226] If the reading *harjand ibn Sām* in Ṭabarī's history, Nöldeke [s. fn. 208] 27, is rightly emended in its second half by him (27²) to *Abarsām*, and in its first half to *harjbad* (Pers. *hargbad*) by Marquart (see Herzfeld, Paikuli 193—an emendation rediscovered by Altheim-Stiehl, Araber [s. fn. 214] II, 1965, 238—that simply means that in Ṭabarī's work we have the Sassanian form.

[227] Cf. Hübschmann 1895, 216-218; Horn 1898, 96. Bartholomae's formulation, o.c. [fn. 217], 42, is too broad.

Iranian of *harkapati* to **arkapati* in any case. In Greek, on the other hand, the loss of aspiration is quite normal in our era, and therefore ΑΡΚΑΠΑΤΗΣ would be the expected representation (apart, perhaps, from the final -ΗΣ) of Iranian *harkapati*. From which it follows that the Talmudic and Syriac forms with initial *ark-* or *alk-* are not directly borrowed from Iranian (Parthian) but *via* Greek.

As concerns the original meaning of the word, Nöldeke assumed, as we have seen, that ΑΡΓΑΠΕΤΗΣ at Palmyra and Tabarī's *arğabed* both reflected an Iranian *argabed* 'Castellherr'. In view of the scanty material at his disposal he could hardly have reached a different solution but it is very much to be doubted whether he would have reached the same conclusion had he known of the Paikuli forms. Seeing that we are so much better placed, it is incumbent on us to re-examine the value of the external evidence.

In the first relevant document, the Greek parchment of Dura dated 121 A.D., it is stated that the loan was made, in the presence of Metolbaissas, a φρούραρχος, by Phraates, εὐνοῦχος, ἀρκαπάτης, a member of the entourage of Manesos, who in turn is described, amongst others, as tax collector (παραλήπτης?), governor of Mesopotamia and Parapotamia, and ruler of the Arabs[228]. Comparing the titles of Metolbaissas and Phraates, Frye stressed the parallelism between the two series and concluded that φρούραρχος, the title given to the first person, was the same as ἀρκαπάτης, ascribed to the eunuch[229]. Altheim was not slow in pointing out that this was no kind of argument, that, if anything at all, the comparison showed that the φρούραρχος was a much higher official than the ἀρκαπάτης, and that the two ranks were in fact quite different, as shown by the difference in the terms used[230]. But we can go a step further[231]. In view of the fact that Phraates appears in the entourage of a revenue-official, that he himself (an eunuch) is anything but a military character, and, last not least, that we are witnesses of a very advantageous financial deal, can we escape

---

[228] For the text see fn. 205 above.

[229] Frye, Oriens 15, 1962, 352.

[230] Altheim-Stiehl, Araber [s. fn. 196] I, 1964, 635 f.

[231] Altheim does not here suggest a counter-solution but in Araber [s. fn. 214] II, 1965, 569 ad I 636f., he thinks that *Ar(a)kadri-* (an old idea, see fn. 214) could be in favour of 'Burg'.

the impression that Phraates himself is a tax official, that is a *harkapati*, and not an *arkapati*? [232].

The next set of documents, which consists of several inscriptions in honour of Septimius Vorodes found at Palmyra, points in the same direction. In the earliest inscription, of April 262 A.D., he is described as a *procurator ducenarius*, in one of April 265 he is in addition an ἀργαπέτης. In the inscription of April 266 we get the full *cursus honorum*: Vorodes was aedile, duovir (στρατηγός), in charge of the safety of caravans, δικεοδότης (iuridicus), finally procurator ducenarius. In the inscription of April 267, he is again a procurator ducenarius and ἀργαπέτης [233]. Again all the titles point to a financial rather than a military career, to Vorodes being a *harkapati*, not a 'lord of the castle'.

Finally, the Semitic sources, when they do not reveal an embarrassment at having to deal with terms incompletely understood, show with their interpretation 'prince', 'high Persian dignitary' that a simple 'commandant of a fort' is hardly enough for the '*rqpṭ*', etc. [234].

It looks, then, as if for the first half of the first millennium A.D., at any rate, we could safely ignore the existence of a dignitary **arkpat* 'lord of the castle'. This result brings one immediate advantage. So far it has been a very puzzling fact that whereas an *arkpat* 'Burgvogt' was known on the periphery of the Sassanian empire, in the core of the realm (e.g. in ŠKZ) he was unknown during the first Sassanids, who however did have a dignitary fitting that description but going by the name of *dizpat*, a term already known in the Nisa ostraca [235]. With the disappearance of the *arkpat* this problem is shown to be a pseudo-problem.

We have all been taught, of course, that the founder of the Sassanid dynasty himself started in life as an *argbed*. Even Herzfeld thought that this was the only case "where the interpretation 'lord of the castle' seems to be well founded" (Paikuli 193B). But is it a fact [236]? What we know is that Pābag, father of Ardašīr,

---

[232] Altheim, Araber I 637, also notes that 'Herr der Grundsteuer' would be excellent in the company of the 'tax collector' Manesos, but thinks that *arkapati* and the Greek forms are against it.

[233] For these data see Altheim, Araber II 255.

[234] Cf. Rundgren [s. fn. 198] 95-96 with footnotes.

[235] See Mlle Chaumont's clear presentation at JA 250, 1962, 12f., and cp. Harnack [s. fn. 212] 543f. The title even goes back to Achaemenid times if the Elamite tablets warrant an OP *didāpatiš*, as is suggested by Hinz 1973, 99.

[236] For the following see Nöldeke [s. fn. 208] 4-5; and Harnack, *l.c.*, 540-541.

took his son, at the age of seven, to King Gōzihr in Istaxr, and asked the king to attach his son to the service of Tīrē so that his son might get an education there and eventually succeed Tīrē in his post. Tīrē was an eunuch and *argabed* of Dārābgird in the eastern parts of the province Pārs, and Ardašīr did in fact succeed Tīrē on his death. Nöldeke's "Commandant von Dārābgird" naturally followed from his earlier discovery that the *argbed* and the ἀργαπέτης of Palmyra represented an *argbed* 'Castellherr'. But with the fall of the 'lord of the castle' there is no reason why we should not interpret the title in this passage also in the usual sense of 'inspector of revenue' [237].

The only remaining trace of an **arkpat* would be the Book Pahlavi form cited by both Bartholomae and Salemann [238], but without giving their source. This point would certainly deserve a special study. But in view of our results we can hardly go far wrong in assuming that, if there be such a form, it must be interpreted as *harkpat*.

This does not, of course, dispose of the late noun *arg* (or *ark*) 'citadel', which is, nonetheless, hardly a late borrowing from an unknown source, nor likely to be extracted from an *arg-bed* [239]. If, in spite of its late attestation, it is of an early date, going back to antiquity, then it would be possible in theory that it should be from an IE root like Lat. *arx*, as used to be assumed before Justi's paper [240]. But since the Latin development is itself rather unusual, I should like to point to a further possibility. Describing the organization of the Persian empire, Xenophon speaks of τοὺς ἐν ταῖς ἄκραις φρουράρχους (Cyr. 8,6,1), i.e. 'guard commanders in fortresses', while, in the Anabasis (7,1,19-20), reporting the violence of his troops in Byzantium, he says that Ἐτεόνικος εἰς τὴν ἄκραν ἀποφεύγει 'Eteonicus takes refuge in the citadel' which is later given its proper name, ἀκρόπολις. The word ἄκρα is the usual military

---

[237] Another personage of the rank of *hargubed* has been thought to be attested in the famous courtier *AburSām*, see Altheim-Stiehl, Araber II 238; Harnack, *l.c.*, 541. But even if the emendation should be correct (s. fn. 226 above), that can only mean that his title was later brought up to date: we know from the ŠKZ that his title was *framādār* (s. fn. 181 above), and came fifteenth in the "honours' list".

[238] See Bartholomae [s. fn. 217] 16; Salemann, in: Grundriss der iranischen Philologie I 1, 1901, 257.

[239] This is suggested by Frye, Heritage [s. fn. 223] 279 fn. 56, but there would be no such Iranian form, only *hargubed*!

[240] See Horn, Grundriß der neupersischen Etymologie, 1893 (repr. 1974), 18. For Justi see fn. 215.

term for 'citadel' even in a later writer like Lucianus. I suggest therefore the possibility that this word was received into Persian where, however, it suffered the metathesis usual in *r*-groups and became *arkā*, later *ark*, *arg*.

To sum up our results concerning the *arkpat* and *hargubed*. The Sassanian world only knew the office of **harkapati*, later *hargubed*; the *arkpat*, allegedly 'lord of the castle' never existed [241], the form is the Greek adaptation (with loss of "aspiration") of *harkpat*, and the Greek form was taken over into the Talmud and Syriac also. The **harkapati* started life as a low-ranking revenue-official—Phraates at Dura was a subordinate of the powerful Manesos, and Ardašīr son of Pābag started his practice in a small place far from the capital—and it is typical of a feudal social structure that an officer of this kind is mentioned neither in Ardašīr's list, nor in Šāpūr's, although the latter has a *ganzvar* 'treasurer', coming 53rd in the list, to be sure, not far from the bottom. It seems obvious that the expensive wars conducted by Šāpūr drove home the importance of state revenue, and that the recognition of this fact manifests itself in the exalted position of the imperial *hargubed* who comes immediately after royalty and may very well have been a member of the Sassanian family.

In the light of these results it would be useful to re-examine the structure of the Sassanian court. Special attention would have to be paid to the no doubt very similar situation prevailing in the later Roman Empire and in the early history of Byzantium [242]. Of particular interest is the fact that, as reported by Theophylactus of Samocatta, at the Persian court seven families held the highest offices, the first being the family of ΑΡΤΑΒΙΔΗΣ which crowns the new king and is itself of royal rank. Nöldeke emended the name to ΑΡΓΑΒΙΔΗΣ, and this, i.e. *hargbed*, would in its rank accord with our conclusions. But in Theophylactus' account the sixth family supplies the official in charge of taxes who is also the keeper of the royal treasure; his office would thus seem to overlap, to say the least, with that of the *hargubed* [243]. This type

---

[241] Note Mlle Chaumont's important observation (JA 250, 1962, 16): "jamais un *argpat* n'apparait à la tête des troupes en campagne".

[242] For the latter a useful starting point could be W. Ensslin's contribution, "The emperor and the imperial administration", in: Byzantium, edd. N.H. Baynes and H.St.L.B. Moss, Oxford 1948, 268-307.

[243] See Christensen [s. fn. 193] 27f.; Chaumont, JA 249, 1961, 305.

of contradiction could perhaps be resolved by a study of the kind suggested above.

Returning to our main problem, the office of *hazārbed* or *hazāruft*, we can see now that, together with the *bidaxš*, he was at the very top of the courtiers' list, immediately after royalty, to begin with; but at the end of the third century the *hargubed* was promoted over their heads. Even so there can be little doubt about their exalted position. In particular, there can be no doubt that the *hazārbed*'s command extended over an army many times larger than a single regiment of a thousand men. And yet this is what the name suggests, this narrowly circumscribed competence is what is borne out by external and internal data.

To begin with, the whole organizational system of the armed forces of Ērānšahr has left its traces in the nomenclature of various neighbouring peoples. In a penetrating study [244], Benveniste pointed out (42f., 53f.) that the Gothic *hundafaþs* 'centurion' and *þusundifaþs* 'chiliarch' are (along with *swnagogafaþs* 'head of the synagogue') a foreign element in the Germanic vocabulary—the Germanic type is represented by Gothic *þiudans*, *kindins*—and represent in actual fact loan-translations of certain Iranian terms [245]. The same applies (ibid. 54f.) to the Armenian term *hariwrapet* 'leader of a hundred', and *hazarapet* 'captain over a thousand' is a straightforward borrowing.

But an even more complete picture is presented by the Greek writers, and one which takes us back to the very beginnings of the Achaemenid state, the early fifth century B.C. [246]. In a famous passage (7,81), Herodotus gives the command-chain of the Persian army as μυριάρχαι — χιλιάρχαι — ἑκατοντάρχαι — δεκάρχαι 'captains over ten thousand, a thousand, a hundred, ten respectively'. Even earlier are the forms used by Aeschylus in the Persae (performed in 472 B.C.): χιλίαρχος and μυριόνταρχος (lines 304, 314); in a fragment he also employs ἑκατοντάρχης. It is interesting that whereas Herodotus uses forms in -άρχης [247], Aeschylus (with the exception of the form last named), and especially Xenophon use forms in -αρχος. And not surprisingly, Xenophon, a military man

---

[244] Benveniste, Interférences lexicales entre le gotique et l'iranien, BSL 58, 1963, 41-57, completed by a chapter in Titres (1966), 67-71.

[245] For the time (third century A.D.?) see Benveniste, BSL 58, 55f.

[246] See Benveniste, *o.c.*, 49f.

[247] Cp. E.H. Rüedi, Vom *Hellānodikās* zum *allantopōlēs*, Diss. Zurich, 1969, 118f.

long in Persian service, gives the most complete list of ranks. He has not only μυρίαρχος, χιλίαρχος, ἑκατόνταρχος, and δεκά-δαρχος, but also πεντηκόνταρχος (although only as an Athenian term), πεμπάδαρχος, and, as two odd men out, the δωδεκάδαρχος and the ἑξάδαρχος. Later the Septuagint will also use these terms, cf. Exodus 18,21: χιλιάρχους καὶ ἑκατοντάρχους καὶ πεντηκοντάρ-χους καὶ δεκαδάρχους.

None of these terms is represented by its Iranian equivalent in the Old Persian records. But the Elamite texts of the Persepolis Treasury and Fortification tablets (509-458 B.C.) have brought to light most of these terms in a thinly veiled transcription. So far the following have turned up [248]:

Elamite	Old Persian
sadabattiš 'centurion'	θatapatiš
dasabattiš 'decurion'	daθapatiš
dašabattiš 'decurion'	dasapatiš?
bašzadasabattiš 'vice-decurion'	pasča-daθapatiš.

The terms for 'centurion' and 'decurion' present the expected type. On the other hand, the term for 'vice-decurion', even if it can be paralleled by later forms like pašāgrīv 'deputy, heir (to the throne)', is nonethless surprising, not least because, if it means 'leader of five men' [249], and thus corresponds to πεμπάδαρχος, one would rather have liked to see *panča-patiš in this function. This expectation is met by Elamite zatturrubattiš which Cameron-Gershevitch (l.c.) no doubt correctly interpreted as čaθru-patiš 'chief of four', although the number is just as odd as in the Greek ἑξάδαρχος, δωδεκάδαρχος. There are no objections to a reconstructed *pančaθatpatiš 'leader of a detachment of fifty', except that its only justification is to be found in Greek πεντηκόνταρχος which does not seem to be used in an Iranian context [250]. Although so far unattested, *hazahrapatiš is no doubt correctly assumed, and is

[248] Cf. G.G. Cameron, Persepolis Treasury Tablets, 1948; Widengren, Orientalia Suecana 5, 1956, 160-162; Benveniste, BSL 58, 1963, 52-53 (with references to Cameron); Brandenstein-Mayrhofer 1964, 125, 139; Cameron-Gershevitch, JNES 24, 1965, 177; Hallock, Persepolis Fortification Tablets, 1969, 676, 680, 749, 773; Harnack, in: Altheim-Stiehl [s. fn. 187] 508, 518; Mayrhofer 1971, 56; Hinz, ZAssyriologie 61, 1971, 294; Hinz 1973, 168B.

[249] See Widengren, l.c., 160-161; Benveniste, l.c., 53.

[250] Widengren, l.c., 161, quotes for his reconstruction Xenophon, Cyrup. II 1, 22, but I can't find the word there.

indirectly supported by the later Armenian loan-word *hazarapet*. For **baivarpati* we can quote, in addition to μυρίαρχος, Avest. *baēvarə.pati-* although its meaning is slightly different (: "der zehntausende beherrscht"? Lommel).

Can we establish the origin of this tightly organized system? Benveniste thinks, no doubt rightly, that the parallelism of the terminology in the four languages surveyed is the result of cultural diffusion from Iran. But he goes even further: "Nous considérons, jusqu'à preuve du contraire, que le principe de cette division en groupes de cent, de mille etc. est né en Perse, dans la Perse des Achéménides... on le trouve là et on ne le trouve ni en Assyrie, ni en Égypte, dans aucune des deux civilisations dont auraient pu s'inspirer les Grands Rois". There are, he says, in the Old Testament chiefs of a thousand, a hundred, fifty, or ten men, but "cette organisation n'a évidemment pas pu influencer celle de l'Empire achéménide" [251].

There can hardly be any doubt that the terminology of Greek, Gothic and Armenian are rightly traced by Benveniste to Iran as the centre of diffusion. We may add as a significant detail Quintus Curtius' well-known statement (V 2,2-3) that Alexander the Great reorganized his forces "*tunc primum in hunc numerum* (sc. 1,000) *copiis distributis: namque antea quingenariae cohortes fuerant*". It can also be maintained that the Israelite organization can hardly have influenced Persia. But it is manifestly wilful to conclude that the Persian system was the product of local parthenogenesis and had not been triggered off in its turn by earlier Near Eastern influence. We would have to postulate such an influence on *a priori* grounds even if there were no specific arguments to bear out our claim. But we need not content ourselves with such general reflexions at all. It is not only the Old Testament facts that resemble the Iranian situation, e.g. the dictum: "choose such men and place them over the people to *be sārē ʾᵃlāpīm, sārē mēʾōt, sārē hᵃmiššīm wᵉsārē ʾᵃsārōt*" (rulers of thousands, rulers of hundreds, rulers of fifties, and rulers of tens) [252]. Much more important is for Iran the fact that we find the same organization in the neighbouring Akkadian civilization; cf. the expressions used for the following groups:

1,000: NBab. *akil līm* "Tausendschaftsaufseher"; LBab. *rab 1 lim*;

---

[251] Cf. for these conclusions Benveniste, Titres, 1966, 68-9.
[252] See Exodus 18,21 (and cp. 25); 2 Kings 1,9f.; and Koehler-Baumgartner, Lexicon in Veteris Testamenti Libros, 1958, 929 and 313B.

100: NBab. *akil 1 me-at* "Hundertschaftsaufseher"; LBab. *rab 1 ME* (*ia*);

50: NAss., NBab. *rab hanšū* "commander of a contingent of 50 soldiers";

10: LBab. *rab ešerti* "Obmann über 10";

5: MBab. *rab hamišti* "foreman of a team of five men"[253].

There can be no doubt that this was the system that determined the military organization of the successor-state, Achaemenid Iran.

It is in this system that the *hazahrapatiš* occupied a distinguished position. But what exactly do we know of this position? According to Marquart, whose results concerning this dignitary are still very largely regarded as authoritative[254], the 10,000 guard troops, called the *Immortals*, formed ten regiments of 1,000 each, each under command of a χιλίαρχος = OP **hazahrapatiš*. But this title usually denoted the commander of the picked body of 1,000 μηλοφόροι or δορυφόροι[255], i.e. of the life-guards, who also had the overall command of the whole corps. When the Persian general Mardonius, who was to stay behind in Thessaly, picked the Immortals as part of his occupation force, their commander, Hydarnes, claimed that he could not leave the king (Hdt. 8,113: οὐκ ἔφη λείψεσθαι βασιλέος), and went home with Xerxes. This, says Marquart, reveals the importance of this confidential post, and, taken in conjunction with the statement of Nepos that the chiliarch held the second position in the realm (Conon 3,2: *qui secundum gradum imperii tenebat*) suggests (p. 228) that: "Der Kommandant dieser Truppe hatte also den Verkehr mit dem Hofe direkt zu überwachen und brachte offenbar auch dem König täglich den Rapport. Jetzt werden wir auch die Glosse des Hesych verstehen: ἀζαραπατεῖς · οἱ εἰσαγγελεῖς παρὰ Πέρσαις". Furthermore, says Marquart (p. 229), name

[253] See von Soden, Akkadisches Handwörterbuch I, 1959-1965, 553Bf.; 318; 254A; 317B; II, 1966-1972, 639.—Chicago Assyrian Dictionary H, 1956, 67, 81; E, 1958, 365; L, 1973, 198A.

[254] Cf. J. Marquart, Hazarapet, Philologus 55, 1896, 227-234.

[255] Marquart thinks (227 fn. 37) that, as stated by Heraclides Cumaeus, only the life-guards, i.e. the members of the first regiment, were called μηλοφόροι. But this is a mistake. For this historian of the fourth century B.C. clearly states (see Fragmenta Historicorum Graecorum, ed. Müller, II 95-6; Fragmente der Griechischen Historiker, ed. F. Jacoby, III C I, 1958, 518 fn. 1) that these guards had *gold* pomegranates at the butt-end of their spear. The other Immortals also had pomegranates but of *silver*, cf. the correct description given by A.T. Olmstead, History of the Persian Empire, 1948, 238-239.

and character of the office are clearly defined by Diodorus Siculus (end of 1st century B.C.) when he states in his Bibliotheca (16,47,3) that Aristazanes "ἦν εἰσαγγελεὺς τοῦ βασιλέως καὶ πιστότατος τῶν φίλων μετὰ Βαγῶαν"[256]. Similarly, Marquart argues, "der Befehlshaber der Leibwache hatte selbstverständlich auch die Hinrichtungen zu vollstrecken", and quotes, amongst others, Prexaspes, who, at Cambyses' command, killed Bardiya (cf. Hdt. 3,74).

This reconstruction is supported by Herzfeld who also holds that "the *hazārapati* of the 1st regiment [of the 'Immortals'] had the special duty never to leave the king, and became, in this capacity, Chief Gentleman Usher. In this way the office, originally military, changed into a civil one. Already during the Achaemenian epoch, this first *hazārapati* was the second in rank after the king"[257]. Further details are added by Christensen: "Von diesen Unsterblichen waren tausend Mann als königliche Leibwache im Palast(!) unter dem Kommando des Chiliarchen (pers. *hazahrapati*) untergebracht. Sie trugen persische oder medische Tracht, Bogen und Köcher und eine lange Lanze, deren Schuh die Form eines Apfels hatte, weshalb die Garden 'Äpfelträger' (μηλοφόροι) genannt wurden". "Wer zum König Zutritt haben wünschte, mußte angemeldet werden". "Sehr wahrscheinlich ist die Vermutung E. Meyers, daß der Chiliarch, der Kommandant der Leibwache, der Oberste der Sieben war. Jedenfalls ist der Chiliarch... in späterer Zeit der erste Minister des Reiches, der Großvezier. Er hatte den *secundum gradum imperii* (Nepos), war der erste im Range nach dem König (Diodor 18,48). Er war der 'Hofmeister', der εἰσαγγελεύς des Königs und der Vollstrecker der Hinrichtungen (Marquart). An Artabanos, den Chiliarchen, wendet sich Themistokles, um beim Perserkönig Audienz zu erlangen (Plut. Them. 27)"[258].

Much more complete and imaginative is the picture drawn in a special study by P.J. Junge[259]. After Justi's pioneering venture[260]

---

[256] Marquart also says that Aristazanes had command of 5000 ἐπίλεκτοι, i.e. of half the guards, but Diodorus merely states that they were 5000 picked troops and breathes no word of the Immortals.

[257] Herzfeld, Paikuli 188B, and cf. 174A (where he repeats Marquart's mistake that only the first regiment went by the name μηλοφόροι).

[258] Christensen, Die Iranier (in: Handbuch der Altertumswissenschaft III/I/III/3/2, 1933, 201-310) 261, 263, 266.

[259] Junge, Klio 33, 1940, 13-38.

[260] Justi, Der Chiliarch des Dareios, ZDMG 50, 1896, 659-664.

—necessarily little satisfying since the reproductions used by him were rather poor—this is the first time that the archaeological evidence is again brought to bear upon our problem. Junge thinks that two reliefs can help us in our efforts more precisely to define the *hazārapatiš* sphere of activity and competence. The first, decorating the Northern gate of Xerxes' Hall of Hundred Columns at Persepolis, had long been known, and had been used by Justi in the study referred to. The second was found in 1936 on the Eastern and Southern porticoes around the central courtyard of the Persepolis Treasury. Since this is the more complete representation of what is essentially the same scene, I shall only discuss this relief very briefly[261]. The central part shows Darius the Great and Xerxes on a dais: the father is seated on his throne, holding in his right the long slender sceptre which rests on the floor, in his left a lotus, the son stands behind him and also carries in his left hand a lotus. Before the king are set two incense burners, in front of a person who is clad in the Median costume, is slightly bent towards the king, holds his right hand to his mouth while his left holds a staff also resting on the ground. "Der eben vor den König tretende Mann muß, wie schon Justi erkannt hat, der Oberste der Einführer, der *hazārapatiš*, sein"[262]—says Junge (17, cf. 24)—; "er wird durch den Stab, der sich vom königlichen Szepter durch Länge und Art unterscheidet, deutlich gekennzeichnet. Dieser Stab nämlich ist das Amtszeichen der Einführer". For that reason the 'announcers', εἰσαγγελεῖς, were also called σκηπτοῦχοι 'wand-bearers' by the Greeks (17). As was shown by Marquart, the Chief Introducer was also the chiliarch of the life-guards (19). But it is curious that these reliefs are set up in the porticoes of the Treasury—where no audience was ever held; this must mean that their placing is connected

---

[261] Cf. Junge, *o.c.*, 24f. It is perhaps useful to refer to some easily accessible works. Olmstead [s. fn. 255] Plate XXX; Ghirshman, Iran, Penguin Books 1954, Plate 19(b); and H.H.v.d. Osten, Die Welt der Perser, 1956, plate 62, give a very good reproduction of the relief as a whole. In Frye's Heritage [s. fn. 223] the relief is shown in two parts in plates 66 and 31—without the reader being told of this fact.—Excellent photos of single figures are to be found in Hinz [s. fn. 202], s. plates 19, 29, 31. Cf. also, for the Hall of Hundred Columns, G. Walser, Die Völkerschaften auf den Reliefs von Persepolis, 1966, plates 6 and 7.—For the following description of the Treasury relief see also Olmstead 216f.; and Feodora Prinzessin von Sachsen-Meiningen, in: Altheim, Geschichte der Hunnen II, 1960, 131f.

[262] This is also Olmstead's view, *o.c.*, 217.

with the person of the *hazārapatiš*: "So muß das Relief also den Verandenraum als Aufenthaltsraum des Hazarapatiš kennzeichnen und demnach eine königliche Ehrengabe darstellen" (27); to put it slightly differently, the place of the reliefs shows that the *hazārapatiš* was "chief of the treasury"! (29). And now the final conclusions: "So viel läßt sich wohl entnehmen, daß der *hazārapatiš* die gesamte Hofhaltung mit den königlichen Einkünften und Ausgaben und dem dazugehörigen Schriftverkehr verwaltete" (30)[263]. "Die ursprüngliche militärische Stellung des *h.* ist... das Kommando einer 1000 Mann starken königlichen Leibwache[264]. Gleichzeitig jedoch war er der Kommandant des aus 10000 Mann... bestehenden Gardekorps" (32). Summing up it can be said: "Dies wohl wichtigste aller Ämter im altpersischen Staat ist... aus der Stelle des königlichen Leibgardekommandanten entwickelt... Er befehligt daher außer der Leibgarde... auch das ganze Gardekorps... Seine Verantwortlichkeit für die Sicherheit des Königs macht es gleichzeitig notwendig, daß ihm auch das Einführerkorps untersteht... er regelt den Audienzverkehr", and is "Chef der zentralen Reichsverwaltung, der königlichen Kanzlei" (35-36)[265]. Essential is also that the *h.* "auch die Kontrolle der Finanzverwaltung und ihrer Einkünfte und Ausgaben durch das Schatzhaus hatte" (37). We can say, then, that "im Achämenidenreich durchweg... die Stellung des *h.* von gleicher, alle anderen überragender Bedeutung ist und daß sie bereits dieselbe Weite aufweist wie die Chiliarchie im Reiche Alexanders des Großen" (38).

These results have been widely adopted by subsequent researchers. Thus, e.g., Olmstead puts much the same view in a nutshell: "as the commander of the royal bodyguard [the *h.*] was the most powerful official at court" (217). According to von der Osten, the *h.* combines the offices of chief of staff, supreme commander of the life-guards, and of premier; his role as an administrator is illuminated by the several thousand cuneiform tablets which have been found in the troops' quarters but which are connected with

---

[263] Junge reports (30⁴) that Hinz had queried the possibility of one person being in charge of the treasury, the state finances and the chancery, seeing that in the very similar Sassanian system these offices are all kept separate. Cf. fn. 265.

[264] Here again (cf. fn. 255) Heraclides Cumaeus is quoted but incorrectly.

[265] Here even Junge admits (36¹) that in the Orient military and civil power are never united in one hand. Cf. fn. 263.

the building of the palace[266]. Bengtson, on the other hand, would like to tone down the military aspect in the sense that the *h.* "unter Abstreifung der ursprünglichen militärischen Befehlsgewalt zum ersten Minister des Reiches, zum 'Großvezir' emporstieg"[267]. Walser expresses himself more cautiously: "Auf den Audienzszenen des 100-Säulen-Saales und des Schatzhauses steht ein gleicher Beamter mit dem Heroldsstab vor dem thronenden Herrscher. Es mag(!) sich dabei um den obersten Chef des Einführerkoprs handeln, den allgewaltigen Hazarpeten, den Vezir des Reiches, der sowohl Kommandant der königlichen Garde als auch Leiter des Audienzdienstes gewesen sein mag(!)"[268].

It seems, then, that a general consensus has been achieved according to which in the early fifth century B.C. the commander of the life-guards, the *hazārapatiš* par excellence, attained to a unique, unequalled position: he was the most powerful person at court, second only to the king; he not only guaranteed the safety of the king through being the commander of the life-guards but also controlled all admissions into the royal presence; what is more, he was in charge of state finances as well. No wonder that this fullness of power should conjure up the vision of the later grand vizier.

But is this construction really tenable? The answer is that there are several features in this picture which must be rejected. To begin with the *relief(s)*, the figure showing reverence to the king *cannot be the hazārapatiš.* Junge observes himself that this person wears the Median costume; and that being the case, we must agree with Hinz that the commander of the life-guards who were all Persians —a fact repeatedly emphasized by Herodotus and others—cannot have been a Mede, he must have been a Persian[269]. Hinz thinks (63,67) that the official is a *Hofmarschall,* a marshal, perhaps even

[266] H.H.v.d. Osten [s. fn. 261] 91.

[267] H. Bengtson, Griechische Geschichte, [2]1960, 130.

[268] Walser (fn. 261) 68.—Walser further makes the interesting observation—which would deserve to be followed up in greater detail—that: "Amt und Abzeichen stammen aus dem assyrischen Hofdienst, wo ein hoher Hofbeamter ebenfalls die Audienzen anmeldet und Besucher vor den Herrscher führt".

[269] Hinz [s. fn. 202] 68. Hinz thinks that the commanders of the other regiments could have been other than Persian, and so the official in question could be a *hazārapatiš* but not *the hazārapatiš.*—On the nationality of the various regiments of the Immortals see also Dandamayev, in: Beiträge zur Achämenidengeschichte (ed. G. Walser), 1972, 55.

a Lord Chamberlain, which is possible. But when he, after Junge (19), suggests that the gesture of the official is simply dictated by hygienic considerations, i.e. to avoid that the king is inconvenienced, he is too much swayed by the advertising media of our day which constantly admonish their victims to, and advise how to, improve their breath. There can be no doubt that the gesture in question simply expresses that the inferior person kisses his hand (i.e. waves a kiss) to his superior. The relief gives the earliest representation of the Iranian προσκύνησις which, in essence, means throwing a kiss, or kissing one's hand, to someone, and does not necessarily imply kneeling down [270].

Junge's argument (27-29) that the place of the second relief shows that the *hazārapatiš* was the chief of the treasury, is only convincing in its second part. If the place suggests anything at all, then surely simply that the recipient was connected with the treasury [271], not that he was the *hazārapatiš*. In point of fact the two offices are probably just as incompatible in Achaemenid times as they will be in Sassanid times.

Turning now to the literary, i.e. Classical, evidence we must stress first of all that Marquart was wrong in using Hydarnes' return as a general argument in favour of the thesis that the *hazārapatiš* could not leave the king for one moment, and therefore was also charged with vetting all his visitors. Obviously the single episode will not stand this kind of straining.

But now the question arises whether there is any positive proof for linking *hazārapatiš* and εἰσαγγελεύς. Frye has already expressed misgivings about this widely accepted thesis: 'to assume that the Greek word εἰσαγγελεύς signified more than 'announcer', and rather was the office of prime minister, is reading too much into it" [272]. His latest pronouncement on the general topic is also relevant: "There is no evidence that Darius or Xerxes had a prime minister, although later the chiliarch or *hazārapati*, literally 'commander

---

[270] On this hotly disputed problem see Marti, Language 12, 1936, 272f.; Altheim-Stiehl, Ein Asiatischer Staat I, 1954, II fn. 1 (: "Zuwerfen einer Kusshand"); Princess Feodora [s. fn. 261]; Bickerman, La Parola del Passato 91, 1963, 241-255; Frye, Iranica Antiqua 9, 1972, 102f.—J. Hofstetter, in: Beiträge zur Achämeniden-geschichte, 1972, 106, has not succeeded in disproving this view.

[271] I learn from Princess Feodora [s. fn. 261], that Ghirshman advanced this view as far back as 1957.

[272] Frye, Heritage [fn. 223] 98.

of a thousand', seems to have assumed powers suggesting those of an official more important than a mere military commander or captain of the guard. But the sources on the chiliarch are post-Achaemenid and one must be careful in reading backwards later conditions"[273]. The last sentence is important but I should like to understand it to mean that, although our evidence for chiliarch, if not for the Old Persian term, comes from the early fifth century (Aeschylus), the combination of the office of *hazārapatiš* and εἰσαγγελεύς is not attested from the Achaemenid period but only much later. A brief survey of the evidence, whether fancied or real, will show this.

The earliest suggestive reference is found in connexion with Themistocles: on the accession of Artaxerxes I to the throne (464 B.C.) Themistocles, ostracized and outlawed, tried his luck at the Persian court in Susa: ἐντυγχάνει πρῶτον Ἀρτοβάνῳ τῷ χιλιάρχῳ, but the statement comes from Plutarch, that is the second century A.D.! The next reference is to the Athenian admiral Conon who, also disgraced, went up to Susa around 395 B.C.: *primum ex more Persarum ad chiliarchum, qui secundum gradum imperii tenebat, Tithrausten accessit seque ostendit cum rege colloqui velle: nemo enim sine hoc admittitur*—this time the source is Nepos (ca. 100-25 B.C.), a friend of Cicero's.

Particularly interesting is the story of Aristazanes under Artaxerxes III Ochus (359-338 B.C). Diodorus Siculus, in the late first century B.C., reports (16,47,3) that he was εἰσαγγελεὺς τοῦ βασιλέως καὶ πιστότατος τῶν φίλων μετὰ Βαγώαν. But Diodorus also reports (16,50,8) that throughout Artaxerxes' reign the all-powerful minister was the eunuch Bagoas, and, what is more (17,5,3), that Bagoas was the chiliarch[274]. These statements imply, to my mind, a clear separation of the two offices. In fact, as far as I can see, the only clear statement in favour of the current view comes from a very late writer. In his *Varia Historia* (I 21), the third-century Greek writer, who worked in Rome, Claudius Aelianus (175-235) speaks of ὁ χιλίαρχος ὁ καὶ τὰς ἀγγελίας εἰσκομίζων τῷ βασιλεῖ καὶ τοὺς δεομένους εἰσάγων. It is the first time, but rather late in the day, to be sure, that the office of chiliarchy appears combined with

---

[273] Frye, in: Beiträge zur Achämenidengeschichte, 1972, 88.

[274] Diodorus also mentions (18, 48, 4-5) that Antipater made his son Cassander χιλίαρχον καὶ δευτερεύοντα κατὰ τὴν ἐξουσίαν, but one would not infer that Cassander also became an introducer!

that of the introducer and reporter of news. The last distinction is, I think, quite important, for it appears already in early Achaemenid times.

Among the earliest testimonies, usually referred to the present context, is the story of Prexaspes, one of Cambyses' closest friends. Herodotus tells us (3,34) that Cambyses ἐτίμα τε μάλιστα καί οἱ τὰς ἀγγελίας ἐφόρεε οὗτος, that is Prexaspes was "a man who was highly valued by the king and used to bring him his dispatches". And almost the same expression is used when Herodotus describes (1,114) how Cyrus at the age of ten, elected king by his mates, assigns them various court offices, to one of them to be his messenger (τῷ δέ τινι τὰς ἀγγελίας ἐσφέρειν ἐδίδου γέρας). It is perhaps right to think of this office as that of "a commissioner armed with a firman for special important services, as e.g. those performed by Prexaspes in the matter of Smerdis"[275]. This office is said by Herodotus (1,99) to have been instituted by Deioces the Mede: μήτε ἐσιέναι παρὰ βασιλέα μηδένα, δι' ἀγγέλων δὲ πάντα χρέεσθαι "admission to the king's presence was forbidden, and all communication had to be through messengers" (A. de Selincourt).

But the other office (or the other aspect of this selfsame office) is described by Herodotus in the same words. When the seven conspirators break into the palace, they reach the courtyard without difficulty but there (Hdt. 3,77) ἐνέκυρσαν τοῖσι τὰς ἀγγελίας ἐσφέρουσι εὐνούχοισι, and were held up by them. After the successful completion of the coup, one day Intaphernes, one of the seven, wanted to see King Darius and wished to make use of the privilege of the seven, i.e. ἔσοδον εἶναι παρὰ βασιλέα ἄνευ ἀγγέλου (Hdt. 3,118). The officer, who here is named by the generic term ἄγγελος, is shortly after described as an ἀγγελιηφόρος, and one might be tempted to infer that this ('announcer') was his official name. But when earlier the agreement on the privilege was mentioned, Herodotus had said (3,84): παριέναι ἐς τὰ βασιλήϊα πάντα τὸν βουλόμενον τῶν ἑπτὰ ἄνευ ἐσαγγελέος "that each one of the seven shall have the right to enter the palace without being announced" (: 'without an announcer'), and it is doubtless the same function that 's at issue.

---

[275] These are J.W. Blakesley's words in fn. 94 to Hdt. 3,34, see his Herodotus with a commentary I, London 1854, 331.

Thus we cannot establish whether there were different Greek expressions for these two offices (or the two aspects of the same office) but it is fairly clear that this office was quite distinct from that of the *hazārapatiš*. How did it, then, come about that the Greeks, later at any rate, confused the two?

Reporting the accession to the throne of Secundianus, or Sogdianus (423 B.C.), Ktesias says[276] : Βασιλεύει δὲ Σεκυνδιανὸς καὶ γίνεται ἀζαβαρίτης αὐτῷ Μενοστάνης "Secundianus ascends the throne, and Menostanes becomes his *azabarites*". In view of the Hesychian gloss on ἀζαραπατεῖς—which served us as a point of departure— several scholars (e.g. Hemsterhuis) concluded very early that ἀζαβαρίτης must be corrupted from ἀζαραπατεῖς[277]. But if we had to do with a simple "metathesis", the result would be expected as ἀζαπαράτης, not ἀζαβαρίτης, so that we have to account for two additional changes: *b* instead of *p*, *i* instead of *a*. In view of the early date of the information—Ktesias wrote in the early fourth century B.C.—the voicing of *p* cannot be admitted, and *i* for *a* also remains difficult. In these circumstances it is perhaps better not to force the equation, i.e. ignore Ktesias' ἀζαβαρίτης[278].

The Hesychian gloss: ἀζαραπατεῖς· οἱ εἰσαγγελεῖς παρὰ Πέρσαις inspires much greater confidence. It presents no phonetic difficulties, and its form, the plural of a singular ἀζαραπατις[279], reveals that we are dealing with an Old Persian *i*-stem, and, to be more precise, with a noun compounded with *pati-* 'master, lord'[280]. We have

[276] For references see fn. 169.

[277] See Henry [s. fn. 169] 124 fn. 3; Marquart, Philologus 55, 1896, 233; Herzfeld, Paikuli 188; Pagliaro, RAL VIII/IX, 1954, 140.

[278] It is perhaps worth mentioning the possibility that ἀζαβαρ- reflects the OP *hadabāra-* "riding together, companion" which in Daniel (3,24.27; 4,33; 6,8) is used in the sense of "high royal official" or even "minister"; -ίτης would be an easily understandable Greek addition. For the Aramaic word and its Iranian source see Herzfeld, AMI 7, 1937, 61 fn.; Henning, BSOS 9, 1939, 844[2]; Jackson Memorial Volume, 1954, 54[1]; BSOAS 23, 1960, 50[1] (but the connection with MPe. *hayyār* is in my view erroneous, see JAOS 70, 1950, 226f., esp. 229A). For a possible Bactrian derivative (from *hada-bāraka-*) see Harmatta, in: Buddijskije peščery Kara-Tepe, Moscow 1969, 105.

[279] It is as well to stress that ἀζαραπατεῖς is the Greek(!) plural of an *-i*-stem in -πατις which exactly reflects the OP stem in -*patiš*; if the Greek noun had ended in -πατης (in itself a possible Hellenization of an Iranian -*pāta-*), its plural would be in -παται not -πατεις.

[280] Benveniste, BSL 58, 1963, 52, also avers that the Greek form is from an Achaemenid noun in -*pati-*.

just established that the εἰσαγγελεύς cannot have been the same person as the *hazārapatiš*[281], and so the last question arises: who can be hidden behind Hesychius' ἀζαραπατις?

The OP *azdākara*, attested in the Aramaic of the Elephantine papyri, and probably signifying 'announcer, messenger', has been suggested by Frye as the source of the OP word rendered by the Greek εἰσαγγελεύς[282]. But Mayrhofer, who shares the growing misgivings about the assumption that the functions of guards-commander and 'announcer' could ever be united in one hand, rightly pointed out that the reduction of an *azdākarapatiš* to *azārapatiš* is unacceptable[283]. In my view, the Hesychian ἀζαραπατις represents an OP *āžarapatiš*, from earlier *ājarapatiš*. The noun *ājara-* is from the verb *ā-gar-*, attested in Avestan *ā-gar-* and paralleled by *abi-gar-*, both of which are taken by Bartholomae to mean 'preisen', by Burrow as *ā-gar-* 'celebrate' (from 'sing') but *abi-gar-* 'welcome, approve'; for the nominal formation note Ind. *abhigara-* 'approval',

---

[281] Rundgren [s. fn. 198] 93, follows the tradition, and assuming that the OP form corresponding to (Medic) *hazārapati* was *hadārapati* thinks that *hadār-* is to be found in the Biblical Aramaic title *ʿᵃdar-gāzərayyā*, in which *-gāzar* could be from a coalescence of Aramaic *gzr* 'cut, decide' and Iranian *gzr* (< v-?). I agree that the Iranian etymology proposed by Andreas and perpetuated by Henning (see F. Rosenthal, A Grammar of Biblical Aramaic, 1968, 58) is difficult since a derivation of *ʿᵃdargāzar-* from *handarza-kara-* demands not only a metathesis but also the replacement of *kar-* by *gar-*. But of course Rundgren's own solution is both formally and semantically difficult, and alternative solutions are not far to seek. A possible source could be, e.g., OP *ādranga-žar*, or *ādrang-āžar-*; the first part could be 'companion' (cf. RAL 18, 1963, 138 fn. 14) or 'Festsetzung' from Av. *ādrənjayeiti* (cf. Schwartz, ZDMG 120/2, 1971, 298), while the second part could be 'announce, invite', see for the Iranian antecedent the text below, for the Aramaic representation Telegdi [s. fn. 209] 203, 222. Finally, it should be noted that there is now, perhaps, proof positive of an "echtpersisch" *hadār-*. In an Aramaic inscription from Hatra (cf. Safar, Sumer 17, 1961, 25f., no. 83; Caquot, Syria 40, 1963, 8) a new title appears: "This is the representation of NN, the *hdrpṭ*, set up by ...". Since Safar had identified the title with Pers. *hērbed* 'fire-priest', it has been suggested (cf. Altheim-Stiehl, Araber 4, 1967, 254; Harnack ap. Altheim-Stiehl, Geschichte Mittelasiens im Altertum, 1970, 497f., 507f.) that it represented ˣ*ātur-pati-* or Av. *aēθrapati-*. But neither antecedent can account for the new form. Not impossible would be *hadār-pati-*, i.e. a *hazārpati-* (in one of the numerous meanings attested) with SW *d*, for general *z*, first found here, outside Iran!

[282] See Frye, Heritage [fn. 223] 267 fn. 69. For the OP word see Szemerényi, Sprache 12, 1967, 202f., esp. 204.

[283] Mayrhofer, Studi V. Pisani, 1969, 663[8].

apagara- 'disapproval'[284]. Thus the Iranian noun *ā-žara-* could mean 'announcement', or possibly 'welcome, approval', so that *āžarapatiš* would be the official in charge of the activity of the εἰσαγγελεύς, and comparable to the Sassanian *nivēd-pat*. If an Iranian *gar-/jar-* 'move' were reliably established[285], we could also start from *ā-žara-* 'approaching, allowing to approach, admission', and *āžarapati-* would be the 'inspector of admissions (into the royal presence)'. But since the Greeks felt in the OP word the notion of 'announcement, introduction', and for this purpose even coined the new word εἰσαγγελεύς[286], it is probably best to derive *āžarapatiš* from 'announcement'.

As concerns the sound-shape of the Old Persian word, we must first of all note that *ājara-*, the palatalized form derived from *ā-gar-*, was in fact *āžara-* as early as the beginning of the Achaemenid era. This is proved not only by the verbal form *nijāyam* which can only represent *niž-āyam*, but, as I showed some years ago, by *Hūja* also since this is developed from indigenous *Sūša*[287]. As to the

---

[284] See Bartholomae, 1904, 512 and 90; Burrow, BSOAS 20, 1957, 133-144, for Avestan esp. 143; Szemerényi, A Gaulish dedicatory formula, KZ 88, 1975, 169f., 179f.—For a Sogdian *niɣrāy-* 'praise, honour' see MacKenzie, The 'Sūtra of the causes and effects of actions' in Sogdian, 1970, 61f.

[285] For this see Bailey, TPS 1956, 95f.; Burrow, BSOAS 20, 1957, 139[3]. But whereas Bailey starts from *gar-* 'take'—which would not illuminate our problem—Burrow assumes a *fra-jar-* 'move', comparing with it his Indian root *gur-/gar-* 'propel'. But Arm. *hražarem* 'dismiss, renounce' should be left out of the discussion; my former student, Dr. P. Considine, of University College London, will show that the meaning of the Armenian verb is 'entreat, deprecate, decline, refuse; take leave of' and derives from Iran. *fra-jāda-*!

[286] Cp. E. Bosshardt, Die Nomina auf -EYC, Diss. Zurich, 1942, 54; and, most recently, J.-L. Perpillou, Les substantifs grecs en -εύς, Paris 1973, 89. As Bosshardt says, ἐσαγγελεύς is only used of the Persian institution, which shows, I would add, that it was coined for this institution. But is is impossible to derive ἐσαγγελεύς *via* an ἐσαγγελιεύς from ἐσαγγελία (Bosshardt 54); it is obviously derived from ἐσαγγέλλω, used by Herodotus at 3, 118, 2!

[287] See Szemerényi, Sprache 12, 1967, 191.—Since the publication of that paper, the result just reported has been widely accepted. But one small point has been laboured unnecessarily (cf. Mayrhofer, Orientalia 40, 1971, 3f.; and Festschrift Scherer, 1971, 50-51), to wit that the Elamite form has identical spirants (*šuša*), and not different spirants as presupposed by my explanation, i.e. *sūša* > *hūša* > *hūža*. But it is an undeniable fact, quite independent of whether the Egyptian form was *s-w-š* or not, and decisive in itself, that the OP form was *Šūšā*, with different spirants as postulated by me for an earlier period of the same millennium. If the Elamite forms of the second millennium also show a difference—albeit in the reverse sequence (see Mayrhofer 3 fn. 18 and 4 fn. 23)—so much the better. But their evidence is in fact superfluous, the OP *Šūšā* is enough to impose our solution.

representation of OP *ž*, later *z*, Greek, like Aramaic [288], failed to make the distinction, and therefore Greek shows simply ἀζαραπατις. In the light of these results, we can answer the question posed above, i.e. "how did it come about that the Greeks, later at any rate, confused the two" terms, i.e. 'the chief of a thousand' and the 'gentleman-usher'. In the early Achaemenid period, and as long as the second term survived, the two words were distinct in Iranian: *hazahrapatiš* and *āžarapatiš*. But in Greek, more exactly in Ionic, where there was no aspiration, the two words must have coincided very early in ἀζαραπατις. Hence the confusion of the late historians who speak of the two offices as if they were performed by one person.

But in Iranian itself the development was different. In the South-West, intervocalic *ž* went to *z*, i.e. *āžarapatiš* went to *āzarapatiš*, and with it the difference between *hazārapatiš* and *āzarapatiš* became too small to be convenient for the speaker. As we know from linguistic geography, such a situation easily leads to an *homonymie fâcheuse*, and to avoid this, one of the colliding terms is often replaced. This certainly occurred in the South-West, but also in the North-West, although we cannot establish when the process started. But it is a fact that the term had been lost before the Sassanian bureaucracy was definitively formed. Accordingly, we find, as a (partial?) replacement for the function, *ādēnīk* in Persian but *nivēd-bed* in Parthian [289]. It is interesting to note that at some later time a further replacement took place (in the South-West only?).

Hübschmann had put together all the material available at the time concerning the MPe. word *(h)andēmān*: Pāzand *andīmāni* 'entgegen, vor (coram)', Arm. *y-andiman* 'gegenüber', *yandiman linel* 'sich vorstellen, erscheinen (vor dem König)', Pahl. *andēmān-kar* 'der empfängt, führt' *andēmānīh* 'das vor Jemand Erscheinen' [290]. Salemann added that *handēmānkar* in the Pahlavi Videvdat must express something like 'Entgegennehmer', i.e. 'derjenige, welcher dem Gaste zum Empfang entgegengehen muss' [291]. At the same time a seal-stone became known whose inscription, *handēmāngarān sardār*, was clarified by Bartholomae: Pahl. *handēmān kartan*, *handēmān burtan*, *handē-mānītan* mean 'jemanden in einem bestimmten Kreis, insbesondere

---

[288] Cp. Telegdi [fn. 209] 203, 222.

[289] See fn. 180 above.

[290] Hübschmann 1897, 141.

[291] Salemann, Ein Bruchstück manichäischen Schrifttums im Asiatischen Museum (Mémoires de l'Académie Impériale de St.-Pétersbourg VIII/VI/6, 1904, 1-26) 26.

an jemandes Hof vorstellen, einführen und aufnehmen', and therefore
handēmānkarān sardār is 'der Chef derer, die mit dem Amt der
Vorstellung und Einführung bei Hof betraut sind' [292]. The Paikuli
inscription brought Pa. *hndymn*, Pe. *'ndymn* 'before, in front of,
opposite', and Herzfeld also confirmed the reading of the seal-stone
mentioned above [293]. The ŠKZ brought both (*h*)*andēmān* 'vor dem
Antlitz' and Pa. *ptydymn* = *patidēmān* 'von Angesicht zu Angesicht',
and the Parthian Paikuli text was recognized to have (at 16′)
the phrase *handēmān būdan* 'come into the royal presence' [294]. The
latest claim [295], that *handēmāngar* is also found on Dura Ostr. 3,1
(= Frye, CII III/III/1, 1968, Plate XXVII No. 24), seems ill-founded:
Frye's photo is of no help for the first word in the upper right-hand
corner, and even Altheim's photos [296], though superior, are not
adequate for reliable decipherment. It is therefore surprising that
Gignoux should have adopted this reading in his Glossary (p. 16).
We must, accordingly, still maintain that Pahl. (*h*)*andēmāngar* 'introducer (into the presence)' [297] is only attested on a seal-stone and
in the gloss of the Pahlavi Videvdat quoted by Salemann.

To sum up. Even the meagre data allow us to perceive that the
notion of 'introducer (into the royal presence)' had several linguistic
expressions in succession. The Achaemenid **āžarapatiš* was replaced
during the Arsacid period by Pa. *nivēdbed*, in the early Sassanian
period by Pe. *ādēnīk*, and the latter was subsequently ousted by
handēmāngar.

To return now to the main subject of this investigation, we may
ignore here the numerous smaller results and concentrate on the
main questions. Having approached the problem of the *hazārapatiš*
along the ascending line of Platonic inquiry, we may now attempt
the summing up of our results along the descending line.

[292] Bartholomae 1906, 159 (and 169). Cp. also Zum sassanidischen Recht IV,
1922, 16-17, where it is suggested that *dēmān kartan* is 'conspectum facere (alicui
seu sibi)' = 'Vorlass, Zutritt (bei einem Hochstehenden) beschaffen, jemand einführen'
oder 'Vorlass erhalten, vorgelassen werden'.

[293] Herzfeld, Paikuli 191 and 138, but the suggestion at the second place that *ns'n*
should be the name of a province is unlikely, see Henning 1958, 45 with fn. 1.

[294] See Henning 1958, 62 with fn. 3; BSOAS 14, 1952, 519. For *bwd hndym'n
'w tw* "standen (in Verehrung) vor dir" see Henning, NGGW 1933, 313.

[295] Harmatta-Pekáry, in: La Persia nel medioevo, 1971, 468.

[296] Altheim, Acta Archaeologica Hung. 2, 1953, 270; Altheim-Stiehl, Das erste
Auftreten der Hunnen, 1953, Plate 7, facing p. 18.

[297] MacKenzie 1971, 42.

During the first half-century of Achaemenid rule only the position of the heir to the throne was constitutionally clarified: by royal proclamation, Xerxes was made 'second king', *dvitīya xšaya*. We have no reason to assume that in his time the position of the *hazārapatiš* was anything more than is indicated by his title: he was the commander of a guards-regiment, and there were at least ten officers of this rank who had the same position at court. It is not until the reign of Artaxerxes I (464-424 B.C.) that the *hazārapatiš* attains to a pre-eminent position, if, that is, Plutarch's story of Artabanus, quoted above, is to be interpreted in these terms. But there can be little doubt that in the fourth century B.C., especially from the fifties on, the position of the *hazārapatiš* was that of the supreme power at court. We can take it for granted that, in the process, the powers of the *dvitīya xšaya* were steadily whittled down until only small royal households of mere local significance kept up the old traditions of the imperial court. This must have been the case especially in the fragmented state of Iran under Greek rule. In consequence, the institution of "second king" survived in Parthia, and when the Parthians reestablished a unified Iran under Arsacid rule, the *bidaxš*—linguistically a Parthian descendant of the Achaemenid *dvitīya xšaya*—regained his exalted position. When, with the Sassanian house, the South came to power again, this Arsacid institution was also taken over—but apparently not with its etymological implications. Well into the sixties or seventies of the third century A.D. the *bidaxš* comes immediately after the members of the royal family, before the *hazārbed*. But towards the end of the century the importance of state finances makes itself felt: the *hargubed*, the 'imperial secretary of revenue', is promoted to the top of the civil list; at the same time, the *bidaxš* is demoted to a peripheral dignity—perhaps even confined to Iberia-Armenia—but the *hazārbed* improves his position as the military counterpart of the *hargubed*. Later, however, at a time which cannot as yet be fixed, the *hazārbed* attains to the most powerful position but his office seems to get amalgamated with another, originally much lower, office. Under Ardašīr I (226-240 A.D.) the famous Abursām came, as *framātār*, 15th in the list (see fn. 181). Under his son, there are even two *framātārs* but one comes 17th, the other, the 54th, almost reaches rock-bottom. But shortly after, the ascent of the *framātār* to the more glorious and influential position of the *vuzurg framādār* must have begun which in the end led to the fusion of this office with that of the *hazārbed*, to the establishment of the post of Grand Vizier or Prime Minister. The *terminus post quem non* for this change is the early fifth century A.D. The Armenian historian Ełišē reporting on Mihrnarse, whose brilliant career began under Yazdgird I (399-421 A.D.), calls him *mec hazarapet Arik' ew Anarik'* "the great hazarbed of Aryans and Non-Aryans" while Mihrnarse himself designates himself as *vzruk hramatar Eran ew Aneran* "the buzurg framadar of Iran and Aniran", and Tabarī also states that Mihrnarse's Persian title was *buzurg framadār*[298]. It is no doubt this pre-eminent position as prime minister that is again reflected on the periphery: the Bactrian *hazāruxt*, discussed above, was doubtless, to use Henning's words[299], the "prime minister".

Andreas-Lommel, Gāthās des Zarathustra, Yasna 43-46. 47-51, Nachrichten der Gesellschaft der Wissenschaften, Göttingen, 1934, 67-169.

Andreas-Wackernagel, Die vierte Ghāthā des Zurathušthro, NGGW 1911, 1-34.

Bailey H.W., Khotanese Texts VI: Prolexis to the Book of Zambasta, Cambridge 1967.

Bartholomae C., Vorgeschichte der iranischen Sprachen—Awestasprache und Altpersisch, in: Grundriß der iranischen Philologie I 1, 1901, 1-248.

Bartholomae C., Altiranisches Wörterbuch, 1904 (repr. 1961).

Bartholomae C., Die Gathas des Awesta, Straßburg 1905.

Bartholomae C., Zum Altiranischen Wörterbuch, Straßburg 1906.

Bartholomae C., Zur Etymologie und Wortbildung der idg. Sprachen, Sitz. Ber. Heidelberg, 1919/10.

Bartholomae C., Zur Kenntnis der mitteliranischen Mundarten VI, ibid. 1925/6.

Benveniste E., Titres et noms propres en iranien ancien, Paris 1966.

Benveniste E., Le vocabulaire des institutions indo-européennes I-II, Paris 1969.

Brandenstein W.-Mayrhofer M., Handbuch des Altpersischen, Wiesbaden 1964.

Brugmann K., Kurze vgl. Grammatik der idg. Sprachen, 1904.

Chantraine P., Dictionnaire étymologique de la langue grecque I (A-K), Paris 1968-1970.

Duchesne-Guillemin, J. Les composés de l'Avesta, Liège 1936.

Duchesne-Guillemin, J. Zoroastre, Paris 1948.

Frisk H., Griechisches etym. Wb. I-III, Heidelberg 1954-1972.

Geldner K.F., Der Rig-Veda I-III, Cambridge Mass. 1951.

Gershevitch I., The Avestan Hymn to Mithra, Cambridge 1959.

Gonda J., Some riddles connected with Royal titles in Ancient Iran, in: Bulletin of the Iranian Culture Foundation 1, 1969, 29-46.

---

[298] Cf. Hübschmann 1897, 25, 174, 182; Herzfeld, Paikuli 188; Tabarī [s. fn. 208] 111.
[299] See fn. 177 above.

Güntert H., Der arische Weltkönig und Heiland, Halle 1923.

Hauri C., Das pentathematische Schema, 1973.

Henning W.B., Mitteliranisch in: Handbuch der Orientalistik I/IV/1, Leiden 1958, 20-130.

Hinz W., Altpersischer Wortschatz, Leipzig 1942.

Hinz W., Zarathustra, Stuttgart 1961.

Hinz W., Neue Wege im Altpersischen, Wiesbaden 1973.

Hoffmann K., Altiranisch, in : Handbuch der Orientalistik I/IV/1, Leiden 1958, 1-19.

Horn P., Neupersische Schriftsprache, in: Grundriß der iranischen Philologie I 2, 1898, 1-200.

Hübschmann H., Persische Studien, Straßburg 1895.

Hübschmann H., Armenische Grammatik I, Leipzig 1897 (repr. Hildesheim 1962).

Humbach H., Die Gathas des Zarathustra I-II, Heidelberg 1959.

Kent R.G., Old Persian—Grammar, Texts, Lexicon, New Haven, Conn. ²1953.

Liebert G., Das Nominalsuffix -ti- im Altindischen, Lund 1949.

Lommel H., Die Yäšt's des Awesta, Göttingen 1927.

MacKenzie D.N., A Concise Pahlavi Dictionary, London 1971.

Mayrhofer M., Kurzgefaßtes etym. Wb. des Altindischen I-III, Heidelberg 1952-1974.

Mayrhofer M., Die Rekonstruktion des Medischen, Anzeiger der Österreich. Akad. Wiss. 1968, Heft 1.

Mayrhofer M., Das Altpersische seit 1964, in: W.B. Henning Memorial Volume, London 1970, 276-296.

Mayrhofer M., Neuere Forschungen zum Altpersischen, in: Donum Indo-germanicum—Festgabe A. Scherer, Heidelberg 1971, 41-66.

Mayrhofer M., Onomastica Persepolitana, Vienna 1973.

Meillet A., Grammaire du vieux perse, Paris 1915.

Meillet A.-Benveniste E., Grammaire du vieux perse, 2nd ed., Paris 1931.

Nagy G., Greek dialects and the transformation of an IE process, Cambridge, Mass., 1970.

Nyberg H.S., Hilfsbuch des Pehlevi II. Glossar, Uppsala 1931.

Nyberg H.S., A Manual of Pahlavi II, Wiesbaden 1974.

Nyberg H.S., Die Religionen des Alten Iran, 1938 (repr. 1966).

Pokorny J., Idg. etym. Wb. I, München 1949-1959.

Reichelt H., Awestisches Elementarbuch, 1909 (repr. 1967).

Risch E., Wortbildung der homerischen Sprache, ²1974.

Schmidt J., Die Pluralbildungen der idg. Neutra, Weimar 1889.

Schwyzer E., Griechische Grammatik I-IV, 1934-1971.

Smith Maria Wilkins, Studies in the Syntax of the Gathas of Zarathustra, 1929 (repr. 1966).

Soden, Wolfram von, Akkadisches Handwörterbuch I, 1959-1965; II 1966-.

Szemerényi O., Einführung in die vgl. Sprachwissenschaft, 1970.

Szemerényi O., Comparative Linguistics, in: Current Trends in Linguistics (ed. T.A. Sebeok) 9, 1972, 119-195.

Thumb A.-Hauschild R., Handbuch des Sanskrit I 1-2, 3rd ed., 1958-59.

Tolman H.C., Ancient Persian Lexicon and the Texts, 1908.

Tolman H.C., Cuneiform Supplement, 1910.

Wackernagel J., Altindische Grammatik I, 1896 (repr. with Nachträge by A. Debrunner 1957).
Wackernagel J., Altindische Grammatik II 1, 1905.
Wackernagel J.-Debrunner A., Altindische Grammatik II 2, 1954.
Watkins C., Etyma Enniana, Harvard Studies in Classical Philology 77, 1973, 195-206.
Weissbach F.H., Die Keilinschriften am Grabe des Darius Hystaspis, 1911a.
Weissbach F.H., Die Keilinschriften der Achämeniden, 1911b.
Wolff F., Avesta—Die heiligen Bücher der Parsen, Straßburg 1910.

Addendum to p. 349 :

Cp. also A²Sa3 *imam apadāna Dārayavauš ... akunaš* no doubt to be interpreted as the masc. acc. sg. *appadān-am* (cf. Henning, TPS 1944, 110[1]), here spelt *appadāna(n)* before Dārayavauš.

AHMAD TAFAZZOLI

ELEPHANT: A DEMONIC CREATURE
AND A SYMBOL OF SOVEREIGNTY

The attitude of the Zoroastrians towards animals as stated in Pahlavi books is well known. According to these sources there are two main categories of animals, namely the good (Ahuric) ones such as the cow, the sheep, the goat, the beaver, the horse and the dog, and the evil (Daivic) ones such as the serpent, the scorpion, the lizard, the frog, the tiger, the lion and the fox [1]. There must have, however, existed a divergence of opinions concerning non-native animals that were introduced to them. One of such cases is that of the elephant. It is reasonable to suppose that most Iranians considered this gigantic frightful animal as a creature of Ahriman, when they first came to know it. That at one time such an attitude existed, can be inferred from the following passage of the *Mēnōg ī Xrad*: [2] *čahārom *kū-š gōspand pad gōhrīg ī* pīl *ō dēwān nē dād*. "The fourth advantage from him (i.e. Jam) was this, that he did not give sheep to the demons in exchange for elephants".

West [3] read the word *pyl* (*pīl*) as *pīr* "old" and translated the last part of the sentence as "in the character of an old man". In this he was followed by Christensen [4] and Bausani [5]. His misreading of the word was apparently due to his misunderstanding of the expression *pad gōhrīg ī*, which is now well established to mean "in exchange for" [6]. It is therefore certain that here there is not a question of exchanging a sheep for an "old man" but more likely the sheep for another animal. Disregarding *pīr* "old (man)", the spelling *pyl* can only represent *pīl* "elephant" [7]. A similar passage occurring in the *Pahlavi Rivāyāt* [8] throws more light on this ambiguous passage. It reads as follows:

[1] See *Bundahišn*, Chapters 13, 22 and 23.
[2] Question 26 (ch. 27) 33a. Ed. T.D. Anklesaria, p. 89; ed. D.P. Sanjana, p. 45.
[3] *Sacred Books of the East*, Vol. 24, p. 60.
[4] *Les types du premier homme et du premier roi*, II, p. 24.
[5] *Testi religiosi zoroastriani*, 1961, p. 125.
[6] See A. Pagliaro, *RSO* 22 (1947), p. 60. A. Tafazzoli, *Glossary of Mēnōg i Xrad*, 1969, p. 254.
[7] I have already adopted this interpretation in the *Glossary of MX.*, p. 96.
[8] Ed. B.N. Dhabhar, Bombay, 1913, p. 102.

(1) *Zardušt ēn-iz pursīd az Ōhrmazd kū Jam pad gēhān nēkīh čē weh kard?* (2) *Ōhrmazd guft kū ān i ka dēwān bē ō mardōmān guft kū gōspand bē ōzanēd tā-tān pīl dahem i sūdōmand, kē-š dāštār ud pānag nē abāyēd,* (3) *mardōmān guft kū tā pad dastwarīh i Jam bē kunem. ušān kard. ud Jam pad nē ōzadan i mardōmān gōspand ud pad nē stadan i mardōmān az dēwān* pīl *abāg dēwān ēdōn paykārd ī-š dēw bē ēraxt hēnd uš margōmand ud pādafrāhōmand kard hēnd:* Zardušt asked Ōhrmazd this, too,: "What good did Jam do in the world?" Ōhrmazd said: "When the demons said to men: 'Kill (all) the sheep, and we will give you elephants, which are useful and do not need a keeper or a guardian', men said: 'We shall do this only by Jam's order'". They consulted him. (lit. they did). In order that men should not kill sheep and accept elephants (instead), Jam fought with the demons in such a way that he defeated them and ʼmade them mortals deserving punishment.

According to the *Bundahišn* [9] the elephant is a creature of Ahriman, but it can be tamed (*rāmīhēd*). It is probably this same concept that has left traces in later Iranian traditions, where the elephant is regarded as sinister, e.g.

ازپیل و بوم شومتر و ناخجسته‌تر دیدار روی اوست به سیصد هزار بار

"To look at his face is three thousand times more sinister and inauspicious than looking at the elephant or the owl". (Suzani-ye Samarqandi) [10].

This hostile attitude, of which reminiscences are preserved in the above passages, does not seem to have persisted long. As the Iranians gradually became familiar with this creature, they altered their older belief. How and when this animal was introduced to them is not known. The Achaemenides, however, made use of this animal in war. According to Arrian [11] a few elephants were among the forces of Dareius III in the battle of Arbela. In Sasanian times elephants usually formed part of their forces and played an important role in their victories. In the siege of Amida the hideous elephants of the Scythians that were among the armies of Shahpur II had an important part in the triumph of this king [12]. According to Ğāḥiẓ there were nine hundred and fifty elephants in the army of Khosrow II,

---

[9] TD2, ed. B.T. Anklesaria, p. 149. 6; TD1, ed. P. Anklesaria, fol. 61 v 1.4.

[10] *Divân*, ed. N. Shah-Hoseyni, Tehran, 1338/1959, p. 41 fn. 8.

[11] *Anabasis Alexandri* III, 8, translated by E. Iliff Robson, London, 1954, p. 247. I owe the reference to Dr. E.S. Shahbazi.

[12] See A. Christensen, *L'Iran sous les Sassanides*, 1944, p. 245.

a hundred and twenty of which served later on in the battle of Qādisiyya[13]. These elephants of Khosrow II are depicted on the great hunting scene of Tâq-e Bostân.

The usefulness and the service that this animal rendered to the Iranians motivated them to modify, probably under the influence of Indian beliefs, their older inimical attitude, to the extent that it became a symbol of sovereignty, as can be inferred from the two following Pahlavi passages:

Kārnāmag ī Ardaxšīr[14] : *anē šab ēdōn dīd čēōn ka Sāsān pad pīl-ē ārāstag ī spēd nišast ēstād... x^warmn-wizārān guft kū ān kē ēn x^warmn padiš dīd, ōy ayāb az frazandān ī ōy mard kas-ē ō pādixšāyīh ī gēhān rasēd, čē x^waršēd ud pīl ī spēd ī ārāstag čērīh ud tuwānīh ud pērōzīh:* "Next night he (i.e. Pābag) dreamt that Sāsān was sitting on an equipped white elephant.... The interpreters of dreams said: 'Either that man himself whom you saw in your dream or somebody from his offspring will obtain the sovereignty of the world, because the sun and the equipped white elephant are (symbols of) triumph, power and victory...'".

Abar madan ī šāh Wahrām[15] :
kay bawād ka payk-ē āyēd az Hindūgān
*kū mad ān šāh Wahrām az dūd ī kayān
*kē pīl ast hazār
abar sarān ast pīlbān
*kē ārāstag drafš dārēd
pad ēwēn ī Xusrōyān

"When may it be that a courier comes from India (and says): 'The king Wahrām from the Kayanian family has come, who has a thousand elephants, upon which are elephant-keepers, and who holds an adorned banner in the manner of the (Sasanian) kings?'"

Vahriz, one of the Sasanian dignitaries of the time of Khosrow I, considered the elephant as the most noble mount for kings[16].

The white elephant appearing as the main figure in one of the Shoshoin screen panels belonging to the Sasanian period deserves attention in this respect. If the interpretations of Phyllis Ackerman[17]

---

[13] *Kitāb al Ḥayawān*, ed. A. Muḥammad Hārūn, Vol. 7, p. 181.
[14] Ch. I. 9, 13, ed. Antia, p. 2-3.
[15] *Pahlavi Texts*, ed. Jamasp-Asana, p. 160.
[16] Ǧāḥiẓ, *op. cit.*, p. 182.
[17] *Iranica Antiqua* IV, 1964, p. 55 and specially p. 66. For a different view see J. Duchesne-Guillemin, "Art et religion sous les Sassanides", *Accademia Nazionale dei Lincei*, 1971, p. 385.

concerning the other figures of the panels as the avatars of Vereθraγna are correct, this animal may also represent another symbol of this god, who is closely associated with royalty in Zoroastrian tradition.

This dual aspect of the elephant is an example illustrating how an old Iranian belief has gradually changed under foreign influence.

BO UTAS

ON THE COMPOSITION
OF THE AYYĀTKĀR Ī ZARĒRĀN*

An edition of the text of the small Book Pahlavi work entitled *Ayyātkār ī Zarērān* (hereafter *AZ*), "Memoir of the Zarēr family", is found in H.S. Nyberg's *Manual of Pahlavi*[1]. Owing to the fortunate fact that Nyberg was able to finish the second part of his *Manual*, the glossary (1974), it is also possible to reconstruct his interpretation of the more complicated passages of this work. On the whole, the text is not especially difficult, but it raises some questions as regards the formal composition and the use of certain verbal forms and tenses. Some observations in these respects will be given below.

This text has a comparatively long history in European Pahlavi studies. W. Geiger published a translation of it and a comparison with the corresponding part in *Šāh-nāmah*, in 1890[2], and Nöldeke contributed a number of remarks in 1892[3]. The Pahlavi text itself was made generally available a few years later, when Jamasp-Asana published it in his renowned *Pahlavi Texts, contained in the Codex MK copied in 1322 A.C. by the scribe Mehr-Âwân Kaî-khûsrû*[4].

The textological situation seems to be quite simple. All known versions are directly descended from Jamasp-Asana's Codex MK, dated 691 A.Y. = 1322 A.D. and, unfortunately, badly worm-eaten[5].

---

* These notes are intended as preliminaries to a forthcoming study on verbs and preverbs in the *Ayyātkār ī Zarērān* which I had the privilege to discuss with Professor Nyberg a few months before his death. They are a quite inadequate tribute to the example and memory of my great teacher.

[1] Part I, Wiesbaden 1964, pp. 18-30; critical notes, pp. 185-186; editorial notes, pp. XII-XIII.

[2] "Das Yātkār-i Zarīrān und sein Verhältnis zum Šāh-nāme", *Sitzungsber. d. philos.-philol. u. hist. Cl. d. k. bayer. Akad. d. Wiss.*, II: 1, pp. 43-84.

[3] *ZDMG* 46, pp. 136-145.

[4] I, Bombay 1897; II [= the same and further texts], with an introd. by B.T. Anklesaria, Bombay 1913.

[5] It is described in detail by B.T. Anklesaria in his introduction to *Pahlavi Texts*, pp. 1-8; according to Nyberg, *Manual* I, p. XI, n. 1, there is uncertainty as to its present whereabouts; on the copyist, Mihrāpān ī Kai Xōsrōi, and the copyist of his model, his grandfather's uncle Rōstahm ī Mihrāpān, see J.C. Tavadia, *ZDMG* 98 (1944), pp. 313-332.

There are in addition a copy of MK, dated 1136 A.Y. = 1767 A.D., designated JJ by Jamasp-Asana[6], and a number of later transcripts (by E.W. West and others)[7]. It has been my objective here to follow as closely as possible the text of MK, as it is represented in Jamasp-Asana's *Pahlavi Texts* (pp. 1-16), with the hope that the critical apparatus there is reasonably complete and reliable. The text of *AZ* is there given with variant readings from MK and JJ, possibly with emendations from a transcript by E.W. West and certainly also with some emendations by Jamasp-Asana himself. The text will be quoted with reference to the paragraph numbers in *Pahlavi Texts*. As for the system of transcription, this our child of sorrow, I am still using the slightly modified version of Nyberg's system employed in my recent article "Verbal forms and ideograms in the Middle Persian inscriptions"[8].

In more modern times the text of Jamasp-Asana has been re-edited in transcription, with introduction, translation, notes and glossary by A. Pagliaro[9], and this edition, in its turn, formed the basis of E. Benveniste's important re-evaluation of the nature of this text in his article "Le mémorial de Zarēr, poème pehlevi mazdéen"[10]. Since the publication of his bold attemt to convert the text of *AZ* into hexasyllabic verse, there has been general agreement on the poetical character of this text, even though the nature of its metrical system has been subject to different interpretations. This verse element is, however, not present to the same extent all through the composition. *AZ*, as we know it, is not a wholly homogeneous work. With regard to the contents, the text may be divided into three sections: §§ 1-34, a summarizing introduction; §§ 35-68, the prophecy of Jāmāsp and its immediate consequences; §§ 69-114, a description of the battle[11].

The section of Firdausī's (i.e. here Daqīqī's) *Šāh-nāmah* which corresponds to *AZ* §§ 1-34 (4 pp. in *Pahlavi Texts*) runs through 271

---

[6] Description by Anklesaria in *Pahlavi Texts*, introd., pp. 8-10.

[7] Cf. *Pahlavi Texts*, introd., pp. 10-11; Geiger, *op. cit.*, p. 44.

[8] *Acta Orientalia*, Copenhagen, 36 (1974), pp. 83-112; on transcription, see p. 85.

[9] "Il testo pahlavico Ayātkār-i-Zarērān, edito in trascrizione, con introduzione, note e glossario", *Rendiconti della Reale Academia Nazionale dei Lincei, Cl. di Scienze morali, storiche e filologiche*, VI: I, Rome 1925, pp. 550-604.

[10] *Journal Asiatique* 220 (1932), pp. 245-293.

[11] The initial invocation, *pat nām ... nipēsihēt*, left without a § number in *Pahlavi Texts*, is not taken into account.

baits or 19 pages of text in the Russian edition of that work[12]. This introductory section in *AZ* is obviously a summary of the full epic version, and seems to be a summary in prose in which verses from a poetical original shine through here and there (esp. in direct discourse). It is on the whole narrated in past tense, although with much direct discourse in present tense. However, some forms cause difficulties: YḤWWNyt: *bavēt* in §3 (a mistake for *būt*?) and Y'TWNyt: *āyēt* in §4 (a form of *frēstītan* would suit the context much better, and a slight emendation of the ideogram to ŠDRWN seems legitimate; *u-šān* first in the § would then furnish the agent of an emended form *frēstīt*). The past tense narration then runs smoothly till the end of §26, although it is possible to see remnants of poetry here and there, e.g. in §20:

šmáh hač ānód āyét	You come from there,
tāi amáh hač ētár āyém	till we come from here,
u šmáh amáh vēnét	and you see us,
[u] amáh šmáh vēném	[and] we see you.

§6 *ēvak vīdrafš yātūk u ditīkar nām-x"āst ī hazārān* also has a very epic ring; compare *Šāh-nāmah*, baits 126-127:

گوی ییر و جادو ستنبه سترگ   یکی نام او بیدرفش بزرگ

که هرگز دلش جز تباهی نخواست   دگر جادوی نام او نام خواست

In the end of §26 something interesting happens. The narration seems to change from past (MHYTWNt: *zat*) to present tense (pzdynd: *pazdēnd*, 'BYDWNd: *kunēnd*) which is kept till the end of §31. With regard only to this passage it might seem that the present indicatives are used in description of simultaneous action, but in the light of the use of tenses further on in the text, this can hardly be the full truth. The explanation is rather that a verse passage is being quoted:

§26 ...] u nái pazdénd	...and they play the flute
u gāž-dúmb[13] váng kunénd	and sound the horn,
§27 u-š kārván ēvárz kunénd	and they muster the troops for him,
u pīlván pat píl ravénd	and the elephant-men ride the elephants,

[12] Firdausī, *Šāh-nāmah*, vol. VI, Moscow 1967, ed. M.-N. O. Osmanov, pp. 68-86, baits 39-312.
[13] Cf. Nyberg, *Manual* II, s.v.

u stōrpán pat stŏr ravénd
u vartēn-dár pat vartén rav[é]nd

and the horsemen ride the horses,
and the charioteers drive the chariots.

§ 28 *vás estét +šif(á)rg(?)* [14]
vás kan-tígr ī purr-tígr
u vás zréh ī rŏšn
u vás zréh ī čahār-kárt
§ 29 *(u) kārván ī ērán(-šahr) ētōn bē-esténd*
ka váng bē ō asmán šavét
u pattán bē ō dōšáx⁻ šavét
§ 30 *pat ráh kú šavénd*
vitárg ētón bē-brīnénd
apāk [súmb?] [15] *áp bē-+š[é]pénd*
ī tāi ē máh [16] *x⁻artán nē-šāyét*

Many a sword(?) appears,
many a quiver full of arrows
and many a bright armour
and many a fourfold armour.
The troops of the Iranians appear so
that the clamour goes to Heaven
and right to Hell it goes.
Wherever on the way they go,
they make their passage so,
they stir up water with [the hoofs?]
which for one month is impossible to drink.

§ 31 *tāi 50 rŏč rŏšn nē-bavét*
múrv-ē-č nišém nē-vindát (for -ēt?)
bé ka ō aspān bášn nēzakān téh [17]

aivāp ō kŏf ī sar-búrz nišīnénd

(*hač gart u dūt šap u rōč nē-paitāk*)

For 50 days there is no light;
not a single bird finds its nest
but on the mane of the horses, the point of the lances,
or they sit down on the lofty mountain.
(Probably interpolated explanation).

Compare *Šāh-nāmah*, baits 305-312:

چو روزی ببخشید و جوشن بداد	بزد نای و کوس و بنه بر نهاد
بفرمود بردن زپیش سپاه	درفش همایون فرخنده شاه
سوی رزم ارجاسپ لشکر کشید	سپاهی که هرکز چنان کس ندید
زتاریکی وگرد پای سپاه	کس روز روشن ندید ایچ راه
زبس بانگ اسپان و از بس خروش	همی نالهٔ کوس نشنید گوش
درفش فراوان بر افراشته	همه نیزه ها ز ابر بگذ اشته
چو رسته درخت از بر کوهسار	چو بیشهٔ نیستان بوقت بهار
ازین سان همی رفت گشتاسپ شاه	ز کشور بکشور همی شد سپاه

---

[14] Cf. Nyberg, *Manual* II, s.v.; or metathesis +*šifigr*?; *ī rōtastahm*, interpolation?
[15] Or *apāk* for adj. *a-pák* and no addition?
[16] *āp*, interpolation?
[17] Two lines?

It is the same and not the same. The poetical ornamentation of the same basic hyperboles is rather differently wrought. Another important difference is the fact that Daqīqī's version is narrated in past tense, while *AZ* here seems to have present tense. A few cases of unexpected present tense in a text like *AZ* could, of course, be explained away somehow, but the occurence of present forms, especially in §§ 35-114, is so consistent and grammatically well integrated that I think we have to accept that the underlying poetical text must have been composed in *praesens historicum*. We know so little about Middle Persian epic poetry that we cannot say if such a use of present tense narration of past events was unusual or otherwise. It is, however, a striking fact that it seems to be unknown in early New Persian epic poetry.

How should the metrical system of the verse passages in *AZ* be defined? That is a difficult question, and it must be admitted that the analysis is not made easier by the archaic transcription used here. But as long as we know so little about the time of composition of the underlying poem[18], other conceivable systems of transcription would also get us into difficulties, especially as regards the number of syllables and the quality of the rhymes. The general discussion of Middle Persian metrics is well-known[19]. Suffice it to mention that W.B. Henning in his two articles "The disintegration of the Avestic studies"[20] and "A Pahlavi poem"[21] convincingly showed that the earlier theories of a purely syllabic metre in Middle Iranian (and Avestan) poetry could not be maintained and that we instead should look for a constant number of stressed syllables (arses) to a line. In "A Pahlavi poem" Henning turns his special attention to the *Draxt ī Asūrīk*, which was the first Middle Persian text to be presented as verse by E. Benveniste[22]. Choosing "a few connected passages, selected at random" (p. 642), Henning managed to show not only that there are four stresses to the line, with a caesura in the middle, but also that "it seems that the limits of variation in the number of syllables are precisely set" (p. 645). He continues: "The differences between the maximum and the average, and between the minimum and

---

[18] Beginning of the 6th century A.D. acc. to Nöldeke, *Das iranische Nationalepos*, 2: e Aufl., Berlin-Leipzig 1920, p. 5; accepted by Benveniste, *JA* 220, p. 291.

[19] A good recent survey is found in S. Shaked, "Specimens of Middle Persian verse", *Henning Mem. Vol.*, 1970, pp. 395-405.

[20] *TPS* 1942 (publ. 1944) pp. 40-56.

[21] *BSOAS* 13 (1949-50), pp. 641-648.

[22] *JA* 217 (1930), pp. 193-225.

the average are apparently equal. Thus, in the *Draxt-ī Asūrīg* the average
number of syllables to a line is 12; the maximum is 14, the minimum
10...". Already in his "Disintegration" (p. 53) he had stated that
"the line of three arses comprised between five and ten syllables, as
a rule, but in this case the average number was seven or eight".

These suggestions by Henning were put into full-scale practice by
Mary Boyce in her *Manichaean hymn-cycles in Parthian*[23], where she
gives a detailed description of the metres in the two hymn-cycles
Huwīdagmān and *Angad Rōšnān* (pp. 45-59). Both cycles use metres
with four stressed syllables to the line (with caesura), but *Huwīdagmān*
is shown to have on the average $1^1/_2$ syllables more in the line
than *Angad Rōšnān*: 12.82 (varying from 10 to 17) as against 11.34
(varying from 8 to 16) syllables (pp. 46-47). There is also statistical
evidence of other differences between the sets of metres, but listing
the different types of distribution of stressed and unstressed syllables,
Mary Boyce comes to a good 25 patterns already for the half-lines
(pp. 49-54), and these with no apparent system. On top of this there
arise occasional difficulties in deciding which syllables take the stress
(p. 54). This must lead us to the conclusion that there are metrical
rules supplementing the general frame set by the number of stresses
(and, in places, caesura). So far these rules seem to have eluded
our recognition[24].

Returning now to *AZ*, it seems safe to assume that the verse found
there is held within the frame of three stresses to the line and that
the line comprises between five and ten syllables having an average
between seven and eight, i.e. exactly as suggested by Henning in the
quotation from "Disintegration" given above[25]. In the present state
of these studies, I am afraid that we must stop there. In this type
of material there are too many factors of uncertainty to allow even
for making statistics, the original form, length and number of the
lines being unknown. If the riddles of Middle Iranian versification
are to be solved, I think this must be done on the basis of texts
where the verse lines are definable with certainty on graphical or
other grounds. Among other things that should mean that the copyists
knew that they were writing verse.

[23] London Oriental ser., 3; London 1954.
[24] Cf. also Shaked, *op. cit.*, pp. 397, 403-405.
[25] The possibility of counting the line as six stresses with a caesura in the middle
should not be completely ruled out, but the distribution of rhymes makes that less likely.

One more aspect of the verse in *AZ* has to be discussed: the rhymes. Of the 24 lines quoted above at least 18 rhyme in some way or other. Considering the unreliability of the text, that might seem sufficient proof in itself, but it is not so certain, after all. All these rhymes are present indicative verbal endings (possibly apart from a ⁺*šifigr*?/*tigr* in § 28), and so it will often be seen to be also further on in the text. According to the common rules of Middle Persian grammar and the obvious poetical aim to finish a clause within the line, this is more or less what could be expected also without rhyming rules. A short look at earlier suggestions and examples of rhyme in Middle Iranian poetry gives a somewhat confusing picture:

H.S. Nyberg, in "Ein Hymnus auf Zervān in Bundahišn" [26], presents a text of lines elegantly rhyming in pairs (p. 223), but Henning in "A Pahlavi poem" (p. 646, n. 5) summarily dismisses the possibility of the passage in question being a poem at all. He does so in connection with a general discussion on rhyme, where he states "that in the whole of the Western Middle Iranian material so far recognized as poetical there is not a single rhyme in the strict sense. There are accidental rhymes and assonances, but the principle of rhyme as such, the deliberate rhyme, seems to have been unknown". Yet, in the next paragraph he publishes an *andarz* text from Jamasp-Asana's *Pahlavi Texts* (p. 54) arranged as a poem rhyming all through in -*ān* (incl. interior rhyme in the *maṭla'* in the manner of Qaṣīda). Commenting upon it, he leaves it an open question if this is a true Middle Persian poem or an imitation of [New] Persian models.

In his article "A rhymed ballad in Pahlavi" [27], J.C. Tavadia finds (p. 30) that the last-mentioned poem may have a Sasanian origin. On the other hand he expresses doubt as to the time of origin of the poem he himself publishes in this article [28]. This text is once more taken from the inexhaustible *Pahlavi Texts* (pp. 160-161) [29], and it is arranged by Tavadia as a poem rhyming in -*ān* all through its 30 lines and with one or two caesuras to the line [30].

S. Shaked, in his already quoted contribution to the *Henning Memorial Volume* (pp. 395-405), seems to disregard rhyme completely

---

[26] *ZDMG* 82(1928), pp. 217-235.

[27] *JRAS* 1955, pp. 29-36.

[28] See also M. Boyce, *JRAS* 1957, p. 41 with n. 2.

[29] Publ. as prose by H.W. Bailey, *Zoroastrian problems*, Oxford 1943, pp. 195-196.

[30] Doubts on this arrangement are expressed by Shaked, *op. cit.* p. 405, n. 37.

as a relevant element in Middle Persian poetic structure, but in
the paper "Andarz ī Wehzād Farrox Pērōz containing a Pahlavi poem
in praise of wisdom"[31], A. Tafazzoli, on much the same text material,
comes to the opposite conclusion. He makes his own arrangement
(independently) of the *andarz* text (from *Pahlavi Texts*, pp. 74-75)
published by Shaked (*op. cit.*, pp. 398-400) as "a hymn to wisdom"
making it rhyme in -*tar* all through. He rearranges the "poem in praise
of wisdom", re-edited by Shaked (*op. cit.*, pp. 400-401) after an earlier
publication by Tavadia[32] of another piece from *Pahlavi Texts* (pp.
165-166), finding in it three strophes rhyming in -*ag*, *xrad* and -*tar*,
respectively, and his conclusion is (p. 58): "Most Pahlavi poems so
far noticed in the Pahlavi works, as well as those preserved in
Persian script in the Islamic books, are consciously rhymed".

It seems as if the problem of rhyme in Middle Persian is about as
complicated as that of metre. Apart from the apparent difficulties
in defining with certainty the end of verse lines embedded in what
is presented as prose in late manuscripts, the relation between
"conscious" and "consistent" use of rhyme seems to be an essential
point. Where is the borderline between accidental and deliberate
rhymes? Rhymes may be used, of course, as a facultative stylistic
device, i.e. "conscious" but not "consistent". Furthermore, "consistent" could mean consistent with rules which we are unable to discern
at present. The conclusion of Benveniste regarding the rhymes in *AZ*
was that the verses "often rhyme" with the cautious addition "sans
être constante ni complète"[33]. On the above material and what is
to be brought forth below, it seems to me that the verses found in
AZ show a deliberate use of rhymes at least as a facultative device,
possibly also consistent with some hidden rules—it must be remembered
that these verses most probably were meant to be sung[34].

The discussion of the text of *AZ* had reached the end of § 31
(supra p. 403). §§ 32-33 are, once more, narrated in past tense, but

---

[31] *Īrān-šināsī* 2(1350/1971): 2, pp. 45-60; also publ. in *Studia Iranica* 1(1972): 2,
pp. 207-217.

[32] "A didactic poem in Zoroastrian Pahlavi", *Indo-Iranian Studies*, I, Santiniketan
1950, pp. 86-95; also publ. in *M.P. Kharegat Mem. Vol.*, Bombay 1953, pp. 271-275.

[33] *JA* 220, p. 251; *ibid.*, p. 293, he speaks, although in a wider perspective, of
"la constance relative de la rime".

[34] See Mary Boyce, "The Parthian *gōsān* and Iranian minstrel tradition", *JRAS* 1957,
p. 28 with n. 1, and passim.

the last paragraph of this first section falls back into present tense, possibly in verse:

§ 34 *pas zanénd 300 méx ī āsēnén* Then they pitch 300 iron poles,
ī pátiš bandénd 300 ⁺xírs(?) [35] to which they fasten 300 rings(?),
kē har ⁺xírs-ē 300 drái ī zarrén in each ring of which 300 golden
                                                          bells
pátiš ākúst-ēstét are hung.

The second section comprises §§ 35-68 (5 pp. in *Pahlavi Texts*), describing the prophecy of Jāmāsp and its immediate consequences. The corresponding passage in *Šāh-nāmah* occupies baits 313-434 in the Russian edition (VI, pp. 87-95). The contents of the two versions are quite similar, at times strikingly similar. The main difference is that *Šāh-nāmah* is almost exclusively concerned with the prophecy, while *AZ* takes the second half of this section to describe King Vištāsp's reaction on the prophecy. Narration in *Šāh-nāmah* is, of course, in past tense. *AZ*, on the other hand, has almost completely present tense narration in this section (the two possible exceptions in § 50 will be treated below), and it is generally rather easy to distinguish the lines of the original poem:

§ 35 *pas vištásp ō kai-gáh nišīnét* Then V. seats himself on the throne
u jāmásp bītáxš ō pēš xᵘāhét and calls J., the Bītaxs, forward.
gōbét kū mán dāném He says (that): "I know
kū tó jāmásp dānák that you, J., are wise
u vēnák [u] šnāsák hé(h) and clear-sighted [and] knowing.
§ 36 *ēn-ič dānēt (?)* Do you also know this:
kū ka 10 róč vārán āyét when it is raining 10 days,
čand sríšk ō damík āyét how many drops fall on the earth,
u čand sríšk apar sríšk āyét and how many drops fall upon
                                                          drops?

§ 37 *u ēn-ič dānē(h) (?)* And do you also know this:
kū [ka] urvarán viškōfét when the plants blossom
katám hān gúl ī roč viškōfét which of those flowers that
                                                          blossoms in the day
u katám hán ī šáp (?) and which one in the night,
katám hán ī fraták (?) which one the next day?
§ 38 *ēn-ič dāné(h) kū ⁺mih(á)rg(?)* [36] Do you also know this: of the
                                                          clouds

---

[35] Cf. Nyberg, *Manual* II, s.v.
[36] Cf. Nyberg, *Manual* II, s.v.

katám hān áp dārḗt	which one has water
u katám hán nē-dārḗt	and which one has not?
§ 39 *ēn-ič dānē(h)* (?)	Do you also know this:
kū fraták-rōč č[ḗ] bavḗt	what will be to-morrow
andar hān aždahák-rázm i vištāspán	in that Dragon-battle of the
	Vištāsps;
háč pusarán u brātarán	among the sons and brothers
i mán kai-vištásp-šáh	of me, K.,
kē zivḗt u kḗ mīrḗt	who will live and who will die?"

The corresponding passage in *Šāh-nāmah*, baits 314-322:

فرود آمد از باره بر شد بگاه   بشد شهریار از میان سپاه

کجا رهنمون بود گشتاسپ را   بخواند اوگرانمایه جاماسپ را

چراغ بزرگان و اسپهبدان   سر موبدان بود و شاه ردان

که بودی بر او آشکارا نهان   چنان پاك تن بود و تابنده جان

ابا او بدانش کرا پایه بود   ستاره شناس و گرانمایه بود

ترا دین به داد و پاکیزه رای   بپرسید ازو شاه و گفتا خدای

جهاندار دانش ترا داد و بس   چو تو نیست اندر جهان هیچ کسی

بگویی همی مر مرا روی کار   ببایدت کردن ز اختر شمار

کرا بیشتر باشد اینجا درنگ   که چون باشد آغاز و فرجام جنگ

The differences in accentuation of the contents seem to be mostly within what could be ascribed to differences in poetical temperament and milieu. The mode of expression is more archaic in *AZ*, and it is especially striking that Daqīqī's version has such a religious tone as opposed to the completely secular spirit of *AZ*.

The main criteria for reading this passage (and others) in *AZ* as verse are: short sentences, often repeating the same structure over and over again; often irregular word order (better examples further on); rhytmically recurring repetitions of words and phrases; use of standing epithets (better examples further on); general rhythmical qualities, very often allowing the text to be scanned in series of three stresses between pauses. In many of these respects, among others the word order, the text is closely related to *Šāh-nāmah*. With this it shall not be claimed that the text arranged as lines of poetry above (and below) necessarily appears in the shape it had in the original epic. Many of the lines are probably close to the original, while others must have suffered considerable corruption during some 7-800 years of oral and written textual history (Codex MK being dated 1322 A.D.)[37].

Considering the narrow textual basis (two interdependent MSS) and the uncertainty as to metrical and other rules applicable to this type of poetry, I have generally made no attempt to reconstruct an imagined original. Furthermore, it would be too cumbersome here to republish the whole text, verse by verse. Such a text would look rather much like the one already produced (although not complete) by Benveniste, the main difference being that it would be possible to put back most of the words he had to exclude in order to follow his own strict rule of six syllables to the line. In the following only verse lines of special interest, for instance in relation to corresponding parts of Šāh-nāmah, will be quoted.

It may be of some relevance here to add a short note on the relation of AZ to the so called Jāmāsp-nāmak or Ayyātkār ī Jāmāspīk, the Jāmāspī of the Parsees[38]. This work is preserved in a fragmentary and confused way, only part of it being known in the original Pahlavi, the rest surviving in Pazand, the so called Parsi (i.e. transcription of Pahlavi in Arabic writing) and New Persian translation[39]. Its chapter XVI (no. as in the reconstruction by Messina), which is the only one fully preserved in Pahlavi, has been analysed as verse (octosyllabic and partly rhyming) by E. Benveniste, who discusses it in detail in his article "Une apocalypse pehlevie: le Žāmāsp-Nāmak"[40]. The main subject matter which AZ has in common with this work is the simple fact that "Jāmāsp bītaxš", being questioned by "Vištāsp-šāh" foretells the future, but there are also some formal similarities. The text is obviously adapted from an original in verse. This is valid for chapter XVI, as argued by Benveniste, but it may also

[37] According to Mary Boyce, Hdb. d. Orientalistik, I: IV: 2: 1, p. 56, AZ was presumably written down after the Arab conquest.

[38] There seems to be but uncertain evidence for the distinction made by Mary Boyce, Hdb. d. Orientalistik, I: IV: 2: 1, p. 50, to the effect that Jāmāsp-nāmak should be just one chapter (XVI) of the longer work Ayyātkār ī Jāmāspīk.

[39] The Pahlavi, Pazand and New Persian (and Gujarati) text material has been published and translated by J.J. Modi, Jâmâspi, Pahlavi, Pâzend and Persian texts, Bombay 1903; partly re-edited in transcription, supplemented with the Parsi text and a reconstruction of the Pahlavi, and translated by G. Messina, Libro apocalittico persiano Ayātkār i Žāmāspīk, Rome 1939.

[40] Revue de l'histoire des religions 106(1932), pp. 337-380; Benveniste uses the text as published by H.W. Bailey in BSO[A]S 6(1930-32), pp. 55-85, 581-600, 822-824.

be so for other parts of the work, although it is difficult to establish the actual verse lines on the basis of the often quite confused secondary material in Pazand and Parsi [41]. In chapter XVI the verse lines are characterized by four stresses with a caesura in the middle and quite frequent rhymes of the same somewhat uncertain verbal type as in AZ [42]. This holds true also for the occasional lines of chapter XVI left out as interpolations by Benveniste.

The first chapter of the *Ayyātkār ī Jāmāspīk* has some apparent connections with *AZ*. Paragraph I.7 (in Messina's reconstruction) is partly an exact parallel to § 1 of *AZ*. It runs (in the transcription used here): *ēn ayyātkār ī jāmāspīk x*ᵘ*ānēnd, pat hān gāh nipišt ka vištāsp-šāh dahyupat būt, u-š dēn ravākēnīt, u-š x*ᵘ*atāyēh spurrīk kart, u-š ōi daxšak mat hān ī vazurg kārēčār ī apāk [uzdēs-]paristišn ī xyōnān būt*, "This they call the Memoir of Jāmāsp. It was written at the time when V. was ruler and the Religion was propagated by him and the dominion was made perfect by him. And to him came the sign, the one of the great which took place with the idol-worship of the X" [43]. The remainder of the first chapter (I.8-14 in Messina's reconstruction) refers to the prophecy of Jāmāsp as described in the second of *AZ*. As a matter of fact I.10-12 render, partly word for word but in some confusion, §§ 35-38 of *AZ* (see above p. 409), although this description of the prophetic gifts of Jāmāsp is not put in the mouth of Vištāsp, as in *AZ*, but is ascribed to Jāmāsp himself.

Another similarity between the *Ayyātkār ī Jāmāspīk* and the second section of *AZ* is found in the standing formulae introducing direct discourse. *AZ* repeatedly uses the phrases /pas/ gōbēt jāmāsp bītaxš kū (§§ 40, 43, 45, 63, 66, 90) and pas gōbēt vištāsp-šāh kū (§§ 42, 68). This corresponds to the use of pursīt (or pursēt?) vištāsp-šāh kū and guft-iš jāmāsp /ī/ bītaxš kū in *Ayyātkār ī Jāmāspīk* (passim). The reversed word order, rhythmic qualities and stereotyped use of these formulae give them an epic ring, but the dependence on Avestic models is also unmistakable (pərəsaṭ zaraθuštrō, āaṭ mraoṭ ahurō mazdå,

---

[41] So e.g. chapter XVII in the reconstruction of Messina, *op. cit.*, pp. 74-77, certainly gives the impression of having been based upon a verse composition.

[42] See above p. 405; cf. Benveniste, *RHH* 106(1932), pp. 365-366.

[43] This parallel further diminishes the probability of the rather arbitrary suggestion by Benveniste, *JA* 220, p. 250, that the corresponding passage in *AZ* should be read with *an gāh* instead of *ān gāh* and translated "ce récit dit de Zarēr a été écrit en un autre lieu" and that this must needs be a reference to another—Parthian version of *AZ*.

etc.)⁴⁴. It is remarkable that these formulae in the metrical parts of the *Ayyātkār ī Jāmāspīk* are in a metre characterized by three stresses to the line while the general metre has four stresses (e.g. XVI.1: *pursít vištásp-šáh / kū ēn dḗn ī apēčák—čand sál ravāk bavḗt / pas hač hán čē āvám—u zamānák rasḗt/*). The somewhat clumsy construction *guft-iš jāmāsp* also raises some doubt: is it a remodelling of a *praesens historicum*: *gōbēt jāmāsp*, as in *AZ*? On the whole, it seems as if *AZ*, at least in some respects, has been a formal model for the version of the *Ayyātkār ī Jāmāspīk* which can be reconstructed from the preserved text material.

In the second section of *AZ* there are many further passages that have close parallels in *Šāh-nāmah*, e.g. *AZ* § 42:

pas gōbḗt vištásp-šáh	Then V. says:
kū́ pat xʷarráh ī ohurmázd	"By the glory of O.
u dḗn ī māzdesnán u ján	and the Mazdayasnian religion and the life
[ī] zarḗr brāt sōkánd xʷarḗt (for -*am?*)	of brother Z. I (?) swear
kū́-t nē-zanám u nē-ōzanám	that I shall not strike and not kill you
u nē tṓ-ič pat dēpáhr dārám	and I shall not either hold you in anger".

and *Šāh-nāmah*, baits 328-330:

بدین و بدین آور پاك رای	جهانجوی گفتا بنام خدای
بجان گرانما‌یه اسفندیار	بجان زریر آن نبرده سوار
نفرمایمت بد نه خود من کنم	که نه هرگزت روی دشمن کنم

AZ § 46:

fraták-rṓč ka patkōfḗnd	Tomorrow when they encounter each other,
nḗv pat nḗv u varáz pat varáz	brave against brave and boar against boar,
vás mát apāk (for *apē*)-*púhr*	many a mother without son
vás.[púhr] apē-pít	many a son without father

---

⁴⁴ This does not necessarily mean that these passages are direct translations from Avestan; they are rather archaic formulae influenced by the Avesta but with specific rhythmic and stylistic qualities in Pahlavi; cf. G. Widengren, *Festschrift Eilers*, 1967, pp. 280-281; cf. also *pas āxēzēt* initially in *Ayyātkār ī Jāmāspīk* XVI. 27 (Benveniste 58) and 41 (Benveniste 84), and comment by Benveniste, *RHH* 106, p. 370.

u vás pít apē-púhr	and many a father without son
u vás brất apē-brất	and many a brother without brother
u vas zán (šōdōmand) apē-šốd bavénd	and many a wife without husband will be

and *Šāh-nāmah*, baits 336, 342:

هوا تیره گردد زگرد نبرد   به پیش اندر آیند مردان مرد

— — —

بسی بی پسر گشته بینی پدر   بسی بی پدر گشته بینی پسر

In *AZ* § 50:

pas vištāsp-šáh ka-š hān sax"án ā́šnŭt	Then V., when he has heard this word,
hač ⁺farrax"ān-gáh[45] *ō damȋk ōpást* (for *ōftēt?*)	falls (?) from the throne to the ground

we meet the two only forms (written 'šnwt and 'wpst) that seemingly
fall outside narration in present tense in this section. However, *ā́šnūt*
may be seen as the predicate of a temporal clause of anterior action
and *ōpast* as a secondary assimilation to that form or as the predicate
of a continuation of the temporal clause[46]. The corresponding verse
(412) in *Šāh-nāmah* runs:

بران گوشهٔ تخت خسپید باز   چو شاه جهاندار بشنید راز

There are also great differences between *Šāh-nāmah* and *AZ* in
this second section. There is, for example, no trace in *Šāh-nāmah*
of the appearance, in turn, of Zarēr (*AZ* §§ 55-56), Pāt-Xōsrōi (§§ 57-58),
Frašāvart (§§ 59-60) and Spandi-dāt (i.e. Isfandiyār; § 61) urging the
king to rise and return to the throne in reliance on their respective
fighting capacity. Instead Daqīqī makes Jāmāsp speak for them all
(baits 425-431):

که ای نیك خو مهتر بافرین   خردمند گفتا بشاه زمین

نهاده بسر برکیانی کلاه   گر ایشان نباشند پیش سپاه

که باز آورد فره پاك دین   که یارد شدن پیش ترکان چین

مکن فره پادشاهی تباه   تو زین خاك بر خیز و بر شو بگاه

---

[45] Cf. Nyberg, *Manual* II, s.v.
[46] Cf. the next verb: *girēt* in § 51.

که داد خدایست و زین چاره نیست خداوند گیتی ستمگاره نیست

زاندوه خوردن نباشدت سود کجا بودنی بود و شد کار بود

مکن دلت را بیشتر زین نژند بداد خدای جهان کن پسند

Compare *AZ* § 53 (lines 2-4 also occur in §§ 55, 57, 59, 61):

pas jāmásp [bītáxš] gōbḗt	Then J., the Bītaxs, says:
hakar šmáh bagán sahḗt	"If it please you, lord,
(u) hač ēn xák apár-āxēzḗt	rise from the ground
u apáč ō kai-gáh nišínḗt	and sit again on the throne,
čḗ šāyēt būtán ka šāyēt būtán	bacause it will be as it will be,
ka ḗn man gúft bavḗt	as it was said by me it will be!"

On the whole, it may be said that this second section of *AZ* gives a far more archaic and much less religious version of the prophecy of Jāmāsp than does Daqīqī in *Šāh-nāmah*.

The third and last section of *AZ*, comprising §§ 69-114, describes the battle against Arjāsp and the Xyōns[47]. It has been remarked already by Nöldeke that the battle description here appears in a very concise form, at least in comparison to the versions found in *Šāh-nāmah* and Ṭabarī[48], and the description in *AZ* certainly gives the impression of a one-day battle, ending with the utter defeat of the Xyōns, leaving only Arjāsp alive and sent back mutilated to his own country as a warning to others. This section takes seven pages in *Pahlavi Texts* (pp. 9-16). The corresponding passage in *Šāh-nāmah* may be considered to run till the first flight of Arjāsp[49] after some two weeks of fighting (see bait 548, p. 103) while the war goes on till the death of Arjāsp much further on (p. 203).

However, this last section of *AZ* is not a summary in the same way as the introductory section. It is true that the beginning is very abrupt, but from § 70 onwards the text has the appearance of a complete and coherent composition standing in a close relationship to an original in verse, although it is not always so easy to distinguish the verse lines here as in the previous section. The first paragraph (69) gives the contents of baits 435-465 in *Šāh-nāmah* in a very concise form. Still it is possible also here, albeit with some difficulty, to arrange the text in lines:

[47] Cf. Avesta, Yt. 9.29-30, Yt. 19.84-87.

[48] See *Das iranische Nationalepos*, 2:e Aufl., Berlin-Leipzig 1920, pp. 5-6; cf. also Boyce, *Hdb d. Orientalistik*, I: IV: 2: 1, 1968, p. 56 with n. 6.

[49] Russian ed., VI, pp. 95-117, baits 435-787.

pas vištāsp-šáh ō kōf-sár nišīnḗt   Then V. seats himself on the
                                          mountain top,

[u-š?] zāvár apák [50] *12 12 bēvár.*   with [him] a force of 12 × 12
                                          thousand;

arjásp [51] *ō kōf-sár nišīnét*   A. seats himself on the mountain
                                               top

u-š zāvár [52] *12 bēvár bēvár*   and with him a force of 12
                                     thousand thousand.

Then there is obviously a gap in the narration [53], corresponding to baits 466-547 in *Šāh-nāmah*, before the introduction of Zarēr in § 70:

u hān táhm spāhpát ī nēv zarḗr   And that brave commander,
                                        valiant Z.

kārēčár ōgōn nḗv kunét   fights so well

čigón ka ātúr dažḗt [54]   as when the fire burns

andár ō nayistán ōftḗt   [and] engulfs the reeds

u-š vát-ič hayyár bavḗt   and the wind also assists it;

ka šamšḗr frāč-zanḗt dáh   when he strikes the sword
                                           forward, ten,

u ka apāč-vēžḗt 11 xyón ōzanḗt   and when strikes back, eleven X.
                                           he kills;

ka gušnák [u] tišnák bavḗt   when he becomes hungry [and]
                                           thirsty,

xū́n [ī] xyōn vēnḗt šāt bavḗt   he sees the blood of the X. [and]
                                           becomes glad.

Šāh-nāmah (baits 549-551) is, for once, a little briefer:

سمند ى بزرگ اندر آورده زير	بپيش اندر آمد نبرده زرير
چو اندرگيا آتش و تيز باد	بلشكرگه دشمن اندر فتاد
مر اورا نه استاد هر كش بديد	همى كشت زيشان همى خوابنيد

And the continuation also runs quite parallel in the two works.

As was the case with the prophecy in the previous section of *AZ*, the battle description is narrated alsmost exclusively in present tense. The exceptions are very few: two instances of *būt* in § 69 have just been mentioned (probably interpolations); the phrase *apar/frāč*

---

[50] *būt*, interpolation?

[51] *ī xyōnān x^uatāi*, interpolation?

[52] *būt*, interpolation?

[53] This is strengthened by the fact that a number of events foretold in the prophecy of Jāmāsp never occur in the battle description.

[54] A probable emendation of d't'; Nyberg reads *yazēt*, "god".

ō pād/pai ēstāt appears thrice: §§ 73, 79 (preceded by *nē-dāt*), 99 (followed by *guft*), where *ēstāt* may be considered a "present prefect" similarly *ēstāt* in § 102) [55] and the accompanying forms, *nē-dāt* and *guft*, cases of secondary form assimilation, but the contexts are a little uncertain in so far as it is difficult to arrange them in verse lines; in § 100 there is the form *apar-nišast* (probably a mistake, emended by Nyberg to *-nišīnēt*) and in § 106 BR' wcyt, to be read *bē-vičīt* or *bē-vazēt*?

Some more parallels with the text of *Šāh-nāmah* may be instructive. Thus *AZ* §§ 76-79:

§ 76 *pas vištásp-šáh hač kōf-sár*	Then V. from the mountain top
nikáh kunḗt u gōbḗt	looks and says:
kū ham [56] *pat ḗt* [57] *dārám ku-mān ōzát*	"I do think that for us has been killed
zarḗr ī ḗrán spāhpát	Z., the commander of the Iranians,
čē nūn nē-āyḗt parríšn ī kamānán	because now the twanging of the bows is gone
u váng [ī] nḗv-martán	and the clamour of the valiant men,
§ 77 *bē hač šmáh ḗrán kē hast k̨ē šavḗt*	but who is there among you Iranians who goes
*u hač zarērán kḗn x*u*āhḗt*	and exacts revenge for the Zarērs,
tái ka-š hān hamák ī man dúxt	so that to him my daughter H.
pat zanḗh áviš dahám	I shall give in marriage,
kē andar hamák šáhr ī ērán	who in the whole land of E.
zán hač ói hu-čihrtár nḗst	no woman is more beautiful than her,
§ 78 *u-š mán [u] katák ī zarḗr*	and to him the family estate of Z.
spāhpatḗh ī ērán aviš dahám	[and] the command over the Iranians I shall give".
§ 79 *hḗč ēr u āzát passáx*u *nē-dát* (for *-dahēt?*)	No Iranian noble replied/replies.

The possible rhymes on other endings that verbal *-ēt* in § 76 are especially interesting. *Šāh-nāmah* is more elaborate. This passage covers baits 594-620, of which the directly parallel ones are the following:

---

[55] The two *kart ēstāt* in §§ 74, 100 are probably interpolations.
[56] ḤWHm.
[57] ḤWHyt.

594	مر اورا بدان رزمگه بر ندید	چو گشتاسپ از کوه سر بنگرید
	که روشن بد ی زو همه رزمگاه	گمانی برم گفت کان گرد ماه
	که شیر ژیان آورید ی بزیر	نبرده برادرم فرخ زریر
	بپاندند گردان ز انداختن	فگندست برباره از تاختن
598	مگر کشته شد شاه آزادگان	نیاید همی بانگ شه‌زادگان

— —

616	که باز آورد کین فرخ زریر	بلشکر بگفتا کدامست شیر
	که باز آورد باره و زین اوی	که پیش افگند باره بر کین اوی
	پذیرفتن راستان و مهان	پذیرفتم اندر خدای جهان
	مر اروا دهم دخترم را همای	که هر کز میانه نهد پیش‌پای
620	ز لشکر نیاورد کس‌پای پیش	نجنبید زیشان کس از جای خویش

The continuation differs considerably in the two works, owing to the fact that in *Šāh-nāmah* the special hero Isfandiyār is made to take over much of the function of Bastvar in *AZ*.

In *AZ* the passage which treats Bastvar's vengenace on Vīdrafš for killing his father Zarēr (§§ 79-108) is in fact the central part of the whole composition, and it has many archaic and interesting features. The beginning of Bastvar's lament at his father's death (§§ 84-87) was discussed already by Chr. Bartholomae [58] who even, but for special purposes, suggested that the text of § 84 might be taken from a song or an epic poem. Benveniste (*JA* 220, p. 280) considers this lament "le passage le plus significatif du texte, celui qui en affirme le plus nettement l'élan épique et la structure métrique". This seems to be a reasonable statement, although he needs some engineering to get hexasyllabic lines all through, but it remains obscure where and how he finds the "dialect elements characteristic of the North-West" mentioned in the same place [59].

It is rather so that the absence of clearly Parthian elements, alien to ordinary Book Pahlavi, is a striking characteristic of this text, which is generally supposed to be an adaptation of a Parthian

[58] *Zur Kenntnis der mitteliranischen Mundarten*, IV, pp. 21-23.

[59] Benveniste refers to Bartholomae, *ibid.*, but as far as I can see, no such conclusion is to be found there; cf., however, Bartholomae, *ibid.*, p. 25, on Parthian elements in the *Draxt ī Asūrīk*.

original. There is one more passage alleged to bear traces of a "northern redaction"[60], Bastvar's incantation of his arrow in §§ 92-93. H.S. Nyberg, too, finds Parthian elements here. He obviously reads the first line differently from the previous editors: $^{+}$nūn, tigr, hač man šavāi[61] / pērōz-āvar ayēh[62], considering ayēh as the Parthian 2nd sing. ind. of "to be" (= Man. Parth. 'yy). This looks an ingenious explanation, but in consideration of the lack of other typically Parthian elements, it remains uncertain. True, there is a genuinely Parthian phrase in the last line of this incantation (end of § 93): yat-ō rōč yāvēt[63], but this yat-ō is also used in the colophon of AZ[64], which can hardly be suspected of having a Parthian model, and its power of evidence is thus considerably diminished.

In conclusion it may be stated that the text of Ayyātkār ī Zarērān has come down to us in a form which betrays much of an original verse composition, narrated in present tense. The original poem has undergone different treatment in different parts of the text. Thus the first section (§§ 1-34) seems to be an abridgement of the original, partly in prose and then in past tense, partly preserving the verses of the poem and with them the present tense narration. The second section (§§ 35-68) gives a coherent description of Jāmāsp's prophecy and may be considered to render the original version in a rather complete way. With one or two possible exceptions it is composed in present tense all through, and it is generally quite easy to divide the text into (approximate) verse lines, each within the frame of three stressed syllables, often rhyming in pairs. The third and last section (§§ 69-114) again seems to be an abridgement or, but less likely, an unintentional shortening of the original. Between §§ 69 and 70 substantial parts of the description of the battle against Arjāsp and the Xyōns are missing. This section, too, is almost completely narrated in present tense. The three or four exceptions may easily be put to the account of the copyists. The verse structure is the same as in

---

[60] Benveniste, JA 220, p. 284, and before that Pagliaro, op. cit., p. 588.

[61] Cf. Manual II, s.v. šutan.

[62] See Manual I, p. 175, under "Parthian forms"; Pagliaro Benveniste read 'YŠ = kas.

[63] Cf. Henning, BSOAS 13, p. 643 n. 5, and Nyberg, Manual II, s.v. yat-ō; Pagliaro and Benveniste read gatān; the same phrase occurs in Draxt ī Asūrik § 20 (Pahlavi Texts, p. 110).

[64] Pahlavi Texts, p. 16, § 4; cf. Henning, loc. cit.

the second section, although the reconstruction of the verses is not always without problems.

What has been called "the original poem" above must have been an epic composition from Sasanian times. Most probably that composition had one or more Parthian models, but it is important to note that there is little or nothing in the actual wording of the *Ayyātkār ī Zarērān* to betray such a dependence. As long as this work was read as prose, the irregularities in the word order were certainly striking and required an explanation, but when we now read most of it as verse, these irregularities are explainable according to the rules of Persian poetical syntax, so well attested in *Šāh-nāmah*. On the whole the state of preservation of this poem within what appears as prose in the text of the *Ayyātkār ī Zarērān* in Codex MK (dated 1322 A.D.) is remarkably good, and this would support the hypothesis that the poem was transmitted orally till a time not far distant from the writing down of the immediate model of this part of MK by Rōstahm ī Mihrāpān in the 13th century A.D.

GEO WIDENGREN

HENRIK SAMUEL NYBERG AND IRANIAN STUDIES, IN THE LIGHT OF PERSONAL REMINISCENCES

Henrik Samuel Nyberg was born 28th December 1889 in Dalecarlia in Soederbaerke, a parish where his father was a curate. The family was rather large and his father's financial situation difficult. Like so many other theological students his father had to bear the expenses of his university studies in Upsala with the help of loans from banks or elsewhere. Heavy debts, with which a man might have to struggle nearly all his life, were the inevitable result. The situation of Nyberg's father was aggravated by the fact that owing to increasing deafness he could not get any promotion in his ecclesiastical career. Nyberg has written in an article that his father's difficulties always were present in his mind.

Nyberg received his first education at home, his father being his teacher for several years. It was not until the age of 13 that he was sent to the famous grammar school in Vaesteraas where he distinguished himself thanks both to his great intellectual capacity and the solid foundation laid by his father.

Having passed his matriculation examination in Vaesteraas, he matriculated at the university of Upsala. It was taken for granted in his family that he like his father would devote himself to the study of theology but his own interests went in the direction of classical and oriental studies. Accordingly he studied Latin with Person, Greek with Danielsson, Sanskrit with Johansson, and Semitic languages with Zettersteen. All these scholars were prominent philologists, well known also outside Sweden, chiefly Jung-grammarians closely associated with the fine philological traditions of Wilhelminian Germany. Danielsson was moreover an outstanding specialist in linguistics.

To some degree it is astonishing that with this background, so well grounded in classical languages and Sanskrit as he was, Nyberg preferred to concentrate on Semitic languages and to present his thesis under the supervision of Zettersteen. That eminent specialist in Arabic actually lacked what was so characteristic of Nyberg during his whole scholarly career: the large views and visions, the deep interest not only in language in itself, but perhaps still more in the content of the texts, written in the many languages for which he had an inborn appetite. Perhaps it was simply for reasons having to do with his academic career. Obviously he must at an early date have felt that he was called to be an academic teacher, but at the same time he perhaps had the impression that it was more difficult to find a position in the field of the other languages, where competition was extremely hard and dependent upon many unforeseeable circumstances. And Nyberg was a penniless student.

At any rate Nyberg specialized in Semitic languages, above all Arabic and Hebrew.

In Semitic languages Nyberg published some outstanding books, articles, and editions of Arabic texts. In 1931 he succeeded his teacher Zetterstéen in the chair of Semitic languages in Upsala, but by that time his chief interest had undoubtedly shifted considerably.

Nyberg's attention had been drawn to the so-called Avroman documents, parchments from the Parthian era, partly bilingual—Middle Iranian and Greek. Possessed of unusually sharp vision and trained in reading difficult Arabic manuscripts he attacked with confidence the task of deciphering these specimens of Parthian Pahlavi, which had remained unreadable in their Iranian part—though the Greek version had been interpreted by Ellis H. Minns who had published these texts.

Nyberg succeeded in his main task, although he was not able to solve all the riddles. He devoted special care to the analysis of the Aramaic ideograms, an analysis to which I shall return. The interpretation both gave Nyberg a fine reputation as a prominent scholar in Iranian studies and stimulated him to pursue his research work in this field. Nyberg had acquired a good knowledge of Avestan thanks to his study of Sanskrit and was supported in these studies by his friend Charpentier, later holder of the Sanskrit chair. Zetterstéen had taught him the elements of New Persian and later he took the opportunity to study that language with an Oriental refugee during the first World War.

Nyberg was therefore well prepared for the study of Iranian languages and with his article "The Pahlavi Documents from Avroman", (*MO* XVII, 1923), he threw himself wholeheartedly on Pahlavi. Here he really was his own teacher, using what books and text-editions he could get hold of. He mentions later Bharucha, *First Lessons in Pahlavi*, but neither in his writings nor in his conversation do I

remember that he referred to *Gujastak abalish*, published by Bar-
thélemy, a text that my teacher in New Persian Arthur Christensen
told me had taught him the first steps in Pahlavi.

The study of Pahlavi had suffered much from the fact that the role
of the Aramaic ideograms had been misunderstood. Pahlavi was
spoken of as a "Mischsprache". This misconception had been eliminated, *inter alia* thanks to the efforts of the great Noeldeke who
included also Pahlavi among the subjects of his studies. But yet
some outstanding Pahlavi scholars, among them Darmesteter and
West, used the traditional and misleading Parsi transcriptions of
the ideograms. Bartholomae, who did so much to promote the study
of Pahlavi, had no first-hand knowledge of Aramaic. The study of
Pahlavi was dominated—and rightly so—by the Turfan discoveries
and the new insights they brought to our understanding of the
Middle Iranian stage of the language. But the study of the ideograms
had been neglected, because the Turfan texts were written in phonetic
script. The fragments of the Psalter were an exception but they
were studied by Andreas in Goettingen, reserved for publication and
not accessible to other scholars.

It was therefore natural that Nyberg should have concentrated
on Pahlavi and devoted special attention to the analysis of the Aramaic
ideograms. Actually he says that he started the study of these ideograms
because of their great interest and importance in Aramaic dialectology
(*op. cit.*, p. 183).

He was eminently well prepared for his task thanks to his outstanding
knowledge of Semitic languages. Very early he started a close examination of the *Frahang i Pahlavīk*, the collection of Aramaic ideograms
published by Junker. This edition suffers from the fact that Junker
obviously lacked all knowledge of Aramaic and for that reason only
presented the material for a study of the ideograms, giving the
traditional Parsi transliterations, but not the correct readings of the
Aramaic words.

Nyberg's occupation with the ideograms brought him at the outset
into contact with the inscriptions in which the ideograms are written
in a less ambiguous manner than in the Zoroastrian texts extant
in Pahlavi, as he himself observed in his article on the Avroman
documents. The well-known archaeologist and specialist in epigraphy,
Ernst Herzfeld, had provided him with a fine photograph of the
Hājjīābād-inscription (which he read with Wikander and me in the
mid-thirties). He published this inscription in the Festschrift for

Arthur Christensen, *Øst og West* (Copenhagen 1945, p. 62-74) and
republished it with some modifications in reading and interpretation
in his *Manual of Pahlavi* (I, p. 122f. and II, Glossary).

Nyberg, as I have said, paid much attention to the inscriptions and
repeatedly discussed various problems connected with some of them.
For the edition of the Persepolis Inscription in his *Manual* (I, p. 126f.)
—in connection with the festivities of the Cyrus Jubilee—he went
to Persepolis and closely examined some readings (cf. *Manual*, II,
p. 284). I remember how pleased he was when he returned to our
hotel in Shiraz.

I also remember from the excursion after the first World Congress
of Iranology in 1966 Nyberg standing before the two Persepolis
inscriptions in the blazing sunshine, his hat pushed back, reading
out the inscriptions in a loud voice, surrounded by an admiring
crowd. I said to him: "H.S. (he was always addressed so by his
friends), how are you able to read the words so fluently, I can
hardly read anything more than *Malkan Malka*?". He answered:
"Well, Geo, as you know I have occupied myself a bit with these
inscriptions". He certainly had.

Already in 1927 the study of Iranian languages was introduced
in Upsala as a possible subject for the B.A. examination and Nyberg
was appointed an examiner. In order to be able to give a proper
place to Middle Iranian studies he created his well-known text-book
"Hilfsbuch des Pehlevi". He wrote the texts himself, a very exacting
and tiresome process which he has described in his preface. However,
Nyberg always was a calligrapher, his handwriting being a model
of beauty and clarity and I think he enjoyed his job even if it claimed
both time and patience.

No one can appreciate the value of his manual unless one remembers
that it was a pioneer undertaking. We should not forget that Nyberg
had access to no more Mir. Manichaean texts than what had been
published. He found himself in a highly disadvantageous position
as compared to the German scholars in Berlin and Goettingen who
were working on the Manichaean fragments brought to Germany
from Turfan. No wonder therefore that Nyberg expressed some
irritation in his preface to vol. I, p. 13.

The glossary suffered from this disadvantage, especially as far as
some readings and, above all, the etymologies are concerned. But
even under the adverse conditions under which he worked Nyberg
could have presented more material, had he paid more attention

to what had been published of older New Persian texts, e.g. Taḏkirat al-Awliyā', Fārsnāmah, the Qur'ān-commentary, the Jewish-Persian literature (to the extent it was accessible at that time) etc. He actually neglected these texts and instead devoted much space to rather complicated and far-fetched etymological explanations. This short-coming in the glossary was partly due to a special trait in his intellectual equipment. He never liked solutions that he found simple, far too simple to his taste. Possessed of a thorough training in the linguistic field it was always a temptation to him to demonstrate his profound learning, a temptation he sometimes was unable to resist. I remember when Wikander and I studied Pahlavi that he sometimes could fill the blackboard almost completely with the hypothetical phonetic changes he had to postulate in order to present an etymology. In this way he finally reached an etymological expla-nation which did full justice to his learning and inventiveness, but which was seldom really convincing. However when referring to some published criticism of his views he invariably gave a very fair account of the arguments presented, adding: "But I haven't said my last word yet". In this connection a great merit in the glossary should be mentioned. Nyberg always paid much attention to the Iranian loan-words in Armenian and introduced many new suggestions into the discussion.

The most positive aspect of the glossary—an aspect neglected by Henning in his over-critical review in *GGA* 1935—is the excellent treatment of syntactic phenomena in Pahlavi texts. Actually Nyberg possessed an extremely fine sense for the syntax of a language. In the glossary of his "Hilfsbuch" we meet with a great many valuable syntactical observations, in fact it would almost be possible to write a syntax of Pahlavi, based on this material.

Another merit in his glossary is that he very often pointed out the dialect differences between NW and SW dialects. In his preface he refers to the differences between the dialects, so his method was fully conscious. Even at that time, however, he could have applied this method with more consistency, for—as it now is—too many entries lack a remark that the word comes from the NW dialect.

In the constitution of the text Nyberg at that time was more prone to emendation than later when his own work on text criticism in the Old Testament field made him much more cautious and conservative in his treatment of the transmitted text.

With its inevitable shortcomings the "Hilfsbuch" filled a gap and was a great achievement. I think that in the history of our studies it will keep a place of honour.

Nyberg had devoted much labour to calendar questions and a result of this work was his collection of texts and translations with some philological commentary, published in *Texte zum mazdayas-nischen Kalender*, 1934. He there contented himself with presenting the material, adding some programmatic commentaries, though from conversations with him I have the impression that from the beginning he intended also to enter upon a detailed discussion of all the problems connected with Iranian calendars. At any rate he was always much interested in the various aspects of these problems.

In his publication Nyberg was able to correct some interpretations of the text T III 260 b II published in *MirM* I, p. 188-191, but above all he gave reliable transliterations and translations of some partly very difficult calendar texts found in Zoroastrian literature.

When tackling the calendar problems Nyberg was a pioneer. It is well known that these questions were discussed later by Taqizadeh and other scholars. It is a matter for regret that Nyberg did not find time to take part in this discussion.

When Nyberg published his calendar texts he was already to a great extent concentrating his research work on the Avesta. When I started my Avestan studies in the spring term of 1931 he used for his lectures Jackson's small *Avesta Reader* which he corrected and supplemented in various ways, being interested above all in the possible restorations of—as one thought at that ime—more authentic forms, based on a reconstructed consonantal text. When Wikander returned from a stay in Paris we started reading the Gathas in Nyberg's seminar as well as following his course in Pahlavi, for which of course his *Hilfsbuch* was used. The Gatha seminars—with some interruptions—continued from the autumn of 1932 to the autumn of 1937. They were held in his home every fortnight and were attended by several older and younger scholars. However, the only regular and really active members of the seminar were Wikander and myself, and for that reason the task of reading and translating the text fell upon us two. The preparation took us exactly a fortnight, and yet many passages were of course quite enigmatic to us. In order to be able to do some other work than the Gathas we divided the task between us, one of us reading every second seminar. We were hardly able to do more than to reproduce the opinions of Bartholomae-Reichelt with some casual references to Andreas-Wackernagel. This was, however, the background against which the superior knowledge of our teacher could unfold itself. At that time as far as I can remember Nyberg's interpretation of the Gathas was concentrated on problems associated with text criticism, lexicography and syntactic observations. It was a strictly philogical interpretation. I did not have the impression that he had arrived at a completely new total view of Zoroaster and the Gathas. This my recollection is probably correct for it is in accordance with what he says in the preface of his Swedish book *Irans forntida religioner*, 1937. In the spring of 1935 he was invited by his friend Tor Andrae to deliver the Olaus Petri Lectures of that year. This invitation, as he observes, provided him with the oportunity to present his views on Zoroaster and Zoroastrian religion. But—as he himself says—"Als die Vorlesungen gehalten wurden, hatte ich bereits alle Fäden zur Lösung des Gatha-problems in der Hand, aber den springenden Punkt sah ich damals noch nicht deutlich", German ed. p. III.

It was only when preparing these lectures for the printing that Nyberg thought he had found the focal point. In its published form his interpretation of Zoroaster is concentrated on some interconnected motifs. Zoroaster is seen as a priestly, i.e. professional ecstatic, using also technical instruments and medicines, singing and drugs, in order to reach a state of ecstasy. Here the *maga*, the circle of his disciples, called by Nyberg "mystery-brethren", of whom Zoroaster is the leader, plays a great role. This radically new interpretation was made possible thanks to an exegesis of the Gatha texts, in many details providing the careful reader with new insights, but in some decisive points hardly convincing. As I have discussed elsewhere—in *Stand und Aufgaben der iranischen Religionsgeschichte* and in *Die Religionen Irans* (improved French edition)—the positions taken by Nyberg I may restrict myself here to saying that I have wholeheartedly accepted Nyberg's views of Zoroaster as an ecstatic with arctic, "shamanistic" affinities and that I have tried to support this interpretation by referring to evidence not adduced by Nyberg. But I have found it difficult to accept the role of the *maga* assigned to it by Nyberg, cf. Widengren, *Die Religionen*, S. 91 f.

In the interpretation of Zoroaster's religious ideas Nyberg was not so much interested in his "theology", though by no means neglecting that aspect, as in the vexed problem of the Amesha Spentas. He interpreted these "archangels", surrounding the High God Ahura Mazdā, as collective entities. This was an interpretation that soon was pushed in the background because of Dumézil's evident solution, which found behind the Amesha Spentas the Zoroastrian reformation of the old Indo-Iranian "functional" pantheon. In his preface to the reprint of his book in its German edition *Die Religionen des alten Iran*, first published 1938, reprint 1966, Nyberg insisted (against Duchesne-Guillemin) that his own interpretation in no way clashed with Dumézil's views and pointed out that these two analyses move on different levels. He defends his linguistic interpretation of these "abstract" deities as based on the relations between abstract and collective notions, p. XVIII.

On this extremely important point I cannot but find that Nyberg was right. Let us for example take his interpretation of *daēnā* (p. 117ff.). Invoking both several passages in the Gathas, in the late-Avestan Hadōxt Nask, and in the Pahlavi treatise Mēnōk i Xrat Nyberg maintains that *daēnā* is *both* the individual (visionary) soul and the totality of all (visionary) souls, i.e. the religious community. He interprets Vohu Manah in the same way, as well as the other Amesha Spentas.

I tried to follow up this line of thought by referring to analogous conceptions in Manichaeism, in which the continuity with older Iranian ideas is conspicuous. Especially I drew attention to the both individual and collective notion of *Vahuman* (< *Vohu Manah*), *ardāyēh* (Mpers.) or *ardāvēft* (Mparth.), and *dēn*. In Zoroastrian Pahlavi translations of Avestan texts we meet with *ahrāyēh*.

Vahman as a collective entity receives the qualification of *vazurg*, great, showing him to be a cosmic figure as seen by Nyberg, *MO* XXIII, 1929, p. 368f. The word *dēn* on the other hand appears in the expression *dēn-sārār* (with parallels), corresponding to Zoroastrian *pēšupāi i dēn*, where in both cases *dēn* clearly means the congregation of religion. In the Coptic Manichaean texts the Greek loanword δικαιοσύνη signifies the totality of all those who are δίκαιος. Behind the Greek term we have of course to surmise all those who are *ardāi*: *ardāv*, cf. *ram ardāvēft* T II D 79:19, and Sogdian *ardāvyā*. At the same time the term δικαιοσύνη with Iranian parallels also means "righteousness".

Nyberg explained the use of the same term in both an individual and a collective sense as due to "primitive" man's inability to distinguish between individual and group, i.e. the group he belonged to. That was an explanation slightly out of date already in the thirties and hardly convincing, because based on the theories of Lévy-Bruhl.

For my part I took my point of departure in the epitheton *vazurg*, great, given to Vahman and his Parthian parallel Manvahmēd, and compared the Indian notion of the individual *ātman*, the soul, and the cosmic *ātman*, *mahātman*, the Great Ātman, also called Brahman, and their actual identity in the Upanishad speculation. For all this cf. my book *The Great Vohu Manah*, 1945.

If we turn to the conception of *daēnā* it would seem to be possible to discover *why* the *daēnā* is both an individual entity, even depicted in mythical colours, and a collective as emphasized by Nyberg, the totality of all *daēnā*-s and for that reason also the heavenly community who speaks to its believing members (Nyberg, *Die Religionen*, p. 119f.). The *daēnā* is both the *daēnā* of the deceased individual, *and* the totality of all *daēnā*-s, and finally an individual deity. That such is the case is also clear from Vendidad 19:30 where a female deity receives the deceased soul (cf. Wikander, *Vayu*, 1943, p. 43). This Zoroastrian goddess is nothing but a transformation of the ancient Iranian Mother Goddess, as Wikander aptly remarks.

In this connection we may refer to Yt. 13:99-100 where Vištāspa liberates the fettered *daēnā*. The Mother Goddess in eastern Iran is Anāhitā. The equation *daēnā* (as the totality of the souls) = Anāhitā is possible to understand if we take into account what Dumézil has demonstrated about the character of Anāhitā as representative of the third function of society and as such representing the collective aspect. She is a collective deity (cf. *Les dieux des indo-européens*, p. 13 and *Tarpeia*, p. 33-66). The *daēnā* may be said to express the non-mythical aspect of the deity of the third function, but meets in Yt. 13:99-100 in a mythic-ritual framework—perhaps due to the influence of Zoroastrian reform (cf. the summary *OLZ* 1963, col. 544-46, which should be developed in more detail).

Against this background it is possible to demonstrate for *daēnā* that the interpretation once given by Nyberg is not in conflict with Dumézil's views. As to the Amesha Spentas we have seen that both Vohu Manah and Aša because of the Manichaean material actually require Nyberg's collective interpretation which provides us with the clue to the incontestable continuity of Iranian ideas in this case. It would of course be desirable to extend the analysis to the other Amesha Spentas, but we have seen that the interpretation is relevant for the representatives of the first function: Aša and Vohu Manah, as well as for the third function: Aramati (*daēnā* = Anāhitā). Lacking is Xšaθra, representative of the second function. From the epitheton *vairya* we get the name *xšaθra vairya*, the desirable kingdom, which is a state of being and possesses an extension in space. Into this kingdom the believers will enter after death, it will be populated by them. Therefore *xšaθra* signifies the heavenly world, Nyberg (p. 135 and Widengren, *Religionen*, p. 90). The collective aspect would therefore seem to be inherent here as well as the abstract idea, for *xšaθra* is also a quality. It is not only a quality belonging to Ahura Mazdā but also to every man who exercises some kind of power (cf. Lommel, *Die Religion Zarathustras*, 1930, p. 55). There is accordingly a correspondence here too between God and man. It should also be observed that Dumézil himself seems rather inclined to lay stress upon points of contact with Nyberg's interpretations, but not to emphasize disagreement (cf. *Naissance d'Archanges*, p. 105, 112, 133, 145).

As a conclusion I should therefore like to state 1) that Nyberg's interpretation of the Amesha Spentas and other "abstract" entities as being also possessed of a "collective" character, at the same time as being "abstract" ideas, is still valid and of great importance for our understanding of a central gnostic idea, i.e. that of "the redeemed Redeemer"; 2) that this interpretation as explaining a "constant" in the Iranian mode of thought, as proved by its continuation above all in Manichaean doctrine, should be further explored, above all in gnostic systems of "Iranian type", more than I was able to do 30 years ago, and 3) that this analysis of Nyberg's is really in no way in conflict with Dumézil's obviously perfectly correct and epoch-making discovery of the Indo-Europaean background of the Amesha Spentas.

A remarkable idea in Nyberg's book was that the Fryāna-tribe with Kavi Vištāspa as its head not only meant to Zoroaster a material support, but that his migration there also carried with it a "theological" reorientation.

This emphasis on the Fryāna-tribe and its special religion—Nyberg considered it above all as a worship of Mithra—inspired Wikander to deep researches, also of a linguistic nature, unfortunately up to now too little utilized in later research (cf. *Vayu*, 1943).

Nyberg was of the opinion that Zoroaster's reorientation led him to the creation of a somewhat "syncretistic" system. This syncretistic trend was accentuated in the history of Zoroastrianism during its expansion westward. Here the role of the Median Magi came into focus. Nyberg convincingly demonstrated that the Magi before the arrival of Zoroastrianism in the West were worshippers of Zervan, the deity of Time and Destiny (cf. *Die Religionen*, p. 388). In this connection he had previously analyzed the Cappadocian Calendar showing it to be Zervanite in its construction. Accordingly he was able to refer to his investigations in his *Questions de cosmogonie*, a work to which I shall return.

This insight of Nyberg's actually had far-reaching consequences, for it refuted the opinion that Zervanism was a late theological speculation of Sasanian times and not a real, living religion. This view was later still held by Zaehner and others. Actually Zervanism after the arrival of the Parthians had its home among them in north-western Iran, where they had occupied the old sites of the Median people (cf. Widengren, *Die Religionen Irans*, p. 215). It should further be observed that the doctrine of Mithraic mysteries placed as the highest deity Aion or Saeculum, behind whom we have to see Zervan. Moreover, the three other higher deities in Zervanism recur in Mithraism (cf. Widengren, *Religionen*, p. 225f.). Mithraism, however, spread from those parts of Iran where Zervanism was firmly established (cf. *op. cit.*, p. 228). And these mysteries were propagated by the Magi (cf. *op. cit.*, p. 177, 225, and Nisa documents No. 2085).

By establishing a close connection between the Median Magi and Zervanism, Nyberg had paved the way for new researches leading to new insights. His insistence on the role played by Zervanism was very fruitful also in other respects, to which I shall return later.

We pass to Nyberg's general description of religious conditions in the West. Here the great problem was and still seems to be the question of the religion of the Achaemenian kings. When I first met Nyberg in 1929 it was when he read a paper in the University of Stockholm, where at that time I was a student. His subject was characteristically enough "The Religion of the Achaemenids". I remember the powerful impression I received from Nyberg's polemic against all those scholars who were of the opinion that the Achaemenids were adherents of Zoroaster's doctrine, and especially against Hertel who was made the target of many sarcastic remarks. We may now read Nyberg's account in *JA* 1931, p. 5f. and in *Die Religionen des alten Iran*, p. 343, though purged of his most trenchant irony. As is well known Nyberg never accepted the hypothesis that the Achaemenids were Zoroastrians. He gave a fine summary of the arguments *pro et contra*, but as I have further developed this theme elsewhere (cf. *Die Religionen*, p. 142ff.), I shall content myself by expressing as my personal opinion that Nyberg both in this case and as regards other difficult problems associated with religious conditions in the West showed himself at his best. When Nyberg had to handle facts on which the light of history is shed, his sound judgement and his historical training provided him with a firm foot-hold.

This fine historical understanding guided Nyberg when he attacked the difficult problem of how the holy canon of the Avesta was collected. This establishment of a canon is associated with the manner of the transmission of Avestan texts and the problem of the literary fixation of Avesta. This question before Nyberg had been treated above all by Nau who, however, lacking knowledge of Pahlavi, had relied exclusively on Syriac sources. Nyberg saw clearly that the Avestan tradition had been handed down since the time of the first community by word of mouth, down into the Sasanian period. He pointed out that the notices preserved in Dēnkart about the existence of a pre-Sasanian Avesta are nothing but a historical legend. Nyberg saw the creation of a Zoroastrian canon as conditioned above all by the struggle between the Zoroastrian Magi and the Manichaean missionaries. The Manichees possessed a written canonical literature to which they referred. The Zoroastrians had none and Nyberg considered this deficiency their weakest point (cf. p. 414). Also the Jews and Christians, being more and more numerous within the borders of the Sasanian empire, had Holy Scriptures which they referred to as the perfect expression of revelation. It was now that the *written* Avesta was brought into existence as an act of self-defence. But the process was a slow one and not finished until the reign of Xosrau I (531-579). Nyberg in this context refers to Dēnkart ed. Madan, p. 412f. where a document is preserved dating back, according to him, to the time of Xosrau I. He is of the opinion that this document really has an official character. His analysis of this very difficult text emphasized the following facts: 1) Ardašēr who is mentioned first did not yet operate with the idea of a written canon, but the notion of a tradition possessed of a canonical character can be traced in the passage devoted to him; 2) Šāpūr I probably added to the old tradition writings in Pahlavi, concerned with medical, astrological, scientific, and juridical questions; these writings obtained an authoritative position; 3) Šāpūr II took a decisive step by ordering all his subjects to follow the doctrine and practice of Zoroastrianism. He further ordered a collection, presentation, and examination of the whole religious tradition, whereupon the leading priestly authority, Āturpāt i Mānsraspandān, underwent the ordeal of molten metal in order to prove the correctness of tradition. Nothing is as yet said of a *book*, but Nyberg concludes that all circumstances presuppose the existence of a written literature. He thinks that the first Pahlavi translations were made at this time.

With these new insights Nyberg had initiated a series of investigations centered around the problem of the creation of the Sasanian Avesta. Bailey in his *Zoroastrian Problems*, 1943, studied the terminology of oral transmission as well as the development of the Avestan alphabet, and the pronunciation of special terms of considerable importance for our understanding of the Avestan language.

Above all, however, it was Wikander who in a decisive manner furthered our knowledge of how a canon was created as a result of the fusion of the Median Magi with their written tradition, having their centre in Šiz, the later Mōbads, and the Hērbads, the priests of Fārs with their oral Zoroastrian tradition, having their centre in Istaxr. In that way Wikander was able to explain *how* the Avesta was created. Nyberg had given the reasons *why* it was created and described the decisive steps in the process of canonization of the Avestan tradition.

Nyberg as we have seen insisted on Zervanism being the religion of the Median Magi. It was therefore only natural for me to advance a step further by asking whether or not parts of the Sasanian Avesta, originating in the homeland of the Mōbads, contained Zervanite texts. The actual Avesta, a fourth part of the original one, does not, but many Pahlavi texts are to some extent either translations of lost Avestan treatises of a Zervanite character or reworked translations, found above all in the Bundahišn and in Zātspram. The method of demonstrating this fact is based on philological and text-critical observations (cf. Widengren, *Festschrift für Wilhelm Eilers*, 1967, p. 278ff.). By adding the recension of the Indian Bundahišn to that of the Iranian Bundahišn it was possible for me in one case to reconstruct the original Pahlavi text which turned out to be based on an epic poem, exhibiting exactly the same stylistic features, i.e. repetitions of fixed formulas, as found in the Parthian epic poem "Abyātkār i Zarērān", cf. Widengren, *Festschrift G. Scholem*, 1967, p. 337ff. These Zervanite texts as coming from northwestern Iran must have been written in NW dialect, Mparthian. The fusion of this literature, containing also Zervanite texts, with the oral tradition, transmitted in SW dialect, Mpersian, led to the creation of a literary language, Book Pahlavi, the language of Zoroastrian literature (cf. Nyberg, *MO* XXXI, 1937, p. 83f. and Widengren, *Die Religionen*, p. 259). Nyberg in his teaching always insisted on the northwestern elements of Book Pahlavi and already in his *Hilfsbuch*, Glossary, indicated the Parthian origin of certain words, a point to which I have already alluded.

It was also possible to follow up Nyberg's ideas about the creation of a canon as coupled with the fight against the religious minorities. All circumstances show that the Zervanite parts of the Sasanian Avesta disappeared when Xosrau I established the final collection of Avestan writings. His accession to the throne coincided with the wholesale massacre of the Mazdakites, a sect actually sprung from Manichaeism. The heretics were called *zandīkān*, people who concentrated on *zand*. Wikander has shown that this term originally denoted the written tradition of the Mōbads. Now it is highly significant that *zand* is a word belonging to the NW dialect. Obviously Zervanites and Manichees—who in their doctrines were closely related to Zervanism—by receiving the stamp of *zandīk* by Zoroastrian orthodoxy were associated with the written tradition of the Magi, the *zand*. This is easy to understand if we remember that the *zand* contained Zervanite doctrines, doctrines which Zoroastrian orthodoxy ultimately purged from the final redaction of the Sasanian Avesta.

It has not been possible to give more than a selection of illustrations of how Nyberg's work has stimulated the investigations carried out by his pupils. Both Wikander and I were convinced that our teacher had created a work that introduced a new era in the study of Iranian religion. We expressed that conviction several times, cf. *inter alia* Wikander, *Vayu*, p. XIV "die Diskussion auf ein Niveau gehoben, das nun von niemandem mehr ungestraft verlassen werden kann", and Widengren. "epochmaking work", Preface, The Great Vohu Manah, 1945, *OLZ* 1963 "Nyberg in seiner eine neue Forschungsära einleitenden Arbeit Die Religionen des alten Iran". In Sweden Nyberg's book was hailed with enthusiasm. His friend Tor Andrae wrote a marvellous article in the newspaper "Svenska Dagbladet", called "The prophet rejoices", alluding to the joy felt by Zoroaster that at last he had found a congenial interpreter. Nyberg received "the Royal Prize" of the Swedish Academy, the finest distinction at the time to be given to a scholar. His German colleague and friend H.H. Schaeder offered to translate this comprehensive volume of 500 pages, and this offer was made already before the manuscript was sent to the printer for the Swedish edition. When Schaeder in the spring of 1938 delivered his Olaus Petri lectures in Upsala he and Nyberg were able to check a great part of the translation. The German edition was rapidly printed and when Nyberg and I went to the Orientalist Congress in Brussels in September Nyberg was much pleased to see the German edition in the book exhibition.

No doubt Nyberg had the feeling that he had produced a work of great value. The first reviews, though not exactly enthusiastic, were also very positive (Kramers, Pettazzoni). Dumézil's review—also positive—was published later. But in Germany the distinguished journal *ARW* had fallen into the hands of the Nazis under the editorship of W. Wüst, a prominent Nazi scholar. Volume XXXVI, 1939-40 devoted pages 215-234 to an article written by one Dr. Paul, and pages 234-249 to an article of the editor himself. Both had the character of a violent attack on Nyberg's book which evidently had deeply offended their feelings. Nyberg had not treated Zoroaster in a proprer way, this "Führergestalt" "an der Zeitwende". In Upsala we considered both authors as fanatical madmen—which they obviously were—and I cannot remember that Nyberg paid much attention to this attack. It was too clearly dictated by political and racial pre-suppositions to be taken as a contribution to scholarly discussion.

However, worse was to come. Herzfeld published after the war his two volume book *Zoroaster and his World*, 1947, from the first line to the last an attack on Nyberg. It is highly regrettable that such a great scholar was to leave behind him as his last major work such a terribly confused and on the whole worthless work. It was left without any effect and did not in any way influence subsequent discussion.

It is more astonishing that the pamphlet now to be mentioned did not meet with the same fate.

In 1951 W. Henning published his Ratanbai Katrak lectures from 1949 with the title *Zoroaster, Politician or Witchdoctor*? Leaving aside the first alternative, which intended to characterize Herzfeld's opinion of Zoroaster, we may say some words about the second alternative, which according to the author purported to be a proper description of Nyberg's views as far as the great founder is concerned. To every unbiased reader of Nyberg's book this is of course nothing but an untrue and ridiculous caricature. In the preface to the second impression of the German edition Nyberg of course protested sharply against Henning's malevolent distortion of his views (cf. p. IX). But I do not think that Nyberg correctly interpreted the motives behind Henning's attack. Nyberg thought that Henning felt himself hurt in his religious feelings, thus ascribing to him something like the "Aryan" Weltanschauung. This motive, though so prominent in the articles of Paul and Wüst, I am absolutely unable to discover in Henning's pamphlet. Therefore I do not think Nyberg's interpretation is justified.

I find Nyberg much more to his advantage in his discussion of Henning's rather wild speculations about a supposed Iranian *aera Alexandri* (cf. p. XI ff.). Henning tried by all means to save the historicity of the date given to Zoroaster, i.e. that he should have lived 258 years before Alexander. In a long discussion Nyberg shows how incredible it is that Alexander who has left no traces in the memory of the Iranian people except as the personification of East-Rome could have played any role in any Iranian chronological system. Nyberg's historical sense and his perfect command of the chronological texts make his position absolutely convincing, whereas Henning in this case—as in others—demonstrates a remarkable lack of sound judgement.

Henning's pamphlet, in which he would seem to have carried with him to England the unfortunate tone used by German Iranists, was greeted with enthusiasm by Zaehner in his book *The Dawn and Twilight of Zoroastrianism* (1961, p. 16). He printed as an Appendix Henning's "admirable critique" and in his bibliography he goes even so far as to call Nyberg's book "a historical novel"! His further statement deserves quoting *in extenso*. "Nyberg originally found disciples among his own Swedish pupils, who, however, now seem to be turning their backs to the embarrassing heritage". He also speaks of "the essentially unscholarly methods employed by Nyberg".

What Zaehner says about Nyberg's pupils can only refer to Wikander and myself (possibly also to Hartman). As far as Wikander is concerned I know of no statement of his that could serve as a pretext for Zaehner's assertion. Moreover it should be observed that Wikander was appointed to the chair of Sanskrit and Comparative Indo-Europaean Linguistics in Upsala in 1953. After that date he as a matter of fact abandoned Iranian studies. He could therefore really not "turn his back" on any "embarrassing heritage". As to myself

I think that my published work in the field of Iranian religion clearly demonstrates that I always gratefully acknowledged the inspiration received from our teacher also when I went my own ways.

Actually World War II isolated Nyberg from his contacts abroad and obviously made research work difficult for him—chiefly perhaps for psychological reasons. I remember that he used to complain that his power was gone. His orientation had been towards France and above all towards Germany. French and German were the languages he used to speak and write. In the thirties during his visits to Germany he observed the influence of Nazi ideology among German scholars in the Oriental field. In the beginning he reacted by mocking such Nazi-influenced colleagues. Once when he returned from a "Deutsche Orientalistentagung" in Bonn he told me that he and Minorsky had found some Germans so ridiculous that—as he said— "we had to step aside and laugh together in French". However, he soon realised how serious the situation actually was. The German invasion of Denmark and Norway made him furious. In May 1940 (when I had a short leave from the army to visit Upsala) he told me that after 9th April (the date of the invasion) he had had a very agitated correspondence with Schaeder (who was no Nazi at all, but rather nationalistic) concerning the German aggression against Scandinavia, whereupon he under protest had left the *Deutsche Morgenländische Gesellschaft*. His example by the way was ultimately followed by the other Swedish members. The connections with Schaeder broke off. After about two years Schaeder came to Stockholm to give a lecture there—probably for propaganda purposes—and asked Nyberg to meet him. Some kind of reconciliation was brought about, but the old friendship was never really restored.

Apart from an article on the verb in Pahlavi to which I shall return it was not until 1955 that anything more substantial was published by Nyberg in the field of Iranian studies. In *Historia Mundi*, III, p. 56-115 he gave an account of the Achaemenian empire, laying stress on political development. Perhaps this short history does not count among Nyberg's best achievements, though of course it is very readable and stimulating. In some cases he shows himself influenced by Olmstead's arguments in his rather insignificant book on the same subject, *History of the Persian Empire*, 1948. Above all Nyberg—though not without some hesitation—accepts Olmstead's curious theory that Gaumāta in reality *was* the brother of Cambyses and Darius an usurper, who started a lying propaganda in order to motivate his assassination of the legitimate king, Gaumāta, the real Bardiya. This theory does not stand the test of a closer examination as I have tried to show *Festschrift für Leo Brandt*, 1970, p. 517-22. This attitude of Nyberg's is rather astonishing as he otherwise admires Darius and his reign (cf. *op. cit.*, p. 92). I also remember the postcard he sent me when he had visited Behistun, expressing how impressed he was. As already hinted, there are on the other hand some pages with excellent opinions and modes of expression.

In this connection mention should also be made of Nyberg's last contribution to Iranian historical studies, his article in the Swedish Cyrus-Jubilee-Volume *Iran through the ages*, 1972, p. 11-19, called "From a Theocratic Imperialism to an Imperium" (also published in Acta Iranica, Vol. I, *Hommage Universel*). Here Nyberg evaluates Cyrus as the founder of an *empire*, different from the earlier Near Eastern theocratic states. The *imperium* was "a political creation in which all the peoples were integrated and were directed by a central power" (p. 18), leaving room for each people to preserve "its individuality and the opportunity to worship its own gods". This article is well written and in a clear form gives us Nyberg's views on the dominant features of the Persian empire.

The difficult problem of the verbal system in Pahlavi and the readings of the Aramaic ideograms was always present in Nyberg's mind. He constantly returned to these questions, for instance in his article "Contribution à l'histoire de la flexion verbale en iranien" (*MO XXXI*, 1937, p. 63-86 (actually printed in 1944). In this article he tackled the problem of the two systems of ideograms for verbs in Arsacid and Sasanid inscriptions, comparing them with the verbal systems of NW and SW dialects in Manichaean literature and in Book Pahlavi as found in Zoroastrian writings. Nyberg here changed some of his earlier positions and modified others, but also developed and defended his main views. He had tried to analyse the use of the ligatures 𐭪, 𐭩 which Bartholomae thought could be employed for whatever verbal form one would substitute according to grammatical rules. Nyberg, on the contrary, argued that this ligature stood either for e.g. *kunēh* or *kunēndēh*, both forms, according to him, optative forms. The latter form he reconstructed with the help of the form *bavēndēh* in Mahrnāmag lines 329, 330, 410. He had offered an ingenious and attractive proposal for the creation of this form, cf. *Hilfsbuch*, I, p. 14f. But he now abandoned the explication of the ligature as **kunēndēh* etc., forms which in his *Manual* have disappeared from the paradigms. Nyberg, however, still was of the opinion that he could demonstrate the existence of optatives in -*ēndēh* in Book Pahlavi, and in his article he transliterated and translated a passage in Dēnkart, ed. Madan, p. 593:11 - 594:4. There, according to him, we meet with three instances of the optative form in question: *ravēndēh*, **zahēndēh*, and *āfrīnēndēh*. The termination -*ēh* was written -*dš* which Nyberg emendated into -*dēh*. However, Molé, *La légende de Zoroastre*, 1967 reads: *ravē(h)*, *zayē(h)*, *āfrīnēnē(h)* and these readings to judge from the facsimile edition of Dēnkart appear to me more probable. It is accordingly highly doubtful whether the isolated forms in NW dialect: *ahēndēh* and *bavēndēh* really represent a form-developing trend in the Middle Iranian stage of the language or only constitute an isolated phenomenon. At any rate Nyberg has the merit of having drawn attention to an interesting problem which, however, cannot be solved with the insufficient and partly doubtful material discussed by him in his article.

In his transliteration of the passage in Dēnkart Nyberg committed a minor slip, completely irrelevant for the solution of the problem under discussion. He read '*YŠ* = *kas*, instead of *HDŠ* = *Hadiš*, the writing being exactly the same. Henning, of course, seized the opportunity of making the most of this insignificant detail, (cf. *BSOAS* XII 1947, p. 60). See note p. 456.

Also Nyberg's *per se* very methodic investigation of how the Aramaic ideograms for the verb-forms should be read suffered inevitably from being based on insufficient material. His point of departure was the Hājjiābād inscription of which he had received, as already stated, a good copy-photograph from Herzfeld. Nyberg on the whole spent much time on the inscription and tried repeatedly to substitute for the ideograms the most probable NW dialect forms in the Arsacid version. The readings and interpretations of the verb-ideograms he revised continually and in his *Manual* he gave final opinion. When more Manichaean texts as well as inscriptions in NW dialect were made accessible it was possible for him to attain more definitive results. It is instructive to compare his article in the Festschrift for Christensen with his presentation of the Hājjiābad-inscription in the *Manual*. Here the rather enigmatic misreading R'MYW-*d* is corrected to *z'mywd*, interpreted as **zāmēd*, instead of his earlier proposal of *afkanēnd*, line 14. His new reading may of course also be discussed, the *W* causing some difficulty. Other points are that in line 9 ḤWY-*ndy* is not *hēndē* but *ahēndē*, and in line 11 ḤWY-*nt*, read as *hēnt* is corrected to *ahānd*, and finally line 14 the last word is not read as Herzfeld's photograph gives: ḤWY-*t*, but as ḤWYN, *ahēnd*.

In the article on the verbal system Nyberg also presented some valuable syntactical observations. In this context I should like to draw attention to another correction adopted by Nyberg in his *Manual* and influencing his syntactical analysis. In line 12 we meet with the ideogram HQ'YMW-*d* preceded by the particle *hyp*. Both in his article and in the Festschrift for Christensen Nyberg proposed to read *hēp avistēnd*, but in *Manual* II, p. 38 b read *avistē(d)*. Nyberg's syntactical approach should of course be continued in new and more comprehensive researches. As to the use of the subjunctive in Book-Pahlavi I have given some supplementary remarks chiefly based on Zervanite texts in *The Zarthoshti Madressa Centenary Volume*, 1967, p. 84-103.

We have seen that Nyberg's philological interests were more and more concentrated on the study of inscriptions with their frequent use of ideograms. This interest, however, dated far back in the past. Already in 1929 he published his observations on the Darband inscriptions, which are unfortunately rather stereotyped. Thirty years and more later he wrote articles devoted to some of the shorter inscriptions such as *ŠVŠ*, *ŠPs* I-II, *ŠMŠ*, *CE*. Some of his findings he published in his *Manual* where in I, p. 122-127 he gave his readings of *ŠH*, *ŠVŠ*, *MNFd* (agrees with Henning) and *ŠPs* I-II. The glossary in *Manual* II presents his readings.

Nyberg was always approached by people who possessed some oriental *objets d'art* provided with some highly conventional inscription in Arabic, usually a quotation from the Qur'ān. It was always a source of astonishment to me that he devoted so much time to the reading of such inscriptions. It was rare that he was asked to examine anything interesting. One exception was, however, provided by the silver bowls in the possession of his friend Kempe, a Swedish industrial magnate.

In this context we should also mention his contribution to the Festschrift offered to B. Karlgren, *Septentrionalia et Orientalia*, 1959, p. 319f., where he discussed a difficult expression found in *ŠE* § 52, read by him *bōr-gil*, written *BWRKL*. In his *Manual*, II, p. 48 b he has also discussed this word *gil*. He derived it from *gṛda*, Npers. *galah* denoting "crowd, herd". On the other hand he assumes the existence of a term *gāl* which he differentiates from *gil*. This *gāl* he derives from the same *grda* (by oversight *Manual*, II, p. 80 b given as *grdha*) and found in OPers *garda*, attested in the Aram. loanword *gardā* and in *garda-pati*, attested as loanword in Late Babyl. *gardupatu* (the final vowel at this time having fallen away the pronounciation was *gardapat*) but also as *gardu* (*AD* Vol. 5, p. 50), which should be added to the references in *Manual*. Now this *gardapati*, the master of the *garda*, is an obvious parallel to sanskrit *grhapati*, master of the house (hold). But this *grha* from the same root Nyberg differentiates from *garda* > *gāl*,—although in connecting it with Avestan *gərəδa* and Armenian *gardastan* "body of servants".—Accordingly *gardapati* and *grhapati* would *not* possess exactly the same Indo-Iranian word as the first element of their composition. This seems rather difficult to accept. Also the meaning of *garda* "villain" needs some qualification and still more research. In this connection a reference may be given to Eilers' hypothetical form **gālbad* (cf. *IIJ* 5, 1961-62, p. 229).

The treatment of this word in Nyberg's *Manual* invites us to a more detailed comparison between his *Hilfsbuch* and his *Manual*. I think it was always in Nyberg's mind to replace the *Hilfsbuch* by a new and improved edition. This new chresthomathy and glossary shows that the author had been continually engaged in digesting the work carried out by himself and other scholars in Middle Iranian studies. It was above all the progressing publication of the Mir. Manichaean texts that meant an advance in Pahlavi, as Nyberg himself observed in his Preface (Vol. II, p. VII).

I shall first consider the principal differences in Nyberg's method of constructing the texts, second his lexicographical work, and third his grammatical, above all syntactical observations.

As to the texts offered we note the absence of Bundahišn Ch. I. In his Preface to Vol. I he gives as the reason for its omission the fact that a new edition was being prepared by Bailey and Barr. However, Zaehner had actually in 1955 published a new edition of this chapter in his book *Zurvan*. It would have been valuable to see Nyberg's attitude to some crucial passages. Zaehner used also the Paris ms., once utilized by Darmesteter for his Avesta commentary. It was certainly the real defect of Nyberg's edition in *JA* 1929 and in *Hilfsbuch* that he had neglected this ms. He was later evidently somewhat uneasy about this negligence. I remember that he once asked me whether I considered the Paris ms. of any special value. I answered of course that from my experience it was valuable to have its readings for comparison and that in some passages the Paris ms. obviously solved some difficult problems. In his edition of Bundahišn I Zaehner—in my opinion rightly—has preferred the readings of the Paris ms. in various passages.

When editing not only Bundahišn I, III but also other texts Nyberg was rather inclined to emend the readings of the text and to suppose the existence of glosses. Obviously he was not aware of this inclination of his for in the Preface of his *Hilfsbuch* I, p. 8* he says that he has removed obvious faults "sonst aber bin ich in textkritischer Hinsicht so vorsichtig und konservativ wie möglich vorgegangen".

Actually he had some less happy proposals in his presentation of the texts—of course together with some obvious improvements. This inclination to suppose faults and glosses more than really necessary I suppose was due to his classical training, for at the time when Nyberg was a student such was the dominant tendency in German scholarship. However, Nyberg's own work on the Hebrew text of the Old Testament made him a convinced opponent of this trend and ultimately he transferred these text-critical principles to Pahlavi studies. A typical illustration is his treatment of the passage *KN* I 7 where we read: *ō virēk ut nihān-ravišnēh ēstāt*. In his *Hilfsbuch*, II, p. 244 Nyberg explained *nihān-ravišnēh* as a gloss. In the *Unvala Memorial Volume*, 1964, p. 66f. I demonstrated that this was not the case at all, *inter alia* comparing the New Persian expression in Fārsnāmah, p. 35:17f. *gurēxtah būd va panhān šudah*. When my article was published—some years after it had been sent in— I received from Nyberg his *Manual*, I, published in the same year 1964. Here I saw that he had independently come to the conclusion that the passage *KN* I 7 contained no gloss. It is also of some significance that Nyberg in his Preface to *Manual*, II declares that he in the interval between the publication of the two volumes I and II had "been able to correct mistakes and premature emendations"! In the "Corrigenda" in *Manual*, II we now find several such cases indexed. It is quite clear that Nyberg's attitude to the question of the general reliability of the Pahlavi texts had changed considerably during his work upon his *Manual*. It is only in *Manual*, II that he has really been true to the principles of text-criticism he claimed to adhere to already in the *Hilfsbuch*. It is indeed admirable that a scholar of his advanced age was able to demonstrate so much freshness in his approach to the text.

Nyberg struggled very hard with his Glossary. The progress as compared with *Hilfsbuch* is very great. Also in comparison with the readings in *Manual*, I he was able to make several improvements. It goes without saying, however, that both in the readings and the interpretations several problems remain. Some of the texts are in my opinion too difficult for a Manual. It would have been more easier to include the whole text of *KN*, the narrative parts concerned with legendary and real history from the Bundahišn, and some selections from the *handarz* literature. As the *Manual* is now constructed it is more a selection of real editions with a full critical apparatus than a Manual for beginners, even if the intention was to provide a textbook sufficient for some years of study of Pahlavi. But Nyberg himself was fully aware of remaining unsolved difficulties (cf. *Manual*, I, p. VI). Sometimes he was moreover rather reluctant to abandon his own earlier interpretations, even when they are obviously wrong. As a typical example I mention the passage *KN* I 17 where Nyberg in his *Hilfsbuch*, II, p. 4 read: *tan pat afzōn kunēh*. In his *Manual*, II, p. 26 b he still gives the same reading (but *apazōn*) though he refers to an article by Wikander, *Orbis* XXXI, 1972, p. 183f. where *āpzan* "bathing vessel" is suggested, referring to the corresponding passage in *ŠN*. Actually in my own copy of the *Hilfsbuch*, I introduced that reading already in the thirties, though without any indication as to its source. And in my *Iranische Geisteswelt*, 1961, p. 296 I translated of course: "Bade deinen Körper"!

On the other hand Nyberg gave up his own reading *KN* I 18 *xvarrē yāmak* for the obviously correct *dast i yāmak*, suggested by Telegdi. There are many other such minor improvements. But he still refuses in the passage *KN* III 4 to change his reading *handrūtak* in favour of *girān grūtak*, suggested by Henning (*BSOAS* IX, 1937, p. 83). In *Manual*, II, p. 95 he has a rather long note in which he defends his reading, asserting that "the idea of lamentation is scarcely to the point in the quoted passage" and demanding more knowledge about the use and purport of *grwdg* (the Manichaean Pahlavi word compared by Henning). However, *handrūtak* is a word *constructed* by Nyberg, he was not able to cite any other passage in which this word is found whereas *grūtak* is found in Manichaean literature.

In *Manual* he still defends his rather unhappy proposal not to interpret 'P in accordance with Frahang XXIV 1-2 as an ideogram for *ut*, *u*, but as *api*. Thus *api-m* and not *u-m* (as indicated by Frahang). In *Hilfsbuch*, II, p. 19 he referred as a support for his reading to

the passage Behistun IV 46, where he read *apiy-may* ... *krtam*.
But already in 1931 this passage was hardly a real support, for this
passage was a *supplemented* reading. The new collation carried out
by Cameron gave as a result *uta-may*! Nyberg further referred to
MX II 197 where he interpreted *aviš* as *apiš*. Both these arguments
are tacitly dropped in *Manual*, II, p. 19 b. There he falls back
instead of them upon the Pāzand readings, such as *avam* and other
such forms in which the enclitic pronoun is found. He also refers
to an isolated *api* occurring in the *Psalter* and in *PRDD*. Nyberg
admits in *Manual*, II, p. 20 a that the word *api* was "obsolete in
the spoken language when the Manichaeans created their own literary
SW language, which was *not* based on the usage of the Sassanian
chancelleries".

It would carry us too far to examine in detail the arguments
adduced by Nyberg. His previous arguments were not accepted, and
it is doubtful whether the new ones will be. We must ask ourselves
whether it is really possible to rely to such a degree on the Pāzand
transliterations. If we take up for examination a long Pāzand text
such as *Ayātkār i Zarērān* we will find that evidently there is no
consistency in the transliteration (and therefore pronunciation) of
the writing 'P + enclitic pronoun. For that reason it seems doubtful
whether such transliterations as *ağišān* XVII 6 = *u-šān* and *ağaš*
XVII 8 = *u-š* are less typical of Pāzand tradition than *avam, avamān*
etc. In the Pārsī version the *regular* transliteration is *azaš* etc. Interesting is III 10 *ō mān* = *u-mān*, going back on 'P-*man*, cf. Messina,
Ayātkār i Zarērān, p. 37 n. 4. This would seem to show that
av-mān was understood as *ō mān* instead of Nyberg's supposed
api-mān, and would therefore speak against his hypothesis. In short,
the tradition is not fixed in this case. Nyberg further supposed that
what he called "allegro forms", i.e. *vem, vat, vaš* were developed
from *avam* etc. He also found a connection with the NW dialect,
assuming that Mparth. preserved -*p(i)*, the enclitic form, and *ap*,
in combination with other particles, cf. *Manual*, II, p. 20 a. I shall
not in this place discuss these facts—which I think may be explained
otherwise, *vem, vat, vaš*, being Npers. *va* if we accept that this *va* is *not*
the Arabic *wa*. At any rate it does not seem very likely that the
Pāzand tradition in just a few cases, quite isolated, but not in the
majority of passages, would have preserved a tradition, called by
Nyberg himself "obsolete", and which had disappeared from the
living language as early as about 250 A.D., the time when Mani had
his writings published in Mir. dialects.

Against the existence of an *api* in the Mir. stage of development we may also adduce the usage of a Sogdian ideogram 'PZY, to be read as *twty* "'P standing for *t-* < *uta* and -ZY for '*ty*, in compounds *-wty*", Gershevitch, *A Grammar of Manichaean Sogdian*, 1954, p. 307.

However, it must be left for future scholarship to discuss the implications of Nyberg's views. It should not be left unnoticed in this connection that Nyberg was not too optimistic about the success of his theories. He did not protest when I transliterated *u-m* instead of *api-m*, but rightly pointed out that such transliterations as *uta-m*, *uta-š* etc. were unacceptable (I had previously, following other scholars, employed them), cf. now *Manual*, II, p. 197 b. With his marvellous sense of humour he observed to my colleague Prof. F. Rundgren (the present holder of Nyberg's chair in Semitic languages): "If you come across a Pahlavi text where you find the reading *api*, then you can be sure that I am the editor, for *api* that's my signature tune".

The lexicographical part of *Manual* clearly demonstrates how intensely Nyberg worked with the vocabulary of Book Pahlavi. The etymologies as given in the Glossary have greatly profited from his evident ambition to provide the reader with as complete a Mir. and Npers. material as possible. It stands to reason that Npers. words could have been adduced to a still greater extent. In the *Unvala Memorial Volume*, p. 66-75 I methodically quoted evidence for lexicographical comparisons with Pahlavi from the oldest extant New Persian literature, such as the Qur'ān Commentary, Fārsnāmah, Taḏkirat al-Awliyā', Jewish Persian texts etc., what was suited to supplement the *Hilfsbuch*, II. Since then Jewish Persian textmaterial has been made accessible to a very great extent. Not all this material has been used in the *Manual*, II, and it is accordingly still possible to supplement it in this regard. I may mention as illustrations the form *aspraγm*, found in Fārs-nāmah, cf. ed. p. XXVII, to be compared with Mparth. *esprahmag*, *vide Manual*, II, p. 178 b. The word *apāč* in the sense of "back" agrees with Npers. *bāz*, cf. *Unvala Vol.* p. 68, and is found denoting "with" not only in Jpers. texts, cf. p. 68. The word *astār*, sin, is met with in Npers. in Jpers. texts, cf. Asmussen, *Cama Inst. Jub. Vol*, 1969, p. 95 to supplement *Manual*, II, p. 32 where no Npers. word is referred to. The form *aškam*, corresponding with *aškamb*, belly, is found not only in Jpers., cf. Asmussen, *Cama Inst. Vol.* p. 95 but also in Fārsnāmah, *vide* ed. p. XXVII (not observed by Asmussen), also *šikamb* in the Qur'ān Commentary.

There are many other interesting forms in Jpers. texts, *ašnidan*, *ōštāb* etc., representing a more archaic stage of development than ordinary Npers. forms, but it would carry us too far to mention all the words which supplement the material given in *Manual*, II. Enough has been said to draw attention once more to this valuable material which is in so many regards a connecting link between Book Pahlavi and New Persian (cf. also Paper, Judeo-Persian deverbatives in -*šn* and -*št*, *IIJ* X, 1967, p. 56-71).

Manual, II, p. 47 a gives as the only existing Npers. form *bi* as corresponding with Pahl. *bē*. However, the Jpers. bible translations provide us with a great many examples of the form *bī*, written *by*, as preverb. Now we have in Mpers. also *ba* in proclitic position, written *b'*. It would therefore be tempting to posit the development *ba* > *bi*, but *bē* > *bī*. It is regrettable that Nyberg demonstrated so little interest in Jpers., for it would have been interesting to have had his opinion on this point.

In the Glossary there are of course some difficult problems to discuss. Nyberg was fully aware of this fact, cf. *Manual*, II, p. VII. I mention just a few examples as illustrations.

There occur some new, rather doubtful interpretations, e.g. the word لو is not emendated into * الو, but read as *sīh*, which is explained as "beauty, splendour", a divine power, *Manual*, II, p. 175, from Opers. **çī-*, Avestan *srī-*. Here I would like to see a reference to at least one other passage where this presumed word is found, for it ought to be met with in Zoroastrian texts.

Another new and interesting interpretation is *kurtīk*, *Manual*, II, p. 120 a f. in the passage *KN* I 7 where it is explained as "villain, slave", and not as "Kurd". This is quite hypothetical, whereas the word Kurd in *ŠN* means also Kurdistan, accordingly Mpers. *kurtīk* corresponding to a New Pers. *kurdī* denotes a man from Kurdistan, a Kurd.

As to transliteration Nyberg still uses a transliteration corresponding to a more archaic stage of Book Pahlavi. I am therefore somewhat astonished that he gives as the form for "believe" *virrōyistan*, *Manual*, II, p. 214 a. He rightly declines to accept Henning's reading *vurravistan*, but the Pāzand readings he invokes are contradictory, presenting both *viravistan* and *varvistan*. That *varn-* could give *varr-* in Mir. is shown by *varrak* < **varnaka*. We are therefore entitled to posit—with Bartholomae, *ZKMM* VI, p. 41f.—a form *varravistan*, or possibly *varrovistan*.

Speaking of transliterations we observe also that Nyberg still as in *Hilfsbuch* transliterates *aivāp*, cf. *Manual*, II, p. 12 a, and not *ayāv*, in spite of Manichaean *ayāb* and ʾPāzand *ayāo*, cf. my remarks *Unvala Vol.*, p. 68, not in *Manual* where we only find *ayå*.

For *vat*, *Manual*, II, p. 206 b we should expect a reference to Bailey, *BSOAS* XIV, 1952, p. 422f. where he suggested a connection with Sanskrit *batá-* found in the Vedas, an etymology I find quite convincing.

Nyberg has provided the reader with a grammatical sketch of 10 densely printed pages. Behind this "skeleton grammar", as he calls it, there lies a great amount of labour. In a condensed form we get a survey of the phonetic development of Pahlavi, of its morphology, and finally some syntactical observations.

In the treatment of the phonetics the author has concentrated on the differences between the two dialects, NW and SW. He refers to the analysis given by Tedesco in *MO* XV, 1926 and maintains that he is recapitulating only its essential features. Tedesco, however, did not examine all the phonetic developments within Pahlavi, partly because his aim was not to present a complete phonology of the Pahlavi language, nor did Nyberg evidently intend to give such a survey. In his Glossary, however, he has actually mentioned or alluded to some phenomena essential to the understanding of the phonetic changes in Pahlavi. In other cases he does not give any such hints, neither in the Glossary (because the typical words in question do not occur in his texts) or in his treatment of the phonology.

Already in his *Hilfsbuch*, II, p. 256 s.v. *zindakīh* Nyberg drew attention to the contraction of NW *-īva-* to *-ī-* in SW. This observation is repeated in *Manual*, II, p. 231 b s.v. *zīvandak*, but not registered in the Grammatical Survey. Another case of contraction is *dipīvar* > *dipīr*, *Manual*, II, p. 63 a, but not found in the Grammatical Survey. As to the etymology I would rather think of **dipi-bara*, like *dāta-bara*, than of Nyberg's **dipi-vara*, **dātavar* > *dāvar* (cf. *Unvala Vol*, p. 69). The same contraction is met with in *dīvān* from **dipi-vahana* > **dipi-vāna* (etymology according to *Manual*, II, p. 64 b). A further case of contraction, though with another first element of the compound, is *dīvār* < **dida-vāra* (etymology according to Hübschmann, *Persische Studien*, 1895, p. 65 No. 599, accepted by Nyberg, *Manual*, II, p. 64 b). I think it would have been to the advantage of the Grammatical Survey if such cases of contraction had received a special treatment in the phonology.

An interesting phenomenon not treated by Nyberg in his phonology is the metathesis -*rg* > *gr*, found in *šagr* Mpers., but *šarg* Mparth. (cf. *Manual*, II, p. 182 b). The development has been pointed out by Bailey, IIJ II, 1958, p. 150 n. 11, who established the change *šagr* > Npers. *šēr*. This development renews the old problem of the phonetic changes behind Mpers. *dēr*. If we compare the developmen *šarg* > *šagr* > *šēr* with the hypothetical development, tentatively suggested by Hübschmann, *Persische Studien*, p. 60, 249: Opers. *darga* > Mparth. *darg* > Mpers. *dagr > Npers. *dēr* (I have inserted the Mparth. form *darg* unknown to Hübschmann as was the development *šarg* > *šagr* > *šēr*) we must admit that Hübschmann's explanation is convincing. However, Nyberg, *Manual*, II, p. 62 b s.v. *dērang* only refers to Bartholomae, *ZKMM* VI, p. 12-14, where the German scholar refuses to accept a development *darg* > *dagr*. In this case it would have been valuable to find a correction of Bartholomae's view and a reference to Hübschmann.

Another metathesis is mentioned by Nyberg, *Manual*, II, p. 12 s.v. *aivēn*, but not registered in his phonology.

Another metathesis has been analyzed by Henning, *TPS*, 1944, p. 110: *apadāna* > *abdān* > *advān > *aivān* > *īvān*. In a similar way he explains *aivēn* as from *abdēn < *abidaina, whereas Nyberg, *Manual*, II, p. 12 a posits a development *aibidēn > *aiviyēn > *aivēn* in SW dialect.

More important is another dialectal change. Nyberg gives in *Manual*, II, p. 150 a s.v. *pāk*, p. 231 a s.v. *zāvar*, and p. 232 a s.v. *zōr* the material for illustrating the alternation between Mparth. -*āva*- and Mpers. -*ā*- (-*ō*- in *zōr*, cf. the discussion Tedesco, *MO* XV, p. 198) but does not mention this shift in his phonology.

It may further be noted that the development -*hr* > *r* after a long vowel is alluded to *Manual*, II, p. 220 a s.v. *xuāhr* and p. 220 b s.v. *xuār*. In his phonology this change is, however, not mentioned. Hübschmann, *Persische Studien*, p. 206, refers to this important change which takes place in the Sasanian period. This fact is also demonstrated by the forms of some Mir. personal names found in Syriac texts.

A related phenomenon, the development -*gn* > -*n* with substitute lengthening of the vowel is not expressly mentioned in *Manual*, II, p. 136 s.v. *nān*, but a reference is given to an article of Gauthiot, *MSL* 19, 1915, p. 129f., where he referred to the Sogdian word *naγn*. Actually this is exactly the form posited by Hübschmann, *Persische Studien*, p. 133 (with question-marks) for the development *naɣna > nān. In this case too-as in so many others—Hübschmann was right and would have deserved a reference. Because the word is so common this development might also have been mentioned in the phonology.

Nyberg often refers to the correspondence y:h or zero in final position of -ai, e.g. gukāi:gukāh (cf. Manual, II, p. 276 § 3.2). This development explains the form dāvar < *dāivar < dādvar (cf. Widengren, Unvala Volume, p. 69).

The many observations found in the articles published by Bailey, Benveniste, Henning and others contain several remarks concerning phonology. It will be a task for future research to supplement Nyberg's sketch of phonetic development in Book Pahlavi by a systematic evaluation of this material.

Nyberg's morphology gives an extremely detailed and valuable survey of the forms found in his texts. These, however, to a great extent are what I should term "translation Pahlavi", i.e. they are either translations of lost Avestan treatises or based on such translations. This circumstance brings with it certain implications from the grammatical point of view.

As to the abstract nouns ending in -ēh it is pointed out Manual, II, p. 278 § 1.10, that they "are also used as collectives". In this connection I refer to what was said above about ardāvēft and ahrāyēh, which confirms Nyberg's opinion.

Concerning the adjectives Nyberg states that the adjective sometimes, together with a cas. obl. pl. takes the ending—ān, referring to two examples, one from Dd Ch. 35 and the other from Dk. VII 2, 19. In the Dk passage the complete text runs as follows: hān man nē Zartušt frōt-barišnēh sahēt apar ō astōmandān gēhān. This passage is a translation from Avesta as we can see from the syntactical construction—and rightly marked as such by Molé, La légende de Zoroastre, 1967, p. 18 (his preliminary analysis is sometimes incorrect). Therefore there can be no doubt that in the Avestan "Vorlage" there was used a casus obliquus, probably accusative, after the preposition avi (= Pahl. ō) and this construction was rendered in Pahlavi in the same way. In Dk VII, VII 4, 26 we have the parallel expression gēhān i astōmandān, the corporeal earthly beings. In Bundahišn p. 102:1 the first couple of mankind are addressed by Ohrmazd as pitar i gēhān, the parents of earthly beings. In all these cases gēhān is a real plural, rendering the Avestan word gaēθā- in different cases. The use of the pl. astōmandān is therefore dependent upon the pl. form of *gaēθā-*, translated as *gēhān*. In order to ascertain whether this is a construction based on the Avestan text or one found in the living language we need a more detailed investigation. In this connection it should be observed that Dd also to some extent seems to be based on Avestan material.

In the treatment of the pronouns Nyberg offers no special observations on *kē* in its relative function, but p. 284 § 7.12 he refers to his treatment of *kē* in the Glossary p. 117 b where he draws attention to what he calls "an imitation of the Avest. idioms *azəm yō Ahurō Mazdå*" etc. Nyberg p. 284 gives a reference to my article in *Festschrift für Wilhelm Eilers*, 1967, where on pp. 282, 287 I demonstrated that the Pahlavi construction *man kē Ōhrmazd ham* etc. appears in texts obviously translated from Avestan texts, lost or still extant. I would not call the Pahlavi construction an "imitation", but an indication of the usual Pahlavi word for word translation technique.

Nyberg's survey of the verbs gives an excellent treatment of the verbal system; here he also returns for the last time to the problem of the ligatures which he calls X_1 and X_2, 𝕎, 𝕏. He says on p. 281 § 5.7 that these endings "added to verbal ideograms involve problems which are not yet solved". This as we have seen occupied Nyberg for nearly 50 years. He is not pessimistic, but asserts that these ligatures "contain the Aramaic letter He [H], the ending *-ēh*, either the 2nd p. sg. pres. ind. or the opt. or the imp. in *-ē(h)*. Some of these forms would seem to stand for the imp. pl.". He admits, however, that there is a certain indistinctness in the use of the imperatives as also in the 1st p. sg. and pl. in the indicative.

It is not clear to me from these formulations whether Nyberg here really denies the use of this ligature for expressing the 3rd p. sg. and pl. However, I do not think such is the case for he says: "they express in a great many cases the ending *-ēh*". From this statement I conclude that he does not deny that in other cases this ligature stands for *-ēt* and *-ēnd*. In this connection I refer to what he said in *MO* 1937, p. 69: "En général, il faut accepter jusqu'à un certain degré l'opinion de Bartholomae. A n'en pas douter, X_1 et X_2 sont assez souvent écrits là où une autre désinence serait de rigueur".

There are many acute and extremely useful observations in the survey of the verbs. In one case I think there is still an unsolved problem to be found. Nyberg reckons with a 3. p. sg. subjunctive e.g. *hāt*, and a 3. p. sg. optative e.g. the corresponding form *hat*, giving a great many illustrations, p. 280 § 5.2-3. In *Zarthoshti Madressa Centenary Volume*, p. 87 ff. I expressed my doubts concerning the existence of an optative 3. p. sg. ending in *-at*, invoking variant readings in Bundahišn and the form ḤWH-*d* in the Psalter (which Barr, *Bruchstücke einer Pehlevi-Übersetzung der Psalmen*, 1933, p. 42 compared with the Book Pahlavi form ḤWH-'*t* and the Manichaean *hād*) as well as the fact that Manichaean Pahlavi has only the subjunctive form *hād*. I further tried to demonstrate that syntactic considerations in some Sasanian inscriptions demand a reading in *-āt*, accordingly a subjunctive in spite of the fact that this form has a *scriptio defectiva*. Gignoux, however, in these passages reads these forms simply as indicatives in accordance with the general rules of orthography, cf. *Glossaire des inscriptions*, but on the other hand this position leads to syntactical difficulties. It is necessary to undertake a thorough examination of a more comprehensive material of Pahlavi texts, not based on translations of Avestan treatises, before a definitive opinion is expressed. At any rate it is remarkable that a presumed optative in *-at* has disappeared already in Manichaean Pahlavi, the only optative form of 3. p. sg. left ending in *-ēh* e.g. *bēh* and *hēh*. The problem originally raised by Bartholomae and then renewed by Nyberg accordingly needs a fresh investigation.

Nyberg's treatment of the preterite is especially detailed and illuminating. He does not, however, give any analysis there of the syntactical use of the preterite in association with the particle *bē*. In this case we have to turn to his glossary, *Manual*, II, p. 46 s.v. *bē*. Here as already in *Hilfsbuch*, II, p. 35 he finds the particle *bē* "denoting the perfective aspect of the act, viz. that it comes to an end, or has its limit: with the *pret.* it gives it the sense of an act completed in the past", p. 46 b. In the *Menasce Volume*, p. 300-302 I have tried to demonstrate that this aspect does not explain exhaustively the usage when *bē* + preterite is employed. To the passages adduced there from *KN* 1 should like to add here KN I 21: *bē dīt – dānist*, "seeing the beauty and quickness... he understood". There is a contrast in this passage between the durative aspect—he was looking at the child—and the single act—he understood. Also *KN* I 32: *gōr-ē andar dašt bē vitart*, "a wild ass was passing over the plain", the aspect is durative for it takes some time even for a wild ass to pass over a plain. KN I 33 is perhaps more difficult to understand for there we read: *tigr-ē ētōn ō gōr zat ku tigr tāi parr pat aškamb andar šut u ditīkar sōk bē vitārt*, "he shot an arrow at the onager in such a way that the arrow went into the belly up to the feather and was piercing through to the other side". There would seem to be a contrast here between the single act that the arrow went into the belly up to the feather of the arrow—which indicates the terrible force of the shot—and the fact that the arrow was even making its way to the other side of the animal, whereupon the wild ass died at once, *u gōr apar gyāk murt*. There is no *bē* here, although this is really a completed action! Evidently the durative aspect is to be explained from the contrast between the swift movement when the arrow went into the belly and the slower pace when it pierced through to the other side.

More easy to explain is *KN* III 9: *u-š pursīt ku hān dō asvār i ō ēn kustak rōn āmat čē zamān bē vitart*, "and he asked: those two horsemen who came in the direction of this region, at what time were they passing away?". Here the durative aspect, *bē vitart*, stands in contrast to the single act, *āmat*, they arrived, because the horsemen did not disappear immediately. The durative aspect is easy to explain here.

Two interesting passages which should be compared one with the other are KN III 10 and 13:

ētōn čigōn vāt i artāi homānak	*ētōn čigōn vāt i artāi*
bē vitašt	*hamē šut hēnd*
KN III 10	*KN* III 13

As Nyberg rightly observed already in *Hilfsbuch*, II, p. 95 s.v. *hamē*, the particle *hamē* + preterite expresses a durative imperfect. This statement is repeated in *Manual*, II, p. 91 b s.v. *hamēv* and *hamē*: "often the original sense has faded and *hamē* serves as a prev. denoting perduration or iteration, as *(ha)mē* in NP". The same durative aspect we find here in the expression *bē vitašt*. We have here a clear proof of the durative aspect, demonstrated in a convincing way because of the parallelism *bē vitašt ō hamē šut hēnd*.

On the other hand it cannot be doubted that in certain texts *bē* + preterite actually denotes a completed act. It was of course not my intention to deny this evident fact. In agreement with Nyberg I referred in my article to *bē* + preterite as expressing a completed act, *op. cit.*, p. 297, 4 b. My intention was to draw attention to the durative-iterative aspect, up to now not observed. Actually I supplemented the observations in *Hilfsbuch* by adducing evidence from other texts where the function of *bē* + preterite as expressing a completed act is extremely prominent. A distinction obviously has to be made between various groups of texts. Actually it is remarkable that there is such a clear distinction between *KN* as a representative of narrative style in SW dialect and a great many other texts containing narrative sections. The next step would therefore be to undertake a close examination based on a more comprehensive text material.

I have tried to show in this "Preface" how Nyberg's *Manual* in various respects stimulates discussion and further research. His excellent Grammatical Survey could easily be developed into a descriptive grammar, based upon the texts presented in his *Manual*. However, he was not too enthusiastic about writing this sketch which he did only at the request of the publisher. I know that it was not only in conversation with me that he expressed his misgivings. Nevertheless as I have stated, it is an excellent point of departure for writing a real Pahlavi grammar. The next step seems to me to be to write a grammar *based exclusively* on those texts that are *not* derived from Pahlavi translations of Avestan original. Then it would be imperative to have a complete grammatical survey of the language of the inscriptions and of the Manichaean texts, observing possible grammatical peculiarities in such texts we know to be translations of Mani's writings in Syriac, in this way trying to achieve *a real historical grammar of Pahlavi*.

We have seen that Nyberg occupied himself for nearly 50 years with the Aramaic ideograms in Pahlavi. I think it was in about 1940 that he told me that he considered his work on "Frahang i Pahlavīk" in all essentials finished, and that he had already made arrangements for the publication of a new edition. But the appearance of Ebeling's transliteration, translation and philological commentary, based on the views of an Assyriologist with some orientation in the Iranian field and supported by an expert in these studies, H.H. Schaeder, made it necessary to revise his work. Ebeling's publication was accessible only in the University Library in Upsala but was ultimately put at Nyberg's disposal for as long as he needed. The examination of Ebeling's highly interesting researches and much other urgent work —as well as many commitments—inevitably delayed his publication of the Frahang. To some extent Nyberg's work on the inscriptions also brought with it a change in his interpretation of the ideograms and in his general views on the character of the Aramaic used by the various scribal systems of Parthian and Sasanian Iran. His declaration in *Manual*, II, p. 1 deserves quoting: "From the Aramaic point of view, most of the forms in which the verbal ideograms appear in Book Pahlavi (as well as in the inscriptions and in the Psalter) are spurious, fabricated as they are by Iranian-speaking scribes and hence without any linguistic foundation. In fact, only impf. forms of the type YKTLWN = YIQT'LWN and some few other forms can claim to be genuine Aramaic. The intricate process by which the Iranian scribes transformed Aramaic forms into purely graphic signs will be dealt with in my new edition of the *Frahang i Pahlavik*".

Nyberg further says that "such ideographical forms as have totally fallen out of the Aramaic verbal system will be explained merely by reference to the triconsonantal root".

He also tells us that for the interpretation of the ideograms in the Frahang he has used to a great extent those found in the Psalter; this he incidentally considered to have been too much neglected (cf. *Manual*, I, p. XXIV, n. 1).

This method surely commends itself as the script of the Psalter is far less ambiguous than the usual Pahlavi writing and much closer to the alphabet of the Sasanian inscriptions.

Not yet having had access to the manuscript left by Nyberg I am unable to say how he on one hand has motivated his opinion about the artificial character of the verbal ideograms, and on the other hand how he has tackled some of the most difficult linguistic problems. To judge from his published work we may assume that he made a better use of the text-critical aparatus than Junker, who did not always choose the best variant reading as the basis of his interpretation.

That the Iranian scribes did not possess any real knowledge of the Aramaic language also goes without saying. This is quite clear from the way in which a determined state of the noun is used instead of a construct state, demonstrating that the Aramaic ideograms were used as conventional signs only. This is a regular phenomenon already in the Parthian period as shown by the Nisa documents.

From Nyberg's published work we are also able to state that in the course of time he had considerably changed his views about the verbal ideograms. In his study of the Avroman documents he was convinced that a great many verbal ideograms were real Aramaic imperatives and his analysis of the ideographical signs proceded from this hypothesis. In *Hilfsbuch* he did not change his views, nothing

being said to this effect. But in *Manual*, II, he has found a completely
new solution, seeing in the ideograms in question not any longer
imperatives but pass. participles. To take one example, Nyberg once
interpreted *'BYDWN-tn* as the Aramaic imperative plur. עבידון, cf.
MO XVII, p. 219, but in *Manual*, II, p. 1 he analyses the same
form as pass. participle of the same verb עבד. In other cases,
however, Nyberg does not give any indication of a special verbal
form. In *MO* XVII, p. 219f. he interpreted *'ḤDWN* and *'ZLWN*
as imperatives. He says: "As they are written with א instead of ע,
they must have had an *e*-vowel in the first syllable, and by this
feature they are unmistakeably marked as imperatives", p. 220. From
the Aramaic point of view this argument is a strong one. But in
Manual, II, p. 1 f. he does not give any indication of what forms they
are in Aramaic. Presumably his edition of the Frahang will give us
further elucidation of his views on this and similar points.

In his article on the Avroman documents he repeatedly referred
to Mandaic for comparison with the Aramaic ideograms of Frahang.
As Mandaic is a dialect of Babylonian Aramaic this approach was,
from the methodical point of view, absolutely correct. When I now
once more examine the ideograms I still find in the orthography
typically Mandaic features as also in the phonetic form of some
ideograms, not least in the nouns *e.g.* 'RK' i.e. *'arqā* as ideogram
for *būm*, and KYN' i.e. *qānā* as ideogram for *gōspand*. For the two
Mandaic words cf. the conflicting views of Schaeder, *Iranische Beiträge*, I, 1930, p. 49 247, and Macuch, *Handbook of Classical and
Modern Mandaic*, 1965, p. 53:20f., 77:18-20 and 95:9 with reference
to Babylonian Talmud Aramaic which is closer to the ideogram.

Schaeder (*op. cit.*, p. 94 [292]) quoted Herzfeld's opinion that the
only true analogy of the Pahlavi system of Aramaic ideograms
"is with the Sumerian ideograms in Babylonian, or the Babylonian
ideograms in Hittite". Of these two analogies only the first one is
correct, in Hittite we have *both* Sumerian and Akkadian ideograms.
In Babylonian business documents of the Hammurabi period we
actually find not only isolated Sumerian words as ideograms for
Akkadian terms but even whole expressions of "verbal" character,
belonging to the legal language. Some documents are so full of
Sumerian expressions that we get an impression of the gradual process
by which Sumerian was replaced by Akkadian in such texts.

Here the documents of Nisa as well as some much discussed
inscriptions offer a perfect parallel. A full discusson of this topic

must, however, be left to the time when Nyberg's edition of the Frahang has been published as he promised to examine this process in his scheduled publication.

In this Preface it has not been possible either to mention all Nyberg's contributions to Iranian studies or to analyze exhaustively the books and articles discussed here. Nevertheless I hope that something of the scope of his interests will stand out clearly. As a philologist he was an expert both in Old Iranian, chiefly the Avestan language, and Middle Iranian, chiefly Book Pahlavi and the language of the inscriptions. In these fields he was an editor of texts, a lexicographer, and a grammarian, most of all interested in syntactical problems, and finally highly competent in epigraphy. A special feature was his absolute mastery of all problems associated with the use of Aramaic ideograms in Pahlavi script.

His achievements in these disciplines alone would have secured him a place of honour in the history of learning. But Nyberg—as already noticed—was a philologist of the type that wants to know what is said in the texts he edits and analyzes from the philological point of view. He was always interested in the content, and he moreover tried to locate the content of a given text within its historical context. Nyberg was a born historian who had learned much of historical method by attending the lectures given by the great historian Harald Hjärne in Upsala. Hjärne he considered as one of his special teachers for whom he felt a great admiration. I have heard him speak of Hjärne as "the old man"—as disciples do—which he never did when he mentioned Zetterstéen whom he used to call "Z".

As a historian Nyberg was in the first place a historian of ideas, both political and religious. His chief interest, however, was concentrated on the history of religions. His first comprehensive work in this field, "Questions de Cosmogonie", grew out of a commentary on the Zervanite texts he edited with philological notes. He accordingly provided the reader with both a philological and a religious and historical commentary. His work in the history of religions was intimately bound up with his work as a philologist.

Also his great work "Die Religionen Irans" to a great extent is founded on the exegetical method, especially his treatment of Zoroaster and the Gathas is on the whole a Gatha exegesis. Other parts of this book are not, however, based to the same extent upon an exegetical method; this was not possible as there was not a sufficient number of texts available to him. He therefore followed a more typical historical method, not proceeding from some special text, but using all texts available. On the whole these parts are excellent and the best in the book. An exception is his chapter on the creation of a Sasanid Avesta where again he takes his point of departure in a special text. This chapter is of fundamental importance.

His work "Questions de Cosmogonie" was hailed with great approval but his major work "Die Religionen" as we have seen met with unjust and partly ridiculous criticism. Enough has been said by me in this connection, both now and on earlier occasions, to show that I have no hesitation in calling it an epoch-making book, epoch-making in the literal sense of the word because introducing a new epoch in the study of Iranian religions.

On the whole Iran was more and more in the focus of his interest and during the last twenty years of his life he devoted all his scholarly work to Iranian studies. In spite of his advanced age he did not hesitate to visit the country repeatedly and made many friends there.

The importance of a scholar cannot be measured only by his literary work, the number of his publications, the texts he has edited, the high percentage of his successful etymologies and the low percentage of committed mistakes. There is something more in the life-work of a philologist. The influence he exercises on his pupils, the inspiration they and other scholars receive from his teaching and his publications, not the least when it stimulates them to discussion and opposition—all this must be taken into account. Nyberg gave a vast inspiration in this way because he was a man of vision. He combined immense learning and knowledge of details with the rare gift of large views and "Mut des Blamierens". All this made him a pioneer in the field.

As a teacher Nyberg was exacting and at the same time extremely inspiring. He opened new ways to us, he taught us to see the problems in a wider context. However, his was a strong personality, and he needed pupils of similar character, admiring and yet independent and critical. For that reason the great period of his life was in the years when the Gatha seminars paved the way for his great book "Die Religionen". At that time he found something of the response he needed, especially from Wikander, as he also says in his preface of the Swedish edition. I remember a dinner-party given by Nyberg some years ago when according to Swedish custom I had to express the thanks of the guests invited. In my little speech

I referred to the "heroic" time when Wikander and I were active in his Gatha seminars and called it "a great time". Nyberg was deeply moved and sighed: "Yes, you are right, it *was* a great time".

Nyberg had bequeathed his library to the University of Upsala as "Bibliotheca Orientalis Nybergiana" but he used it and did all his work in the two rooms annexed to his private apartment. Every time he was in Iran he bought large numbers of books and paid heavy sums for overweight in the plane. In his will he expresses the hope that his library might serve as a basis for a future insitute of Iranian studies—rich Sweden being too poor to have been able to create such an institute or rather, the government being completely indifferent to such studies.

Nyberg worked to his very last minute. There was left at his death on his desk the handwritten and signed preface of his *Manual*, II. As already mentioned he had also finished his edition of Frahang.

It is always difficult to give a just evaluation of a scholar who has been an intimate friend. Nyberg has been part of my life since 1929 and has influenced me more than any other of my great teachers. Nevertheless I am quite sure that I do not exaggerate when I say that this great scholar will always be mentioned as one of the very few really great names in the field of Iranian studies.

Additional note. Henning correctly referred to the fact that already West, SBE XLVII, p. 7, had given the proper reading and that it had been repeated by Christensen.

G.L. WINDFUHR

ISOGLOSSES:
A SKETCH ON PERSIANS AND PARTHIANS,
KURDS AND MEDES*

This is not a linguistic study in the sense that a theoretical problem is focussed on; rather it follows the line of the 'traditional' approach to the complex dynamics of W Iranian dialectology, and should be understood as a reanalysis and a sequel to two outstanding studies, Tedesco (1921) and Mackenzie (1961), by asking more or less the same questions. To these, of course, one must add Lentz (1926).

The 'Median' bands

The Kurdish dialects are found in the center of the Middle East, the Fertile Crescent, and in the adjoining areas of Anatolia and NW Iran. Besides, Kurdish speakers are found scattered in smaller groups, the largest of which is located in the NE of Iran.

In Iran, there is a continuous band of Kurdish dialects extending from Azarbayjan south along the Zagros covering the Western parts of what once was Media Atropatene (or Minor) and Media Major, i.e. Azarbayjan and Central W Iran. Adjacent and parallel to this 'diagonal' Kurdish band there is an eastern band of so-called Median dialects, i.e. Talishi and Tati (so called recently by Yarshater 1969). Today, this formerly continuous band consists of larger and smaller pockets of Iranian dialects amidst a continuum of Turkish dialects.

Both bands must have been in contact for a considerable time which is evidenced e.g. by Vafsi located roughly in the middle of the contact line, or area, of the two bands. Vafsi is basically a Tati dialect with some distinctive Kurdish features (e.g. the change of

[The following was written under pressure of time. The request for this contribution left only some 2 months to work intermittently on this paper. Therefore much had to remain in an unfinished state. It is hoped that the basic arguments brought forward here still make some sense.]

* I would like to acknowledge the continuing support of Iranian dialect studies from the Center for Near Eastern and North African Studies, U of M, and support from the Rackham School of Graduate Studies, U of M, as well as support from the John S. Guggenheim Memorial Foundation and the American Council of Learned Societies/the Social Science Research Council.

wordinternal $m \rightarrow v$); more conspicuously, that long contact is evidenced by a number of rather smooth continua of features such as the *ezâfe* and 'ergative' constructions in Iran.

Since both bands cover roughly equal halves of what once was Media, both should be called 'Median dialects', not only the Talishi-Tati band, as long as there can be found evidence that both had moved into Media before or during Median and Achaemenian times, i.e. prior to about 300 B.C.

State of the Art

The main arguments for such movements are essentially linguistic features of change and innovations, and of lexical items shared with other dialect groups. As mentioned, Kurdish shares a number of features with the 'Median' band of dialects. However, it also exhibits a cluster of innovations, and lexical items which it shares with dialect groups not now adjacent to Kurdish, namely Persian and Baluchi. Tedesco (1921) consequently concluded that all three must at one time have been in closer contact; since he located Persian in the SW, in the province of Fars (knowing that the Achaemenids spoke Persian) he reconstructed a map on which Pre-Kurdish was located between Persian in Fars and Pre-Baluchi in the center of W Iran. Therefore, I presume, he located Kurdish either in NE Lurestan or in the Esfahan province of Media.

Geographically, at least, Tedesco's reconstruction would make Pre-Kurdish a Southern Median dialect.

However, it should be noted that neither the 'Median' band of dialects (Talishi-Tati) nor the Kurdish dialects have the single peculiarly *Median* feature we know of, namely the change of $*hw \rightarrow f$ as evidenced by names of (Median) nobles containing *farnah* < **hwarnah-* 'glory, etc.' Thus, either dialect band would qualify only geographically as 'Median', but not linguistically.

Tedesco (1921: 253 fn. 1) suggested in a footnote the following sequence of dialectal layering and movements: the oldest groups of non-Persian ('Northwestern') dialects in W Iran are Pre-Baluchi and the 'Caspian' dialects (Talishi, Gilaki, Mazanderani) and Semnani. These were pushed either NW (Talishi), or N (Gilaki, Mazanderani), or SE (Baluchi), pushed aside by the 'Central' dialects (now found mainly on the Kashan-Esfahan region) to which also belong Gorani (now in Central Kurdish Areas) and Zaza (now in E Anatolia).

As the most recent layer he identified the Kurdish dialects which overlaid the western 'Central' dialects, namely Gorani and Zaza.

MacKenzie (1961) ingeniously detailed this Kurdish overlay, largely utilizing his own extensive data on Iraqi Kurdish and Gorani. At the end of his study, in agreement with Tedesco, he suggested the following more specific sequence of movements:

1) Persian in Fars, Kurdish adjacent to it to the N or NE, Baluchi in Central West Iran.

2) Zaza in Azarbayjan/Armenia or Deylam; the Goran north of the Baluch;

3) Kurds move northward into Armenia, perhaps expelling the Zaza westward into Anatolia; the Goran occupy the southern Zagros

4) more recently, expansion of the Kurds, from the north, gradually absorbing all but the surviving Goran.

MacKenzie does not mention any move of the Baluch, but since he refers to Tedesco, he seems to imply, like the latter, an early SE movement of the Baluch.

The major isoglosses which link Persian with Kurdish and Baluchi are (Tedesco 1921: 255):

$$*tr \rightarrow s \qquad \text{vs. } \theta r \rightarrow hr \text{ elsewhere}$$
$$*dw \rightarrow d \qquad \text{vs. } d\beta \rightarrow b$$
$$*\#y \rightarrow j \qquad \text{vs. } y$$
$$*\#w \rightarrow b/g(w) \qquad \text{vs. } v$$

However, none of these are found as regular changes in the central dialects, i.e. in the area where Tedesco placed Pre-Kurdish and Pre-Baluchi. In fact there is no evidence that there was at any time a widespread Baluchi speaking area in W Iran or a widespread Kurdish speaking area near Fars. It is true that one can recognize Kurdish and, perhaps, Baluchi features in certain areas, such as among some of the *Râ(ye)ji* dialects of the Kashan-Natanz region, or Sivandi and Kalun-Abdui in Fars; yet, the considerable linguistic difference among them as well as their size suggest the influence of various incoming groups of speakers rather than a lost continuum of dialects. There is not sufficient evidence to assume with Tedesco a move out from W Iran of Pre-Baluch to the SE and of Pre-Kurds to the NW, an assumption, which implies that the two groups must somehow have moved through each other, unless a movement of the Baluch, emptying the area, preceded the NW movement of the Kurds. Even then the course of the movement is not quite evident given the fact that the northern parts of the area are occupied by the Talishi-Tati dialects which MacKenzie did apparently not consider.

One should recall here one of the most peculiar conclusions by Tedesco (1921). On pages 220-221 he identified the NW dialect of Turfan, i.e. Parthian, as a now lost member of the 'Baluchi-Caspian' group in the Zagros! and as a transitional dialect between Kurdish and the Central dialects. Since this would place Kurdish in the north(-west) of the Zagros in Tedesco's reconstruction, the constellation of Kurdish-NW Turfan (Parthian)-Central dialects must have developed after the supposed move of the Kurds from an area near Fars, and thus after the bulk of the 'Baluchi-Caspian' dialects had emptied the Median Zagros, which would make Parthian a last holdout of these groups.

The Eastern Connection

Tedesco located his triangle in central West Iran in spite of the fact that he found certain features of Old Persian (OP) which are not pure (*echt*) Persian. As to OP, Andreas had noted (acc. to Henning 1958: 108) at least five features of OP which it shares with Sogdian, and suggested that both must have been in contact at some time; I assume, prior to the movements of the Achaemenids into Fars in the SW and somewhere in Xorasan. The features are:

1) *tr → sibilant, i.e. ç in OP, š in Sogdian
2) both have *$gaub$-, 'speak' in OP, 'praise' in Sogdian
3) *$kṛnau$ → kun- in both
4) *kar used as modal 'can' in both
5) *$haca$ + pronominal suffix 'from X' in both.

Isoglosses

Given these observations the question of the Persian-Kurdish-Baluchi 'triangle' and its part in the 'dynamics' of West Iranian dialectology must be reconsidered.

This will be done on the basis of twelve major features; seven phonological changes and five morphological differences. The major dialect groups considered include 1) old dialects: Old Persian of the Achaemenid inscriptions (OP) and Avestan; 2) middle dialects: Middle Persian, Parthian, Sogdian, and 3) modern dialects: Persian/Fars dialects, Kurdish, Baluchi, Tati, Talishi, Gorani, Harzani, Zaza, Gilaki, Mazanderani, Sangesari and 'Central' dialects. Only some of the latter will be specified at various points since in most features discussed they constitute a complex unit.

Most of the changes considered are discussed by Tedesco (1921). He did not include the changes and differences * #fr → š, *šm → hm, *haca + pronominal suffix, *kar as modal, the distinctiveness of which became only known after his study[1].

The features considered and their distribution are:

phonological changes

1) *tr → s: Pers, [OP] Kd, Bal.
   [→ š under certain conditions in Sogdian and Xwarezmi],
   (in remnants in) Sangesari
   → θr → hr: elsewhere in W Iranian

2) *dw → d: Pers., Kd., Bal.
   duv: [OP]
   [→ dβ/b: Avestan texts]
   → b: elsewhere

3) * #y → j: Pers., Kd., Bal., Zaza?
   [→ ⟨ⱬ⟩/⟨ⱬ⟩ (= [dž?]) in Avestan orthography]
   → y: elsewhere

4) * #w → b/g Pers., Kd.
   → g before front vowel/ → gw elsewhere in Baluchi; Xori,
   Bashakardi
   [→ ⟨ⱬ⟩ (= [β]?) in Avestan orthography]
   → v elsewhere

5) *hw → w: Zaza, Gorani
   → h before front vowel/ → v elsewhere in Baluchi
   → wh: [Parthian]
   → f: Xori, Sivandi (under certain conditions), [O 'Median']
   → x(w), h elsewhere

6) * #fra → fra/far: Pers., [OP] Kd., [Parthian], [Avestan]
   → fa: Gilaki, [conditionally in Sogdian]
   → ša: Baluchi, (remnants in) Sangesari, [Xwarezmi]
   → hr: elsewhere

7) *šm → hm: Kd., Zaza, Vafsi, Gor., Bal., Gil., Bashakardi,
   Bandar Abbas, Kešei, Ormuri, Parachi, [Chr.
   Sogdian]
   → šm: elsewhere

---

[1] The data on Sangesari, Tati, Harzani and Xori is from more recent sources (Azami-Windfuhr 1972; Yarshater 1969; Mortazavi 1954, 1962-63; Ivanov 1929).

morphological differences

1) **â-gatá:*   Bal., Kd., [Parthian], Xori, Sangesari (remnant in
                        ptcpl.: *ê-v-ə* < *ât-* < **âxt-* besides, regular *mê-v-ə*
                        'having come'), all E Iranian
   *â-gmatá :   remainder of W Iranian
   *ima/*hau: Kd., Xori, Gabri, Kešei, Talishi, Tati, [Parthian],
                        [OP], [Sogdian, but Chr. Sogd. *înê*]
   *aina/âna: Pers., Zaza, Gor., Central (except Gabri, Kešei),
                        Semnani, Gil., Maz.
   *ai/*a: Baluchi, Gorani [3]

3) **hai:*   Kd., Xori, Kohrudi-Soi, Harzani, Bal., Bashakirdi,
                        Bandar Abbas, [Xwarezmi], [Avestan (besides **šai*)] [4]
   *šai: Pers., [OP], remainder of W Iranian except Kohrudi-
                        Soi), [Sogdian]

4) *haca* + pron.: Talishi, Tati, Harzani, [OP], [Sogdian], (remnants
                        in) Semnani, Zaza

5) **kar*   used as model 'can' plus participle/past stem; in
                        Bal., [Sogdian], [Saka], [Xwarezmian], [OP], with
                        transitive verbs (best summary, Gershevitch 1954:
                        131), with all verbs in subjunctive in Sangesari.

Significance

   The preceding list of dialectologically significant criteria seems to
be an *ad hoc* selection. In fact, it is based on the largely intuitive
recognition of their distinctive importance by Tedesco and his predecessors, and followed by scholars to this date. Such approach to
dialectology may be questioned exactly because of its seemingly
intuitive and unsystematic character. This is not necessarily true.
E.g. the difference of the demonstrative pronouns is in fact part of
a more comprehensive difference of pronominal systems, which are
not detailed here [5]. Similarly, most of the phonetic changes listed
are part of some systematic tendency rules, i.e. chains of extension

---

[2] Xori has *âwad* (probably < *âwat* < '*ayat*, since no regular change *-m-* → *v*);
Kurdish *hât-* on the other hand could be derived from **â-xt*, as assumed so far,
or from **âwat* < **â-mat* with the regular change of *-m-* → *w*.

[3] Further pronominal systems with *n-* are not considered here.

[4] Sangesari and Zaza, and Northern Kurdish, have lost their pronominal suffixes.

[5] Cf. Tedesco (1921: 248), Henning (1955: 98), and most recently the excellent
comparative study of the pronominal system in Old Persian and Sogdian by Qarib
(1974).

of rules through time. The most conspicuous of these is the tendency rule which may be formulated as follows: in SW Iranian/Persian the postconsonantal glide *w tends to be elided while in non-Persian the glide tends to be preserved or strengthened: the earliest evidence for this is sw/zw → Persian s/z; but sp/zb elsewhere. Of the changes mentioned in the list above, the changes of *hw and *dw belong to this tendency rule; possibly also the change *#w → b in Persian where *pause* can be considered an extension of the condition 'post-consonantal'. At the same time, the latter change is part of a rule that defricativizes initial glides, i.e. (first) *#y and (then) *#w. The latter change, or pair of changes, occurs exactly in those dialects, i.e. Persian, Kurdish, Baluchi where voiceless non-strident fricatives before r do not (partially) merge, i.e. where *θr/fr/xr not → hr. To this tendency rule belong the changes of *θr and *fr of the list.

The traditional seemingly arbitrary selection of criteria for comparative historical dialectology does reflect more than *ad hoc* insights.

Dating

The preceding list combines old, middle and modern dialects. It appears, however, that, based on the evidence of Old Persian, the larger part of these changes and differences go back to about the sixth century B.C.

*dw → d, *#y → j, and *#w → b/g :

The earliest evidence for these changes is Middle Persian, which has d, j, but only the change *wṛ-/wim → gur-/gum- is attested, not yet *w → b. Still, the first two changes had taken place before Middle Persian, i.e. before the 3rd century A.D. and somewhere during the Parthian period [6].

*hw: This cluster was early susceptible to change as evidenced by the Old Median change to f, i.e. about 600 B.C. In, or before, Parthian it had changed to (written) wh. This, in turn, is the change from which w developed in Baluchi, Zaza, and Gorani (and f in

---

[6] This assumption runs, of course, counter Hübschmann's (1895: 150-166) brilliant analysis of the history of these changes, based on comparison with loans in Armenian mainly. However, it seems to me that there is no real proof that those loans are 'Persian'. The fact that since about the 5th century one finds these changes reflected in loans in Armenian indicates that these changes were becoming accepted in the official literary language of the empire, but they say little about the local Fars dialects. In fact, it is not improbably that the earlier Sasanians (and the Zoroastrians) adopted and perpetuated an archaizing style of language (see also Bolognesi 1960).

Xori and Sivandi). These dialects should have been in contact at least during Parthian times in Parthia, i.e. NE Iran.

The evidence of Baluchi suggests that the change of *$w \rightarrow$? $\rightarrow g(w)$ must have preceded that of *$hw \rightarrow wh \rightarrow w$ (or v); otherwise both would have merged. One may tentatively infer that the change of *$w \rightarrow$? ($\rightarrow$ later b/g) occurred fairly early also in Persian and Kurdish.

The change hinted at by '?' assumes the change of *w to an as yet unspecified labial fricative in the three dialects. This assumption is not necessary. It is simpler to assume that the bilabial *w had *not* changed in these three dialects, while it did change to a labio-dental [v] elsewhere in W Iranian [This would also explain why in Zaza and Gorani *$hw \rightarrow w$ did not merge with *$w \rightarrow v$]. The change from the bilabial fricative to a bilabial or a velarized stop *could* only happen, so-to-speak, in Persian, Kurdish and Baluchi.

*$\check{s}m \rightarrow hm$: in *$ca\check{s}man$- 'eye', a widely spread change is already attested in Christian Sogdian. It may be part of the isogloss of 'sonorization' or *$\check{s}$ in SE Iranian (Morgenstierne 1926:53). This change indicates contact of the dialects which share this feature with Eastern dialects, and thus should have developed in Kurdish prior to their move to the West.

As observed by MacKenzie (1961: 70-71) this change must have preceded that of $m \rightarrow w$ in Kurdish, as evidenced by Kurdish $\check{c}aw < *\check{c}am < *\check{c}a\check{s}m$-. The change *$m \rightarrow w$, which is also found regularly in Vafsi and sporadically in Lori, N Baluchi and Gabri, is first attested as a sporadic change in the Manichean-Parthian dialect of Turfan.

The change * #$fr \rightarrow hr$ is found throughout W Iranian, except Kd, Pers. far; Gil. fa and Bal. $\check{s}a$. Likewise the literary languages Middle Persian and Parthian show fr, as do O Persian and Avestan. Bal. $\check{s}$ can only have developed in contact with E Iranian, i.e. not in central western Iran, just as the $\check{s}$ found remnants in Sangesari.

*$tr \rightarrow c \rightarrow s$ is already found in OP.

Avestan

With regard to these features, the only other known old Iranian language, Avestan, has the following: *fra, *ima/*hau, *hai (besides *$\check{s}ai$) both *$\hat{a}$-$gat\acute{a}$ and $\hat{a}$-$gmat\hat{a}$; *$tr \rightarrow \theta r$; and, according to special orthographic symbols, it shows the incipient changes *$dw \rightarrow b$ (written $dv/d\partial b/tb/b$), * #$y \rightarrow j$ (written ⲙⳏ/Ɫ [=[d$\check{z}$]?]); * #$w \rightarrow b$ (written ζ [=[β]?]). This orthography has to be related to one of the redactions of the texts, and should go back at least to Pre-Islamic times.

The people from the East

Thus, one can reconstruct a triangle of contact in the NE, in Parthia, of Persian-Kurdish-Baluchi, or, more cautiously, of those earlier dialects which constituted the distinctive fond of the three dialects.

Most of the changes must have occurred there during Parthian times, if not earlier. The only change not attested for that time is that of $*\#w \rightarrow b$ (while $*\#w\underset{.}{r}\text{-}/wim\text{-} \rightarrow gur\text{-}/gum\text{-}$ is). Even so, the earlier preservation of $*\#w$ in these three dialects, against $*\#w \rightarrow v$ elsewhere, as suggested above, is an additional argument for the NE triangle of those three dialects.

Given the existence of the triangle of Persian-Kurdish-Baluchi in the NE, and not in central W Iran, the features shared by these three dialects can only have been introduced into the West by migration. One of the changes, $*tr/\hat{k}r \rightarrow$ a strident symbolized by a special sign (ς), was introduced into Fars by the Old Persians. But the changes of $*\#y \rightarrow j$ and $*\#w \rightarrow b/g$ are not found in Old Persian, and are later that dialect; nor are they found in dialects other than the mentioned three (except for $*\#y \rightarrow j$ in Semnani). Consequently, they must have been introduced into the older Persian of Fars by superstrate, by one of various groups from the NE, perhaps the Pre-Sasanians, who established themselves in Fars; and the two changes mentioned are major shiboleths of the Fars dialects. Similarly, as indicated earlier in this study, such features as the change of $*\check{s}m \rightarrow hm$, $*\check{s} \rightarrow h$ in some words, the existence of the 3rd sg. pronominal suffix $*hai$, and $*k\hat{a}m\text{-}$ used as future auxiliary (as in Sogdian) found in some groups of Râ(ye)ji-dialects in the Kashan-Natanz area are best explained by superstrate over essentially Western-Central dialects.

The Kurds, it seems, first established themselves in Azarbayjan or near there; the latest to establish themselves were the Baluch in the mountains of the Kerman area, the wild *Kûč o Balûč* tribes ($k\hat{u}\check{c} < q\hat{o}f\underset{.}{s} < \hat{a}kauf\check{a}\check{c}iya$).

The conclusion reached here, namely that the change of $*\#y/w \rightarrow \#j/b \sim gw$ occurred in the NE of Iran, together with other changes, recalls repeated observations by Morgenstrierne of isoglosses between western dialects, mainly Kurdish and Baluchi, and eastern dialects, most prominently Parachi-Ormuri. E.g. the latter have the changes $*\#y \rightarrow$ Par. $\check{z}$, Orm. j and $*\#w \rightarrow \gamma(w)$ in both, as well as

* #*fra* → *ša* (and preserve the initial voiced stops vs. the partial fricativation elsewhere in E Iranian; Morgenstierne 1958: 159, 169). One should also mention *Saka*, where * #*y* and * #*w* → #*j* and *v*/*b*/*g*. As of now, one can hardly go so far as to suggest that this pair of distinctive changes (as some others) are directly related to the Saka invasion of NE Iran. Nevertheless, these changes appear to be an 'eastern' and not a 'southwestern' Iranian, i.e. Persian, phenomenon.

Parsa and Parsua

The dialects of the first Persians in Fars is a 'transitional' dialect (Tedesco 1921: 248); it is not (yet) Persian/SW Iranian to a considerable degree.

Those non-Persian features have been explained as influenced by the language of their predecessors as rulers of Iran, i.e. as Median (cf. the succinct discussion by Mayrhofer 1968).

The particular 'Median' dialect from which those features in OP are supposed to derive has not been specified so far. However, there is one dialect group which can be related to OP, namely Tati-Talishi, i.e. the band of 'Median' dialects, mentioned in the earlier part of this paper. These dialects share with OP at least:

1) 3rd sg. *šai
2) *haca* + pronominal suffix
3) the demonstratives *ima/*hau

In addition, there is one peculiar feature found in one SW dialect, in Lari, which Lari shares only with Tati-Talishi and with Sogdian, namely the ending of 2nd sg. *-iš* [7].

This is additional evidence for the NE triangle, in contact with Sogdian. Adjacent to which, as we see now, were the (Pre-) Talishi-Tati dialects [8].

It is intriguing to link the (Pre-) Tati-Talishi/ Old Persian isolosses with the *Parsua* mentioned in the Neo-Assyrian sources. (cf. Levine 1974: 106-112). In that case one can reconstruct a westward movement of bands of Iranians called *Parsua* from the east, from the province

---

[7] This similarity between Lari and Talishi was first observed by Henning (1954: 153).

[8] Morgenstierne (1958: 174) noted that the dialects of Laristan are very peculiar (*ganz eigenartig*), and refers to the fact that durative present is constructed with the past stem. He did not remark on the fact that the same is true for the Talishi dialects, as he briefly described on the same page. This similarity may be considered an additional link between the NW and the SW of Iran.

of *Parthawa* (< **Parsu/awa*). One group, the Talishi-Tati dialects, began to establish itself in the north of Median central West Iran, and the *Parsua* found in Mahidasht can be viewed as one daring sub-group of them, which crossed or by-passed 'Medians' in the area, the Kangavar valley, and established itself as a rather loose confederation for some 150 years (Levine 1974: 110 and T. Cuyler Young, Jr. 1967).

Another group of people from *Parsu/awa* in the east moved into the SW probably through the Esfahan province, the people first called *Pârsumaš* by 640 B.C., later *Pârsa*[9]. Archaeological-historical arguments for a direct move of Persians into Fars have been brought forward recently by Stronach (1974)[10].

'Parsuan' dialects

The major suggestions of the preceding sketch are 1) that there existed in NE Iran, an early 'triangle' of dialects which constituted the distinctive fond of what later became Persian, Kurdish and Baluchi (and other dialects) from where first, as early as the 9th century B.C., a group of Persians moved westward and then south; 2) that this triangle of contact continued to exist at least into Parthian times in that area; this as an alternative to Tedesco's (1921) Persian-Kurdish-Baluchi triangle in W Iran; 3) that Kurds and Baluch began to move from the NE into West from that period on[11].

For want of a name for this triangle of West Iranian dialects in the Northeast of Iran, adjacent to East Iranian dialects, I suggest

[9] The change from *Parsumaš* (=/pârs(u)waš/) to *Parsa* (=/pârsa/) evidences one of the only two 'typical' SW Iranian, i.e. Persian, changes, namely (*$\hat{k}w/\hat{g}w$ →) *sw/zw → s/z. The change in the names allows one to date it between 640-500 B.C. This change must be later than the other 'typical' Persian change (*$\hat{k}/\hat{g}$ →) s/z → θ/d under specific conditions, as in *pârsa/uwa → Parthava*, which did not affect *sw/zw. Still later is the change of the strident (ς) to s, since it had not occurred yet in the language of the inscriptions (for all three changes, cf. Windfuhr 1972: 58-59).

[10] This spread of *Parsua* from the east into the N and NW of Medianized territory, occasionally entering the Zagros, and into Fars in the South is quite similar to the moves of closely related, but different groups of Turkic speakers into the very same areas of W Iranian territory some 1500-2000 years later).

[11] In fact, there are sufficient reasons to investigate whether this triangle ever ceased to exist. So far the existence of Kurds in Xorasan has been explained by the fact that Kurds from Kurdestan were exiled to Xorasan in Safavid times. However, there is no proof that there were no Kurds in Xorasan prior to that time; on the contrary, people and tribes called Kurds are reported in that area much earlier.

identifying them 'geographically' by the old name of the province
and to call them *Parthian* or better *Parsuan* (rather than calling them
'North-east Western' dialects which is what they really are in terms
of our current understanding, and terminology, of Iranian dialectology).

As to Parthian itself, it obviously is a well-defined member of that
isoglossic area in the NE exibiting a specific cluster of isoglosses
both phonological:

1) *hr*, 2) *b*, 3) *y*, 4) *w*[or *v*?], 5) *wh*, 6) *fra*, 7) *šm*, and morphological:
1) **â-gatá*, 2) **ima/hau*, 3) **šai* [12].

The Median bands again

This sketch began with the description of two bands of dialects
in the area of former Media.

The preceding discussion suggests that one of the bands, the band
of Kurdish dialects, was established later in or after the Parthian
period, overlaying a band of other dialects, such as Gorani, which
can be regarded as one of the original Median (*Madai*) dialects.
Consequently, one hesitates to identify the Kurdish band as 'Median'
dialects, not even geographically (rather one may call them 'Parthian'
considering the time and the fact that many non-Persian dialects in
W Iran once were called *pahlavi/fahlav*-dialects) [13].

The other band of Median dialects, i.e. the Talishi-Tati dialects,
was probably in northern Media already during, if not before the
time of the Median empire. This would make them Median dialects,
geographically and politically. However, as soon as they are identified
with the northern *Parsua*, as suggested above, they cannot be related
to the *Madai* mentioned in Assyrian sources. Moreover, the only
known peculiarly Median feature, the very early change of $*hw \rightarrow f$
found in the language of the elite of the Medes in Achaemenid times,
is not found in the Talishi-Tati dialects. Nor is it found in other
dialects in the area such as Gorani. This lack could be explained
by loss under the influence of later dialects. If so, the entirety of

---

[12] One may add such features, not yet discussed in this context, as optative *-ēn*
in Kurdish, Baluchi and Parthian, or the lengthening of the root vowel in the causative
found in Baluchi, Sangesari and Parthian.

[13] One may add that the overlay of a strong superstrate by a dialect from the
eastern parts of Iran does not imply the conclusion that ethnically all Kurdish speakers
are from the east, just as one would hesitate to identify the majority of Azarbayjani
speakers as ethnic Turks. The majority of those who now speak Kurdish most likely
were formerly speakers of Median dialects.

dialects in Western Iran must have been under such influence. But there is no known dialect such as to have effected the loss.

Consequently, the f < *hw in the language of the Median elite appears as a superstrate feature, and the dialect from which this originated must be sought outside of W Iran. There are two dialects only which have this change, Sivandi in Fars and the oasis dialects of the Xor- region in the Kavir desert. In fact, Sivandi, better Pre-Sivandi, has been suggested as the origin of the Median (elite, one should repeat) dialect. Only, in Sivandi the change of *$hw \rightarrow f$ is conditional and not a general rule, and applies also to 'secondary' clusters such as fit < *$whît$ < *$vîxt$ 'sifted' (cf. Morgenstierne 1958: 171).

Sivandi has long been recognized as a 'NW'–enclave in Fars. Its origins remain unknown. It may have originated from a dialect area where, among others, the change of $hw \rightarrow f$ was developing. In its present state, Sivandi is a 'central' dialect except for this one change. (It also has, of course, a number of words and changes reminiscent of Kurdish).

In Xori, however, the 'Median' change in question is unconditional. Based on the little data we have on this dialect, Xori is a peculiarly interesting member of the 'Parsuan' dialects. E.g.:

phonological changes:

1) tr → s in *pusu* 'small'
        (but θr in toponym *Mihregân*)
2) *dw → d in *der* 'door'
3) * #y → $g(y)$ in *gyus* 'walnut',
4) * #w → $g(w)$ in *gud* 'bad'
5) *hw → f in *for* 'sun', 'eat'
6) *fra → hr in *ruš* 'sell'
Besides, it shows the regular 'NW' changes
*$\hat{k}/\hat{g}$ → s/z in *keysu* 'small' and *zun* 'know'
*$\hat{k}w/\hat{g}w$ → sp/zw in *ispidi* 'white' (but *sag* 'dog'), and *hizun* 'tongue'

morphological:

*$\hat{a}$-gatá-: ôwad- 'come (past)'
*pronominal system *ima/ava*: em/ev (besides în and ân)
*3rd sg. suffix *hai*: e(y) [14].

---

[14] Moreover, there are 'typical' Kurdish features like $x \rightarrow k$, as in *kirus* 'rooster', *âsun* 'iron', *hek* 'egg', and the imperfective prefix *de-*.

Today, Xori must be considered a 'central' dialect, based on other
phonological and morphological features which cannot be detailed here.
As an oasis-refuge dialect it evidently has been subject to a series
of superstrates.

Nevertheless, the origin of the Median elite dialect must have been
the same as or adjacent to at least one of the ancestors of Xori
(and, perhaps, of Sivandi). This implies a dialect area in the NE where
the 'Median' change developed, and implies, as well, that it was
undone there later, except in the two-exclaves Xor and Sivand, undone
by the combined influence of the other 'Parsuan' dialects: Parthian,
Persian, Kurdish and Baluchi.

The dialect of the Median elite appears thus as the dialect of
newcomers from the east of Iran-implying, as it were, that, with
few interruptions, pre-Islamic Iran was ruled by dynasties originating
from the northeast, by 'Medes', Achaemenids, Parthians and perhaps
the Sasanians[15].

The observations of this paper focus on one particular complex
of isoglosses, the one which is shared by the dialects most discussed,
namely Persian, Kurdish, Baluchi, Parthian and Avestan. Little
could be said here about other complexes of isoglosses shared by
lesser known and/or discussed dialects, such as the 'Central' dialects
which even now appear to be ill defined except that they do not share
the features of the other groups, or the isoglottic area that stretches
SW-SE from Fars over Larestan and Bashakard parallel and along the
Gulf up to Baluchestan, or the former cluster of dialects in the N which
is now widely scattered, namely Tabari (Mazanderani), Sangesari
with Afdari and Sorxe'i-Lazgerdi, Harzani in Azarbayjan and Zaza
in E Anatolia.

Tedesco was the first to demonstrate practically that the notion
of 'dialect' has to be defined both in terms of time and geography as
well as socially, subject to a dynamic process of changing systems,
changes developing under a host of conditions such as intrastructurally
conditioned innovations, innovations by diffusion from neighboring
dialects or from dialects and languages symbiotic in the same area,
or by superstrate brought in by immigrant groups. Here is not the
place to discuss these and other parameters to be considered. The aim
of this paper was to show that with our present knowledge we are

---

[15] Just as it was ruled, with few interruptions, by (mostly) Turkish dynasties
from the east thereafter, until 1925 when the Pahlavids began their rule in Iran.

in a position to attempt a renewed analysis and interpretation of the stages and the history of Iranian dialectology with the as yet distant goal to contribute with our material not only to Iranian studies but to general linguistics, to the theory of 'glottodynamics' which appears to be evolving.

BIBLIOGRAPHY

A·ẒAMI, Čerāq ʿAli - Gernot L. Windfuhr, A Dictionary of Sangesari. With a Grammatical Outline. [Vāženāme-ye Sangesari] (Tehran : Franklin), 1972.

BOLOGNESI, Giancarlo, Le fonti dialettali degli imprestiti iranici in armeno (= Publ. dell'Univ. Cattolica del Sacro Cuore, serie 3, scienze fil. e lett.) Milano, 1960.

GERSHEVITCH, Ilya, A Grammar of Manichean Sogdian. (=Publications of the Philogical Society.) Oxford: Blackwell, 1954.

HENNING, Walter B., "The Ancient Language of Azerbaijan", TPhS 157-77, 1954.

—, "Mitteliranisch", in Handbuch der Orientalistik 1.4.1 (Ed.: B. Spuler) (Leiden/Köln: E.J. Brill), pp. 20-130, 1958.

IVANOV, W., "Notes on the dialect of Khur and Mihrijan", [1. Khuri phonology and morphology. 2. Addnl. notes on Anaraki. 3. Notes on Naini article by O. Mann] Acta Orientalia 8: 45-61, 1929.

LENTZ, Wolfgang, "Die nordiranischen Elemente in der neupersischen Literatursprache bei Firdosi", ZII 4 :251-316, 1926.

LEVINE, Louis D., Geographical Studies in the Neo-Assyrian Zagros. Toronto: Royal Ontario Museum-Tehran: British Institute of Persian Studies, 1974.

MACKENZIE, David Neil, Kurdish Dialect Studies, I (= London Oriental Series 9) (London : Oxford University Press), 1961.

MAYRHOFER, Manfred, "Die Rekonstruktion des Medischen", Anzeiger der Österreichischen Akademie der Wissenschaften 105. 1: 1-23, 1968.

MORGENSTIERNE, Georg, "Neu-iranische Sprachen", in Handbuch der Orientalistik 1.4.1 (Ed.: B. Spuler) (Leiden/Köln: E.J. Brill), pp. 155-78.

—, Report on a Linguistic Mission to Afghanistan (= Inst. for Sammenlignende Kulturf., Ser. C. 1.2.), Oslo-Leipzig, 1926.

MORTAẒAVI, Manučehr, "Nokte-i čand az zabân-e harzani", [Some notes on Harzani] Našriye-ye Dâneškade-ye Adabiyât, Tabriz 6: 304-14, 1954/1333.

—, "Feʿl dar zabān-e Harzani", [The verb in Harzani] Našriye-ye Dâneškade-ye Adabiyât, Tabriz 14: 453-88; 15: 61-97 (republ. Tabriz 1963/1342, with errata), 1962-63/1341-42.

QARIB, Badr oz-zamân, "An Old Persian-Sogdian Isogloss". Melanges Jean de Menasce, ed. by Philippe Gignoux and Ahmad Tafazolli, Louvain, 1974.

STRONACH, David, Achaemenid Village I at Susa and the Persian Migration to Fars. Iraq 36, pts. 1-2: 239-248, 1974.

TEDESCO, Paul, "Dialektologie der westiranischen Turfantexte", Le Monde Oriental 15. 1-3: 184-258, 1921.

WINDFUHR, Gernot Ludwig, "Some Avestan Rules and their Signs", JAOS 92.1: 52-59, 1972.

YĀR-SHĀṬER, Eḥsān, A Grammar of Southern Tati Dialects (The Hague/Paris: Mouton), 1969.

YOUNG, T. - CUYLER Jr., "The Iranian Immigration into the Zagros", Iran 2. 11-34, 1967.

PLANCHES

Fig. nº 1

Fig. nº 2

Fig. nº 3

Fig. nº 4

Fig. n° 5

Fig. n° 6

Fig. n° 7